Handbook of Measurement Issues in Family Research

Handbook of Measurement Issues in Family Research

EDITED BY

Sandra L. Hofferth
University of Maryland at College Park

Lynne M. Casper
University of Southern California

LEA LAWRENCE ERLBAUM ASSOCIATES, PUBLISHERS
2007 Mahwah, New Jersey   London

Copyright © 2007 by Lawrence Erlbaum Associates, Inc.
All rights reserved. No part of this book may be reproduced in
any form, by photostat, microform, retrieval system, or any other
means, without prior written permission of the publisher.

Lawrence Erlbaum Associates, Inc., Publishers
10 Industrial Avenue
Mahwah, New Jersey 07430
www.erlbaum.com

Cover design by Tomai Maridou

Library of Congress Cataloging-in-Publication Data

Handbook of measurement issues in family research / edited by
Sandra L. Hofferth and Lynne M. Casper.
    p.   cm.
    Based on a conference held in Bethesda, Md. in Nov. 2003 on
"Measurement Issues in Family Demography".
    Includes bibliographical references and index.
    ISBN 0–8058–5617–X
    1. Family—Research—Methodology—Congresses. 2. Family life
surveys—Methodology—Congresses. 3. Family demography—United
States—Congresses. I. Hofferth, Sandra L. II. Casper, Lynne M.
HQ10.H24   2006
306.85072—dc22   2005044691

Books published by Lawrence Erlbaum Associates are printed on acid-free
paper, and their bindings are chosen for strength and durability.

Printed in the United States of America
10 9 8 7 6 5 4 3 2 1

Contents

Preface

The Federal Interagency Forum on Child and Family Statistics, which comprises 20 federal agencies, was established to promote "coordination, collaboration and integration . . . of Federal data on child and family issues and conditions."

To carry out this mission, the Forum initiates activities to improve federal statistics on children and families. The Forum's Data Collection Committee, in collaboration with many researchers and policymakers, undertook a detailed review of federal statistics on marriage, divorce, remarriage, and cohabitation, holding a conference titled "Counting Couples: Improving Federal Statistics on Marriage, Divorce, Remarriage, and Cohabitation," on December 13–14, 2001 (Federal Interagency Forum on Child & Family Statistics, 2001).

Over the past several decades, dramatic changes have reshaped America's families. Young adults have delayed marriage. Cohabitation before marriage has become more commonplace. One in three women giving birth is now unmarried, up from 5% in 1960. The proportion of children under 18 living in single-parent families rose from 23% to 31% between 1980 and 2000, reflecting increased rates of both nonmarital childbearing and divorce.

This transformation in U.S. families has profound implications for policymakers, but our data collection systems have not been sufficiently modified to keep pace with this transformation. It is clear that family trends have had important effects, both positive and negative, on the lives and well-being of children and adults and on the ways in which families function. Effective economic and social policy depends, in part, on the ability to understand and address the changing shape and needs of American families. This, in turn, requires valid and reliable data on marriage, divorce, remarriage, cohabitation, and the family situations of children over time at the national, state, and local levels.

Policymakers use statistical data for a variety of purposes. Data provide basic point-in-time descriptions of the current composition of families and households in the United States; they map trends in family formation and structure; and they help audiences understand the causes of family change and how they affect the well-being of children. Statistical data are used for developing and targeting policies and intervention strategies, such as those currently envisioned to strengthen marriage, and for evaluating whether programs and strategies are working properly and meeting intended goals.

In December 2001, the Federal Interagency Forum on Child and Family Statistics convened the Counting Couples conference chaired by Lynne Casper and Jason Fields to assess how some of the major agencies in the federal statistical system were meeting the need for data on marriage, divorce, and cohabitation. More than 90 professionals from federal and state statistical agencies, policy organizations, and academic and research organizations participated.

Workshop participants overwhelmingly agreed that the federal statistical system can and should improve consistency and accuracy in how it measures family structure and family transitions such as marriage, divorce, and cohabitation. Basic information is needed not only at the national level, but also at the state and local levels, where responsibility for policymaking is increasingly shared. Participants also emphasized the need to better understand why family change occurs and the consequences it has for the well-being of families, couples, and children. They called for improved data on several topics related to this need, including the role and presence of fathers in the family, the relation between family structure and child well-being, the quality of couple relationships, family attitudes and norms, and the causes and consequences of family change.

The conference identified 14 "Targets of Opportunity" for improving data on marriage, divorce, and cohabitation and on the causes and consequences of union formation, dissolution, and family change. These 14 targets evolved from a synthesis of the independent working group discussions among conference participants. These targets of opportunity are outlined in Table 1.

This volume builds on the work begun by the Federal Interagency Forum on Child and Family Statistics. Academic researchers led by the National Institute of Child Health and Human Development (NICHD) Family and Child Well-Being Network teamed up with staff from the Federal Interagency Forum on Child and Family Statistics to continue this important work. These chapters address most of the topics in the targets of opportunity and have greatly moved the agenda forward by critically analyzing concepts and measures and their adequacy for describing families today.

TABLE 1
Targets of Opportunity Identified by Working Groups
at the Counting Couples Conference

I. Measuring Marriage, Divorce, Remarriage, and Cohabitation

- Develop cost-effective systems using vital registration and/or survey methods for providing marriage and divorce data at the national, state, and local levels.
  Conduct a feasibility study to assess the relative costs and benefits of vital registration and survey methods for tracking trends in marriage and divorce and providing data at the state and local, as well as national levels, and implement recommended systems.
- Standardize marital status information across surveys.
  Collect comparable information on the marital status of people, with cohabitation included as a category.
- Collect summary measures of marriage and cohabitation history.
  Ascertain the number of times married and the date the current status began in surveys whose major focus is not marriage and the family.
- Collect full marital and cohabitation histories.
  Ensure that complete cohabitation and marital histories are collected on a consistent basis and provided in a user-friendly format.
- Include special populations.
  Develop and study the feasibility for implementing strategies to conduct reliable marriage- and family-related research on specialized populations such as institutionalized or group quarter populations, ethnic and racial minorities, gays and lesbians, and adopted and foster children.
- Share existing questionnaires and knowledge.
  Place examples of good questionnaire items from existing federal surveys on the childstats.gov Web site to be used as templates for surveys seeking to improve data collection. Include methodological reports that examine measurement quality.
- Improve tabulation and publication of marriage and family formation data.
  Expand, improve, and standardize categories presented in tables and publications to reflect the diversity of union status and family forms.

II. Measuring the Causes and Consequences of Marriage, Divorce, Remarriage, and Cohabitation

---

- Increase the detail of household relationship information.
  Identify the specific relationship of children to the adults in the household.
- Develop and test key concepts.
  Undertake small-scale cognitive and qualitative studies to improve the measurement of important concepts, including cohabitation, social fathering, men's fertility, father involvement, and reasons for mother or father absence. Issue a report of the findings.
- Include measures of family-related values and attitudes.
  Add a core set of attitudinal variables assessing attitudes, perceptions, and values toward family and family life to surveys whenever possible.
- Obtain information for all fathers and mothers in studies of children.
  When appropriate, expand survey(s) to include information on all parents or guardians in the household and all nonresident parents.

(Continued)

TABLE 1 *(Continued)*

- Develop standard sets of variables to track indicators of the causes and consequences of family change.
  Form a research group to identify and test important explanatory and outcome variables that should be added to surveys as time permits and as appropriate to the goals of a particular survey; and compile a report of specific recommendations.
- Develop a plan for a new family study to examine the causes and consequences of family change.
  Form a research group to conduct a feasibility study to set specific goals and design data collection strategies with the ultimate goal of fielding a comprehensive marriage and family study.
- Field a couples study.
  Develop and field a couples study, including information from both partners for cohabiting, married, and dating couples.

The chapters also provide concrete recommendations to improve measures in family research.

Many of the data sets the authors examine are not part of the federal statistical system. However, most of them are collected with funds from federal sources. Many of the changes needed to improve family measures are more easily obtained in data collections that fall outside the purview of federal statistical agencies. Nevertheless, examining these surveys provides helpful hints for researchers, policymakers, and federal agencies to improve data and measures should the opportunity arise.

This authoritative volume provides a blueprint for addressing some of the most important measurement issues in family research. It points out potential pitfalls for researchers and students who may not be familiar with data quality issues. Finally, the volume is a testament to the manner in which the government and the research community can partner to improve the capabilities of our national information system.

—V. Jeffery Evans
Lynne M. Casper

Acknowledgments

This volume grew out of a conference held in Bethesda, Maryland, in November 2003 on "Measurement Issues in Family Demography," which was organized by Lynne Casper and Sandra Hofferth, and which served as a follow-up to the 2001 conference, "Counting Couples: Improving Marriage, Divorce, Remarriage, and Cohabitation Data in the Federal Statistical System." The 2003 conference was sponsored by the National Institute of Child Health and Human Development (NICHD) Family and Child Well-Being Research Network; the U.S. Department of Health and Human Services, Office of Planning, Research, and Evaluation, Administration for Children and Families; the Federal Interagency Forum on Child and Family Statistics; the Demographic and Behavioral Sciences Branch, NICHD; and the Maryland Population Research Center. We thank these organizations for the investments they made in the research contained within this volume.

The purpose of the conference was to describe why and how the measurement of family-related demographic phenomena matters and to discuss and recommend how best to improve current data collection practices to more accurately depict family change and behavior. The conference was organized around many of the recommendations that emerged from the 2001 conference. We acknowledge the work of the Federal Interagency Forum on Child and Family Statistics and the individuals who organized and participated in this conference. A report on this workshop can be found on the following Web site: http://www.childstats.gov/countingcouples/report/ccr.pdf.

The specific goals of the Measurement Issues in Family Demography conference were to:

- Describe the problem or issue of measurement to be addressed and why accurate measurement is important.

- Summarize how the demographic phenomenon is measured currently in both public and private survey data collection.
- Discuss limitations in current measurement, including whether measures accurately reflect the diversity in, and causes and consequences of, family behavior.
- Make concrete recommendations for improving measures.

The conference brought together an interdisciplinary group of stellar scholars, researchers, and policymakers to identify methodologies, key concepts, and constructs and to explore the existing research on data in the area of family research. The conference drew presenters and discussants from a wide range of disciplines, including child development, demography, economics, family studies, psychology, and sociology, as well as from federal statistical agencies, other federal agencies, and nonprofit organizations with an interest in family issues. Scholars, researchers, and policymakers covered many topic areas, including marriage and cohabitation; the quality of couple relationships; men's fertility; divorce and separation; household composition; father involvement and social fathering; family relationships across time; and nonresident parenting.

Conferences and edited volumes do not just happen: They are the result of the support and efforts of many individuals. We would like to acknowledge the members and associates of the National Institute of Child Health and Human Development's Family and Child Well-Being Research Network for their help in organizing the conference, including V. Jeffery Evans, the NICHD program officer of the Network, Peter Brandon, Randal Day, Jeanne Brooks-Gunn, Greg Duncan, Jacqueline Eccles, Kathleen Mullan Harris, Dennis P. Hogan, Kristin Moore, Elizabeth Peters, Gary Sandefur, and Freya Sonenstein. Naomi Goldstein of the Office of Planning, Research, and Evaluation, at the Administration for Children and Families, also assisted in organizing the conference.

A number of Maryland Population Research Center staff members, including Hoda Makar, Barbara Hillinger, and Sarbartha Bandyopadhyay, handled the logistics for the conference. They were assisted by Janice Wahlmann of the Demographic and Behavioral Sciences Branch at the NICHD. Wainani Au of the Department of Family Studies assisted during preconference planning. Megan Fitzgerald, Department of Family Studies, put together the extensive reference list.

The chapters in the volume benefited from review by researchers who critiqued them and made suggestions to authors for improvements. These reviewers include Alison Aughinbaugh, Andrea Beller, Peter Brandon, Susan Brown, Maria Cancian, Marcy Carlson, Randal Day, Kathleen Harris, Donald Hernandez, Wendy Manning, Brent McBride, Philip Morgan, William Mosher, Frank Mott, Kelly Musick, Martin O'Connell,

Joseph Pleck, Kelly Raley, Bob Schoen, Judith Seltzer, Freya Sonenstein, Stephanie Ventura, and Maureen Waller. The chapters also benefited from presentations and discussion comments from a number of researchers and policymakers beyond those whose chapters appear in the volume. We thank the following individuals for these intellectual contributions: Alison Aughinbaugh, Johanne Boisjoly, Philip Cohen, Barbara Downs, Jason Fields, Frances Goldscheider, Rosalind King, Linda Mellgren, Donna Morrison, Seth Sanders, Pamela Smock, Matt Stagner, Koray Tanfer, Linda Waite, and Maureen Waller.

Finally, the editors are indebted to Barbara Ray who handled communications with the authors, shepherded the many drafts through the review process, and copy edited each chapter.

—Sandra L. Hofferth
Lynne M. Casper

PART I

Introduction

1

Playing Catch-Up: Improving Data and Measures for Family Research

Lynne M. Casper

University of Southern California

Sandra L. Hofferth

University of Maryland at College Park

During the last third of the 20th century enormous demographic and economic changes occurred in American families. These include (a) declines in marriage among some groups, delays in marriage in most groups, and increases in cohabitation; (b) increases in marital dissolution due to divorce; (c) increases in nonmarital births but concomitant increases in childrearing in cohabiting unions; (d) increases in single-parent families; (e) increases in maternal employment and changes in fathers' roles; and (f) increases in same-sex households. Although children's living arrangements have changed, increased parental education, increased earnings, and smaller families have improved the lives of children during the past few decades. In addition, changes in attitudes and values toward parenting have led to children in two-parent families spending increased time with their parents in the late 1990s compared with the early 1980s.

We often compare today's families with families during the 1950s, right after World War II. That was the peak of what we know as the baby boom, when men and women were marrying and rearing children in large numbers and economic times were good. However, the baby boom was unique in breaking what was a long-term trend toward increased age at marriage and lower fertility (Cherlin, 1992). Thus, many of the trends that we describe herein are continuations of trends from the past hundred years rather than brand-new developments. Yet it is convenient to compare these numbers with numbers from the 1950s because that was the most recent peak in family building.

OBJECTIVES OF THE VOLUME

Changes in the type and quality of family relationships affect future policies and the nature of children's and parents' lives for years to come. Yet our data collection systems have not kept pace with these changes in the family, and researchers are left playing catch-up, often inventing ways of improving data that were collected according to a method devised in the 1950s to reflect the reality of the American family at that time. For example, our federal surveys do not ask about cohabitation in any depth. Only recently have surveys added the category of "unmarried partner" to the list of categories that describe the relationships of people in a household. The lack of an appropriate category for cohabitation makes it hard to establish whether the family is actually two-parent or one-parent. The lack of these data would not have had a profound impact on estimating family trends in the 1950s, when very few adults cohabited. However, now that more than one half of adults have cohabited at some point, the lack of such data leads to an unrealistic picture of the American family.

The accuracy of poverty statistics also is plagued by a lack of cohabitation data. In calculating family income, the poverty rate does not include the income of a person who is not related by blood or marriage to the head of the household. Thus, cohabitating partner income is not included in family income for the purpose of calculating family poverty. Some of these partners are biological parents of the children, and their income probably should be counted. However, it is unclear that unmarried partner income always should be included in family income, given that the beginning and ending of cohabiting relationships are not well demarcated and that cohabitation is usually a short-lived relationship that carries different meanings for different couples. To accurately determine whether partner income should be included in calculating the poverty rate, researchers would need to know whether, for how long, and how much partners contribute economically to running the household. But data sets do not contain this type of detailed information, and we are left to make the best estimates possible, even though we know they are riddled with inaccuracies.

Given rapid social change, it is important to regularly evaluate key concepts and measures in the federal statistical system and in other national data collections and to identify areas in need of improvement—areas in which to play catch-up—so that the concepts and measures reflect the reality of today's families. The goal of this volume is to review research that has used existing data to estimate the prevalence of cohabitation, marriage, divorce, and separation; changes in household composition and relationships within and outside the family; male fertility; and the involvement of resident and nonresident fathers with children. We asked the authors of these chapters to (a) describe the problem or issue of measurement to be addressed and why accurate measurement is important; (b) summarize how the demographic phenomena are currently measured in both public- and private-survey data collection; (c) discuss limitations in current measurement, including whether measures accurately reflect the diversity in, and causes and consequences of, family behavior; and (d) make concrete recommendations for improving measures. This volume not only identifies both the gaps in data collection and the implications of these gaps for our understanding of families, but also can be used to guide policymakers and researchers in designing new surveys that enable us to better describe the American family in the new millennium.

MARRIAGE AND COHABITATION

One of the most profound changes in families during the past several decades has been the rise of cohabitation and the delay of marriage. Cohabitation is becoming a common precursor to marriage. One half of all men and women ages 25 to 29 have cohabited (U.S. Census Bureau, 2000a). Although delaying legal marriage, young men and women are not delaying coresident sexual unions. When we sum the proportions who have ever cohabited and those who have ever married, rates of first union formation have declined only slightly. Three quarters (76%) of women born in 1960 to 1964 had formed a union by age 25, compared with 83% of those born in 1940 to 1944 (Moore, 1995).

Compared with the 1950s, more men and women are delaying marriage. In 1955, 11% of women ages 25 to 29 had never married. By 1999, that figure was 39%. Sixty percent of Black women in this age group had never married in 1999, compared with 29% of White women. Among men ages 25 to 29, in 1955 28% had never married. By 1999, that figure was 52%. Sixty-five percent of Black men ages 25 to 29 had never married, compared with 46% of White men (U.S. Census Bureau, 2000a).

Another way to look at marriage is to examine the age at which one half of young people have married. In 1890, the median age of first marriage was 22 for women and 26.1 for men. It dropped to 20.1 and 22.5, respectively, in the 1950s and rose again to 24 and 26 in 1990. In the late 1990s, the median age at first marriage continued to rise, to 25 for women and 27 for men (Casper & Bianchi, 2002).

The significance of these trends for family life and the need for better measures of marriage and cohabitation to understand these changes was underscored at the 2001 conference "Counting Couples: Improving Marriage, Divorce, Remarriage, and Cohabitation Data in the Federal Statistical System." (See the Preface for more information about this conference.) Participants in the conference noted that no survey exists that collects a full cohabitation history from a nationally representative sample of all adults in the United States. They also remarked that although some federally sponsored surveys conducted at universities collect detailed data on cohabitation, the data are collected differently in each survey and may not measure exactly what it means to cohabit. Finally, they noted that relationship quality plays a crucial role in relationship stability and that most surveys do not adequately measure relationship quality.

The first objective of Part II, Marriage and Cohabitation, is to identify the surveys and questions used to identify cohabitation, and to compare the estimates obtained on marriage and cohabitation using the different questions and methods. The chapters in this part draw on current qualitative and quantitative studies that collect information on relationships to explore the ways in which cohabitation is measured and to contrast relationship quality and commitment in cohabiting and marital relationships. The data sets and studies presented in these chapters represent the most recent developments in this field.

In chapter 2, Jean Tansey Knab and Sara McLanahan walk us through the various ways in which surveys have measured cohabitation and conclude that although cohabitation appears to be a straightforward concept, the boundaries and the meaning of cohabitation for couples are ambiguous. They argue that these ambiguities cause problems for researchers trying to measure cohabitation. Using data on new parents from the Fragile Families and Child Wellbeing Study, they demonstrate that survey results differ depending on how, when, and whom you ask about cohabitation. They also show that the way cohabitation is measured is likely to affect our understanding of the characteristics and behaviors of cohabiting couples.

In chapter 3, Michael S. Pollard and Kathleen Mullan Harris use data from the National Longitudinal Study of Adolescent Health (Add Health) to demonstrate a variety of ways to measure cohabitation, both qualitatively and by the length of time a couple has lived together. They investigate the difficulties associated with collecting accurate data on the beginning and ending dates of cohabitation. They also discuss the fact that couples attach different meanings to their cohabiting relationships. They conclude that couples can live together in varying degrees, including spending the entire night together several times a week, living together, or living together in a marriage-like relationship. Like Knab and McLanahan, Pollard and Harris find that it is extremely difficult to demarcate exactly when a couple began living together. They also demonstrate that cohabitors are not a homogenous group by providing different descriptions of cohabiting relationships.

The second objective of Part II is to assess the conceptualization and operationalization of relationship quality. Chapters 4–7 discuss how measures of relationship quality are or can be designed to capture the effects of interventions, how they apply across a range of relationship types, how they apply to diverse populations, and how they relate to child well-being. In chapter 4, Paul R. Amato explains why, if we want to understand what keeps couples together, it is important to know more about marriage than just the demographic characteristics of the marital partners and their marital happiness and satisfaction. He shows that although negative interaction may lead to marital breakup, positive interaction may be even more important in determining whether a marriage survives. He also argues that marital commitment may be the most important factor, particularly when a relationship is troubled. Amato recommends that measures of interaction and commitment be included on surveys, but he also notes that it is important to find and develop valid and reliable measures that can be added to large-scale surveys.

In chapter 5, Alan J. Hawkins, Blaine J. Fowers, Jason S. Carroll, and Chongming Yang emphasize the importance of marriage as a social institution rather than as solely an individually satisfying relationship. Instead of the love/communication/satisfaction model of marriage based on individual needs, this chapter emphasizes the importance of group virtues such as generosity, loyalty, and justice. Rather than focusing on individuals, Hawkins et al. argue that researchers must pay more attention to the "corporate" model—the friend or partner model in which the unit of the partnership is important. The authors also develop and examine the psychometric properties of several scales that fit into this revised conceptualization of marriage.

In chapter 6, Scott M. Stanley also proposes a new model of healthy marriage that builds on the early satisfaction model and later communication/conflict models by incorporating commitment, attachment, sacrifice, support, acceptance, and forgiveness. As in chapter 5, the framework presented in this chapter contains a substantial element of group loyalty. Stanley's conceptualization of healthy marriage includes three elements: interaction safety, personal safety, and commitment safety. This chapter includes a discussion of moderating factors—characteristics that may alter the effectiveness of interventions meant to strengthen marriages. Couple characteristics such as premarital cohabitation, religiosity, attachment security, and commitment may determine whether an intervention to improve marital quality will be effective.

In chapter 7, Kristin A. Moore, Jacinta Bronte-Tinkew, Susan Jekielek, Lina Guzman, Suzanne Ryan, Zakia Redd, Jennifer Carrano, and Greg Matthews add a third complexity to the study of relationship quality: a focus on low-income couples. These couples may face unique challenges as they struggle to remain in healthy relationships. Yet most studies of relationship quality have focused on married, biological-parent, middle-income couples. In addition, there are a variety of types of couples about whose relationships we know very little, including cohabiting, step- and remarried parents, non-resident coparenting divorced couples, military families, and incarcerated parents. In this chapter, the authors develop a set of 10 concepts that apply in various ways to these different types of low-income couples. They argue that these concepts can be used as the basis for a new measure of healthy relationships that is appropriate for these groups.

SEPARATION AND DIVORCE

Divorce is a 20th-century phenomenon. Until the 1940s, the most common reason for ending a marriage was the death of a partner. However, following World War II, divorce increased dramatically as death rates fell. Divorce rates rose in the 1960s and 1970s but began to level out in the 1980s. After 1985, the divorce rate per 1,000 married women 15 and older declined in very small increments, from 21.7 in 1985 to 19.8 in 1997 (Casper & Bianchi, 2002). The most recent estimates indicate that about 50% of first marriages for men younger than age 45 and between 45% and 50% of first marriages for women of this age may eventually end in divorce (Fields & Kreider, 2000).

Our understanding of this important family experience and its causes and consequences depends on how well we measure marital instability. Not all divorces happen in the same way. Important questions to address include the following: When does a marriage end? Does it end at separation, divorce, or a new cohabitation? Does the picture of family instability change if we consider the dissolution of cohabiting relationships along with marital relationships? The Counting Couples conference pointed out that it is important to know about all of these pathways and that researchers have not focused enough attention on separation. In the first chapter in Part III, chapter 8, Larry Bumpass and Kelly Raley provide an overview of existing measures of separation and divorce available in many major data sets and discuss several issues affecting the quality of these measures. They assess the quality of different estimates from retrospective histories, vital statistics, and longitudinal measures. They also discuss the conceptual and methodological difficulties involved in gathering information on separation and divorce, and they propose ideas for improvement.

In chapter 9, Martin O'Connell provides an extensive commentary from the view of the federal statistical system on the issues raised in chapter 8. He uses marital history data from the Census Bureau's Survey of Income and Program Participation (SIPP) to illustrate the magnitude of imputed data, explain how missing data are imputed and edited, and compare the final edited data with vital statistics data. He concludes that nonresponse rates may be less problematic than researchers think, given that marital paths often have "an internal structure of regularity that aids in providing the answers to patterns of missing data."

HOUSEHOLD COMPOSITION AND FAMILY RELATIONSHIPS

As statistically defined, a family is a group of two or more persons who are related by birth, marriage, or adoption. A household consists of all the persons who occupy a housing unit, often defined by shared cooking facilities or direct access to outside. A housing unit can be a house, an apartment, a group of rooms, or a single room, but it is intended as separate living quarters and can include related and unrelated persons. Generally, income is assumed to be shared by family members but not by unrelated household members. For the most part, data that describe families refer to what are often called "family households," persons sharing living quarters who are all related in some way to the householder—the person in whose name the home is owned or rented. Defining and measuring the family has become more difficult given increased cohabitation, the increased proportion of same-sex families, and the increased tendency for family members to be scattered throughout several households. Increasingly *the* family is being replaced by complex cross-household families that can include married or cohabiting opposite-sex or same-sex couples; single parents; biological, step-, half-, and unrelated siblings; and other related and unrelated individuals.

One of the key recommendations from the Counting Couples conference was that family surveys collect detailed data about household relationships, including identifying the resident biological and nonbiological parents of children. However, the methods for determining who is related to whom are still in their experimental stages and are not widely used in survey research. In addition, households do not remain the same over time. Their composition changes as children leave home, families break up, and members leave and return.

The aim of Part IV is to better understand the strengths and weaknesses of existing surveys for measuring household and interpersonal relationships and relationships that span households. Chapters 10 to 13 focus on the measurement of household relationships through the household roster, the measurement of cross-household family ties and family trajectories, and the policy implications of how family units are defined within a household.

In chapter 10, Peter D. Brandon focuses on what we can learn about household and interpersonal relationships from current rosters and, in particular, from the household relationship matrix, an improved method for collecting information about family and household structure in the United States. Many studies identify a focal child and obtain information on the relationship of that child to every other child. This technique works and is minimally burdensome if the focus is on children. However, this chapter shows that the relationship matrix provides a richness of detail about the structure of families and households in the United States that is impossible to obtain from any other technique.

Martha Hill and Paul Callister examine family ties across households in chapter 11. The authors demonstrate the decreased usefulness of a concept such as "single-parent family" and make an innovative attempt to emphasize the importance of measuring cross-household family ties. Many family members are coparenting children who reside in other households. However, these "invisible parents" are often missed in conventional household-based surveys. The authors argue that these parents are involved in their children's lives and should be identified in all of our surveys.

In chapter 12, Wendy D. Manning and Ronald E. Bulanda address the importance of considering the transitory nature of families. Families are not static, nor do they always involve marriage. In this chapter, the authors examine static and dynamic measures of families and conclude that examining family status at any particular point in time most likely underestimates the breadth of family experiences. They also demonstrate that it is important to measure the cumulative effects of family experiences, including cohabitation, by examining the impact of cumulative levels of family instability on adolescent well-being.

In chapter 13, John Iceland describes one problem with the current definition of the poverty threshold: It is based on the traditional model of a family related by blood, marriage, or adoption. This method of calculating poverty assumes that cohabiting parents are not pooling income, an unlikely scenario in some types of households. The chapter shows that the measured poverty of the mother–child unit would be much lower if the cohabiting partner's income were taken into account in a "cohabiting couple unit." In addition, the poverty level of unrelated persons sharing living quarters, such as roommates or housemates, also would be reduced if the definition of poverty were based on the household. Although overall poverty estimates are not reduced substantially by altering the family unit for determining poverty, the estimates for those families affected are greatly altered. Iceland cannot determine, however, whether families actually pool income/resources, a problem that must be resolved if we are to better measure poverty.

Another recommendation that emerged from the Counting Couples conference was to "Develop and study strategies for conducting research on specialized populations such as institutionalized populations or those in group quarters, ethnic and racial minorities, gays and lesbians, and adopted and foster children." A number of new studies include information on minorities and low-income populations to test whether questions that researchers usually ask about relationships make sense for these populations. Less is known, however, about gay and lesbian families and the military, incarcerated, and college-attending populations.

In chapter 14, Gary J. Gates and Randall Sell examine the increasingly important issue of identifying and enumerating gay and lesbian couples. The chapter examines two strategies for accomplishing this: (a) direct enumeration through questions about sexual orientation and (b) examining gender and "partner" designation provided in the household roster. The authors conclude that both strategies are likely to result in underestimates; however, the latter may be the most complete at the present time. The chapter points out that the Census Bureau may have contributed significantly to errors in classifying gay and lesbian couples through its practice of reclassifying as unmarried those same-sex couples who claim they are married.

In the final chapter in this part, chapter 15, William D. Mosher points out that as we begin to study low-income and minority male populations, it becomes less justifiable to ignore institutional populations, particularly incarcerated and military populations. One third of Black men could be incarcerated at some time in their lives; therefore, researchers studying Black men ages 18 to 39 should consider including such populations in their surveys. Mosher describes four options for including these groups: (a) direct personal interview, (b) telephone interview, (c) interviewing household members about incarcerated members, and (d) obtaining information once the men have returned to their households. He also points out the advantages and disadvantages of each approach.

BECOMING A FATHER

Between 1920 and 1935, the total fertility rate dropped dramatically, from about 3.2 children per woman to about 2.2 children per woman. It rose dramatically in the 1950s to a high of 3.7 children per woman in 1957, but dropped again to a low of 1.7 in 1976. Since then, it rose to about 2.0

and has been relatively stable at this level for the past decade. The number of births has risen because of the large number of women of childbearing age born during the baby boom and because childbearing is being delayed. Despite this delay, however, childlessness has risen only slightly; in 1980 10% of women were expected to be childless, and today 19% may be.

But what about men? Until recently, fertility data have come from women mainly because of the difficulty in establishing a high degree of confidence in the links between men and their biological offspring. However, because of the growing complexity of families, researchers have identified male fertility as an essential topic of study to understand changes in the American family. Surveys have begun to collect data on births from men. Yet concerns remain regarding the quality of fertility data collected from male respondents. The first two chapters in Part V, chapters 16 and 17, document the problems with collecting accurate male relationship and fertility data and offer different techniques for improving the data quality. Chapter 18 uses qualitative methods to provide suggestions for altering surveys that can improve our understanding of the nuances of male fertility. Chapter 19 provides a good discussion of the need for male fertility data and an overview of the state of data collection in the area of male fertility.

In chapter 16, Frank L. Mott, Dawn S. Hurst, and Thomas Gryn use data from the 1979 and 1997 National Longitudinal Survey of Youth to explore the willingness and ability of young men to accurately report earlier relationships and related fertility events. The authors evaluate the quality of existing data to provide better estimates of fertility among young men. They find that the major reason men have discrepancies in their reported fertility over time is that large proportions of younger men are not living with their children. They also find that event history information is very important in filling the between-survey gaps. The authors argue that without event history data even high-quality panel survey data with frequent collection can contain fertility data of suspect quality.

In chapter 17, Scott Boggess, Gladys Martinez, Carolyn Bradner Jasik, and Laura Duberstein Lindberg use data from the National Survey of Adolescent Males. Similar to chapter 16, this chapter examines the validity of young men's reports of fertility and explores ways of improving these estimates. The authors conclude that more accurate estimates of fatherhood can be obtained for certain types of fathers, particularly nonresident and unmarried fathers, by using longitudinal rather than cross-sectional data.

In contrast to chapters 16 and 17, which use quantitative methods to examine male fertility, William Marsiglio in chapter 18 uses qualitative methods to show how this method of analysis can inform survey strategies for studying male fertility and produce unique insights about men's subjective fertility experiences. He provides convincing evidence to suggest that existing surveys must be improved to understand the nuances of male fertility. He recommends that survey questions be expanded to include measures of paternity confidence, fatherhood readiness, and paternal claiming. Other recommendations include adding questions to address three forms of men's knowledge of their reproductive abilities: basic understanding of their own reproductive physiology, perceptions of personal potency, and confirmed paternity status.

In chapter 19, Christine Bachrach assesses the current state of male fertility data, including a discussion of the data available in several data sets. She first provides a convincing case for studying male fertility and lays out exactly what we need to know. She then describes the progress that researchers have made in measuring male fertility. The chapter concludes with a discussion of the well-known problems in the quality of male-fertility data and offers some suggestions for improvement.

FATHERS AND FATHERING

Many changes in the family have illuminated the importance of research on fathers and fathering and of collecting the appropriate data to conduct such research. Increases in cohabitation, divorce, separation, births to single mothers, and maternal employment have altered how families function and the roles mothers and fathers play within them.

The proportion of children born to unmarried mothers has increased, partly as a result of declines in marital fertility. From 1960 to 1964, 8.5% of births to White women, 42.4% of births to Black women, and 19.2% of births to Hispanic women were to unmarried women. In 1998, 33% of all births were to unmarried women (26% for White women, 69% for Black women, and 42% for Hispanic women; U.S. Census Bureau, 2000a). Marital fertility is lower than nonmarital fertility for Blacks. In 1998, the birthrate per 1,000 unmarried women was 44 for all women, 38 for White, 73 for Black, and 95 for Hispanic women. The birthrate for all women was 64 for White, 71 for Black, and 104 for Hispanic women. Out-of-wedlock fertility rose during the 1980s but has been declining in the late 1990s for all racial-ethnic groups.

Just because the mother is not married does not mean that the father is uninvolved. About one quarter of out-of-wedlock births occur to cohabiting couples. This includes 29% of births to non-Hispanic Whites, 18% to Blacks, and 40% to Mexican Americans (Moore, 1995). Although children in these relationships may be better off than if they were living with only their mother (Hofferth & Anderson, 2003), the relationships are less stable. Fewer than 40% of cohabiting parents marry within 3 years, and rates of divorce are higher for marriages that begin as cohabitations.

One major family change has been the sharp increase in levels of maternal employment (Casper & Bianchi, 2002; Hofferth & Philips, 1987). In the 20th century in the United States, married mothers were traditionally less likely to work than unmarried mothers. Their labor force participation rose in the 1970s and 1980s, leveling off in the 1990s. Whereas 40% of married mothers with children younger than age 18 were in the workforce in 1970, 70% were in the workforce in 1999 (U.S. Census Bureau, 2000a). Rates traditionally have been lowest for married mothers of children younger than age 6, but these rates rose as well, from 30% in 1970, to 45% in 1980, to 59% in 1990, to 62% in 1999.

In the 1980s, single mothers were least likely to work. The availability of public assistance as a source of economic support has been cited as the reason for the relatively low levels of employment among this group of women. In the 1990s, public policies that were implemented to increase work effort and improve the economy resulted in large increases in employment of unmarried mothers. Labor force participation rates for unmarried mothers rose from 44% in 1980, to 48% in 1990, to 68% in 1999—an increase of 50%. The labor force participation of these mothers is now above the level of married mothers with young children. These trends have led to a record proportion of the mothers of infants in the workforce—59% in 1998 (U.S. Census Bureau, 2001).

Although men's and women's roles have changed drastically since the 1970s, with more women participating in the labor market and more men participating in unpaid labor within the home, our data sets have not kept pace in collecting the information we need to assess how these changes have affected family life (Sayer, Cohen, & Casper, 2004). Fathers are undoubtedly part of all these processes but little information is obtained from or about them. In most data collections, the presumption has been that the mother is the most knowledgeable about children; however, this may be less true today. Recent studies point to increased father involvement and to the unique contribution fathers make to their children's development (Hofferth & Anderson, 2003; Sandberg & Hofferth, 2001). Given the increased likelihood that one of the parents in two-parent families is not the biological father of at least one of the children, variation in father involvement is critically important to understand.

Nonmarital childbearing, separation, divorce, and the breakup of cohabiting households create ties between parents across households and have drastically altered fathers' and mothers' lives and their involvement in their children's lives. For example, when parents split up, fathers are important to the economic viability of mothers and children. Paternity, not marriage or other legal status, is what entitles children to the earnings of the father. Because of the difficulty of collecting data across households, we know relatively little about how families function when they do not share households.

As a result of the work done in 1998 by the Federal Interagency Forum on Child and Family Statistics in the report "Nurturing Fatherhood: Improving Data and Research on Male Fertility, Family Formation, and Fatherhood" (1998), the past decade has witnessed a dramatic increase in research on fathers and fathering. However, the Counting Couples conference acknowledged that although we have made much progress, many gaps remain, particularly in data collection. One of the recommendations from the workshop was: "When appropriate, expand survey(s) to include information on all parents or guardians in the household and all nonresident parents." In this volume, one chapter focuses on residential fathers and two focus on nonresident fathers.

Paternal involvement has been growing, but increasingly fathers are involved with children who are not biologically related to them and with children with whom they share no formally recognized social relationship (e.g., children of a partner). Little research has examined resident father involvement in these "other" father types and the consequences for children of this type of involvement or lack of it. In the first chapter of Part VI, chapter 20, Sandra L. Hofferth, Natasha Cabrera, Marcia Carlson, Rebekah Levine Coley, Randal Day, and Holly Schindler use five recent data sets to examine six constructs of father involvement: engagement, activities, accessibility, responsibility, warmth, and monitoring/control. The chapter concludes with several recommendations to improve data in this area of research, including measuring the biological relationship between parent and child and the relationship status of parents, including father figures; getting direct reports from fathers and mothers about their own behavior; getting reports from mothers about fathers' behaviors; obtaining similar measures for mothers and fathers; making sure that each parent's involvement is measured separately; and finally, improving the measurement of responsibility.

In chapter 21, Laura Argys, Elizabeth Peters, Steven Cook, Steven Garasky, Lenna Nepomnyaschy, and Elaine Sorensen examine contact between children and their nonresident parent, which the authors conclude is not well defined. The chapter discusses the types of information collected that relate to contact with nonresident fathers and notes problems with these data and their collection methods. The authors note that different types of contact may matter and that the timing of contact also may be important, both over a single year and throughout the child's life. Legal agreements specify legal custody and often physical custody and visitation. The authors conclude that although compliance with child support has been studied extensively, little is known about compliance with visitation agreements. They recommend that we examine information on barriers to contact as well as types of visitation agreements that could structure contact. They also argue that because parents' perspectives differ, information must be gathered from both parents. Finally, quantifying the nature of the relation-ship between nonresident parent and child and their activities is crucial.

Steven Garasky, Elizabeth Peters, Laura Argys, Steven Cook, Lenna Nepomnyaschy, and Elaine Sorensen examine child support provided by nonresident fathers to their children's current household(s) in chapter 22. In 2000, about one quarter of children younger than age 21 had a non-resident parent. Of their custodial parents, 62% had a child support order. This chapter first examines formal cash support provided in response to an established legal support order as well as informal cash and in-kind sup-port. Second, it examines the complexity of the families. Third, it examines the extent to which legal orders are modified over time. It recommends gathering data on child support provision from all parents, capturing the amount and regularity of informal and formal support, including children not necessarily living with a biological parent, and gathering data for each eligible child in a household.

CONCLUSION

The authors of this volume provide a wealth of data, information, and anal-ysis that can be used by statistical agencies and researchers during the next decade to improve the reliability and validity of family research. In the final chapter (chap. 23), Sandra L. Hofferth and Lynne M. Casper discuss the specific recommendations for improvement made throughout the volume and assert that they are critical in playing catch-up—in ensuring that our measures and methods reflect the reality of families in the 21st century.

PART II

Marriage and Cohabitation

2

Measuring Cohabitation: Does How, When, and Who You Ask Matter?

Jean Tansey Knab
Sara McLanahan
Princeton University

In response to the dramatic increase in cohabitation during the 1980s and 1990s and the growing interest in this new family form, researchers have increasingly included measures of cohabitation in large-scale surveys. Although many national surveys now contain questions designed to identify cohabitors, they differ in their wording and format of the questions. Not only do these differences affect estimates of the prevalence of cohabitation (Casper & Cohen, 2000), they also likely shape our understanding of correlates and outcomes (Knab, 2005).

Inconsistent measurement across surveys occurs, in part, from the different goals of and constraints on particular surveys. It also reflects a lack of consensus in the research community about how to define cohabitation. Although living together seems like a fairly straightforward concept, recent research highlights ambiguity in the boundaries and meaning of cohabitation for many couples. Cohabitors are diverse in their marriage intentions (S. L. Brown & Booth, 1996; C. Osborne, 2002), residence patterns (Binstock & Thornton, 2003; Knab, 2005), and reasons for living together (Casper & Sayer, 2000; Manning & Smock, 2005; Sassler, 2004). Because of these differences, cohabitation estimates may vary depending on how and when the question is asked.

Measurement is complicated even further when we consider that cohabitation consists of two individuals who may have different perceptions of the same relationship (Waller & McLanahan, 2005). Moreover, couple reports have been known to vary on a variety of subjective and objective issues, including father–child contact and fertility intentions (Auriat, 1993; Coley & Morris, 2002; R. Williams & Thomson, 1985). Therefore, cohabitation rates may also vary, depending on whether it is the man or the woman who is asked to report on the couple's living arrangement.

Most previous research on measuring cohabitation compares the correspondence between direct and indirect measures of cohabitation across different surveys (Baughman, Dickert-Conlin, & Houser, 2002; Casper & Cohen, 2000). In this chapter, we examine variation in direct cohabitation measures within a particular survey. We use data from the Fragile Families and Child Wellbeing Study (FF) to construct multiple measures of cohabitation and to determine how these different measures affect estimates of the prevalence of cohabitation and estimates of the composition and behavior of cohabitors. The major advantage of the FF data is that cohabitation is asked in various ways at different points during the survey. The major limitation of these data is that all the respondents are new parents, and thus our results can be generalized to this population only.

BACKGROUND ON COHABITATION

Rates of heterosexual cohabitation increased dramatically during the latter part of the 20th century. Cohabitation rates for unmarried women tripled, from 3% to 9% between 1978 and 1998 (Casper & Cohen, 2000) and today, more than one half of U.S. heterosexual women live with a man before they marry (Bumpass & Lu, 2000). Much of the research on cohabitation attempts to understand the meaning of cohabitation by examining the characteristics of cohabitors and by trying to situate cohabitation along a continuum of romantic relationships. Fitting cohabitation into a single theoretical construct has proved difficult, however, as cohabitation appears to serve different purposes for different couples. Whereas some couples appear to use cohabitation as an alternative to marriage, others treat is as a precursor to marriage, a trial marriage, or an alternative to dating (Casper & Sayer, 2000).

As noted, the diversity in the form and function of cohabiting unions has implications for clarity and consistency when measuring cohabitation, and, as a result, estimates of its prevalence. Casper and Cohen (2000) examined variation in cohabitation rates across major nationally representative surveys, including the National Survey of Families and Households (NSFH), the National Survey of Family Growth (NSFG), the Survey of Income and Program Participation (SIPP), the National Longitudinal Survey of Youth,

1979 (NLSY79), and the Current Population Survey (CPS). Because each of these surveys measures cohabitation slightly differently, cohabitation rates vary across surveys (e.g., up to 13 percentage points between the NSFG and CPS for some age groups [Casper & Cohen, 2000]).

Rates of cohabitation also vary within the subsample of unmarried parents. Using data from the 1995 Cycle of the NSFG (NSFG-5) and looking specifically at cohabitation at the time of a child's birth, Bumpass and Lu (2000) estimated that 40% of nonmarital births during the early 1990s were to cohabiting couples. Using FF data, however, and looking at births at the end of the 1990s, McLanahan and her colleagues (2003) estimated that 51% of nonmarital births were to cohabiting couples. The 11-percentage-point difference between these cohabitation rates may stem from geography—the FF sample is restricted to large, urban areas, whereas the NSFG is representative of all areas of the country—or it may stem from the time differences. Cohabitation increased throughout the 1990s (Acs & Nelson, 2001), and it is possible that the prevalence at the end of the decade is 11 percentage points higher than the prevalence at the beginning of the decade.

Differences in cohabitation rates may also result from how and when the questions were asked. The FF survey asked parents about their cohabitation status soon after their child was born, whereas the NSFG survey asked retrospective questions about births during the last 5 years. Asking about cohabitation at the "magic moment" of the child's birth may inflate reports of cohabitation either because couples feel more loving toward one another or because they respond in a more socially desirable way. Retrospective questions may underestimate prevalence if couples fail to recall less serious cohabiting relationships (such as short-term or part-time).

Casper and Cohen (2000) reviewed many of the reasons why cohabitation prevalence rates vary across surveys. This chapter extends their work by examining how these rates vary within a single survey. In what follows, we focus on how cohabitation questions are asked (specifically, what criteria are used to determine household membership), when questions are asked (whether respondents are asked concurrently or retrospectively), and of whom the questions are asked (whether the respondent is a man or a woman). Examining reports of cohabitation within the same survey by the same respondents can inform us about the reasons cohabitation rates may differ so dramatically across surveys.

HOW SURVEYS TYPICALLY MEASURE COHABITATION

One approach to measuring cohabitation is to ask respondents a direct question about their current relationship status or household membership.

However, the criteria for household membership differ across and even within surveys. For example, Cycle 6 of the NSFG, the SIPP, and the CPS limit household membership to persons who have the same "usual address"; Cycle 5 of the NSFG limits household membership to individuals who "live and sleep here most of the time"; and the first wave of the NSFH asks about persons living in the household "half of the time or more." Questions that ask about cohabitation in terms of current relationship status often present no guidelines for household membership. Some surveys ascertain cohabitation status from multiple questions (household roster and relationship questions), which may boost cohabitation rates.

Variation in the criteria for household membership may lead to different couples being counted as cohabiting across surveys or across questions. Manning and Smock (2005), in recent qualitative research, described a "slide" into cohabitation for many young couples, with couples gradually moving in together over a period of time while maintaining multiple residences (see also Manning and Bulanda, chap. 12, this volume). Therefore, some couples are cohabiting part-time and would be classified as cohabitors in one survey but not another. In addition to their deliberate inclusion or exclusion across surveys via household membership criteria, couples who are cohabiting part-time may be uncertain whether to label themselves as such when provided with no formal guidelines (or even despite formal guidelines).

If the slide into cohabitation were fairly common, it would have important implications for measuring and interpreting cohabitation in large-scale surveys. Questions that set more stringent criteria for cohabitation will produce lower prevalence rates. Based on the FF study, Knab (2005) showed that, among unmarried mothers, a significant minority is cohabiting part-time when their child is age 1. Between 5% and 11% of mothers who were unmarried at their child's birth report living together part of the time 1 year after the birth. Therefore, including all or some of these couples as cohabitors would have a significant effect on the cohabitation rate. Including or excluding part-time cases not only affects prevalence estimates, but also affects the demographic characteristics of cohabitors and the effects of cohabitation on union transitions, income pooling, and father involvement.

A related (and somewhat overlapping) issue is whether respondents understand the terminology used to identify cohabitation or whether they even subscribe to the idea that they are "living together" with a partner. Manning and Smock (2005) found that the term "unmarried partner," which is often used in household rosters, does not resonate with many couples (see also Manning and Bulanda, chap. 12, this volume). These labels are not terms that couples commonly use to refer to each other and may imply a different level of commitment than what is perceived by respondents. Another issue is that of intention, given that some couples report having moved in together without having made a conscious decision to do so. That these couples never decided to live together (Manning & Smock, 2005) may lead to ambiguities regarding the labeling of their relationship.

Knab (2005) found substantial variation in the labeling of living arrangements across mothers. Although some respondents who spend two to six nights together per week report themselves as not cohabiting, others do consider themselves cohabiting. These relationship labels may be tied to a couple's marriage intentions, religious beliefs, or the quality of their relationship at a given moment.

WHEN COHABITATION IS MEASURED

Another approach to measuring cohabitation is to collect retrospective information. For each previous relationship, cohabitation histories ascertain the dates the couple started (and stopped) living together. The manner of collecting cohabitation histories also varies across surveys. Some surveys allow for a single relationship to have multiple start and end dates, whereas others allow for only a single start and end date.

The retrospective approach has long been used to collect data on marriage and fertility. However, research has documented discrepancies between current and retrospective reports of marital transitions and has found that these differences can influence estimates of divorce and remarriage (Lillard & Waite, 1989; Peters, 1988). One might expect the discrepancies between current and retrospective reports of cohabitation to be even greater, given the ambiguities described previously. For example, if couples have lived together part-time, they may find it more difficult to recall or pinpoint start dates in retrospective surveys.

Teitler, Reichman, and Koball (forthcoming) used data from the FF study to examine the correspondence of reported cohabitation over time. They found that 16% of mothers change their report of whether they were cohabiting when their child was born between the baseline and 1-year follow-up interviews. The authors find that mothers' individual characteristics (but not fathers') and a couple's current relationship status are strongly related to changes in reported cohabitation.

High rates of residential separations among cohabitors also have implications for cohabitation histories. Binstock and Thornton (2003) found that a substantial proportion of cohabiting couples spend time living apart (for reasons other than relationship discord). It is unclear whether during this time these couples should and do consider themselves "living together" and how they would respond to a cohabitation history table that asked for only one start and end date per partner.

WHO REPORTS ON COHABITATION

Finally, surveys differ with respect to who is asked to report on cohabitation status, with some surveys (e.g., CPS) targeting any knowledgeable respondent, others targeting women (NSFG-5), and still others collecting data from both partners (FF, NSFH-1). Given the ambiguities surrounding the meaning of cohabitation and the frequency of part-time cohabitation and short-term separations, it is easy to see how couples might disagree about their status. It is also possible that men and women differ in their understanding of cohabitation, which could lead to gender differences in prevalence.

Substantial research reports differences in both subjective and objective measures across couples, such as father–child contact and fertility intentions (Auriat, 1993; Coley & Morris, 2002; R. Williams & E. Thomson, 1985). A recent study that examined the living arrangements of children of divorced parents found fairly substantial differences in reporting between mothers and fathers (Lin, Schaeffer, Seltzer, & Tuschen, 2004). These authors highlighted the subjective nature of this type of reporting and how living arrangements can be complex and responses highly sensitive to the wording of the question.

At least two studies detail couple disagreement in the FF study. Waller and McLanahan (2005) found that one fourth of the romantically involved couples differed in their expectations about future marriage to their partner. If cohabiting partners have different levels of commitment, they may also choose to label their relationship differently (in terms of cohabiting or not), particularly if this is a subjective (and residential) distinction as alluded to in earlier research. Teitler and Reichman (2001) also found that 11% of couples disagreed on their cohabitation status at the child's birth, a measure we reexamine here.

A NEW LOOK AT COHABITATION AMONG UNMARRIED PARENTS

The FF is a birth cohort study of about 5,000 children born between 1998 and 2000 in large U.S. cities. The study oversampled nonmarital births and includes about 3,700 births to unmarried birth parents and about 1,200 births to married parents. Researchers interviewed new mothers at the hospital shortly after the child's birth, and they conducted interviews with new fathers at the hospital or as soon as possible thereafter. Both mothers and fathers were reinterviewed when the child was about 1, 3, and 5 years old.

This analysis focuses on whether parents were cohabiting at the time of the child's birth. For two of the analyses—those addressing the *how* and *when* questions—we use a sample of mothers who were unmarried at baseline and who completed both the baseline and 1-year interviews. The original sample of unmarried mothers was 3,712. Of these mothers, 88.7% responded to the 1-year follow-up interview, yielding a sample of 3,294 mothers. We dropped 9 cases in which the baseline interview occurred more than 1 month after the child was born, and we dropped another 25 cases in which the mothers were not asked about their cohabitation at birth. The final sample contains 3,260 mothers.

For the third analysis—the comparison of mother–father reports—we further restrict the sample just described to mothers for whom we have baseline and 1-year follow-up interviews with the father. First we examine whether reported cohabitation at birth (using the baseline interview) differs across mothers and fathers. Then we examine whether using the mother or father as the reporter of cohabitation would change our estimates of the demographic characteristics and union transitions (as of the 1-year follow-up). Union transitions come from the follow-up interview, necessitating this sample restriction. Sixty-five percent of mothers interviewed at both waves had a corresponding father interview at both waves, yielding a sample of 2,153 couples. After dropping 20 mothers who were not asked the question about cohabitation status at baseline, and after dropping 307 cases in which the couple was interviewed more than 1 month apart at baseline, the final couple sample is 1,826. At baseline, we asked parents whether they were living together "now"; a difference of 1 month could affect couple agreement. As it turns out, including these cases or the cases we lose because of father attrition at the 1-year follow-up would change the prevalence of reported cohabitation at the child's birth, but interestingly would not change the reported levels of agreement within couples.

The cohabitation rates presented are unweighted and, therefore, are not nationally representative of urban births. We have run the results with the preliminary sampling weights, and they are similar to those presented here.

How the Fragile Families Study Asks About Cohabitation

We begin by examining the effect of part-time cohabitors on the prevalence of cohabitation at the child's birth. At the 1-year interview, the survey asked mothers whether they and their baby's father were living together "all or most of the time," "some of the time," "rarely," or "never" at the time of the child's birth. One half of the mothers said they were living with the father "all or most of the time" at the child's birth (Table 2.1). An additional 9% of mothers reported living with the father "some of the time." If

TABLE 2.1
Prevalence of Cohabitation at Birth Based on *How* Question Is Asked

When child was born, were you and baby's father living together . . . ?[a]	
All or most of the time	50%
Some of the time	9%
All/most/some of the time	59%

Note. Sample includes mothers interviewed at baseline and 1-year follow-up (*N* = 3,260) in the FF. Cohabitation at time of birth as reported at the 1-year follow-up.

[a]Three percent of mothers, those who reported in the follow-up but not the baseline interview that they were married at the child's birth, are counted as "not cohabiting."

we treat living together "some of the time" as cohabitation, the prevalence increases by nearly 20%, from 50% to 59%, a nontrivial increase. These findings demonstrate quite clearly that part-time cohabitation is a relatively common phenomenon among unmarried parents, and we suspect that it is equally, if not more, common among childless couples. Thus, treating part-time cohabitation as part of the definition of cohabitation is likely to increase estimates of prevalence.

Whether we should count adults who are living together part-time as cohabiting is unclear. Knab (2005) suggested that couples living together part-time are more similar to dating couples than to full-time cohabitors in terms of their union stability and income pooling. Later in the chapter, we reexamine this conclusion to determine whether it holds for other characteristics and outcomes.

When the Fragile Families Study Asks About Cohabitation

Next we examine whether the prevalence of cohabitation is sensitive to when the question is asked. That is, does it matter whether cohabitation questions are asked retrospectively or concurrently? At the baseline interview, mothers were asked (yes/no), "Are you and (baby's father) living together now?" By this "current" measure, 47.7% of mothers reported that they were cohabiting with the child's father at the time of the birth (see Table 2.2). (As discussed earlier, the nationally representative estimate is that 51% of mothers were cohabiting at the child's birth.)

At the 1-year follow-up interview, researchers asked these same mothers a retrospective question about whether they were living with the child's father at the child's birth. Mothers who indicated they were living with the father at least part of the time were then asked, "When did you and (baby's father) start living together?" This date was compared with the child's birth date to determine whether the parents were cohabiting at the child's birth.[1] According to this retrospective question, 51.6% of mothers were cohabiting with the child's father at birth (see Table 2.2).

That we find higher rates of cohabitation in retrospective reports than in current reports is contrary to what we expected. We had anticipated that some less serious cohabitations would be forgotten, resulting in a lower prevalence rate for the retrospective report. One reason for the unexpected result may be that the retrospective question explicitly incorporates part-time cohabitation, whereas the concurrent question does not. If we estimate that roughly one half of part-time cohabitors would have included themselves in a yes/no question about cohabitation (see Knab, 2005, for an estimate of this), the retrospective reports of cohabitation would be 48.6%, compared with 47.7% for concurrent reports. This makes the concurrent and retrospective rates quite similar.

Similar rates of prevalence do not mean researchers would get equivalent results, however. Although the overall prevalence may be similar, the composition of the group of cohabitors may change over time. Indeed, we observe substantial reporting changes within mothers over time. Only 39% of mothers reported cohabiting with the father at birth in both the baseline and 1-year follow-up interviews (see Table 2.2). In total, 21% of

TABLE 2.2
Prevalence of Cohabitation at Birth
Based on When Question Is Asked

	Percent
Current report: question asked at child's birth:	
Are you and (baby's father) living together now?	
Responded "yes"	47.7
Retrospective report: question asked 1 year after birth:	
When did you and (baby's father) start living together?[a]	
Date preceded focal child's birth	51.6
Agreement (within mothers over time)	
Yes, both waves	39.1
Yes, current; no, retrospective	8.6
No, current; yes, retrospective	12.6
No, both waves	39.8

Note. Sample includes mothers interviewed at baseline and 1-year follow-ups (*N* = 3,260) in the FF. Cohabitation at time of birth as reported at the 1-year follow-up.

[a]Asked of mothers who reported at Year 1 living together at least "some of the time" at the time of the child's birth. Three percent of mothers, who now report being married at the child's birth, are counted as "not cohabiting."

mothers' baseline reports disagree with their inferred cohabitation at the 1-year follow-up.[2] Discrepancies are not evenly dispersed; mothers are more likely to "upgrade" their relationship (12.6%) than "downgrade" it (8.6%) (see Table 2.2). Given the systematic differences in reporting changes, this difference could affect the associated characteristics and union transitions.

The panel data allow us to uncover the sources of the discrepancies in reporting. Among mothers who downgraded their relationship status (reported cohabiting at the child's birth in the baseline interview, but reported not cohabiting at the child's birth in the retrospective report), we find three primary sources for the discrepancy. First, approximately 20% of the mothers report they were married at the child's birth, perhaps in an attempt to legitimize the birth; thus, they were not cohabiting, as reported. Second, 18% of the mothers report that they did not know the month or year (primarily the month) they started living with the father (see Endnote 1 for a description of how and when dates were imputed). Finally, 26% of the mothers report that they started living together after the birth, with most of the clustering occurring around 1 to 3 months following the birth. The remaining mothers (about one third) report that they were rarely or never living together at the time of the child's birth. If cohabitation begins because of an impending or recent birth, rates of cohabitation may be highly sensitive to imputation strategies and whether the question is asked currently or retrospectively.

Among mothers who upgraded their relationship status, 29% said at one year that they had been cohabiting part-time at birth. This implies that these mothers did not count themselves as cohabiting at baseline when the question required a yes/no response but did count themselves as cohabiting when the question explicitly allowed for part-time cohabitation.

Another interesting finding is that the mothers who upgraded their status had a mean cohabitation "start date" of 27 months prior to the child's birth. Only a small percentage of mothers reported a start date for living together within 3 months of the birth. The high rate of discrepancy between these measures may be the result of transitions into and out of cohabitations alluded to by Binstock and Thornton (2003), perhaps related to temporarily ending cohabitation around the time of the birth because of relationship issues or other support received by the mother. If this is true, cohabitation histories that ask only the start date of the relationship may overestimate prevalence at a given point in time.

Who Responds

Finally, we examine if the prevalence of cohabitation is sensitive to whether the mother or the father is the respondent. As noted earlier, for this part of the analysis we restrict our sample to mothers for whom we have baseline and 1-year follow-up interviews with the baby's father. This sample is more

TABLE 2.3
Prevalence of Cohabitation at Birth Based on *Who* Is Reporting

	Percent
Mother	
Are you and (baby's father) living together now?	
Responded "yes"	63.5
Father	
Are you and (baby's mother) living together now?	
Responded "yes"[a]	66.2
Agreement	
Both report cohabiting	59.7
Mother reports cohabiting, father reports not cohabiting	3.8
Father reports cohabiting, mother reports not cohabiting	6.5
Neither reports cohabiting	30.1

Note. Sample includes couples with both mother and father interviews at the baseline and 1-year follow-up (N = 1,826).

[a]One percent of fathers who reported being married at the child's birth (but for whom the mother reported being unmarried) are counted as "not cohabiting."

selective of committed couples than the sample used for the previous two analyses, and therefore we would expect the overall prevalence rate to be higher for this group. Because the purpose of this analysis is to compare gender differences rather than prevalence levels, we should not pay much attention to estimates of the latter. According to Table 2.3, 63.5% of mothers and 66.2% of fathers reported that they were living with the other parent when their baby was born.

Although the aggregate rates imply only a 2.7-percentage-point difference in mothers' and fathers' reports of cohabitation, the within-couple comparison indicates that approximately 10% of couples disagreed about their status. Thus, although the gender of the respondent may not greatly affect overall prevalence estimates, the reporter can potentially affect the characteristics and outcomes associated with cohabitation, which we examine in the next section.

CHARACTERISTICS AND OUTCOMES OF COHABITORS

In the previous section, we showed that estimates of the prevalence of cohabitation are sensitive to the ways in which cohabitation is measured. In this section, we illustrate how different measures can lead to different estimates of the characteristics and behaviors of cohabiting adults. Table 2.4

TABLE 2.4
Variation in Prevalence of Cohabitation at Birth and Related Outcomes Depending on *How*, *When*, and *Whom* Is Asked Question

	Percent Cohabiting	Are Black	Completed Any College	Are Married at 1-Year Follow-Up	Are Separated at 1-Year Follow-Up
			Percent of Cohabitors Who:		
What question is asked (N = 3,260)					
Cohabiting all/most of time	50.0	47.5	26.2	12.0	18.3
Cohabiting all/most or some of time	59.0	50.6***	25.7	10.9***	21.7***
When question is asked (N = 3,260)					
Current report	47.7	44.2	27.1	14.7	20.8
Retrospective report (date)	51.6	48.8***	25.9	11.1***	20.9
Who is reporting (N = 1,826)[a,b]					
Mother only	63.5	41.9	27.5	16.0	17.9
Father only	66.2	43.3*	26.8	17.1***	14.9***

Note. Asterisks represent results from *t* tests of mean differences: $*p \leq .10$. $**p \leq .05$. $***p \leq .01$.
[a]Includes only cases with both mother and father interviews at the baseline and 1-year follow-up.
[b]Characteristics and outcomes are of the mother/father as reported by mother/father.

reports the percentage of cohabiting parents who are African American, have completed any college, and have married or separated 1 year postbirth, using the various measures of cohabitation. We chose these demographic characteristics and relationship transitions because they commonly appear in the cohabitation literature. We use t tests to determine whether the difference between the measures is statistically significant.

Looking first at how cohabitation is asked, we find that when respondents are offered the more inclusive option (all/most or some of the time), the proportion of African American cohabitors rises from 47.5% to 50.6%. (T tests represent the difference in means between those cohabiting all/most of the time and those cohabiting some of the time.) The proportion of cohabitors who have attended college, however, does not vary by measure (see Table 2.4). Other characteristics that vary include immigrant status, parity, and whether the couple plans to marry (not shown in Table 2.4). Most striking, the more inclusive definition lowers the percentage of cohabitors who report being married at the 1-year follow-up, and raises the percentage who report being separated.

Looking at when the question is asked—either at the birth of the child (concurrently) or 1 year later (retrospectively)—those reporting cohabitation retrospectively are considerably more likely than those reporting cohabitation at the birth of the child to be African American (48.8% vs. 44.2%) (see Table 2.4). (Again, t tests represent the difference in means between those cohabiting based on the retrospective report only and those cohabiting based on the current report only.) Using the retrospective report, we also find lower rates of marriage (by 3.6 percentage points), but similar rates of union dissolution (21%). Again, there are no statistically significant differences in the percentage of mothers who completed any college across measures of cohabitation.

Finally, looking at whom we ask about cohabitation yields some differences as well. We find differences in the proportion of cohabitors who are African American and differences in union transitions across reporters. Fathers who report cohabiting at the child's birth are more likely to report marriage 1 year later than mothers (17.1% vs. 16%, respectively) (see Table 2.4). Cohabiting fathers are also 3 percentage points less likely to report union dissolution than cohabiting mothers (15% vs. 18%, respectively).

CONCLUSION

This chapter documents how the prevalence, characteristics, and behaviors of cohabiting couples may depend on how, when, and of whom cohabitation questions are asked. Cohabitation rates are lower when survey questions do not include part-time cohabitation, when they ask about current status, and when mothers rather than fathers are the respondents.

Reporting differences do not appear to be random. Consequently, different cohabitation questions are likely to affect our understanding of the characteristics and behavior of cohabiting couples. We expected that at the 1-year follow-up, mothers might "forget" short-term or part-time cohabitations, resulting in a lower rate of cohabitation retrospectively and perhaps explaining observed differences in cohabitation rates at the time of the child's birth between the FF and the NSFG. However, compared with the NSFG, we found similar to higher rates of cohabitation using the retrospective report and very high rates (greater than 20%) of changes in reports between the two waves. Given that the average time between interviews was only 1 to 1.5 years and many of these couples were still together, perhaps it was too soon for the "forgotten" cohabitations to emerge as a problem. It is clear, however, that mothers have difficulty recalling dates of cohabitations that began only within the previous year and a half and that occurred around the birth of a child, an important life event. "Land marking" life events usually aids in recall (Belli, 1998), but perhaps cohabitation starts are too "fuzzy" to pinpoint. Difficulties in reporting dates resulted in mothers both forgetting cohabitations and reporting cohabitations they had not reported at the baseline interview. Because of the inconsistencies in date reporting, even over this short period of time, imputations of dates in cohabitation histories may influence reported cohabitation at birth.

Although this study has provided some important insights into the difficulties of operationalizing and measuring cohabitation, it is important to recognize the limitations of our analyses. First, *when* we measure cohabitation is somewhat confounded by *how* we measure cohabitation. Our 1-year question about cohabitation at birth is not entirely parallel to our baseline question, insofar as the baseline question required a "yes" or "no" answer; whereas the 1-year, retrospective question explicitly included part-time cohabitation. However, the magnitude of the reporting changes was very large and common even among mothers who said they were living together all the time at baseline. Thus, we do not believe the problem is entirely because of the change in the question.

Finally, the sample is limited to parents and to births in urban areas, which makes us cautious about generalizing beyond this population. The meaning of cohabitation clearly differs between parents and nonparents, which suggests that our results would not apply to nonparents. That said, we suspect that cohabitation may be an even looser institution for nonparents, in which case our results would underestimate the problems associated with measuring cohabitation more generally. Unlike marriage and divorce, which are legal events with well-defined beginning and ending dates, cohabitation is a subjective concept. The more we learn about cohabitation, the more we recognize the variety that underlies this new family form.

Notes

1. If the month was missing, but the year was prior to the child's birth, the couple is counted as cohabiting. If the month was missing and the year was the same as the child's birth, the couple is counted as not cohabiting (or unconfirmed cohabitation). Most surveys would likely allocate a portion of these couples via imputation. If the mother reported at the 1-year follow-up that in fact she was married at the child's birth, this is counted as not cohabiting (or disagrees with baseline reported cohabitation).
2. The discrepancy rate reported here is approximately 5 percentage points higher than that found by Teitler et al. (forthcoming). We use the partially imputed (see earlier discussion) date report as our retrospective report of cohabitation, which potentially includes part-time cohabitors. Teitler et al. limited their comparisons to mothers who responded they were living together "all/most of the time."

3

Measuring Cohabitation in Add Health

Michael S. Pollard
RAND Corporation

Kathleen Mullan Harris
University of North Carolina–Chapel Hill

Changes in union formation in the United States over the last four decades are well documented but poorly understood. The U.S. Census Bureau and various national surveys have tracked high but currently stable rates of divorce, postponement of and recent declines in marriage, and the relatively recent rise in cohabitation (Bumpass, 1990; Cherlin, 1992; Fields & Casper, 2001; Fitch & Ruggles, 2000; Raley, 2000). The trends also indicate that young people continue to establish intimate relations with romantic partners, as rates of union formation, including marital and cohabiting unions, have remained fairly stable (Bumpass, Sweet, & Cherlin, 1991; Raley, 2000). Furthermore, although most individuals eventually marry at least once, more than one half of marriages formed between 1990 and 1994 began as cohabitations (Bumpass & Lu, 2000).

Because the rise in cohabitation has been swift and relatively recent, it has taken some time for federal statistics to officially measure and track these unions (see Casper & Cohen, 2000). Therefore, surveys have supplied the majority of data for documenting and interpreting trends in cohabitation (see Smock, 2000).

Although the problems of measuring cohabitation have been discussed with regard to census data (Casper & Cohen, 2000), measurement issues rarely arise in reviews of research on cohabitation using other types of survey data (see, e.g., Smock, 2000). Yet researchers routinely compare married and cohabiting couples in an effort to understand differences and similarities in these two union types (see, e.g., Brines & Joyner, 1999; S. L. Brown & Booth, 1996; Nock, 1995; Rindfuss & VandenHeuvel, 1990). Before we can better understand the significance of cohabitation for young couples today, we must assess the measurement and quality of data on cohabitation.

A new wave of cohabitation research examines the concept of cohabitation itself and the ramifications of its measurement (e.g., Casper & Cohen, 2000; Hunter, 2003; Knab, 2004; Manning & Smock, 2003; Teitler & Reichman, 2001; see also chap. 2, this volume). With the exception of Casper and Cohen's pioneering effort, which examined differences in cohabitation rates across five national surveys stemming from differing survey measures, all of the research cited previously relies on either qualitative research using small, nonrepresentative samples (e.g., Hunter, 2003; Manning & Smock, 2003) or the Fragile Families and Child Wellbeing Study (Fragile Families), composed of a birth cohort of children and their parents from the late 1990s with an oversample of nonmarital births. Although Fragile Families may be ideal for studying cohabiting parents, only one third of cohabitators have children under age 15. In addition, the majority of women in the Fragile Families study were poor, and 40% had less than a high school education and were racial-ethnic minorities (Teitler & Reichman, 2001). It is unclear whether results from the study apply to cohabitors in general.

In this chapter, we document cohabitation data from the recent third wave of the National Longitudinal Study of Adolescent Health, or Add Health, a nationally representative longitudinal study of adolescents and young adults beginning in 1995 that was funded by the National Institute of Child Health and Human Development (NICHD) and 17 other federal agencies. Add Health respondents were aged 18 to 26 in Wave 3 (2001–2002), a time of life when romantic relationships tend to become more serious and intimate as young people take on adult roles and responsibilities. Add Health employed several innovative methods to measure cohabitation and better understand relationship dynamics of cohabiting unions in ways that are similar to marital unions.

We present a variety of ways to measure cohabiting unions, both qualitatively and by the length of time a couple has lived together, and discuss the implications of these different definitions for the levels of cohabitation in the Add Health sample. Following work that suggests there is a gradual slide into cohabitation, rather than a discrete decision to cohabit (Manning & Smock, 2003), we provide a context for the murky transition into cohabitation among young adults. Finally, we distinguish four types of cohabitors (following Casper and Sayer's, 2002, argument that cohabitation may serve different purposes for different couples) and demonstrate the implications of treating these distinct types as a homogenous group when describing qualitative aspects of relationship intimacy.

THE NATIONAL LONGITUDINAL STUDY OF ADOLESCENT HEALTH

As noted, Add Health is a nationally representative study of adolescents in Grades 7 to 12 in 1995 who have been regularly interviewed over the years into young adulthood. The study selected a sample of 80 U.S. high schools and 52 middle schools with unequal probability of selection. Systematic sampling methods and implicit stratification ensured that this sample is representative of U.S. schools with respect to region of country, urbanicity, school size, school type, and ethnicity. The study selected a sample of adolescents and one of their parents from school rosters for in-home interviews, which were conducted between April and December 1995, yielding Wave 1 data for 20,745 adolescents aged 12 to 19. One year later, in 1996, all adolescents in Grades 7 to 11 in Wave 1 were reinterviewed in their homes for Wave 2.

In 2001 to 2002, the original respondents from Wave 1, now aged 18 to 26 and entering adulthood, participated in Wave 3 in-home interviews. The Wave 3 interview collected data on attitudes, behaviors, and outcomes in late adolescence and young-adult life, with particularly rich data on romantic relationships and union and family formation. Wave 3 interviewed more than 15,000 Add Health respondents, with longitudinal data over the various waves of interviews. See Harris et al. (2003) for more details on the Add Health design and longitudinal data.

For the present analysis of cohabitation data in Add Health, we do not impose any sample restrictions and use data from the Wave 1 and Wave 3 interviews, yielding a sample size of 15,197 men and women. We base our analyses, however, on varying samples of relationships, given that an individual may have multiple relationships and, therefore, contribute multiple observations to a sample of relationships. In all analyses, we use the Wave 3 sampling weights, which adjust for the complex sampling design and attrition to Wave 3.

Data on Cohabitation

Data on cohabitation come from two different sections of the Wave 3 interview in Add Health. One section uses the traditional approach of asking respondents for a history of all marriage and "marriage-like" (up to 10) relationships. This approach asks respondents to report beginning and ending dates of all such relationships, and, if they ended, how they ended. With the beginning and ending dates, event history data can be assembled and survival analysis of entry into cohabitation or marriage and durations of cohabitation and marriage can be conducted. It is important to note that Add Health identifies cohabitations by positive response to the question, "Have you ever lived with someone in a marriage-like relationship for one month or more?"[1]

A second set of data on cohabitation comes from the relationship section of the questionnaire. Add Health collected a relationship history at Wave 3 by asking respondents to list all romantic and sexual relationships in which they were involved for 3 months or longer in the last 6 years; the 6-year time period extends back to Wave 1, when data on romantic and sexual relationships were collected. The Wave 1 interview asked a series of questions about each relationship, including dates and length of relationship, the partner's demographic characteristics, whether the relationship was sexual, a detailed pregnancy and fertility history within the relationship, and the type of relationship (i.e., cohabitation [here assessed by "ever lived together"], marriage, or dating).

PLAN FOR DESCRIPTIVE ANALYSIS

We first construct life table estimates of the entry into cohabitation from the complete marriage and cohabitation history data available in the Wave 3 questionnaire. In addition to data concerns, we show that the way Add Health defines cohabitation (in terms of minimum coresidence duration and phrasing of the question) affects cohabitation estimates.

Much of the demographic work on union entry and exit (including the life table estimates here) assumes that the start and end dates of a relationship can be clearly situated within an individual's life course. However, determining the beginning of cohabitation is not simply a case of noting the date when partners "move in" together, as virtually all large surveys that include cohabitation do. Following Manning and Smock's (2003) qualitative work based on 115 individuals in Toledo, Ohio, who recently cohabited, we investigate the extent to which young cohabiting couples "drift" into cohabitation over an extended period of time, rather than move in together at a certain date.

Finally, Casper and Sayer (2002) noted that to compare cohabitors with married or single individuals, as is often done, is to conceptualize cohabitors as a homogenous group. Several authors have argued that this is not the case and that cohabitation does not necessarily serve the same purpose for all couples (Bianchi & Casper, 2000; Casper & Bianchi, 2002). Some cohabitors may view cohabitation as an alternative to legal marriage, some as a precursor to marriage, others as a trial marriage to evaluate a partner's marriageability, and others as an expression of being serious dating partners (S. L. Brown & Booth, 1996; Bumpass, 1990; Casper & Bianchi, 2002; Manning, 1993; McLanahan & Casper, 1995; Rindfuss & VandenHeuvel, 1990). Following Casper and Sayer's criteria, we are able to distinguish four distinct groups of cohabitors according to several measures of relationship intimacy.

ENTRY INTO COHABITATION

Using weighted data from the complete cohabitation histories, we are able to construct life table estimates of first cohabitations, cohabitation being defined as "living with someone of the opposite sex in a marriagelike relationship." Among women, we find differences by race and ethnicity. Figure 3.1 plots, by race-ethnicity, the life table cumulative probability curves for women by age (N = 8,123), that is, the proportion of females who, from age 12, have ever cohabited.[2] Figure 3.1 illustrates a considerable diversity in cohabitation experience. One half of the White women have cohabitated by age 23, whereas for Black and Hispanic women, the comparable age is 25. By age 25, only 40% of "other" women (primarily Asian) have cohabited. Although cohabitation is increasingly expanding at ages beyond that of the young adults included in the Add Health sample (Casper & Bianchi, 2002), the survey indicates that more than 16% of people aged 18 to 27 (men and women combined) were cohabitating at the time of interview, and that most had cohabited at least once by age 27. Although

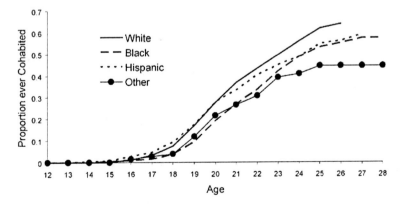

FIG. 3.1.   Entry into any cohabitation—women.

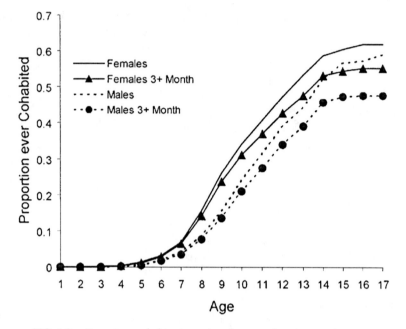

FIG. 3.2.   Entry into cohabitation using alternate duration requirements:
men and women.

the Add Health sample consists of younger respondents than other surveys
that address cohabitation, clearly these are crucial ages for cohabitation
experience.

It is important to take into account what minimum relationship duration
is used when defining a cohabiting union. The probability curves calculated
earlier were based on the respondents' reports of living "in a marriagelike
relationship" with someone for a month or longer. Figure 3.2 presents probability curves for men and women using both "1 or more" and "3 or more"
month restrictions. From these curves, it is obvious that increasing the
minimum length of cohabitation from 1 month to 3 months substantially
reduces estimates of cohabitation. With the 3+-month definition, the median age of cohabitation entry for women increases by 1 year, from age 24
to 25. Furthermore, under this definition, slightly less than one half (49%)
of the men enter cohabitation by age 28 compared with a median age of 25
when considering cohabitations of 1 or more months.

Figure 3.2 shows that there are many short-term cohabitations. The differences in probability curves of 1-month and 3-month minimum durations
are quite large, with 1- to 2-month cohabitations composing 15% of all
reported cohabitations. Further, these extremely short cohabitations are

neither cohabitations begun within 3 months of the interview date, and therefore censored by the survey, nor brief periods of cohabitation immediately prior to marriage; 10% of all cohabitations reported (weighted) by Add Health respondents lasted less than 3 months. Cohabitation is often described as a brief or unstable form of union because most cohabitations dissolve or convert into marriage within 5 years (e.g., Booth & Crouter, 2002; Bumpass & Lu, 2000). However, clearly the ephemeral nature of many of these cohabitations is still underestimated.

Finally, the probability curves in Figure 3.2 also demonstrate that these very short-term cohabitations occur for all the ages considered, rather than being characteristic of only young people. For both men and women, the divergence between all cohabitations and only 3+-month cohabitations grows across age, indicating that all age groups experience these short-term cohabitations. If these short-term cohabitations were associated solely with teenagers, for example, the probability curves would stop diverging and continue to run parallel beyond the teen years.

Figures 3.1 and 3.2 also call attention to another point: Some individuals report entering cohabiting relationships as early as age 13, reminding us that cohabitation, unlike marriage, has no legal age restrictions. Although these particular cases may represent a small segment of the population, 5.7% of men and 7.2% of women enter their first cohabitation by age 17. By age 18, the legal age of marriage, 11.3% of men and 16.5% of women have entered their first cohabitation. Thus, neglecting to measure entry into cohabitation from at least age 16 fails to account for a significant segment of first cohabitation experience.

Because, unlike marriage, no formal ceremony signifies the beginning of a cohabitation, couples themselves may be unsure of when they "officially" began living together (Macklin, 1972; Manning & Smock, 2003; Rindfuss & VandenHeuvel, 1990). Figure 3.3 presents the weighted "don't know" responses by men and women to the question of when the most recent cohabitation or marriage began and ended (month and year). More than 6% of applicable men and 3% of women could not recall the specific month they began to cohabit, and nearly 1.5% of men did not know the year. Levels of uncertainty regarding end dates were half those of start dates. In contrast, uncertainty regarding marriage dates is roughly 1% for men and negligible for women.

The relatively large percentage of respondents who did not know their cohabitation start date suggests caution when using dates in cohabitation research; in addition, these uncertain respondents were significantly more likely to be men and have only a high school education or less. However, there was no clear indication that cohabitors who did report specific dates were "heaping" on particular months (results not shown).

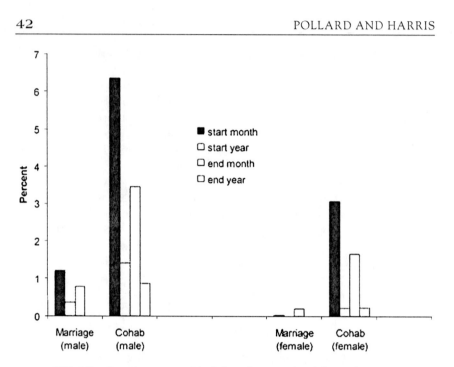

FIG. 3.3. Percent reporting "don't know" start and end dates of most recent marriage and cohabitation.

DEFINITIONS OF COHABITATION

Thus far, we have focused on the method Add Health uses to identify
cohabiting relationships, asking its survey respondents, "Have you ever
lived with someone in a marriage-like relationship?" Table 3.1, Panel A,
summarizes the responses for men and women (aged 18 to 27) in Wave 3.
Bumpass and Lu (2000) noted that cohabitation rates vary by age, race, and
educational attainment. This is replicated in the Add Health data, with
those with education beyond high school and Black or Hispanic respondents (relative to Whites) significantly less likely to report having "ever
lived in a marriage-like relationship," whereas age is positively associated
with the likelihood of an affirmative response (results not shown).

Studies have indicated that the wording of questions about cohabitation affects measurement (e.g., Casper & Cohen, 2000; see also Knab &
McLanahan, chap. 2, this volume). As definitions become more stringent,
cohabitation rates decline, especially for Blacks (Teitler & Reichman,
2001). In addition to the question identifying "marriage-like" relationships, the most qualitatively stringent measure of cohabitation in Add
Health, the study also asks respondents two less stringent questions about

relationships: "Have you ever spent the night together?" and "Have you ever lived together?" The data in Panel B in Table 3.1 are the percentages of those who have "ever lived together," given that they also report "having spent the night together," the least stringent identifier. Panel C presents the percentage having "ever lived in a marriage-like relationship" among those who also reported having "lived together." These questions were asked about *each* romantic or sexual relationship an individual reported. Contrasting these differing approaches to identifying cohabitation reflects the range of meaning individuals assign to cohabitation, and also enables a comparison of Add Health's primary cohabitation measure ("marriage-like relationships") with the measure ("live together") commonly found in other surveys, such as the Fragile Families.

Panel B clearly indicates that "spending the night together" does not equal cohabitation. Two thirds of the women and three quarters of the men who indicated having ever spent the night with someone did not report ever having lived with the person.[3] Men and individuals with some

TABLE 3.1
Prevalence of Cohabitation Using Alternate Definitions

Panel A. Reports of "Ever lived in a marriage-like relationship for one month or more" (Ages 18–27)

	% Women	% Men
Never	55.7	62.5
Yes	44.3	37.5
Unweighted N	8,008	7,149

Panel B. Reports of "Ever lived together" with someone for those reporting they have previously "ever spent the night together" with someone

	% Women	% Men
Never	66.2	74.5
Yes	33.8	25.5
Unweighted N	1,010	756

Panel C. Reports of "Ever lived in a marriage-like relationship" for those reporting they have previously "lived together" with someone.

	% Women	% Men
Never	7.1	9.0
Yes	92.9	91.0
Unweighted N	2,257	1,699

Note. Percent of respondents is weighted.

postsecondary education were less likely to say they had lived together, despite reporting they had spent the night in a relationship, whereas older respondents were more likely to have reported both (data not shown).

Panel C shows substantially greater correlation between reports of having "lived together" and "lived together in a marriage-like relationship" (93% of women and 91% of men said both about their relationships), but, as we might anticipate, the overlap is not complete; at least some respondents distinguish between living together and living together in a marriage-like relationship. Age was positively associated with reporting both, whereas those with higher education and those who were Black or Hispanic (relative to Whites) were less likely to state both (data not shown). It has been suggested that the meaning of cohabitation may vary by race or ethnicity, age, and education of the respondent (Bumpass & Lu, 2000; Manning, 1993; Raley, 1999; Smock, 2000). Our results offer some support for this notion; non-Whites and those with more education distinguish between "living together" and "living together in a marriage-like relationship," consistent with Teitler and Reichman (2001). Blacks, Hispanics, and those with more education are less likely to describe relationships as both "living together" *and* "living together in a marriage-like relationship," which may mean that they view cohabitation more formally than Whites and those with less education.

If researchers are interested in assessing strictly coresidential relationships, then relying on information about "marriage-like" relationships will likely underestimate the number of non-White relationships. Figure 3.1, for example, may underestimate Black and Hispanic cohabitations (strictly defined by coresidence). These factors are also associated with the likelihood of a cohabitation transitioning into marriage or dissolving (Manning & Smock, 1995; Z. Wu & Balakrishnan, 1995), and thus operationalizing "cohabitation" will affect estimates of these processes as well. However, if researchers are interested in relatively more significant personal cohabiting relationships, relying on "live-together" relationships may overestimate the prevalence among non-Whites.

"SLIDING" INTO COHABITATION?
COHABITATIONS AS DISCRETE HOUSEHOLDS

Manning and Smock's (2003) qualitative research describes the transition to cohabitation as more often a "slide" or "drift" into coresidence while maintaining multiple residences than a conscious decision to begin living together. Research based on the Fragile Families study indicates that 30%

of romantically involved mothers who were unmarried at their child's birth reported cohabiting part-time (Knab, 2005). Part-time cohabitation is not uncommon for couples with young children, but we do not know a substantial amount about the living circumstances of cohabitors as a whole. However, using Add Health, we can generate a comprehensive picture of these coresidential households.

Table 3.2 illustrates the "drift" and current living situations of cohabitors according to the "living with someone in a marriage-like relationship" definition. Panels A, B, and C reflect cohabitors' responses to questions about the period before they "lived together" with their partner. Respondents were not given specific definitions of when living together started, which provides an opportunity to determine how cohabitors view their own circumstances. Panel A indicates that the majority of men and women kept clothing or toiletries at their partner's residence before moving in. Logistic regression (controlling for age, race and ethnicity, gender, and education, not shown) indicates that older respondents and Hispanics (relative to Whites) were less likely to do so.

As shown in Panel B, cohabitors distinguish between "spending the entire night" and "moving in." Roughly 86% of cohabiting men and women spent the entire night together prior to moving in with each other. Panel C indicates that couples spent one to two nights (median) per week together prior to moving in (46% of men and 50% of women indicated they spent one to two nights together). More than 20% of men and women indicated spending five to seven nights together per week prior to moving in, a frequency at which most of the unmarried mothers in Knab's (2005) research reported as "living together all/most of the time" (p. 13). Again, older respondents were less likely to report spending the night together prior to moving in, as were Hispanics and Blacks (logistic regressions not shown).

Panels D, E, and F refer to maintaining other residences. Panel D indicates that 17% of male and 12% of female cohabitors maintain an additional residence where they "keep clothes or toiletries and sometimes spend the night." In contrast, panel E indicates that cohabitors thought that only 10% of their female partners and 8% of their male partners maintained such a residence. Men and non-White cohabitors were more likely to report maintaining an additional residence and to think their partner did the same (not shown). Add Health contains (self-reported) information on who lives in these additional residences, summarized in Panel F. Respondents primarily listed living with their parents or other relatives at their additional residences, although 3% reported living with another romantic partner. Indeed, 17% of female and 27% of male cohabitors indicated they were not "exclusively dating" their cohabiting partner. When we contrast the respondent reports of who lives at their additional residence with the

TABLE 3.2
Current Cohabitors: The Slide Into Cohabitation[a]

Panel A. Kept clothing or toiletries at the other's residence
before started to live together

	Men (N = 938)	Women (N = 1,431)
Yes	54.6	57.1

Panel B. Spent the night together before started to live together

	Men (N = 943)	Women (N = 1,434)
Yes	86.2	85.8

Panel C. "In an average week before moving in together, how often
did you spend the entire night together?" (If "yes" in Panel B)

	Men (N = 787)	Women (N = 1,200)
0	6.9	3.6
1 to 2 nights	45.9	50.3
3 to 4 nights	27	23.7
5 to 7 nights	20.2	22.4

Panel D. "Do you have another residence where you keep clothes
or toiletries and sometimes spend the night?"

	Men (N = 795)	Women (N = 1,194)
Yes	17.2	12.3

Panel E. "Does your partner have another residence?"

	Men (N = 795)	Women (N = 1,194)
Yes	10.4	7.9

Panel F. "Who else lives at the other residence?"[b]

	Respondents		Partners	
	Men (N = 153)	Women (N = 163)	Women (N = 93)	Men (N = 108)
No one	0	0	10.1	6.1
Parent	43.6	57.8	74.4	70.8
Relative	21.1	19.6	20.4	22.7
Roommate	18.7	10.3	12.3	11
Other romantic partner	2.6	2.8	7.1	2.2
Other	17.4	18.1	5	4.2

[a]Unweighted Ns and weighted percentages are shown.
[b]Respondents could identify any combination of other residents, and thus columns total over 100%.

TABLE 3.3
Living Arrangements of Current Cohabitations

Panel A. "Living on Own"—77.6% of current cohabitations (N = 1,798)
    "Alone"   2.7
    "With others"   97.2 (58.2% indicate more than one other person)

Panel B. "Living With Parents"—13.4% of current cohabitations (N = 313)

Panel C. "Living With Others"—9% of current cohabitations (N = 225)

Spouse	45.7%
Friend	19.2%
Relative	17.6%
Employer	0.8%
Other	16.8%

85.1% indicate more than one other person
68.5% indicate more than two other people

respondent reports of who lives at their partner's additional residence, we see a much higher identification of "parents" and "no one."

Manning and Smock (2003) noted that much of the current research on cohabitation is based on the major population surveys and, therefore, only infers cohabitation status from household roster membership. For instance, the POSSLQ method assigns a status of cohabitation when a household head lives with a person of the opposite gender, with no other adults aged 15 or older in the household (Casper & Cohen, 2000). Therefore, in situations in which cohabiting partners live with roommates or the household head is not a member of the couple, cohabitations remain uncounted (Baughman et al., 2002; Casper & Cohen, 2000; Manning & Smock, 2003).

Manning and Smock's (2003) qualitative research suggests that it is not uncommon for cohabitors to share a household with adults, such as parents or roommates. Table 3.3 presents a description of the types households in which cohabiting respondents currently live.[4] Among those who reported currently living with someone in a marriage-like relationship, 13% indicated living at their parents' home, 78% at their own place, and 9% at another person's home. Of those living at their own place, 58% reported the presence of people in addition to their cohabiting partner. Of those "living at another person's home," 85% reported that more people lived in the household than just their partner. Further, accounting for couples with children in the household (not shown) leaves only roughly 60% of currently cohabiting couples under the age of 27 in households with no other members apart from children; identifying cohabitations using POS-SLQ measures would fail to identify more than one third the households containing cohabiting couples.

TYPES OF COHABITATION

Discussions of cohabiting couples very often draw contrasts between co-habitors and singles, or more often, cohabitors and married couples (e.g., Smock & Gupta, 2002). Indeed, one of the common motivations given for studying cohabitation is to determine how it fits in the larger family system in the United States: whether it functions as an alternative to marriage, an alternative to singlehood, or in some other intermediary capacity (see Smock, 2000). Casper and Sayer (2002) made the important observation that "comparisons of cohabiting and married [or single] individuals rest on the assumption that cohabiting relationships are homogenous in terms of their purposes, goals, and meaning" (p. 4). As noted earlier, Casper and Sayer distinguished four types of cohabiting relationships, which we follow here: (a) as a substitute for marriage (the relationship will not likely end in marriage, but is unlikely to dissolve), (b) as a precursor to marriage (the couple has definite plans to marry), (c) as a trial marriage (the couple has no definite plan to marry and is evaluating their compatibility), and (d) as coresidential daters (see also Casper & Bianchi, 2002). Using nationally representative data from 1987 for cohabitors aged 19 and older, Casper and Sayer identified 46% of cohabitations as precursors to marriage, 29% as coresidential dating, 15% as trial marriages, and 10% as substitutes for marriage. Casper and Sayer also demonstrated the association between union transition probabilities and these different types of cohabitations.

Using Add Health, we can sort current cohabitors into these four catego-ries and contrast qualitative aspects of the relationships across these types to further describe differences among cohabitors. We identify cohabitation as a *substitute for marriage* when cohabitors are not engaged, do not want to marry, and are "almost certain" that the relationship is permanent.[5] We identify a *precursor to marriage* when cohabitors are engaged. We identify a *trial marriage* when cohabitors do not oppose marrying their partner, but are not engaged. The residual group we define as *coresidential daters*.

Using these operationalizations, we find that 11.6% of cohabitors are substitutes, 42% are precursors, 30.4% are trials, and 16% are coresidential daters ($N = 871$). In other words, our figures for substitutes and precursors are very similar to Casper and Sayer (2002), but we are unable to distinguish between trial marriages and coresidential daters using the same questions as Casper and Sayer. (The data Casper and Sayer used include a question ex-plicitly referring to cohabitation as a trial marriage period, which we do not have; we approximate the conceptual categories with the data at hand.)

Table 3.4 illustrates how several qualitative aspects of relationships vary across the types of cohabitation just identified. Add Health respondents were asked to indicate how close they felt to their current partner by select-ing an image from a series of seven pairs of overlapping circles representing

TABLE 3.4
Relationship Characteristics, by Type, Ages 18–26 (%)

| | Relationship Type[a] | | | | | |
	Substitute	Precursor	Trial	Coresidential	All Cohabitors	Marriage
Max. closeness	52.6	73.2***	55.8	20.4***	57.1	61.3***
"Completely" committed	79.1	89.0***	82.9	39.9***	78.1	89.1***

[a]Significant differences are compared with the "Substitute" category.
***$p \leq .001$

"self" and "other." The images ranged from no overlap to nearly complete overlap. Here we focus on respondents who selected the image indicating maximum closeness. Respondents were also asked, "How committed are you to your relationship with [partner]?" The responses ranged from 1 (completely committed) to 5 (not at all committed). We focus on responses identifying "completely committed."

Table 3.4 shows that closeness and commitment are highest for those cohabitations serving as a precursor to marriage and lowest for coresidential daters, whereas substitute and trial marriages assume a median position. Although this sequencing is not surprising and supports the validity of the categorizations, the diversity across types of cohabitation is noteworthy. Only 20% of coresidential daters reported maximum closeness compared with 73% of the precursor-to-marriage group. Similarly, 40% of coresidential daters reported being completely committed to their relationship in contrast to 89% of the precursors. The final column in Table 3.4 summarizes responses from all cohabitors as a single group, and although the responses approximate those of the substitute and trial marriage cohabitors, the 58% of cohabitors who are precursor and coresidential daters are poorly represented. Furthermore, unless we distinguish between types of cohabitation, we fail to recognize that some cohabitations (precursor and trial marriage) are as committed as marriages. We also fail to recognize, alternatively, that reports of closeness fall significantly below those of married couples, with the exception of precursors, who report being significantly closer than married couples.

DISCUSSION

Cohabitation is swiftly and increasingly becoming a normative experience, and researchers have been forced to respond quickly to keep up with the rapid changes. However, it is also important to step back and contemplate precisely what it is that is being studied. As an "incomplete institution," cohabitation lacks clear normative standards for participants, but also for those who study it in terms of how it is defined and measured.

Clearly, identifying a cohabiting couple is not as simple as noting whether they live together. In contrast to marriage, where couples are likely to live together on their own, the majority of young cohabiting couples appear to live with additional adults in the household. Furthermore, couples can live together in many degrees, ranging from spending the entire night together several nights a week, to living together, to living together in a marriage-like relationship. Cohabitation can be recorded differently for the same individuals using each of these approaches.

Individuals also vary in how they describe their own circumstances; those who are non-White, less educated, and younger are generally less likely to meet the more stringent criteria for cohabitation. For instance, although we may focus our research on individuals who live in "marriage-like" coresidential relationships, there is a sizable, nonrandom group of respondents who will say they "live together" but that their relationship is not "marriage-like."

We also cannot easily demarcate the beginning of cohabitation as when individuals move in together. A large portion of those who cohabit experience a protracted period of cohabiting only part-time and they do not necessarily consider themselves to be living together, despite spending five to seven nights together in an average week. It is therefore not surprising that asking respondents to provide dates for when they started living together entails a great deal of uncertainty. Finally, even after deciding how to identify cohabitors, we must keep in mind that they are not a homogenous group, that within the rubric of cohabitation exists a variety of distinct groups with distinct characteristics, and that making generalized contrasts to other groups (such as married couples or singles) can be misleading.

It is important to note that the respondents to Wave 3 of the Add Health study are still relatively young. Although results are representative at these ages, it is unclear whether they apply to all cohabitations. This is particularly an issue with the rising popularity of cohabitation following divorce. However, the results are still relevant in their own right, as a sizable proportion of people (roughly 20%) under the age of 27 currently cohabit and most have already cohabited at least once.

ACKNOWLEDGMENTS

An earlier version of this chapter was presented at the Counting Couples Conference II, National Institutes of Health, Bethesda, Maryland, November 13–14, 2003. Please send all correspondence to Michael S. Pollard,

RAND Corporation, 1776 Main Street, P.O. Box 2138, Santa Monica, California, 90407-2138. E-mail: mpollard@rand.org. We thank several anonymous reviewers for their comments. We gratefully acknowledge research support from the Carolina Population Center to Pollard through a postdoctoral fellowship and from the National Institute of Child Health and Human Development to Harris through Grant P01 HD31921 as part of the Add Health program project and Grant U01 HD37558 as part of the NICHD Family and Child Well-Being Research Network. This research uses data from Add Health, a program project designed by J. Richard Udry, Peter S. Bearman, and Kathleen Mullan Harris, and funded by Grant P01-HD31921 from the National Institute of Child Health and Human Development, with cooperative funding from 17 other agencies. Special acknowledgment is due Ronald R. Rindfuss and Barbara Entwisle for assistance in the original design. Persons interested in obtaining data files from Add Health should contact Add Health, Carolina Population Center, 123 W. Franklin Street, Chapel Hill, North Carolina 27516-2524 (http://www .cpc.unc.edu/addhealth/contract.html).

Notes

1. Unless otherwise noted, the term cohabitation refers to people who identified living "in a marriage-like relationship" with someone, but who were not legally married.
2. Cohabitation entry patterns for men are similar to those for women, although slightly delayed in comparison.
3. Although "ever lived together" is a less qualitatively stringent measure than "ever lived together in a marriage-like relationship," a smaller proportion of total *relationships* in Panel B report "living together" than the proportion of total *respondents* report "living together in a marriage-like relationship" in Panel A.
4. Respondents were asked "Where do you live now? That is, where do you stay most often?" Response choices included "your parents' home," "another person's home," "your own place," "group quarters," "homeless," and "other."
5. Respondents were asked how likely their relationships with their partners were permanent, ranging from 1 ("almost certain") to 5 ("almost no chance").

4

Studying Marriage and Commitment
With Survey Data

Paul R. Amato
Pennsylvania State University

Studies based on existing survey data offer a solid understanding of the demographic factors that predict marital dissolution. For example, one's own parents' divorce, early age at marriage, low socioeconomic status, and various forms of marital heterogamy (i.e., marriages between spouses who differ in terms of race, religion, education, or other important characteristics) are consistent predictors of divorce (Bramlett & Mosher, 2001; Bumpass, Martin, & Sweet, 1991). Attitudinal variables also are related to marital disruption. For example, religious individuals and individuals who voice strong support for the norm of lifelong marriage tend to have relatively low rates of divorce (Amato, 1996; Heaton & Pratt, 1990). Despite these advances, existing data sets have been less useful in describing the internal dynamics of marriage and individuals' subjective views of their marriages.

Although demographers understand the demographic and attitudinal factors that provide a context for marriage, the field knows relatively little about the proximal processes that cause some marriages to last and others to end in divorce. (Fig. 4.1 shows the current state of knowledge.) These processes in marriage largely represent a "black box" to demographers. In general, survey researchers have been content to leave these processes to family and clinical psychologists, assuming that once the demographic

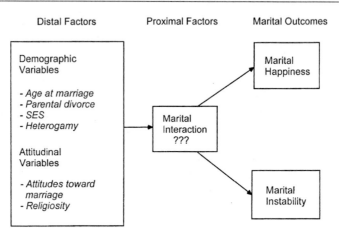

FIG. 4.1.   Distal factors, proximal factors, and marital outcomes.
SES = socioeconomic status.

predictors of divorce are understood, their work is finished. Indeed, some observers may argue that studying these processes is tautological. That is, once we know that individuals who marry at young ages are prone to divorce, for example, it is redundant to demonstrate that these relationships are troubled.

There are several problems with this line of reasoning. First, not all troubled marriages end in divorce, and many marriages appear to function reasonably well prior to marital disruption (Booth & Amato, 2001). Moreover, the various demographic and attitudinal factors that predict divorce may do so for different reasons. For example, individuals who marry at young ages may be especially likely to engage in infidelity (Booth & Edwards, 1985); parental divorce may lead children to reach adulthood with poor interpersonal skills (Amato & Booth, 2001); and holding nontraditional attitudes toward marriage and divorce may make it easier for individuals to leave troubled relationships (Heaton & Albrecht, 1991). To understand why demographic and attitudinal variables predict divorce, we must know more about the interpersonal processes that mediate these associations. (That is, we need a better understanding of the mechanisms through which demographic and attitudinal variables affect marital quality and stability.)

Although sociologists and demographers have not, in general, focused on the internal workings of marriage, many data sets contain information on marital happiness. For example, items on marital happiness (or satisfaction) appear in the National Survey of Families and Households (NSFH), the National Longitudinal Study of Adolescent Health (Add Health) (Wave 3), and the annual General Social Survey. This variable is important for two reasons. First, longitudinal studies show that marital happiness is a good predictor of divorce (Booth, Johnson, White, & Edwards, 1985). Second, marital unhappiness is linked to a variety of problematic outcomes, including inept parenting (Hetherington & Kelly, 2002), psychological distress (Bradbury, Fincham, & Beach, 2000), and poor physical health, especially among wives (Kiecolt-Glaser & Newton, 2001). Nevertheless, items on marital happiness provide only a partial understanding of how individuals subjectively evaluate their marriages. Moreover, knowing that individuals are happy or unhappy with their marriages reveals little about the patterns of interaction that serve as precursors to these subjective evaluations.

I suspect that family sociologists and demographers have tended to focus on marital happiness in prior surveys because they have not had a clear understanding of the interactional patterns that predict marital success and failure. I argue in this chapter, however, that family sociologists and demographers should build on the research conducted by family psychologists during the last two decades. Family psychologists, using largely observational methods with small samples, have produced a rich set of constructs related to marital functioning, and many of these constructs are good predictors of divorce. Moreover, many findings from this research tradition have been replicated by multiple studies, which indicates that we have a strong enough understanding of some of the key interactional processes to justify incorporating these variables into large-scale surveys. Developing survey-based measures of these constructs (i.e., reliable measures of marital process that require relatively few items) would substantially enrich our understanding of marriage.

I also argue in this chapter that the construct of marital commitment is underdeveloped, both theoretically and empirically. Moreover, studying marital commitment may prove to be as central to our understanding of marital quality and stability as the study of marital happiness has been. Although I frame my comments in terms of married couples, the same considerations apply to cohabiting (and perhaps dating) couples.

MARITAL INTERACTION

Most studies of marital interaction are based on observations of married couples discussing a problem in their marriage. Researchers typically videotape these interactions, and teams of independent coders later rate spouses' behaviors using objective coding schemes. These schemes often include categories for communication content (disagreement, showing support), tone of voice, and facial expressions. Some labs also include physiological measures, such as heart rate. The ability to study sequences of behavior makes it possible to identify recurring patterns of interaction that distinguish happily married couples from unhappily married couples. Moreover, these studies demonstrate that observations of interaction early in marriage can reasonably accurately predict subsequent divorce.

Several longitudinal studies have shown that the interactions of couples headed for divorce tend to involve more expressions of negative affect than do the interactions of stable couples (Gottman & Notarius, 2000). In fact, during interactions, happily married couples tend to exhibit about five positive behaviors for every one negative behavior. Unhappily married couples, in contrast, exhibit about as many negative behaviors as positive. These results suggest that it takes five positive comments to make up for the damage inflicted by one negative comment. Moreover, distressed couples tend to engage in long chains of reciprocated negativity (e.g., responding to anger with anger). Gottman, Murray, Swanson, Tyson, and Swanson (2002) pointed out that all couples, even happily married ones, engage in cycles of reciprocated negativity. Happier couples, however, frequently attempt to repair the situation by expressing humor, exchanging information, sharing feelings, finding areas of common ground, or appealing to larger expectations about the marriage. These attempts are most likely to succeed early in a disagreement, when negativity is still at a relatively low level.

For distressed couples, reciprocated negativity tends to be an absorbing state, one that is difficult to exit once entered. Spouses in distressed marriages appear to become so focused on the negative that they are unresponsive to other possibilities, even when their spouses use repair strategies. Moreover, distressed couples tend to escalate (rather than de-escalate as happier couple do) negative affect during episodes of conflict. This escalation often reflects a rejection of influence on the part of one (or both) partners. For example, when one spouse criticizes the other, the second partner may angrily reject the point or counter the criticism. In many distressed marriages, the escalation of negativity during conflict can be viewed as a power struggle between spouses.

Gottman (1994), in longitudinal research, identified four negative behaviors that are particularly good predictors of marital disruption. The first behavior involves expressing contempt (e.g., insults, mockery, sarcasm, and hostile humor); contempt can be communicated through facial expressions and tone of voice, as well as words. The second behavior is criticism, especially criticism that is harsh in tone. The third behavior is defensiveness, which involves an attempt to ward off or protect oneself from perceived criticism. Defensiveness can take the form of denying responsibility for a problem, engaging in counterattacks, or "whining." The latter involves statements such as, "Why are you always picking on me? I didn't do anything wrong." The final behavior is "stonewalling," that is, avoiding disagreements by emotionally or physically withdrawing from one's spouse.

Spouses in troubled marriages often exhibit a "demand–withdrawal" or "pursuer–distancer" pattern (Gottman, 1994; Hetherington & Kelly,

2002). In these marriages, one spouse (generally the wife) is habitually critical of the other's behavior. In response, the other spouse (generally the husband) denies the existence of the problem and physically or emotionally withdraws from the interaction. Withdrawal leads wives to intensify their criticism, resulting in even more withdrawal on the part of husbands. Eventually, many wives grow tired of this routine and become contemptuous of their husbands. Gottman and colleagues view this pattern as one in which wives engage in "negative start-up," and husbands refuse to accept influence from their wives (Gottman, Coan, Carrere, & Swanson, 1998).

Most observational studies have focused on negative interactions, based on the assumption that these behaviors are better predictors of divorce than are positive interactions. Nevertheless, some observational studies have shown that social support within marriage (showing affection, expressing agreement, and providing practical assistance) predicts subsequent marital outcomes, even after controlling for negative behaviors (Pasch & Bradbury, 1998). Indeed, some researchers believe that studies have underestimated the importance of positive interaction in predicting the long-term success of marriages (Bradbury et al., 2000).

Although the results of observational studies are intriguing, these data are difficult, time-consuming, and expensive to collect. It may take 6 to 12 months to train a team of coders to rate behaviors with an acceptable level of intercoder reliability. Furthermore, once trained, it requires about an hour to code 10 minutes of interaction (Rogge & Bradbury, 1999). Although observational methods are ideal for identifying the interpersonal dynamics that predict later marital outcomes, applying these methods on a large scale is impractical.

Given these constraints, some family psychologists have measured marital behaviors using questionnaires, mainly focusing on styles of communication and methods of problem solving. A few longitudinal studies indicate that questionnaire measures of interaction predict subsequent marital outcomes about as well as do observational measures (C. T. Hill & Peplau, 1999; A. S. Larsen & Olson, 1989). Rogge and Bradbury (1999) found that self-report measures and observational measures of marital interaction were equally successful in predicting marital happiness and stability during a 4-year period.

In summary, prior research suggests the utility of adapting or developing survey questions to measure behaviors such as contempt, criticism, defensiveness, withdrawal, cycles of escalating negative reciprocity, and the pursuer–distancer pattern. Measures of social support and positive interaction within marriage also may be useful. Although the findings from observational studies may advance our understanding of marriage, this research is severely limited by its reliance on small, convenience samples. Moreover, observational studies tend to overrepresent White, middle-class couples. Few large, representative data sets contain such measures. The NSFH contains a short series of items addressing disagreements and the manner in which couples respond to conflict. The Marital Instability Over the Life Course (Booth, Johnson, White, & Edwards, 1981) contains a series of items on the frequency of conflict and the existence of problems in the marriage. These data sets, however, do not contain items that directly measure the constructs that have emerged from observational studies.

Given the cost of large-scale surveys, family sociologists and demographers face the challenge of including measures of marital interaction that involve relatively few items. In a recent attempt to measure some of these dimensions within the context of a social survey, C. Johnson and colleagues (2001) included the following items in a telephone survey of 3,344 individuals in Oklahoma and three adjoining states:

1. My spouse criticizes or belittles my opinions, feelings, or desires. (*criticism*)
2. When we argue, one of us withdraws, that is, does not want to talk about it anymore or leaves the scene. (*withdrawal*)
3. Little arguments escalate into ugly fights with accusations, criticisms, name calling, or bringing up past hurts. (*escalation of negative reciprocity*)

Response options were *never or almost never* (1), *sometimes* (2), and *frequently* (3). Correlations between these items ranged from .38 to .55.

Table 4.1 shows the associations between several demographic variables and each of the three measures of negative marital interaction. Note that education was negatively related to criticism but not to escalating negativity or withdrawal. African Americans (compared with Whites) reported more escalating negativity and withdrawal in their marriages, but not more criticism. Latinos reported more escalating negativity than did Whites. Age at marriage was associated with less escalating negativity and withdrawal, but it was not associated with criticism. Duration of marriage was associated only with escalating negativity. These associations indicate that particular demographic variables are linked only with certain problematic marital behaviors. In contrast, cohabitation prior to marriage, use of public assistance, and religiosity were associated with all three forms of negative behavior.

To show the links between these behaviors and marital outcomes, I created a scale of marital quality based on two items, one referring to marital happiness and the other to marital satisfaction (alpha = .73). I created a second scale of perceived marital instability, based on five items that assessed whether individuals thought their marriage was in trouble, were thinking about divorce, had discussed divorce with their spouses, had discussed divorce with a friend or relative, or had consulted an attorney (alpha = .85).

TABLE 4.1
Unstandardized Regression Coefficients Showing Associations
Between Demographic Variables and Three Negative Forms
of Marital Interaction

	Escalating Negativity	Criticism	Withdrawal
Female	−.046	−.050	−.008
Education	−.008	−.027**	−.002
African American	.232***	.089	.283***
Latino	.129*	−.006	.070
Age at marriage	−.006**	.000	−.011***
Duration of marriage	−.006*	.001	−.003
Cohabitation	.124***	.104**	.085*
Government assistance	.247***	.200***	.226**
Religiosity	−.054***	−.072***	−.081***
Constant	1.812	1.620	2.224
R squared	.071***	.045***	.051***

Note. N = 1,920. Data are from C. Johnson et al. (2001).
$*p < .05.$ $**p < .01.$ $***p < .001.$

Table 4.2 shows the associations between demographic variables and
these two marital outcomes (happiness and instability), with and without
the three negative behaviors (criticism, escalation, and withdrawal) included in the equations. Comparing Model 1 (in the first column, with
negative behaviors excluded) with Model 2 (in the second column, with
negative behaviors included) reveals that the negative marital behaviors
reduced many of the associations between demographic variables and the
marital outcomes. With respect to marital happiness, adding the negative
marital behaviors to the model reduced the coefficient on happiness for
African Americans by about one half, and the coefficient for Latinos declined by about one fourth. The behavioral items completely accounted for
the association between prior cohabitation and marital happiness, as well
as the association between use of public assistance and marital happiness.
The coefficient for religiosity also was reduced substantially. These results
indicate that the three negative behavior items accounted for much of the
associations between demographic variables and marital happiness.

The results were comparable for perceived marital instability. The behavioral items accounted for most of the estimated effects on marital instability
of being African American, of cohabiting prior to marriage, and of using
public assistance. The coefficients for age at marriage and religiosity also were
reduced substantially. Once again, these results suggest that negative marital
behaviors help to explain why demographic variables are related to marital
quality and stability. It is impossible in this chapter to interpret each of the

TABLE 4.2
Unstandardized Regression Coefficients Showing Associations
Between Demographic Variables, Negative Marital Behaviors,
and Marital Outcomes

	Marital Happiness		Marital Instability	
	Model 1	Model 2	Model 1	Model 2
Demographics				
Female	−.126**	−.167***	.053	.094
Education	.015	−.003	−.023	−.008
African American	−.435***	−.216*	.336**	.138
Latino	−.375***	−.298**	−.036	−.120
Age at marriage	−.006	−.011**	−.017***	−.012**
Duration of marriage	−.020***	−.021***	.004	.006
Duration squared	.001***	.001***	−.001**	−.001***
Cohabitation	−.117*	−.017	.225***	.106*
Gov. assistance	−.292***	−.023	.363***	.115
Religiosity	.207***	.130***	−.185***	−.117***
Negative Marital Behaviors				
Escalating negativity	—	−.383***	—	.445***
Criticism	—	−.506***	—	.385***
Withdrawal	—	−.209***	—	.218***
Constant	−.113	1.998	1.033	−.874
R squared	.065***	.348***	.051***	.344***

Note. N = 1,920. Model 1 includes only the demographic and attitudinal predictors of marital happiness and instability, whereas Model 2 includes the marital behavior measures. Data are from C. Johnson et al., 2001.
*$p \le .05$. **$p \le .01$. ***$p \le .001$.

individual findings, and the results in Tables 4.1 and 4.2 are suggestive rather than definitive. For example, it is unclear whether results from the Oklahoma region can be generalized to other parts of the country. Nevertheless, these results suggest that including a broader range of marital behaviors in statistical models may explain why certain demographic characteristics place individuals at risk of having unhappy marriages or seeing their marriages end in divorce. More detailed research, especially work that attempts to distill the insights of family psychologists into survey questions, eventually may delineate the specific behavioral mechanisms (proximal factors) that link broad demographic factors to problematic (or successful) marital outcomes.

MARITAL COMMITMENT

Marital commitment implies an underlying set of related beliefs and feelings about one's partner and the marriage. It can be defined as the extent to which individuals hold long-term perspectives on their marriage, make sacrifices for their relationship, take steps to maintain and strengthen the cohesiveness of their union, and stay with their spouse even when their marriage is not rewarding. Commitment implies an obligation to others that can be abandoned only under extreme circumstances. Implicit in the notion of marital commitment is the sense that marriage has value that extends beyond the happiness of the individual spouses.

Many researchers define marital quality primarily in terms of marital happiness or satisfaction (Bradbury et al., 2000; Glenn, 1990). According to this view, marital happiness is the sine qua non of a high-quality marriage. Other dimensions of marriage, such as spending time together, the level of conflict, or perceptions of relationship problems, are sources of marital quality rather than forms of marital quality. A good argument can be made, however, that commitment is as central to what we mean by marital quality as is happiness. Consider a marriage in which both spouses are reasonably happy, but one spouse decides to leave the marriage because he or she has found an even more attractive partner. Most observers would not consider this to be a successful marriage. Now consider a marriage in which both spouses are unhappy with the marriage but want their marriage to work, reject the option of divorce, and decide to attend counseling with the goal of improving the relationship. Most observers would likely consider the second marriage to be in better shape than the first, despite the fact that spouses in the second marriage are unhappy. It is likely that the current focus among family scholars on marital happiness as the defining characteristic of a high-quality marriage reflects the culture of expressive individualism and self-growth that has become pervasive in American society since the 1960s (Bellah, Madsen, Sullivan, Swidler, & Tipton, 1985). Seen in this light, a focus on commitment as a central feature of marital quality represents a necessary corrective to the individualistic and hedonistic slant of much contemporary research on marriage.

Exchange theory recognizes that stability and happiness are different dimensions (Levinger, 1976). According to this perspective, a stable relationship might arise because spouses enjoy each other's company. In this case, the rewards of the relationship lead to marital cohesion. In contrast, other relationships remain together despite the fact that both partners are unhappy. In these cases, spouses may remain in the marriage because of barriers (e.g., not wanting to give up one's home or standard of living, concerns about one's children, or religious beliefs) or because no viable alternatives are apparent. Some exchange theorists view barriers and the absence of alternatives as factors that promote relationship commitment (M. P. Johnson, Caughlin, & Huston, 1999). One can question, however, whether it makes sense to say that individuals are "committed" to a relationship only because they feel constrained to remain in it. According to this latter view, actions that reflect commitment are engaged in willingly and reflect more than the existence of internal or external constraints on leaving the relationship.

Commitment to a relationship requires what psychologist Caryl Rusbult calls *accommodative behavior* (Rusbult, Bissonnette, Arriaga, & Cox, 1998). Accommodative behavior is when partners sacrifice their short-term well-being for the long-term stability of the relationship. Accommodation can take a variety of forms, such as dealing with unpleasant in-laws, accepting faults in one's partner, forgiving a partner for a transgression, or curbing an urge to retaliate when a partner criticizes. Individuals are accommodative because they are committed to the stability of their relationships, not because they are maximizing self-interest. Indeed, sacrificing one's self-interest makes sense only when individuals believe in the long-term viability of the relationship (Stanley, Markman, & Whitton, 2002). Accommodation is not the same as commitment, but it occurs frequently in committed relationships.

The measurement of commitment is not well developed. Researchers have developed several commitment scales that include items such as, "How likely is it that your relationship will be permanent?" (Lund, 1985), "To what degree to you feel committed to maintaining your marriage?" (Rusbult et al., 1998), and "I want to grow old with my partner" (Stanley & Markman, 1992). These scales, however, are generally highly correlated with measures of relationship happiness, and factor analytic studies show that questionnaire items assessing happiness and commitment tend to load on the same factor. In other words, marital happiness and commitment appear to be measures of the same construct. These studies demonstrate that commitment is difficult to disentangle from happiness when individuals' relationships are progressing smoothly. Under these circumstances, individuals will say that they are "committed" to their partners because their relationships are rewarding.

It is only when relationships are troubled, and spouses are unhappy with their marriages, that commitment comes into sharp focus. When confronted with unhappiness or tension in a relationship, individuals can respond in four ways. One possibility is to leave the relationship, a response that reflects the absence of commitment. A second strategy, one that reflects a minimal level of commitment, is to remain in the marriage but to disengage from one's partner or deny the existence of problems. A third strategy, which reflects a stronger level of commitment, is to stand by one's partner and optimistically wait, trusting that the relationship will improve. The final strategy, and one that reflects the highest level of commitment, is for couples to work actively on their disagreements with the goal of making their marriages satisfying again. In other words, commitment is reflected primarily in how couples react to stress in their marriages (see Rusbult et al., 1998, for a discussion).

TABLE 4.3
Percentage of Respondents Who Discussed Divorce With Their
Spouses During the Previous Year, by Level of Marital Happiness

	Marital Happiness			
Discussed Divorce	Low	Below Average	Above Average	High
No	90	98	99	100
Yes	10	2	1	0
Total	100	100	100	100

Note. N = 2,034. Each marital happiness category contains about one fourth of the sample. Data are from Booth, D. R. Johnson, White, and J. N. Edwards (1981).

Some large-survey data sets contain items on perceived instability or propensity toward divorce. For example, the NSFH includes a series of questions about whether one is thinking that the marriage might be in trouble, whether spouses have discussed separation or divorce, and the perceived chances of splitting up. The Marital Instability Over the Life Course Study, designed by Booth and colleagues (1981), contains the best measure of its kind: a 13-item scale that assesses cognition (thinking about divorce) and behavior (talking with one's spouse about separation, consulting an attorney, or having a trial separation). This scale is an excellent predictor of divorce; spouses who score in the top 10% of the distribution are eight times more likely to divorce within the next 3 years than are those in the bottom 50% of the distribution (Booth et al., 1985). Nevertheless, perceived instability (or divorce propensity) is related to, but not the same as, marital commitment.

Consider the data in Table 4.3, which come from the first (1980) wave of the study of Marital Instability Over the Life Course. Marital happiness is based on an 11-item scale that taps specific aspects of the relationship (happiness with the spouse as a companion, happiness with the sexual relationship) as well as an overall evaluation of the relationship. For presentation, I divided this scale into quartiles. The row variable refers to whether respondents have raised the issue of divorce with their spouses during the previous year. Note that when marital happiness is high (in the top quartile of the distribution), no one reported talking about divorce. (After all, why should they?) In contrast, among those in the bottom quartile (indicating they were relatively unhappy), 10% had talked with their spouse recently about divorce. The key question is why the figure is as low as 10%. (The results are nearly identical when I selected "thinking about divorce" rather than talking about it.) Some individuals may not have wanted to admit that they had discussed divorce. Other individuals probably felt constrained to stay in their marriages, because of either barriers or the lack of good alternatives. Others, however, were not considering divorce because they were committed to their marriages.

What happened to these relatively unhappy individuals 3 years later (in 1983)? Some—mainly those who were thinking about divorce—ended their marriages. Among those who stayed together, two thirds were still unhappy with their marriages. One third, however, were happier at the next interview, and 10% were substantially happier, shifting from the bottom quartile of the happiness distribution to the top 50%. One hypothesis is that unhappily married individuals who remained unhappily married were stuck in their marriages because of perceived barriers or the lack of good alternatives. Correspondingly, those whose happiness improved may have engaged in accommodative behaviors associated with high levels of commitment. They expressed loyalty and stayed with their partners, waiting for the bad times to pass, or they actively sought solutions to their problems. It is impossible to test these ideas with the existing data. However, the hypothesis that commitment can provide an engine not only to maintain marital stability, but also to recover from periods of unhappiness, is one that could be explored in the future.

Future surveys can measure marital commitment in two ways. First, it should be possible to develop a short sequence of questions that taps individuals' feelings of commitment. Previously developed scales could represent useful starting points, although it will be necessary to distinguish commitment to one's spouse from the barriers to leaving the marriage or the lack of good alternatives. To provide content validity, it will be necessary to delineate the central components of commitment, and to design at least one survey item to represent each component (Carmines & Zeller, 1979). In addition to more rigorous thinking, information on these components could be obtained from focus groups or from interviews in which spouses are asked to explain their views on commitment.

Second, survey items could assess the extent to which spouses engage in accommodative behaviors when addressing marital disagreements. As noted earlier, these behaviors (e.g., working to find solutions as opposed to ignoring problems or disengaging from one's partner) can be considered indicators of underlying commitment. Because commitment and relationship satisfaction are positively correlated, it would make sense to control for marital happiness in analyses to provide purer estimates of commitment effects.

CONCLUSION

The next generation of survey research on marriage (and cohabitation) would benefit from developing and incorporating measures of relationship interaction and commitment. Observational studies have revealed patterns of interaction that are good predictors of subsequent marital unhappiness and divorce. Furthermore, the construct of relationship commitment is underdeveloped, both theoretically and empirically. Incorporating valid and reliable measures of these variables into future data sets should make it possible to describe the behaviors and processes that link particular demographic variables to specific marital outcomes. Taking these steps would not only promote a closer dialogue between family demographers and family psychologists, but also provide a stronger basis for interventions to strengthen marriage, an important concern in an era in which promoting marital quality and stability has become an explicit goal of social policy.

5

Conceptualizing and Measuring Marital Virtues

Alan J. Hawkins
Brigham Young University

Blaine J. Fowers
University of Miami

Jason S. Carroll
Brigham Young University

Chongming Yang
Social Science Research Institute, Duke University

One of the most unmistakable features of the study of marriage is a reliance on self-report measures of marital satisfaction, happiness, or adjustment as indicators of the quality of marriage. This feature can be viewed as an attempt to allow research participants to define what is and is not a high-quality marriage. By leaving quality assessment to the research participants, investigators believe they can avoid making value judgments about marriage. Indeed, the received view of science is one of objectivity. Many social scientists, policymakers, and citizens hope that this objectivity can lead to professional practices that enhance marriages and reduce divorce.

An equally plausible explanation, however, is that the majority of marital researchers live in cultures that stress individualism. Within this worldview, individual happiness and fulfillment are paramount, and the autonomy to pursue self-chosen ends is essential. Individualism portrays marriage as a choice based on present satisfaction and perceived future gratification within the relationship. Commitment to the relationship largely depends on the rewards that it offers compared with alternatives. However, there is, in fact, no well-documented research that establishes this key premise; social scientists have simply assumed it from the beginning.

In this chapter, we present early findings from our attempt to measure the construct of marital virtues, one that provides an alternative lens to view marital quality. We draw on data from a larger study of a self-guided intervention to strengthen couple relationships during the transition to parenthood. The intervention emphasized the importance of marital virtues and their role in assuaging common challenges during the transition to parenthood.

INDIVIDUALISM AS A MODEL FOR STUDYING MARRIAGE: THE COMMUNICATION-SATISFACTION MODEL

Individualism focuses on the benefits that partners derive from the relationship, and views the contributions that partners make to a relationship as investments that will provide a return of satisfaction, intimacy, support, and reward. In the predominant social scientific understanding, these contributions occur primarily through communication and interaction and take the form of providing each other rewards, communicating feelings, using positive conflict resolution tactics, and so forth. Although there is some recent debate about the importance of developing relationship skills (Fowers,1998, 2000; Gottman, Driver, & Tabares, 2002), some researchers (e.g., Markman, Resnick, Floyd, Stanley, & Clements, 1993) see the ability to communicate well as a technical matter, where spouses learn positive communication and conflict resolution skills in order to foster a satisfying pattern of interaction that leads to relationship commitment. We refer to this as the communication-satisfaction model of marriage.

The focus on communication and satisfaction is so commonsensical in individualist societies that it is seldom questioned. It may even be difficult for many investigators to imagine a reasonable alternative perspective on marriage. The predominance and the naturalness of this approach, however, should not blind us to the fact that it is not the only model of marriage in human culture. The importance of romantic love, communication, emotional intimacy, and relationship satisfaction as central to the quality of marriage is a relatively recent development in the history of marriage (E. J. Carlson, 1994; May, 1980; Mintz & Kellog, 1988; Phillips, 1988; Stone,

1979). The widespread practice of arranged marriages makes it clear that a love-communication-satisfaction model of marriage is culturally and historically relative.

Of course, humans no doubt are, at least in part, motivated by pleasurable experiences, and contemporary marriage is one of the most important sources of feeling good. The real problem arises from the fact that researchers by and large present the individualistic perspective as a comprehensive and sufficient description of marriage, rather than as one framework among many.

Evidence that researchers favor a communication-satisfaction model comes from a study by Fowers, Bucker, Calbeck, and Harrigan (2003), who analyzed more than 2,200 quantitative studies spanning 10 years of marital research. They also analyzed the measurement procedures in a subset of 200 of these studies. By a very wide margin, the most frequently referenced terms and most frequently measured constructs were satisfaction and other measures of subjective evaluation. The second most common set of terms and measures was related to communication (communication, conflict, interaction, problem solving). Other terms identified included, in descending order, gender, power/violence, general affective terms (emotion, love, feelings, anger, etc.), cohesion/intimacy, sexual, cognitive (attribution, belief), and, in ninth place, commitment.

The relative lack of attention to relationship commitment is particularly illuminating, given its importance in marriage. The content analysis revealed that relationship satisfaction was mentioned and measured between 12 and 26 times as frequently as relationship commitment. In addition, the studies rarely mentioned any personal strengths that spouses might bring to the marriage, such as maturity, devotion, loyalty, generosity, dedication, goodwill, or sacrifice. Similarly, the studies seldom mentioned or measured features of the relationship that transcend individual satisfaction (e.g., "we-ness," cooperation, teamwork).

Of course, several studies have confirmed the associations between communication, positive affect, positive cognitions, intimacy, marital satisfaction, and marital stability, which supports the plausibility of the communication-satisfaction model of marriage (Bray & Jouriles, 1995; Fowers & Olson, 1986; Gottman, 1999; Larsen & Olson, 1989). The empirical support for associations among these variables is relatively well established and may tempt one to ignore the narrowness in the commonsense definition of a good marriage.

Yet, the overwhelming emphasis on personal emotional experience as the sine qua non of a good marriage raises the question of how this model of marriage came to predominate. Why is there such a strong consensus about the communication-satisfaction approach to marriage? Why has research placed such a premium on individual satisfaction in marriage? What are the other models of marriage against which the communication-satisfaction model has been compared? On what basis should we assume that the communication-satisfaction model is the best model?

Contemplating the prevalence of satisfaction, communication, and intimacy in marital research might well lead the field to recognize the strong similarity between the communication-satisfaction model of marriage in the research and the cultural ideals, especially for emotional gratification, surrounding marriage in individualist-based societies (Fowers, 1993, 1998, 2000; Furstenberg & Cherlin, 1991; Popenoe & Whitehead, 2001; Richardson, Fowers, & Guignon, 1999).

To the degree that the social science of marriage is focused on the personal satisfaction of the spouses, researchers may find themselves in the problematic position of perpetuating this cultural view of marriage rather than providing a more reflective perspective on it. To the extent that disappointments and overly high expectations in marriage play a role in divorce decisions, the professional emphasis on the emotional side of marriage may even exacerbate the already inflated expectations of marriage. Moreover, researchers' view that rewards are spouses' primary motive might encourage individuals to operate primarily from self-interest, concerned with maximizing their personal fulfillment. In other words, social scientists may be throwing gasoline on the fire with our obsession with marital happiness rather than providing an independent account of marriage.

Some scientists will cry foul at this reasoning. They might argue that it is not their place to question or criticize social mores or values. They are only attempting to describe and explain the social world as it is. Their job is to simply work within those social realities and let people make their own decisions about values.

This scientific disclaimer misses the point, however. Many authors believe that the prevalence of individualism is at the heart of the confusion and problems we are currently experiencing with marriage (Bellah et al., 1985; Fowers, 2000; Furstenberg & Cherlin, 1991; Popenoe & Whitehead, 2001; Richardson et al., 1999; Whitehead, 1997). Not only do social scientists fail to question individualism, they actually endorse it by conducting research that assumes the centrality of the individual and sees marriage primarily as a source of individual benefit. To the extent that the science of marriage adopts an individualistic understanding of marriage as a reality, researchers convey the idea that individual benefits *are* the ultimate reality. In so doing, they fail to recognize that the importance of emotional fulfillment in marriage is a historical construction rather than the real truth about marriage.

Some research has offered alternatives to the predominant model of marriage that portray a more complete and somewhat less culturally biased view of marriage. Fowers (1998, 2000) argued that personal strengths or virtues, such as generosity, loyalty, and justice, are key to good marriages. Other personal strengths include marital competence (L'Abate, 1997), goodwill (Gottman, 1999), self-control, wisdom, and humility (Strom, 2003), and dedication and commitment (Stanley, 1998). These personal strengths may foster a willingness to sacrifice for the sake of the relationship (Hargrave, 2000; Van Lange et al., 1997). Characteristics that reflect these personal strengths include generosity, loyalty, sacrifice, devotion, maturity, and goodwill. Attention to spousal strengths such as these expand our understanding of marriage by devoting greater attention to the ways that the partners contribute to the quality of the relationship as well as the benefits they derive from it.

A second conceptualization of marriage emphasizes the corporate aspects of marriage, described variously as "we-ness" (Buehlman, Gottman, & Katz, 1992; Carrere, Buehlman, Gottman, Coan, & Ruckstuhl, 2000; Hargrave, 2000), character friendship or partnership (Fowers, 2000), communal relationships (Clark, Mills, & Powell, 1986), and cognitive interdependence (Agnew, Van Lange, Rusbult, & Langston, 1998). Characteristics of this conceptualization include partnership, teamwork, cooperation, collaboration, and coordination.

Current research is identifying components of spousal interaction that are quite consistent with a spousal-strength view. Character friendship is a spousal strength that disposes spouses toward teamwork and concern with their spouse's well-being (Fowers, 2000). Communication is particularly conducive to a high-quality relationship when spouses treat each other as friends and seek to work together on problems rather than approach difficulties as adversaries. Gottman and his colleagues (Gottman, 1999; Gottman et al., 1998) have identified actions they call "turning toward" and "repair attempts" that exemplify a friendship approach to communication. The ability to maintain goodwill and seek common ground is essential to good communication.

Generosity, or the willingness to give of oneself freely to the partner, is another important spousal strength. Several studies have shown that being generous with one's spouse in small ways is strongly related to relationship strength. Spouses who see the best in their partners are happier with their relationships (Fowers, Lyons, & Montel, 1996; Murray, Holmes, & Griffin, 1996). Similarly, spouses who accommodate their partners (Wieselquist, Rusbult, Foster, & Agnew, 1999), who are willing to sacrifice for the relationship (Van Lange et al., 1997), who feel understood and appreciated (Hawkins, Marshall, & Allen, 1998; Reis, Sheldon, Gable, Roscoe, & Ryan, 2000), and whose accomplishments are met with celebration (Gable, 2003) have stronger, happier relationships.

In a recent study of relationship competence, Carroll (2004) found that respondents' reports of loving, kind, and compassionate actions on behalf of their partners and their perceptions of their mate's loving, kind, and compassionate actions on their behalf were central to their ability to negotiate with each other and to their relationship satisfaction. This suggests that partners' personal strengths, goodwill, and generosity may play a critical role in the quality of relationships. In a qualitative investigation of family strengths among dual-earner couples, valuing family time and the existence of partnership in the marriage emerged as the most prominent theme in how these couples maintain their relationships (Haddock, Zimmerman, Ziemba, & Current, 2001). Respondents described partnership in terms of mutual decision making, respect, and appreciation for each other. These studies highlight the possibility that marital quality may be as dependent on what the partner gives to the relationship as to what spouses receive from it.

An intriguing possibility worth exploring is that personal strengths and virtues that individuals offer to the relationship may be strongly related to parenting behavior and children's well-being. A substantial body of research confirms that marital quality, as measured by reports of satisfaction and the emotional quality of the rewards of the relationship, affects the quality of parenting, especially for mothers, and the quantity of parenting, especially for fathers (M. Carlson & McLanahan, 2002; Cummings & Davies, 1994). However, the behavioral elements captured by measures of marital virtues, such as generosity and loyalty, may generalize easily to positive parenting behavior, and may be a stronger predictor of parenting behavior than are the psychological elements and emotional feelings about the marriage captured by most measures of relational quality. If this hypothesis is confirmed by future research, interventions targeting marital virtues may also translate more readily into better outcomes for children, a critical goal for marriage education.

These spousal strengths appear to contribute to a stronger relationship, and marital research must begin to focus more on the relationship itself rather than on the partners' self-reports of satisfaction and intimacy only and self-reports or observations of communication behaviors. The relationship itself can be studied in terms of the emergence of the couple's identity as a unit and in terms of the degree to which partners coordinate their activities. Investigations of concepts such as we-ness, couple identity, and cognitive interdependence would focus more on the strength of the bond between spouses than the individuals' emotional states as indicators of marital quality.

There are hints in current research that spousal strengths or virtues are an integral aspect of high-quality marriages. This topic, however, is in its infancy and requires much more research. It is one thing to offer a conceptual critique of a hole in the research on marriage. It is another to offer a few shovels of dirt to begin filling the hole. The first few shovels will need to build measurement tools capable of reliably and validly capturing the construct of interest, in this case, marital virtues.

We offer a first attempt to operationalize some key constructs consistent with a marital-virtues model. Virtues are traits that make it possible to pursue worthwhile goals. Several virtues seem important in pursuing the goal of having a high-quality marriage. Marital researchers are beginning to recognize the importance of the virtue of friendship, which includes having shared goals and engaging in teamwork (Buehlman et al., 1992; Carrere et al., 2000). Generosity is another key virtue for marital quality. Generosity involves giving more than is required to one's spouse or relationship. Instances of generosity include seeing what is best in one's spouse, the gifts of forgiveness and acceptance (Christensen & Jacobsen, 2000), making sacrifices for the relationship, and giving appreciation (Fowers et al., 1996; Gable, 2003; Van Lange et al., 1997). Similarly, being characteristically fair and loyal with one's spouse seems crucial to having a good marriage (Hawkins et al., 1998). These virtues are evident in the characteristic actions of spouses who have devoted themselves to a high-quality marriage. Thus, these character strengths should be observable to others, including the spouse.

With improved measurement techniques, we can move on to studies that compare a marital-virtues model with the communication-satisfaction, or individualistic-rewards model, helping to advance our understanding of marriage and relationships.

METHODS

Sample and Procedures

As noted in the introduction, the data reported here are from a larger study of an intervention designed to strengthen couples' relationships as the birth of their first child approached. Over a period of about 9 months, the study recruited 155 couples who were enrolling in childbirth education classes at three hospitals in Utah County, Utah. The childbirth class fee of $45 was waived for study participants.

Couples agreed to complete a battery of assessments at four points: before the childbirth class (T1), immediately following the class (T2), at 3 months (T3), and at 9 months (T4) following the birth of their child. (Data for this measurement study are from the first three waves.) Trained research assistants surveyed couples in their homes.

Table 5.1 summarizes various characteristics of the sample. The age range of individuals in this sample was from 19 to 41 years for the men and from 19 to 33 years for the women. Average age among husbands was 25, and

TABLE 5.1
Demographic Data for Sample

Demographic Variable	Mean N = 310	SD	Range
Age:			
Men	25.3	3.21	19–41
Women	24.0	2.83	19–33
Ethnicity:			
White (%)	91		
Hispanic (%)	5		
Asian/Islander (%)	3		
Native American (%)	1		
Education:			
Some high school (%)	1		
High school degree (%)	7		
Some college (%)	52		
College degree (%)	37		
Graduate degree (%)	3		
Current students:			
Men (%)	62		
Women (%)	17		
Current employment:			
Men (%)	94		
Women (%)	77		
Occupational category:			
Managerial, specialty (%)	22		
Technical, sales (%)	26		
Service occupation (%)	18		
Other (%)	35		
Hours per week in paid employment:			
Men	35.4	14	0–84
Women	32.1	11.6	0–55

average age for wives was 24. Compared with national reports, our sample of first-time parents is young. According to the U.S. Census Bureau (2000b), the average age of parents at the birth of their first child is 29 for husbands and 27 for wives. Nearly three fourths (73%) of the husbands in our sample were 26 or younger at T1; 61% of the wives were 24 or younger.

The relative lack of racial and ethnic diversity (91% were White) reflects the study's communities. More than 90% of residents in Utah Valley are members of the Church of Jesus Christ of Latter-day Saints (Mormons). Approximately one half (52%) of the sample indicated that they had completed some college education, with 40% indicating they had a college degree. Only a small proportion (1%) of our sample did not receive a high school diploma. Utah Valley has a large population of college students, and 62% of the husbands and 17% of the wives were students at the first interview. A large percentage of the sample (94% of men and 77% of women) was employed at the time of the first interview. The average reported number of hours spent in paid employment each week at T1 was 33.9 for our entire sample; 35.4 hours for men and 32.1 hours for women.

Measuring Marital Virtues

Because we found no existing instrument to adequately assess the construct of marital virtues, we developed a new measure. We designed the Marital Virtues Profile (MVP) to capture a profile of individual and relationship virtues, as articulated by Fowers (2000), that contributes to marital quality and stability.

Although direct observation of marital behavior generally produces stronger effects in studies of marriage (Markman et al., 1993; Stanley et al., 2001), it proved too challenging for this study. First, observational studies require clearly defined behaviors that can be observed by trained researchers in a limited period of time. Observational studies of marital interaction, for example, typically create a situation for couples to discuss, such as a problem they are currently experiencing, and researchers carefully and systematically observe communication and personal interactions. These communication patterns certainly would reflect, in part, underlying constructs of marital virtues, but it is unlikely that they are the most important manifestations of strengths and virtues. A wider range of situations and time frames seemed necessary to adequately measure the construct.

Yet we were also dubious about the value of a self-report measure of personal strengths and marital virtues. It is not that individuals are incapable of honestly reporting these characteristics, but they are certainly biased, bathing their actions in a positive light and giving themselves the benefit of the doubt. Hence, we settled on a strategy of spousal reports of partners' strengths and virtues. Although spouses' ratings also can be biased, they were more likely to produce greater variation. Moreover, a spouse's report seems more consistent with the construct of marital virtues and is a more demanding way to assess it. That is, a marital virtue should manifest itself to the spouse, not just reside in one's head and heart. Asking the partner to report requires an "outsider" to see or feel the spouse's virtuous behavior. Partner-report items, moreover, often correlate more strongly with outcome measures than self-report measures (Busby, Holman, & Taniguchi, 2001; Strom, 2003). Using partner reports also offers the benefit of reducing the potential for method variance in correlational analyses.

Measurement Structure.   We included in our survey 32 partner-report items intended to capture various indicators of marital virtues, and 8 items assessing relationship constructs, such as sense of partnership and shared vision. Initial exploratory factor analyses indicated that about 14 of the 40 items did not work particularly well in our pilot study. An interpretable factor structure did emerge from the remaining 26 items. Six factors, with acceptable to good internal consistency reliability, emerged from a promax rotation that corresponded reasonably well with many of the virtues that Fowers (2000) discussed. (More details on these subconstructs are presented in the Discussion.) The factors were highly correlated, however, indicating that a second-order model, with the six factors as indicators of a global relational-virtues construct, would likely fit the data well.

With some initial confidence that our instrument was measuring these relationship virtues, we proceeded to a more rigorous, confirmatory test of the MVP's factor structure, as well as tests of spouse and time invariance. We tested a second-order factor model based on the exploratory analysis described previously. To examine the measurement invariance between husbands and wives as well as measurement invariance across time, we conducted a set of confirmatory factor analyses using structural equation modeling. (In all these models, we correlated the error terms of husbands' and wives' corresponding items to model the likely dependency in the data.)

Measurement Invariance. To examine measurement invariance between husbands and wives, we estimated the measurement of the constructs for both husbands and wives with the first three waves of data. These three models had no equality constraints on the factor loadings for husbands and wives. We next estimated three models with equality constraints. We compared the constrained model for each wave of data with its unconstrained model in terms of chi-square differences corresponding to the differences in degree of freedom. A significant increase in the chi-square indicated that certain factor loadings did not vary across the two informants. Wherever we found a significant chi-square increase, we compared additional models with certain release of the equality constraints on the factor loadings with the unconstrained model to identify which items had variant loadings between the two informants. The first- and second-order standardized factor loadings are listed in Table 5.2.

We found only two items with significantly different factor loadings between husbands and wives at T1; we found no significantly different factor loadings between husbands and wives at T2 or T3. Accordingly, we concluded that the measure worked similarly for both husbands and wives (spousal invariance).

Furthermore, to examine measurement invariance across time, we separated husbands and wives. We then specified the measurement models to include T1 and T2 measures, and then T1 and T3 measures, respectively. (The relatively small sample size constrained our ability to estimate all these parameters simultaneously.) We did not constrain the first set of models to have equal factor loadings between T1 and T2 or between T1 and T3. We did constrain the second set of models across the two waves. The model comparisons based on the chi-square difference tests indicated certain factor loadings changed at T3 for wives and at T2 for husbands. We further compared models with more release of the equality constraints with unconstrained models to identify individual items that changed in factor loadings. The goodness-of-fit indices of the unconstrained models and chi-square increase for the constrained models are listed in Table 5.3. The results indicate that only three items changed significantly over time in their factor loadings. The relative invariance of the vast majority of factor loadings between the two measurements indicates that the measures are also reliable over a time period of about 6 months (time invariance).

Measurement Reliability.   We then calculated Cronbach's alpha coefficients as an estimate of internal consistency reliability for the six first-order factors and the single second-order factor composing the MVP for husbands and wives for the first three times of measurement (see Table 5.3). Cronbach's alphas for the six first-order factors ranged from 0.77 to 0.89 for husbands across the three times of measurement (average alpha = 0.82), and from 0.61 to 0.91 for wives (average alpha = 0.81). An overall Cronbach's alpha for a global relational-virtues scale that is composed of all items ranged from 0.92 to 0.94 for husbands and from 0.92 to 0.93 for wives.

Overall, the MVP subscales and overall scale appear to have good internal consistency. A more stringent test of instrument reliability, however, is test–retest reliability. Hence, we computed correlations between the overall MVP scale at T1 and T2 (about 8 weeks apart) for husbands and wives in the control group. (Because this study was part of a program evaluation study, about 100 couples were assigned to two treatment groups. These couples received an intervention after the initial assessment at T1 that attempted to strengthen these marital virtues. Accordingly, we deemed it inappropriate to include treatment-group participants' scores in this test–retest reliability analysis.) The stability coefficient for the overall MVP for husbands was 0.80, and for wives, 0.83.

Measurement Validity.   We also tested the construct validity of the MVP. First, we looked at simple correlations between the MVP and theoretically related measures. For instance, the MVP Total scale (T1) was strongly correlated with the Revised Dyadic Adjustment Scale (RDAS) (Busby, Crane, Larson, & Christensen, 1995), a common measure of marital quality (husbands' reports of wives' virtues, $r = 0.78$; wives' reports of husbands' virtues, $r = 0.70$). Similarly, the MVP Total was strongly correlated with a reliable marital-satisfaction scale (husbands, $r = 0.73$; wives, $r = 0.74$) and a reliable marital-instability scale (thoughts about ending

TABLE 5.2
Confirmatory Factor Analysis of the Marital Virtues Profile: Standardized Factor Loadings, Alpha Reliability Coefficients, for Husbands and Wives across Measurement Times for Various Models

Factor/Contents	Model 1 (Time 1)		Model 2 (Time 2)		Model 3 (Time 3)	
	Wives	Husbands	Wives	Husbands	Wives	Husbands
Factor I: Other-centeredness (fairness, understanding, sacrifice)	Alpha = .84	Alpha = .79	Alpha = .86	Alpha = .85	Alpha = .85	Alpha = .80
My partner recognizes when I am feeling that things are unfair in our relationship	0.61	0.72	0.81	0.78	0.82	0.80
My partner is familiar with my likes and dislikes	0.54	0.63	0.87	0.90	0.92	0.94
My partner knows my preferred ways of receiving love	0.57	0.68	0.90	0.89	0.89	0.91
My partner makes time to be with me	0.65	0.73	0.93	0.88	0.92	0.87
My partner makes personal sacrifices for the good of the relationship	0.72	0.61	0.92	0.87	0.92	0.88
My partner drops some personal activities to be more available to me	0.68	0.67	0.89	0.76	0.90	0.82
Factor II: Generosity (forgiveness, acceptance, appreciation)	Alpha = .81	Alpha = .82	Alpha = .82	Alpha = .84	Alpha = .83	Alpha = .81
My partner is forgiving of my mistakes	0.78	0.51	0.92	0.93	0.94	0.94
My partner is able to truly let go of negative feelings toward me	0.72	0.42	0.93	0.89	0.89	0.92
My partner brings up my past offenses when we are arguing (R)	0.66	0.51	0.80	0.88	0.84	0.90
My partner is able to look past my shortcomings	0.54	0.81	0.93	0.93	0.94	0.94
My partner expects me to change (R)	0.53	0.57	0.69	0.73	0.79	0.81
My partner appreciates all the work I do for our relationship	0.73	0.75	0.90	0.85	0.91	0.88
My partner struggles to recognize the things I do for him (R)	0.46	0.70	0.78	0.81	0.73	0.84

Factor III: Admiration	Alpha = .90	Alpha = .84	Alpha = .88	Alpha = .88	Alpha = .89	Alpha = .90	Alpha = .86
My partner sincerely compliments me on a regular basis	0.88	0.82	0.92	0.84	0.84	0.89	0.91
My partner recognizes my positive qualities	0.80	0.90	0.96	0.93	0.93	0.96	0.97
My partner admires me	0.86	0.90	0.94	0.96	0.96	0.97	0.96
Factor IV: Teamwork	Alpha = .80	Alpha = .81	Alpha = .81	Alpha = .83	Alpha = .83	Alpha = .84	Alpha = .77
My partner and I have a number of shared life goals we are working toward	0.64	0.56	0.92	0.94	0.94	0.93	0.96
My partner and I work together as a team to accomplish our goals	0.88	0.74	0.93	0.94	0.94	0.94	0.97
Our relationship is based on a deep sense of teamwork	0.79	0.72	0.91	0.91	0.91	0.95	0.96
Factor V: Shared vision	Alpha = .70	Alpha = .80	Alpha = .71	Alpha = .78	Alpha = .71	Alpha=.77	
My partner and I are headed in different directions in life (R)	0.59	0.70	0.93	0.90	0.91	0.93	
My partner and I want the same things from life	0.75	0.74	0.95	0.96	0.97	0.98	
My partner and I have a shared vision of what makes up a good life	0.77	0.61	0.85	0.93	0.98	0.98	
Factor VI: Loyalty/backbiting	Alpha = .61	Alpha = .83	Alpha = .85	Alpha = .82	Alpha = .91	Alpha = .89	
My partner talks about me behind my back (in a negative way) (R)	0.89	0.56	0.96	0.98	0.98	0.98	
My partner talks about my faults with others (R)	0.81	0.74	0.94	0.98	0.97	0.98	
Second-Order: Global relational virtues	Alpha = .92	Alpha = .92	Alpha = .93	Alpha = .94	Alpha = .93	Alpha = .93	
FI Other-centeredness	0.82	0.91	0.98	0.94	0.98	0.96	
FII Generosity	0.85	0.81	0.97	0.97	0.99	0.99	
FIII Admiration	0.66	0.72	0.93	0.93	0.95	0.92	
FIV Teamwork	0.85	0.89	0.97	0.99	0.95	0.97	
FV Shared vision	0.68	0.76	0.97	0.98	0.93	0.98	
FVI Loyalty/backbiting	0.58	0.66	0.95	0.94	0.92	0.95	

TABLE 5.3
Confirmatory Factor Analysis of the Marital Virtues Profile: Goodness-of-Fit Indices for Husbands and Wives Across Times of Measurement for Various Models

Spouse invariance (time 1—time 3)

Goodness-of-fit indices of models without equality constraints on factor loadings	$\chi^2 = 1297.79$ $df = 1047$ CFI = .93 TLI = .92 RMSEA = .04	$\chi^2 = 1616.94$ $df = 1057$ CFI = .95 TLI = .95 RMSEA = .06	$\chi^2 = 1728.43$ $df = 1053$ CFI = .95 TLI = .94 RMSEA = .06
Chi-square increase of models with equality constraints on factor loadings	$\chi^2_{dif} = 38.39$, $df_{dif} = 16$, $p < .05$	$\chi^2_{dif} = 4.29$, $df_{dif} = 18$, $p > .05$	$\chi^2_{dif} = 5.19$, $df_{dif} = 18$, $p > .05$

Time invariance (for wives and husbands)

	Time 1 + Time 2	Time 1 + Time 3
Wives		
Goodness-of-fit indices **without** equality constraints on factor loadings of two measurements	$\chi^2 = 1465.18$ $df = 1029$ CFI = .90 TLI = .90 RMSEA = .05	$\chi^2 = 1404.84$ $df = 1025$ CFI = .91 TLI = .90 RMSEA = .05
Chi-square increase **with** equality constraints on factor loadings of two measurements	$\chi^2_{dif} = 13.94$, $df_{dif} = 18$, $p > .05$	$\chi^2_{dif} = 36.15$, $df_{dif} = 18$, $p < .05$
Correlation between two measurements	$\phi = .78$	$\phi = .73$
Husbands		
Goodness-of-fit indices **without** equality constraints on factor loadings of two measurements	$\chi^2 = 1378.76$ $df = 1031$ CFI = .92 TLI = .91 RMSEA = .05	$\chi^2 = 1440.45$ $df = 1021$ CFI = .90 TLI = .89 RMSEA = .05
Chi-square increase **with** equality constraints on factor loadings of two measurements	$\chi^2_{dif} = 30.70$, $df_{dif} = 18$, $p < .05$	$\chi^2_{dif} = 19.06$, $df_{dif} = 18$, $p > .05$
Correlation between two measurements	$\phi = .79$	$\phi = .68$

the relationship) (husbands, $r = -0.59$; wives, $r = -0.57$). (See Busby et al., 2001, for information about these marital-satisfaction and marital-instability measures.) In addition, the MVP Total was modestly and negatively correlated with a measure of depression (CES-D) (Devins & Orme, 1985) (husbands, $r = -0.34$; wives, $r = -0.29$). Accordingly, the MVP produces reasonable construct validity, both with proximal measures of marital relationships and with a more distal measure of psychological well-being (depression).

Next, we compared the correlations of the MVP subscales with our outcome measures to a similar set of correlations of measures of couple communication behavior with the outcome measures. These measures of couple communication reliably assessed such things as spouse's negative conflict behavior, spouse's stonewalling, and spouse's flooding (Busby et al., 2001), constructs that researchers have identified as crucial to marital quality (Gottman & Silver, 1994), and central to the communication-satisfaction model of marriage.

How did the MVP stack up with the couple communication measures as correlates of marital quality, marital satisfaction, and marital instability? In 16 of 18 separate comparisons, the MVP was a significantly stronger correlate compared with the couple communication constructs. In the other two comparisons, the correlations were virtually equal (see Table 5.4). Negative conflict behavior is a particularly potent correlate of marital outcomes, but the MVP was a significantly stronger correlate in four of the six comparisons. Accordingly, our measure of marital virtues appears to outperform measures common to the communication-satisfaction model of marriage in terms of their association with common outcome variables. This set of findings, then, strengthens the case for good construct validity for the MVP.

These analyses suggest that marital virtues can be identified and reliably measured with partner-report data. In addition, the distinct virtues appear to indicate a more global construct of relationship virtues in marriage. Moreover, husbands and wives appear to respond to the MVP items in similar ways, facilitating comparisons between their responses. Also, the MVP has good construct validity. Therefore, we conclude that the MVP has potential as an instrument in marriage studies employing the construct of marital virtues.

DISCUSSION

We have argued for alternative models in understanding marriage. Specifically, we have argued for the potential utility of a spousal-strengths or marital-virtues model in addition to the hegemonic communication-satisfaction

TABLE 5.4
Construct Validity Analyses:
Comparison of MVP to Communication Behavior Measures

Measure	First-order correlations (N = 150)					
	MQ-W Wife Marital Quality	MQ-H Husb Marital Quality	MS-W Wife Marital Satisfaction	MS-H Husb Marital Satisfaction	MI-W Wife Marital Instability	MI-H Husb Marital Instability
MVP-W. MVP-Total (w→h)	.70		.74		−.57	
MVP-H. MVP-Total (h→w)		.78		.73		−.59
NCB-W. negative conflict behavior (w→h)	−.50		−.51		.59	
NCB-H. negative conflict behavior (h→w)		−.57		−.62		.59
STW-W. stonewalling (w→h)	−.10		−.19		.34	
STW-H. stonewalling (h→w)		−.31		−.05		.47
FLD-W. flooding (w→h)	−.33		−.34		.28	
FLD-H. flooding (h→w)		−.36		−.47		.36

Comparison of Correlation Coefficients (overlapping, correlated)	
MRR z-statistic test[a]	z
MVP-W/NCB-W w/MQ-W	3.53**
MVP-H/NCB-H w/MQ-H	4.88**
MVP-W/STW-W w/MQ-W	6.57**
MVP-H/STW-H w/MQ-H	5.60**
MVP-W/FLD-W w/MQ-W	4.82**
MVP-W/FLD-H w/MQ-H	6.75**
MVP-W/NCB-W w/MQ-W	4.24**
MVP-H/NCB-H w/MQ-H	2.51*
MVP-W/STW-W w/MQ-W	6.44**
MVP-H/STW-H w/MQ-H	7.34**
MVP-W/FLD-W w/MQ-W	5.44**
MVP-W/FLD-H w/MQ-H	4.22**
MVP-W/NCB-W w/MQ-W	−.34 (ns)
MVP-H/NCB-H w/MQ-H	.00 (ns)
MVP-W/STW-W w/MQ-W	4.33**
MVP-H/STW-H w/MQ-H	5.77**
MVP-W/FLD-W w/MQ-W	3.41**
MVP-W/FLD-H w/MQ-H	3.20**

[a]Tests done with the Meng, Rosenthal, and Rubin (1992) z-statistic for comparing overlapping correlated correlation coefficients.

$* = p < .05.$ $** = p < .01.$

model. As a first step in comparing the value of these models, we designed an instrument to measure marital virtues, the MVP, which consists of about 25 spouse-report items.

Empirically, and not too surprisingly, the various dimensions of marital virtues we explored did not align perfectly with the dimensions that Fowers (2000) discussed. For instance, fairness, understanding, and sacrifice clustered together in a construct we labeled "other-centeredness." We anticipated that fairness items would cluster with loyalty items. The loyalty construct, however, was reduced to a few items that emphasized a specific behavior—backbiting. (Frankly, our initial attempt to measure the loyalty construct was not well done, or there was too little variation to yield to analytic inspection.) Forgiveness, acceptance, and appreciation clustered predictably in a construct we labeled "generosity." The construct of "admiration," however, which Fowers discussed under the rubric of generosity, remained empirically distinct from acceptance and appreciation. "Teamwork" and "shared vision" also were empirically distinct dimensions, even though conceptually they seem intimately related in a construct of partnership. Of course, saying that these constructs were empirically distinct is overstating the reality. The second-order factor model revealed that they were highly correlated, suggesting that marital virtues is an effective, overarching rubric for the various components.

This study is a first attempt, and as such, it suffers from notable weaknesses. First, our sample is narrow in terms of age (20s) and family life cycle (transitioning to parenthood). Participants were predominantly White and religious (Mormon). In addition, our loyalty construct must be measured more effectively, and other potential marital virtues, such as courage, maturity, and goodwill, should be included. The wording of several items also must be simplified for survey populations with less formal education. The MVP needs further testing with a more diverse national sample to stretch these initial findings.

The take-home message, however, is that marriage researchers have both a reason and a tool to examine their reliance on the communication-satisfaction model. Researchers should explore their own assumptions about the motives individuals bring to their marriages, and the foundation of a healthy, stable marriage. Although future work will produce better measurement tools, we provide researchers willing to challenge their assumptions with at least one tool that can begin to illuminate a contrasting model of marriage, one rooted in a marital-virtues framework, and how it might compare with or supplement an individualistic framework. This approach will likely revise our understanding of strong and healthy marriages and lead to better interventions.

6

Assessing Couple and Marital Relationships: Beyond Form and Toward a Deeper Knowledge of Function

Scott M. Stanley
University of Denver

Both the public and private sectors are increasingly interested in helping more couples enter into and maintain strong marriages (Horn, 2003; Ooms, 1998). Although there has been a growing marriage movement in the United States since the early 1990s, public-sector interest in marriage burgeoned with the passage of the Personal Responsibility and Work Opportunity Reconciliation Act of 1996 (PRWORA). Although little known and less emphasized, the act included the goal of increasing the number of children living in stable, two-parent families.

Various efforts consistent with these goals are under way, and efforts are likely to increase since the law has been reauthorized. These efforts will likely encompass everything from changes in existing programs to make them more marriage friendly, to relationship and marriage curricula that provide individuals and couples with strategies to improve their odds of remaining together, to policy changes that remove disincentives to marry.

As public- and private-sector efforts to help couples navigate marriage accelerate, it becomes increasingly important to gauge the overall effectiveness of the ongoing efforts. I review several constructs and variables that may be useful in such evaluations, as well as in the larger goals of improving the basic science and understanding of relationships.

THE CONCEPT OF "HEALTHY" MARRIAGE

The public discourse surrounding marriage promotion policies and goals has been refined in recent years, as reflected in the words of Wade Horn, Assistant Secretary for Children and Families of the Administration for Children and Families, U.S. Department of Health and Human Services (Horn, 2003) in a keynote address: "We're going to support activities that help couples who choose marriage for themselves to develop the skills and knowledge necessary to form and sustain healthy marriages."

Perhaps the most important word in the context of this chapter is *healthy*. As stated on numerous occasions by Horn and others, the goal of government initiatives to foster healthy marriage is to help couples interested in marrying to have a better chance of a healthy marriage. This has led to important discussions in a variety of sectors about what constitutes a healthy marriage. I do not draw any firm conclusions on such matters here, except to note the dimensions that I and colleagues such as Howard Markman believe could help gauge the effects state and community programs have on healthy marriages. Some variables discussed here are, of course, more fundamental to measuring healthy marriage than others.

Based on existing research, a healthy marriage has three dimensions. All dimensions extend from two types of safety found in the best relationships and marriages (Stanley et al., 2002). First is the safety of the day-to-day interaction of the relationship, including emotional safety and a sense of positive connection in the absence of chronic fear of criticism, negativity, or danger. This type of safety includes safety from physical or psychological injury.

Second is the safety that comes from having a clear commitment to the future, which provides an overall sense of security and a reason to believe that it is worth investing oneself in the relationship. Hence, three elements of safety, in my view, create a foundation for a healthy marriage: emotional or interactional safety, personal safety, and commitment safety.

Essential Elements of Healthy Marriage: Emotional Safety

A tremendous amount of evidence suggests that relationships characterized by chronic negative interaction can be damaging to adults and the children living with them. Negative patterns of interaction clearly differentiate happy couples from unhappy couples (e.g., Birchler, Weiss, & Vincent, 1975; Christensen & Heavey, 1990; Clements, Stanley, & Markman, 2004;

Fincham & Beach, 1999; Gottman & Notarius, 2000; C. A. Johnson et al., 2002; Stanley et al., 2002). They are one of the best determinants of chronic distress, breakup, or divorce (e.g., Gottman, 1993; Karney & Bradbury, 1995; Markman & Hahlweg, 1993).

Negative patterns of interaction are also associated with a variety of negative outcomes for children, including mental health risks, declining school performance, and various forms of acting-out behavior (Cummings & Davies, 1994; Emery, 1982; Grych & Fincham, 1990). Finally, such patterns are associated with negative mental health outcomes for adults, such as depression and anxiety (Beach & O'Leary, 1993).

A reduction in negative interaction patterns would be one indication that interventions were effective in promoting healthier marriages and family relationships. Likewise, promoting positive dimensions of interaction, such as supportiveness and friendship, would likely foster a sense of safety and connection in a marriage (see later discussion of these and other dimensions).

Essential Elements of Healthy Marriage: Personal Safety

The obvious may not need to be stated, but domestic violence puts adults—and especially women and children—at great risk for mental health problems, health problems, and death (Straus & Gelles, 1990). Interventions ought to promote healthy marriages as a way of reducing domestic violence, existing violence, and the number of abusive relationships overall, especially those characterized by the most dangerous forms of violence.

Essential Elements of Healthy Marriage: Commitment Safety

Marriage functions in many ways like a long-term investment (Stanley, 1998; Stanley, Lobitz, & Dickson, 1999). It is the expectation of longevity that makes the day-to-day investment and sacrifice that characterize good marriages rational. In contrast, having no clear sense of a future increases pressure for performance in the present, which can result in a score-keeping mentality (Murstein & MacDonald, 1983). Although data directly addressing the effects of long- versus short-term views are thin, and causality is no doubt bidirectional, evidence suggests that couples do best when they see a longer future for their relationships (Amato & Rogers, 1999; Stanley & Markman, 1992; Waite & Joyner, 2001). Simply put, couples do best when they have a clear sense of an "us" with a future (Stanley & Markman, 1992). This does not mean that it makes sense for all couples to have a future. Some relationships are destructive and would be better ended than continued. I believe that the average couple stands to benefit from the protective commitment of marriage.

VARIABLES AND CONSTRUCTS

The following list of variables and constructs that show potential for evaluating healthy marriage interventions is certainly not exhaustive, but it is useful for portraying the potential of existing measurements. I would not expect that all or even most studies would attempt to measure all of these constructs, but I do believe that the constructs exemplify what can be assessed to advance knowledge and offer a level of richness beyond the simplicity of assessing mere relationship satisfaction or stability.

The Movement Toward Larger Meanings and Depth in Marital Research

Just as great changes have been occurring in the public-policy arena, major changes have been taking place in the field of marital research, perhaps none more relevant than the growing interest in a range of constructs that capture what I have called the larger meanings of marriage and relationship dynamics (Stanley & Markman, 1998). Whereas a focus on marital satisfaction dominated the early days of marital research, the focus shifted in the mid-1970s to a sustained, intense, and productive focus on communication and conflict (led by researchers such as Robert Weiss, John Gottman, Howard Markman, and Clifford Notarius)—a focus that may have been overdone (e.g., Fincham, 2003).

However, beginning in the mid-1980s, and greatly accelerating into the 1990s and beyond, the focus shifted dramatically toward richer constructs that have potential to elucidate important aspects of how couples form and function. Hence, such constructs as support, commitment, attachment, acceptance, and forgiveness, and intervention research are regular features of the landscape of basic research on marriage and family relationships. Such dimensions also move research closer to a broader conception of marriage that has the potential to uncover deeper values and beliefs that affect marriages and how people behave in them (Fowers, 2001). Furthermore, the team in which I participate believes such dimensions are important and quite measurable among couples from a variety of economic, ethnic, and cultural backgrounds.

Moderators and Outcomes

When considering constructs and variables, it is useful to distinguish between *moderators* of effects and their *outcomes*. As Holmbeck (1997) noted, moderators are variables that "affect the relationship between two variables, so that the nature of the impact of the predictor on the criterion varies according to the level or value of the moderator" (p. 599; see also

Baron & Kenny, 1986). In contrast, I use the term *outcome* here to describe possible dimensions that interventionists and policy interests may wish to affect. Mediators specify how or by which mechanisms an effect occurs (Holmbeck, 1997). Doubtless, many important moderators and outcomes are yet undiscovered or tested, and I make no attempt to be exhaustive. Furthermore, one study might conceptualize certain variables as moderators and another study as outcomes. Indeed, many constructs might be important to study in a number of roles in different models.

I do not cover moderators that obviously should be measured in virtually all intervention evaluations, such as education, income, economic potential, ethnicity, and so forth. Likewise, although mediators of effects are important to study in this field—particularly in the studies examined—mediators and theories of change are not my focus here.

Finally, I do not attempt a review of the outcome research on various couple curricula. (For such reviews, see Carroll & Doherty, 2003; Giblin, Sprenkle, & Sheehan, 1985; Halford, Markman, Kline, & Stanley, 2003; Silliman, Stanley, Coffin, Markman, & Jordan, 2001; Stagner, Ehrle, Kortenkamp, & Reardon-Anderson, 2003.)

Possible Moderators

I use the word *possible* in the subheading because we are in only the earliest stages of understanding which moderators are likely to matter most in studying marriage interventions. Yet there are reasons to believe that certain moderators deserve careful attention. The moderators I include are family background, premarital cohabitation, religiosity, attachment security, and commitment.

Moderators are important in this context because they represent variables that might alter the effectiveness of interventions but may be relatively unalterable in their own right (e.g., religiosity; see later subsection). Hence, moderators such as those discussed here are associated with risk, but many are also relatively unchanging. This is in contrast to risk factors, which are more dynamic and, therefore, can plausibly be changed (Stanley, 2001).

My colleague Howard Markman and I believe that static moderator variables are less interesting as targets of intervention but are of central interest as possible determinants of who might benefit most from different interventions. In many cases, what we call static risk factors, such as parental divorce, express their risk through a dynamic risk, such as poorer communication skills or a diminished sense of commitment in marriage.

Family Background. The first moderator is family background, given the evidence that several family background variables increase risks among couples. For example, parental divorce experienced as a child is associated with subsequent risks for relationship problems in adulthood (Amato & Booth, 1997; Amato & DeBoer, 2001). Evidence also suggests that exposure as a child to violence between parents is associated with negative affect and communication in engaged, male adults (Halford, Sanders, & Behrens, 2000). In a longer term study of premarital education, couples defined as high risk based on these family background characteristics did better with fully developed skills and cognitive-based curricula (Halford, Sanders, & Behrens, 2001). Low-risk couples taking the eclectic, less intense curricula faired somewhat better than the higher risk couples. Such findings on family background moderators, however, have yet to be replicated; we have not obtained these results with similar analyses.

Some, yet unmeasured variables that might be interesting to pursue as moderators include the number of successful marriages participants have witnessed in their communities, whether these experiences have affected their own aspirations and risks, and any lessons they have learned.

Premarital Cohabitation. A vast amount of evidence exists that couples who live together prior to marriage are, on average, at greater risk for marital distress (e.g., Cohan & Kleinbaum, 2002; DeMaris & Rao, 1992; Stanley, Whitton, & Markman, 2004). Furthermore, evidence from our own work suggests that couples who began living together prior to becoming engaged faced the clearest risk (Kline, Stanley, et al., 2004). Preliminary analyses of the Prevention and Relationship Enhancement Program (PREP) (Markman, Stanley, & Blumberg, 2001) showed that higher risk couples (those cohabiting prior to engagement compared with those cohabiting after engagement or marriage) made the greatest gains in communication quality from taking PREP (Kline, Stanley, & Markman, 2002).

Religiosity. Although the influence of religious faith and practice on public life in the United States has somewhat diminished, there is little doubt that religious beliefs and backgrounds continue to exert a strong influence on the marriage prospects of many couples. Religious faith and practice affect couples' decisions about cohabitation prior to marriage (Axinn & Thornton, 1992; Lillard, Brien, & Waite, 1995; Stanley, Whitton, et al., 2004), and are associated with marital quality and stability (Call & Heaton, 1997; C. A. Johnson et al., 2002). Furthermore, joint involvement of partners in beliefs and practices of faith is strongly associated with marital quality (Mahoney et al., 1999).

Mahoney and colleagues (1999) are studying richer constructs related to religiosity and marriage. Such constructs might assist in some evaluations of healthy marriage interventions. One potentially useful construct is a "sanctification of marriage" measure. This measure assesses the degree to which a couple holds religious beliefs that marriage is of particular spiritual significance (Mahoney et al., 1999). Not only may such beliefs protect a couple's marriage in the present, but they may increase a couple's motivation to build and sustain a marriage, especially during difficult times.

Attachment Security. There are compelling reasons to believe that attachment security and insecurity could be important moderators of outcomes. Compared with happily married individuals or those who divorce, people who are most likely to remain in unhappy marriages tend to score lower on attachment security (Davila & Bradbury, 2001). Davila and Bradbury stressed the importance of attachment as a potentially important risk factor and the need for interventions that target security. One might predict, for example, that interventions that boost a mutual sense of commitment between partners might particularly benefit those who have chosen a partner well, but struggle with strong feelings of insecurity in relationships. As such, attachment might moderate risk; thus the need for intervention. However, it may also moderate the effectiveness of an intervention (e.g., moderating the relationship between intervention and outcomes), given that a person who is highly insecure in attachment style may benefit less from programs that do not overtly enhance the reality or perception of security. In other words, such relationships offer less sense of safety to begin with; it is also harder to make them safer as a result of intervention.

Commitment. Although commitment would seem a logical choice as an outcome of marriage enhancement curricula and government programs, we have thus far seen few effects on this dimension in our own outcome research (Stanley et al., 2001). Yet basic research on commitment has yielded an impressive array of meaningful results (Jones & Adams, 1999). It is likely that commitment variables may function as moderators of program outcomes with certain populations. (As noted earlier, some variables might be moderators, mediators, *and* outcomes in this line of research, and this is likely nowhere more true than with dimensions of commitment.)

Researchers often measure commitment in terms of either commitment to the institution of marriage or intention to marry. Generally, commitment theory makes an important distinction between forces that draw people together and sustain connection and forces that increase the costs of leaving. In our own work, we call the higher order level of these constructs dedication and constraint. I briefly elaborate on these and other distinctions.

Partners who share a stronger level of dedication (or interpersonal commitment) tend to have a stronger sense of couple identity, or a "we-ness" in their approach to life. They also are more likely to say they have a strong desire for a future together. Committed couples make the needs of their partners and the relationship a high priority and are willing to sacrifice for one another (Stanley & Markman, 1992; Whitton, Stanley, & Markman, 2002).

In contrast, constraint may offer insight into why some individuals remain in unhappy relationships. Constraint can take many forms (Stanley & Markman, 1992). The forms for which we have developed measures include concern for children's welfare, the morality of divorce, social pressure, structural investments (financial investments, combined resources, etc.), and termination procedures (the difficulty involved in ending the relationship) (M. P. Johnson et al., 1999).

Alternatives overlap the concepts of dedication and constraint. Alternatives have played a prominent role in exchange theory and other theories (Thibaut & Kelley, 1959). Alternatives can function as a type of constraint; couples who perceive their alternatives to be limited and less desirable than their current situation are constrained. Alternatives play an equally important role in understanding dedication. The degree to which one seriously evaluates alternative partners correlates with less commitment (dedication) and greater dissatisfaction (D. Johnson & Rusbult, 1989; Stanley et al., 2002).

In terms of moderation of outcomes, one could predict that higher levels of dedication would correlate with greater gains from interventions, assuming that other relationship quality variables remain constant. Conversely, high levels of constraint with lower levels of dedication might lead to a poor prognosis. Discrepancies in level of dedication between partners could also moderate outcomes in important ways. Because premarital cohabitation (without engagement) is associated with higher relationship risks and less male dedication to female partners (Stanley, Whitton, et al., 2004), cohabiting couples might be good candidates for preventive interventions (with cohabitation seen here as a moderator of risk). Yet they may be less likely to respond ideally to existing inventions because of lower male dedication (a potential moderator of program effectiveness or participation). Under these conditions, an intervention that positively influences male dedication might affect future marital quality, in part, via the mediating effect of changes in dedication (hence, a possible mechanism of change). Again, I am generally not focusing on mediation here; however, I would note that there is little hope for understanding mechanisms of change without measurement of possible candidates.

Many other potential moderators may affect interventions to promote healthy marriage and relationships. These include substance abuse, domestic violence, economic status, and mental health. Mental health and domestic violence could also constitute outcomes of some intervention efforts.

Outcomes

Researchers have assessed many outcomes to detect the effects of relationship education interventions. Others, which I list in the subsection Miscellaneous Outcomes, have not been used to my knowledge, but may warrant future research.

Satisfaction. The most widely used outcome in studies of relationship and marriage education is, not surprisingly, global relationship satisfaction. This is an important outcome variable because it matters to people. However, it is less theoretically interesting because it reveals almost nothing about the dynamics in a relationship. Nevertheless, it remains an important outcome in assessing healthy marriage.

Evidence from many studies indicates that participation in various relationship education classes can help couples gain or preserve satisfaction for at least a short time (Carroll & Doherty, 2003; Markman, Floyd, Stanley, & Storaasli, 1988; Wampler, 1990). On the other hand, probable ceiling effects in some samples make it difficult to detect short-term differences in measures of global adjustment and satisfaction (Hahlweg & Markman, 1988). This limitation makes it important to include measures of other dimensions that may be more sensitive to change.

Negative and Positive Interaction. Despite 30+ years of outcome studies on relationship education, debates still arise about effects and strategies (e.g., Gottman et al., 1998; Stanley, Bradbury, & Markman, 2000). However, that couples can learn to communicate less negatively and more positively—and that such changes can be lasting—seems relatively clear (Giblin et al., 1985; Hahlweg, Markman, Thurmaier, Engl, & Eckert, 1998; Markman et al., 1993). In general, research using objective coding of couple interaction has demonstrated such intervention effects more clearly. However, research on young Army couples, who appear to have room for improvement on self-report measures compared with extremely happy premarital couples, has demonstrated some strong self-reported communication effects (Stanley et al., 2005). Overall, the assessment of interaction—and especially negative interaction—is crucial in efforts to assess healthy marriage intervention.

Most curricula for couples target communication processes, either alone or with other dimensions. Programs such as Couple Communication (S. Miller, Wackman, & Nunnally, 1976) target communication almost exclusively; whereas PREP targets communication, conflict, negative-affect management, and other dimensions, such as commitment, friendship, spirituality, expectations, and core beliefs (Markman et al., 2001; Stanley, Blumberg, & Markman, 1999). Relationship Enhancement (Guerney, 1977), another intervention, targets communication and empathy, but has demonstrated effects on various other dimensions as well (Ridley, Jorgenson, Morgan, & Avery, 1982).

Evaluations of healthy marriage efforts should include one or more measures of negative interaction. Many ways to measure interaction are available to researchers, including brief self-report (Stanley et al., 2002), theoretically derived self-report, such as demand–withdraw patterns (Christensen & Heavey, 1990), and objective coding of couple interaction (see Heyman, 2001, for a review; see also Gottman, 1993; Gottman & Notarius, 2000; Kline, Julien, et al., 2004; Markman & Notarius, 1987). Although objective coding of couple interaction may be too expensive and cumbersome to deploy in many contexts, the payoff can be great. Brief measures also can be effective, yielding findings that have solid overlap with those from much more rigorous, objectively coded research (Stanley et al., 2002). However, it has been our experience that objective coding is more sensitive to change, especially in the short term with couples who are generally very happy, such as with premarital couples where ceiling effects can affect interpretation of self-reported patterns. Researchers need to consider the relative pros and cons of using objecting coding and be aware that in some contexts using only self-report measures may compromise the detection of effects.

Relationship Confidence. I believe that confidence in the future viability of a relationship may become an important variable in understanding couple formation, couple dynamics, and outcomes resulting from efforts to help couples build healthy marriages. There is relatively little research on this construct, although we have begun to regularly assess it in various aspects of our work. Others have focused on the specific efficacy a couple may possess for handling conflict (Doherty, 1981; Notarius & Vanzetti, 1983). Confidence is important because it may directly relate to persistence over time in efforts to maintain or improve the quality of a relationship.

I and my colleagues have assessed confidence in terms of efficacy in handling issues in life and in one's general confidence in the future of a relationship. We have found confidence to strongly differentiate couples who cohabited prior to engagement from those who cohabited after engagement; these differences hold important meaning in our theories of cohabitation risks (Kline, Stanley, et al., 2004). In outcome research with premarital couples, we found no short-term effects of interventions on confidence, which we believe is likely due to ceiling effects (Stanley et al., 2001). In our research with young married couples in the Army, we found strong short-term effects, with couples who participated in PREP showing increased confidence (Stanley, Allen, et al., 2004). We also found an association between female relationship confidence prior to marriage and depressive symptomatology in the 1st year of marriage (Stanley, Prado, et al., 2000).

Positive Connection. Beyond measuring satisfaction, research has focused surprisingly little on the positive connection between partners in marriage. This is a noteworthy gap given how important dimensions such as friendship and fun are to healthy marriages in our culture. Such dimensions have drawn increasing attention in curricula (Jordan, Stanley, & Markman, 1999; Markman et al., 2001; Stanley, Trathen, McCain, & Bryan, 1998) and in marital theories (Gottman, Ryan, Carrere, & Erley, 2002).

Measuring these dimensions seems fairly straightforward. Based on two large-sample surveys that assess friendship and fun in marriage, we have observed that thoughts of divorce among women correlate with a lack of positive connection in the marriage; whereas among men, thoughts of divorce correlate more with the levels of negative interaction (C. A. Johnson et al., 2002; Stanley et al., 2002). Such findings suggest that women and men may respond differently to different intervention targets.

Propensity for Divorce. Many studies suggest that individuals can reliably report the degree to which they have been thinking about, talking about, or planning to divorce. Valid and brief measures exist for these precursors to divorce (Booth, Johnson, & Edwards, 1983; R. L. Weiss & Cerreto, 1980). These types of measures are valuable because they are sensitive to shifts toward divorce without necessarily requiring knowledge of actual dissolution.

Domestic Violence. Domestic violence clearly signals an unhealthy marriage. Researchers can measure domestic violence with longer, multi-dimensional measures (e.g., Conflict Tactics Scale; Straus, 1979) or simple one- or two-item measures asking if, for example, a person has pushed, shoved, or hit his or her partner in the past year. It would be very valuable in this field not only to regularly assess outcomes related to domestic violence, but to measure typologies of domestic violence. Marital researchers agree that domestic violence differs in type and that these differences have varying implications for prevention, treatment, and safety potential (Holtzworth-Munroe & Stuart, 1994; M. P. Johnson & Ferraro, 2000). The issues and complexity of this topic exceed what can be covered in this chapter. But I believe that reliable, valid, and economically employable measures of various types of domestic violence would be of great value in outcome research with couples.

Forgiveness. Driven largely by funding from the Templeton Foundation, forgiveness as a process in adult, romantic relationships has garnered much attention in recent years. Research by Fincham (2000) and Mc-Cullough, Worthington, and Rachal (1997) exemplifies the advances in this area. Researchers have developed measures that could be used in outcome research (Gordon & Baucom, 2003). Gordan, Baucom, and Snyder (2003) found, in a preliminary study, that couples changed their attitudes on forgiveness as a result of treatment for marital infidelity. Forgiveness might be a very important outcome to measure in interventions for couples struggling with significant distrust, as the case has been for couples in the Fragile Families research project (England, Edin, & Linnenberg, 2003).

Sacrifice.   Another construct garnering attention is sacrifice in romantic relationships. Counter to the word's pejorative connotation, a greater willingness to sacrifice, satisfaction with sacrifice, and sacrifice without a sense of personal loss all correlate with happier and better functioning relationships and marriages (Stanley & Markman, 1992; Van Lange et al., 1997).

Evidence points to some potentially significant differences between women and men in how commitment to a long-term future with a partner affects willingness to sacrifice without resentment (Whitton et al., 2002). Specifically, males' willingness to perform daily sacrifices without experiencing personal loss strongly correlates with their commitment to a future; whereas the correlation is much smaller for females. Such findings could explain, in part, why marriage regulates male behavior so highly (consistent with much data provided by Nock, 1998, marriage being the strongest emblem of commitment to a future together); whereas women tend to willingly sacrifice themselves regardless of marital status. A man's willingness to sacrifice in appropriate ways for his female partner may help researchers gain insight into healthy relationships.

Social and Spousal Support.   Researchers not only link supportive behaviors to marital health, but believe they likely can be taught. Supportiveness may take on added importance in research on interventions targeted to fragile families, where the perceived supportiveness of the man (by the woman) is among the stronger determinants of which couples go on to marry (Carlson, McLanahan, & England, 2003).

Attributions.   One solid goal for future work would be testing and refining the ability to modify the attributions individuals make about their partners (Bradbury & Fincham, 1990). As an example, Bradbury and Fincham (1992) found that maladaptive attributions for marital difficulties related to less effective problem solving, more negative behavior overall in communication, and a greater tendency to reciprocate negatively, especially for wives. Although outcome research has not studied attributions to my knowledge, some curricula do target negative interpretations (e.g., PREP; Markman et al., 2001), a type of maladaptive attribution.

Miscellaneous Outcomes.   Researchers can assess a variety of straightforward yet important outcomes, especially in evaluations of specific relationship education efforts. Some of the more obvious are:

• *Program satisfaction.* Do individuals like the education program? Do they believe it is valuable?

- *Most useful aspects or components of relationship education curricula.* Participants can provide valuable information on which aspects of the program were most useful to them (Silliman & Schumm, 1989; Stanley et al., 2001; K. Sullivan & Anderson, 2002).

- *Barriers to participation.* Barriers may be especially important to assess for the most disadvantaged participants.

- *Connection with other resources.* One of the more useful things that programs might do is to make participants aware of other programs and resources that may help them function well in life (Stanley, 2001), such as substance abuse treatment, mental health treatment, couples' counseling, economic supports and training, and domestic-violence treatment or prevention services. Evaluators can assess the secondary benefits of participation in relationship interventions.

- *Program leader characteristics.* Characteristics of program leaders, especially leaders of education efforts, likely play an important role in participants' gains. Therefore, it is useful to measure the characteristics of leaders to better determine fit and effects related to matching or training.

- *Attitudes and beliefs.* It is important in some contexts to assess attitudes and beliefs about marriage, cohabitation, nonmarital childbearing, and so forth, because such beliefs can significantly affect relationship decisions.

THE MEASUREMENT TENDENCIES OF DIFFERENT DISCIPLINES

I have focused on constructs and measurement approaches that psychologically trained marital researchers typically use. I therefore emphasize a rich set of constructs that can be useful for advancing understanding of societal changes in marriage and family structure, and for evaluating outcomes of interventions designed to foster healthy marriages. Although the backgrounds of researchers in marriage and family are many (e.g., sociology, psychology, economics, social work), sociology and psychology are the two dominant groups, and there are important differences in their traditions. Sociologists frequently use large samples with brief measures, with often one or two items measuring a variable. Psychologists, in contrast, typically use smaller samples but more detailed and richer measurement, probably owing to their theoretical interests and the need to have more robust measures to compensate for the lower power available in smaller samples.

A great need persists for ongoing multidisciplinary collaboration. Given the range of different experiences and expertise, it is immensely useful to have researchers from a variety of backgrounds working together on measure selection and development when evaluating studies of healthy-marriage initiatives. It would be simplistic to say that sociologists have focused more on family structure (form) and psychologists more on dynamics (function). However, greater blending of such emphases in research can only strengthen mutual efforts to expand knowledge.

Brief Measures Can Still Tell Us a Lot

In many contexts, complex measurement may be desirable, yet hampered by pragmatics such as the limited time of participants. Fortunately, researchers can measure many important variables relatively briefly, even if initial research used longer term measures of those variables for psychometric reasons. For example, a long and impressive line of studies on religiosity has used Allport and Ross's (1967) multi-item Religious Orientation Scale. Yet three items among the many on the original scale capture most of the essential variance associated with the constructs (Gorsuch & McPherson, 1989). Similarly, we have found that four self-report items assessing negative interaction yield results entirely consistent with studies employing objective coding of couple interaction (C. A. Johnson et al., 2002; Stanley et al., 2002). Although in some studies excluding objective coding of couple behavior would sacrifice sensitivity, in many other studies brief self-report measures reveal an adequate amount of information. Measuring variables not typically assessed in outcome research does not necessarily introduce cumbersome procedures for participants. Multidisciplinary teams can achieve the best balance of depth and breadth to yield useful information for informing policies and programs.

CONCLUSION

I have presented some variables that might contribute to evaluations of initiatives and interventions promoting healthy marriages. This is only a sampling of what is possible. Various moderators and outcomes can provide a detailed understanding of who participates in interventions and who gains the most from them. Policymakers and curriculum developers can use this information to refine efforts over time, a process invaluable to the field. We have much to learn about how to most effectively meet the needs of individuals and couples who aspire to healthy marriages. Yet we have learned a great deal and possess many tools to continue to learn.

A diverse and rich measurement approach is crucial for evaluating interventions in this new policy environment. This measurement approach also reduces bias (not to mention increases statistical power), which arises from researchers' failure to observe or discuss what they do not measure. In a politically and philosophically charged environment, where public policy, public costs, and private behavior can ignite a storm capable of producing more heat than light, the job of good research is to shed light. Broad, high-quality measurement sheds light on the depths of important phenomena. Our knowledge base must provide a rich understanding to ground our efforts and accurately portray the dynamics that affect real couples struggling to live well.

ACKNOWLEDGMENTS

Preparation of this chapter was supported in part by a grant from the National Institute of Mental Health: Division of Services and Intervention Research, Adult and Geriatric Treatment and Prevention Branch, Grant 5-RO1-MH35525-12, "The Long-Term Effects of Premarital Intervention" (awarded to Howard Markman and Scott Stanley).

Notes

1. An extensive appendix on various available measures, including summaries of findings and a large set of references, can be obtained from the author or at the following Web site: http://www.prepinc.com/main/docs/countingcouples.pdf.

7

Developing Measures of Healthy Marriages and Relationships

Kristin A. Moore
Jacinta Bronte-Tinkew
Susan Jekielek
Lina Guzman
Suzanne Ryan
Zakia Redd
Jennifer Carrano
Greg Matthews
Child Trends

Research indicates that adults and children are most likely to prosper in a family formed by married biological parents in a low-conflict marriage (Amato, 2000; Seltzer, 2000). Such marriages have come to be called "healthy marriages," and their creation and support represent a major public-policy goal. A series of government-sponsored evaluations are under way to examine educational, counseling, and other approaches to strengthen the quality and duration of marriages, particularly for low-income couples. Months or even years later, researchers will assess their effectiveness. Thus, increasing the prevalence of healthy marriage is a critical goal for the interventions, and by attaining that goal, policymakers and others expect to see improvements in outcomes for adults, children, and families. The goal of the project discussed in this chapter is to create a scale or index that measures the health of a marriage or relationship, which will be used as an outcome measure in random-assignment intervention evaluations. Although this work can also be of use in other research, our primary purpose is to develop a dependent variable for use in experimental evaluations of marriage interventions.

Creating a scale or index that measures the health of a marriage or relationship is an outgrowth of research under way in the Conceptualizing and Measuring Healthy Marriage for Empirical Research and Evaluation Project. This project started with a conceptual question: What is a "healthy marriage" or a "healthy relationship"? and has moved from conceptualization to measurement.

To inform this work, Child Trends compiled a compendium of relationship quality measures. In addition, the project commissioned short papers from scholars on measuring healthy relationships, and we have drawn from them heavily for the conceptual work discussed in this chapter. The authors of this chapter have also synthesized research on the conceptualization and measurement of healthy marriages and relationships, highlighting gaps for critical populations. The project has also developed and tested concrete measures in cognitive interviews. These detailed materials are available on Child Trends's Web site (http://www.childtrends.org).

Although the focus of the work described in this chapter is on healthy marriage, couples who are planning to marry are also targets of the intervention. Accordingly, we use the terms *healthy marriage* and *healthy relationship* interchangeably in discussing relationship quality of both married couples and couples who are planning to marry.

In the following sections, we first outline our working assumptions and discuss the underlying reasons for focusing on low-income couples. We then describe the various groups who will be measured. Based on prior research and theory, we describe the components of a healthy marriage. We also define how the definition of a healthy marriage is distinguished from the antecedents and consequences of a healthy marriage. Finally, we summarize the strategy we have implemented to develop and refine new measures for low-income couples in varied groups based on these activities.

WORKING ASSUMPTIONS

The first working assumption of the project is that a healthy marriage is a continuum. It is not a yes/no construct, but a scale or index. Thus, it is not something that a couple definitely has or does not have, but something that couples have to varying degrees.

Second, we assume that the elements of a healthy marriage can be learned. As yet, we do not know the exact details about whom the programs will target or what their content will be. However, our assumption, based on the available research and theory, is that healthy-marriage constructs can be identified, and these constructs can be affected by marriage education interventions.

Third, we assume that healthy relationships should be assessed differently for different populations. It seems likely that intervention evaluations will focus primarily or solely on couples with children; but some couples may not have children. Also, even in a study of married couples and couples planning to marry, family structure and living arrangements will vary over time. For example, some married couples will divorce, and a number of couples will never marry. Also, some couples live apart, yet are a romantic couple. In anticipation of this variability, measures are needed that will work for various family subgroups: two-resident, biological parents; married or cohabiting couples; resident couples who are not parents; (re)married or cohabitating couples with stepchildren; nonresident, estranged couples with children in common; visiting couples who are parents; couples who do not reside together because of incarceration; and couples who do not reside together because of military service. Much of the research conducted on marriage to date has focused on White, middle-class couples. However, federally funded interventions are likely to focus primarily on low-income couples, many of whom will be non-White. Accordingly, it is important to develop constructs and measures appropriate for these populations.

A fourth working assumption is that a healthy marriage has multiple elements. Of those elements, satisfaction is the most frequently studied, followed by couple communication (Fowers, 2003; Fowers et al., 2003). Like Fowers, most scholars argue that other dimensions are important to include when conceptualizing healthy marriage, and we follow this advice.

WHY FOCUS ON LOW-INCOME COUPLES?

Research on marital relationships among low-income couples has been lacking, despite acute marital stresses within this population. Reflecting this reality, a new generation of interventions is planned for low-income couples. Fein (2004) created a profile of the population of economically disadvantaged married couples from published reports and new tabulations of the Current Population Survey (CPS). The findings indicate that the focus on this group is well warranted. We review some of these reasons next.

Marriages Among the Economically Disadvantaged Are More Unstable

Analyses of the 1995 National Survey of Family Growth (NSFG) suggest that the likelihood of marrying at some time does not vary by level of education or by neighborhood income level. However, the odds of staying married are substantially lower for couples who are economically disadvantaged (Bramlett & Mosher, 2002). The fragile nature of marriages among low-income couples suggests the need to focus intervention efforts on disadvantaged couples.

For Disadvantaged Newlywed Couples, First Births Often Precede Marriage

Using CPS data on the timing of women's first births relative to first marriages, Ellwood and Jencks (2004) found that among couples who married in 1990, one third of those in the lowest educational category had their first child before marriage compared with one tenth in the top education category. Other studies indicate that nonmarital childbearing and multiple-partner fertility reduce the probability of marriage because fathers are reluctant to assume responsibility for a new mother's previous children. Also, mothers are reluctant to marry a father who has previous obligations for children because these obligations reduce the disposable income available to the new family, and unpaid obligations undermine the economic contributions of parents (especially fathers) to their children (DaVanzo & Rahman, 1993; Willis, 1999).

Disadvantaged Married Couples Are Young

Low-income married women are substantially younger than their middle- and higher income counterparts. Estimates from the 2003 March CPS, for example, suggest that, among poor married women, 47% were still in their prime childbearing ages (under 35), compared with only 18% of those with incomes at least six times the poverty threshold. In addition, young couples are less likely to have intended births (S. S. Brown & Eisenberg, 1995). Young married couples are typically less established financially and emotionally to undertake the responsibilities of marriage, and they have higher rates of marital disruption (Bramlett & Mosher, 2002).

A Marital-Quality Gap Exists Between Low-Income and Other Married Couples

Some studies suggest that marital quality is slightly lower for low-income couples (incomes less than 200% of the poverty threshold) than for more advantaged couples. If public assistance is used as an indicator of disadvantage, the marital-quality gap between low-income and other couples is larger (Fein, 2004). One explanation is that weaker supports and cultural norms coupled with more stressful external circumstances lead to more negative outcomes for low-income couples who experience distress. The most pressing concern is not only relationship quality at a given point in time for low-income couples, but rather, the rapidity with which relationships deteriorate in the face of stressful events.

To summarize, the risk factors experienced by low-income couples reduce marital stability and increase fragile marriages (McLaughlin & Lichter, 1997). Accordingly, low-income couples represent a population that could benefit from marriage education efforts. Because research on marriage has tended to ignore disadvantaged couples, it is necessary to consider how constructs and measures might differ for them.

MEASURING HEALTHY MARRIAGES AMONG DIVERSE POPULATION GROUPS

One notable deficiency in current work is the lack of measurement tools crafted for couples in a variety of relationships. Studies of healthy marriage or relationships often use the measures developed for intact, two-parent families to assess the quality of marital relationships within different populations, such as estranged couples or couples with a partner in prison. In this section, we highlight the limitations of using existing measures for a variety of populations.

Cohabiting and Visiting Couples

Cohabiting couples represent an increasingly common family form in the United States. Although cohabiting and visiting couples face challenges that differ from those of married couples, studies generally use the same measures (Ryan, 2004). Clearly, measures are needed that more accurately reflect the unique circumstances that cohabiting and visiting couples face and that include the understudied dimensions of relationships most salient to these family forms, namely, the frequency and nature of contact.

Step- and Remarried Families

The defining feature of stepfamilies is the presence of children from a previous union. In addition, the ex-partner or -spouse may affect the current relationship. However, as with cohabiting and visiting couples, for the most part, these marriages are conceptualized and measured similarly to first marriages (Guzman, 2004). Although the theoretical and substantive understanding of what stepfamilies are like and how they function has grown in recent decades, measures still lag in both theory and research findings.

Couples Coparenting After Relationship Dissolution

Coparenting occurs both when parents are together and when they are apart. The nature of the coparenting relationship can change over time as new unions are established and additional children are born to either partner. Research suggests that those who have positive coparenting relationships prior to divorce are more likely to be satisfied with their shared physical custody (Hetherington & Stanley-Hagan, 1995), and low conflict prior to divorce is also related to cooperative coparenting. Most research on coparenting after relationships end has focused on divorce and its effects on children. Few studies have addressed the couple relationship after the dissolution of a nonmarital relationship, and few measures currently exist for such couples (Jekielek, 2004).

Military Families

A growing body of research explores marital relationships in military populations, many of which involve lower income couples. Researchers have examined both deployment and family reintegration following prolonged involuntary separation (Bronte-Tinkew, 2004b). The most common separation likely to influence marital relationships is when one spouse leaves for active duty. Other separations can involve two active-duty members of the same family. Research indicates that stress in the marital relationship occurs at three stages: preparation, during service, and reunion. Each stage has its own emotions and problems. Most available measures of marital relationships in military populations have used measures from research on marriage and family relationships, although it is difficult to determine their validity and reliability because psychometric analyses for the military sample have not yet been published.

Incarcerated Parents

Incarceration remains one of the leading causes of marital noncohabitation and occurs disproportionately among low-income persons. Research on incarcerated partners is limited and inconclusive (Bronte-Tinkew, 2004a). Although it is becoming more apparent that incarceration can have negative consequences for marriages and families, measures to capture the quality of relationships among the incarcerated are still lacking.

Families With Children

Marriages with children are quite different from marriages without children, yet many studies of marital relationships explore conflict over children or the implications of becoming a parent on marital quality without distinguishing marriages with and without children. Given this distinction, it is important to construct items that apply to both parents and nonparents.

In sum, existing measures of relationships and marriages are important to informing new studies conducted among diverse populations. However, as low-income couples become the focus of research, available measures should be reconsidered. Also, given the complex realities of family life, it is necessary to expand the set of items assessing healthy marriages or relationships for use among varied population groups, such as those outlined earlier, and for low-income couples. A set of reliable, valid measures of healthy marriages or relationships that are appropriate for varying populations should increase the potential of researchers to examine the broad range of factors believed to affect the well-being of couples and children.

In the following section, we describe the components of a healthy marriage that have been identified in the course of our review of previous research, measures, and databases, as well as the perspectives of leading scholars in the field.

COMPONENTS OF A HEALTHY MARRIAGE

Based on an extensive review of previous research, we have identified 10 domains that should be measured to fully encompass the concept of a "healthy marriage." These include marital satisfaction, couple communication, interaction and time together, commitment to the children, emotional intimacy, conflict resolution, violence, fidelity, commitment to the couple, and the duration of legal marital status. We describe each domain in more detail.

Domain 1: Marital Satisfaction

Measuring marital satisfaction is one of the most common approaches to assessing marital quality (Booth, Amato, Johnson, & Rogers, 2003). Marital satisfaction is typically assessed as both global satisfaction and satisfaction with specific aspects of the marriage, such as a couple's standard of living and time together. It can also take the form of overall happiness with marriage (Booth et al., 2003). Marital satisfaction has been found in numerous studies to be related to marital stability and dissolution (see Bradbury et al., 2000, for a review). Evidence also suggests that marital satisfaction is important in the marriages of African Americans, as well as middle-class White samples. For example, Murry, Brown, Brody, and Cutrona (2001) found that a warm, supportive, and satisfying relationship helped buffer the negative effects of experiencing racist incidents on depression or anxiety.

Analyzing a sample of rural African Americans, Murry (2003) also found husband and wife reports of marital satisfaction to be moderately correlated with marital stability.

Domain 2: Couple Communication

Based on our review, important elements of communication include the quality and style of communication (such as honesty, openness, or a respectful tone); the type and content of communication (such as talking about one's day, making joint decisions, or laughing together); and minimizing negative aspects, such as feeling inundated by attacks. Quantity seems less critical than quality, although some minimal amount of communication seems crucial. For couples who are separated because of military service or incarceration, such communication could involve telephone, letters, or e-mail (Day, 2003). Communication overlaps somewhat with conflict resolution, and research links couple communication patterns to marital stability (Gottman, 1994). However, communication covers a broader range of topics, from simple chatting to decision making to sharing beliefs and concerns. Couple communication has been measured mainly through responses to survey questions, but also through direct observation.

Domain 3: Interaction and Time Together

Marital interaction includes day-to-day activities and social activities (Booth et al., 2003). Some evidence indicates that couple interaction has declined during the past several decades and has contributed to declining marital satisfaction over time (Amato, 2000). Booth and colleagues find that marital quality stems mainly from the dyadic properties of the couple, such as their interaction, and not their individual traits (with the exception of individual antisocial behaviors, such as drug use or heavy drinking, which harm marital quality). Accordingly, to measure interaction, items should assess the amount and frequency of couple interaction, the quality of interactions, and the type and diversity of interactions.

Domain 4: Commitment to Children

Numerous researchers suggest that positive or supportive relationships outside the couple dyad are indicators of a healthy marriage or relationship, with a particular emphasis on the fulfillment of parenting roles (Cowan & Cowan, 2003; Fagan, 2003; Fowers, 2003; Ganong & Coleman, 2003; Heyman, 2003; W. E. Johnson, 2003; Kitzmann, Nicholson, & Schum, 2003; Nock, 2003; Olson & Knutson, 2003). Cowan and Cowan included the ability to coparent effectively as a critical dimension of healthy and satisfying relationships. This includes both partners being involved in decision making, being satisfied with the division of labor, and supporting each other's parenting. E. A. Anderson (2003) emphasized the fulfillment of paternal responsibilities, given the influence of children on marriage. Given these recommendations, and that the overarching goal of enhancing healthy marriage is to enhance child well-being, we consider the commitment of the couple to his/her/their children as an important construct in defining healthy marriage.

For couples who live with only their biological children, commitment to children is a fairly straightforward construct that incorporates financial, social, and emotional support over time. However, for couples whose legal or romantic relationship has ended, or for couples who live apart, the quality of their commitment to their children, though still crucial, is more complicated. For divorced couples, the coparental relationship ceases to be one of commitment to each other, but is one that allows parents "to meet their childrearing responsibilities" (Kitzmann et al., 2003). Although some elements of coparenting might remain similar for both intact and divorced couples—for example, positive and supportive communication—the topics of communication might be different. For example, a parent's satisfaction with child custody compliance or with a partner's flexibility surrounding reasonable changes in arrangements are commonly measured elements of coparenting after relationship dissolution (Ahrons, 1981). The Quality of Coparental Communication developed by Ahrons is one of the most commonly used scales and shows evidence of reliability and validity (Kitzmann et al., 2003). The items from this scale, however, were not developed with unmarried couples in mind. Also, incarceration impedes couple communication and child contact, and given the higher rates of incarceration among low-income individuals (W. E. Johnson, 2003), measures should be considered that are valid for couples that may be committed to the relationship but not living together.

Children from previous relationships are often a source of conflict in new relationships, leading several researchers to recommend measuring couple communication on stepparenting (E. A. Anderson, 2003; Cowan & Cowan, 2003; Ganong & Coleman, 2003; W. E. Johnson, 2003; Kitzmann et al., 2003). Arguments over how finances are spent on children from a prior relationship are one of the main sources of conflict in stepparent families (Ganong & Coleman, 2003).

Domain 5: Emotional Intimacy

Emotional intimacy has been referred to by Gottman (1999, 2003) as the quality of the couple's friendship. Couple friendship includes the notion of feeling known, knowing each other, expressing interest in hearing what the other has to say, closeness, emotional support, and feelings of trust. This construct can also include negative aspects of intimacy, such as feelings of loneliness (Gottman, 2003), which may be a particularly salient construct to measure for married individuals who are incarcerated (Rokach & Spomenka, 1997; Segrin & Flora, 2001) or where one spouse has been activated for military duty. We distinguish sexual intimacy as an aspect of emotional intimacy.

Domain 6: Conflict and Conflict Resolution

Conflict is a predictor of adult unhappiness and marital breakup and is associated with diminished child development (Bradbury et al., 2000); therefore, low conflict is an important aspect of a healthy marriage or relationship. Conflict resolution skills are also "changeable" (Fagan, 2003), and therefore represent a reasonable target for a healthy marriage intervention.

Conflict and conflict resolution are elements that should be distinguished from violence (see the next subsection). Any relationship, including family, work, and community relationships, involves some disagreement. The ability to resolve differences is a critical skill. Not surprisingly, a review of the research shows a positive link between marital satisfaction and the frequency with which each spouse uses positive conflict resolution tactics (e.g., agreement, compromise, and humor), and a negative link between marital satisfaction and the use of negative strategies, such as conflict engagement and withdrawal (Kurdek, 1995). This suggests that how a couple handles negative affect and disagreements in their interactions is an important aspect of a healthy marriage.

Domain 7: Violence

Violence (both mental and physical) goes beyond disagreement. Research suggests that spousal violence is often not an isolated event: Men who are physically violent toward their partners are also likely to be violent toward their children (Straus & Gelles, 1990). Initial definitions of family violence focused on physical assaults against children, spouses, and other family members; over time, research has come to view family violence to also encompass sexual abuse, neglect, and psychological abuse (Straus, 1992). M. P. Johnson (2003) conceptualized violence as comprising both the context of the violence and the act of violence itself. For example, violence embedded in a general pattern of coercive control is different from violence that occurs in the absence of such control or as resistance among women trying to cope with their partner's "intimate terrorism."

Domain 8: Fidelity

Fidelity (faithfulness to the partner) looms large as a component of healthy marriage. Qualitative work by Smock and Manning (2003a) indicates that infidelity is a "deal breaker." In other words, when partners are unfaithful, the relationship tends to end. Even the presence of a past romantic partner may threaten the current romantic relationship, and can be a concern, especially for those who have children with prior partners (W. E. Johnson, 2003). Ongoing involvement in coparenting with an ex-partner is a reminder of a previous romantic relationship, which can challenge trust and fidelity in one's current relationship. This may pose a particular challenge when the end of a past relationship is not clearly marked by a divorce (a common pattern among low-income couples), and yet that couple still must maintain contact owing to their children.

Domain 9: Commitment to the Couple

Fowers (2003), Nock (2003), and Cowan and Cowan (2003) argued for including commitment among the constructs that compose marital health. In Nock's view, "A healthy marriage (or relationship) is one in which partners are sufficiently committed to their union" (p. 2), which is the key to withstanding inevitable bouts of disaffection in marriage. Fowers viewed commitment as an essential individual contribution that partners must develop to maintain enduring relationships. This construct includes a number of elements, including a sense of "we-ness" and obligation, a feeling that there are costs and barriers to leaving the marriage, a willingness to sacrifice for the spouse, minimal monitoring of alternatives to the marriage, and an expectation that the relationship is long-term. Stanley and Markman (1992) described commitment as including both dedication and constraints, with dedication being the desire to invest, improve, and sacrifice for a relationship (see chap. 6, this volume, for further discussion). Constraints are a separate construct from dedication, involving such aspects as standard of living or social relationships that may change for the worse as a result of divorce.

In his longitudinal study, Nock (2003) found that commitment correlates with several measures of marital quality, and in fact, is a stronger predictor of divorce than other indicators of marital quality. Commitment to the couple, therefore, should be a central construct in the definition of a healthy marriage or relationship.

Domain 10: Duration and Legal Status

Finally, we note two elements, duration and legal status. Numerous studies in the United States indicate that marriage should be distinguished from cohabitation because the two have different implications for children. Specifically, although most children who are not reared by both biological, married parents turn out well (Hetherington & Kelly, 2002), children who

have lived with cohabiting parents are more likely to be worse off economically than children with married parents (Manning & Lichter, 1996), they
are at a higher risk of experiencing family structure changes, and they have
fewer legal claims to child support or other sources of family income (Graefe
& Lichter, 1999). They also generally have poorer outcomes than children
reared by biological parents who are married (S. L. Brown, 2004).

Assessing whether the couple is legally married is not an enormous
challenge. Duration since marriage is also relatively straightforward to
conceptualize and measure. Moreover, a legal marriage of longer duration
can be considered a good outcome. However, measuring the duration of
a nonmarital romantic relationship is more complex, with considerable
ambiguity about when a relationship starts and ends. These difficulties are
less pressing for our work, though, given the clear focus on legal marriage in
the intervention studies.

DISTINGUISHING THE COMPONENTS
FROM THE ANTECEDENTS OF A
HEALTHY MARRIAGE

Multiple studies have identified other factors that are strongly associated
with marriage, its dissolution, and quality, such as finances, social support,
mental and physical health, substance use, incarceration, religiosity, children from prior relationships, and community context (see later discussion;
M. Coleman, Ganong, & Fine, 2000). Advocates regularly note that ignoring such factors in programs to support healthy marriage is unrealistic and
undermines their effectiveness. Others argue that such factors do not equate
with healthy marriage per se, but are antecedents to a healthy marriage.

Defining a healthy marriage or relationship is a controversial task,
especially when the focus is on the relationships of low-income couples.
Low-income individuals face many challenges known to place couples at a
higher risk for marital disruption, lower quality marriage, or no marriage at
all. Smock and Manning (2003a) found that financial constraints influence
whether and when cohabitors decide to marry. Job loss is a stressor to individual and family well-being, particularly when emotional and economic
resources are already strained (Conger et al., 1990; Liker & Elder, 1983),
and economic insecurity appears to take a particular toll on a husband's
provider-role anxiety (Ganong & Coleman, 2003; W. E. Johnson, 2003;
Menaghan, 1991; Murry, 2003; Smock & Manning, 2003a).

Social networks can also influence marriage and marital quality. Many
researchers argue that measuring social support from relationships outside
the couple dyad—such as multigenerational households or peer and family
networks—may be better indicators of family health than those that focus
only on the couple (E. A. Anderson, 2003), especially when considering

young, low-income, or unwed couples (Fowers, 2003; W. E. Johnson, 2003; Kitzmann et al., 2003; Lichter, Batson, & Mellott, 2003; Murry, 2003).

We see this controversy as an important consideration in developing a conceptual model and framework for measurement work. We address this issue by explicitly distinguishing between factors that are correlated with or predict a healthy marriage (i.e., antecedents) and the definition of a healthy marriage for several reasons.

The first reason for distinguishing the antecedents of healthy marriage is conceptual. Many of the elements mentioned previously may be related to a healthy marriage, but not necessarily define a healthy marriage. For instance, lacking a job and experiencing economic strain can predict marital difficulties (Conger et al., 1990; Hernandez, 1993; Liker & Elder, 1983; Menaghan, 1991), but lacking a job defines unemployment, not an unhealthy marriage. Similarly, although a higher income can buffer difficult circumstances (Bolger, Zuckerman, & Kessler, 2000; Waite, Bachrach, Hindin, Thomson, & Thornton, 2000), lack of economic strain does not necessarily define a healthy marriage. Accordingly, antecedents should be conceptually distinguished from the definition of a healthy marriage.

The second reason for distinguishing the antecedents from the definition of healthy marriage is also conceptual. A healthy marriage is a couple construct, whereas many of the antecedents are measured at the individual level, or other contextual levels. Physical health and education, for example, are characteristics of individuals. Social support, on the other hand, reflects involvement of a larger community of family, friends, and neighbors, over whom couples may have little influence. Instead, when defining a healthy marriage or relationship, research should incorporate elements that are centered in the relationship of the couple.

The third reason is practical. Distinguishing etiological factors from outcomes helps to clarify some potential points of intervention. In other words, antecedents differ from the elements of a healthy marriage because they cause problems for couples or pose barriers to healthy marriage and thus might be targets for intervention. The measure of healthy marriage then assesses the success of those interventions. Perhaps some would not consider a conceptual model as a "practical" reason, but others would argue that nothing is as practical as a good theory or model (Heyman, 2003; Holman, 2003).

DISTINGUISHING THE COMPONENTS FROM THE CONSEQUENCES OF A HEALTHY MARRIAGE

As with the antecedents of a healthy marriage, the consequences must be distinguished from the definition of a healthy marriage. Such consequences include social, personal, economic, and family outcomes, both for parents and for children. Some antecedents and consequences assess the same domain because some factors are both antecedents and consequences. For example, on the one hand, a good income can increase the prospects for marriage (see White & Rogers, 2000, for a review), and economic difficulties can strain a marriage (McLaughlin & Lichter, 1997). On the other hand, marriage can contribute to earning a higher income (Waite, 1995). Similarly, positive mental and physical health can enhance a marriage (Booth & Johnson, 1994; C. Johnson, 1985; Whisman & Bruce, 1999), and at the same time, those who are married have more optimal health than those who are not (Horwitz, Raskin, & Howell-White, 1996; Links & Stockwell, 2002; Mirowsky, Goldsteen, & Ross, 1990; Sacco & Phares, 2001; Waite, 1995).

Marital processes are also associated with adult and child well-being. Supportive behaviors displayed by one's spouse help to buffer against distress during stressful events (Bolger et al., 2000). Certain communication patterns, such as a demand for change followed by spousal withdrawal from confrontation, place couples at higher risk of divorce (Gottman, 1994). Marital conflict is associated with a deterioration in parent–child relationships (Amato, 1993; Grych & Fincham, 1990; P. E. Peterson & Zill, 1986). Hetherington, Cox, and Cox (1982) found that parental conflict leads to stress, which leads to less effective parenting.

Research on the effects of relationship quality for children's well-being typically focuses on well-being in either childhood or early adulthood, often with the goal of understanding the divorce process. These studies find that parental conflict undermines children's emotional and behavioral well-being (Amato, 1993; Emery, 1988; Grych & Fincham, 1990), even in young adulthood (Amato & Rogers, 1997). The critical point is that researchers have distinguished the elements of a healthy marriage and found that they predict numerous consequences, and measures should preserve this important distinction.

These principles and the 10 healthy marriage constructs are depicted in Fig. 7.1. In this measurement framework, we distinguish background, antecedents, and consequences from the definition of a healthy marriage or relationship.

OPERATIONALIZING A HEALTHY MARRIAGE

In operationalizing the definition of a healthy marriage, we ultimately seek to develop a single scale or index of the health of a marriage or relationship. A single measure, which might range from 0 to 100, would be most efficient. Such a measure would provide a straightforward dependent variable

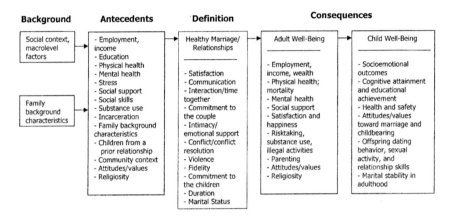

FIG. 7.1.   Measurement framework.

for an evaluation study. Creating such a measure is a challenge, however, for several reasons.

To illustrate these challenges and offer a heuristic device, we combined the subgroups with the healthy marriage elements in a matrix and posited the index to total 100 (see Table 7.1). In this matrix, a cell represents the intersection of a construct with a particular population, and each cell contains a measure. It could be a single item, a scale, an index, or a battery of observational measures. Ideally, the measure would be reduced to a single score, say a 10 for that cell, and, ideally, adjacent cells in a row would contain identical measures and they would all be scored on a scale from 0 to 10.

However, reading across each row, it is clear that the meaning of a given construct differs across the columns, that is, across family structure types. For example, communication is quite different for couples who do and do not live together and for those with a partner who is in the military or who is incarcerated. Fidelity also is very different for coresident couples and nonresident, estranged couples. Similarly, time together and commitment are less relevant for estranged couples than coresident couples.

Obviously, developing measures of the constructs across types of families on the same metric represents a substantial challenge. In particular, it may be impossible to assess healthy marriage among couples who are estranged, necessitating a dummy variable. Thus, couples who are estranged would be coded 0, and only couples in a current relationship would be assigned a numerical score. (Similar variables have been created for wages, designating those who are not working with a dummy variable and calculating wages only for those who are working.)

For a variety of reasons, we prefer to allow all types of couples the possibility of scoring the maximum (say a 10) on each construct. Thus,

TABLE 7.1
Healthy-Marriage Constructs and Subgroups, With One Potential Scoring System

Constructs	(Re)Married or Cohabiting Biological Parents	Residential (Re)Married or Cohabiting Couples With Any Stepchildren	(Re)Married or Cohabiting Couples Without Children	Institutionalized Populations (e.g., Couples With a Partner in Prison)	Nonresidential Visiting Couples or Couples Planning to Marry, With or Without Children	Couples Who Become Estranged, With or Without Children
Satisfaction	10	10	10	10	10	10
Communication	10	10	10	10	10	10
Interaction/time together	10	10	10	10	10	10
Commitment to children	10	10	10	10	10	10
Emotional intimacy	10	10	10	10	10	10
Conflict resolution	10	10	10	10	10	10
Violence	10	10	10	10	10	10
Fidelity	10	10	10	10	10	10
Commitment to the couple	10	10	10	10	10	10
Marital status/duration	10	10	10	10	0	0
Total =	100	100	100	100	90/100	90/100

an estranged couple would not automatically be assigned a 0 on communication or interaction. This allows for the possibility that a marriage intervention may improve communication and interaction skills, even among couples who split up. It also acknowledges the limits of the current knowledge base. Specifically, it is yet unclear which constructs should be truncated and which should not. Marital status and duration represent an exception. Unmarried couples would presumably receive a 0 on marital status and duration, whereas estranged couples would score less than 10 on marital status and duration. Reflecting, however, the possibility that couples who have participated in marriage interventions have gained relationship skills that enhance their coparenting despite the breakup of their marriage or relationship, it seems appropriate to develop a measure that gives all couples the possibility of scoring the maximum on the other constructs. If this fails, the solution adopted by studies of wages represents a fallback.

In addition, as shown in Table 7.1, ideally a total score is envisioned for each column. This total score would be useful for an evaluation that seeks an answer on the overall impact of the healthy-marriage intervention. It is critical to reiterate, though, that the separate constructs can be examined individually as well. In addition, a subset of constructs can be combined into a subscale; for example, intimacy, interaction, and communication could be combined for analyses. In addition, difference scores could be computed. In the illustrative matrix shown in Table 7.1, each column totals to 100. If couples cannot score 100 (e.g., they have no children), their score could be multiplied by a constant to put it on a comparable metric. As with rows, the cases in a column (or cases in several columns), which correspond to specific groups, could be examined separately. However, selecting cases based on their characteristics several years after random assignment, when healthy marriage outcomes would be assessed, would be a nonexperimental analysis. Our goal is to create a robust but flexible set of measures that can be used in a number of types of analyses.

Another difficult question is how to weight the various components. It cannot be presumed that each cell down a column would have the same weight. That is, if violence counts as 10, it should not be presumed that satisfaction also counts as 10, and that intimacy is a 10 as well. If domestic violence is scored as a 10, then perhaps satisfaction should be scored 5 or 8. Unfortunately, an empirical basis for assigning such weights is lacking. For this reason, in this matrix, we have given each construct an equal weight. It would be optimal to establish weights empirically, for example, by including the elements identified as constructs central to the definition of a healthy marriage in a multivariate regression analysis predicting child outcomes. Even a cross-sectional analysis would inform the absolute and relative importance of the several constructs.

Having empirical data would help address a number of additional measurement questions. For example, it is unclear whether varied components are linear. Are gains to adult and child well-being larger at the bottom of the index, or are the increments similar across the index?

Whether to define cutoffs for a healthy marriage is another question. Policy audiences and journalists appreciate having a yes/no outcome; common examples are whether a family is in poverty or not, or has health insurance or not. For this reason, it would be desirable to sharply distinguish between healthy and unhealthy marriages. As noted, however, we view healthy marriage as a continuum and it seems inherently difficult to define cut points for healthy, unhealthy, or "good enough" relationships. We suspect that a consensus might be reached that an "unhealthy" marriage or relationship involves one or both of the deal breakers of violence or infidelity. However, it is far less clear what is "healthy enough." Again, empirical analyses predicting, for example, child, family, and adult well-being would be helpful. In the absence of such empirical evidence, we designed an ordinal index with cutoffs to be considered at a later date as data become available.

Because the goal of federal healthy-marriage interventions is to enhance outcomes for children, it would be helpful to measure all of these constructs in the same survey and prospectively examine their individual and cumulative association with child outcomes, as well as adult and family outcomes. Such a study would provide evidence to help decide how to weight various components, to explore nonlinearities and cutoff points, and to assess which components have the greatest effect on child, adult, and family well-being.

Developing Survey Items

Clearly, the task of developing and testing specific items to measure healthy-marriage constructs across populations is a major challenge. Although observational measures are possible, the primary focus of our work has been to develop items for surveys. We have developed a number of guidelines for this purpose.

Specifically, the components of the healthy-marriage or relationship measure should be sufficiently broad in scope to capture the varied outcomes that different programs will conceivably target (e.g., communication strategies, conflict resolution, and commitment to marriage). In addition, measures should tap into aspects of relationships that are malleable; in particular, aspects that might change as a result of an intervention. Items should be applicable and meaningful to diverse racial-ethnic and socioeconomic groups, including disadvantaged couples, given that interventions will disproportionately include economically disadvantaged couples.

As noted, couples are also likely to differ in terms of family type (e.g., cohabiting vs. married stepfamilies; nonresidential vs. residential couples), the presence of children, and the stage of their relationship. Therefore, where possible, questions should apply appropriately across family types. Moreover, because the ultimate goal of this project is to promote child well-being, higher priority should be given to items that tap aspects of a healthy relationship that are most closely associated with child well-being.

The time frame is also a consideration. In the Supporting Healthy Marriage evaluation, outcome data collection is scheduled for 2 and 5 years after random assignment. If some dimensions of a healthy marriage are likely to be affected more quickly than others, we must measure those dimensions sooner rather than later. Certain items (e.g., conflict and violence) will need a specified time frame, such as the past year or the past month; and the time frame should be as consistent as possible throughout the instrument to reduce respondent burden, increase accuracy of reporting, and provide comparable measures that can be scaled.

In addition, because positive behaviors in marriage are attributes of long-term satisfying relationships (Cutrona, 1996), researchers should take care to include constructs and items that capture positive aspects (e.g., commitment, intimacy, and satisfaction). Items should also be designed to reflect both male and female perspectives, as well as the couple's perspectives. Care should be taken to ensure that response scales across (final) items are compatible so that items can be cumulated. Finally, instruments should limit the number of response scales to decrease respondent burden and interview length and to increase the ability to create composite scales.

Cognitive interviews provide insight into how well instruments work for the target population of economically disadvantaged couples who are married or planning to marry. Cognitive testing for healthy-marriage items is critical, given that most prior research on relationship quality has been based on White, middle-class married couples. Does the language in the items make sense to the respondents? Are the issues covered salient to the respondents? Cognitive interviews will help identify items that are likely to be appropriate and relevant to the population targeted for the Supporting Healthy Marriage evaluation; however, as noted, a full pretest would be needed to confirm that a measure of healthy marriage is reliable and valid among economically disadvantaged respondents who are married or are planning to marry.

DISCUSSION AND CONCLUSIONS

The goal of the project discussed here is to devise a healthy-marriage or -relationship measure that can be used to evaluate the impact of interventions that support healthy marriages. Although we draw on an extensive research base, including both tried-and-true and more innovative approaches, the measures that we develop can be distinguished from past approaches in several ways. First, it is important not only to measure marital status or marital stability, but also to measure whether the couple relationship is a healthy relationship. Also, the measure we develop must be appropriate and applicable for diverse, low-income populations; and it should encompass aspects of healthy marriage that are related to child well-being, an ultimate concern of this endeavor.

We have described several challenges we face in devising a final measure of a healthy marriage or relationship. Primary among these is creating a measure that is appropriate for diverse and low-income populations. Another challenge is measuring the influence of social support, income, stress, and additional adults in the households. In addressing this challenge, we have developed a conceptual model that defines healthy marriage as a distinct construct from factors that we consider to be antecedents or consequences of a healthy marriage.

An additional challenge is that some couples may be cohabiting, living apart, or estranged at follow-up surveys. For certain constructs, it will likely be necessary to develop items specific to that population; for example, questionnaire items measuring the construct of commitment will differ if the couple is estranged. Overall, comparable items on the same metric represent an ideal, but there is a real and as yet unresolved tension between addressing diversity and seeking a comparable measure across groups.

Another challenge is how to combine constructs into a scale of healthy marriage. Some dimensions of a healthy marriage may matter more than others. For example, we suspect that violence in a marriage may appropriately be weighted more heavily than other dimensions, such as interaction, because of the clear concern for a person's immediate health and safety. Ideally, it would be useful to empirically examine the relative associations between other constructs (such as satisfaction, communication, fidelity, interaction/time together, intimacy/emotional support, conflict and conflict resolution, commitment to the couple, commitment to the children, and marital status/duration) and child well-being to establish guidelines for scale construction. In the meantime, cognitive interviews can help assess the meaning of constructs and the wording of items.

Policies to support healthy marriages are expected to strengthen families, reduce poverty and out-of-wedlock births, and improve the well-being of American children. A critical departure for this policy is its emphasis on marriages that are healthy for the well-being of couples and their children, and not just marriage per se. Although evidence suggests that a low-conflict marriage between two biological parents is optimal for child well-being, only minimal evidence to date suggests that an intervention can improve the likelihood of a child living with two parents who share a healthy marriage. To our knowledge, there is no evidence from an experimental evaluation that such an intervention can be beneficial for low-income couples who face multiple stressors. Thus, it is crucial that the measures we develop are conceptually and empirically solid, because they will be used to answer an extremely important question: Are interventions to support healthy marriages effective?

ACKNOWLEDGMENTS

This chapter was prepared with support from the Interagency Agreement between the U.S. Department of Health and Human Services, Administration for Children and Families (ACF), and the U.S. Department of Health and Human Services, National Institutes of Child and Human Development (NICHD), through the NICHD Family and Child Well-Being Network (Grant HD30930 awarded to Moore).

PART III

Separation and Divorce

8

Measuring Separation and Divorce

Larry Bumpass
University of Wisconsin–Madison

Kelly Raley
University of Texas–Austin

Marital instability is a central aspect of the American family system. The proportion of all first marriages that ended in divorce increased exponentially for more than a hundred years (Cherlin, 1992), and over the last quarter of a century about one half of all first marriages have been expected to disrupt. The consequences of this high level of marital instability for the well-being of both adults and children are well documented (Amato, 2000; Seltzer, 1994). Even during the plateau since 1980, social inequality in family life has continued to increase as a consequence of divergent trends (Raley & Bumpass, 2003). Our understanding of this important family experience is obviously dependent on how well we are able to measure marital instability. This is true for the monitoring of trends, as well as for research on the causes and consequences of disruption, and on the potential effects of social policy.

We begin with a discussion of different measures of family instability and review several issues affecting the accuracy of those measures. We then compare the quality of estimates from retrospective histories, vital statistics, and longitudinal measures across surveys with varying times since events

and with different substantive focuses. Finally, we consider the data needed
to improve measures of family stability. In all but one section of this chapter,
we focus solely on reports from women, both because of the lower quality
of reports from men (McCarthy, Pendleton, & Cherlin, 1989), and because
many of the surveys we examine are limited to women.

CONCEPTUAL ISSUES

Divorce Versus Separation as Dissolution Date

Recent estimates suggest that 43% of all first marriages will end in divorce
(Schoen & Standish, 2001). This is not, as might be assumed, a revision
of common estimates that one half of all marriages will break up (Cherlin, 1992; Raley & Bumpass, 2003). The difference between the estimates
results from the distinction between separation and divorce. The first estimate is of divorce; the second includes separations that have not resulted in
divorce. Indeed, separation is the more appropriate measure because some
couples separate permanently but never get divorced (Sweet & Bumpass,
1987). Although legal issues are defined by divorce, a marriage effectively
ends from a social perspective when a couple separates permanently. Hence,
using the date of separation rather than divorce has become a common
practice in analyses of family instability (Andersson & Phillipov, 2002;
Sweet & Bumpass, 1987; Teachman, 2002).

One potential, but minor, complication is that some who are separated
at the time they are interviewed will subsequently reconcile (Bumpass,
Sweet, & Castro Martin, 1990). Because almost all of the separations that
reconcile do so within a year, only separations that occur within a year of
the interview are likely to affect the results. We estimate that less than
5% of the separations measured for the 5-year marriage cohort immediately preceding the interview are likely to reconcile. The proportion will
be slightly higher when estimates are based completely on events closer to
the interview, as, for example, in period life-table estimates for the prior
year. Even then, however, reconciliations will affect estimates of disruption timing more than the ultimate proportion of disruptions because most
of those who reconcile eventually separate permanently. (Nonetheless, to
avoid potential bias owing to separations that will be at least temporarily
reconciled, the estimates in this chapter have been censored a year prior to
the interview.)

Using the date of separation versus the date of divorce to mark the end
of a marriage can significantly affect measures of both the timing and level
of marital disruption, and these differences are particularly important when
comparing population subgroups, especially African Americans and Whites

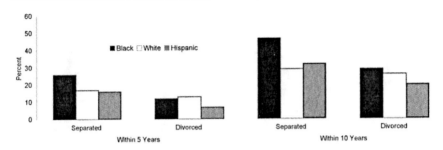

FIG. 8.1. Percent of first marriages disrupted within 5 and 10 years, as measured by divorce and by separation, by race-ethnicity: women, 1995 NSFG.

(McCarthy, 1978). Figure 8.1 illustrates the consequences of this measurement difference, based on marriages occurring between 1980 and 1994 using the 1995 National Survey of Family Growth (NSFG). When divorce is used to define the end of marriage, there appears to be little difference in marital stability by race. When separation is used to mark the date of disruption, however, a much higher rate of disruption is seen for African American marriages. These differences are large, and by 10 years after marriage almost one half of African American marriages had separated, compared with about 30% of those of Whites. Bramlett and Mosher (2001) clearly demonstrated why this is so. They estimated that virtually all separations will culminate in divorce within 10 years of separation among non-Hispanic Whites compared with only 79% among African Americans.

Marriages Versus All Unions

Marriage dissolution has long been used to define family instability. Although recognizing that many cohabiting unions are not "like marriage" (Rindfuss & VandenHeuvel, 1990), we must consider both marital and cohabiting transitions if we are to understand family instability (Bumpass & Lu, 2000; Bumpass & Raley, 1995; Bumpass, Raley, & Sweet, 1995). For this purpose, we combine both married and cohabiting unions, and we define the risk of breaking up as beginning when the couple begins living together (whether or not they subsequently marry). The difference between focusing just on marriages and including all unions is illustrated in Fig. 8.2, which presents life-table estimates of family instability by race and ethnicity for two cohorts, those formed in 1980–1986 and 1987–1994 (Raley & Bumpass, 2003).

The first two sets of columns represent only *marital* stability. In the more recent cohort, about one third of African American marriages ended within 5 years compared with about one fourth of White marriages. Nonetheless,

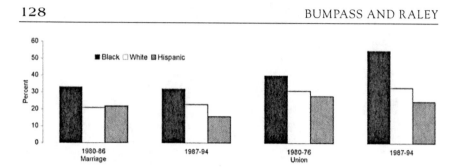

FIG. 8.2.   Percent of first marriages/unions (cohabitations and marriages) separated or divorced within 5 years, by race-ethnicity: women, 1995 NSFG.

race differences in *union* instability are much greater. Whereas one third of White unions ended within 5 years, more than one half of African American unions did so. Hence, African American marriages are 39% more likely than White marriages to end within 5 years, but when married and cohabiting unions are combined, African American *unions* are 67% more likely to do so. Looking at all unions, including cohabitations, we see that family instability increased much more rapidly among African Americans than among Whites. This change is missed if one examines only marriages.

Including transitions into and out of cohabitation is important for research documenting children's experiences as well. Life-table estimates from the 1995 NSFG show that if one counts only marital transitions, the average child experiences only 0.69 transitions by age 12, but if cohabitation is included, the average child experiences 0.92 transitions. (Note that the transition from a union to marriage is not counted in the second estimate.) As we would expect from the previous discussion, including cohabitation has a much larger effect on estimates for African American children than for Whites. The average African American child experiences fewer changes to his or her parents' marriage than the average White child (0.55 compared with 0.69, respectively). However, African American children experience many more changes in family composition when both the mother's cohabitations and marriages are considered (1.18). Put another way, more than one half of the family instability that African American children experience occurs from transitions in and out of unmarried unions (Raley & Wildsmith, 2004).

First Versus All Marriages

Finally, most of the research on trends and differences in divorce (including our own) focuses on a first marriage, even though about one third of all brides have been married before, and almost one half of all marriages are remarriages for at least one spouse (National Center for Health Statistics [NCHS], 1996). It is well known that second and subsequent marriages are less stable than first marriages (Bramlett & Mosher, 2002; Castro Martin & Bumpass, 1989). For example, among marriages formed between 1985 and 1994, 40% of second marriages disrupted within 10 years compared with about 32% of first marriages (based on life-table calculations using the 1995 June Current Population Survey).

Although the estimated proportion of all marriages that will break up is only slightly higher than that of just first marriages, including these higher order marriages can make a larger difference among populations with less stable marriages. The ability to separately consider marriages by their order is often restricted by sample size or sample design issues, but researchers also likely focus on first marriages when addressing more general objectives either out of habit or because it is easier. One understandable reason for this habit is the importance of first marriage as a part of life-course development, and the focus on this marriage tends to carry over into the analysis of separation and divorce.

DESIGN ISSUES

Retrospective Versus Longitudinal Measurement

It seems evident that longitudinal surveys provide more accurate data on transitions than retrospective histories because the time interval to be recalled is much shorter. Nonetheless, we know very little about the extent to which this is so for the various dimensions of family stability. Differences in the quality of data collected from these two measurement approaches very likely depend on factors such as the definitiveness of the transition being measured and the time that has elapsed since the event. In addition, longitudinal measurements necessarily either are dated inexactly by current statuses at successive interviews, or are themselves retrospective reports, albeit for shorter time intervals.

In the first instance, the range of error in the interval between events can be almost 2 years in the case of annual interviews, and 4 years if interviews are biannual. A respondent who was single at one interview, married at the next, and separated at the next may have married immediately after the first interview and separated just before the last, or married just before and separated just after the middle of these three waves.

In addition, spells that began and ended between interviews are missed altogether, as was the case with cohabitation intervals in the National Longitudinal Survey of Youth (NLSY) in earlier waves (Gryn, Mott, & Burchett-Patel, 2000). It is for this reason that the Panel Study of Income Dynamics

(PSID) and NLSY now ask about the dates of transitions since the prior interview. Mott and colleagues note in chapter 16, this volume, that male reports of fertility can be inconsistent between interviews, even when asked at 1- or 2-year intervals. It is plausible that these differences can be introduced by life circumstances that affect reporting at one interview, but that may be irrelevant when events are reported from a longer range perspective.

In some instances, longitudinal surveys have included a supplement in a single year that collects a retrospective history spanning prior interview waves. This was true for the PSID in 1985 and for the National Longitudinal Study of the High School Class of 1972 (NLS72) in 1986. These histories provide dates of transitions that were missed when only changes in statuses between interviews were measured. Because the period spanned in these retrospective histories included interview waves that had asked respondents to recall dates of events that had occurred since the prior interview, these data sets provide unique opportunities for comparing retrospective and longitudinal data.

Question Format and Sample Coverage

It should be clear from this discussion that we think it is essential to ask the dates couples start and stop living together in addition to dates of marriage and divorce. Beyond this, however, a key issue has little to do with the wording of questions per se, but with whether researchers collect the dates of marriage, separation, and divorce as a separate history, which entails collecting the sequential dates of formation and dissolution of each marriage, or whether they collect these dates in the context of surrounding life events, that is, a life-history calendar (Freedman, Thornton, Camburn, Alwin, & Young-DeMarco, 1988). In a life-history calendar, researchers record events on a sheet laid out before the respondent so that responses about the dates of events in one domain can be used as reference points for recalling others. Suppose a respondent moved in with his girlfriend during the fall after he graduated. He might be better able to report when this cohabitation began if placed in the context of his month and year of graduation already recorded on the calendar.

The life-history calendar works very well for a young cohort, such as the study of 1961 births in Detroit (Thornton, Axinn, & Teachman, 1995), but it is more difficult to apply in a study with a broad cross section of ages, such as in the National Survey of Families and Households (NSFH), or even the NSFG. There are practical limits to the length of a life-history calendar (in the absence of a scroll). Furthermore, although adaptations can be made, such as sending the respondent a calendar before the interview, life-history calendars are more difficult to employ in telephone surveys.

In any application of this approach, however, researchers must make choices about the domains to be used as cues for transitions in other domains. With this point in mind, it becomes clear that the format in which cohabitation histories are collected vis-à-vis marriage histories is simply a more limited version of the issues relating to life-history calendars. The NSFH approach, for example, keys questions about cohabitation to the marriage history, given that marriage histories are more clearly defined, with marriage dates being particularly salient. After the marriage history has been recorded, respondents are then asked about each interval before the first marriage, between marriages, and after the last, as applicable. Each sequence before a marriage begins by asking whether the respondent lived with his or her spouse before the marriage, and if so, when they began living together. An alternative is to ask about each cohabiting union sequentially, recording whether the couple was married when they started living together, whether they ever married, and if so, the date they married. This was the procedure followed in the National Health and Social Life Survey (NHSLS) and in the 1986 wave of the NLS72.

Upper Age Limits on Samples

We conclude this section by elaborating on a well-known, but often forgotten, observation about the effects of upper age constraints. This is illustrated most clearly by the NSFG with a sample that targets women of reproductive age, with an upper age limit of 45. Among a single-year marriage cohort married 20 years before the 1995 survey (in this case women marrying in 1975), only those who married before age 25 are represented in the 1995 survey because of the upper age limit of 45. This censoring on age at marriage obviously becomes progressively more severe for each earlier cohort. Hence, trends can be evaluated in a single survey only for a relatively recent past, and for marriages initiated before the youngest age represented in the earliest cohort. The problem is more severe the older the ages at which initiating events occur, one example being the risk of divorce after second marriage. Furthermore, this limitation affects life-table estimates such as the cumulative proportion divorced by a given duration since marriage, given that the estimates of the probability of divorce at successively longer durations are limited to persons who married at progressively younger ages. When a survey has been repeated periodically over several decades, this problem can be resolved by pooling the data across survey years, as both Bramlett and Mosher (2002) and Teachman (2002) have done with the NSFG.

COMPARISONS EVALUATING DATA QUALITY

We now turn to the issue of whether survey data accurately depict these experiences at the population level. We examine estimates derived from the 1980, 1985, 1990, and 1995 June Current Population Surveys (CPS), the 1987–1988 NSFH, the NSFG pooled across years, the 1979 NLSY, the Survey of Income and Program Participation (SIPP), and vital statistics in addition to the NHSLS. These surveys represent a wide range of dates and central topics, and they employ different questioning approaches and interview modes.

For example, the main objective of the CPS is to collect information about employment and the labor force, whereas the focus of the NSFG is sex, fertility, and contraception. The NSFH explores family life. The NSFH, NSFG, and early CPS surveys were all in-person interviews, but the 1995 CPS was a telephone survey. Although we base most of our estimates on retrospective histories, those from NLSY79 are longitudinal. These differences enable us to examine the robustness of estimates of divorce across a variety of approaches to data collection.

Time Since Event

We can assess whether reporting accuracy deteriorates with passing time by comparing estimates for cohorts as they were represented in successive quinquennial June CPS surveys. There is little evidence in Fig. 8.3 that marital separation is reported less accurately in surveys further removed in time

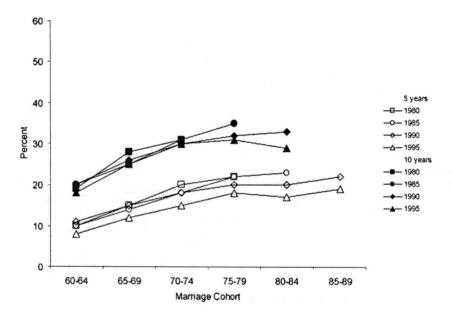

FIG. 8.3.   Percent of first marriages separated or divorced within 5 and 10 years, by marriage cohort and survey year: women, June CPS 1980, 1985, 1990, and 1995.

from the events being reported. Two patterns should be noted, however. First, estimates of separation by both 5 and 10 years after marriage tend to be about 3% higher in the survey closest to a marriage cohort than in later surveys. These differences are not likely a consequence of better reports of events just before surveys, given that these reports are for events that occur 1 to 10 years before surveys for separations of 5 years, and 10 to 20 years before surveys for separations of 10 years. Furthermore, the estimates are almost identical across surveys for earlier cohorts.

Second, estimates from the 1995 CPS are about 3 percentage points lower across all cohorts than those from the other survey years. The complete shift from personal to telephone interviewing in the 1995 survey does not explain this because two thirds of the 1990 June CPS interviews were completed by telephone. All of these differences are relatively small, and the key point is that the CPS data seem to provide consistent estimates even when events are measured as long as 30 years after their occurrence.

Survey Context

The preceding information has demonstrated rather remarkable agreement across surveys using the same questions, the same format, and the same survey context. As noted earlier, the NSFH, NSFG, and SIPP provide varying contexts, ranging from a study dedicated to family issues, to one heavily concerned with contraception and fertility, to one focused almost solely on economic issues. When we compare estimates of separation by 10 years from these surveys with those we have observed from the 1990 CPS (Fig. 8.4), we again find rather high agreement. (We select 10 years because the estimates from the NSFG are reported for this duration, and we use the 1990 CPS because of the systematic deviation seen in Fig. 8.3 for the 1995 CPS.)

There are, however, some inexplicable deviations: The NSFG estimate is about 6 percentage points below the others for the 1965 to 1969 marriage cohort, and the SIPP estimates for the 1980 to 1984 cohort are about 5 points below that from the 1990 CPS. There is further evidence of consistency across surveys, in that using data pooled across all of the NSFG years, Teachman (2002, and personal communication, October 26, 2004) found no interactions between survey year and disruption during the first 10 years of marriage. We therefore conclude that the surveys examined here are in striking agreement. Indeed, this agreement is even more remarkable because of the high levels of proxy reporting and imputation in the CPS. (For example, McCarthy et al., 1989, indicated that in the June 1980 CPS about one fourth of the marriage histories were reported by someone other than the interviewee, and that dates were imputed for about 13% of the

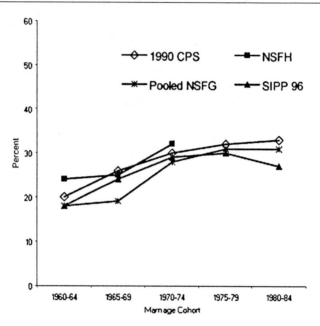

FIG. 8.4.   Percent of first marriages separated within 10 years, by marriage cohort and survey: women, CPS, NSFH, NSFG, and SIPP.

marriage dates, for about one fourth of the divorce dates, and for more than one third of the separation dates.)

We can examine two surveys—the NHSLS and NLS72—for marriage histories as part of a sequential partner history, although we must examine each from the perspective of birth cohorts rather than marriage cohorts. The 1986 wave of NLS72 included retrospective marriage histories embedded in partner histories. (Hence, although the study is longitudinal, the marriage history was collected through retrospective reporting.) Of those who had married by 1986, life-table estimates indicate that 25% had seen their marriage dissolve within 6.5 years (Teachman & Paasch, 1991). The 1990 CPS shows that 24% of the marriages dissolved among 1972 high school graduates. Once again, despite the difference in question design, the estimates are amazingly comparable.

The results are different when we examine the other survey that collected marital histories as a part of partner histories. Laumann, Gagnon, Michael, and Michaels (1994) reported the proportion that had divorced within 10 years of marriage for three birth cohorts, those in their 30s, 40s, or 50s at the time of the NHSLS survey. These estimates differ substantially from those obtained for these cohorts from the June 1990 CPS, and the difference is greater the longer the time before the survey. The NHSLS estimates are 12% higher for the youngest cohort, 27% higher for the middle cohort, and 33% higher than those from the earliest cohort of the 1990 June CPS. A decline in quality of reporting with passing time is not the cause, as might be assumed, because the same time had elapsed for both the CPS and NHSLS reports. Nor is the focus on sexual topics in the NHSLS a likely reason, given that the survey asked only background questions, such as education and employment, before the partnership histories. We are unable to evaluate this difference further given that these divorce figures are reported in a brief section without an elaboration of the procedures used.

We have only one instance in which we compare retrospective histories with longitudinal data. The NLSY79 is obviously a single cohort, but we can compare the marital separation history of this birth cohort, assembled from longitudinal data, with estimates from the 1995 CPS. We chose 1995 data because we wanted to match the longest durations possible, and we have censored the NLSY79 observations at 1995 (which makes little difference). Once again, we are impressed with the high level of agreement across data sources.

Figure 8.5 represents the cumulative proportion separated by years since first marriage. The longitudinal estimates fall only about 2 percentage

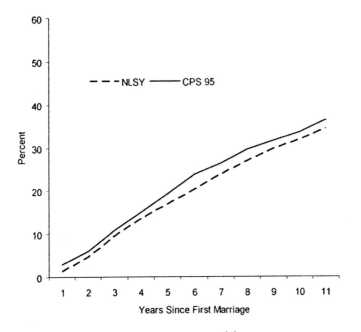

FIG. 8.5. Percent of first marriages separated, by years since marriage, women born 1957–1964: NLYS79 and 1995 CPS (NLSY79 censored at 1995).

points below those from the 1995 CPS at all durations. In itself, this would be a trivial discrepancy, but recall that the 1995 CPS itself consistently fell below the other sources in the estimates for all the marriage cohorts considered. Although not a big difference, these results may suggest some effect of even the modest attrition in the NLSY79 sample, given that those who have separated and divorced are more difficult to locate and interview than others. In any event, these results do not support an argument that longitudinal data provide a more complete account of marital histories than do retrospective reports.

Estimates From Survey Marital Histories and From Vital Statistics

The publication of annual national tabulations on marriage and divorce ceased in 1990 (*Federal Register Notice*, 1995), although age-specific rates continued to be published annually through 1995. State-level counts of marriages and divorces are sent to the NCHS. States in the marriage registration area (MRA) and the divorce registration area (DRA) forwarded either samples or complete files which included characteristics with varying content and completeness across states. These records (or samples of them) were then tabulated to produce national estimates. Even though they are no longer current, vital statistics on marriage and divorce have generally been regarded as the gold standard against which other sources can be evaluated. They have, however, always been far short of such a lofty standing because not all states have participated, and the number participating has varied over the years. In 1995, the MRA included 41 states and the DRA included 31, the latter covering only 47% of the population (Schoen & Standish, 2001). In addition, vital statistics data have been of little use for assessing social differences in divorce rates, especially at the national level, because few characteristics are recorded on divorce certificates, and even these are collected unevenly across states and often with very low response rates.

Given the demise of national vital statistics on marriage and divorce, we now depend completely on survey data (Bramlett & Mosher, 2002). It is nonetheless important to evaluate the extent of agreement between surveys and vital statistics. Early estimates suggested that survey results fell as much as 25% below vital statistics; these estimates are by Preston and McDonald (1979), comparing the 1970 census, and McCarthy et al. (1989), comparing the June 1980 CPS. More recently, Goldstein (1999) concluded that survey data provide estimates consistent with the crude divorce rate. We have two pieces of evidence on this question. As we noted earlier, Schoen and Standish's (2001) estimate of lifetime divorce is highly consistent with survey estimates that one half of all marriages will end in divorce or separation. They drew their numerators from vital statistics and their denomina-

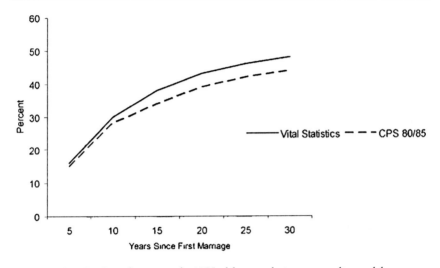

FIG. 8.6.   Period estimates for 1975 of the cumulative percent divorced, by years since first marriage: vital statistics and 1980/85 June CPS.

tors from the March 1995 CPS, with adjustments for the states not covered in the DRA. We replicate their period estimate of divorce (44% compared with 43%) even though they use vital statistics and we use the CPS. This is impressive agreement across sources and methods, especially because their life table was based on age-specific rates and ours used rates specific to marriage duration.

Weed (1980) provided the only source that allows us to compare survey estimates with marital-duration life tables from vital statistics. Using pooled 1980 and 1985 CPS data, we calculated a period life-table estimate for 1975 of the cumulative probability of divorce by successive marital durations. The CPS estimates are derived from the duration-specific experience during 1975 of the 1945–1975 marriage cohorts. Figure 8.6 shows the comparison of these estimates to Weed's. The two sources are virtually identical over the first 10 years of marriage. A slight difference then emerges, with the CPS estimates becoming about 2 percentage points lower. The cumulative proportions estimated to have divorced within 30 years are about 8% lower in the CPS than in vital statistics. This difference contrasts with about 25% in the earlier estimates and our almost exact replication of Schoen and Standish's (2001) estimate from 1995. It does seem that surveys and vital statistics had been drawing closer over time.

Vital statistics rates can also be used to calibrate survey data before they are used in other calculations, as Krieder and Fields (2002) did in their analysis based on the 1996 SIPP. They estimated that 53% of married persons are likely to divorce if the age-specific divorce rate of the early 1990s were to persist over a lifetime. When separations not resulting in divorce are taken into account, this implies a rate of marital disruption considerably higher than other estimates, closer to 60%. Consistent with our earlier assessments of general agreement across sources, our period life-table estimates approximate the commonly understood level of "about one-half" ever separating, whether we use the June CPS data or the 2001 SIPP. It seems likely that the difference results from Krieder and Fields adjusting SIPP weights based on age-specific rates from vital statistics. Hence, Krieder and Field's result could be a very important finding both substantively and methodologically. In addition to documenting a higher level of marital disruption than thought, it would highlight the need to adjust survey data for undercounts in comparison with vital statistics. In the process, it would underscore the significance of the demise of a national vital statistical system on marriage and divorce.

Direct conflict exists, however, between the estimate of the proportion ever divorcing from Krieder and Fields (2002) (53%) and Schoen and Standish (2001) (43%). The estimates are for the same period and are both based on rates specific to age rather than duration. They both took vital statistics into account, adjusting for differential coverage, the first by scaling the weights in survey data and the second by using adjusted vital statistics rates. We are unable to adjudicate this difference, but it warrants careful attention in the future because of its implications for our understanding of levels of marital disruption. This difference raises the question of whether vital statistics should be used to calibrate survey estimates, given the extent to which adjustments are needed for the one half of the population not covered in the DRA. We are skeptical that such adjustments to survey data are appropriate, both because of our replication of Schoen and Standish's (2001) estimate from vital statistics and because of Goldstein's (1999) conclusion that survey and vital statistics agree. If, however, we decide this calibration is necessary, we then must evaluate the robustness of various procedures for adjusting vital statistics for coverage and for calibrating surveys to these adjusted vital statistics estimates.

Mode Effects and Reporting Accuracy

In part because of fiscal constraints, surveys are increasingly moving to computer-assisted telephone interviewing (CATI). This raises the obvious question of whether our measures of marital instability are affected by this change in interview mode. We noted this issue in passing when comparing estimates across the various years of the June CPS. In contrast to personal interviews in the June CPS until 1985, the CPS conducted two thirds of the interviews by phone in 1990 and all in 1995. Yet estimates of the proportion separating by 10 years across the first three marriage cohorts were very close across all of the CPS years, whether or not they were conducted by phone.

To further address this question, and to evaluate the accuracy of reporting, Call and Bumpass conducted a 1996 survey based on a sample of divorce certificates in four counties in Wisconsin. The authors designed the "Life Events and Satisfaction Survey" explicitly to evaluate mode effects. A description of the study can be found in Colter (2003).

Call and Bumpass randomly selected one member of each divorcing couple to be interviewed either in person, by telephone, or by a mail questionnaire. They also drew the divorces from 1989 and 1993 to evaluate any effect of time between the divorce and the interview. Even though parameters from this sample, such as the proportion misreporting various dates, cannot be generalized to the U.S. population, the patterns speak to the issue at hand.

On the one hand, the date of divorce is a legal record and can thus be evaluated with the most certainty. On the other hand, both marriage and separation dates are subject to errors on the certificates, in addition to misreporting by respondents in surveys. Nonetheless, as we would expect, dates of marriage showed the greatest agreement between the survey report and the divorce certificate, and dates of separation the least. Allowing for 6 months on either side of the date on the divorce certificate, women reported marriage dates that agreed in about 90% of the cases, and divorce dates that agreed in about 75% of the cases (Coulter, 2003). If we widen the band to within a year on either side of the divorce, agreement rises to almost 90% for divorce dates and to more than 95% for marriage dates. Hence, we find a considerable amount of "noise" in this measurement of divorce rates, but the error does not appear to be large.

Consistent with our observation from the comparisons across the June CPS years, we find no significant differences in reporting accuracy between phone and personal interviews, although the well-known lower quality of data from men is evident. At variance with our previous findings, however, respondents reported both separation and divorce dates more accurately for events that occurred nearer the interview. The contrast between these results and the agreement across surveys for marriage cohorts suggests that this deterioration with time likely attenuates rather quickly after the first few years. Furthermore, underreporting of marriage and divorce may be offsetting to some degree in the estimation of divorce rates.

DISCUSSION AND RECOMMENDATIONS

The results show strengths and weaknesses in the data. On one hand, we have found surprising agreement across a number of surveys with different focuses, formats, and designs. Furthermore, the estimates in these surveys are consistent with vital statistics for the most recent periods. On the other hand, dates of divorce are sometimes misreported by as much as a year. These results suggest little bias in the reporting error, but perhaps more serious implications for the relative dating of events over the life course.

How well should we expect respondents to remember the dates we are asking them to report? Both the clarity and the saliency of dates to respondents are key factors affecting research, and in research analyzing family stability, these essential dates vary systematically on these factors. On the one hand, dates of marriage and of children's births are unambiguous, and they often remain salient to the respondent throughout life. On the other hand, divorce decrees often occur as part of an extended process and may be less clearly remembered as an exact date. Unlike births and marriages, few divorced respondents mark their divorce anniversary.

Similarly, substantial variation likely exists in the ability to specify the beginning and end of cohabitation. For some, these are single and clearly defined events and are solidly anchored in memory. Others may move in or out of a shared household multiple times, a process interwoven with the evolution or dissolution of their relationship (Smock & Manning, 2003b). When asked in a retrospective survey, such respondents may be unable to assign a clear date even if an event is recent and the question highly specific.

In our attempt to understand the role of family instability in the lives of children and adults, we need cohabitation histories, dates specific to months, samples that cover the respondents across the older ages when children are under age 18, and samples large enough to allow attention to details such as ages of children when marriage or cohabitation begin and end. We offer three recommendations. The first two concern the data available for studying family instability. Significant advances could be made with changes to SIPP and NSFG.

It was a major loss when the June CPS ceased collecting full marital histories every 5 years. Although the absence of cohabitation data had become increasingly serious as cohabitation increased, these marital histories at least allowed researchers to document trends. These included important variation in trends by demographic characteristics and analyses of the effects of these variables on marital stability. The SIPP has partially filled this gap and it has the advantage of having more relevant variables and more frequent observations. These data will allow trends to be better documented than in the past. However, two changes could be made to the SIPP to greatly improve its usefulness.

As is the case with the June CPS, the absence of cohabitation histories is a major limitation. In a time when the majority of marriages begin with the couple living together and almost one half of all cohabiting couples have children present, our ability to understand changing family life is seriously impaired by this omission. We must emphasize how essential it is to obtain cohabitation and marital histories. In their absence, important family transitions of both adults and children are missed, with particular implications for our understanding of low-income and minority families (McLanahan, Garfinkel, & Mincy, 2001). It is critical in this regard to remember that two fifths of all births to unmarried mothers are born into two-parent, though unmarried, families (Bumpass & Lu, 2000; Bumpass & Raley, 1995). We are well aware of the difficulties in implementing this change, but decisions in this regard must consider the consequences of not doing so.

Second, SIPP data are much less than desirable for analyses at the individual level between marital instability and variables such as education, economic well-being, and ethnicity. This is so because the public data include only years, and not months, in which events occurred. We have noted how reporting difficulties create noise in measures of cohabitation, marriage, separation, and divorce dates. To this has now been added a much larger noise component. For example, suppose a marriage began in November of one year and separated in March of the next. With only 1 year of occurrence, we would not know whether this 4-month duration was 2 months (December to January) or almost 2 years (January of one year to November of the next).

Consequently, it would be a major contribution to include months as well as years of events in the SIPP public-use data. This is not done because of potential problems with maintaining confidentiality, but with considerable loss to analyses of family stability. Not having the months in which events occur can introduce errors of almost 2 years in the duration between events such as marriage and divorce and lead to serious misclassification of family statuses on the basis of these dates. At the very least, it is important that some mechanism be in place that will allow users access to these data under secure conditions.

The NSFG has become our major source for periodic data on cohabitation and divorce histories. Nonetheless, these data are limited by their upper age constraint. An older sample is needed if we are to analyze more than first marriages, and if we are to follow the life course of children who are affected by their mothers' transitions after age 45. It is important to remember that the mission of NSFG explicitly includes family and fertility, and its value for this objective could be markedly enhanced by adding a panel of older respondents, aged 45–64. Interviews with this supplemental sample should be much shorter than the present NSFG, covering explanatory variables, birth histories, and marriage and cohabitation histories.

Our second recommendation is to examine error at the individual level to determine, for example, whether it is possible to improve the quality of reported dates through changes in survey questions or procedures. This should include attention to transitions occurring later in the family life course, such as remarriage and the stability of higher order unions.

Obviously, a relevant body of research on measurement must underlie this effort, but that is beyond the scope of this chapter. There is rather little evidence on the superiority of life-history calendars in collecting marital histories. In connection with moving from a 1-year to a 2-year interval between interviews, both the PSID (Belli, Shay, & Stafford, 2001) and the NLSY (Dugoni, Lee, & Tourangeau, 1997) report better correspondence between retrospective and panel data with life-history calendars than with conventional formats. However, neither addressed marital histories. Freedman and colleagues (1988) compared data collected in their Detroit birth cohort study with a reinterview with the same respondents soon after the main interview, but the results were only suggestive of correspondence because of the small size of the follow-up sample.

Several potential designs come to mind. As in the Call and Bumpass (Wisconsin) study described earlier, factorial designs are needed in which respondents are randomly assigned to alternative questioning formats. The design of alternative approaches will necessarily involve variations on life-history calendars, and it must be informed by the kind of qualitative explorations Smock and Manning are doing (2003b).

A major difficulty in this line of research is finding a standard against which to measure "accuracy." This can be relatively straightforward by sampling from lists of marriages or divorces, but it is exceedingly elusive for cohabitation and separation dates for the very reasons they are the most problematic in the first place. Interviewing both partners would allow the extent of agreement to be used as an approximate standard, although design difficulties arise even with this approach. Preliminary work can be done with the data from both partners in the NSFH.

It does seem possible that alternative procedures for retrospectively measuring cohabitation and separation dates can be evaluated reasonably well in ongoing longitudinal studies. As has been done for short intervals and recent experience with the PSID and NLSY, alternative experimental retrospective modules can be collected and compared with the month and year of events that have been collected between waves spanning several years.

Although it is important that we better understand the extent of erroneous reporting and how it varies by characteristics, it is most critical that we evaluate the effect of this misreporting on our substantive analyses. It is obvious that measurement error affects the predictive ability of our models, but that is not what is at stake at the moment. Rather, a first issue concerns the extent to which the ordering of life events is misclassified, affecting our retrospective identification of family contexts, such as children's experience in single-parent families. A second issue concerns whether the differences in intervals between events affect substantive conclusions about transition rates. It may be worth noting that events misdated by even a year in retrospective surveys may yield data of comparable quality to longitudinal data without dates of between-wave transitions.

All of this is not just toolmakers' fascination with their trade. As we noted at the outset, our concerns with the effects of marriage and divorce on the lives of children and adults must be expanded to include cohabitation—and it is the dating of the beginning and ending of cohabitation that is most problematic. Ultimately, to better understand family life, and to better design social policy, we need improved tools and materials.

9

The Visible Hand:
Editing Marital-History Data
From Census Bureau Surveys

Martin O'Connell
U.S. Census Bureau

When I first read the chapter in this volume by Larry Bumpass and Kelly Raley (chap. 8), I was quite pleased that they had "surprising agreement across several surveys with different focuses, formats, and designs," regarding overall trends and patterns in marriage and divorce from retrospective marital histories. A notable finding was the agreement of data from privately conducted surveys, such as the National Survey of Families and Households (NSFH), with the Census Bureau's Current Population Survey (CPS), and the Survey of Income and Program Participation (SIPP), despite the latter two surveys' focus on labor force and economic issues.

Replicating demographic patterns across surveys is important for several reasons. First, not all researchers have access to all surveys, and it is assuring to researchers that their findings will not be challenged simply because they have access only to one particular survey. Second, some surveys may have more detailed covariates than others (economic or psychological) and are selected for analysis on that basis. Data users should take comfort in knowing that their more specialized analysis will not be biased by the basic demographic patterns collected in different surveys. Third, retrospective surveys are, by nature, costly and, hence, may be collected at infrequent intervals. The technique of pooling several surveys to enhance sample size and extend historical periods can be an important resource, as demonstrated by Bumpass and Raley, so long as the pooled surveys can remain comparable over time.

Retrospective surveys are also notorious for the memory lapses of respondents. In surveys with high response levels, allocating missing data is often not attempted, and the cases with missing data are simply deleted from analysis. For surveys that have relatively high nonresponse, the allocation process is very important and often very complicated. Why, then, did Bumpass and Raley find the surveys they examined so comparable in their results? Bumpass, in an informal telephone conversation in October 2003, suggested a rather unscientific, but magical, explanation—that an "invisible hand" was behind all of this.

As the principal magician behind the editing process for much of the SIPP's marital-history data collected since the early 1980s, I will make this "invisible hand" a little more visible to data users by describing the basic tenets that are used to edit and impute marital-history data in Census Bureau surveys. I attempt to allay the fears of those who may be wary of using marital-history data with high rates of nonresponse, and I describe some simple allocation techniques that can be adapted for use in other surveys with significant missing data.

Using the marital-history module from the SIPP, which has been, since 1996, the Census Bureau's primary source for these data, I illustrate the magnitude of imputed data, demonstrate how these missing data are handled, and compare the final edited data with vital-statistics estimates of marital events. The SIPP panels have used the same editing techniques since the survey was first conducted in 1984. These procedures, in fact, were adapted from routines originally devised for the marital-history supplements to the CPS beginning in June 1980.[1]

SURVEY OF INCOME AND PROGRAM PARTICIPATION: 1996

The 1996 SIPP panel is a nationwide sample survey that collected marital-history information for 51,342 men and women aged 15 and older in 1996. The survey obtained the month and year of marriages, separations, widowhoods, and divorces for up to three marriages—the first two and the last marriage. If the respondents are unable to give an exact date, they are asked to provide the best possible estimate of when the marital event occurred. The survey collects no cohabitation histories.

Among ever-married individuals in the SIPP, 78% were married once, 18% twice, and 4% three or more times. The most commonly reported marital path (58%) taken by ever-married individuals was to be married once and still be married (excluding those currently separated). Among individuals married twice, the most common sequence was divorced and remarried (65%). Among those married three or more times, the most common path was divorced twice with a third marriage still intact (59%).

Bumpass and Raley warn of relatively high allocation rates often encountered in retrospective surveys, and the SIPP is no exception. SIPP data are flagged to be allocated for a variety of reasons:

1. *Missing data.* Individuals may not report marital dates because of memory lapse and uncertainty of reports for other household members, among other reasons. (In the SIPP, a household respondent may report on data for other members of the household. Recollection of specific dates of events by a household respondent may result in missing data, especially if it involves marital events for one's current spouse for a prior marriage.)

2. *Aborted interviews.* Interviews may also be broken off by the respondent, leaving entire sections of the survey with no response.

3. *Chronologically incorrect events.* During the preliminary phases of the editing routine, dates are scanned for correct chronology and correct spacing of events. Events that are out of sequence are flagged for allocation. In general, the first reported date beginning with the first marriage is considered the benchmark date, given that internal computer verification during the interview proceeds chronologically with each response.

4. *Marriage dates between spouses.* A final check ascertains that the current marriage dates for currently married spouses living in the same household match exactly. Because data are collected for husbands and wives individually in different sections of the instrument, inconsistencies may occur during the reporting stage by interviewer. If this occurred, the most recent date reported by either spouse was the date that was accepted.

ALLOCATION LEVELS

Allocation rates for men and women vary by number of marriages, the type of marital event, and type of marital path taken. Figure 9.1 shows that among individuals married once, dates of first marriage are best reported by currently married individuals and by women rather than men. Individuals married once constitute about four out of every five ever-married individuals. Among those married only once, about three quarters are still in their first marriage. The marriage dates of about 10% of these husbands and wives were allocated. For the remaining individuals married only once, allocation rates for the date of first marriage can exceed 20% for those separated or divorced, despite their relatively simple marital histories. Apparently, marital disruptions may even affect response levels among those married only once and having only one marriage date to remember.

Figure 9.2 shows allocation rates for twice-married individuals who were first divorced and then remarried and are still married. This is the second most frequently mentioned marital path in the 1996 SIPP panel, representing 12% of all ever-married respondents. Compared with first-marriage allocation rates of 10% (Fig. 9.1), the allocation rates for first-marriage dates among twice-married couples were 26% for men and 16% for women. Allocation rates for first separations and divorces were as high as 35% for men and 25% for women. However, allocation rates for the second marriage were 11% for both men and women, which is the same as marriage data for couples married only once. Overall, slightly more than 60% of individuals in this marital path reported good data for all required dates; only 7% had all of their dates allocated. Almost one third of cases still remained with a patchwork of reported dates requiring more complex allocation techniques.

Among individuals with two divorces and who had married a third time, allocation rates again were lowest for the date of the last marriage (12%) but reached levels as high as 50% for intervening dates among men, and 35% among women. For individuals in this marital path, about one half reported acceptable data for all seven of the required dates, whereas 1 in 10

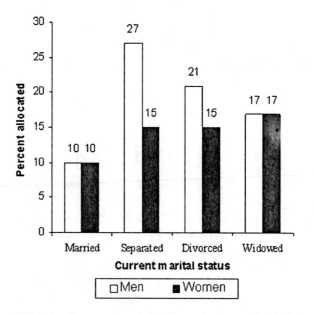

FIG. 9.1.   First-marriage dates allocated among individuals married once, 1996.

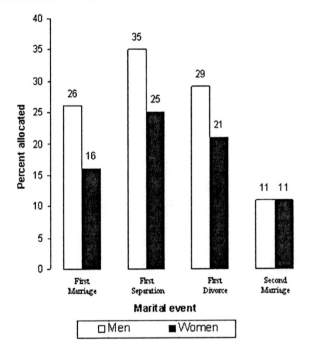

FIG. 9.2. Marital dates allocated among individuals divorced and then remarried, 1996.

did not and the event dates were allocated, leaving about 40% of individuals with incomplete histories. These high rates must be tempered by the fact
that this group (married three times) composed fewer than 3% of all survey
respondents

Table 9.1 summarizes the overall performance of the survey, showing
how many individuals had allocated dates, categorized by the number of
dates required given their marital path. For example, individuals married
once and still married are required to report only one date, and individuals
divorced twice and currently divorced are required to report six dates.

Overall, 80% of respondents reported all dates required of them, 9%
reported some, and 11% reported none. Allocation rates climbed as more
dates were required, but most of the increase occurred in the partially
completed category rather than in the totally incomplete category. Overall,
allocation rates were highest for separation dates, lowest for marriage dates,
with divorce and widowhood dates at intermediate levels.

In determining how to allocate these observations, the question to be
asked is not how to fill in the missing dates, but rather, how to connect
the existing dates. The solution to this problem is analogous to a game of
connecting the dots to form a picture. By establishing the path of existing

TABLE 9.1
Distribution of Respondents by Number of Event Dates
Required and Allocated: 1996

		Percent of dates allocated		
Dates required[a]	No. of respondents	None	Some	All
Total	51,342	80	9	11
1	29,809	90	NA	10
2	5,287	81	7	13
3	5,514	71	14	15
4	6,263	63	30	7
5	942	59	32	9
6	1,522	59	28	13
7	1,361	47	46	7
8	227	43	46	11
9	417	38	46	17

Note. NA = not applicable. From 1996 Survey of Income and
Program Participation, Wave 2 marital-history module.
[a]Dates required as determined by respondent's marital path.

dates, one can create a model set of marital timetables that, when constructed, provides approximations of the intervening and missing dates
along the path.

MODEL MARITAL TIMETABLES

The following section describes the general procedures used to edit and
allocate missing marital-history dates in Census Bureau surveys, including
the SIPP. The missing dates along a marital path produce a pattern that
conceptually resembles a train timetable, with missing arrival dates at stops
along the route of the train. Suppose we wanted to estimate the arrival
times along a known route between Washington, DC, and New York from a
sample of passengers who took a wide variety of trains along the route at different times, from the slow train at night to an express train during the day.
Most passengers could probably tell you when they left Washington and
arrived in New York, and some could even remember when they entered
the underground station in Philadelphia. Most, however, would not know
when they arrived at every station along the route, even though they might
know the names of the all cities they passed.

However, with a good deal of confidence, one could develop a model
timetable to fill in these missing times. The route (and hence the stops) is
known and the stops must be sequentially encountered on the trip. If times

between different stations could be generated even from partial responses, then intervals between all stations could be estimated for individuals who traveled the same route.

For example, if someone responded that it took 1 hour and 15 minutes to get from Philadelphia to New York, but another person could remember only that it took 15 minutes to get from Newark, New Jersey, to New York, then a good guess would be that it took an hour to travel between Philadelphia and Newark, given that one must pass through Newark en route from Philadelphia to New York.

As the passengers who travel along a known route are able to report when they begin and end a journey (but are asleep for all other stops), individuals who travel along a marital path may remember some dates but not others. Table 9.2 shows the analytical similarities between the train routes and marital paths. It is this comparability that enables one to develop model marital timetables to fill in the missing dates by connecting the intervals between the known and reported dates. The key point in Table 9.2 is Item 3, the establishment of a set of required and sequentially ordered marital dates that permits one to develop the model marital timetables.

The following five steps briefly outline how we develop allocation routines that handle the problem of missing data:

1. *Identify marital path.* Once the marital path of a person is known, the required number of marital events can be identified. Marital paths are established by asking respondents how each marriage ended. The 1996 SIPP includes 28 separate marital paths for ever-married individuals.

TABLE 9.2
Conceptual Development of Model Marital Timetables

Train Table Concepts	*Marital Table Concepts*
1. Different times of departure/arrival	1. Different ages at marital events
2. Different routes to travel	2. Different marital paths to experience
3. Once train taken, all stops are known and traveled in sequence	3. Once path determined, all dates are required and are in chronological order
4. Accidents/delays occur and cause deviations in schedule	4. Love and the legal system cause variations in intervals between events
5. Travel time ends when final destination is reached	5. Final anchor date is current age of the respondent
6. Intervals between stops are derived from times traveled	6. Marital intervals are derived from respondent experiences

2. *Validate dates.* All dates are initially scanned for missing or chronologically incorrect values and must meet minimum/maximum tests. For example, no person could marry before age 12 or report an age at a marital event older than their current age. Invalid dates are flagged for allocation.

3. *Identify anchor dates.* Good dates that meet chronological tests are used to bound missing dates to ensure only allocation of consistent intervening dates.

4. *Allocate dates based on model marital timetables.* Using reported and accepted anchor dates, the person's "age at marital event" is derived by interpolating dates from model marital timetables specific to that marital path. Models are developed from nonallocated responses and from historical data in previous surveys to develop sufficient observations for marital paths "less traveled."

5. *Final verification and consistency checks.* Final allocated values are checked for chronological consistency and consistency of last marriage dates between currently married spouses.

A principal concern of this allocation routine is to develop the database to produce the model timetables. Two different methods are used to develop the timetables, depending on the number of times the person has been married. Given that 78% of the individuals in the 1996 SIPP panel were married only once, the age-at-event patterns for these individuals were continuously updated throughout the data processing. Actual dates were drawn from the existing file, given that there were many cases available to provide an average picture of the four marital patterns (married, separated, divorced, and widowed). In other words, the pattern was not static.

For the 20% of ever-married individuals married more than once, obtaining enough cases from those with complete dates to provide patterns for the two dozen possible marital paths each for men and women would prove daunting. Instead, to provide a stable set of ages at each event, the timetables for these individuals were developed from the final set of patterns from prior panels, thus providing more stable models, albeit from a recent past. However, the key point is that the timetables only provide a basis for filling in the missing gaps and are not a substitute for the entire set of marital events. In addition, for those married more than once, the majority of all earlier marital events more often than not occurred many years prior to the survey and, therefore, were not subject to recent trends.

The following example illustrates how this procedure works, based on data for twice-married (and still married) individuals. Figure 9.3 shows the overall average ages[2] at events from the fully allocated 1996 SIPP panel for the most common marital path among individuals married twice, namely,

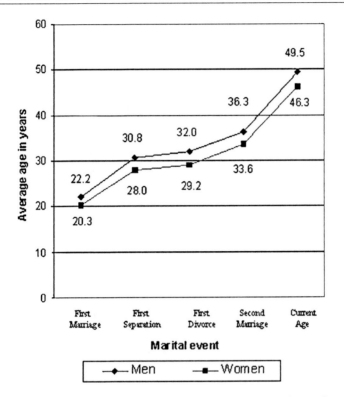

FIG. 9.3.   Average age at marital events among individuals divorced
and then remarried: final 1996 estimates.

those who were first divorced and remarried who remain married. Excluding
their current age, which provides closure to the sequence, four marriage
dates are required for this particular path. Although the average age for men
at these events is about 2 to 3 years older than for women, the shapes of the
paths for men and women are virtually identical.

When allocating a missing date along this path—say, for example, the
separation date—the first step would be to anchor the interval around the
missing separation date with valid and acceptable marriage and divorce
dates in the initial pre-edit scan of the data. The next step would be to draw
from the timetable an initial estimate of where the missing date would fall,
estimate the allocated age at event, and bound it by the valid dates reported
by the respondent, thus preserving the reported interval and acceptable
data, but approximating the intervening missing date. Similar model timetables have been developed for men and women for the 28 different marital
paths (including the 4 marital paths for individuals married only once),
resulting in a set of 56 different timetables.

SURVEY AND VITAL-STATISTICS
COMPARISONS

Table 9.3 compares the resulting allocated data from the SIPP with annual, national vital-statistics estimates based on data derived from states in
the marriage and divorce reporting areas. Overall, SIPP marriage data for
women differ by only a few percentage points from vital-statistics data from
the 1970s to the mid-1990s. Data for men deteriorate more rapidly into
10- to 15-percentage-point shortfalls and the number of marriages in the
early 1970s are 20% less than vital-statistics estimates.

Divorce statistics fare worse, falling below vital-statistics estimates by
10% for women, even in recent periods, and even lower for men. Of course,
large shortfalls for periods some 20 to 30 years before the survey date are
affected by mortality, and are especially problematic for divorce statistics
because individuals are more likely to divorce at older ages.

It is also necessary to remember that for the present time, vital statistics
on marital events are limited to gross national estimates, given that even
state estimates of marital events are often incomplete. The National Center
for Health Statistics ceased publishing detailed characteristics of annual
marriages and divorces in 1996 (see http://www.cdc.gov/nchs/releases/

TABLE 9.3
Comparison of SIPP and Vital Statistics Marital Events:
1970–1974 to 1990–1994

Marital Event and Period	SIPP		Vital Statistics
	Men	Women	
Marriages			
1990 to 1994	11,706	12,113	11,872
1985 to 1989	11,399	12,124	12,022
1980 to 1984	11,019	11,767	12,192
1975 to 1979	9,631	10,624	11,100
1970 to 1974	9,109	10,030	11,145
Divorces			
1990 to 1994	4,561	5,057	5,964
1985 to 1989	4,713	5,224	5,858
1980 to 1984	4,497	4,832	5,899
1975 to 1979	3,481	4,213	5,521
1970 to 1974	2,553	2,990	4,218

Note. Numbers in 1,000s representing 5-year aggregates of
events. From 1996 Survey of Income and Program Particiaption
(SIPP), Wave 2 marital-history module, and annual volumes of Vital
Statistics of the United States, Vol. III: Marriage and Divorce.

96facts/mardiv.htm for an explanation). Currently, it is impossible to even annually derive the median age at marriage from the data.

Therefore, if we are to turn to survey data, we face two problems: How do we get better data, and how do we know when we really have better data? Is a bigger number always a better number?

Reviewing the 1996 SIPP data, despite high allocation rates, the invisible hand that haunts the allocation schemes of surveys appears to be a kindly spirit. The resulting SIPP data are very accurate for deriving aggregate national estimates of marriages for almost 20 years prior to the survey date, albeit more accurately for women than for men. We find greater differences between survey and vital-statistics estimates for divorce data, which substantially deteriorate for time periods of more than a decade in length.

With the absence of annual vital-statistics data, we must now depend on surveys to a greater extent for even basic estimates. Fortunately, Bumpass and Raley show that most surveys produce similar aggregate patterns and trends. That similarity persists despite the different ways that surveys deal with missing data, which implies that nonresponse may be less critical than formerly believed.

Surveys are costly, and the costs increase when nonresponse follow-up is required, and nonresponse will always be an issue when it comes to retrospective surveys. This suggests that further research in allocation techniques may become a more integral component of basic survey research and, as shown, an important determinant in data quality when large proportions of data must be allocated. However, the behavioral characteristics of marital-history data suggest that nonresponse may be less problematic than originally thought, given that marital paths often have an internal structure of regularity that aids in providing the answers to patterns of missing data.

ACKNOWLEDGMENTS

This chapter is intended to provide the results of research and to encourage discussion of methodological issues. The views expressed on technical issues are those of the author and not necessarily those of the U.S. Census Bureau. The author would like to acknowledge the comments of Rose Kreider and Jason Fields on previous drafts of this presentation.

Notes

1. James Weed, now Deputy Director of the Division of Vital Statistics, National Center for Health Statistics, worked jointly with me to initially develop the marital-history edit specifications for the June 1980 CPS. The marital-history supplement to the CPS ended in June 1995. Thereafter, only the SIPP would contain retrospective marital-history

items. The 1984 SIPP panel contained the first marital-history topical module. The most recent 2004 panel, in the second interview wave or cycle, continues this tradition.

2. The averages in this figure represent the final average ages for each marital event from the fully edited 1996 panel. These data will then serve as model pattern for this specific marital path when editing the 2001 SIPP panel.

PART IV

Household Composition and Family Relationships

10

Mapping Children's Living Arrangements With a Relationship Matrix

Peter D. Brandon
The Australian National University

Many reports and much scholarly research document the dramatic changes that have reshaped America's families since the 1970s (Bumpass & Lu, 2000; Bumpass & Sweet, 1989b; Casper & Bianchi, 2002; Teachman, Tedrow, & Crowder, 2000; U.S. Census Bureau, 1999a, 1999b). Undoubtedly, the profound changes that American families have undergone in the past three decades have significant implications for studying children and families and for a range of future social policies (Federal Interagency Forum on Child & Family Statistics, 2001). Because relationships among children and adults in a family have become more complex and can change rapidly, sophisticated methods are needed to accurately describe children's living arrangements and circumstances. Without more advanced methods for measuring household composition, American society will fail to fully comprehend the diverse needs of today's children, and families and will fall short of developing effective social and economic policies for the most vulnerable among them.

This chapter focuses on one advanced method for collecting data on children's relationships to adults within a household. The method involves using "relationship matrices" to collect data on the specific relationships of children to all adults in a household at a point in time. The method also permits inverting a matrix of data so that analyses from the children's perspective are possible. Two caveats, however, are in order. First, other advanced techniques exist for collecting data on children's relationships to adults within a household, such as randomly selecting a focal child and studying his or her relationships to adults in a household (Hofferth, Davis-Kean, Davis, & Finkelstein, 1999), or distinguishing how children in a household are related to the adult heading the household. It would be useful in the future to compare several methods for collecting relationship data on children using household survey data. A second caveat is that, despite its many attractive features, the relationship matrix has drawbacks, which I expand on in the conclusion.

With these caveats in mind, I concentrate on showing the usefulness of the relationship matrix for depicting the diversity of American children's living arrangements, identifying the numbers of children in those arrangements, identifying demographic variation across arrangements, demonstrating how data from relationship matrices have policy relevance, and for promoting cross-country comparisons of children's living arrangements.

ANALYSIS PLAN, DATA DESCRIPTION, AND MEASUREMENT STRATEGY

Analysis Plan

Because relationship matrix data depend on the type of survey being used, understanding the nature of the survey itself is crucial. I first describe the Survey of Income and Program Participation (SIPP) and the manipulations that were required to use the data gathered from the relationship matrix. Tables 10.1 and 10.2 demonstrate that although these relationship data can produce very precise categories of children's living arrangements, it makes more sense, both theoretically and statistically, to combine categories based on the presence or absence of parents and parental marital status. Table 10.3 shows that even with fewer living arrangement categories, combined categories can still be profitably employed with other relationship matrix data to identify the children who are most likely to live with different types of relatives. Finally, Tables 10.4 through 10.6 highlight the policy relevance of relationship matrix data and the promise the data offer for detailed, cross-country comparisons of children's living arrangements.

Sample

The primary source of data for this study is the 1996 SIPP. The sample selected for the 1996 SIPP is a stratified, multistage probability sample that is nationally representative of households in the civilian, noninstitutionalized U.S. population. Respondents are interviewed every 4 months for 48 months. At each interview, a household informant is asked to provide demographic, employment, income, and program participation information for every member of the household in each of the past 4 months (U.S. Census Bureau, 2001). Included in the demographic information are the number of families in the household and the composition of each family in each of the preceding 4 months. Children under age 15 are counted, and information is gathered on their age, gender, race, and ethnicity. Original sampled members aged 15 and older who move are located, if possible, and retained in the sample (U.S. Census Bureau, 2001). This study only uses SIPP cross-sectional data collected on children under age 15 at Month 4 of Wave 2, but the survey design permits identifying the month children enter or leave the panel. SIPP panels are divided into waves, with the household relationship matrices usually, although not always, inserted into the Wave 2 data collection period.

The 34,287 sampled households interviewed in Wave 2 included 91,216 persons. Of the 34,287 sampled households, 22,574 (65.8%) contained no children under the age of 15 and were, therefore, ineligible for this study. This left 11,713 households containing 19,267 children under the age of 15. Of the 19,267 children, 117 children were immediately excluded because the household relationship matrix contained missing relationship codes (13.6%), or parent imputations were inconsistent with parent identifiers (61.3%), or other data inconsistencies were irreconcilable (25%). Thus, the relationship matrix could describe the relationships among 19,150 children and the adults with whom they shared a dwelling. Although the study could describe the relationships between 19,150 children and adults in the same dwelling, it could only describe household socioeconomic characteristics for 18,950 children. In other words, another 200 children were lost to the study because information from the core data on their parents, families, and households could not be accurately appended to their records, even though identifiers in the household relationship matrix and "core" data were created to do so. Notwithstanding, the SIPP remains a high-quality survey that permits collecting a rich amount of household sociodemographic data on children younger than age 15, including information on their exact relationships to adults in a household at Wave 2.

Measuring Intrahousehold Relationships

Although the main focus of the SIPP is collecting information on labor force participation, jobs, income, and participation in federal assistance programs, information on other topics, such as household relationships, is also collected in topical modules on a rotating basis (U.S. Census Bureau, 2001). Generally, the finer-grained data on household relationships has been collected in Wave 2, which has—by design or by chance—meant collect-

TABLE 10.1
Distribution of Living Arrangements Among American Children Under Age 15

Child lives With:	Unweighted	Weighted	Est. Weighted Percent[a]	Standard Error of Estimate[b]
1. Adoptive father only, N.M.P, N.P.P	4	11,212	0.021	0.0109
2. Foster parents, N.P.P	76	201,508	0.377	0.06
3. Grandparents, N.P.P	405	1,021,494	1.915	0.1287
4. Siblings older than 15 but younger than 18, N.P.P	18	36,994	0.069	0.0219
5. Nonsiblings older than 15 but younger than 18, N.P.P	1	3,213	0.006	0.006
6. Biological father only, N.M.P	279	782,921	1.467	0.1201
7. Biological father with female partner[c]	39	97,378	0.182	0.0412
8. Biological father with unrelated female[c]	67	168,471	0.315	0.0486
9. Biological mother only, N.F.P	2,782	7,246,1251	13.590	0.3631
10. Biological mother with male partner[c]	229	560,028	1.050	0.0979
11. Biological mother with unrelated male[c]	612	1,453,585	2.725	0.1589
12. Two biological parents	12,611	36,472,619	68.383	0.4849
13. Biological mother and stepfather	584	1,555,626	2.916	0.1599
14. Biological mother and adoptive father	59	163,909	0.307	0.0459
15. Biological mother, grandparents, N.F.P	809	2,046,199	3.836	0.1825
16. Biological father and stepmother	111	306,916	0.575	0.0671
17. Adoptive mother only, N.F.P, N.P.P.	39	105,755	0.198	0.0344
18. Biological father and adoptive mother	3	9,325	0.017	0.0101
19. Adoptive mother and stepfather	3	8,936	0.016	0.0129
20. Two adoptive parents	106	314,999	0.590	0.0665
21. Biological father, grandparents, N.M.P	74	179,001	0.335	0.0474
22. Relatives older than 18 other than grandparents, N.P.P	137	339,483	0.636	0.0782
23. Nonrelatives, no family members present	102	249,771	0.468	0.0556
Totals	19,150	53,335,469	100	

Source: SIPP (1996 panel, Wave 2, Topical Module on Household Relationships).
[a]Estimated weighted and unweighted proportions of children in each living arrangement are similar. [b]Standard error of the weighted estimated percent based on primary sampling units. [c]Partner or unrelated person of the opposite sex sharing household is reported to be aged 18 years or older. N.M.P = no mother present; N.P.P = neither parent present; N.F.P = no father present.

ing data on household relationships over the summer months. (This data collection period could create lower estimates of household composition if children are away during the summer months for one reason or another.)

After contacting members of a household, the exact relationships between all household members are pinpointed and recorded.[1] The relationship matrix establishes a grid of specific and detailed relationships of each household member to all other members, including children. For example, a sibling is identified as full sibling, step- or half-sibling, adoptive sibling, or foster sibling. In-law relationships are also identified, as are adult relationships. From the elaborate roster of relationships, children in a household in Wave 2 can be identified as living with both biological parents who may or may not be married; living with only one biological parent who may or may not live with a partner, or who may be a lone parent; or living with no biological or adoptive parents. In the latter case, children can be identified as living with a grandparent or other relative, or a nonrelative, such as a foster parent. Hence, the household relationship matrix permits researchers to construct measures of intrahousehold relationships, including intergenerational ones. Undoubtedly, a household relationship matrix that potentially encompasses 31 relationship categories surpasses a standard one-dimensional survey item that indicates the relationship of a household member to the householder or reference person.[2]

Using the sampling weight provided in the topical module, I was able to estimate the proportions of children living in particular living arrangements in the summer of 1996 and to compare their demographic and household circumstances.[3] With only limited aggregation, Table 10.1 shows that the 19,150 children were spread across 23 different living arrangements. Adding row 1 to rows 6–21 of Table 10.1 suggests that about 96% of children live with at least one parent, and among children living with two parents, only 1.3% had one or more adoptive parents. Among children living with one biological parent who shares a household with an adult of the opposite sex, 71.1% of those adults are recorded as "unrelated" rather than the "partner" of the children's parent. Thus, by exploiting the SIPP household relationship matrix, a more precise and illuminating picture of the diversity in children's living arrangements is gained.

DESCRIPTIVE AND MULTIVARIATE ANALYSES

Descriptive Analyses

Although informative, comparing each category in Table 10.1 is impractical and unnecessary. Fortunately, without any great loss of detail, aggregating categories in Table 10.1 into higher level, yet still instructive, categories is possible. (Before reviewing Tables 10.2 and 10.3, the factors guiding category creation are: (a) distinguishing biological from nonbiological relationships between children and adults; (b) identifying the marital status of children's parents; and (c) establishing the presence or absence of parents. Therefore, terms such as "stepparent," "stepfather," or "stepmother" strictly refer to a nonbiological, married parent.)

Table 10.2 shows the distribution of the combined living arrangement categories among the estimated total from Table 10.1 of 53.3 million children younger than age 15. The data confirm the finding that 96.5% of children in America live with at least one biological parent (Casper & Bianchi, 2002; Hernandez, 1993). What is also essential to know is which other adults besides a parent share the household and what are their exact

TABLE 10.2
Distribution of Living Arrangements Among Children Under Age 15

Child lives With:	Weighted Ns	Weighted Percent	SE[c]
1. Lone biological mother only, no grandparent present[a]	8,805,465	16.51	0.3883
2. Lone biological mother only, a grandparent present	2,046,199	3.84	0.1825
3. Lone biological father only, no grandparent present[a]	962,604	1.80	0.1299
4. Lone biological father only, a grandparent present	179,001	0.34	0.0474
5. Married biological or adoptive mother and father	36,085,868	67.66	0.4918
6. Married biological mother and a stepfather	1,556,048	2.92	0.1603
7. Married biological father and a stepmother	304,078	0.57	0.0669
8. Cohabiting biological mother and father	874,984	1.64	0.1287
9. Cohabiting biological mother and male partner[b]	568,542	1.07	0.0995
10. Cohabiting biological father and female partner[b]	100,217	0.19	0.0422
11. Foster parents only, neither parent present	201,508	0.38	0.06
12. Grandparents only, neither parent present	1,021,494	1.92	0.1287
13. Other relatives only, neither parent present	376,477	0.71	0.0812
14. Nonrelatives only, neither parent present	252,983	0.47	0.0559
Total	53,335,468	100	

Note. This table was created by combining the following categories from Table 10.1: rows 9, 11, and 17 form "lone biological mother only, no grandparent present"; rows 1, 6, and 8 form "lone biological father only, no grandparent present"; rows 12, 14, 18, and 20 form "married biological or adoptive mother and father"; rows 4 and 22 form "other relatives only"; and rows 5 and 23 form "nonrelatives only." Sampling weights were applied from the topical module file to produce weighted counts and percentages presented in Table 10.2. Source: SIPP (1996 panel, Wave 2, Topical Module on Household Relationships, N = 19,150).

[a]Other adult relatives are possibly present. [b]Partner of the opposite sex sharing household is reported aged 18 years or older. [c]Standard error of the weighted percent based on primary sampling units.

relationships to the children. The type of relationship between them, for example, might affect the resources available to the children or their developmental outcomes.

By adding the weighted sample sizes in rows 6, 7, 9, and 10 of Table 10.2, for instance, it is clear that among the roughly 2.5 million children with only one biological parent who is "partnered," meaning the parent had a married spouse or a cohabiting partner, more of these children (73.5%) live with a biological parent who has a married spouse (i.e., a child's stepparent) than with a biological parent who has a cohabiting partner (26.5%). Interestingly, the gender of the biological parent does not influence the likelihood of a child having a stepparent. Adding rows 6 and 9, which yields the number of children with only biological mothers who are "partnered," and adding rows 7 and 10, which yields the corresponding number of children with only biological fathers who are "partnered," reveals that children with only one biological parent are much more likely to find themselves with a stepmother or stepfather than with an unrelated male or female cohabitor who may or may not exercise a parenting role that stepparenthood at least implies. The percentages with stepparents are 73.2% for children with only biological mothers and 75.2% for children with only biological fathers, respectively.

Interestingly, if partner status versus unrelated status is not misreported, approximately 3% of children ($N = 1{,}543{,}743$) live with cohabiting adults. For nearly 57% of them, both adults are their biological parents. Thus, if a child lives with a cohabiting couple, chances are a little greater than 50:50 that that couple is the child's biological father and mother. Clearly, the chances that a child lives with both biological parents who are cohabiting are smaller than living with both biological parents who are married—the latter being about 95%. Nevertheless, these SIPP data show that among children who live with cohabiting couples, the majority live with both biological parents.

No more striking example of the changes in families since the 1970s exists than the number of children living with lone parents. Table 10.2 indicates that nearly 12 million children under age 15 live with lone parents, or more than one in five children. What is surprising is that when children live with lone fathers or mothers, they are nearly equally likely to live with at least one grandparent as well. Among the 10,851,664 children living with lone mothers, about 18.9% also have grandparents present; similarly, for the 1,141,605 children living with lone fathers, about 15.6% also have grandparents present. Also, reflecting trends that have caused a rethinking of family policies (Brandon, 2003; Casper & Bryson, 1998a; Dench & Thomson, 1999), among the children who live with neither parent present in the household (rows 11 to 14 in Table 10.2), 55.4% live with grandparents.

TABLE 10.3
Some Selected Characteristics of the Living Arrangements of Children Under the Age of 15 Years

Panel A: Living Arrangement When at Least One Biological Parent Present

	Single Mothers Only	Single Fathers Only	Married Biological Mothers & Fathers	Married Biological Mothers & Stepfathers	Married Biological Fathers & Stepmothers	Two Biological Cohabiting Parents	Biological Parents Cohabiting with Partners[a]
Proportion living with at least:[b]							
One grandparent	0.189	0.156	0.032	0.035	0.081	0.019	0.000
One uncle or aunt	0.139	0.090	0.022	0.017	0.000	0.034	0.007
One non-relative adult	0.062	0.086	0.007	0.005	0.000	0.021	0.801
One biological sibling	0.639	0.569	0.780	0.495	0.429	0.553	0.644
One cousin	0.047	0.039	0.005	0.000	0.000	0.000	0.000
Proportion males	0.500	0.575	0.512	0.469	0.592	0.514	0.481
Proportion non-Hispanic White vs. other racial categories[c]	0.572	0.830	0.867	0.836	0.853	0.759	0.836
N	4,242	424	12,458	584	110	321	272

Panel B: Living Arrangement When Neither Biological Parent Present

	Grandparents	Other Relatives	Nonrelatives	Foster Parents
Proportion living with at least:[b]				
One grandparent	1.000	0.000	0.000	0.000
One uncle or aunt	0.337	1.000	0.000	0.000
One nonrelative adult	0.068	0.047	1.000	0.615
One biological sibling	0.007	0.300	0.316	0.291
One cousin	0.000	0.000	0.000	0.000
Proportion males	0.522	0.517	0.522	0.585
Proportion non-Hispanic White vs. other racial categories[c]	0.487	0.559	0.856	0.626
N	405	155	103	76

Note. Weighted tabulations. Source: SIPP (1996 panel, Wave 2, Topical Module on Household Relationships, N = 19,150). [a]Combines groups of children living with male or female biological parent cohabiting with partner of the opposite sex. [b]Indicates the presence of at least one or more. [c]Other racial categories defined in the core data of the SIPP are black, American Indian, Aleut, or Eskimo, and Asian or Pacific Islander.

The diversity in American children's living arrangements is associated with great differences in the compositional characteristics of their households. Table 10.3 shows some of the differences across 11 different living arrangements.

Panel A of Table 10.3, based on living arrangements with at least one biological parent present, suggests that children in single-mother households, followed by children in single-father households, were the most likely to live in households that also contained a grandparent. Children in single-mother and single-father living arrangements were also the most likely to have an aunt or uncle living with them as well. Children living with one biological parent who cohabits with a partner were less likely than children in other arrangements to also live with grandparents, uncles or aunts, or cousins. By definition, however, children living with one biological parent and a cohabiting partner were the most likely to live with a nonrelative, that is, the partner who is not biologically related to children. In this living arrangement, even if the partner acts as a parent and is perceived by the child as "my parent," the household relationship matrix records the partner as unrelated to the child.

Panel A also reveals that children in arrangements with one (married) biological parent and a stepparent were the least likely, compared with the other five arrangements in panel A, to have biological siblings present in the household. Possibly, some of the siblings could have been living with their noncustodial biological parent. By contrast, children living with both married biological parents were the most likely to also have biological siblings present than were children in the other six arrangements.

Panel B of Table 10.3 shows aspects of household composition for children living with neither biological parent. More than one in three children living with grandparents with neither parent present were also living with an aunt or uncle. That proportion is higher than for any other group of children in any other living arrangement in Panel A or B. Compared with children living with other nonbiological surrogate parents (i.e., relatives other than grandparents, nonrelatives, or foster parents), children living with grandparents rarely shared the house with siblings. By contrast, one third of children living with other parental substitutes had at least one other sibling living with them. Comparing Panels A and B, the children living away from their parents are less likely to have siblings in the same house than are children living with at least one parent.

Finally, Table 10.3 shows that the gender and race of children differ across living arrangements. Larger proportions of boys than girls live with single fathers, married biological fathers and stepmothers, and foster parents. Among the arrangements shown in Table 10.3, boys, compared with girls, are less likely to live with married biological mothers and stepfathers. Turning to racial differences, compared with all other arrangements, fewer than half of the children living only with grandparents are non-Hispanic White. Also, the proportion of non-Hispanic White children living with single fathers only is much higher than the proportion of those living with single mothers only: 83% and 57%, respectively. The proportion of non-Hispanic white children is highest among children living with two married biological parents.

The Utility of Relationship Matrix Data for Policy Analyses: An Example

Tables 10.1, 10.2, and 10.3 reveal that children's living arrangements are diverse and that categories of children's living arrangements that incorporate parental presence or absence, the marital status of parents, and biological relationships are very informative. However, information on children's living arrangements generated from a relationship matrix can also help policymakers and program administrators gauge the likelihood of public assistance programs being received by children in various living arrangements.

Previous research has shown that household structure and relationships among household members are associated with eligibility for and receipt of public assistance (Brandon & Bumpass, 2001; McLanahan, 1988; McLanahan & Sandefur, 1994; Moffitt, Reville, & Winkler, 1998). However, many questions remain about whether public assistance use varies by relationships between children and adults in a household. In the following example using food stamp receipt, Tables 10.4 and 10.5 explore the associations between specific types of relationships among children and adults in a household and the odds of receiving food stamps,[4] controlling for other demographic and economic variables. The three multivariate logistic regressions in each table demonstrate how models predicting food stamp receipt become progressively more informative as measures of children's living arrangements become increasingly more exact.

Table 10.4 shows results of fitting three logistic models predicting the odds of food stamp receipt among children living with at least one parent. Models 1 through 3 contain alternative measures of children's living arrangements that become progressively disaggregated to better reflect the exact relationships between children and adults in a household. Model 1's measures are imprecise because they only distinguish three living arrangements: children living with: (a) a single parent, (b) a cohabiting parent, or (c) a married parent. By comparison, the eight measures in Model 3 distinguish among children living with: (a) a single mother, (b) a single father, (c) a mother and a stepfather, (d) a father and a stepmother, (e) a mother and cohabiting partner, (f) a father and cohabiting partner, (g) two biological cohabiting parents, or (h) two married biological parents. The presence of grandparents and aunts and uncles are also specified in the models.

Likelihood-ratio (LR) tests performed between pairs of the logistic models shown in Table 10.4 suggest that Models 2 and 3 better explain the odds of food stamp receipt among children than does Model 1. Drawing on Long and Freese's (2003) description for testing multiple coefficients using the LR test, hypotheses that the effects of more precise measures of children's living arrangements are simultaneously equal to zero are rejected at the

TABLE 10.4

Coefficients From Regressions Estimating the Odds of Food Stamp Receipt Among Children Living in Different Living Arrangements With at Least One Parent Present

| | Logit Regressions | | | | | |
| | Model 1 | | Model 2 | | Model 3 | |
Independent Variables	Coefficient	SE	Coefficient	SE	Coefficient	SE
Single parent	6.37***	0.45	—		—	
Cohabiting couple	3.31***	0.52	—		—	
Married, a biol. parent and a step	—		1.38*	0.28	—	
Single mother	—		7.20***	0.53	—	
Single father	—		1.69**	0.38	—	
Cohabiting, both biological parents	—		3.12***	0.60	—	
Cohabiting, one biol. parent only	—		4.02***	1.01	—	
Married mother and step father	—		—		1.54**	0.32
Married father and step mother	—		—		0.64	0.43
Single mother	—		—		7.20***	0.53
Single father	—		—		1.69***	0.38
Cohabiting, both biological parents	—		—		3.12***	0.60
Cohabiting, a biol. mother only	—		—		4.28***	1.09
Cohabiting, a biol. father only	—		—		2.72	1.85
Log-likelihood	−4,055.54		−4,026.05		−4,024.72	
Number of observations	18,282		18,282		18,282	

Note. Dash = not applicable to particular model being estimated; controls include number of children, poverty status, household income, education attainment of household head, ethnicity and gender of children, presence of adult relatives, and for state fix effects; these results are available on request. Source: SIPP (1996 panel, Wave 2, Topical Module on Household Relationships and core data from fourth reference month).

*$p \leq .10$. **$p \leq .05$. ***$p \leq .01$ (two-tailed tests).

0.001 levels (χ^2 = 61.65, df = 5, p < .001 for Model 3 relative to Model 1; and, χ^2 = 58.98, df = 3, p < .001 for Model 2 relative to Model 1). Yet the LR test failed to reject the hypothesis that measures distinguishing between married stepfamilies and cohabiting biological parents and partners are simultaneously equal to zero (χ^2 = 2.68, df = 2, p < .2625). Thus, Model 3 fails to outperform Model 2.[5]

Models in Table 10.4 also indicate that the presence of relatives and nonrelatives in a household is associated with the odds of food stamp receipt. Children living with grandparents or adult nonrelatives are at least one third more likely as children not living with grandparents or adult nonrelatives to receive food stamps. However, children living with uncles or aunts are one third less likely than children not living with uncles or aunts to receive food stamps. The results could indicate that grandparents and nonrelatives are unemployed, thereby increasing the chances of the household needing government assistance. By contrast, aunts and uncles may be more likely to work and contribute to the household's economic self-sufficiency.

Because the SIPP relationship matrix provides much information about the types of relationships between children and adult relatives in the household, we fitted another set of logistic regression models to test whether the generational structure in single-parent families changes the odds of food stamp receipt. A lack of precise measures about which types of adult relatives share a household with children has prevented testing this possibility, even though research suggests that the generational structure of households is correlated with economic outcomes, such as poverty status and welfare receipt (Brandon, 2003; Casper & Bryson, 1998).

Models 1 through 3 in Table 10.5 use alternative measures of children's living arrangements when they live with a single parent only. Measures are gradually disaggregated to better reflect the exact generational structure of the relationships among children, single parents, and other adult relatives in a household. For example, measures in Model 1 are inadequate given that they only distinguish between children living with a single mother or single father. By comparison, the more detailed measures in Model 3 distinguish among children living with a: (a) single mother only, (b) single mother and her adult siblings, (c) single mother and her mother, (d) single mother living with her siblings and mother, (e) single father only, (f) single father and his adult siblings, (g) single father and his mother, and (h) single father living with his siblings and mother. Thus, the possible generational structures in children's households include first, second, and third generations.

The LR tests performed between pairs of the logistic models shown in Table 10.5 suggest that Model 3 better explains the odds of food stamp receipt among children than do Models 1 and 2. The hypothesis that the effects of more precise measures of children's generational living arrangements that include identifying particular types of relatives are simultaneously equal to zero are rejected at the .01 level or below ($\chi^2 = 17.33$, df = 6, $p < .01$ for Model 3 relative to Model 1; $\chi^2 = 14.28$, df = 4, $p < .01$ for Model 3 relative to Model 2). The LR test failed to reject the hypothesis that measures distinguishing the presence of adult relatives in households with children and single parents are simultaneously equal to zero ($\chi2 = 3.06$, df = 2, $p < .2171$). Hence, these findings support past research arguing that studies of children living with single parents should more seriously consider the specific generational structures of these particular living arrangements.

Models in Table 10.5 also indicate that the presence of nonrelatives in a household is associated with increased odds of food stamp receipt. Children

TABLE 10.5
Coefficients From Regressions Estimating the Odds of Food Stamp Receipt
Among Children in Different Generational Living Arrangements
With Only Single Parents

	Logit Regressions					
	Model 1		Model 2		Model 3	
Independent variables	Coefficient	S.E.	Coefficient	S.E.	Coefficient	S.E.
Single father only	0.26***	0.06	—		—	
Single mother and adult relatives	—		1.21	0.15	—	
Single father only	—		0.28***	0.06	—	
Single father and adult relatives	—		0.25***	0.13	—	
Single mother, adult sibling only	—		—		1.08	0.23
Single mother, mother only	—		—		1.67***	0.28
Single mother, both[a]					0.85	0.16
Single father	—		—		0.28***	0.06
Single father, adult sibling only	—		—		0.10*	0.14
Single father, mother only					0.30*	0.21
Single father, both[a]					0.30	0.25
Log-likelihood	−2,038.79		−2,037.26		−2,030.12	
Number of observations	4,602		4,602		4,602	

[a]"Both" meaning child lives with mother's mother and aunts or uncles as well; dashes = not applicable to particular model being estimated; controls include number of children, poverty status, household income, education attainment of household head, ethnicity and gender of children, presence of adult relatives, and for state fix effects; these results are available on request. Source: SIPP (1996 panel, Wave 2, Topical Module on Household Relationships and core data from fourth reference month).
$*p \leq .10. **p \leq .05. ***p \leq .01$ (two-tailed tests).

living with adult nonrelatives are at least 35% more likely to receive food stamps than children not living with adult nonrelatives. Results could again indicate that nonrelatives are more likely to be unemployed, which might increase need.

The food stamps example illustrates the usefulness of using relationship matrix data to identify which children in which type of living arrangement are mostly likely to receive food stamps. Obviously, these data are potentially applicable to other public programs, such as Medicaid, that aim to safeguard the well-being of children.

Potential Cross-National Comparisons of Children's Living Arrangements

The comprehensiveness of the SIPP relationship matrix shows that American children live in a variety of arrangements that differ along social and economic characteristics. These data also have potential for cross-national comparisons. An Australian survey, the Household, Income, and Labour Dynamics in Australia (HILDA) contains a relationship matrix in Wave 1 that collects complete information about how each member of the household is related to every other member of the household (Watson & Wooden, 2002). A few caveats are in order, however. First, SIPP data predate by about 3 years the HILDA data. Second, slight differences exist in the relationship matrices' questions. In HILDA, the term "de facto" spouse is used to describe a romantic, ongoing relationship between two unrelated adults; in the SIPP, the term "partner" is used to describe such a relationship. Notwithstanding these cautions, analyses remain valid and reliable.

Table 10.6 reveals that Australian and American children under age 15 have equal chances of living with two married biological parents. However, Australian children were more than 3.5 times as likely to live with both biological parents in a cohabiting relationship than were their American counterparts. Further, Australian children were more than twice as likely to live with a biological parent and her or his partner than are American children. These two significant differences perhaps reflect more liberal Australian attitudes about adults living together or the more inclusive Australian social welfare system that, unlike public assistance programs in the United States, does not determine eligibility for income support based on marital status or paternity (Moffitt et al., 1998). Two other notable differences are shown in Table 10.6. First, American children are more likely to live with grandparents when they live with neither parent than are Australian children. Second, whereas 20.3% of American children younger than age 15 live with lone mothers only, 17.3% of Australian children live with lone mothers only.

TABLE 10.6
Distribution of Living Arrangements Among Children
Under Age 15 Years in Australia and the United States

	Source of data	
Child Lives With:	HILDA (%)	SIPP (%)
Two married biological parents	67.79	67.66
Two cohabiting biological parents	5.80	1.64
A married biological parent and a stepparent	2.83	3.49
Unmarried biological parent and partner	3.04	1.26
Lone biological mother only	17.33	20.35
Lone biological father only	2.00	2.14
Grandparent only	0.72	1.92
Foster parents only	0.30	0.38
Other relatives only	0.19	0.71
Other nonrelatives	0.00	0.47
Total	100	100

Note. Weighted comparisons; totals rounded up. HILDA = Household, Income, and Labour Dynamics in Australia; SIPP = Survey of Income and Program Participation. Sources: HILDA (N = 4,711) and SIPP 1996 (N = 19,150).

CONCLUSION

In implementing in 1996 the recommendation of the National Research Council (NRC) that the SIPP "ascertain the relationships of children to all adults in the household and to add the category of 'partner' to identify consensual unions" (Citro & Kalton, 1993, p. 76), more accurate measures of cohabitation are available and important topics, such as paternity establishment and fatherhood outside of marriage, can be studied. Overall, the improvements to the 1996 SIPP and its successors will greatly enhance our understanding of children's living arrangements and the circumstances associated with those arrangements.

Although the redesign of the SIPP offers researchers more opportunities to better understand children's relationships to adults and household composition, further improvements are needed. Presently, the relationship matrix is included only once per SIPP panel and overlooks housing units with fewer than three persons. Depending on the length of a panel, the relationship matrix should be included annually rather than only once per panel and should be inserted into Wave 1 instead of Wave 2, which suffers from sample attrition.

Advantages of an annual accounting of all relationships within a household include the possibility of measuring changes in child-to-adult relationships over time and generating an additional set of longitudinal statistics based on relationships within households. Other benefits of annual, supplementary relationship matrices are that they would augment cross-sectional measures of children's family types and month-to-month measures of changes in their relationships to a household head, as well as further promote a primary aim of the SIPP, which is to provide data on children's eligibility for and participation in government assistance programs. (See Citro & Kalton, 1993, for a discussion of using the SIPP to track the dynamics of children's living arrangements using monthly data.)

Also, more methodological work is needed to understand whether the categories for partner and unrelated individual suffer from reporting bias. This study shows that single parents distinguish between the two categories, but the accuracy of the reports are prone to misreporting. This latter issue, in addition to the problems of imputing certain types of relationships, of missing data on adults' records contained on the core data file, and of losing about 13% of the original sample from attrition between Waves 1 and 2, signifies that the quality of the SIPP data is still compromised.

Notwithstanding problems and recommendations, if relationship matrices offer so much, why are they used so little? Relationship matrix data have been available for every SIPP panel since 1984, yet, with few exceptions, (Baughman et al., 2002; Brandon & Bumpass, 2001; Furukawa, 1994; Hernandez & Brandon, 2002), they have seldom been exploited by nongovernmental personnel. One reason why relationship matrices are underused is that manipulating them is computationally daunting and prone to programming errors, which includes programming errors when changing the unit of analysis from adult to child. Added to this problem is a severe lack of "user-friendly" documentation (e.g., prototypes of successful programming code), and no preexisting derived variables from the relationship data in a public use file that could guide analysts. With attention by the U.S. Census Bureau, such problems are correctable.

A second major reason why relationship matrices are avoided in household surveys is that it is possible to gain much information by randomly selecting only a focal child from a household and investigating that child's relationships with everyone else in a household. This data collection method is less expensive to implement in a survey than a full relationship matrix, and the data are less cumbersome to process. The trade-off is a smaller amount of information on all the children in a household and the entire array of specific relationships among all household members. Impediments to using relationship matrices are unfortunate, because there is the potential for more informed policies and better studies than ones that are generated from studies that use a standard one-dimensional survey question that asks about children's relationships to the head of the household.

Clearly, a variety of multivariate approaches are feasible using the relationship matrix data, but the aim of this chapter was to demonstrate the versatility of these data using only the most unpretentious of techniques. Certainly, more sophisticated analyses are needed to provide deeper insights into how America's children are faring and to develop effective social and child welfare policies. At least the prudent decision to regularly collect relationship data through a relationship matrix once per SIPP panel permits researchers to consider relationship matrix data and use it to depict American children's living arrangements; estimate how many children are in each arrangement; identify the impact of particular types of relationships between children and adults in the household on socioeconomic outcomes; and, compare American children's living arrangements with those of children in selected other countries.

Overall, data from the relationship matrix provide strong evidence that America's children can grow up relating to many different adults. Future research should examine whether the exact type of relationship between children and adults in a household affects their access to household resources. Also underscored are the vast differences in the socioeconomic conditions confronting children. Whether child outcomes, from school achievement, to teenage pregnancy, to drug use, to behavioral problems, are associated with the broader array of living arrangements is yet an unresolved question. Finally, compared with children in the United States, Australian children are more likely to live with adults who, for one reason or another, decide to remain unmarried. Interestingly, the choices of Australian adults to stay unmarried while rearing children may be of no consequence to the amount

TABLE 10.7
Estimates of Children's Living Arrangements Calculated
From Two Alternative Methods Within the 1996 SIPP

Child Lives With:	Question Asks Household Members' Relationships to the "Household Reference Person" [a] (%)	Question Asks Household Members' Relationships to All Other Members of the Household [b] (%)
At least one parent	88.42	96.52
Grandparent only	7.09	1.92
Other relative only	2.30	0.71
Foster parent only	0.43	0.38
Other nonrelative only	1.75	0.47
Number of observations = 19,150		

[a] The variable in the core wave files of the SIPP is "ERRP." It has 13 categories that describe how each person is related to the household reference person. [b] There are numerous variables measuring household relationships, (e.g., "RELAT1" and so on), with a beginning statement in the module, "Now I would like to ask you a few questions about how persons in this household are related to each other." Source: SIPP (1996 panel, Wave 2, Topical Module on Household Relationships and core data from fourth reference month).

of government income they receive. These sorts of questions spawned from the relationship matrix in the SIPP deserve further research.

Finally, the standard household survey method that distinguishes how children in the household are related to the head of the household is outmoded and should be replaced. Table 10.7 shows that because the standard method is based on children's relationships to household heads only, who may not be relatives, it provides less information and produces inaccurate estimates of children's living arrangements compared to information gathered from a relationship matrix, even though both methods use the same source of data. Thus, there is little doubt that, now more than ever before, the standard approach renders it difficult to assess with any precision whether a child lives with none, one, or two parents and whether that child is the biological child of the parents. The federal statistical system would benefit enormously from the more energetic use of the SIPP relationship matrices. Federal agencies needing national-level data on children and families should encourage the adoption of multidimensional relationship matrices for collecting data on relationships between children and adults in a household.

ACKNOWLEDGMENT

The author wishes to thank colleagues from the National Institutes for Child Health and Development's Family and Child Well-Being Research Network for their encouragement on this project, as well as Sandra Hofferth for comments on a previous draft of this chapter.

Notes

1. An underestimate of the total count of children is introduced because SIPP pinpointed only the exact relationships for households of three or more members (www.sipp.census .gov/sipp/chap3-4.htm). Interviewers show a respondent, who must be the reference person, a flashcard defining the various possible specific relationships, but only for households of three or more members. Thus, a child living with a single mother or a grandmother is omitted. The number of children is probably small, but they are a group that designers of the SIPP relationship matrix should plan to include in future SIPP household relationship matrices.
2. Many other surveys (e.g., the British Household Panel Survey and the Panel Study of Income Dynamics) ask how each household member is related to a reference person, usually the person who maintains the household. The Household, Income, and Labour Dynamics in Australia (HILDA) survey and the SIPP are notable exceptions, given that they directly code relationships between all household members.
3. The appropriate weight is the person cross-sectional weight for the fourth reference month. According to national intercensal estimates of the resident population of the United States on July 1, 1996, there were 58,703,911 children under age 15 (U.S. Census

Bureau, 2000b). Using the cross-sectional weight for the fourth reference month in Wave 2, the estimated number of children in this age range, before loss of cases, is smaller, numbering 53,635,079, which is 8.6% lower than the U.S. Census Bureau estimate. Many factors could explain the difference between the estimated population counts, including sample attrition that averaged about 14.5% between Waves 1 and 2 of the 1996 panel (U.S. Census Bureau, 2001). For more information see: http://eire.census.gov/popest/data/national/tables/intercensal/US-EST90INT-04.php

4. The Food Stamp program provides benefits in the form of food coupons or electronic cards that allow low-income, eligible households to increase their food purchasing power. In most cases, the food stamp recipient unit is the same as the census household. Sometimes, however, subfamilies and multiple families within a household are eligible (Doyle, Czajka, Boldin, Beebout, & Hirabayashi, 1987). To a large extent, controlling for the array of relationships of children to adults (their own "subfamilies"), and the number of children within a household remedies this possibility, although the approach cannot redress instances in which adults do not purchase or share meals.

5. LR tests are for selected coefficients all simultaneously equaling zero. Clearly, other statistical tests are possible of individual coefficients or pairs of coefficients equaling one another. Because this study examines a collection of relationship measures among adults and children, tests of individual coefficients are unreported, although possible.

11

Is *Single-Parent Family* a Misnomer Misdirecting Research and Policies?

Martha Hill
University of Michigan

Paul Callister
Wellington, New Zealand

The meaning and experience of *family* have been transformed over the past half century by increased divorce, separation, and repartnering. Yet in constructs and terms used to characterize family, research and policy worlds cling to the idea of a stable uniform building block—the single-household nuclear family—as the underlying model defining family. This oversimplified image tends to limit awareness of newer forms of family, at times orchestrating scores out of tune with today's children, parents, and family life.

Families commonly known as single parent, mother only, lone mother, sole father, or fatherless are focal points in policy discussions, political debates, social science research, and everyday conversation. Underlying these terms and the images they convey is the assumption, explicit or not, that children have but one reliable biological parent. In truth, most such children have not just one, but two living biological parents. One is the *single parent*. The second lives in another household. Some children see only the single parent, but some see both. Researchers and policymakers, though, rarely see the second parent and tend to label that parent as *absent*, *nonresident*, or *noncustodial*, even though these terms can be misleading when children spend time with both parents.

We offer the term "invisible" as a more apt characterization of the second parent. The double quotes are intended to convey underlying ambiguity and the very real possibility that such parents are more invisible to researchers and policymakers than to children. Some "invisible" parents are entirely unseen by children, but some are seen every day. The common assumption that single parent means a struggling young mother with little support from the father of her children is fostered by the image of "invisible" parents posing a danger through domestic violence, drug use, or mental illness. That image is but one possibility among many. This chapter focuses on a different possible image, that of "invisible" parents as active, positive agents in children's family lives.

Although research and policies in the United States have been paying increasing attention to "invisible" parents (see, e.g., Coley, 2001; Garfinkel, McLanahan, & Hanson, 1998; Hofferth, Pleck, Stueve, Bianchi, & Sayer, 2002; Lamb, 2002; Lerman & Sorensen, 2000; Marsiglio, Amato, & Day, 2000; Seltzer, 1991; Seltzer & Bianchi, 1988; Stewart, 1999; see also chap. 20, this volume), data about "invisible" parents are relatively scarce and come almost exclusively from potentially biased reports of the parent living with the children (Pasley & Braver, 2004; Schaeffer, Seltzer, & Dykema, 1998; Sorensen, 1997). Data are seldom collected from the "invisible" parent and almost never from the children themselves.

A family spread across multiple households is rarely recognized in its entirety and from the perspective of all its biological members: father, mother, and child(ren). It is this perspective that we speak to in efforts to orient research and policies more closely to 21st-century realities and the potential for complex family constructs to be a positive force. A special focus is on concepts and terms for characterizing family when a critical member, usually the father, becomes "invisible" (invisible, at least, in most past and some current research and policymaking) because bonds of a conjugal nature and coresidency no longer hold.

It has long been understood that the constructs we develop and the descriptive terms we use are important in shaping our understanding of the world. Literature on transformation of identity offers pointed lessons on thoughtful attention to the way we speak and to the transformative nature of words: "Any name is a container; poured into it are the conscious or unwitting evaluations of the namer. . . ."; altering names is a "rite of passage" to a "new self image" (Strauss, 1959, pp. 15–17). Introducing new, more accurate descriptive terms and constructs merits thoughtful attention in a rite of passage to better acknowledgment of "invisible" parents actively engaged in beneficial activities.

In this chapter, we first address the nature of family ties then document the rise of "invisible" parenting and note examples of issues inadequately addressed owing to lack of knowledge about across-household connectivity. Next, we offer thoughts on new approaches to family that facilitate recognizing across-household connectivity involving "invisible" parents. We then propose new terms for characterizing the across-household connectivity, striving for wording less judgmental of the overall nature of "invisible" parenting. This is an exploratory expansion of vocabulary aimed at prompting discussion and debate about the constructs and terms we use and how they shape our perspectives of the world. In discussing these issues, we place the United States at center stage and, at times, compare other countries, notably New Zealand, to the United States in ways that expand the perspective.

TIES THAT BIND

An important reason for the limited research and policy considerations of "invisible" parenting is a disconnect between definitions of family and the unit that is usually observed. Household—the collection of individuals in a dwelling unit—is the focus of data gathering by most statistical agencies. With a dwelling unit as the visible skin of a household, and dwelling units unlikely to move as one counts them, problems of omission or double-counting seem less problematic than trying to count people constantly in motion. Hence, censuses have gathered information about individuals living in households, and this practice has received international support. For example, in its *Principles and Recommendations for Population and Housing Censuses*, the United Nations (1998) stated that a family cannot constitute more than one household. Surveys of family life, on large and small scale, have tended to follow that pattern by sampling households to gather information about the individuals living there.

Defining family is more problematic than defining household, which is one reason researchers have tended to focus on households. Although family and household are often assumed to be the same, they can be very different. This difference is particularly important when considering research on fathers (Cherlin & Griffith, 1998). Whereas a household is composed of individuals sharing the same dwelling, family is conceptualized as a collection of related individuals, and what is meant by related can vary widely.

Many social scientists tend to think of family structurally as bound by kinship ties, forged by blood or formal connections of marriage or adoption. Family, however, can be conceptualized as transcending structural kinship boundaries, built instead through common goals and goal-attaining strategies, with boundaries established by level of commitment. It is from this perspective that the family process field of research directs attention to functions, processes, and dynamics that underlie family (see, e.g., Day, Gavazzi, & Acock, 2001). From this perspective, groups of caring individuals bond and form alliances with collective (though possibly unstated) goals, ideologies, and strategies. Potential members have some choice about whether to participate, subscribe, or contribute to the family: "Some families have members who are more vested in the family entity than others, and some families have members so disengaged from one another that the family entity is barely visible" (Day et al., 2001, p. 105). The definition of family, be it an entity defined by social scientists structurally or an entity defined by family process scholars through functions, goals, or motivations, can span across households or even countries.

Wide diversity in what defines family in people's everyday lives is poignantly revealed in qualitative studies of children's perceptions of family after parents have parted (e.g., Pryor & Rodgers, 2001; Smart, Neale, & Wade, 2001). With such diversity both conceptually and in everyday lived realities, current approaches to defining and studying families leave statistical agencies, researchers, policymakers, and the general public struggling to make sense of family life. The chapters by Brandon and Iceland (chaps. 10 and 13, respectively), in this volume address within-household challenges. Lack of information on cross-household connections, though, contributes an added set of challenges, and this chapter attends to the incomplete visualization of possibilities that result.

THE RISE OF "INVISIBLE" PARENTING

Until relatively recently in our history, disease, war, accidents, starvation, abandonment, and death during childbirth meant that many children grew up without a mother, a father, or either parent (see, e.g., Ellwood & Jencks, 2002; Uhlenberg, 1980). At the start of the 21st century, although death and abandonment continue to remove parents from their children's everyday lives, the most common pathways for that are through parental divorce or separation or by a union failing to form when a child is born (although a prison sentence has increasingly become another route).[1] If a union fails to form, the mother typically assumes custody, although the names of the father and mother have been increasingly appearing on birth certificates (Argys & Peters, 2001; Marcil-Gratton, 1998). When a union dissolves, children are typically allocated a primary caregiver via a decision by the parents or through a court order. In all these cases, the child still has two biological parents, a striking change from the historical model in which death claimed one or both of them. In the United States, as many as one half of all children are expected to spend part of their childhood living apart from at least one of their parents, usually their father (Furstenberg & Cherlin, 1991; Zill, 1996), and children with an "invisible" parent have become a solid feature of everyday life throughout the industrialized world.

The family picture can be even more complex: One or both of the biological parents may repartner, thus creating step relationships; in addition, "invisible" parents may have a second or even third set of children (Manning, Stewart, & Smock, 2001), and two or more single parents with children present may be sharing the same household. The proliferation of these new family types has, in part, promoted a shift by many social scientists from a biological construction to a social construction of parenthood. Indeed, for some aspects of family life, indications are that residence sometimes supercedes biology (e.g., Harris & Ryan, 2004, showed involvement with children higher for stepfathers than for nonresident fathers). Complexities such as this merit careful consideration and, indeed, are discussed in other chapters in this volume (see Brandon's discussion of within-household relationship matrices, chap. 10, and Hofferth et al.'s discussion of social fathering, chap. 20).

That biology still matters for attachment and caring, however, also is supported by evidence. Quantitative research indicates that biological fathers in coupled (married or not) families tend to invest more heavily in children than do stepfathers, and that biological fathers contribute time and attention to their children even when they are nonresident (Harris, Heard, & King, 2000; Hofferth & Anderson, 2003). Qualitative research in New Zealand shows children often retain strong bonds to blood links, even when parents hardly communicate (Fleming & Atkinson, 1999). In addition, evidence suggests that many children separated from a biological parent want to establish contact (Hertz, 2002). In fact, U.S. research supports the idea that many children would like a high level of contact with both parents postseparation (Fabricius, 2003), and Australian research estimates that more than one third of teenagers of separated parents favor arrangements with equal time with each parent (Parkinson, Cashmore, & Single, 2003). That many adults also consider biology to matter is reflected in the societal expectation (codified in child support laws) that an "invisible" parent has an ongoing financial obligation to support his or her children. There is also an expectation, although at times more contested, that an "invisible" parent provide ongoing care and attention to his or her children (Sarre, 1996).

Although some notable fraction of "invisible" parents is disengaged from their children, a sizable number is active in parenting. Joint-custody arrangements are one way of identifying those likely to be engaged in active parenting (although having custody does not guarantee active and positive parenting, just as life in two-biological-parent homes does not guarantee it). Joint custody is not the most common arrangement, however; the most common arrangement is still sole-parent custody, usually by the mother (Child Trends, 2002). Nevertheless, joint custody (physical if not legal) has become increasingly common, especially among states that encourage its application.[2] Joint physical custody, with the child spending roughly 25% or more time at each parent's home, is the arrangement in more than one in five postdivorce U.S. families, although somewhat more common for higher income children (Child Trends, 2002). Physical custody by the father is an arrangement for about 10% of households with a nonresident parent elsewhere; it is again somewhat more common for higher income children.

Child custody is but part of the picture; "invisible" parents can have contact with their children living elsewhere even if they do not have custody. Although mothers' proxy reports and fathers' self-reports tend to differ, both show that the degree of contact on the part of "invisible" fathers is nontrivial. Indications are that the majority of U.S. children with "invisible" parents are in contact with them. About one half see the "invisible" parent once a month or more (Child Trends, 2002; Hofferth et al., 2002); almost 15% live with them for a month or more during the year (Child Trends, 2002). Even fathers separated at the time of the child's birth usually are not absent at that point (M. Carlson et al., 2003; Padilla & Reichman, 2001; Teitler, 2001). Contact, like custody, however, varies over the economic spectrum, with more contact for higher income children (Child Trends, 2002). Yet, even for low-income children with access blocked by mothers, "invisible" fathers appear to express a widespread desire for contact with their children (M. Carlson, McLanahan, & Brooks-Gunn, 2003; Lin & McLanahan, 2001; Padilla & Reichman, 2001; Teitler, 2001). These patterns also appear in other industrialized countries. In Australia, for example, among children aged 0 to 17 with a biological parent living elsewhere, one half saw their other parent frequently (at least once per fortnight), whereas 31% saw their other parent either rarely (once per year, or less often) or never (Australian Bureau of Statistics, 2004).

Although contact is not necessarily indicative of involved parenting, studies show a notable portion of "invisible" parents engaging with their children. Research suggests that among children of divorce, roughly one half of those in contact with their father are actively engaged with him on a steady basis (Seltzer & Brandreth, 1994). For children up to age 12, contact with the "invisible" father is likely to involve presents and working or playing together (Hofferth et al., 2002). In addition, roughly one third of "invisible" fathers in contact with their children are involved in the children's school activities, 10% at a high level of involvement (National Center for Education Statistics, 1998).

How beneficial is the involvement of "invisible" parents in children's lives? This part of the picture is particularly underdeveloped and challenging to clarify. Perceptions are clouded by data based largely on resident parents' proxy reports and limitations in the measured dimensions of involvement. Early studies registered meager positive and some negative influences of "invisible" parents. However, more recent meta-analyses and reviews of research and key research projects show "invisible" parents making important positive contributions to children via child support, authoritative parenting, and children's feelings of closeness (Amato & Gilbreth, 1999; Dunn, 2004). In addition, recent findings show benefits of "invisible" parents' involvement in children's school activities (National Center for Education Statistics, 1998).

ISSUES MISSED OR MISREPRESENTED

The United States in recent decades has substantially expanded data on parenting to better measure fathering (see, e.g., Peters & Day, 2000) and out-of-marriage parenting as well as parenting after divorce (see, e.g., Smock, 2000). Although describing studies with data on "invisible" parents and their children is beyond the scope of this chapter, Table 11.1 provides a list of U.S. studies that illustrate the wide array of methodological approaches in use.

Despite this long list in Table 11.1, data on "invisible" parenting continue to lag far behind data on intact, two-parent families, and some issues are clouded or virtually unseen because across-household links are inadequately recognized. Characteristics of "invisible" parents and interactions with their children, for example, are prone to biased measurement (e.g., Pasley & Brave, 2004; Shaeffer et al., 1998; Sorensen, 1997). In addition, assessments of "invisible" parents' contributions to their children could be missing significant amounts of support, both cash and in-kind, not reported in formal systems (Coley, 2001). It is not widely acknowledged, for example, that the U.S. census, like censuses in many industrialized countries, may (a) undercount some children (ones who, because they are visiting their "invisible" parent on census day, are away from their usual home), (b) overcount other children (ones evenly splitting time between parents with joint physical custody), and (c) provide no indication of "invisible" parents (Callister & Hill, 2002). Furthermore, failure to identify "invisible" parents devalues them as parents and can lead to misunderstandings if census data, or surveys modeled on them, are used to study issues such as income adequacy and distribution, housing size and adequacy, job mobility, child care, and characteristics and behavior of parents.

Resources "invisible" parents provide their children can be missed, along with important aspects of family environment. For example, a standard approach to collecting data on child support (in the United States and other industrialized countries, such as New Zealand) involves gathering data on

TABLE 11.1
U.S. Surveys Relating to "Invisible" Parents

American Time-Use Survey (ATUS): www.bls.gov/tus/home.htm
Current Population Survey Child Support Supplements:
   www.census.gov/hhes/www/childsupport/prevreps.html
Early Childhood Longitudinal Study (ECLS-B): http://nces.ed.gov/ecls/Birth/studybrief.asp
Early Head Start (EHS):
   www.acf.hhs.gov/programs/core/ongoing_research/ehs/ehs_intro.html
Fragile Families and Child Wellbeing Study (Fragile Families):
   www.researchforum.org/project_general_28.html
National Children's Study: http://nationalchildrensstudy.gov/about/
National Household Education Survey (NHES): http://nces.ed.gov/nhes/
National Longitudinal Study of Adolescent Health (Add Health):
   www.cpc.unc.edu/addhealth
National Longitudinal Survey of Youth (NLSY): www.bls.gov/nls/home.htm
National Survey of Families and Households (NSFH):
   www.nichd.nih.gov/about/cpr/dbs/res_national4.htm
Panel Study of Income Dynamics (PSID):
   http://psidonline.isr.umich.edu/Guide/Overview.html
PSID Child Development Study (PSID CDS-I and CDS-II):
   http://psidonline.isr.umich.edu/CDS/
Survey of Income and Program Participation (SIPP): www.sipp.census.gov/sipp/
Survey of Inmates in State Correctional Facilities (SISCF):
   www.la.utexas.edu/research/crime_criminaljustice_research/siscf.html
Welfare, Children, and Families: A Three-City Study:
   www.researchforum.org/project_printable_19.html

Note. See Callister and Hill (2002) and Cherlin and Griffith (1998) for brief descriptions of many of these studies.

payments received by a parent (as part of gross income) but no information on the transfer of that income (expenditure) by an "invisible" parent. Furthermore, in the United States, as in New Zealand, it is not uncommon for an invisible father to spend time with his children on weekends and holidays or overnight stays on weekdays, and this involves direct expenditure on the children. It could also mean additional household resources, such as an extra bedroom, are required in the "invisible" parent's household for these visits (Reichert, 1999). Based on simple household data, measures of disposable income and costs of living for the "invisible" parent's household and the resident parent's household can be inaccurate (see Birks, 2001, Hodgson & Birks, 2002, and O'Dea, 2000, for a discussion of these issues in New Zealand). As a result, some households classified as single-mother households appear worse off and some male-headed households (those with "invisible" fathers) appear better off than they actually are. That a child could spend time in the "invisible" parent's household and the resident parent's household tends to be poorly represented in the data.

Lack of information on across-household links also can bias assessments of the ability of the "invisible" parent to support children. Missing data on nonresident fathers have prompted researchers (e.g., Garfinkel & Oellerich, 1989) to base measures of characteristics of nonresident fathers on those of resident mothers by assuming homogamy (mating of like with like). However, the validity of this assumption is suspect. As Garfinkel, Glei, and McLanahan (2002) noted, a nontrivial portion of nonresident fathers are in prison when mothers are not, or vice versa (for detailed estimates, see Mumola, 2000; and chap. 15, this volume). Furthermore, the resident and nonresident parent may differ substantially in the presence in their household of a new set of children from a new union, and such children affect the levels of child support that are forthcoming (Manning et al., 2001). In addition, analysis of matched former-couple data for resident and nonresident ("invisible") parents indicates that information on nonresident parents substantially improves prediction of child support beyond what is possible with only measures of the characteristics of resident mothers (Smock & Manning, 1997).

Invisibility of across-household links also fosters other partially valid, or even false, assumptions. For example, moves to other locations for job opportunities can be assumed to be easy for adults living on their own, or even adults living in couple households. However, adults may be dissuaded from a move for job-related reasons because it would mean loss of regular contact with their nonresident children (S. D. Stewart, 1999). Equally, a resident parent may be constrained, sometimes under court order, not to move too far from the nonresident parent. Likewise, child-care possibilities can be unseen by researchers and policymakers. An "invisible" parent living nearby his or her children could even be a good source of child care, willing and able to care for the children after school or at other times.

Failing to recognize cross-household ties can also limit the vision of policymakers in other ways. Currently, U.S. policymakers and researchers are focused on marriage as a policy prescription for addressing several social and economic challenges, including child poverty (see, e.g., Garfinkel et al., 2002; Mincy, 2002; Thomas & Sawhill, 2002). There can be, however, circumstances when strengthening children's interaction with an "invisible" parent (most often a father) provides a better alternative than introducing additional father figures through marriage. Possibilities of involved "invisible" parents (mothers and fathers) working effectively for their children's good merit concerted attention, as does the link between "invisible" parents' circumstances and the assistance they are able and willing to give to their children. Prior to the recent adoption of marriage as a policy prescription, U.S. policymakers were initiating policies for enhancing "invisible" parents' earnings as a means of increasing child support payments (Blank & Ellwood, 2002). Should these policies be rekindled and expanded to encourage additional parenting roles for "invisible" parents? Are there aspects of "invisible" parenting that contribute to children's well-being and thus should be encouraged?

PONDERING THE "INVISIBLE"

In pondering questions such as these, it is important to give careful thought to ways to reveal "invisible" parenting. In this vein, this section discusses some reorientation of theoretical and analytical perspectives, focusing as well on a relatively new construct for conceptualizing family and a critical examination of descriptive terms relating to "invisible" parenting.

Adding Children's Perspectives

Research and policies have tended to focus on adults as the major players in families. However, instead of centering the statistical family around one or two adults, it is important to include children as well. Concerns about complying with the 1989 United Nations Convention on the Rights of the Child (United Nations, 1989) are influencing the formulation of family policies in other parts of the world, including New Zealand and Sweden. This convention supports giving children a greater voice in policymaking, and, based on concepts of best interests of the child, it also supports the concept of shared parental responsibility. Although not yet ratifying this convention, the United States has been shifting toward greater inclusion of children's perspectives and greater recognition of fathers' as well as mothers' parenting roles. Melding the perspectives of children with that of their parents offers the potential of a clearer focus on the well-being of all family members.

We recognize that such a comprehensive melding of the perspectives is not without complications. These complications involve treatment of social and biological parenting, siblings in a family, and overlap between families (e.g., siblings being part of different families; Nolan, 2001). In addition, although young children can be the center of family connections, it is often the parents who determine the relationships that are actively pursued. Furthermore, when gathering data from children, consent and other ethical issues must be confronted, including gauging the age when a child is a capable reporter. Such complexities are beyond the scope of this chapter and are reserved for future investigation. Here, we introduce underlying concepts in a simplified context.

Mother–Child–Father Triad

Following in the footsteps of Cherlin and Griffith (1998) and family process researchers, we look to network and complex systems approaches and focus the spotlight on the mother-child-father triad. This approach enables expansive visions of family that can include "invisible" parents in a beneficial parenting role. The mother-child-father triad construct draws attention to the family as a network and, in the language of social network analysis, to connectivity among all its members (Wasserman & Faust, 1999). At a minimum, the two biological parents and the child constitute the family network. Ideally, other important family members, such as partners of parents, siblings, and grandparents, should be taken into account also, but a manageable start for obtaining a better view of biological family is to concentrate on the triad, whether or not father, mother, and child reside in the same household.

Underlying the triad is a vision of family as a network or system of actors with some overlapping sense of goals and the potential to be engaged in processes oriented to achieving shared goals. In accordance with a family process perspective and network and complex systems analysis, the focus is on the connections between the family members, not the attributes of the people in the network. The family takes its shape from the way individuals interact with one another. The nature, texture, and effectiveness of the strategies potential members use to achieve individual and collective goals are the defining aspects of the connectivity between family members.

The triad takes us beyond the traditional approach of seeing separate dyads of mother-father, mother-child, or father-child. These dyads are not ignored, but rather are the building blocks nested in the triad, which allows for the simultaneous consideration of all three dyads. In the triad, each parent can exhibit a parenting role and a partnering role, and the child is an active agent, able to react to parenting and to initiate actions. The nature of the biological family is shaped by how all three actors play their roles, although, as Dunn (2004) stressed, the quality of the mother–father and the mother–child relationship can be crucial in shaping the child–father relationship, especially when fathers are no longer living full-time with their children. How the parents interact with each other (as in marital interactions such as those discussed in chap. 4, this volume) and how each parent interacts with the child—intersections of all three actors—shape the triad.

The triad concept is beginning to enter U.S. literature, bolstered by growing recognition of fathers' active parenting and increased attention to the voices of children. In the triad context, research thus far suggests an important structural element regarding "invisible" parenting: a gatekeeper (M. Carlson et al., 2003; Coley & Chase-Lansdale, 1999). With parents' residence in separate households, the resident parent is often in a position to make or break connections between the nonresident parent and the child, and thus potentially make or break researchers' ability to know anything about the nonresident ("invisible") parent. The quality of ties (e.g., extent of trust and respect) between resident and nonresident parents appears to determine the extent of this gatekeeping (National Center on Fathers and Families, n.d.), with ongoing romantic attachment, rather than a desire to spend time with the child, often the driving motivation for contact (Mc-Lanahan, Garfinkel, & Mincy, 2001).

Active "Invisible" Parenting

Although the family processes of the mother–child–father triad merit most attention for understanding how families function, structural considerations are frequently taken as indicators of family function. Residency ties, for example, loom large in tests of child development theories. Comparisons are often made between children reared in one-parent households and two-parent households (e.g., Blankenhorn, 1995; M. S. Hill, Yeung, & Duncan, 2001; McLanahan, 1988), with an underlying, unstated assumption that parenting by an "invisible" parent is either irrelevant or identical to that of the resident parent. The triad construct opens our eyes to potential diversity in "invisible" parents: It explicitly allows room for "invisible" parents and the possibility of distinguishing those engaged in constructive parenting.

Defining active or involved parenting is, of course, a major challenge, especially with "invisible" parents (see, e.g., Harris & Ryan, 2004; chap. 20, this volume). Active interaction could range from as little as sending a birthday card to parents spending equal amounts of time with their children. Furthermore, interaction is but one form of child care; accessibility and responsibility, which are especially difficult to measure, are additional forms of child care (Lamb, 1987). Difficulty in gauging responsibility is evidenced by time-use research showing parents claiming child-care responsibility while the child is sleeping at night or playing at a neighbor's house; parents make these claims because they are still ultimately responsible for the child (Schwartz, 2002). Ideally, assessments of active parenting would measure both quantity and quality of time devoted to children. Although delving further into what constitutes active, quality parenting would take us beyond the scope of this discussion, it is important to recognize that parents living in separate households heighten the challenges of defining parenting.

Seeing "Invisible" Fathers

Central to problems of gauging the extent and value of active parenting by "invisible" parents (typically fathers) is the fact that they are rarely asked if they are parents. The common approach in estimating the activity of "invisible" parenting is to rely on a resident parent (typically the mother) for information about the nonresident parent's activities (Cherlin & Griffith, 1998; National Center on Fathers and Families, n.d.; Schaeffer et al., 1998; Seltzer & Brandreth, 1994). This is the predominant approach taken in past research, in part because mothers have been considered children's major socializing agent (Coley, 2001) and in part because resident parents are readily identifiable as parents (Schaeffer et al., 1998).

However, limiting the perspective on parenting to a single parent is particularly problematic when parents do not constitute a couple. Research indicates wide disparities between resident mothers' and nonresident fathers' reports about the parenting behavior of the nonresident parent (Braver, Wolchik, Sandler, Fogas, & Zvetina, 1991; Coley & Morris, 2002; Pasley & Braver, 2004; Schaeffer et al., 1998; Seltzer & Brandreth, 1994). Each parent tends to report less in the way of the other parent's contributions to the child, and the child's report tends to fall between the two. However, there are exceptions. In reports of the child witnessing domestic violence before a divorce, children are less likely than either parent to report such an experience. Little is known about the extent to which biases misrepresent the nonresident father's impact on child well-being (Pasley & Braver, 2004).

When men have been asked to identify themselves as nonresident fathers, many have declined, further compounding assessments. Estimates indicate that a little more than one half of nonresident fathers respond affirmatively when questioned about having children elsewhere, and when questioned separately about number of biological children and number of children in the household about three quarters reveal their status as nonresident fathers (Sorensen, 1997). The undercount is largely rooted in the tendency for men to underreport their fertility (Cherlin, Griffith & McCarthy, 1983; Rendall, Clark, Peters, Ranjit, & Verrapoulou, 1999). Chapters 16 and 18 in this volume offer insight into reasons behind this and strategies for more accurate data.

Noncoverage is also a problem. Surveys fail to include sizable numbers of "invisible" fathers (and some "invisible" mothers) in samples because "invisible" parents often live in group quarters, notably prisons but also military barracks, and group quarters are not included in household-based surveys (Garfinkel et al., 1998; Sorensen, 1997; see also chap. 15, this volume). In addition, some subgroups (e.g., African American males in their early 30s) who are especially likely to be nonresident fathers tend to be missed in surveys and censuses (Sorensen, 1997).

Following mother-child-father triad members through time in a panel study, the approach taken by many recent data sets (e.g., Fragile Families, Early Childhood Longitudinal Study [ECLS-B], Three-City study, and Panel Study of Income Dynamics, Child Development Supplement [PSID-CDS]) is helpful in identifying "invisible" fathers. The time of birth seems to be the best time to enlist biological fathers in a panel study; nearly 80% of fathers are present at the birth of the child or visit the hospital, and at that time both parents typically indicate a strong desire that the child's father be known (Fragile Families and Child Wellbeing, 2000). The Fragile Families study takes this approach, having a particular interest in fathers and issues such as expectations about fathers' rights and responsibilities, mother–father relationships, and how many fathers want to be involved in rearing their children. Similarly, the ECLS-B enlists fathers via children's birth certificates. Enlisting fathers at the birth of children does, however, mean a long wait before much is known about fathers' involvement across the course of childhood. It is important to find ways to identify "invisible" fathers with children at later childhood stages as well.

FITTING DESCRIPTORS

When what constitutes family is evolving rapidly, descriptive terms for accurate characterizations may not keep pace. Examples of incorrect descriptors, most notably *single-parent family*, abound, even in prominent official publications that support the idea of collecting data on "invisible" parents and in the authors' own publications. Yet descriptors of families shape existing problems and visions of potential solutions. If single-parent family connotes but one parent available to a child, then circumstances and possible contributions of a second, less visible parent do not spring to mind.

The shorthand that has developed for use in research and policy debates, especially as loosely employed by the popular media, works against acknowledging such complexity. It is much easier, for example, to describe children as simply being reared by lone mothers or in single-parent families than it is to talk about the real complexity in parenting arrangements and children's lives. Phrases such as "father who no longer lives with the mother of his children" are appearing, though they are cumbersome. Terms such as *absent father*, though potentially an incorrect descriptor for many "invisible" fathers, are easier to use. Similarly, *fatherless family* is a term that has been used by some groups when promoting the return to living in traditional families (see, e.g., Blankenhorn, 1995).

With a sympathetic view toward differing family arrangements, Duncan and Edwards (1997, p. 30) used the term *lone mothers*, a term long in use in Europe for "all mothers bringing up children without a resident partner." With a less sympathetic view, researchers, policymakers, and the general public refer to invisible fathers as *deadbeat dads* (Reichert, 1999; Sorensen, 1997) because a sizable portion are not paying child support. *Dead broke* is also a term used for low-income "invisible" fathers (Talvi, 2002). These terms are punitive, aimed at prodding enforcement of child-support awards, rather than looking to "invisible" fathers' low income as a notable source of child-support shortfalls for poor children (see, e.g., M. S. Hill, 1992). A neutral to positive descriptor might more effectively turn creative energies to envisioning research and policies directed at this source of the problem and to recognizing contributions of social involvement between "invisible" fathers and their children. Indeed, the fathers themselves may be more willing to participate in their children's lives and more willing to participate in surveys that call for them to self-identify if terms such a deadbeat dad and fatherless family were used less.

Terms long in use are listed in Table 11.2, along with proposed ones that take more of a cross-household perspective. The list at a minimum reveals a need for new terms, as some newly coined ones improve accuracy and some fill a void.

Central to this discussion and at the top of the list, *single-parent household* is usually technically more accurate than *single-parent family, lone-parent,* or *fatherless* family. When the "invisible" parent is actively parenting, this reality is better reflected by terms such as *binuclear* family (Ahrons & Perlmutter,

TABLE 11.2
Terms Relating to "Invisible" Parenting

Currently in Common Usage	*Cross-Household Suggestions*
Single-parent family (OR) lone-parent family (OR) fatherless family	Single-parent household (OR) lone-parent household (OR) fatherless household
No comparable terms	Two-parent, two-household family (OR) two-household family (OR) two-home family (OR) separated family (OR) binuclear family
No comparable terms	Two-parent, two-household child (OR) two-household child (OR) two-home child (OR) separated child
No comparable term	Mother-child-father triad
Resident parent (OR) custodial parent (OR) single parent (OR) lone parent	"Visible" parent (OR) near parent
Nonresident parent (OR) noncustodial parent (OR) absent parent	"Invisible" parent (OR) elsewhere parent (OR) far parent (OR) separated parent
No comparable term	In-common child
Nonresident child (OR) noncustodial child (OR) absent child	"Invisible" child (OR) elsewhere child (OR) far child (OR) separated child

Note. In some instances, *single-parent household* is an inaccurate substitution for *single-parent family*, as with a household containing two single parents each with their children present.

1982), *separated* family, and, most especially a term starting to be used in the United States and other countries—*two-parent, two-household* family (or simply *two-household* or *two-home* family) (see, e.g., Birks, 2000, 2001; Dubow, Roecker, & D'Imperio, 2001; Kauffman Early Education Exchange, 2002). It is useful to consider applying such terms to children as well, as they tend to capture children's perspectives of alternating between the residences of two parents. What differentiates two-household from two-home, at least in the authors' minds, is that two-home conveys a high level of shared parenting. Not all children with separated parents would be classified as two-household or two-home children, only those with two active biological parents.

We also ask researchers and policymakers to ponder the construct *mother-child-father triad* and the connectivity that binds the component members. Holding this construct in mind, we suggest using the descriptors "*visible*," "*invisible*," and *in-common*—one "visible" parent, one "invisible" parent, and their in-common child. We avoid negative connotations with these terms, and the perspective of researchers and policymakers is drawn into the discussion. As a point of comparability, "invisible" is a descriptor applicable to children as well when viewed from the "invisible" parent's perspective.

Contrast these terms with those in common use. *Nonresident* and *noncustodial* appear frequently in publications and everyday speech, often in contexts that give no clear justification for one over the other. Noncustodial is a legal term and reflects a legally sanctioned unequal division of custody, which some argue discriminates against fathers (Braver & Griffin, 2000). There are also parents who truly share custody and the care of their children for whom noncustodial is an inaccurate term. (Parallel problems apply to terms such as *primary caregiver*.) The term nonresident has problems as well, in that it implies the family is where the child lives most of the time, and the other parent is an outsider. When that child is with the nonresident parent, the nonresident parent becomes resident. Furthermore, the prefix of "non" with both terms is negative and suggests deviance. We considered the terms *inside* and *outside* parents, but these also have negative connotations of exclusion. In some situations, these terms reflect reality, but in others, they are misleading. *Absent* parent is a term with less negative connotation, but it implies that "invisible" parents are out of the picture entirely. With many "invisible" parents actively involved in their children's lives, a term such as *elsewhere* parent avoids that misconception and offers a natural counterpart—elsewhere child.

Separated parent is a term with the appeal of being neutral in designating primary or secondary parenting status; it also more readily lends itself to complementary terms for parent and child. Separated child is a fitting term for the child no matter in which parent's home the child is residing at the time. It carries no information about where the child usually resides, however. In addition, separated, when applied to parents, poses the problem of implying that the parents live apart but have not yet reached divorce, which could be inaccurate.

From the child's viewpoint, the terms *far* and *near* parent are worth pondering. They are complementary with relatively weak connotations regarding primary and secondary parenting status; however, the terms could be thought to convey strength of emotional connection. The terms "visible" and "invisible" are less fraught with potentially inaccurate connotations.

CONCLUSION

In research and policy debates, families with children are still commonly portrayed as either two-parent (biological or stepparent) or single-parent families. Yet parenting arrangements are highly diverse, and one major group often overlooked is children with "invisible" biological parents who, to varying degrees, have two active parents and two households. Despite the prevalence of such families in all industrialized countries, much is unknown about them, especially from the perspective of the children and the "invisible" parent.

There are many aspects relating to "invisible" parenting that researchers and policymakers need to better understand. Specific public-policy issues, such as determining income adequacy for children and designing child-care support systems, would benefit from better understanding of "invisible" parenting. Understanding the influences of "invisible" parenting on child development, the time "invisible" parents devote to their children's lives, and what child custody arrangements really are in the best interest of the child, also hinge on improved visibility of "invisible" parenting. Entire areas of research, such as identifying what works well and what works poorly in terms of the interactions and parenting strategies and behaviors in families with "invisible" parents, could evolve with the availability of information that bridges separate but related households.

The mother-child-father triad is a construct we advocate as providing useful insight into two-parent, two-household families. At a minimum, it is an expansive conceptualizing tool, and, with further development to address a variety of complications insufficiently considered here (such as taking account of multiple children in the family and repartnering of parents), it seems to offer possibilities for bringing innovative analysis approaches to bear on the complexities of family. These approaches may require a wide array of data, assessing family from the perspective of children, fathers, and mothers and measuring active parenting in its diverse forms. In both intact and nonintact families, it is possible that mothers, fathers, and children all have significantly different perceptions of the central figures in their lives and the flows of emotional and financial connectivity across the mother-child-father triad. Mother reports, father reports, and, where possible, children's reports may be crucial for obtaining a clear picture of the dynamics of family ties. Such a triangulated approach, along with innovative analytical methods, could help researchers and policymakers better understand how increasingly complex families operate.

The issues of cross-household families are becoming better understood, and data on shared parenting arrangements are becoming increasingly available in the United States. Still, the triangulated approach is rarely taken. More attention to this type of approach might well spur innovative use of existing analytical techniques (e.g., complex systems approaches and network analysis), development of new analytical techniques, and possibly development of new software for researching complex cross-household family networks and what they mean for their members.

Rethinking the descriptive terms used in research and policy debates is also in order. The terms are lagging behind changes in family structuring and functioning. Although most researchers try to differentiate between single-parent households and single-parent families, and the language of children in two-parent households is entering into print, the term single-parent family can still be found in many research publications (as well as the media and in policy debates), even when it is quite clear that the children involved have two active parents.

Recognizing that certain literature and fields of discourses are inherently tied to terms long in use, this chapter suggests an expansion of descriptive terms, not a complete substitution of a new set for the old. We advocate careful attention to constructs and terms. Parsimonious use of terms such as deadbeat dad in research and popular language is one step for bringing discussions to more neutral ground. Neutral terms such as "invisible" father, the often more accurate construct mother-child-father triad, and terms such as two-parent, two-household family, or two-home child, create images in our collective consciousness of "invisible" fathers and children as positive elements in one another's lives, despite living apart.

Policy changes and changes in nomenclature may be needed for fostering cross-household mother-child-father triads that are nurturing to members. Consider the example of a law change in Norway that recognizes that some resources flowing from an active "invisible" parent may be unknown by the "visible" parent (Reichert, 1999). Norway has instituted a new law regarding maintenance payments by "invisible" parents that gives more consideration to the time children spend with each biological parent and to the parents' relative financial situation. With pre- and postimplementation surveys measuring time in-common children spend with each parent and the economic well-being of the two households, Norway will track baseline information about the extent of single responsibility that single parents really have and changes in behavior resulting from the policy change. From this, researchers and policymakers can learn how well such approaches succeed in gathering information and motivating "invisible" parents to claim their "invisible" children.

ACKNOWLEDGMENTS

The initial idea for the chapter arose in conversations with Stuart Birks, of Massey University, New Zealand, and we thank him for comments on earlier versions as well. We also wish to thank Mary Corcoran and student participants in the University of Michigan Ford School of Public Policy's Joint Doctoral Research Seminar, Marit Rønsen, Christine Bachrach, and Sandra Hofferth. Initial work was supported by Grant 96-6-9, 99-6-23 from the Alfred P. Sloan Foundation as well as visits by Paul Callister to the Cornell Employment and Family Careers Institute, Cornell University, and by Martha Hill as a Fulbright Senior Specialist adviser to the Ministry of Social Development, Wellington, New Zealand. Correspondence should be directed to Martha Hill.

Notes

1. At year end 1999, an estimated 667,900 fathers and 53,600 mothers of minor children were prisoners in the custody of U.S. state and federal prisons (Mumola, 2000). This meant an estimated 1,372,700 minor children had a father in state or federal prison, whereas 126,100 children had a mother in prison (Mumola, 2000). These numbers are, no doubt, higher at the time of this writing, given the persistent and striking trend of increase in U.S. prison population numbers: The 1999 incarcerated population was double the number in 1990 and quadruple the number in 1980 (Radosh, 2002). The prison population of parents is also strikingly African American or Hispanic. In 1997, more than two thirds of parents in state prisons and nearly three quarters of parents in federal prisons were African American or Hispanic (Mumola, 2000). A reviewer of this chapter noted that although many fathers will be in jail for a short time, these families experience an "ambiguous presence." That is, their presence is undetermined, malleable, and transient.
2. The shift toward joint custody is attributable to concepts of custody based on the *best interests* of the child, as well as changes in the gender division of child care, household work, and labor market work, for both men and women, pushing lawmakers and family courts toward gender neutrality and shared parenting. Because some parents pose a danger to their children, there are major complexities in developing family law supportive of shared parenting and in the best interests of the child. A meta-analysis of research on child adjustment in joint-custody versus sole-custody arrangements, however, provides support for the joint-custody model (Bauserman, 2002).

12

Cohabitation and Measurement of Family Trajectories

Wendy D. Manning
Bowling Green State University

Ronald E. Bulanda
Miami University

Cohabitation has become a dominant family form in the United States, one that is increasingly likely to include children (Smock, 2000). Two fifths of children will likely spend some time in a cohabiting family (Bumpass & Lu, 2000). Yet children's experiences in cohabiting families are often short-lived (Manning, Smock, & Majumdar, 2004; Raley & Wildsmith, 2004). Researchers have begun to examine how cohabiting parents influence the well-being of children. However, to date, much of the research uses snapshot or static measures of family structure rather than measures encompassing cumulative childhood experiences.

We examine the potential benefits of measuring cumulative family experiences, which takes the often transitory nature of families into account, especially those that cohabit. To illustrate the implications of various measurement strategies, we examine how childhood experiences within cohabiting families influence suspension or expulsion from school, a school-based indicator of child well-being.

BACKGROUND

Cohabitation and Family Trajectories

Recent research focuses on cohabitation in an attempt to better understand the effects of family structure on the cognitive, social, behavioral, and psychological well-being of children (see, e.g., Acs & Nelson, 2002; S. Brown, 2002; DeLeire & Kalil, 2002; Dunifon & Kowalski-Jones, 2002; T. L. Hanson, McLanahan, & Thomson, 1997; Hao & Xie, 2001; Manning & Lamb, 2003; E. Thomson, McLanahan, & Curtin, 1992). Much of this work draws on measures of family structure at the time of interview, yet this form of measurement may be problematic for several reasons.

First, cohabiting unions are relatively more unstable and shorter than marriages (e.g., Manning et al., 2004; Raley & Wildsmith, 2004). For example, although only 6% of children were living with cohabiting parents in 1999 (Acs & Nelson, 2001), 40% of children are expected to spend some time in a cohabiting family (Bumpass & Lu, 2000). Therefore, using a single point in time to measure family structure substantially underestimates children who have ever experienced (or will experience) cohabitation.

Second, accounts of the biological status of the cohabiting partner are often underdeveloped in measurements of family structure. Research on family structure recognizes the importance of biological ties and argues that children living with both biological parents fare better than children living with a stepparent (see M. Coleman et al., 2000). Yet prior work that includes full cohabitation family trajectories has not made this distinction (e.g., Dunifon & Kowalski-Jones, 2002; Hao & Xie, 2001). DeLeire and Kalil (2002) used the National Educational Longitudinal Survey to compare late-adolescent well-being within cohabiting biological and stepparent families; however, data limitations abbreviated the family history to events after eighth grade. They found some indication of different effects, but they were unable to establish whether the differences were statistically significant. Using cross-sectional data from the National Survey of American Families, S. L. Brown (2004) found no relationship between children's well-being and their biological relationship to the cohabiting partner.

Third, the age of the children likely influences the type of cohabiting union. Overall, nearly one half of children with cohabiting parents live with two biological parents, and the other one half live with one biological parent and a cohabiting partner (Fields, 2001). However, most very young children living with cohabiting parents are living with two biological parents, whereas most teenagers living with cohabiting parents live with one biological parent and a cohabiting partner (S. Brown, 2002). Failure to account for the age of the child when measuring cohabitation may therefore yield inaccurate representations. Static measures of family structure at any age of the child are likely to include select samples of cohabiting unions.

Recent research supports the need to examine trajectories of family structure to better illustrate the effects of family experiences on child and adolescent well-being (see, e.g., Bumpass & Lu, 2000; M. Carlson & Corcoran, 2001; Cooksey, 1997; Graefe & Lichter, 1999; M. S. Hill et al., 2001; L. Wu & Martinson, 1993; L. Wu & Thomson, 2001). However, most accounts of family trajectories have not adequately incorporated cohabitation. These accounts either incorrectly label children's experiences in cohabiting families as single-mother or stepparent family experiences or exclude cohabiting families altogether from accounts of family structure (e.g., Albrecht & Teachman, 2004; M. S. Hill et al., 2001; Sandefur, McLanahan, & Wojtkiewicz, 1992; L. Wu & Thomson, 2001). Researchers have excluded cohabiting families because of small sample sizes, lack of measures for cohabitation, or a substantive focus on other family types. In some instances, studies have described childhood experiences in cohabiting families, but they have not examined the implications of these trajectories for child well-being (Bumpass & Lu, 2000; Graefe & Lichter, 1999).

Only a few researchers have measured the influence of cumulative experience in cohabiting families from birth to adolescence on child well-being (Dunifon & Kowalski-Jones, 2002; Hao & Xie, 2001; Morrison & Ritualo, 2000). Using the National Survey of Families and Households, Hao and Xie found an association between time spent in cohabiting families and misbehavior, but their sample of cohabiting-parent families in both waves of the survey was small. Using the National Longitudinal Survey of Youth (NLSY), Dunifon and Kowalski-Jones studied early adolescents (aged 10–14) and found that the effect of time spent in cohabiting families depends on the outcome considered and the race-ethnicity of the child. This work, however, did not distinguish between cohabiting biological and stepparent families. In addition, there are some complexities when considering exactly how to measure and analyze children's cumulative experience in varying family types.

CURRENT INVESTIGATION

Our primary aim is to assess whether relying on static rather than dynamic measures affects our understanding of children's experience in cohabiting families. We therefore compare the implications for children of measuring parental cohabitation at a single point in time with measuring cohabitation throughout childhood, until age 14. To do so, we analyze family history questions targeted to adult women about their living experiences through age 14. The 1995 National Survey of Family Growth (NSFG) asks women aged 15 to 44 about a wide range of topics, including sexual behavior, fertility, and family formation. It is one of the few national data sources to ask respondents about their complete childhood family histories and to include cohabitation as a family type. The NSFG also distinguishes between cohabiting biological parents and cohabiting stepparents. These data allow us to move beyond current family structure measures and the relatively crude measure of family structure at age 14, which is the only measure of family structure available in the latest cycle of the NSFG (2002). Hence, the 1995 NSFG represents the most current data source available to compare outcomes between biological and stepparent cohabiting families, and to assess the long-term dynamic experiences of cohabitation.

To illustrate the effects of the respondents' family trajectories, we evaluate how prior and current experience in a cohabiting family influences rates of suspension or expulsion from school. Suspension or expulsion represents a gateway to later problematic behaviors, and previous research indicates that family experiences influence school outcomes (e.g., Garasky, 1995; M. S. Hill et al., 2001; Manning & Lamb, 2003; Sandefur et al., 1992; Wojtkiewicz, 1993).

First, we determine whether being born to cohabiting parents is negatively associated with being suspended or expelled from school. We anticipate that children born to cohabiting parents will fare worse than those born to married parents. Several potential factors link cohabitation and a diminution in child well-being: higher rates of instability in cohabiting families, preexisting differences between cohabiting and married parents, and lack of institutional support for raising children in cohabiting unions. First, research indicates that family stability positively affects child and young-adult behavior and child development (e.g., Hao & Xie, 2001; M. S. Hill et al., 2001; L. Wu & Martinson, 1993). Cohabiting parents, however, experience higher levels of instability than married parents, which potentially explains why children fare worse in cohabiting-parent families (Manning et al., 2004; Raley & Wildsmith, 2004). We therefore compare both stable and unstable married and cohabiting relationships. Second, cohabiting parents have less education and lower incomes than married parents (Manning & Lichter, 1996). Thus, children in cohabiting-parent families, on average, experience greater disadvantage, which may affect their well-being. Third, cohabitation has not received strong institutional support (Casper & Bianchi, 2002; Nock, 1995; Smock & Gupta, 2002). As a result, cohabiting partners' (particularly those not biologically related to the child) responsibilities and relationships to children may not be clearly specified, which may negatively influence children's behavior.

Second, we assess how living with cohabiting parents (both biological and stepparents) at age 14 influences child behavior. This type of snapshot measure informs us about family life at only a single point in time and does not reflect experience in other family types prior to age 14. For example, measures of single-mother families exclude any of a child's prior experience in a married or cohabiting family structure. Because nearly 20% of our sample has experienced at least two transitions, static measures do not capture any of the family dynamics those transitions entail.

Third, we examine the cumulative effect of living in cohabiting families on adolescent well-being. We address some analytic concerns about how to measure and interpret cumulative family experience. We expect that children with experience in cohabiting families are more likely to be suspended and expelled from school. Based on the stepfamily literature, we also expect that children in cohabiting families with only one biological parent will fare worse than those with both biological, cohabiting parents. Children living with two biological parents fare better than children living with a stepparent (M. Coleman et al., 2000). These findings suggest that children living with a cohabiting stepparent may fare worse than children living with two biological cohabiting parents. From a family stability perspective, it may appear more important for a child to experience family stability than a specific family structure (Hao & Xie, 2001; Wojtkiewicz, 1993; Wu & Martinson, 1993). We may find that family instability more accurately predicts adolescent well-being than family type.

DATA

We rely on the 1995 NSFG. This survey, unlike others, asks respondents directly about their own cohabiting family histories as youth and, thus, is the most appropriate for our analyses. The National Survey of Families and Households (NSFH), which was conducted in 1987 and 1988, only asks parents about their fertility and union histories. Children's family histories have been constructed but reflect the experiences of children during an earlier time period. Furthermore, the sample size from the NSFH of children who experienced parental cohabitation is quite limited (see Hao & Xie, 2001). Another relevant data set, the NLSY, until recently did not distinguish married from cohabiting parent families. Furthermore, the most recent NSFG (2002) contains only a single-item question about family structure at age 14.

We limit our analyses to 2,897 respondents who were born between 1970 and 1981 and were aged 14 to 25 in 1995. This sample restriction minimizes recall error and limits family experiences to recent periods. As noted, we focus on suspension and expulsion from school. In our sample, 15.8% were expelled or suspended.

We measure family experience in several ways. Two questions identified the male and female parental figure at the time of respondents' birth.

The response categories used to describe the female parental figure covered a broad spectrum of choices, including no female parent, natural mother, stepmother, adoptive mother, father's girlfriend, foster mother, grandmother, aunt, other female nonrelative, other female relative, or guardian. Parallel categories identified the male parental figure. These two items identified several family structures, but did not allow us to positively distinguish between married biological parents and cohabiting biological parents. The NSFG asked respondents to identify whether their biological parents ever married, and if so, when. We then matched the marriage date to the respondent's birth date and the presence of both biological parents in the household to identify the family form. We code family structure at birth as two married biological parents, single mother, two cohabiting biological parents, or other. We code the family type of children born to married or cohabiting stepfamilies as other because these family types are relatively rare at birth.

In addition to family structure at birth, the NSFG collects information that can identify up to 11 more possible family forms and the nature of the transitions that led to these new family forms. The primary question used to identify a change in the respondents' living situation (repeated up to 11 times) asks if and how the respondents' prior family living situation ever changed. Answers to these questions reflect whether adults moved in or out of the household. Examples of the response categories to this series of questions include: separation, divorce, death of one or both parents, family problems (illness, drugs, etc.), separated people got back together, marriage of parent, remarriage of parents to each other, remarriage of one parent, a parent or guardian started living with someone, went to live with a different parent, and other.

Because our purpose is only to identify a change in living circumstances, any valid response to this item is coded as a family transition. Unfortunately, we could not identify the marriage of cohabiting partners as a transition because the lack of change in family structure prevented respondents from identifying a change in subsequent questions. We also code the number of times parents or stepparents moved in or out of the household, a variable indicating family instability. For respondents experiencing a change, we obtained the identity of both the male and female parental figures in the subsequent family form. We analyzed this information in the same manner as family structure at birth. In turn, our coding identifies whether a respondent has ever experienced specific family structures.

As with family structure at birth, we use this static indicator of family structure at age 14 to identify six family types: those with two married biological parents, a single mother, two cohabiting biological parents, a married stepparent, a cohabiting stepparent, and other.

We also used more complex family trajectory coding schemes to capture whether respondents had ever experienced those same family structures between birth and age 14. The six cumulative family experiences include having ever lived with two married, biological parents, a single mother, two cohabiting biological parents, a married stepparent, a cohabiting stepparent, and another family type. Because the NSFG includes the beginning and ending dates of each family structure, we can track when children experienced each family type.

Unlike the static family measures, these measures are not mutually exclusive. For example, a respondent born to two married biological parents who divorced and never formed another union has experienced two family types and would be categorized as having ever lived with two married biological parents and having ever lived with a single mother.

Given the high rates of family transition, many children will have experienced more than one family type. As a result, we must analyze the reference categories and interpretations of the family type categories carefully. If we simply included dummy variables for each family experience, the reference group would consist of children who never experienced any of the family types. For most analyses, this is typically not the appropriate reference group.

One strategy is to redefine samples to enable explicit comparisons between respondents with two different family experiences. For example, limiting analyses to respondents who ever lived with an unmarried mother (e.g., having ever lived with a single mother or with two cohabiting biological parents) allows researchers to compare children who lived with two cohabiting biological parents with children who lived with a single mother and never lived with two cohabiting biological parents.

An alternative strategy is to use the entire sample and include only one family experience. For example, if we include the experience "ever cohabiting, two-biological-parent family," the reference group consists of respondents who have never experienced a cohabiting, two-biological-parent family. However, this strategy results in a reference group that combines relatively advantaged children (those whose biological parents ever married) and disadvantaged children (those who ever had a single mother).

A third option, which we do not examine in this chapter, is to establish extremely refined family structure categories, categories that might include two married parents whose marriage remained intact, two married parents who broke up and never formed a new union, two married parents who broke up and cohabited, and so forth. This strategy may be desirable when testing very specific hypotheses about family change. However, the family categorizations may become unwieldy, and sample sizes may prevent use of some family definitions.

We include additional covariates that various researchers have found to influence adolescent behaviors (e.g., M. S. Hill et al., 2001; Manning & Lamb, 2003; McLanahan & Sandefur, 1994; Sandefur et al., 1992),

TABLE 12.1
Distribution of Dependent
and Control Variables

Dependent Variable	%
School suspension	
No	84.2
Yes	15.8

Control Variables	%
Race-Ethnicity	
White	67.4
Black	14.7
Hispanic	12.7
Other	5.3
Birth cohort	
1971–1975	49.4
1976–1981	50.6
Religiosity growing up	3.2
Mother's education — years	12.8
Mother's employment	
None	26.6
Part-time	18.4
Full-time	55.0
Number of siblings	2.1
Mother had teenage birth	
No	85.4
Yes	14.6
N	2,897

Note. Weighted percentages and
unweighted N. From NSFG 1995.

including race and ethnicity, birth cohort, religiosity while growing up, mother's education, mother's employment, number of siblings, and whether the mother had a teen birth. We present the distribution of these variables in Table 12.1.

We use a series of models employing binomial logistic regression to assess the cumulative effects of family structure at birth on school suspension or expulsion for adolescents aged 14. We initially test multivariate models to determine how family structure at birth (age 14) influences the dependent variables. We then incorporate the measure of family instability to evaluate its ability to account for the effect of family structure at birth (age 14). Given the differentials in family instability according to family structure, we also test interactions to determine whether a change in family type from that recorded at birth affects suspension or expulsion from school. We focus on whether children born to and reared by two stable, cohabiting biological parents fare better or worse than children born to and reared by two stable, married biological parents.

Our second set of analyses focuses on the dynamic measures of family structure. We present multivariate models assessing the relation between cohabiting family structures and school suspension or expulsion. First, we contrast specific family experiences. We test whether children who lived with single mothers fared better or worse than children who lived with two cohabiting biological parents and cohabiting stepparents. We also compare the well-being of children who share the same basic family configuration (e.g., two biological parents) but whose parents possess a different legal status (e.g., married parents vs. cohabiting biological parents). In addition, we examine the significance of biological status among cohabiting parents. Finally, we test a strategy that makes a simpler comparison between respondents who ever versus never experienced cohabiting two-biological-parent families and ever versus never experienced cohabiting stepparent families. Throughout, we test whether the number of family transitions explains the effect of cohabitation.

RESULTS

Measuring Family Structure

Table 12.2 presents our key static family structure variables and shows the stability of these family types. The first column shows that 6.5% of children were born to single mothers. The majority of youth were born to married biological parents (83.2%). Substantially fewer respondents, 3.9%, were born into cohabiting families with two biological parents. Our results mirror those from other studies; Bumpass and Lu (2000) found that nearly two fifths (38%) of respondents born to unmarried mothers were born to women who were cohabiting.

Family structure at age 14 reveals a considerable shift from that at birth. At age 14, 16.8% of respondents were living with single mothers. The percentage of respondents living with two married biological parents declined by age 14 to only 58.4%. At age 14, we find that only 1.5% of respondents were living in cohabiting families with two biological parents. One in eight respondents were living in married stepparent families, and 2.2% were living in cohabiting stepparent families. These results suggest that many children experience family change.

The third panel of Table 12.2 shows that 64.6% of respondents experienced no family transitions between birth and age 14, whereas 16.4% experienced one transition, and 19% experienced two or more. Overall,

TABLE 12.2
Distribution of Family Structure Measures

| | | Number of Transitions | | |
	Total	0	1	2+
Family structure at birth				
Single mother	6.5	58.6	26.6	14.8
Married two biological	83.2	66.9	14.5	18.6
Cohabiting two biological	3.9	43.9	31.0	25.1
Other	6.4	52.7	22.1	25.2
Family structure at age 14				
Single mother	16.8	22.7	56.9	20.5
Married two biological	58.4	95.8	1.2	3.0
Cohabiting two biological	1.5	100.0	0.0	0.0
Married stepparent	12.7	5.9	19.5	74.6
Cohabiting stepparent	2.2	10.3	15.2	74.5
Other	8.4	28.4	39.2	32.3
Number of family transitions				
0	64.6			
1	16.4			
2+	19.0			
N	2,897			

Note. Weighted percentages and unweighted N. From NSFG 1995.

more than one third of the children experienced at least one change before they turned 14.

We next show how these measures of stability differ according to family status at birth and age 14. Among children born to single mothers, we find that 58.6% remain in that family type until age 14 and do not experience any family change. More than one quarter experience one change, and 14.8% experience two or more family transitions. Children born to two biological married parents face similar levels of family change. Consistent with prior work, we find that children born to cohabiting biological parents more often experience family transitions than children born to married biological parents. We find that fewer than one half (43.9%) of children born to cohabiting biological parents experience no transition, approximately one third experience one transition, and approximately one quarter experience two or more transitions.

Next we view family stability through the lens of a 14-year-old. Among those living with single mothers at age 14, approximately three quarters experienced some family change. Most children experienced only one family change (most often marriage or cohabitation), but approximately one in five experienced two or more family transitions. Children living with both biological parents in married or cohabiting families at age 14 experienced relatively few transitions. Most transitions involve single parents marrying after the birth of the child. As expected, almost all children living in married and cohabiting stepparent families experienced some family change, typically two or more family transitions.

Table 12.3 presents children's cumulative family experiences. Overall, 29% spent some time—on average, 6 years—living with a single mother (results not shown). The overwhelming majority spent some time in a married, two-biological-parent family, with an average duration of 11 years. By age 14, nearly 10% had lived with cohabiting parents. These experiences were evenly divided between living with two biological parents and living with one biological parent and a partner (4.6% and 4.7%, respectively). We find that 1 in 20 children had lived with two biological, cohabiting parents by age 14, and the average duration was 7 years. Similarly, 1 in 20 children had lived with a cohabiting stepparent by age 14 for an average of nearly 5 years (results not shown). Thus, youth spend relatively less time with cohabiting stepparents than cohabiting biological parents. A much higher percentage of children (16%) spent time in married stepparent families by age 14 and the average duration was 6 years (results not shown).

The final panel of Table 12.3 uses cumulative rather than static indicators of family structure at age 14. To examine the static and dynamic measurement strategies, we compare the percentage of respondents living in a particular family structure at age 14 with their cumulative family

TABLE 12.3
**Distribution of Cumulative
Family Structure Measures**

	Total %
Cumulative family experience	
Ever single mother	29.0
Ever married two biological	85.0
Ever cohabiting two biological	4.6
Ever married stepparent	15.9
Ever cohabiting stepparent	4.7
Experiences missed with age-14 measures	
Single mother	42.0
Married two biological	31.4
Cohabiting two biological	66.9
Married stepparent	20.3
Cohabiting stepparent	53.2
N	2,897

Note. Weighted percentages and unweighted N.
From NSFG 1995.

experiences from birth through age 14. Table 12.3 shows that relying on the age-14 measure misses one half the experiences of living in cohabiting families, compared with the cumulative experience measure. Two thirds of the experiences in cohabiting families with two biological parents are overlooked using the static measure, and one half of the experiences in cohabiting-stepparent families are excluded. Our results show that measures of family structure at age 14 fail to account for two fifths of experiences in single-mother families; one third in biological, two-parent, married families; and one fifth in married stepparent families. Thus, cohabitation experiences are disproportionately underrepresented using age-14 indicators of family structure. We expect to find similar results for any cross-sectional measure of cohabiting-parent families.

Family Structure and Suspension From School: Bivariate Relations

Table 12.4 presents bivariate relations between family structure and suspension or expulsion from high school for girls in the family. The first panel shows the prevalence of school suspension according to the family structure at birth. Girls born to single mothers were more than twice as likely as those born to married biological parents to be suspended or expelled. Nearly two fifths of the respondents with cohabiting biological parents at birth were suspended or expelled. Overall, children born to biological cohabiting parents are significantly more likely to be suspended or expelled than children born to single or married mothers.

The second panel of Table 12.4 shows the prevalence of school suspension or expulsion by family structure at age 14. Approximately 11% of children living with married biological parents at age 14 were suspended or expelled, which is the lowest percentage of expulsions or suspensions for any family structure at this age. A similar percentage of children living with single mothers (24.3%) and cohabiting biological parents (20.6%) had been suspended or expelled. Nearly 19% of the children living with married stepparents and more than one third of young women living with cohabiting stepparents at age 14 had been suspended or expelled. Overall, school suspension at age 14 is greatest among children of cohabiting stepparents, although the difference between children of cohabiting stepparents and biological cohabiting parents is only marginally significant owing to small sample sizes ($p = .08$).

The final panel of Table 12.4 shows the frequency of school disruptions by children's cumulative family experiences. Similar to the first two panels, living with married biological parents is associated with the lowest frequency of school suspensions or expulsions. More than one fifth of children who had lived with a single mother had been either suspended or expelled from school. The rate is similar among those who have ever lived with

TABLE 12.4
Bivariate Relation Between Family Experiences
and School Suspension or Expulsion

Family Experience	Suspension or Expulsion (%)
Family structure at birth	
Married two biological	13.4
Single mother	29.9[a]
Cohabiting two biological	37.8[ab]
Other	19.3[ac]
Family structure at age 14	
Married two biological	11.3
Single mother	24.3[a]
Cohabiting two biological	20.6[a]
Married stepparent	18.5[ab]
Cohabiting stepparent	36.5[abd]
Other	20.3[ae]
Childhood family experience	
Ever married two biological	13.7
Ever single mother	22.7[a]
Ever cohabiting two biological	34.8[ab]
Ever married stepparent	18.8[abc]
Ever cohabiting stepparent	31.1[abd]

Note. Weighted percentages and significance tests are based on comparisons of the two specified family types. From NSFG 1995.
[a]Significantly different from married biological at $p < .05$. [b]Significantly different from single mother at $p < .05$. [c]Significantly different from cohabiting biological at $p < .05$. [d]Significantly different from married stepparent at $p < .05$. [e]Significantly different from cohabiting step at $p < .05$.

either cohabiting biological parents or cohabiting stepparents (34.8% and 31.1%, respectively). The level of school suspension among children of biological cohabiting parents is likely higher in this panel than the prior panel because the age-14 measure is composed of stable biological cohabiting families. Young women who had lived with married, stepparent families are more likely to be suspended or expelled than those who lived with married biological parents. However, both of these groups had been suspended less often than those who had lived with single mothers or cohabiting parents.

Family Structure and Suspension From School: Multivariate Models

Family Structure at Birth. Table 12.5 charts a child's odds of being suspended or expelled from school based on family structure at birth. Children born to single mothers are 44% more likely to be expelled or suspended

TABLE 12.5
Odds Ratios of Suspension or Expulsion According to Family Structure
at Birth and Age 14

	Birth		Age 14	
Family Structure	Model 1	Model 2	Model 3	Model 4
Family structure at birth (Married two biological)				
Single mother	1.44*	1.43*		
Cohabiting two biological	2.39***	2.31***		
Other	1.28	1.25		
Family structure at 14 (Married two biological)				
Single mother			1.85***	1.79***
Cohabiting two biological			1.48	1.48
Married stepparent			1.50*	1.43
Cohabiting stepparent			4.14***	3.91***
Other			1.53*	1.47*
Number of transitions		1.15***		1.03
Race-ethnicity (White)				
Black	2.23***	2.30***	2.37***	2.39***
Hispanic	1.37*	1.39*	1.43*	1.43*
Other	0.92	0.95	1.00	1.01
Birth cohort (1970–1974)				
1976–1981	1.07	1.05	1.03	1.03
Religiosity	0.82***	0.83***	0.83***	0.83***
Mother's education	0.94***	0.94***	0.94***	0.94***
Mother's employment				
None	0.82	0.86	0.87	0.88
Part-time	1.02	1.04	1.07	1.07
(Full-time)				
Number of siblings	0.96	0.96	0.97	0.97
Mother teenage birth	1.83***	1.77***	1.76***	1.76***
−2 log likelihood	2,503.0	2,492.4	2,482.3	2,482.0
N		2,897		

*$p \leq .05$. **$p \leq .01$. ***$p \leq .001$.

from school than are children born to married biological parents. Children born to cohabiting parents are 139% more likely to be suspended or expelled than children born to married parents.

We next measure family instability (Model 2). Including this covariate contributes to the fit of the model but does not alter the direction or magnitude of the family structure variables. Children born to single or cohabiting mothers are at greater odds than children born to married biological parents of being suspended or expelled from school. Children who experienced more family transitions face a significantly higher risk of being suspended or expelled. We next test for interactions between family structure at birth and family instability.

Including the series of dummy variables that accounts for stable and unstable family trajectories from the time of birth improves the fit of the model (results not shown). Ultimately, children reared in stable environments, regardless of family structure, face similar odds of being expelled or suspended from school. Children who experience family transitions (measured as unstable) are more likely to be expelled or suspended than children who remain within their respective family type (measured as stable). However, this does not mean all children's experiences of family transitions are comparable. Having been reared in an unstable, cohabiting family with two biological parents is associated with higher odds of suspension or expulsion than having been reared in an unstable family with both biological married parents (results not shown).

Family Structure at Age 14. The final two columns of Table 12.5 (Models 3 and 4) directly connect family structure at age 14 and school disruptions. Model 3 shows the effects of family structure at age 14 on the odds of being suspended or expelled from school without controlling for the number of transitions. We find that children living with single mothers are 85% more likely to be suspended or expelled than children living with married biological parents. In the multivariate models, children living with cohabiting biological parents share similar odds as children living with married biological parents. This result reflects the continuity of children's experiences living in stable families with biological cohabiting parents, given that these relationships most often begin in early childhood or at the child's birth. Hence, this indicator does not include children born to cohabiting parents who eventually separated, which accounts for nearly one half of all children born to cohabiting parents. In addition, some of the covariates reduce the comparison between biological cohabiting parents and biological married parents to nonsignificance. Race-ethnicity, maternal education, and having a teen birth explain the effects of growing up in a biological, cohabiting-parent family on school suspensions. It is important to note that the coefficient remains large, and the sample sizes may be too small for differences to reach statistical significance.

Model 3 also indicates that children reared in stepfamilies (married and cohabiting) have higher odds of being suspended or expelled than children living with married biological parents. However, recall that the age-14 indicator of living in a cohabiting-stepparent family overlooks about one half of children's experiences in cohabiting-stepparent families (Table 12.3). Furthermore, 14-year-olds living with a cohabiting stepparent face higher odds of being suspended or expelled than their counterparts living with two cohabiting biological parents (results not shown).

The final model of Table 12.5 incorporates the number of family transitions into our measurement of family instability. The addition of this indicator does not contribute to the fit of the model nor does it substantially change the direction of the family structure variables. It does, however, somewhat affect the comparison between married stepparents and married biological parents (p = .06). However, net of the transitions, 14-year-olds living with cohabiting stepparents are still at higher risk of being suspended or expelled than those living with cohabiting biological parents (results not shown).

Cumulative Family Experience.   Table 12.6 presents models predicting suspension or expulsion from school based on cumulative family experience. We begin with children who ever lived with unmarried mothers. The first column shows that respondents who ever lived with cohabiting biological parents experienced higher odds of suspension or expulsion than respondents who lived with single mothers who never cohabited with the father of their child. The next column shows that children who lived in cohabiting-stepparent families faced greater risk of suspension or expulsion than children who lived with single mothers who never cohabited with the child's biological father. To evaluate whether the greater instability of cohabiting parent families explains these differences, we included a covariate measuring family instability (results not shown). We find that the inclusion of the instability indicator alters little the effects of living in cohabiting-parent families.

Our next set of models focuses on children who share similar family configurations but differ in terms of the legal status of their parents' union. Respondents who lived with cohabiting biological parents faced higher odds of suspension or expulsion than those who lived with married biological parents who never cohabited. Similarly, children who lived with cohabiting stepparents experienced greater odds of expulsion or suspension than those who lived with married stepparents who never cohabited. The inclusion of the instability measure does not explain the effect of cohabitation in either model (results not shown).

Finally, we compare different groups of children who lived in cohabiting-parent families. Children who lived with cohabiting biological parents and never lived with cohabiting stepparents share similar odds of being expelled or suspended from school. These results do not support our argument for the importance of distinguishing cohabiting-biological and cohabiting-stepparent families. Again, including an instability measure does not alter these findings (results not shown).

Based on these findings, it appears that children who spent some time in cohabiting-biological or cohabiting-stepparent families fare worse (in terms of suspension or expulsion) than children who lived in other family types. This evidence supports distinguishing between children who have and have not lived in each type of cohabiting-parent family. Table 12.7 shows that children who ever lived with cohabiting biological parents were nearly 100% more likely to be suspended or expelled than those who had not experienced this family type. Table 12.7 also shows that children who ever lived with cohabiting stepparents faced substantially greater odds of being suspended or expelled than children who never lived within this family structure.

TABLE 12.6
Odds Ratio of Suspension or Expulsion According to Cumulative
Family Experience: Specific Family Contrasts

	Unmarried Mother Families	Two Biological Parent Families	Stepparent Families	Cohabiting Parent Families
Family experience				
Single mother never cohabit	RG	RG			
Married two bio never cohabit			RG		
Stepparent never cohabit				RG	
Ever cohabiting two biological	1.58*		2.11***		0.85
Ever cohabiting stepparent		1.94***		2.31***	RG
Race-ethnicity					
(White)					
Black	2.45***	2.67***	2.38***	2.48***	2.80**
Hispanic	1.35	1.58*	1.41*	1.95*	1.89
Other	0.81	0.59	0.99	0.56	0.84
Birth cohort					
(1970–1974)					
1976–1981	1.00	0.89	1.10	0.72	0.77
Religiosity	0.86**	0.88*	0.80***	0.86	0.84
Mother's education	0.95*	0.96***	0.94*	0.96	0.97
Mother's employment					
None	1.09	1.27	0.77	1.02	1.14
Part-time	0.94	1.47	1.01	0.87	1.25
(Full-time)					
Number of siblings	0.94	0.97	0.97	1.05	0.95
Mother teenage birth	1.71**	1.78**	1.97***	2.17**	1.29
−2 Log likelihood	1,048.0	986.3	2,018.1	527.4	363.0
N	989	942	2,475	536	293

Note. RG = Reference group. From NSFG 1995.
*$p \le .05$. **$p \le .01$. ***$p \le .001$.

TABLE 12.7
Odds Ratios of Suspension or Expulsion:
Cumulative Cohabitation Family Experience

	Suspension or Expulsion	
Cohabiting family experience		
Ever cohabiting two biological[a]	1.98***	
Ever cohabiting stepparent[b]		2.36***
Race-ethnicity		
(White)		
Black	2.51***	2.74***
Hispanic	1.43*	1.50**
Other	0.93	0.98
Birth cohort		
(1970–1974)		
1976–1981	1.08	1.06
Religiosity	0.81***	0.82***
Mother's education	0.94***	0.94***
Mother's employment		
None	0.83	0.85
Part-time	1.03	1.04
(Full-time)		
Number of siblings	0.95	0.96
Mother teenage birth	1.90***	1.86***
−2 Log likelihood	2,510.5	2,505.7
N	2,897	2,897

Note. From NSFG 1995.
[a]Reference group is never lived with cohabiting two biological
parents. [b]Reference group is never lived with cohabiting stepparents.
*$p \leq .05$. **$p \leq .01$. ***$p \leq .001$.

DISCUSSION

Much of the research on the effects of cohabitation on child well-being
relies on measures that track family status solely at the time of the interview
or for relatively short periods. Our aim in this chapter has been to demonstrate the importance of dynamic and detailed measures when examining
families.

In 1995, the NSFG included complete family histories that allow us to
determine the timing and existence of family change. Our results indicate
that about one half of children born to cohabiting parents experience some
family transition by age 14. These levels are higher than those experienced
by children born to single mothers (40%) or married parents (33%). Also,
the vast majority of children who ever lived with cohabiting or married stepparents experienced some family change. Efforts to characterize children's

experiences of family structure should account for the potentially important role of instability and change.

These high levels of family change suggest that indicators of family status at any one particular point will most likely underrepresent the breadth of their experiences, particularly experiences in those family types that have greater instability. Looking only at a youth's family structure at age 14, for example, overlooks two thirds of children's experiences in cohabiting, biological-parent families. Similarly, when we use a measure of cohabiting-stepparent families at age 14, we miss one half of children's experiences in this family structure. Thus, static measures of family life do not capture the full range of children's experiences in families.

Our chapter is one of the few to examine how cumulative experiences of living with cohabiting parents are tied to one measure of adolescent well-being. We discussed some of the challenges associated with using cumulative rather than static measures of family experience. Researchers must consider the meaning of the cumulative family categories net of the other variables in the model and select a measurement strategy that addresses their research question. Our findings suggest that children who ever lived with cohabiting parents (biological and stepparent) are at higher risk of being expelled or suspended from school than children who never lived in a cohabiting-parent family, including children who lived with single mothers.

In addition, children who lived in cohabiting-stepparent families face no higher risk of being expelled or suspended than children who have lived in cohabiting, biological-parent families. This finding runs counter to our expectation and may suggest that biological status is not an important factor among cohabiting-parent families. Given the strong empirical and substantive evidence for distinguishing between biological children and stepchildren in married-parent families, this topic may warrant further investigation among cohabiting-parent families.

In models that include family structure measures, the instability of parental relationships is often unrelated to suspension or expulsion. We also find that accounting for transitions does not contribute to the fit of the models. The two exceptions are that instability has a negative effect when examining family structure at birth. Children who experience a stable relationship among their two biological, cohabiting parents face similar odds of being suspended or expelled from school as children whose biological parents are married. Also parental instability is related to higher odds of suspension or expulsion among children who have ever lived with two biological parents. However, this does not mediate the effect of cohabitation. Finally, including the instability measures does not alter, nor explain, the effects of cohabitation on our illustrative measure of well-being. This suggests that factors other than family instability explain why cohabitation may negatively affect child well-being.

We must note several limitations of the study. First, we base our analyses on older cohorts, which do not necessarily reflect the nature and prevalence of children born into cohabiting families today. Second, we examine family change only through age 14. We make this restriction to compare our results to the traditional family structure measure at age 14. We expect to find even higher levels of family change with an older (through age 17) sample. Third, we limit these analyses to girls. Some evidence suggests that family stability affects boys more than girls (Katzev, Warner, & Acock, 1994; Morgan, Lye, & Condron, 1988). Prior work suggests changes in family structure influence boys and girls differently (see, e.g., Buchanan, Maccoby, & Dornbush, 1996; Morrison & Cherlin, 1995; Powell & Parcel, 1997). Future research should address the possibly different effects for boys and girls. Fourth, family histories may contain considerable error, as respondents must recall past events of their family life in detail. Finally, we consider only one outcome. We intend for our analysis to illustrate the importance of accounting for the dynamics of family life, and we expect that this may relate to other measures of adolescent well-being. Future research may supplement our findings by expanding the scope of child outcomes.

Taken together, these results suggest that any assessment of the relation between family structure and child well-being should include cohabitation. Our findings indicate that cohabitation has a unique association with an important school behavior, expulsion or suspension. We stress the importance of distinguishing between stable and unstable cohabiting-parent families at birth. Our work does not empirically support distinguishing cohabiting-biological from cohabiting-stepparent families, but we believe there is still a strong theoretical case for making this distinction based on biological status.

In terms of measurement issues, full family histories are ideal and permit one to analyze timing of family change. We show how relying on measures of family structure at age 14 results in the omission of important family experiences. The most recent NSFG (2002) adopts this strategy, and researchers should recognize the shortcomings of relying on this as a measure of children's family experience. However, collecting data that include full family histories remains expensive and time-consuming. Collecting data on the occurrence of family transitions is an alternative, more cost-effective strategy. Another way to incorporate some indicators of timing would be to collect additional information about whether respondents lived in these families after a particular age or grade. In addition, researchers could modify family change indicators to address the specific type of family change. Family change includes the formation and dissolution of parental relationships. As children increasingly experience new family forms and face greater family instability, we must adjust our measurement and analytic strategies to keep pace.

ACKNOWLEDGMENTS

This research is supported in part by the Center for Family and Demographic Research, Bowling Green State University, which has core funding from the National Institute of Child Health and Human Development (R21 HD042831-01). The authors thank Susan Brown, Al DeMaris, I-Fen Lin, Kelly Raley, Pamela Smock, and Susan Stewart for their input and thoughts about the measurement of family change.

13

Measuring Poverty
With Different Units of Analysis

John Iceland
University of Maryland at College Park

The increasing diversity of family and household arrangements in the United States during the past few decades compels us to rethink how family units should be conceptualized and defined. In the area of poverty, the debate revolves around the most appropriate unit of measure—the family, the household, or some other group. Complicating the issue is the fact that cohabiting couples are not counted as families using "official" family definitions in most government surveys and statistics, although many argue they should be treated as such when assessing individuals' economic well-being.

Using the family as the basic unit—as in the official U.S. poverty measure—suffers from two substantive problems. First, cohabiting couples and any of their children are treated as if they did not pool resources at all, a debatable assumption. Second, unrelated individuals, such as roommates, boarders, and lodgers, are treated as if they have the same economic needs as those living alone, despite their much lower housing costs.

The rapid growth in the number of cohabiting couples and individuals living in nontraditional housing arrangements (Casper & Bryson, 1998b; Casper & Cohen, 2000) has magnified the effect of these problems over time. Although a consensus is growing that cohabitors should be treated more like other families when measuring poverty (National Research Council,

1995), it is less clear whether other unrelated individuals in a household should be considered part of a single unit. Relatively little evidence exists on whether such individuals pool their income and share resources. Yet, even if unrelated individuals in a household do not share resources, they still benefit from lower housing costs associated with living with others (i.e., economies of scale).

The key questions that guide this analysis are: How do poverty estimates vary by unit of analysis chosen? For whom does this variance matter the most? Do patterns of family change support treating cohabiting couples as families? How does individual poverty status change when household structures change, and how does this vary by unit of analysis used?

Using data from the 1996 Survey of Income and Program Participation (SIPP), this analysis estimates poverty rates using alternative units of analysis. It also examines poverty rates for people who experience changes in their household composition during the course of a year. Finally, it discusses how poverty estimates for people experiencing household changes differ when using alternative units of analysis.

FAMILY STRUCTURE, STABILITY, AND THE SHARING OF RESOURCES

Most people would agree that official statistics should take into account changes in society. A growing number of people have lived in cohabiting relationships, a smaller proportion are marrying, and many people continue to live in households with nonfamily members, such as housemates (Bumpass & Raley, 1995; Bumpass & Sweet, 1989a; Casper & Bryson, 1998b; Lichter & Graefe, 2001; Smock, 2000). The percentage of marriages preceded by cohabitation rose from about 11% between 1965 and 1974, to 56% between 1990 and 1994 (Bumpass & Lu, 2000; Bumpass & Sweet, 1989a). Furthermore, an increasing proportion of children are born into and reared by cohabiting couples. In 2002, about 16% of children under age 15 lived in households with a parent residing with an unmarried partner (Fields, 2003), and between 25% and 40% of children will spend part of their childhood in cohabiting unions (Bumpass & Lu, 2000; Graefe & Lichter, 1999). African American and Hispanic children are more likely to ever live with a cohabiting mother than non-Hispanic White children, and African American children living in cohabiting families are slightly less likely to transition into married-couple families than non-Hispanic White children (Graefe & Lichter, 1999).

Two important issues arise when considering how to treat individuals living in nontraditional household arrangements in measuring poverty. First, for a group of persons to be considered a unit, most would agree that there should be some stability in arrangements. Cohabiting-couple unions are certainly less stable than married unions (Bumpass & Lu, 2000). Graefe and Lichter (1999) described how children in cohabiting families usually experience rapid subsequent changes in family status, with some unions ending in marriage and others dissolving altogether. Other research indicates that about 55% of all cohabiting couples marry. Another 40% end the relationship within 5 years of moving in together (Bumpass & Lu, 2000; Smock, 2000). Manning et al. (2004) found that children born into cohabiting families face significantly higher odds of instability than children born to married parents. For example, about 15% of children born into cohabiting unions experience the end of their parents' union by age 1, and 50% do so by age 5. The comparable figures for children born to married parents are 4% and 15% by ages 1 and 5, respectively.

Nevertheless, although married families are more stable, cohabiting arrangements do appear to last, on average, for several years. Because the accounting period for poverty estimates is generally 1 year (although it can be as short as a month; see Iceland, 2003), treating cohabiting couples as a unit makes most sense if these unions last for more than half a year, if not more—and the preceding research indicates that they do.

A second issue is the extent to which individuals share resources in various household types (National Research Council, 1995), even in conventional family units (Findlay & Wright, 1992). At the very least, individuals in larger households benefit from economies of scale, and this argues for adopting a more inclusive unit of measurement. Regarding shared resources and expenses among cohabiting couples, Kenney (2003) found that cohabiting partners with children tend to split household expenses. Her findings suggest that, although cohabiting families may not blend income as much as in married families—as each person's income in a cohabiting couple is more likely to be earmarked for particular expenses—they nevertheless share a common set of expenses. Oropesa, Landale, and Kenkre (2003), in a study of mainland Puerto Ricans, found that only about 40% of cohabiting fathers pool their incomes with the mothers or pay for all expenses, indicating some limits to resource sharing. The authors believe more research on irregular contributions and "allowances" would be helpful in determining whether cohabiting couples should be considered a unit when measuring poverty.

DeLeire and Kalil (2005) did not look at the issue of resource sharing directly, but they examined how spending patterns vary across family types. They found that, on the one hand, cohabiting parent families spend more on "adult" goods (such as alcohol and tobacco) and less on children's education than married families, but on the other hand, the two groups do not differ much on the share of their expenses devoted to other child-related goods. They concluded that cohabitation is a distinct family type from marriage, with somewhat less investment in children, which could be interpreted as indicating somewhat less resource sharing in cohabiting families than in married families. Bauman (1999) examined resource sharing among unrelated individuals in households more generally by looking at reports of hardship across different family units in a household. His findings suggest that, although some resources are shared, nonfamily members, as traditionally defined, share less.

In summary, evidence on resource sharing indicates that cohabiting couples share resources to some extent, but not as much as married-couple families. It would be safest to say that poverty rates for such families based on the official family definition and the cohabiting-couple unit of analysis (described in more detail later) represent upper and lower bounds, respectively, of material deprivation. However, because cohabiting couples do share resources to at least some extent, and they also benefit from economies of scale by living in a single household, I would venture that poverty rates based on the cohabiting-couple unit of analysis are more accurate than those based on the official family definition, although more research is clearly needed. Future study of resource sharing among other nonrelatives living in the same household, such as housemates, is also needed.

DEFINING ALTERNATIVE UNITS OF MEASUREMENT WHEN MEASURING POVERTY

I consider three alternative units of measurement in the following analysis: the family as defined in the official poverty measure, the cohabiting-couple family, and the household. These represent viable alternatives discussed in the National Academy of Sciences (NAS) panel's report on poverty and family assistance (National Research Council, 1995). The official *family* currently used in poverty measurement consists of persons related to one another by birth, marriage, or adoption. This definition includes siblings and other kin. According to this definition, multiple families may reside within a household. It should be noted that although a family in Census Bureau publications refers specifically to a unit with two or more individuals related by blood, adoption, or marriage, a family with regard to the family poverty unit used in the official poverty measure can also consist of a single, unrelated individual. That is, even though these individuals are not a "family," per se, they are counted as a separate unit for the purposes of poverty measurement.

In the *cohabiting-couple* unit of measure, family units are defined exactly as they are in the official family unit of analysis with one exception: In households in which a person is identified as an unmarried partner, the householder's family and the unmarried partner's family are combined into a single unit. The incomes of the two families are combined, and a new threshold is devised based on the size and composition of the combined unit.

The third unit of measurement—*households*—consists of all persons who occupy a housing unit. A *housing unit* is defined as a house, an apartment, a mobile home, a group of rooms, or a single room that is occupied as separate living quarters. Separate units are those in which the occupants live separately from any other individuals in the building and that have direct access from the outside or through a common hall. Therefore, in addition to family members and cohabiting couples, the household unit includes all housemates, roommates, boarders, and foster children who share the housing unit.

In using any of these three units of measure, poverty is calculated by comparing the unit's aggregate income with the unit's poverty threshold. The dollar amount of the poverty threshold depends on the number of adults and children in the unit, which, in turn, varies by the unit definition (i.e., family, cohabiting couple, household), and dollar amounts are provided each year by the Census Bureau (for the full set of thresholds, see http://www.census.gov/hhes/poverty/threshld.html). Unit incomes are calculated by summing the income of the members of each unit, and poverty is then calculated by comparing the unit income to the unit poverty threshold. If the unit's income is less than the unit's poverty threshold, all the individuals in the unit are considered poor.

IMPLICATIONS OF USING ALTERNATIVE UNITS FOR POVERTY ESTIMATES

Previous work has shown that, as expected, estimated poverty rates are lower when using more inclusive units of measure that assume greater pooling of resources and that are affected more by economies of scale (Iceland, 2000; Lichter, Zenchao, & Crowley, 2004; Manning & Brown, 2003). In an earlier study (Iceland, 2000), I used 1997 Current Population Survey (CPS) data and an NAS recommended poverty measure (see National Research Council, 1995) to estimate poverty rates with different units of analysis. (The NAS measure improves on the official poverty measure in a few ways not as relevant to this analysis, such as a more complete measure of income that includes in-kind government transfers, and poverty thresholds devised in a more refined manner.) I found, for example, that the overall poverty rate was 15.4% using the "official" family unit of analysis, which is slightly higher than the poverty rate (14.9%) when the cohabiting-couple unit of analysis is used, which was, in turn, somewhat higher than the poverty rate using the household unit of analysis, 14%.[1]

In general, although differences in poverty rates using different units of analysis are modest, they are greater for persons living in nontraditional household arrangements, such as cohabitors and nonfamily members. The poverty rate for individuals in cohabiting families, for example, was 31.8% when using the official family definition (where the cohabitors are treated as separate units who do not pool income), but only 16.9% when treated as a single unit with pooled income using the NAS poverty measure (Iceland, 2000). Manning and Brown (2003) reported similar findings and also broke results down by race. Among White children, 61% of those who are poor when using the traditional family definition are lifted out of poverty with a more inclusive unit of analysis; for Blacks and Hispanics, the respective figures are 31% and 35%.

Among unrelated individuals who live with others in a household, such as housemates, the largest effect occurs when moving to the household unit of analysis, as would be expected. Their poverty rates under both the official family and cohabiting unit of analysis were 30.9%, but only 13.5% under the household unit of analysis, where their incomes are added together (based on the assumption of complete resource sharing) and the thresholds are proportionally lower owing to economies of scale (Iceland, 2000).

CALCULATING POVERTY RATES FROM SIPP USING DIFFERENT UNITS OF ANALYSIS

The following analysis builds on this previous work not only by calculating poverty rates using different units of analysis, but also by looking at how the effect of using different units of analysis differs among people who experience changes in their household composition in a given year. For example, I calculate poverty rates for individuals who were in a cohabiting-couple arrangement for only part of the year, and examine how their poverty status differs from those who did not experience change. I also examine how this difference varies when using alternative units of analysis.

The analysis uses data from the 1996 SIPP, a 4-year panel survey. The NAS panel on Poverty and Family Assistance recommended that the SIPP become the basis of official U.S. income and poverty statistics because of its detailed data on demographics, labor force, and income. The SIPP is appropriate for this analysis because it reinterviews households every 4 months (collecting monthly data) and thus is able to capture the timing of household composition changes. As described earlier, the association between household composition changes and poverty (estimated in various ways) is one of the focal points of this study.

In the SIPP, each interview in the panel consists of a core interview, with additional topical questions on specialized topics. The 1996 SIPP panel had

TABLE 13.1
Composition of Households and Patterns of Change, 1999

Present in Household	Every Month in 1999	6–11 Months in 1999	1–5 Months in 1999	% of Household Type That Changed During Year
Cohabiting couples	2.2	0.4	0.5	27.8
Housemates, room-mates, foster children & other nonrelatives	2.8	0.5	0.6	28.6
Roomers and boarders	0.3	0.1	0.1	29.5

Note. The unit of observation consists of all householders in Month 1. From 1996 Survey of Income and Program Participation.

a sample size of 36,000 households, making it a large, nationally representative survey of the civilian noninstitutionalized U.S. population. Most of the following analysis examines poverty in 1999, the last year of the 1996 SIPP panel. I examine patterns of household change during this 12-month period and its effects on poverty estimates using different units of analysis. The analysis had valid information for the duration of the SIPP panel on 82,017 individuals.

Table 13.1 provides descriptive statistics on the composition of households during 1999. The proportion of households with cohabiting couples is small—only 2.2% had a cohabiting couple in each month of 1999, whereas another 0.9% had a cohabiting couple for part of the year. Similarly, only 2.8% of the households had a housemate, roommate, foster child, or other nonrelative present during the entire year, and another 1.1% had such individuals for part of the year. Only 0.5% of households had a roomer or boarder for even part of the year. A minority of each type of household in the table—close to 30%—experienced change over the course of the year. These findings suggest that, in terms of the stability of arrangements (and without reference to the issue of resource sharing), cohabiting couples and even housemates and roomers and boarders should be considered part of a single unit of analysis, given that these arrangements are likely to last for the entire year, which is the usual time unit used in poverty measurement.

Table 13.2 examines the implications of using alternative units of analysis for poverty estimates by family type, relationship to householder, race-ethnicity, and age. Overall, 11.5% of the population is poor using the official family definition. When moving to a cohabiting-couple unit of analysis, where the incomes of the cohabitors are pooled (under the assumption of complete resource sharing) and a new threshold based on the unit's size and composition is used, the poverty rate declines slightly to 11.1%.[2] This

TABLE 13.2
Poverty Rates by Unit of Analysis
and Demographic Characteristics, 1999

| | Unit of Analysis | | |
	Official Family	Cohabiting Couple	Household
All persons	11.5	11.1	9.2
Family type			
In married couple family	5.1	5.1	4.8
In male householder family	7.6	7.6	6.2
In female householder family	31.2	31.2	25.3
In cohabiting couple family	26.5	10.2	10.0
Unrelated individual	19.0	19.0	13.4
Relationship to householder			
Householder	10.3	9.9	9.5
Spouse	5.2	5.2	3.8
Child	14.4	14.1	11.9
Other relative	19.8	19.5	12.4
Foster child	na	na	2.9
Unmarried partner	23.1	8.0	7.3
Housemate/roommate	17.3	17.3	6.1
Roomer/boarder	30.7	30.7	1.9
Other nonrelative	39.2	35.4	6.4
Race-ethnicity			
Non-Hispanic White	6.9	6.6	5.2
Non-Hispanic Black	25.2	24.6	20.6
Hispanic	24.2	23.5	20.8
Other	15.8	15.2	13.1
Age			
<18	17.6	17.2	14.2
18–64	9.2	8.7	7.1
65+	9.9	9.8	9.0

Note. Poverty is based on summed monthly incomes and thresholds. Individual characteristics are measured in last month of the year. Universe consists of people in the SIPP sample in all months of 1999. From 1996 Survey of Income and Program Participation.

small difference is not unexpected, given that, as Table 13.1 showed, only a small proportion of households have a cohabiting couple. When the unit is expanded to the household, when every person in the household's income is pooled, the poverty rate falls to 9.2%.

As would be expected, changes in poverty when using alternative units of analysis vary considerably by the group considered. For individuals in married families, a change in the unit of analysis has little effect, given that these families are unlikely to live with nonfamily members. For individuals in cohabiting families, however, the difference is larger. For example, the poverty rate is 26.5% using the official family unit, but only 10.2% under the cohabiting-couple unit, where incomes are pooled. For unrelated individuals—those who do not live with family members (and who often live alone)—the largest difference occurs when shifting to a household unit of analysis from the official or the cohabiting unit of analysis; the poverty rate declines to 13.4%, from 19% under the official and cohabiting-couple units of analysis.

Likewise, differences in poverty estimates vary by relationship to householder. The poverty rate for the unmarried partner, for example, declines from 23.1% under the official family unit to 8% using the cohabiting-couple unit of analysis. Among housemates, the poverty rate declines from 17.3% (which assumes no resource pooling or economies of scale) under the official family unit to 6.1% when assuming complete resource sharing. The results do not appear to vary significantly by race and ethnicity or age.

Table 13.3 focuses on poverty rates for unmarried partners and their children and housemates and roommates. Results indicate that the poverty rate among unmarried partners and their children is high for Blacks and Hispanics and for children when using the official family definition. The poverty rate of elderly unmarried partners is relatively low, at 10.2%. For all groups, the poverty rate is considerably lower when using the cohabiting-couple unit of analysis. The changes are quite large for Blacks and the elderly, although because of the relatively small sample sizes for these groups, the exact point estimates should be viewed with some caution.

For the other groups of individuals—housemates, roommates, foster children, and other nonrelatives—most of the difference in poverty occurs when moving to the household unit of analysis. Sizable reductions in poverty are evident for all racial-ethnic and age groups.

Table 13.4 shows how poverty rates vary by the length of time in a particular household arrangement in 1999 and by unit of analysis. A person's poverty status is based on his or her family's monthly income and thresholds summed over the course of the year. For example, a woman residing in a married-couple household for 5 months but who lived alone for the other 7 months would have an income during the year that is the sum of the 5 months of family income registered while she lived in the married-couple family, plus the 7 months of income she earned or received when she was living alone. Her annual threshold would be determined as the sum of the 5 monthly thresholds while she was in a married-couple family and the 7 monthly thresholds when she lived alone.

As would be expected, those in married families for the entire year have lower poverty rates than those in such families for part of the year, regardless of the unit of analysis. Poverty rates for individuals in married families the entire year do not differ much when using alternative units of analysis mainly because such families typically do not live with other unrelated household members, who would alter their units' incomes or thresholds.

TABLE 12.3
Poverty Rates by Various Characteristics, 1999

	Total (%)	Non-Hispanic White (%)	Non-Hispanic Black (%)	Hispanic (%)	Other (%)	Less Than Age 18 (%)	Age 18–64 (%)	Age 65+ (%)
Poverty rates for unmarried partners and children of unmarried partners								
Using official family unit of analysis	26.5	20.3	28.5	46.3	38.6	37.6	23.3	10.2
Using cohabiting couple unit of analysis	10.2	6.2	3.2	28.1	17.7	19.7	7.3	0.6
Using household unit of analysis	10.0	5.4	4.8	29.6	15.7	19.3	7.2	0.0
Poverty rates for housemates, roommates, foster children, other nonrelatives								
Using official family unit of analysis	29.0	23.7	46.5	42.3	39.3	45.1	23.8	48.3
Using cohabiting couple unit of analysis	27.1	21.7	45.8	41.1	35.8	34.4	23.8	48.3
Using household unit of analysis	6.0	3.7	12.1	11.1	11.7	7.9	5.4	3.3

Note. Poverty is based on summed monthly incomes and thresholds. Individual characteristics measured in last month of the year. Universe consists of people in the SIPP sample in all months of 1999. From 1996 Survey of Income and Program Participation.

TABLE 13.4
Poverty Rates by Unit of Analysis and Family Type, 1999

	Unit of Analysis		
	Official Family	Cohabiting Couple	Household
In married-couple family			
12 months	5.0	5.0	4.8
6–11 months	9.0	9.0	6.9
1–5 months	16.0	16.0	7.1
0 months	24.4	23.1	18.2
In male-householder family			
12 months	7.5	7.5	6.7
6–11 months	5.7	5.7	5.0
1–5 months	12.4	12.4	8.2
0 months	11.6	11.2	9.3
In female-householder family			
12 months	31.9	31.9	26.2
6–11 months	23.7	23.7	12.8
1–5 months	10.9	10.9	7.9
0 months	8.0	7.5	6.4
In cohabiting-couple family			
12 months	27.3	10.2	10.7
6–11 months	20.8	8.2	5.0
1–5 months	16.1	12.2	2.6
0 months	11.3	11.3	9.2
Unrelated individual			
12 months	20.0	20.0	14.0
6–11 months	13.1	13.1	8.4
1–5 months	10.8	10.8	7.9
0 months	10.3	9.8	8.6

Note. Poverty is based on summed monthly incomes and thresholds. Universe consists of people in the SIPP sample in all months of 1999. From 1996 Survey of Income and Program Participation.

Single-parent, male-householder families, though experiencing higher poverty rates than married families, still had lower poverty rates than other family types. Thus, those who had lived in such a family for the entire year had lower poverty rates than those in the arrangement for none of the year, again regardless of the unit of analysis. Those in single-parent female households the entire year have higher poverty rates than those living in such an arrangement for either part or none of the year.

Different patterns emerge for individuals in cohabiting-couple families. Under the official family definition, those who have been cohabiting the longest (i.e., the entire year) have the highest poverty rate (27.3%), and those who were never in such an arrangement have the lowest rate (11.3%). However, when using the cohabiting-couple unit of analysis, where resources are assumed to be pooled, poverty rates are relatively low and do not vary much by length of time in this arrangement, given that the poverty rate for individuals in cohabiting couples (using the cohabiting-couple unit of analysis) was near the overall average. For unrelated individuals, poverty rates are the highest among those in that arrangement for the entire year (20% using the official measure and the cohabiting-couple measure). Using the household unit of analysis, poverty rates are still fairly high (14% for those in that arrangement the entire year), but lower than when using the official family definition.

CONCLUSION

This analysis examined poverty rates using three alternative units of analysis—the family, the cohabiting couple, and the household—and looked at the dynamics of poverty and household change for different types of households. Results show modestly lower poverty rates among more expansive unit definitions, with the largest difference found for persons living in nontraditional households, such as living with cohabitors and nonfamily members. Although individuals in cohabiting arrangements appear to have relatively high poverty rates under the official family definition, those rates are considerably lower when using the cohabiting unit of analysis, which assumes complete resource sharing among the cohabitors.

Poverty rates are low for individuals who were in married families for all 12 months of the year analyzed, in this case 1999, and high for individuals in female-householder families for the entire year. For individuals in cohabiting-couple families, results depend on the unit of analysis. Using the official family definition, the longer the duration in a cohabiting-couple family, the worse off individuals are in terms of poverty. Using the cohabiting-couple unit of analysis, however, poverty rates do not vary significantly by duration in that arrangement, although the rates are, in general, about twice those found among individuals in married-couple families. The finding that individuals in cohabiting families are more likely to be poor than are those in married-couple families—despite the smaller differential when assuming that cohabiting couples share resources—is consistent with other research on related issues (Iceland, 2000; Lichter et al., 2004; Manning & Brown, 2003).

One important next step for research is to gauge how much resource sharing occurs across different household arrangements. As is, poverty rates using the family and cohabiting units of analysis should perhaps be viewed as upper and lower bounds of the deprivation faced by individuals in cohabiting arrangements. With more research on resource sharing, we could arrive at a more informed decision about which unit is most appropriate. In the meantime, based on the evidence in this chapter and in other research, the cohabiting-couple unit of analysis likely captures experiences of poverty more accurately than the other units of analysis. It should be noted, however, that even if one assumes no resource sharing among unrelated individuals living in the same households (as is done in the official family definition and the cohabiting unit of analysis), methods are available that allow one to adjust poverty thresholds to at least take into account the benefits from economies of scale (see Iceland, 2000). I recommend that these methods be adopted into any new poverty measure as well.

Notes

1. I also applied a novel, perhaps more refined, unit of analysis that falls between the cohabiting couple and household ones. This unit assumes income pooling among family members, including cohabiting couples, but not among nonrelatives, but takes into account the benefits from economies of scale for all household members even when they live with nonrelatives. The overall poverty rate when using this unit of analysis was 14.7%.
2. Because the percentage point comparisons here for a given group are a result of using alternative accounting procedures for estimating poverty (i.e., alternative units of analysis) using the same sample—rather than cross-group or cross-sample comparisons—conventional statistical significance tests are unnecessary.

14

Measuring Gay and Lesbian Couples

Gary J. Gates
University of Caifornia–Los Angeles

Randall Sell
Columbia Unversity

Intense public policy debates, coupled with the availability of data that allow researchers and others to better identify sexual minorities, have enhanced interest in social science research on gay men and lesbians. Policy debates regarding marriage rights, civil unions, domestic partnership, and adoption rights highlight the critical need for research that focuses specifically on gay and lesbian couples.

Challenges associated with identifying and enumerating all cohabiting couples are inherent in studying gay and lesbian couples. For example, distinctions between casual relationships and more formal "marriage-like" relationships can be difficult to capture in surveys. Studies of cohabitation must also consider the changing cultural norms that have lessened the stigma of cohabitation and childrearing outside of marriage. Similarly, the status and acceptance of gay and lesbian couples in society is increasing at an extraordinary pace. The notion of the normalcy of homosexuality and same-sex coupling is quite recent, and cultural norms associated with same-sex coupling continue to be both dynamic and far from uniform. This almost certainly affects the expectations of those entering into same-sex relationships as well as how and if same-sex couples prefer to identify themselves in surveys.

Enumerating gay and lesbian couples is further exacerbated by the myriad options for the sanctioning of these relationships. Same-sex couples in Canada, Belgium, the Netherlands, and the state of Massachusetts can now legally marry. Couples in Vermont can register their partnerships as civil unions, while several European nations and some U.S. states and municipalities have initiated different types of partnership registries. Increasing numbers of religious communities are willing to conduct marriages and commitment ceremonies for same-sex couples, regardless of governmental recognition of the relationships.

Research attempting to understand the dynamics of gay and lesbian coupling must confront the difficulties associated with measuring sexual orientation. Are same-sex couples necessarily gay, lesbian, or bisexual people? Are different-sex couples necessarily heterosexual or bisexual people? Just as other demographic constructs, such as race and gender, lack universal standardized definitions and measures, the construct of sexual orientation lacks a single definition agreed on by researchers and society. Sexual orientation is generally measured by assessing sexual attractions, sexual behaviors, or sexual orientation identities (Sell & Petrulio, 1996). However, Laumann, Gagnon, Michael, and Michaels (1994); Sell, Wells, and Wypij (1995); and Black, Gates, Sanders, and Taylor (2000) demonstrate that individuals do not always report "consistent" responses to questions in these three areas, and each area yields different samples of individuals with different characteristics. Further complicating matters, there are multiple ways to measure each of these domains, which can produce dramatic variation not just between but also within them. Same-sex or different-sex couple status is therefore not simply related to the construct of sexual orientation; however, understanding this relationship is important in conducting research, interpreting and presenting findings, and developing policies that affect these populations.

This chapter offers an overview of issues associated with enumerating and studying gay and lesbian couples. We consider how varied methods of identifying sexual orientation complicate such analyses, explore some of the primary data sources used to study these couples, and consider potential methodological and measurement issues associated with these data.

MEASURING SEXUAL ORIENTATION

Sexual orientation is generally measured by selecting a single category from a list of a few discrete categories provided as responses to a single question about either: (a) the sex of people to which the respondent has been sexually attracted, (b) the sex of those with whom they have had sexual contact, or (c) how they identify their sexual orientation (sexual orientation identity; Sell & Petrulio, 1996). Not surprisingly, these correspond with the three most common dimensions of sexual orientation included in definitions of the sexual orientation construct: sexual attraction, sexual behavior, and sexual orientation identity. A fourth, and arguably less precise, way to identify sexual orientations is by assessing coupling status (that is, same-sex or different-sex).

It would be convenient if measures of sexual attraction, sexual behavior, and sexual orientation identity (or even coupling status) identified the same population. Unfortunately, they do not. The National Health and Social Life Survey (NHSLS), which was one of the largest surveys to ever collect sexual orientation data in the United States, demonstrated this. Laumann et al. (1994) found that of the 8.6% of women reporting any same-sex sexuality, 88% reported same-sex sexual desire, 41% reported some same-sex sexual behavior, and 16% reported a lesbian or bisexual identity. Of the 10.1% of men reporting any same-sex sexuality, 75% reported same-sex sexual desire, 52% reported some same-sex sexual behavior, and 27% reported a gay or bisexual identity. Other surveys have had similar results; unfortunately, the relation between these measures and coupling status has not been explored thoroughly (Sell et al., 1995; Russell & Joyner, 2001).

Examples of questions that can be used to assess each of these three dimensions of sexual orientation are provided in Table 14.1. The identity and behavior questions, with slight modification, are taken from the Massachusetts Youth Risk Behavior Survey (YRBS; Massachusetts Department of Education, 2004). The YRBS researchers have examined the properties of these questions extensively and have modified them based on six waves of the survey beginning in 1993. Sexual attraction questions are rarely included in data collection instruments, and the sexual attraction question included in Table 14.1 was consequently created to mirror the sexual behavior question. A summary of questions used in additional research studies is available elsewhere (Sell & Becker, 2001a).

No matter how sexual orientation is assessed, the validity and reliability of the measure should be investigated. Few, if any, measures of sexual orientation have ever been as seriously examined as, for example, questions on race and ethnicity (K. Miller, 2002). Sell and Becker (2001b) have recommended that research on measures should include (a) cognitive studies in diverse populations to provide guidance on the interpreted meaning, wording, and ordering of questions and responses; (b) studies to investigate the impact of the mode of data collection (in-person, telephone, self-administered, etc.) on the validity and reliability of the questions and categories; (c) studies of the significance to validity and reliability of item nonresponse to questions and response categories; (d) studies examining

TABLE 14.1
A Framework for Gay and Bisexual Health Research and Practice

Dimensions of Sexual Orientation	Example of Assessment
Sexual orientation identity	*Which of the following best describes you?* a. Heterosexual (straight) b. Gay c. Lesbian d. Bisexual e. Not Sure
Sexual behavior	*During the past year, the person(s) with whom you have had sexual contact is (are):* a. I have not had sexual contact with anyone b. Female(s) c. Male(s) d. Female(s) and male(s)
Sexual attraction	*During the past year, the person(s) to whom you have been sexually attracted is (are)?* a. I have not been sexually attracted to anyone b. Female(s) c. Male(s) d. Female(s) and male(s)

the implications of measures on data tabulation and analysis; and (e) studies examining the skills and training required for researchers who are collecting and maintaining data.

The questions in Table 14.1 are practical for measuring sexual orientation because they are brief; however, these single-item measures contain inherent limitations that may oversimplify the assessment of a complex construct. The three chief complaints with these types of sexual orientation measures are that they do not recognize sexual orientation as a complex continuum between heterosexuality and homosexuality; they may inappropriately combine the constructs of heterosexuality and homosexuality, which would be better measured independently; and such measures may not adequately reflect the cultural differences in the interpretation or expression of same-sex sexuality (Sell, 1997; Silenzio, 1997). Addressing some of these concerns, others have developed more complex measures (see, e.g., Berkey, Perelman-Hall, & Kurdek, 1990; E. Coleman, 1990; Herdt, 1998; Kinsey, Pomery, & Martin, 1948; Klein, Sepekoff, & Wolf, 1985; Sambrooks & MacCulloch, 1973; Sell, 1998; Shively & DeCecco, 1977). Unfortunately, the complexity of these assessments usually makes them impractical for most research purposes, and their validity and reliability remain unexamined. The development and testing of sexual orientation measures remain relatively unexplored.

Yet, even without consensus on how the construct of sexual orientation should be measured, researchers and others have ventured forward and measured sexual orientation. In fact, we may never reach consensus on how to best measure these constructs, and arguments over measurement standards may never be settled conclusively (as is the case with race and ethnicity). Researchers presenting their results should, therefore, explicitly outline and discuss how they measured sexual orientation, and what they believe are the limitations of the methods they chose to assess the construct.

MEASUREMENT OF SAME-SEX COUPLES USING THE HOUSEHOLD ROSTER

Perhaps the most widely used technique for identifying gay and lesbian couples, or more precisely same-sex couples, involves using a household roster to identify the nature of couples' relationships. Use has become widespread with the introduction of various "partner" categories to household rosters on national census forms and related governmental surveys. National censuses have the advantage of yielding very large samples of same-sex couples, a rare situation in gay and lesbian research. They also provide comparable samples of different-sex couples, both married and unmarried, along with a wide range of demographic and economic variables.

The U.S. Census Bureau first added the term "unmarried partner" to the household roster for its decennial census in 1990 and retained the category in the Census 2000. Considering both the household roster and the sex of respondents provides a mechanism to identify same-sex couples. Several other nations have added similar categories to their censuses. Among English-speaking countries, Australia, New Zealand, Ireland, and the United Kingdom have all added a partnership category to the household roster. Ireland and the United Kingdom use the term "partner" while Australia uses "de facto partner." New Zealand uses a broader category of "partner or de facto, boyfriend, or girlfriend."

The 2001 Canadian census included a category designed to collect information on both opposite-sex and same-sex "common law" partnerships (this was prior to the introduction of marriage rights for same-sex couples in some provinces and territories). Unlike the U.S. census, the household roster on the Canadian census combines sex and partnership status variables into two distinct categories for "common-law partner (opposite sex)" and "common-law partner (same-sex)." Canada's decision to combine the sex and partnership variables stemmed, in part, from concerns about measurement error from sex miscoding among different-sex couples, which we explore later in this chapter (Turcotte, Renaud, & Cunningham, 2003).

Using household structure to identify gay and lesbian couples avoids the difficulties associated with measuring sexual orientation. However, researchers still cannot say with complete certainty that the sample is comprised of gay or lesbian couples. Black et al. (2000) demonstrate that same-sex "unmarried partners" in a census share many demographic traits with individuals identified in the General Social Survey (GSS) and NHSLS as gay or lesbian based on questions about their sexual behavior and sexual orientation. For example, same-sex couples in the census and gay men and lesbians in the GSS and NHSLS all infrequently report having ever been married and they report relatively high education levels. Another study using public health data shows that these same-sex unmarried partner couples exhibit sexual and family planning behaviors that are consistent with a gay or lesbian sexual orientation (Carpenter, 2004).

Carpenter and Gates (2004) compare census same-sex couples with gay and lesbian couples identified in two other surveys, the Urban Men's Health Study (UMHS) and the California Health Interview Survey (CHIS). The UMHS includes both self-identified gay men and men who report having ever had sex with men since age 14. Gay men and lesbians can be identified in the CHIS through a question about sexual orientation. Some differences are observed between census same-sex partners and cohabiting gay men and lesbians in the CHIS and UMHS. The census sample is more racially and ethnically diverse, has a broader education distribution (not as skewed toward higher education levels), and is more likely to report the presence of children under 18 in the home. It could be that the "indirect" method of measuring same-sex couples using the household roster provides a broader sample of this population. It could also be that couples who identify as gay or lesbian are systematically different in some ways from those who do not report their sexual orientation or same-sex sexual behavior in a survey.

Spouses Versus Partners

In surveys that collect household rosters, same-sex couples are often given the choice of identifying one partner as either a "spouse" or a "partner." In final data preparation, survey administrators must decide how to treat these two different groups, and these decisions have potential consequences for the accuracy of measuring same-sex couples.

In the 1990 U.S. census, a household record that includes a same-sex "husband/wife" was edited such that, in most cases, the sex of the husband or wife was changed and the couple became a different-sex married couple in publicly released data (Black et al., 2000). This decision is reasonable if one believes that most of the same-sex husbands and wives were a result of the respondent checking the wrong sex for either himself or herself or his or her spouse. However, in Census 2000, officials decided that same-sex husbands and wives may not be a sex miscoding, but rather an indication that some same-sex couples may consider themselves married, regardless of the legal recognition of their marriages. Because federal law precludes the Census Bureau from reporting statistics on same-sex married couples, the decision was made to alter these household records such that the same-sex "husband/wife" was coded as an "unmarried partner" for all enumerations and for public data releases.

Although this decision may appropriately reflect changing realities in how gay and lesbian couples structure their relationships and identify themselves in surveys, it likely inadvertently creates a potentially serious measurement error issue. It can be assumed that some very small fraction of the different-sex couples make an error when completing the census form and miscode the sex of one of the partners. Under Census 2000 editing procedures, all these miscoded couples would be included in the counts of same-sex unmarried partners. Because the ratio between different-sex married couples and same-sex couples is so large (roughly 90 to 1), even a small fraction of sex miscoding among different-sex married couples adds a sizable fraction of them to the same-sex unmarried-partner population, possibly distorting some demographic characteristics. Gates and Ost (2004) found that if 1 in 1,000 different-sex married couples miscodes the sex of one of the partners (and gets reclassified as same-sex unmarried partners), then approximately 10% of the same-sex unmarried partner couples are actually miscoded different-sex married couples. Although this same error could occur among different-sex unmarried partners, the smaller ratio between them and same-sex unmarried partners greatly reduces the effects of this form of measurement error on the same-sex couple population.

Black, Gates, Sanders, and Taylor (2003) propose a method for at least identifying the direction of the bias when considering various demographic characteristics of same-sex couples. They note that same-sex, unmarried partner households where one member of the couple was identified as "husband/wife" are most at risk for this form of measurement error. There is no simple way to identify this group, but one way to isolate same-sex "spouses" is to consider the marital status variable allocation flag (a variable indicating that the original response had been changed). Census Bureau officials confirm that their editing procedures altered the marital status of any unmarried partners who said they were "currently married." (Changes in marital status occurred after editing all of the same-sex "husbands" and "wives" into the "unmarried partner" category.) A large portion of the same-sex unmarried partners who had their marital status allocated likely originally responded that they were "currently married" given that one of the partners was a "husband/wife." Same-sex couples who have not had their marital status variable allocated are likely free of significant measurement error. Of course, eliminating same-sex partners with a marital status allocation from analyses also likely eliminates the genuine same-sex couples in which one partner was identified as a "husband/wife."

Using the Black et al. (2003) procedure, Carpenter and Gates (2004) offer some evidence that the census same-sex couple sample may suffer from some "contamination" with different-sex couples. Depending on how statistical agencies decide to treat households where a same-sex partner is identified as a spouse, other enumerations of same-sex couples could suffer from the same measurement error issues identified here.

Undercounting

Nearly all research on gay men and lesbians must face the issue of under-reporting and the potential undercounts and sample biases that this presents. Although most surveys find that attitudes toward gay men and lesbians and their families are moving in the direction of greater acceptance, incidents such as the 1998 murder of Matthew Shepard provide a grisly reminder of the stigma still attached to sexual minority status. This stigma likely leads sexual minorities to be cautious in reporting information that could imply that they are gay or lesbian on surveys, resulting in potential undercounting and sample bias. It is therefore generally assumed that samples contain the subjects most open about their sexual status or living arrangement. However, when sexual orientation identity is assessed (rather than sexual attraction, sexual behavior, or relationship status), the counts in some cases may be considered accurate. Identities are very situation-dependent. That is, a person may identify as gay in one setting, bisexual in another, and heterosexual in another. Sexual orientation identities assessed in research settings are valid measures of the prevalence of sexual orientation identities in such research settings. However, if similar data were collected in other settings or for other purposes, the prevalence of specific identities would be expected to vary.

Evidence of undercounting also exists even when household roster questions avoid asking directly about sexual attraction, behavior, and orientation. Concerns about the confidentiality of their responses may have led many gay and lesbian couples to camouflage the true nature of their relationship by identifying a partner as a "housemate/roommate" or an "unrelated adult." Some couples may also believe that "unmarried partner" or "husband/wife" does not accurately describe their relationship. A study of the undercount of same-sex unmarried partners in the Census 2000 indicates that these were the two most common reasons that gay and lesbian couples chose not to designate themselves as unmarried partners (Badgett & Rogers, 2003). Estimates of the undercount in that census range from 15% to 50% (Badgett & Rogers, 2003; Gates & Ost, 2004).

Marital Status

Many surveys include a question on current marital status of respondents. Response categories most often include *currently married, separated, divorced, widowed,* and *never married.* This item as it is most often constructed can be problematic for same-sex couples because the item rarely includes the distinction between marriage and legally recognized marriage. Among census forms in the United Status, Canada, Australia, the United Kingdom, Ireland, and New Zealand, only New Zealand and Canada ask about the respondent's "legal marital status." Canada's census also includes a question about whether the couple is in a "common-law" union, a status with legal recognition there.

Gay and lesbian couples can be married or consider themselves married regardless of legal recognition. It is unclear how these couples might respond to the marital status question, especially if it lacks any reference to legal status. Including response categories that reflect the legal status of gay and lesbian couples or acknowledge some of the unique ways they form their relationships could provide another mechanism for enumerating this group. The increasingly complex legal climate for same-sex couples, particularly in the United States, does not make this a simple proposition. Adding items such as "domestic partnership" or "civil union" could begin to address this issue. Another approach might be to separate this question into "legal" marital status or a union regardless of legal status.

CONCLUSION

Efforts to overcome the many challenges associated with enumerating gay and lesbian couples begin with survey research methodology. Adding questions about sexual orientation, or changing items such as household rosters and marital status, is hardly a simple process. Much work is necessary to formulate well-constructed and reliable questions that are sensitive to the cultural and legal climates in which sexual minorities function. Until more surveys—especially large surveys that use probability sampling techniques—begin to make these changes, research on gay and lesbian couples and their families will be highly constrained by small sample sizes and many of the measurement issues discussed earlier. With limited data available to assess the characteristics of these couples and their families, researchers often lack the ability to consider how robust findings are across different surveys.

An increasing number of health-oriented surveys and large data collection efforts such as the GSS now include questions about sexual orientation or sexual behavior that permit analyses of sexual minorities, albeit sometimes with relatively small sample sizes. These data, coupled with national censuses and other large surveys that include options that permit respondents to identify themselves as same-sex couples via the household roster, offer an opportunity to remedy a gap in our understanding of the characteristics of gay and lesbian couples and their families. Although researchers must confront and address the methodological and measurement issues noted in this chapter, it is nevertheless possible to inform important policy debates that affect the lives of sexual minorities with more than anecdotes and stereotypes.

15

Including the Military and the Incarcerated in Surveys of Families

William D. Mosher
National Center for Health Statistics

Survey designers face many issues at the outset of a survey on families. One of these issues is whether to include active-duty members of the U.S. armed forces or inmates of jails or prisons in the survey in some way. These groups could be included in surveys of family life when they are important for theoretical or policy reasons, or when their responses may significantly affect statistics for the general population or important groups of the population.

Decisions to include or exclude active-duty military personnel and the incarcerated should be based on an assessment of their value for the substantive focus of the survey and the cost and complexity of including them, compared with the value and cost of studying other topics or subpopulations. When we decided to include men as well as women in the National Survey of Family Growth (NSFG), we wrote language into the survey contract to make it possible to pursue any of the following five options:

- Include samples of the active-duty military, the incarcerated, or both.
- Increase sample size in the civilian noninstitutional population, particularly for those aged 15 to 44, to improve statistics on teenage pregnancy, sexually transmitted diseases, and other issues.

- Include men and women aged 45 to 54 in the civilian noninstitutional population to improve statistics on infertility and infertility treatment, adoption, stepchildren and stepfathers, and to improve measures of the lifetime probability of divorce.
- Conduct weekly follow-up interviews with women for 12 to 16 weeks to improve data on the frequency of sexual activity and the consistency of contraceptive and condom use.
- Collect selected biomarkers, such as urine or saliva samples or pregnancy tests, to improve data on sexually transmitted diseases, pregnancy outcomes, and other health-related variables.

The agencies designing the NSFG thought that any or all of these innovations could improve the survey and our knowledge of family life, family growth, and public health in significant ways. This chapter reports how the inclusion of the military and the incarcerated was assessed. This account may be useful to others who study families as they consider including these populations in their own studies.

There are at least four possible approaches to including the active-duty military and the incarcerated in studies of the family:

- These groups may be included directly and interviewed in person. Researchers can attempt to sample the incarcerated in prisons and jails or sample the active-duty military on military bases as they sample the civilian noninstitutional population.
- Questionnaires can be shortened and simplified, and limited information can be obtained with a brief telephone interview.
- More limited but still useful data may be obtained by interviewing members of the households they lived in before they went into the military or to prison or jail.
- Military and prison or jail experience can be included by asking survey respondents if they have been in prison, jail, or the military.

This chapter touches on all of these approaches, primarily as they apply to in-person surveys such as the NSFG. The NSFG is conducted using face-to-face interviews with a national sample of men and women aged 15 to 44. National fertility studies began in the United States in 1955 and were conducted again in 1960, 1965, 1970, 1973, 1976, 1982, 1988, and 1995 with national samples of women during their reproductive ages, operationally defined as aged 15 to 44 (Mosher, 1998; Mosher & Bachrach, 1996; Westoff, 1975). They were also limited to the civilian, noninstitutional population. At the time, these restrictions were thought reasonable because the survey was primarily about fertility and marriage, and the number of women aged 15 to 44 who were in the military or in prisons and jails was small.

Three important things about these surveys, however, have changed. First, the 2002 NSFG now includes men. Other surveys of families and fertility (such as the National Longitudinal Survey of Youth [NLSY] and the Current Population Survey [CPS]) also include men and women. Second, the number of men in prisons and jails in the United States increased markedly in the 1980s and 1990s. Third, most surveys of families oversample African American and Latino persons, and, as is shown later, those in the military and those incarcerated are disproportionately Black or Latino men aged 18 to 39 (Bonzcar, 2003; Harrison & Karberg, 2004). Surveys, particularly longitudinal surveys or those focused on low-income populations, may find it increasingly important to consider the impact of these missing men on their estimates.

On the other hand, the costs of interviewing in general, and interviewing these populations in particular, can be high. Most surveys in the United States are already facing rising costs and declining response rates (Groves & Couper, 1998; Groves, Dillman, Eltinge, & Little, 2002). Krosnick (2003) observed that, "a series of factors have made it more difficult to contact potential respondents, driving up costs. During the same time period, respondents' willingness to participate in surveys has declined slightly. Taken together these shifts have led to lower response rates than those of 20 years ago" (p. 1).

These issues of costs and response rates in surveys are not limited to the United States, as De Leeuw and de Heer (2002) showed. Using multilevel logistic models on data from government surveys in 16 developed countries, they showed that the proportion of potential survey respondents who cannot be contacted after repeated attempts is increasing in all 16 countries regardless of type of survey. Refusal rates are also increasing in some surveys and some countries.

Survey management is a process of balancing virtually infinite wants for data against limited—often severely limited—resources. Interviewing the incarcerated or those in the military may not be feasible or affordable unless it is a primary objective of the study or the survey sponsors are willing to sacrifice other survey goals.

Survey designers may reach different conclusions on the feasibility of including these populations, depending on the type of study being planned and the substantive issues being studied. For example, studies in local areas, and other studies that do not aspire to make national estimates, may be able to choose prisons and jails or military facilities that are willing to cooperate with a study without worrying about whether they are statistically representative. Some of the substantive questions that might determine inclusion are whether the survey will be designed to apply to the national population or whether it will focus on a particular locale or population; whether the study is cross-sectional or longitudinal; and its length, complexity, or sensitivity.

The example used in this chapter, the NSFG, is a cross-sectional, general-population survey with sensitive content.

WHY INCLUDE THESE POPULATIONS?

Including the military or incarcerated individuals in family surveys can be justified on several grounds. Most of these factors will have a greater impact on men than women, but may affect both to some extent. First, incarceration and active-duty military service can separate husbands, wives, and children, often for long periods, and the separation will likely have some effect on the family. Second, these populations are not static; some leave jail, prison, or the military each year and return to the civilian, noninstitutional population. This circulation may be particularly important in longitudinal surveys. For example, only about 1% of the adult U.S. population was incarcerated in 2003 (Harrison & Karberg, 2004), but given current rates of incarceration, an estimated 2% of women and 11% of men may be incarcerated at some point in their lives. If current rates of incarceration continue, 32% of Black men could be incarcerated at some time in their lives (Bonczar, 2003). For those in the military, the number of veterans is much greater than the number on active duty in the military at any given time.

Third, many men in the military and in prisons and jails are fathers. Recent U.S. Department of Defense (DOD) data show that about 49% of active-duty military personnel have one or more children (U.S. Department of Defense, 2002a). Data on state prisons show that in 1997, 55% of male state prisoners and 63% of male federal prisoners were fathers; similar proportions of female prisoners also had children (Pastore & Maguire, 2002). How and whether these men can support their children or maintain contact with their children may affect both their own lives and their children's outcomes. Finally, men and women in these populations may be at risk of infectious diseases or injuries and may carry these back with them to their households. These conditions have potential implications for public health and for health care costs (Maruschak, 1999).

HOW LARGE ARE THESE POPULATIONS?

Approximately 288 million people lived in the United States in 2002. Of these, about 1.4 million were in the active-duty military (about 0.5%), and about 2.1 million were incarcerated (about 0.7%). In 2000, approximately 2.26 million individuals aged 18 to 64 were living in institutions (excluding group quarters such as college dorms) (see Table 15.1). The population in group quarters is different from those in institutions; in 2000, about 2 mil-

TABLE 15.1
U.S. Institutionalized Population
Aged 18 to 64, 2000 (in Thousands)

	Male	Female	Total
Total	1,968	292	2,260
Jails, prisons	1,773	166	1,939
Nursing homes	88	75	163
Mental hospitals	37	18	55
Other institutions	70	33	103

Note. Statistical Abstract of the United States, 2002, Table 61, from the 2000 Census of the United States. Totals exclude those living in group quarters, such as college dorms.

lion individuals were living in college dormitories, but college students in dormitories are routinely interviewed in surveys of the general population, either in the dormitories themselves or in their other residences. Among persons aged 18 to 64 in institutions, about 86%, or 1.94 million, were in jails or prisons. In other words, only 320,000 people aged 18 to 64 were in institutions other than prisons and jails (such as nursing homes, psychiatric hospitals, etc.) in 2000. These 320,000 were about 0.1% of the U.S. population. Therefore, for most surveys of the general population below the age of 65, the numbers in institutions other than jails or prisons are too small to affect survey estimates significantly.

Prisons and Jails: The Incarcerated Population

Between 1980 and 2003, the number of people in prisons and jails in the United States quadrupled to more than 2 million (Table 15.2). As of June 30, 2003, about 91% of prison and jail inmates in the United States were male and 85% were under age 45 (Harrison & Karberg, 2004, Table 13). For sources of data on incarceration, see the Appendix. Inmates were also disproportionately Black or Hispanic. Approximately 36% were non-Hispanic White, 43% were Black, and 19% were Hispanic (Harrison & Karberg, 2004).

Table 15.3 shows the percentage of the population aged 18 and older that was incarcerated in local jails and state and federal prisons in 2003 by age and race-ethnicity. Only 0.1% of women were incarcerated in 2003. Approximately 0.7% of White men were incarcerated compared with about 1.8% of Hispanic men and 4.8% of Black men. The patterns by age among Black men are more striking: 11.3% of Black men aged 20 to 24, 12.8% aged 25 to 29, and 10.6% aged 30 to 34 were incarcerated in 2003.

Survey planners should consider including the incarcerated if Black men aged 20 to 39 are a critical part of the study. For White men and for

TABLE 15.2
Jail and Prison Inmates in the United
States, 1980–2003 (in Thousands)

Year	Jail	Prison	Total
1980	184	320	504
1990	405	743	1,148
2000	621	1,316	1,937
2002	665	1,368	2,033
2003	691	1,381	2,079

Note. Data for 1980–2002 are from
http://www.ojp.usdoj/bjs/glance/Tables. All
ages included. Counts for prison populations are as of December 31 of each year.
Counts for jail populations are as of June
30. Data for 2003 are from Harrison and
Karberg (2004).

TABLE 15.3
Percent of the U.S. Resident Population Aged 18+
Incarcerated In Local Jails or in State or Federal Prisons,
by Race, Origin, and Age: June 30, 2003

	All Women (%)	All Men (%)	White Men (%)	Black Men (%)	Hispanic Men (%)
Total	0.1	1.3	0.7	4.8	1.8
Age					
18–19 years	0.1	1.7	0.9	5.4	1.9
20–24	0.3	3.3	1.6	11.3	3.6
25–29	0.3	3.4	1.6	12.8	3.7
30–34	0.3	2.9	1.5	10.6	3.5
35–39	0.3	2.6	1.5	9.6	3.0
40–44	0.2	2.1	1.2	7.6	2.5
45–54	0.1	1.1	0.6	4.4	1.8
55+	0	0.2	0.2	0.8	0.5

Note. Data are from Harrison and Karberg (2004).

all women, very small proportions are incarcerated, and their inclusion or
exclusion will have little effect on survey statistics.

Active-Duty Military

In October 2002, about 1.4 million men and women were on active duty
in the U.S. armed forces, and the vast majority were men (1.2 million vs.
0.2 million women). Looking at it another way, about 2% of the 63 million

TABLE 15.4
Number of Active-Duty Members of the U.S.
Armed Services (in thousands), Aged 15 to 44,
by Gender and Residence: October 31, 2002

	Total	Men	Women
On a military base	729	626	103
Elsewhere	666	559	107
Total	1,395	1,185	210

Note. From special tabulation, Defense Manpower Data
Center, and personal communication with Barbara J. George
and others, April 2003.

U.S. men aged 15 to 44 in 2002 were in the armed services, and about 0.3%
of women aged 15 to 44 were (see Table 15.4) (U.S. Census Bureau, 2002,
Table 11). Of the 1.4 million active-duty members on October 31, 2002,
about 729,000, or 52%, lived on military bases in the United States, whereas
the remaining 666,000, or 48%, lived among the civilian population. These
48% of the active-duty military who do not live on military bases can be
interviewed as part of conventional household surveys. The CPS, for example, interviews this population. The 2002 NSFG also interviewed men
who worked in the active-duty military but who lived in the household
population. Tabulations from the March 2002 CPS Public Use Files, as well
as tabulations provided by the Defense Manpower Data Center (DMDC),
measure the size of this population, so they can be included in weighted
national estimates. (For other sources of data on military personnel, see
the Appendix.) However, given that the population of active-duty military
living in civilian housing is about 666,000 (or less than 0.25% of the U.S.
population), most surveys would be unable to produce reliable statistics for
this group unless they were heavily oversampled.

ISSUES IN INTERVIEWING
THESE POPULATIONS

The issues involved in interviewing the populations discussed here focus on
in-person surveys, such as the NSFG. The following questions suggest the
range of issues that survey designers should consider in approaching these
populations:

- What data are needed on this population? At one extreme, does the
  study require simple, descriptive data that can be obtained in a few
  minutes of nonsensitive questions, or does the study require detailed
  event history or other in-depth data?

- Can the data be collected by proxy, by telephone, or by Internet, or does it need to be collected in person?
- Will the sensitivity of the questions asked be an issue for these populations?
- Will the grade level of the questionnaires need to be revised?
- Will financial incentives to complete the survey be acceptable—or useful?
- Using a given data collection method, what approvals or clearances are required to include this population in the study?
- If the study intends to interview hundreds or thousands in this population, will there be economies or diseconomies of scale?

Active-Duty Military

The NSFG is conducted using face-to-face interviewing in a private setting (only the interviewer and the respondent are present) because of the complexity and sensitivity of its content. The interview typically lasts 60 minutes for men and 85 minutes for women. In contrast, surveys in the military typically last only about 45 minutes and are typically self-administered. Thus, in-person interviews would be outside the norm for military personnel, as would interviews lasting an hour or more.

Active-duty military personnel are often surveyed by the DOD, most often in self-administered surveys. The DMDC, for example, draws samples from a list of all active-duty members to conduct self-administered (mail or Internet) surveys on behalf of the Office of the Under Secretary of Defense for Personnel and Readiness. In the 1990s, the DMDC conducted a survey of 90,000 active-duty military members on sexual harassment, a survey of 76,000 members on equal-opportunity topics, and a survey of 41,000 members and civilians on financial services provided by the DOD on military bases. Separate health-related surveys are sponsored by the Office of the Assistant Secretary of Defense for Health Affairs and its TRICARE Management Activity (TMA). These are also primarily self-administered surveys, often filled out on a military base with a civilian contractor collecting the completed survey forms. In the late 1990s, the TMA conducted a "Survey of Health-Related Behaviors Among Military Personnel" to collect data on 45 of the *Healthy People 2000* objectives.

Obtaining Cooperation. Finding military respondents at home may be the greatest challenge for surveys. Summer is often a difficult time to do interviews with military personnel because many are moving to new duty stations. In addition, in times of war, many personnel may be absent for extended periods because they are deployed overseas. In such cases, samples may have to be redrawn or survey fieldwork postponed.

Sensitive Content.   The NSFG and other surveys of family and household topics often contain sensitive content. The DOD reviews surveys intended to be administered to military personnel; the department is concerned about oversurveying its members. Sensitive content is not necessarily ruled out if three conditions are met: if the sensitive content is well justified; if adequate precautions are taken to protect the confidentiality of the individuals involved, during data collection and after data files are prepared; and if the bases or facilities where the individuals are stationed are contacted in advance.

Literacy.   Ensuring that respondents understand the questions is always a concern of surveys. With the military, this is less an issue, given that an enlistment test is required for admission to the armed forces, and therefore literacy in English is virtually universal. In 2002, 77% of the active-duty military population had at least some college training, and 20% had a college degree (U.S. Department of Defense, 2002b).

Incentives.   Like many large, complex surveys in the United States, the NSFG uses monetary incentives (also called "tokens of appreciation") to thank respondents for their participation. The DOD does not currently use incentives in any of its surveys of active-duty members because they are employees of the DOD, and paying for a survey is considered double compensation. However, if a survey sponsored by an outside organization (such as the NSFG) is longer than most DOD surveys, has sensitive content, and is not sponsored by the DOD, the DOD would weigh the usefulness of incentives against the prospect that they might create the expectation for incentives in future DOD surveys. On the other hand, incentives may not always be necessary. Active-duty military members typically have high cooperation rates, and if the base commander or the DOD approves the survey, they will usually try to cooperate.

The Incarcerated Population

The federal regulations governing the protection of human subjects in federally funded research are found in Title 45 of the Code of Federal Regulations, Part 46 (45 CFR 46), at the Office of Human Research Protection's Web site (http://www.hhs.gov/ohrp/humansubjects/guidance/45cfr46.htm). These regulations single out certain groups who are likely to be vulnerable to undue influence and thus have a reduced capacity for giving truly voluntary, informed consent. These groups include children, prisoners, pregnant women, and mentally disabled persons. For these populations, "additional safeguards" are required "to protect the rights and welfare" of respondents so that they are not harmed by research (45 CFR 46.111). Researchers should expect that Institutional Review Boards (IRBs) will carefully review proposals to interview prison and jail inmates. This means that some IRBs may resist, refuse, or demand significant changes to a given research proposal, and some jail or prison administrators may prohibit particular studies in their facilities. In contrast, others may encourage or welcome such research.

The differences between prisons and jails must also be taken into account when designing a survey. Jails are usually locally run, and their inmates are typically held for 1 year or less (Harrison & Karberg, 2004). As a result, inmates will return to the noninstitutionalized population sooner than those in prisons. In contrast, state prisons typically hold inmates for a year or longer. The fact that prisons hold inmates for longer amounts of time has important implications for their families; jail inmates are usually back to their families and children in a year or less, but prison inmates may be away from their families for years. Federal prisons hold only about 160,000 of the most serious criminals nationwide, and thus might be excluded from surveys if resources are limited.

The Bureau of Justice Statistics (BJS) sponsors surveys of inmates using face-to-face interviewing. The Census Bureau hires and supervises the interviewers for the BJS surveys. The surveys include stratified samples of jails, state prisons, and federal prisons. For state prisons, permission is needed from the state's department of corrections. For jails, which are locally administered, permission is needed from the administrator of each jail sampled (one recent survey sampled 460, and 431 participated.) Arrangements for access, security clearances, and space must be made with the administrator of the jail or prison. The interviews are arranged in advance.

In-person Interviewing. Prisoners are usually willing to be interviewed; the response rate in one recent national survey was 86% for jail inmates and 92% for prison inmates (Caroline Harlow, personal communication, 2003). The usual practice in household surveys of interviewing respondents in person and in private, however, must be altered in prisons and jails. Interviews with prison or jail inmates are often conducted in an office or other room provided by the prison or jail administrator. To protect the safety of the interviewer, interviews cannot usually be conducted in private. Sometimes, the interviewer and the inmate are separated by a wall or transparent window and speak to each other over a telephone. This allows interaction but also protects the interviewer's safety. The NSFG interview for men in 2002 was 60 minutes on average and may be an appropriate maximum length for interviews with inmates.

Sensitive Content. The questionnaires for the NSFG, and probably for most surveys of families and households, would have to be rewritten for incarcerated populations to ensure that all sections of the questionnaire are relevant to the incarcerated population, to reduce its sensitivity, and to simplify its language for the lower level of literacy of the incarcerated population. Questions on sexual behavior, for example, would likely need to be recast. Most incarcerated individuals have little or no opportunity for heterosexual intercourse; therefore, most recent sexual behavior, if it occurs, is likely same-sex contact, and some of it would be involuntary. The likelihood of collecting accurate data is low. In addition, the most important determinant of an inmate's sexual behavior may be the length of his or her imprisonment, and questions on "recent" sexual or contraceptive behavior may have to be revised or eliminated (Caroline Harlow, personal communication, 2003). Questions on fatherhood or child support may also be sensitive for some inmates, and questions on contact with children may also have to be rewritten to make them relevant to inmates.

Literacy.   Approximately 40% of prisoners have not completed high school or obtained a GED (general equivalency diploma). Two thirds are members of minority groups (Harlow, 2003). Literacy, therefore, may be a significant problem. Moreover, the grade level of many questionnaires may be too high for most inmates. Questionnaires such as the NSFG would likely need to be revised with a simpler vocabulary. Spanish translation would also be important in some jails and prisons.

Incentives.   In most facilities, the prison and jail directors would not allow the use of cash incentives or any other token of appreciation for participating in surveys. Some IRBs and prison and jail directors view incentives as coercive to the surveyed inmates and as unfair to nonsurveyed inmates. For example a $10 or $20 incentive may be seen by an IRB as coercive if an inmate makes $30 or $40 a month on a prison job. In addition, incentives may be seen by an administrator as divisive if inmates who were not sampled resent the incentives being received by inmates who were chosen for the survey. On the other hand, incentives may not be necessary or cost-effective, given the already high response rates in inmate surveys. However, prisons and jails may incur extra costs in cooperating with a survey because prison guards may have to work overtime to provide security for the interviewers. In-person surveys may need to allocate funds to defray some of the costs of this extra staff time.

OTHER APPROACHES: USING RETROSPECTIVE OR PROXY DATA

For some surveys—particularly longitudinal surveys and those focused on communities with many low-income Black and Hispanic men—it may be important to include active-duty military and prisons and jail inmates in some way. As stated in the introduction, these populations can be included in surveys in one of at least four ways:

- Sampling military bases, prisons, and jails directly and interviewing in person.
- Interviewing by telephone, which removes interviewer safety issues, but may still require many of the other arrangements discussed earlier.
- Obtaining proxy information from spouses, relatives, and friends.
- Asking retrospective questions on past experiences in the military and in prisons and jails.

The majority of this chapter has concentrated on the first method, but researchers should also consider whether it is possible to obtain the needed data by telephone, proxy, or retrospective questions. Survey sponsors should weigh the substantive benefits of including these populations, which may be considerable, against the costs in money, time, and labor, including the opportunity costs of not attaining other goals of the study.

The NSFG as an Example

In the 2002 NSFG, survey designers were concerned that interviewing in prisons, jails, and on military bases would increase the cost and complexity of the survey, delay the fieldwork, and increase the risk that the study would fail to gain approval or be delayed by the IRB. Thus, they decided that some proxy and retrospective data on these populations should be included, but interviewing full samples on military bases or in prisons and jails would not be attempted until the study had been carried out successfully with men and women in the civilian, noninstitutionalized population at least once.

It was, however, also necessary to learn as much as possible about these populations and their effects on survey statistics. Therefore, designers included several features in the 2002 NSFG to generate useful information and keep options open for future surveys. First, the NSFG contract was written to include an option giving the National Center for Health Statistics (NCHS) the right to include a pretest and a main study of a military sample, an incarcerated sample, or both, in Cycle 7 or 8 of the NSFG. Second, in the 2002 survey, all men aged 18 to 44 were asked questions about experience in the military:

JC-1. Have you ever been on active duty in the armed forces for a period of 6 months or more?

JC-2. (If yes) In what month and year did that period of active duty begin?

JC-3. What was the month and year of your last separation from active duty (if any)?

Third, the audio self-administered section of the survey asked men about incarceration:

KB-2. In the last 12 months, have you spent any time in a jail, prison, or juvenile detention facility?

KB-3. (If no) Have you *ever* spent time in a jail, prison, or juvenile detention center?

Women were not asked these questions because the NSFG sample of women (7,600 in 2002) is too small to generate reliable statistics on military experience or incarceration among women.

Fourth, researchers asked married or cohabiting women whose husbands were not currently living in the household where their husband currently lived. The answer categories included armed forces and correctional institutions (jails and prisons). The fifth step toward including these populations was to interview military personnel not living on military bases when normal screening procedures found them. Given that the sample of men in the 2002 NSFG was only 4,928, the sample size of those currently in the military was not large enough to profile it separately with adequate statistical reliability.

Further consideration could be given to interviewing military or incarcerated individuals directly. This would involve consulting with staff of the Department of Justice (DOJ) or the DOD, writing a questionnaire for incarcerated or military respondents, and determining whether the questionnaire should be administered in person or by telephone and whether it should be administered only in English or also in Spanish. The questionnaire would likely require approval by the DOJ or DOD. IRB and Office of Management and Budget (OMB) approval would also be required. As noted previously, prison and jail inmates are a protected population under human subjects rules, and special justification is necessary to interview them.

Other Family Surveys

Most of the issues discussed herein would likely be applicable to many surveys on family-related topics. For nonfederal surveys, OMB approval would not be required, but IRB approval would usually be necessary. In addition, some kind of clearance or approval from the base commander, jail director, or state corrections department may also be required. Survey directors should consider all of the alternatives—in-person data collection, telephone data collection, using proxy data, and retrospective reporting. If direct data collection from these populations is necessary, we recommend consulting with the staff at the DOJ or DOD, or both, during the study design stage. Sources of information and procedures for contacting these staffs are discussed in the Appendix.

CONCLUSION

Decisions to include or exclude active-duty military personnel and the incarcerated populations should be based on an assessment of their value to the survey and the cost and complexity of including them.

The 2002 NSFG, a nationally representative, cross-sectional survey of men and women 15 to 44 years of age, surveyed 7,643 women and 4,928 men, representing the 125 million persons aged 15 to 44 in the United States. Survey sponsors recently decided that the most urgent priority was to increase the sample size of the survey and to collect the data more frequently than every 6 to 7 years. Once this was accomplished, the lack of coverage of the incarcerated and military populations would be weighed against the other proposals listed at the beginning of this chapter for improving the survey. The information in this chapter suggests that additional efforts to include these populations merit serious consideration in many, but perhaps not all, surveys focused on families.

Assessments such as those presented here can be undertaken case by case for each survey or study. Some survey planners will conclude that they must include military or incarcerated populations; for example, surveys that focus much of their sample on Black men aged 18 to 39 should seriously consider obtaining data in some way on the military and incarcerated populations, especially because more than 10% of Black men in their 20s and 30s are incarcerated and 30% spend some time in prison during their lifetimes (Bonczar, 2003). Survey data—especially longitudinal data—for Black (and perhaps Hispanic) men aged 18 to 39 may have significant limitations if they exclude the military and the incarcerated. To interview successfully in these settings, however, extensive revisions in the survey approach may be needed, and these revisions may be expensive. Depending on the priorities and resources of the survey in question, some may conclude that telephone, retrospective, or proxy data are the most cost-effective approach to including military and prison experience in survey data on families; others may conclude that military personnel and those in prison must be interviewed in person.

ACKNOWLEDGMENTS

The views expressed in this chapter are those of the author and do not necessarily reflect those of any government agency. The author gratefully acknowledges the comments of Dr. Caroline Harlow of the Bureau of Justice Statistics, and of Dr. Timothy Elig and Anita Lancaster of the Defense Manpower Data Center on earlier drafts of this chapter. The author also benefited from discussions with them and with other federal statisticians on interviewing the incarcerated and the active-duty military populations; these included Dr. Cynthia Mamalian of the National Institute of Justice, Tracy Snell of the Bureau of Justice Statistics, and Janet Hassan, then of the Tri-Care Management Activity, Office of the Assistant Secretary of Defense for Health Affairs. Stephanie Ventura of NCHS made many useful suggestions on an earlier draft of this chapter. Cycle 6 of the National Survey of Family Growth was jointly planned and funded by the following programs with the U.S. Department of Health and Human Services: CDC's National Center for Health Statistics (NCHS); the Office of Population Affairs; the NIH's National Institute for Child Health and Human Development (NICHD); the CDC's Division of HIV/AIDS Prevention; the CDC's Division of Reproductive Health and the CDC's Office of Women's Health; the Children's Bureau of the Administration for Children and Families (ACF); the Office of Planning, Research, and Evaluation of ACF; and the Office of the Assistant Secretary for Planning and Evaluation (OASPE).

APPENDIX: DATA SOURCES

Data on the incarcerated and military populations can be useful for survey planning, and several sources are noted here. The annual *Statistical Abstract of the United States*, published by the Census Bureau, includes some data on these populations (available at http://www.census.gov). General sources of federal statistics can be found at http://www.fedstats.gov and at http://www.whitehouse.gov/news/fsbr.html, the "Federal Statistics Briefing Room."

Incarcerated Populations

The Web site of the Bureau of Justice Statistics contains extensive statistical data on the incarcerated population (http://www.ojp.usdoj.gov/bjs). This site also includes links to the "Sourcebook of Criminal Justice Statistics Online" (http://www.albany.edu/sourcebook). See particularly section 6, "Correctional Statistics."

Active-Duty Military

A comprehensive source of information on the military population can be found at the Web site of the Department of Defense (http://www.defenselink.mil), including the annual "Department of Defense Selected Manpower

Statistics" (located in the "Personnel Statistics" section). "About the Department of Defense" is a guide to the various DOD Web sites, including statistical data from the Statistical Information Analysis Division (SIAD). Additional information can be requested from the Defense Manpower Data Center (http://www.dmdc.osd.mil), or by writing to the Director, DMDC, 1600 Wilson Boulevard, Arlington, VA 22209-2593.

PART V

Becoming a Father

16

Male Relationship and Fertility Data in the NLSY

Frank L. Mott
Dawn S. Hurst
Thomas Gryn
Ohio State University

OBJECTIVES

Historically, research regarding fertility has primarily limited itself to women because of the difficulty in establishing confident links between fathers and their biological, often nonresident, children (Cherlin & Griffith, 1998). Our previous research suggests the most important reason that female fertility reports are more accurate than those of men is that mothers are more likely to be living with their children (Mott, 1998). Accurate information about adult relationships, particularly male relationships, has also been more difficult to obtain, reflecting the greater complexity of contemporary relationships, in part the result of increased ambivalence among couples about the beginning and ending points of more casual unions, such as cohabitations. Gaining accurate information is also more difficult to obtain because of couples' tendencies to reinterpret the meaning of prior relationships. These issues inform a major theme of this chapter, the willingness and ability of young men to accurately report earlier relationship and related fertility events.

In this chapter, we use the 1979 National Longitudinal Survey of Youth (NLSY79) (spanning 1979 to 1998) to clarify fertility-reporting issues for a contemporary national sample of men. We also partially clarify the utility of the relationship event history in the 1997 NLSY for men during their adolescent years, a life stage during which reporting issues may be a particular concern. We then analyze and compare these two data sets to describe relationship (e.g., cohabitation, marriage, and parent–child living arrangements) and fertility profiles for these two distinctively different national populations of men. The availability of comprehensive male fertility information in the NLSY, in conjunction with the full family histories for the male respondents, permits far more comprehensive analyses of the links between fertility, family, and paternal events than other data sets have allowed.

THE DATA SETS

The NLSY79 data set consists of a nationally representative sample of 12,686 young men and women surveyed on a variety of topics related to employment, family, health, and education. The participants were interviewed annually between 1979 and 1994 and are currently interviewed every 2 years. In this study, we follow the men in this cohort beginning in 1979 when they were aged 14 to 22 through 1998, when those still being interviewed were aged 33 to 41 (Center for Human Resource Research, 1999).

We also examine a more recent national cohort of men from the 1997 NLSY, who ranged in age from 12 to 17 at the first interview in 1997 and from 16 to 22 at the fifth interview in 2001 (Center for Human Resource Research, 2003). This omnibus survey is wide-ranging and includes a comprehensive record of the family, education, early employment experiences, and attitudes of these youth as they aged through adolescence. By examining and comparing these two data files, we are able to gain significant insight into generational differences. We are also able to compare, to some extent, the validity of cross-sectional and longitudinal measures of early relationship and fatherhood trends.

Evaluating Data Quality

Using the 1979 Cohort for Evaluating Fertility Data Quality, How Confident Are We About Child Reporting? The depth of information available in the 1979 national sample allows us to use a variety of checks internal to the data to determine which factors are associated with better fertility reporting. There are, however, a few weak links in the 1979 NLSY data set. First, many of the respondents have incomplete adolescent and early-adult relationship and fertility profiles, in part because many of the early fertility–relationship events occurred prior to the first survey in 1979. In addition, even at its best, the quality of adolescent birth reporting is far from perfect. Before proceeding, we should acknowledge one important point. Our current investigation of male fertility is limited to those men who indicate they have biological children. We recognize that biological ties are not essential for establishing a paternal–child relationship, and that some relationships may be more meaningful than their biologically related counterparts (Furstenberg, 1995a; Marsiglio, 1998). Indeed, our previous research (Burchett-Patel, Gryn, & Mott, 1999) affirms that a sizable number of men assume fatherly responsibilities for nonbiological children, even when the children live elsewhere. However, exploring the subjectivities surrounding nonbiological fatherhood, although important, is beyond the scope of this chapter.

Relatively recent research based on the National Survey of Adolescent Males (Boggess, Martinez, & Bradner, 1998; see also chap. 17, this volume) suggests that more than one third of adolescent fathers reported their fertility inconsistently at some point during three survey rounds. Although these inconsistencies had no significant overall effect on estimated rates of teen fatherhood, they allowed researchers to identify several characteristics associated with the likelihood of providing conflicting information, such as younger age, nonresident location, African American self-identification, and being unmarried. When examining the NLSY fatherhood data, we too found discrepancies in reporting (Mott, 1998) and identified convincing factors that signal a man's tendency to alter his willingness to acknowledge biological paternity of specific children (a more detailed analysis is included in Mott & Gryn, 2001).

Methods

The information collected by the NLSY79 provides a wide range of cross-year checks on fertility-related responses and can resolve some inconsistencies with varying degrees of confidence. Between 1979 and 1998, the NLSY79 repeatedly interviewed male respondents on a wide range of topics (Center for Human Resource Research, 1999). For instance, the men regularly completed a fertility history that, in some years, was an update from the preceding survey round and, in other instances, was a complete relisting of births. In addition, the respondents completed a roster each year that specified the ages and names of all biological and nonbiological children in the household. Also, in many of the more recent years, the interview included rosters of all nonbiological children not in residence. This provided important corroborating evidence about what happened to children who had previously or subsequently been defined as biological children, either inside or outside the father's home.

However, the primary utility of the NLSY79 data set for evaluating fertility quality rests on the availability of a significant amount of relationship and other sociodemographic information that permit one to intuit the likelihood that related fertility reports are more or less valid. In particular, we used the considerable body of relationship information to determine the presence or absence of specific partners and spouses between 1979 and 1998. Our ability to do this was significantly enhanced by our knowledge of the names of spouses and partners in the household record and information such as educational attainment, age, and even employment status at each point in time. We were thus able to make very strong inferences about partner-spouse living arrangements at each survey point and about the likelihood that children in the household either "belonged" or did not "belong" to the male respondent. This information also permitted us to clarify why, in some instances, men might redefine their paternal status with respect to a particular child (Mott & Gryn, 2001; Mott, Gryn, & Burchett-Patel, 2002).

By considering all of the aforementioned possible factors and the comprehensive relationship profiles, we categorized each child according to our confidence or certainty that he or she was indeed a biological child of the man. The primary reason we were able to clarify a large proportion of these births was that we had repeated measurements for the "same" event, something that is possible only with a panel data set such as the NLSY. It is also useful to note that one important way to clarify female records—minimal gaps between births—is obviously not feasible for men. In addition, perfectly consistent but inaccurate reports across survey years, whether intentional or inadvertent, are typically impossible to identify.

The Importance of Stable Residence and Relationships

Tables 16.1 and 16.2 provide results based on this evaluation, and we supplement this information with a few notable conclusions from our more extensive paper (Mott & Gryn, 2001). In Table 16.1, a "code" of 1 or 2 implies that we are very comfortable (based mainly on record consistency over time) that the child claimed as biological is indeed the man's child. A code of 3 means that we cannot resolve the issue in any reasonable way, and codes 4 and 5 indicate that the child is in all likelihood not the man's biological child. Overall, we believe that approximately 92% of the births are accurately reported as "belonging" to the man (dating misreports are much more substantial, but beyond the scope of what we highlight here). To assess where the largest numbers of misreports are found, we consider only those children born between the first interview in 1979 and 1998. It

TABLE 16.1
Distribution of Confidence Level for Selected Relationship Patterns,
1979 to 1998 (Unweighted, NLSY79)

	Paternity Likely (Code 1 or 2)	Paternity Unclear (Code 3)	Paternity Not Likely (Code 4 or 5)	N
Father present at birth (1979–1998)	97.3	0.7	2.0	6,819
Child always present	96.0	0.8	3.2	5,282
Child has one entry *or* one exit	90.1	2.9	7.0	1,792
Child has multiple entries *and* exits	89.0	2.3	8.7	345
Child never present in home	82.1	15.0	3.0	1,216
Child has one entry *and* one exit	82.0	5.1	12.9	606
Father not present at birth	81.4	9.9	8.7	1,742
Child appears belatedly on fertility roster	51.7	26.8	21.6	486

is among this subgroup of children who were ever reported as being born to the men that we are best able to resolve inconsistencies in reports, given that the full lifetime of the child is encompassed in our reporting window. Overall, 90% of children fall into this category. Although more details are available, we focus here on the link between child presence or absence in the father's home and our estimate of paternity likelihood. As presented in Table 16.1, in instances where a father is present in the home at the child's birth, we are comfortable (after examining the complete longitudinal record) that 97.3% of reported children are indeed biological. Our estimate is 96% when a child is in the home at all survey points.

We are far less confident about reported paternity in most of the other residence permutations. The greatest uncertainty surrounding paternity is when a child appears belatedly in the fertility roster at some point post birth. The net result is that we are comfortable assuming paternity for only about one half of this category of children. The status of nonresidential fatherhood can, at times, be highly unstable and fluctuate between survey rounds (Mott, 1998; Nord & Zill, 1996). Where a reported biological child is never in residence (which constitutes a rather substantial group at these young-adult ages), substantial ambiguity exists. Also, when a child has one or more entries or exits from the home, or when a father was not present at the birth interview point, paternity statuses are less definitive.

Table 16.1 indicates that the major paternity reporting issues relate to complex relationship patterns, be they paternal, maternal, child related, or some combination of the three. This, of course, is an oversimplification, given that paternal acknowledgment, or lack thereof, undoubtedly reflects complex family processes.

In Table 16.2, we take this evaluation a step further by clarifying the independent importance of child and parent variables as predictors of

TABLE 16.2
Odds of Having "Low Confidence" (Unweighted Logit Estimates) in Paternal Fertility Reports for Selected Samples by Race (NLSY79)

		Odds Ratios				
	All Children			*All Children Born 1979–1998*		
	Total	*White*	*African American*	*Total*	*White*	*African American*
Father h.s. dropout	1.032**	0.671**	1.259	1.156	0.800	1.306
Father has 12 years of school	0.973	1.036	0.865	1.153	1.186	1.066
Father's age at birth <20	5.849***	9.291***	4.202***	2.321***	3.471***	1.920***
Father's age at birth 20–24	1.727***	1.924***	1.743***	1.528***	1.544**	1.596***
African American	1.287**	—	—	1.454***	—	—
Hispanic	0.865	—	—	0.958	—	—
No. yrs. spouse present	0.923***	0.916***	0.931***	0.937***	0.939***	0.934***
No. yrs. partner present	0.923***	0.956	0.909***	0.928***	0.957	0.921**
No. yrs. interviewed	1.050***	1.073***	1.048*	1.054***	1.117***	1.002
No. spouses & partners	1.146**	1.085***	1.091	1.185***	1.241**	0.976
Child never in father's home	1.301*	2.313***	0.817	2.281***	4.562***	1.245
Child enters & leaves once	2.083***	3.644***	1.238	2.373***	4.020***	1.555*
Child enters & leaves >1	1.123	1.653*	0.556*	1.117	2.303**	0.446
Child enters or leaves once	1.551***	1.760***	1.153	1.836***	2.036***	1.381
Gender of child	1.006	0.930	0.941	1.061	1.013	0.960
No. of children (last point)	1.210***	1.207***	1.202***	1.245***	1.169***	1.277***
N	9,149	5,787	2,704	8,234	5,277	2,356

*p ≤ .10. **p ≤ .05. ***p ≤ .01.

268

reporting confidence by controlling for a variety of social and demographic factors that may be closely associated with the child residence variables. Confidence categories 3 through 5 are recoded as "1," or low confidence, in the Table 16.2 outcome measure, and 1 or 2 are recoded as "0," or high confidence. In these logit equations, higher odds ratios indicate lower confidence in paternity. There are parallel equation sets, one including all children ever identified and the second limited to children born after the first (1979) survey. It is useful to note that for the large majority (more than 90%) of these children, the 1979 to 1998 survey window encompasses their entire life. We briefly focus here on that subset.[1]

Focusing first on the total race group, we find that several demographic and socioeconomic distinctions are generally consistent with expectations. Low confidence in reporting is associated with younger ages at childbirth, being African American, and having had more children. We now shift to factors more directly linked with family structure and family transitions. The first factor that increases our confidence that paternity records are accurate, after controlling for the number of relationships a man has been in (with larger numbers linked with lower confidence in paternity), is the number of years a man has been with a spouse or a partner. More years spent in either a spousal or partner relationship is associated with greater confidence in the fertility reports. Family stability, not surprisingly, is a major factor predicting high-quality reporting on births and children.

Confidence in paternal-fertility reports becomes less certain when the child's residential patterns are erratic, independent of paternal relationship status and socioeconomic and demographic characteristics. Compared with a child who is always present, the least confident scenario is when a child enters and leaves the father's home exactly once. A typical scenario occurs when a mother and child jointly arrive in a father's household and also leave together, and the child status change is indicated (sometimes significantly after the exodus), yet only limited corroborating evidence is available to clarify paternity. This disengagement can evolve from uncertainty stemming from many factors that follow a separation or divorce (Nord & Zill, 1996), including geographic distance, remarriage, an uncooperative relationship with the former spouse, visitation or communication deterrents, a new "father figure" living with the child and his mother, an attempt to lessen the emotional pain, or a lack of financial resources (Furstenberg & Cherlin, 1991; Furstenberg & Harris, 1993; Seltzer & Bianchi, 1988; Umberson & Williams, 1993). Also, some uncertainty surrounds a child who is never in residence, largely because contradictions in reports about that child over time are less easily resolved.

We uncovered some interesting racial distinctions, but space considerations limit our discussion here. (These data, however, are presented in Table 16.2.) Briefly, although we find similarities in some patterns across

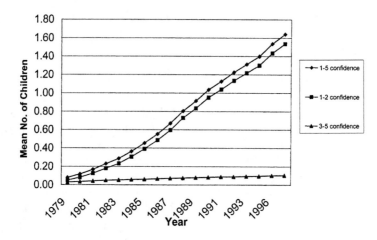

FIG. 16.1.   Mean number of children, by confidence level, men interviewed all years 1979–1998, weighted.

race and ethnicities, other distinctions may be important. In particular, we found child residence to be a less relevant predictor of confidence in paternity for African American children. This is true, perhaps, in part because fewer African American children were "always present" (the reference group), so those not always present represent a more mainstream group of African American children than of other racial groups.

Figure 16.1 synthesizes the net impact of all corrections (child acknowledgment and dating accuracy) to the male fertility records highlighted previously with their fertility profiles between 1979 and 1998. Three curves are presented, one based only on children we are confident "belong" to the men (code 1 or 2), one that includes all children ever reported by the men as their own (codes 1 through 5), and one representing the children for whom we have low paternity confidence (codes 3 through 5). It should be noted that the revised curve, which includes only codes 1 or 2, also incorporates all the date changes we made to the file and the deletion of children for whom we believed expressed paternity was dubious at best.

The net impact of our evaluation reduced fertility for men aged 33 to 41 (in 1998) by about one tenth of a child—with most of that difference already evident at much younger ages. We readily acknowledge that year-specific changes at the individual-dynamic level can reveal changes not evident in this aggregate, cumulative profile. However, the modest aggregate effect on the overall fertility profile is consistent with our finding that the actual change in paternity acknowledgment—less than 10%—was quite modest. We should note that although any misplacement of births owing to inaccurate dating may affect the shape of the fertility curve, by the 1998 endpoint, these misdates will have "come out in the wash."

Using the NLSY97 Cohort for Evaluating
Young-Adult Relationship Data

We now focus specifically on relationship and fertility issues related to the NLSY97 cohort, a data set that represents a national cohort of youth who were aged 12 to 16 at the end of 1996, and who were almost all aged 12 to 17 when interviewed in the latter part of 1997. By the fifth interview in 2001, the youth were between ages 16 and 22.

Methods.   Our primary objective was to explore the value of comparing event history cohabitation and marriage information with a series of survey point estimates. The availability of five annual waves of NLSY97 data permitted us to explore relationship quality issues in ways not possible with the NLSY79, which in the early survey years did not include a relationship history. Although the 1997 cohort clearly represents a different generation than the earlier NLSY cohort, the considerable depth of relationship and fertility information for these men permits us to make several useful substantive and methodological clarifications.

The Value of Event Histories.   To assess the extent to which we may have understated our cumulative estimates for cohabitation using the NLSY79 (which were based only on survey point information), we explore the association between cumulative point estimates and complete retrospective histories for respondents from the 1997 NLSY as of the fifth wave in 2001. Because we do not have retrospective cohabitation histories for the 1979 young men, but only estimates based on survey point information, comparing the relationship between cumulative estimates based on full histories with point estimates over time may enable one to infer the potential magnitude of the cohabitation undercount for the 1979 men. We then present, in a preliminary fashion, comparative findings for male youth through age 22.

Table 16.3 describes the relationship status of our respondents as they age into adulthood. Until age 19, few have been in a cohabiting relationship or married. Only for the 20- to 22-year-old age group does the percentage in a relationship (either married or cohabiting) reach double digits, at 16.3%; approximately 10% are cohabiting and 6.4% are married as of the 2001 survey point. Table 16.3 also shows the considerable extent to which marital status at a young age can be a reliable proxy for longer term marital status. This is because very few of the youth married more than once, and only a small number left a marriage.

However, parallel links do not hold for cohabitation, as the cross-sectional cohabitation information substantially underrepresents cohabitation propensities, defined generally as living in a romantic or sexual relationship

TABLE 16.3
Summary of Relationship and Fertility Measures by Age in 2001
(NLSY97 Youth-Weighted Estimates)

Age	% Married	% Cohabited	% Married or Cohabited	% Ever Married	% Ever Cohabited	% Ever Married or Cohabited	% Father	Mean Children Ever Born
20–22	6.4	9.9	16.4	7.2	22.3	26.0	11.9	0.14
19	2.0	6.9	8.9	2.1	10.9	12.1	6.5	0.08
18	0.4	2.6	3.0	0.4	5.7	6.1	1.5	0.02
16–17	0.0	0.7	0.7				1.3	0.01

Note. Limited to men interviewed every year.

TABLE 16.4
Comparing Cumulative Survey Point and Event History Statistics
(NLSY97)

	Event History Report	Survey Point Cumulation
% Ever married by age:		
18 and over (total)	4.3	4.3
20–22	7.2	7.1
19	2.1	2.2
18	0.4	0.4
% Ever cohabited by age:		
18 and over (total)	15.4	10.7
20–22	22.3	15.5
19	10.9	8.1
18	5.7	2.9
% Ever married or cohabited by age:		
18 and over (total)	17.7	13.9
20–22	26.0	20.7
19	12.1	10.0
18	6.1	3.4

with a member of the opposite gender for at least one month. However, this definition is subject to considerable "fuzziness."[2] For example, among those aged 20 to 22, nearly 10% report they are currently cohabiting, whereas 22% report having cohabitated at some point between 1997 and 2001. Overall, for this 20- to 22-year-old population, about one in four men report being in a cohabiting relationship or having been at some point in time. Having said this, it is clear that these numbers become substantial only by age 20 or so.

Table 16.4 highlights the considerable importance of collecting a continuous longitudinal record on relationships, even in a panel survey where cross-sectional status is frequently asked. To the extent that relationship histories are typically unavailable, using a series of survey point estimates as a first approximation for measuring longer term cohabitation can lead to a substantial underreporting of longer term patterns. Table 16.4 contrasts "ever-cohabited" statistics drawn from the full relationship history with "ever-cohabited" statistics obtained from cumulative cohabitation status at the various survey points between 1997 and 2001. From age 18 onward, the differences based on using these two approaches are quite substantial. By ages 20 to 22, the relationship history indicates that 22.3% had ever co-habited compared with only 15.5% when using the survey point approach. In separate race results, a similar pattern unfolds for African American and White 20- to 22-year-old men (not shown in table).

Relationships and Fertility for Men: Results From NLSY79 and NLSY97

We have explored several issues of male relationship- and fertility-reporting quality. To the extent possible, we have adjusted the 1979 cohort data, and they now reflect what we believe to be significantly improved quality. The analyses that follow include those cases that we have defined earlier as confidence codes 1 and 2. The 1997 data set permits us to partially evaluate the extent to which event history data more effectively measure cumulative relationship histories than do discrete event data or even more limited retrospectively collected information. Although none of the aforementioned clarifications come with a guarantee, they nonetheless provide important insights, and in all likelihood significantly improve data quality. In the remaining sections, we use the revised fertility data and the relationship insights to synthesize recent trends in male relationships and fertility that are as yet unavailable from other data sources. We first synthesize patterns for men from adolescence in 1979 to middle age in 1998 using the NLSY79 data. We then summarize adolescent relationship and fertility patterns for young-adult men between 1997 and 2001. Finally, we provide selected comparative relationship and fertility patterns for young adults approximately two decades apart, in 1979 and 2001. To some extent, we are able to suggest changes and similarities in the determinants of early fatherhood during the two-decade period.

Fertility Trends and Determinants for NLSY79 Men. The pattern and progression of contemporary male fertility is summarized in Table 16.5 with select fertility indicators as of 1985, 1990, and 1998 for men aged 14 to 17 at the first survey point in 1979. Thus, Table 16.5 shows fertility trajectories for these men from incipient adulthood through ages 33 to 37. For all indicators, at all survey points, Hispanic fertility is the highest and non-Hispanic White fertility is the lowest. The pace of minority fertility is

TABLE 16.5
Fertility Summary for NLSY Men Age 14 to 17 in 1979
(NLSY79 Weighted Estimates)

	% Ever Father			% With 2+ Children			Mean No. of Children		
	1985	1990	1998	1985	1990	1998	1985	1990	1998
Total	15.8	42.3	68.9	3.5	20.0	48.0	0.20	0.69	1.42
White	12.6	38.6	67.0	2.5	17.3	47.1	0.16	0.60	1.35
African American	28.9	57.9	75.4	7.2	29.1	49.2	0.38	1.02	1.64
Hispanic	26.5	56.9	79.4	7.3	34.4	57.1	0.36	1.07	1.82

clearly more rapid than White fertility, although the gap narrows somewhat by 1998, when approximately three quarters of minority men and two thirds of White men have become fathers (although White fertility remains well below replacement level).

Tables 16.6 and 16.7 highlight the determinants of fatherhood (from zero to one parity) and from first to second birth for this same sample of men from age 14 to 17 in 1979 to age 20 to 24 in 1985, and 33 to 37 in 1998. We briefly consider transitions into fatherhood, that is, movement from not being a father in 1979 to having had a child by ages 20 to 24, and then by ages 33 to 37.

Regardless of whether one controls for relationship—marriage and co-habitation histories—separately, race and ethnicity are independent predictors of progression to first birth at both outcome points. This finding is noteworthy given the racial disparities in nonmarital and marital childbearing documented in past research (Brien & Willis, 1997). At both the 1985 and 1998 survey points, African American (but not Hispanic) movement from one to two births is significantly below that of the White majority, suggesting some compensation for African Americans' earlier, more rapid initial fatherhood.

Finally, many of the variations in predicting fatherhood by 1985, such as paternal education, single parenthood, and church attendance, are no longer relevant by 1998. This is consistent with expectations. As the proportion of men who become fathers ultimately reaches high levels, one can anticipate that the motivations for ever becoming a father (although not necessarily having several children) will equalize across groups, reflecting the normative importance of attaining fatherhood in our society.

Progression Into Relationships and Fertility for Adolescents: Trends Over Time. In this section, we use first-wave data from the NLSY79 and fifth-wave data from the NLSY97 in 2001 to compare early relationship and fertility patterns between young men aged 20 to 22 in 1979 with men who

TABLE 16.6

Odds Ratios: Parity Progression to First and Second Births by 1985 by Race-Ethnicity
(Sample Limited to 14- to 17-Year-Old NLSY79 Nonfathers in 1979)

	Total				Non-African American, Non-Hispanic				African American				Hispanic			
	0→1	1→2	0→1	1→2	0→1	1→2	0→1	1→2	0→1	1→2	0→1	1→2	0→1	1→2	0→1	1→2
Yrs married by 1985	—	—	3.96***	1.41***	—	—	4.17***	1.66***	—	—	2.55***	1.33*	—	—	6.57***	1.14
Yrs cohabited by 1985	—	—	2.88***	1.37***	—	—	3.02***	1.56**	—	—	2.29***	1.42	—	—	3.84***	1.18
Age 1979	1.42***	1.35	1.11*	1.24*	1.59***	1.61***	1.03	1.34	1.44***	1.14	1.26**	1.06	1.20*	1.48*	1.04	1.47
African American	1.72***	0.79	5.42***	0.42***	—	—	—	—	—	—	—	—	—	—	—	—
Hispanic	1.93***	0.85	2.03***	0.84	—	—	—	—	—	—	—	—	—	—	—	—
Rural 79	0.98	1.02	0.84	0.92	1.25	0.99	1.00	0.75	0.73	1.29	0.73	1.38	0.65	0.68	0.68	0.61
Mother is hs dropout	2.77***	1.19	2.61***	1.14	3.43***	1.12	2.56***	0.96	2.00**	0.76	2.41**	0.78	3.68***	—	2.84	—
Mother has 12 yrs. school	1.96***	0.77	1.97***	0.75	1.56*	1.06	1.41	0.87	2.13**	0.38	2.53**	0.40	3.51**	—	2.05	—
Mother alone 1979	1.31***	1.18	0.84	1.07	1.66**	1.27	0.80	1.12	1.00	1.08	0.91	1.08	1.10	1.11	0.65	0.99
Mother & step	1.18	1.25	1.21	1.38	1.31	1.77	1.69*	2.63*	0.91	1.31	0.88	1.27	1.57*	1.09	2.24**	1.14
No. of siblings 1979	0.83	1.25	0.91	1.04	0.98	1.91	1.09	1.35	0.55	.001	0.64	<.001	0.73	2.88	1.33	2.85
1 or 2 sibs 1979	0.75**	0.76	0.86	0.80	0.71**	0.70	0.77	0.83	0.87	0.83	1.04	0.98	0.84	0.58	0.80	0.58
Catholic	0.67***	1.22	0.94	1.36	0.74	1.12	1.08	1.40	0.60	4.12	0.55	3.25	0.66	0.80	1.40	0.84
Regular church attendance	0.76***	1.00	0.78*	1.03	0.70**	1.18	0.73	1.41	0.69**	1.13	0.70*	1.12	1.10	0.82	1.33	0.82
Traditional attitude	1.06**	1.07	1.05	1.06	1.07*	1.14	1.08	1.13	1.04	1.01	1.04	1.00	1.05	1.03	1.00	1.03
N	2,503	532	2,503	532	1,403	224	1,413	224	673	193	673	193	417	115	417	115

Note. Sample interviewed all survey points, 1979 through 1985.
*p ≤ .10. **p ≤ .05. ***p ≤ .01.

TABLE 16.7
Odds Ratios: Parity Progression to First and Second Births by 1998 by Race/Ethnicity (Sample Limited to 14- to 17-year-old NLSY79 Nonfathers in 1979)

	Total				Non-African American, Non-Hispanic				African American				Hispanic			
	0→1	1→2	0→1	1→2	0→1	1→2	0→1	1→2	0→1	1→2	0→1	1→2	0→1	1→2	0→1	1→2
Yrs. married by 1998	—	—	1.48***	1.25***	—	—	1.52***	1.31***	—	—	1.41***	1.19***	—	—	1.45***	1.37***
Yrs. cohabited by 1998	—	—	1.33***	1.17***	—	—	1.33***	1.20***	—	—	1.37***	1.16***	—	—	1.34***	1.24***
Age 1979	1.10	1.07	0.90*	0.93	1.10	1.14	0.82**	0.92	1.24**	0.94	1.11	0.85	0.91	1.09	0.80	0.96
African American	1.33**	1.41**	3.69***	0.68**					—	—	—	—	—	—	—	—
Hispanic	1.62*	0.97	1.73***	0.87	—	—	—	—	—	—	—	—	—	—	—	—
Rural 1979	0.91	1.31	0.79	1.25	0.96	1.67**	0.72	1.54*	0.99	0.91	1.05	0.97	0.55	1.50	0.70	1.34
Mom is hs dropout	1.27	0.70	1.14	1.00	1.47*	0.97	1.10	0.70	0.93	2.34**	1.15	2.75***	2.06*	0.47	1.50	0.47
Mom has 12 yrs school	0.99	1.00	0.91	0.96	0.99	0.83	0.89	0.74	0.91	1.96*	1.09	2.26**	1.67	0.75	1.05	0.66
Mom alone 1979	1.30	0.89	1.28	0.86	1.11	0.80	0.96	0.69	1.80*	1.08	1.95	1.16	1.34	0.82	1.36	0.73
Mother & step	0.84	1.17	0.91	1.23	0.85	0.92	1.33	1.31	0.87	1.26	0.81	1.20	0.89	1.26	0.86	1.20
No. siblings 1979	0.60**	0.42**	0.60	0.38**	0.81	0.41**	1.00	0.37**	0.31*	0.21*	0.30**	0.18**	0.61	0.95	0.52	1.03
1 or 2 siblings 1979	0.80*	0.72**	0.93	0.80	0.80	0.58**	0.89	0.60**	0.73	1.75*	1.07	2.33***	0.86	0.42**	0.83	0.38**
Catholic	0.90	1.14	1.22	1.25	0.75*	1.27	1.00	1.40	1.76	1.39	1.55	1.30	1.65	0.78	2.50*	0.93
Regular church attendance	0.95	1.05	0.88	0.90	1.08	0.89	1.15	0.93	0.73	0.91	0.57**	0.73	0.99	1.86**	0.91	1.92*
Traditional attitude	1.10***	1.01	1.11***	1.02	1.04	1.02	1.03	1.01	1.08	0.95	1.14**	0.97	1.30***	1.10	1.28*	1.12
N	1,744	1,237	1,744	1,237	924	619	924	619	499	366	499	366	321	252	321	252

Note. Sample interviewed all survey points to 1998.
*p ≤ .01. **p ≤ .05. ***p ≤ .10.

TABLE 16.8
Current Relationship and Fertility Statistics for 20- to 22-Year-Olds
in 1979 and 2001, by Race

	% Cohabiting	% Married	% Married or Cohabiting	% Father
1979 (NLSY79)				14.5
African American	2.5	8.3	10.7	31.3
Non-African American	1.2	16.0	17.0	12.2
2001 (NLSY97)				11.9
African American	10.9	2.8	13.7	19.6
Non-African American	9.8	7.1	16.9	10.5

Note. Non-African American category includes all except African American sample.

were the same ages in 2001. Table 16.8 provides summary statistics, and Table 16.9 reports multivariate results that suggest similarities and changes in the factors that appear to independently predict early fatherhood.

An important caveat in these two tables is the possibility of unspecified systematic biases between the two data collection efforts, given that we are comparing estimates for 20- to 22-year-olds from the first interview in 1979 with those from the fifth-wave interview in 2001. Because we do not have appropriate cumulative cohabitation statistics for the 1979 cohort, our relationship comparison draws on estimates from 1979 and 2001 for youth who were age 20 to 22 at that point. Clearly, even these cross-sectional cohabitation estimates may reflect somewhat different concepts. However, we can likely conjecture that cumulative cohabitation estimates for the 1979 group were quite low, given that the point estimates were only 2.5% for the African American youth and 1.2% for their White counterparts. The fertility data summarized in Table 16.8 have been subject to somewhat different processing, and in our preliminary multivariate comparison, some of the explanatory variables do not precisely match. That said, some of the results are nevertheless sufficiently robust to warrant comparison.

Table 16.8 summarizes relationship and fatherhood status by race-ethnicity for youth who were aged 20 to 22 in 1979 and 2001, respectively. Clearly the mix between marriage and cohabitation has fundamentally changed during the two decades. Marriage by these ages has declined sharply, and there is nearly a one–to-one increase in cohabitation. This finding, of course, also parallels the reality of increasing age at marriage in recent decades. Later marriages by definition leave young adults with more years to consider involvement in other forms of relationships, including cohabitation.

In our multivariate analysis of early childbearing for the 1979 cohort, we noted that for White youth, years in a marriage were more closely linked

TABLE 16.9

Estimating Fatherhood for Male Youth Ages 20 to 22 in 1979 and 2001, by Race-Ethnicity (Log Odds Estimates, Unweighted Samples)

	Total		African American		Hispanic		Non-African American Non-Hispanic	
	1979	2001	1979	2001	1979	2001	1979	2001
Age	1.41***	1.58***	1.33*	1.04	2.22***	2.08	1.34**	1.78**
African American	1.76***	1.35	—	—	—	—	—	—
Hispanic	1.47*	1.71**	—	—	—	—	—	—
Rural residence	0.96	1.07	0.59	1.79	—	0.28	1.41	1.06
Military residence	1.02	—	0.66	—	0.78	—	1.26	—
Mother has < h.s. degree	1.46*	1.85**	1.35	0.62	1.76	4.09***	1.47	2.67***
Mother has 12 yrs. of school	1.23	1.54*	1.44	1.09	1.01	3.12*	1.17	1.36
Lived w/ both biological parents	0.76**	0.77	0.89	1.57	0.75	0.72	0.63**	0.52**
Youth has no siblings	1.01	0.60	1.12	1.35	1.05	0.54	0.81	0.34
Youth has 1 or 2 siblings	0.84	1.05	0.50**	1.15	2.01	0.38	0.87	1.14
Religious services at least monthly	1.09	0.59**	1.18	0.53*	1.11	0.49*	1.09	0.70
Raised Catholic	0.77	0.61**	0.58	—	0.90	0.72	0.83	0.59
Respondent has < h.s. degree	3.95***	5.34***	1.86*	6.80***	5.51***	3.04***	5.09***	6.42***
Respondent has h.s. degree only	2.54***	1.79***	1.58	2.70***	2.15	0.88	3.60***	2.06**
Pseudo R2	0.08	0.13	0.04	0.11	0.12	0.14	0.08	0.17

*p ≤ .10. **p ≤ .05. ***p ≤ .01.

with fatherhood than years in cohabitation—something that was not as true for young African American men (Table 16.6). Given the sharp rise in cohabitation for both White and African American young adults, if this relationship status–fertility link remains for today's youth, cohabitation could be one reason for the diminishing fertility gap between African American and White youth in recent decades.

From a methodological perspective, given that a larger proportion of youthful fertility may now be taking place among individuals who are neither cohabiting nor married or who are in cohabiting relationships, data quality investigations (as we did for the 1979 cohort) may point to lower contemporary data quality. This would be because a larger proportion of children are perhaps being born in less stable family situations. This topic warrants further investigation.

Overall, little change has occurred in the rate of fatherhood during the period, declining from 14.5% to 11.9%. However, this slight change masks significant racial convergence. This convergence parallels national statistics for women. During the two decades, the rate of fatherhood for non-African American men declined from 12.2% to 10.5%, whereas the rate for African Americans declined from 31.3% to 19.6%.

The preceding is a brief summary of fertility trends. Perhaps of greater interest is whether the characteristics of these young fathers have changed in ways that can inform potential policy interventions. For this, we employ a multivariate perspective. Although not quite reduced in form, we include only a limited set of explanatory variables that were available for both cohorts and that, with limited exceptions, may be considered exogenous to the early fatherhood process, or at least measured at points prior to fatherhood. As a general comment, we recognize the tendency to view endogeneity issues in fertility analyses as gender neutral. In all likelihood, this is at least partially inappropriate, given that the "disconnect" between employment and education-linked behaviors and childbearing is undoubtedly greater for men.

Previous research (S. Hanson, Morrison, & Ginsburg, 1989; Lerman, 1993; Marsiglio, 1987; Pirog-Good, 1992, 1995) suggests many factors that can increase the likelihood of early fatherhood, such as being African American, going steady, having more tolerant views regarding illegitimate births, growing up in poor or unstable conditions, having less education, participating in illegal activities, and having lower self-esteem.

Although the patterns in Table 16.9 are somewhat erratic, several results that are partially consistent with the aforementioned literature may be of interest. Most generally, respondents with less than a college education are more likely to become fathers at an earlier age in both years. Connected to this finding is evidence that young adults who have mothers with less education are also more likely on average to become fathers. Having lived with both parents while growing up is linked with fewer instances of early fatherhood, as is being reared Catholic. Finally, although not overwhelming, minority youth are more likely than the average to become fathers at early ages in 1979 and 2001.

Although frequent church attendance shifts substantially toward predicting less fatherhood by 2001, this shift was largely driven by large changes among the two minority groups during the 22-year period. However, although the church attendance coefficient among non-African American, non-Hispanic youth was not significant in 2001, the direction of the effect is similar—church attendance was associated with less early fatherhood. Why church attendance has emerged as a factor is uncertain, but it is certainly consistent with the premise that the meaning of church attendance for young men, and perhaps the characteristics of those who attend, may be different today than a generation ago. This issue also warrants further investigation.

In many respects, the patterns for White men mirror the overall patterns of male fertility. Also, although limited education is associated with a higher than average likelihood of early fatherhood for all groups, the propensity for early fatherhood was stronger in 2001 than in 1979 for the least educated African American youth, perhaps because they may now represent an even more select group than in 1979. This is consistent with the notion that the meaning of low education (which now characterizes a much smaller proportion of the population) has perhaps changed considerably. This low-education group may represent an even more disadvantaged group than in earlier decades. The results may parallel, in some ways, the apparent increased association between a mother's education and her son's early onset of Fatherhood for white and Hispanic youth. In general, the basis of the connection between low education and early fatherhood, and how it appears to be changing over time, warrants more careful evaluation and analysis.

CONCLUDING COMMENTS

In this chapter, we have considered several closely linked objectives. We have used two national longitudinal data sets to explore issues related to the quality of male fertility and relationship data collection. We then synthesized selected recent male fertility and relationship trends, which have not previously been available for nationally representative samples, with insights we gained from our evaluation process.

The first of these two data sets, the NLSY79, enabled us to clarify, to some extent, male fertility patterns for a national cohort of men aged 33 to 41 by 1998 and well into their "fathering" years. We were able to clarify a number of fertility and relationship reporting issues during the 19-year survey window because of the many data checks on the reported events internal to the data collection effort. Our revised estimates are based on data that, on the surface, appear reasonably accurate.

We found only a modest percentage of cases in which we believe the man was misrepresenting paternity at some point. For approximately 92% of all births during the 1979 to 1998 survey window, we are quite comfortable about the indicated paternity. For the remainder, we are either quite certain that the man is not the biological father, or, for a small percentage, still uncertain. An important caveat is that some inconsistency over time must appear before a birth can even become suspect. Thus, a child who is consistently reported or not reported could fly under the radar screen.

It would appear that using our revised fertility estimates, which include only confidence levels 1 and 2, modestly reduces our fertility profile. Several caveats are in order, however. First, younger adults disproportionately fall into the group that initially acknowledges a child only to deny paternity later, and thus the magnitude of the difference in profiles between the original and revised data reflects these discrepancies from earlier points. Not acknowledging a child is less common among older men. Furthermore, the issue of incorrectly assigning dates of events, which we do not address in this chapter, is certainly significant in that it can modestly alter the shape of the cumulative fertility profile. However, it has little effect on final levels. It is important to be mindful, however, that cumulative fertility as of any *specific* year in a longitudinal survey can be affected by dating errors, and more important, can influence the dynamics of microlevel analyses. The same can be said for the dates of cohabiting and marital relationships because relationship acknowledgment or relationship dates can significantly affect various issues surrounding fertility.

The NLSY97 data set has permitted us to make a few preliminary statements about youthful male fertility and how it has changed during the past two decades, and to begin to clarify some methodological caveats on relationship data quality. First, from a data quality perspective, although perhaps intuitive, it was useful to quantify the very large proportions of younger men who are not living with their acknowledged children. This, of course, is a major reason they have trouble reporting precise demographic information about their children. It also represents a red flag regarding the probability that some significant portion of these children will vanish from the men's radar screen down the road.

A second methodological point relates to the substantial number of youth who reported having ever cohabited at a relatively early age but who do not report this cohabitation at any survey point. If this had indeed been true when we developed our cohabitation profile for the 1979 men, then our analyses for that cohort will have understated cumulative relationship probabilities at younger ages. Whether this is significant for our early fertility analyses for that cohort remains in question. What is clear is that, without event history information to fill in the between-survey gaps, even a high-quality panel survey with fairly frequent data collection can miss the boat in important respects.

From a substantive perspective, the combined availability of the NLSY79 and NLSY97 data permit us to describe and compare male relationship and fertility patterns for contemporary nationally representative cohorts. The NLSY79 is admittedly cohort bound, and as such excludes new additions to the cohort over the 19 years, a nontrivial exclusion. Having said that, one can still generalize from this group to a very large segment of men who are currently in their peak childbearing years. We have also been able to use these two data sets to highlight some changes and similarities over time in male adolescent cohabiting and marital relationships and fertility trends.

Acknowledging all the possible methodological constraints, even our fairly perfunctory comparisons of relationship and fertility profiles for young men aged 20 to 22 across two decades suggest some important changes and similarities over time. By these ages, the proportion in a relationship has changed little; what has changed is the type of relationship. Marriage has declined substantially whereas cohabitation has risen sharply. The modest decline in fatherhood for this group is evident for both White and non-White youth, although the rate for African American men remains substantially higher than for White men. Our preliminary multivariate results suggest that even though levels of early childbearing have declined sharply, for the most part similar factors predict early fatherhood in both 1979 and 2001.

The 1979 data reveal a much earlier entrance into fatherhood for minority men, although this gap had narrowed considerably by 1998, reflecting a sharp African American decline in early childbearing during a period when White male fertility stayed largely unchanged. Analytically, many of the factors predicting fatherhood by ages 20 to 23 are no longer relevant predictors by ages 33 to 37, reflecting the reality that ultimately, most men in most social and demographic categories attain fatherhood.

Other potentially important changes, however, relate to the apparently increasing importance of religion for delayed fatherhood and the apparent increased connection between very low education and early fatherhood for African American youth. Both of these factors may be linked with the increasing selectivity of youth who remain in these categories. These findings warrant further investigation.

Of importance for future research would be a careful exploration of male fertility data quality issues using the NLSY97 data once those youth have a few more survey rounds under their belt. As our evaluation of the 1979 cohort has demonstrated, many of the factors linked with poor data quality are related to the adolescent and early-adult life cycle stage, where fertility is more commonly linked with measures of relationship instability, such as fertility that occurs in a cohabiting relationship or outside of a marital or cohabiting relationship. Given the increase in the proportion of non-marital unions in recent years, it may well be that the data quality issues we have noted may be even more prevalent for this generation than for earlier adolescent cohorts.

ACKNOWLEDGMENTS

The authors acknowledge the support of National Institutes of Health (NIH) grants RO1 HD 25702 and RO1 HD37078 and the Bureau of Labor Statistics (BLS) Contract J-9-J-9-0029, which included NIH funds as part of an interagency agreement between the NICHD and the BLS. Additionally, we would like to acknowledge the considerable assistance of Diane Burchett-Patel on earlier versions of our research on male fertility as well as the very useful comments we have received from anonymous reviewers.

Notes

1. In earlier research (Mott, 1998) we documented conclusively how the earliest reports for the 1979 cohort had substantial misreporting inconsistencies that were not easily re-solved. This, in part, reflected the fact that many of those births preceded the first survey round and, in addition, that fertility information collected prior to the 1982 survey round was much more perfunctory.
2. A definition was not provided unless the respondent asked for clarification.

17

Counting Dads: Improving Estimates of Teen Fatherhood

Scott Boggess
U.S. Census Bureau

Gladys Martinez
National Center for Health Statistics

Carolyn Bradner Jasik
University of California San Francisco

Laura Duberstein Lindberg
Alan Guttmacher Institute

Public concern about teenage childbearing has been fueled by concern about the negative consequences for teen mothers and their children, and the related social and economic costs to society (Maynard, 1997; for an alternate view, see Nathanson, 1991). The majority of research and policy discussion has centered on teen mothers and their children, with little attention to teen fatherhood, its magnitude, causes, and consequences for the father and his child. Previous research indicates that teen fathers are more likely to leave school early and to have unstable marriages than men who delay fatherhood, which, in turn, has potential economic, social, and developmental consequences for the young men, their children, and their partners (Brien & Willis, 1997; Card & Wise, 1978; Elster, Lamb, & Tavare,

1987; Gibbs, 1988; Lerman & Ooms, 1993; Marsiglio, 1987; Spingarn & Durant, 1996; Thornberry, Smith, & Howard, 1997).

Data collection and analysis on the factors that place teens at risk for fatherhood have recently begun to expand, as have efforts to include adolescent males in teen pregnancy prevention efforts (Brindis et al., 1998; Resnick et al., 1997; Sonenstein, Stewart, Lindberg, Pernas, & Williams, 1997). Growing interest in the role of men in teenage childbearing, and in fathers more generally, argues for improved understanding of teenage fatherhood (Federal Interagency Forum on Child and Family Statistics, 1998; Goldscheider & Kaufman, 1996; Moore, Driscoll, & Ooms, 1997).

The relative lack of research on teen fatherhood results in limited knowledge of the scope of the issue. Key ethnographic studies of teen males have explored the experience of teen fatherhood in community settings, but the ability to generalize the results to larger populations is unknown (E. Anderson, 1990, 1993; Sullivan, 1993). National data show that young men age 19 or younger father only about one third of births to teenage girls (aged 15–19); adult men father the rest (Lindberg, Sonenstein, Ku, & Martinez, 1997). What is less clear is how many men are teen fathers. Birth certificate data show that the number of 15- to 19-year-old fathers has remained relatively constant since 1990 at 23 to 25 per 1,000 (Ventura, Martin, Curtin, & Matthews, 1998). Nevertheless, this is substantially higher than the 1988 unmarried-teen fatherhood rate of 16.4 births per 1,000 found in the National Survey of Adolescent Males (NSAM) and 14.1 births per 1,000 in the National Maternal and Infant Health Survey (NMIHS) (Lindberg et al., 1997). These cross-sectional estimates of teen fatherhood underestimate the prevalence of teen fatherhood in a cohort because they are censored observations of the full exposure to risk. That is, the data do not capture fatherhood that occurs after the year of measurement but before an individual's 20th birthday.

In contrast to the cross-sectional estimates of a teenage fatherhood rate of 1% to 3%, retrospective reports from the National Longitudinal Survey of Youth (NLSY) estimate that, in 1983, 1.3% of all teen males became fathers prior to age 18, and 5.9% became fathers prior to age 20 (Mott, 1985). There was significant variation in rates of teen fatherhood by race-ethnicity; more than 14% of Black males reported becoming fathers prior to age 20 compared with 9.4% of Hispanic males and 4.4% of White males.

Data quality concerns plague these estimates, however. In the NLSY79, nearly one half of the personal reports of fatherhood among young men aged 17–24 showed discrepancies across the survey time span. The age-specific birth rates may be biased given that they rely heavily on imputed data for the substantial proportion of birth certificates on which the father's age is missing. Approximately 42% of mothers aged 15 to 19 did not report their partner's age on their child's birth certificate (Bachrach, Ventura, Newcomer, & Mosher, 1995). The direction of potential bias of the imputed data is unclear. Mothers may be less likely to report the age of younger fathers, given that these relationships are less likely to involve marriage or cohabitation (Lindberg, Sonenstein, Martinez, & Marcotte, 1998). Alternatively, mothers may be less likely to report the age of older fathers for fear of legal or social sanctions owing to large age differences.

More generally, research finds that, compared with women, men underreport their own fertility. Both inconsistent reporting and underreporting appear to be greater problems for never-married men, for nonresident fathers, and for African American men (Bachu, 1996; Cherlin et al., 1983; Garfinkel et al., 1998; Mott, 1983; Rendall, Clarke, Peters, Ranjit, & Verropoulou, 1999; Sorensen, 1997). Given that these groups are likely to compose a substantial proportion of teen fathers, estimates of teen fatherhood may be particularly sensitive to problems of misreporting. However, paternal reports of unmarried teen fatherhood in the 1988 NSAM were found to be consistent with maternal reports of unmarried teen fatherhood in the 1988 NMIHS (Lindberg et al., 1998), suggesting that it is possible to collect valid fertility data from teen fathers.

In the present study, we estimate the prevalence of teen fatherhood and examine how sensitive these estimates are to inconsistent reports of fatherhood across survey waves using data from a recent, nationally representative, longitudinal survey of young males. We hypothesize that the quality of reporting is not random, but is correlated with certain paternal characteristics, particularly the father's age, marital status, and living arrangements. Older fathers, fathers who are married to their child's mother, and fathers who also live with their child will likely provide more consistent reports of their fertility than younger, unmarried, and nonresident fathers.

This analysis provides recent national estimates of the scope of teen fathering overall and for key subpopulations beyond what can be examined in vital statistics. It also extends studies of the validity of young men's reports of fatherhood by examining the reliability of reporting across multiple survey waves. Identifying individual and survey characteristics associated with inconsistent reporting can assist in the burgeoning efforts to accurately collect data on children directly from men (Cherlin & Griffith, 1998). New federal efforts to collect information directly from men include the National Survey of Family Growth 2000 and the Early Childhood Longitudinal Study, Birth Cohort (ECLS-B).

STUDY DESIGN

Data

The data for this study are drawn from the first three waves of the NSAM. The first wave surveyed a nationally representative sample of 1,880 noninstitutionalized, never-married males aged 15 to 19 living in the contiguous United States in 1988. The original wave was drawn as a multistage area probability sample that oversampled both African Americans and Hispanics, making detailed racial-ethnic analyses possible. The initial sample contained 820 White males, 680 Black males, and 390 Hispanic males. The follow-up was administered in 1991 and had a response rate of 89%. The third follow-up was conducted in 1995, at which time the respondents were aged 22 to 26, and the survey had a follow-up rate of 75% (Sonenstein, Ku, & Pleck, 1997).

We restrict our analytical samples to those males observed at least until age 18 and age 20, resulting in unweighted samples of 1,768 and 1,554 males, respectively. We constructed longitudinal sample weights to compensate for probability of selection and nonresponse, and all analyses presented in this chapter are weighted. We used SUDAAN to compute all tests of significance, owing to the complex sampling design of the NSAM (Research Triangle Institute, 1993).

The NSAM offers four primary advantages when studying teen fatherhood. First, unlike some other data sources, the information in the NSAM is obtained directly from the young males and not through indirect sources, such as sexual partners. Second, the NSAM is nationally representative, in contrast to city-, county-, and clinic-based samples used in past studies (Spingarn & Durant, 1996; Thornberry et al., 1997). Third, because the NSAM is a longitudinal data set, we can follow the respondents through their teen years. This is an improvement over cross-sectional data that observe adolescents at only one point during their teen years or that rely completely on retrospective data collected during their 20s or 30s. Finally, by asking questions about pregnancy and fatherhood in the context of sexual behavior, the NSAM may do a better job than other data sets of eliciting more complete reporting, given that, at the time they are asked about fatherhood, respondents will already have been asked to recall a significant amount of related information on sexual activity and relationships.

Methods

We calculate the prevalence of teen fatherhood by using the respondent's age at first birth, which is determined using his date of birth and the reported date of birth for his firstborn child. Because we are interested only in when the respondent first became a father, we do not incorporate information about subsequent births.

Because of concern over the accuracy of self-reported fatherhood and the effect that inaccurate or inconsistent reporting may have on the estimated rate of teen fatherhood, we begin by estimating the frequency of inconsistent reports of teen fatherhood within the NSAM. The three waves of the NSAM asked about any past or current partner pregnancies, giving respondents multiple opportunities to provide a birth date for their firstborn child; it also, however, offered respondents multiple opportunities to revise their reports. As a result, the inconsistencies or gaps in these reports are not surprising. Inconsistencies between these reports are classified into one or more of the following categories: missing information, "lost" children, "found" children, and different dates.

Missing information occurs when the respondent reports a live birth but fails to provide a birth month or year for the child. "Lost" children are those who are reported in the 1988 or 1991 surveys (or both), but who are not reported in one or more subsequent waves. Assuming no interviewer or data entry errors, there are several possible explanations for lost children. The initial report of fatherhood may be incorrect. Respondents may be reporting children in 1988 who do not exist. Respondents may believe they are fathers in 1988 only to find out that the child is not theirs. Respondents may fail to report their own children in later survey waves because their children have died, they have lost contact with them, or the mother has (re)married, or because they fear that admitting paternity may legally bind them to the child's support.

"Found" children correspond to children reported in the 1991 or 1995 surveys (or both) who, based on their reported birth dates, should have been reported in one or more of the previous waves. Likely explanations for found children include respondents who may not learn they are fathers until several months or years after a child's birth. As a result, they do not report the child in the first survey wave after the child's birth. Respondents may also be misreporting the child's birth date. For example, in the 1991 survey, a respondent may report a child being born in 1987—prior to the base-year survey—when the child was actually born in 1989. The respondent may also know he is a father in the early survey waves but fail to report the child out of embarrassment or fear. (A child reported only in the 1991 survey wave who, based on the reported date of birth, should have been reported in both the 1988 and 1995 surveys is classified as both "lost" and "found.") The problem of different dates involves fathers reporting either different birth months or different birth years for what appears to be the same child in different waves of the survey.

In the first part of this study, we examine how the rates of inconsistent reporting vary by the respondent's age, race-ethnicity, and marital status at the time of the birth, and by the child's residence at the date of the first interview in which the father reports the child.

In the second, and central, part of this study, we estimate the percentage of young males who report becoming fathers prior to ages 18 and 20. Because the estimated rate of teen fatherhood will differ depending on how we choose to handle the four types of reporting inconsistencies, we calculate three separate estimates of teen fatherhood: a best estimate, a low estimate, and a high estimate.

The best estimate uses all available information to calculate what we believe to be the most likely age at first birth. We assume that all lost and found children are the biological children of the respondent, given that previous research suggests that young males are more likely to underreport than overreport their fertility. For missing birth dates, we imputed dates. In those instances in which we know the month and year the respondent learned about the pregnancy, we impute the child's birth date as 7 months from the date, which is the mean length of time between these two dates for those respondents with complete birth and pregnancy information. If the respondent is missing only the child's birth month, and we have no information on when he learned of the pregnancy, we set the child's birth month to June. In all other cases, we set the child's birth date as equal to the date of interview for the first survey in which the child is reported. For lost and found children and others with different dates, we assume that they were born on the date given in the earliest survey wave in which they are reported; we make this assumption because the ability to recall exact dates diminishes over time.

To produce the low and high estimates, we use the earliest date of birth reported in each survey wave to calculate three separate ages at first fatherhood. The age at first birth calculated from each of the three survey waves, coupled with the best estimate, resulted in up to four different ages at first birth for each respondent. We then calculated the low estimate for the percentage of males who became teen fathers by using the oldest of the four ages, whereas we calculated the high estimate using the youngest of these ages. In those cases in which we imputed the child's birth month, we substituted December when calculating the low estimate and January when calculating the high estimate.

In addition to the overall estimates, we also estimate rates of teen fatherhood for important demographic subgroups: race-ethnicity; region and whether an urban, suburban, or rural residence; and whether the respondent was behind in school in 1988 as determined by his age and grade. Family characteristics include the education of the respondent's most educated parent, family structure at age 14, family welfare receipt in the 12 months prior to the 1988 survey date, and whether the respondent's mother was a teen mother. We use chi-square tests to determine whether observed differences in the best estimates are statistically significant across these groups.

To test whether the bivariate correlations represent true associations or whether they result from other underlying relationships, we compare the bivariate estimates of fatherhood by age 20 with multivariate estimates from a logistic regression model. The dependent variable in the logistic regression model is a dichotomous variable equal to 1 if the respondent reported a birth prior to age 20, based on our best estimate of age at first birth. In addition to the aforementioned individual and family characteristics, the logistic regression model also includes control variables for family income, mother's employment status while the respondent was growing up, religious attendance at age 14, early alcohol and marijuana use, and the strictness of family rules at age 14. Our choice of independent variables was heavily influenced by the work of Thornberry et al. (1997), Sonenstein, Pleck, and Ku (1993), and S. Hanson et al. (1989). A complete description of the variables used in the multivariate model appears in the Appendix.

To produce the estimated prevalence of fatherhood for a particular demographic group, we assign all individuals in the sample the characteristic of interest and, holding all other characteristics constant, we calculate the predicted probability of fatherhood for each individual using the estimated coefficients from the logistic regression equation. We then average the individual probabilities to obtain the overall predicted probability for the characteristic.

As mentioned earlier, one advantage of the NSAM is that it is longitudinal rather than cross-sectional. Because of the shorter recall period, cohort data may provide more complete reporting of fatherhood than cross-sectional data. In the final phase of the analyses, we test this assumption by comparing the best estimate of teen fatherhood with three alternative cross-sectional estimates. Alternative 1 estimates the teen fatherhood rate using data from the first interview after the respondent's 20th birthday; 777 respondents turned 20 prior to the 1991 wave, whereas the remainder turned 20 between the 1991 and 1995 waves. In this case, the recall period varied from 0 to 4 years. Alternative 2 estimates the rate of teen fatherhood using only data from the 1991 follow-up; in this case, the denominator for the fatherhood rate includes only men who turned 20 prior to the 1991 interview. This estimate has a recall period of 0 to 2 years. Alternative 3 is similar to Alternative 2 but only employs data from the 1995 follow-up, by which time all the respondents had reached age 20. This estimate has a recall period of 2 to 6 years and is limited only to those men who participated in the second follow-up. We used t tests to test for significant differences between the best estimate and each of the three cross-sectional estimates. This analysis is performed for the full sample and separately by race-ethnicity.

THE PROPORTION OF FATHERS
WHO PROVIDE INCONSISTENT REPORTS
OF FATHERHOOD

Among the 1,554 twenty-year-old respondents in our sample, 196 reported a birth prior to age 20 in at least one wave. Of these individuals, 86 had evidence of one or more data problems in relation to the date of birth of

TABLE 17.1
Factors Associated With Inconsistent Reports of First Births by Teen Fathers

Variable	N	Inconsistent[a]		Type of Inconsistent Report[b] (No. of Cases)			
		No. of Cases	Weighted %	Lost Child	Found Child	Different Dates	Missing Info.
Number of teen fathers	196	86	34%	41	26	21	19
Age at first birth							
Under 16	15	15	100	10	3	2	8
16	14	10	72	7	1	6	2
17	28	14	44	7	5	2	5
18	55	25	40	11	5	8	2
19	84	22	19	6	12	3	2
p value			(0.001)				
Race							
Non-Hispanic White	47	19	27	8	5	6	7
Non-Hispanic Black	104	54	50	28	19	10	7
Hispanic	35	8	18	4	1	2	3
p value			(0.035)				
Marital status at first birth							
Married	20	5	17	2	1	2	0
Unmarried	176	81	38	39	25	19	19
p value			(0.054)				
Child's residence at first report of birth							
In same household as father	39	4	17	0	3	1	1
Not in same household as father/other[c]	122	70	48	39	20	17	13
Missing	35	12	25	2	3	3	5
p value			(0.005)				

[a]An individual's fertility report is classified as inconsistent if they have one or more of the following: lost child (child reported in one wave and then not in a subsequent survey), found child (child reported in a later survey who should have been reported in an earlier wave), different dates (different birth dates for the same child in different waves), or missing information (all or part of the child's birth date is missing). [b]Lost, found, different dates, and missing information do not add up to 196 because respondents could have more than one type of inconsistent report. [c]Other includes babies that died ($N = 3$) or were adopted ($N = 2$) in addition to those who live with the mother and/or other relatives.

their firstborn child (Table 17.1). Using our sample weights, we estimated that more than one third of all teen fathers misreported the date of birth of their first child across the three waves of the survey. The most common problem was a lost child ($N = 41$), followed by a found child ($N = 26$), different dates ($N = 21$), and missing information ($N = 19$).

FATHERS WHO ARE MOST LIKELY TO PROVIDE INCONSISTENT REPORTS

The younger an individual was at first fatherhood, the more likely he was to have inconsistent reports. Every respondent who reported having his first child prior to age 16 had at least one data inconsistency issue, the most common being lost children. This compares with fewer than one in five males who reported becoming a father at age 19. However, some caution is warranted when interpreting these results because those who reported becoming fathers at an earlier age had, on average, more opportunities to experience data problems than older fathers. Individuals who had a first child prior to the 1988 base survey and who reported this birth at the time of the base survey could lose, find, or misreport the birth date of their first child either between the first and second waves or between the second and third waves of the survey. They could also have missing information in either of the three survey waves. On the other hand, an individual who had a first birth between the second and third waves of the survey could not, by definition, have had a lost child or inconsistent dates and could only have had missing information in Wave 3.

To determine whether the increased opportunity to misreport a birth was responsible for the results in Table 17.1, we separated the fathers into three groups based on the survey in which they first reported a birth, thus controlling for the opportunity to misreport information. We then tested whether there were still significant differences in the quality of reporting by age at first birth for each of the three groups. For two of the three groups—those who first reported a birth in Wave 1 and those who first reported a birth in Wave 2—we found significantly higher rates of misreporting for younger fathers than for older fathers. In the third group—those who first reported a birth in Wave 3—there was too little variation in age at first birth to perform a meaningful test of significance. We also find significant differences in the rates of misreporting by race-ethnicity. One half of the African American fathers gave inconsistent reports compared with 27% of White and 18% of Hispanic fathers.

The results for marital status suggest that married fathers are less likely to misreport their child's birth information than unmarried fathers. Among fathers who were married to the child's mother at the time of the birth, only 17% had one or more reporting inconsistencies, compared with 38% of fathers who were not married to the child's mother. Again, these results should be viewed with caution given that unmarried fathers have, on average, more opportunities to misreport information than married fathers. Analyses performed separately for those who first reported a birth in Wave 2 and those who first reported a birth in Wave 3 reveal the same pattern of misreporting. In this case, however, the differences cease to be significant owing, at least in part, to the small number of sample cases.

Finally, we find that individuals who reported living with their child when they first reported the birth were significantly less likely to have reporting inconsistencies than fathers who did not live with their children (17% vs. 48%). In addition, none of the 39 fathers who reported living with their child shortly after birth failed to report that child in a subsequent survey wave (i.e., a lost child).

THE PERCENTAGE OF MALES WHO BECOME TEEN FATHERS

Table 17.2 presents the estimated prevalence of teen and early-teen fatherhood for the population as a whole and for various demographic groups. Using our weights to adjust for the sampling design, our "best" estimate is that 1.9% of males became fathers prior to age 18, and 8.3% became fathers prior to age 20. The first row of Table 17.2 shows that using different approaches to the various data problems does not have a large effect on our estimates of teen fatherhood. The low and high estimates are 1.3% and 2%, respectively. The low and high estimates for the percentage of males who became fathers prior to age 20 are 6.6% and 8.4%, respectively.

DEMOGRAPHIC CORRELATES OF TEEN FATHERHOOD

Table 17.2 also presents estimates of the prevalence of teen fatherhood for various demographic groups. We used chi-square tests to test for significant differences in the rate of fatherhood across these groups. Because the trends are similar for fatherhood prior to age 18 and fatherhood prior to age 20, we focus, for simplicity, primarily on the latter.

We find significant differences in the prevalence of teen fatherhood by race. The highest teen fatherhood rates are reported by African American males; 17.9% report having a child prior to age 20. African American males are three times more likely to report a teen birth, and six times more likely

TABLE 17.2
Estimated Rates of Teen and Early Teen Fatherhood,
Bivariate and Multivariate Results

	Bivariate Results				Multivariate Results
	% w/ child by Age 18		% w/ Child by Age 20		
Variable	Best	Low–High	Best	Low–High	% w/ Child by Age 20
All	1.9	1.3–2.0	8.3	6.6–8.4	8.3
Race					
White	1.0	0.7–1.0	5.9	4.6–5.9	6.8
African American	5.9*	3.2–5.9	17.9*	13.4–18.3	13.7*
Hispanic	1.6	1.1–1.6	9.9	8.8–10.1	9.7
Region					
Northeast	1.4	1.0–1.4	5.7	4.9–5.7	7.0
Midwest	1.8	1.6–1.8	11.3*	10.2–11.3	11.7*
South	2.6	1.4–2.7	9.9*	6.4–10.1	7.8
West	1.4	0.9–1.4	4.7	4.3–4.7	6.4
Urbanicity					
Urban	4.3*	2.9–4.3	10.2*	8.2–10.4	8.7
Suburban	0.9	0.8–0.9	7.0	6.1–7.0	6.9
Rural	2.2*	1.1–2.2	9.1	6.5–9.3	10.0
Parent education[a]					
Less than high school	3.3	1.0–3.3	13.3	9.4–13.5	6.3
High school	2.0	1.2–2.0	12.6	10.5–12.7	11.8*
Some college	2.4	2.1–2.6	5.5*	4.5–5.6	6.5
College graduate	0.9*	0.9–0.9	2.7*	2.3–2.7	4.6
Missing	6.1	3.4–6.1	16.4	7.9–16.9	9.7
Family structure					
Lived with both parents at 14	1.5	1.2–1.5	6.2	5.3–6.3	7.5
Did not live with both parents at 14	3.1*	1.4–3.1	13.5*	9.7–13.6	9.7
Welfare receipt					
Received assistance in last 12 mos.	6.9*	4.5–7.0	19.8*	14.9–20.3	10.9
Did not receive assistance	1.1	0.8–1.1	6.2	5.0–6.2	7.4
Missing	3.2	0.6–3.2	15.5*	12.1–15.5	12.0
Teen mother					
Mother was a teen mom	4.4*	3.0–4.4	15.4*	12.9–15.5	10.3*
Mother was not a teen mom	0.8	0.5–0.8	4.9	3.8–4.9	6.7
Missing	2.6	0.6–2.6	12.4*	3.3–13.2	7.5
Own education					
Behind in school[b]	4.2*	3.4–4.4	15.4*	11.3–15.6	8.2
Not behind in school	1.6	1.0–1.6	7.4	5.9–7.5	8.4
N (unweighted)	1,768	1,768	1,554	1,554	1,554

[a]Education level of most educated parent. [b]Respondent is 2 or more years behind in school for their age (among those in school) or they have not graduated high school (among dropouts). [c]Multivariate regressions also controlled for family income in 1988, the strictness of family rules while growing up, religious attendance at age 14, mother's employment status while the respondent was growing up, and early alcohol and marijuana use.

*Wald chi-square test of significant difference from comparison group, $p < 0.10$.

to report an early-teen birth, than are White males. Hispanic youth have prevalence rates (9.9%) nearly twice those of White youth (5.9%).

The prevalence of teen fatherhood is highest for those living in the Midwest and South and outside suburban areas (Table 17.2). However, the regional differences are only significant for fatherhood prior to age 20, whereas the urbanicity differences are only significant for early-teen births. We find a significant negative association between parental education and teen fatherhood. As parental education rises, the prevalence of teen fatherhood falls, from 13.3% to 2.7%.

Males living with both biological parents at age 14 are significantly less likely to become young fathers than those living with only one parent. Among those living with one parent, those living with their fathers had a lower prevalence of teen fatherhood than those living only with their mothers (results not shown). (At this point, cell sizes were too small to conduct meaningful tests of significance.) Teen fatherhood was also more prevalent for males who lived in a household that received income from welfare at any time in the 12 months prior to the 1988 interview. Having a mother who herself was a teen mother also significantly increased the likelihood of teen fatherhood; 15.4% of the sons of teen mothers became teen fathers, compared with only 4.9% of sons of nonteen mothers. Finally, males who were at least 2 years behind in school in 1988 showed a higher prevalence of teen fatherhood than other males.

Once again, we observe little difference between the low and high estimates for nearly all demographic groups. The only exception is the small group of males who are missing information on whether their mother was a teen mother. In this case, there is a large difference between the two estimates, 3.3% versus 13.2%.

MULTIVARIATE ANALYSIS

The final column of Table 17.2 presents the multivariate predicted probabilities of teen fatherhood by age 20, generated from the logistic regression model. These estimates display much less variability than the corresponding bivariate estimates. In several cases, differences that were statistically significant in the bivariate analysis are no longer significant after controlling for other individual and family characteristics. This is true for urbanicity, family structure, welfare receipt, and own education. In other cases—race-ethnicity, region, and mother who was a teen parent—the differences, though smaller, are still significant. The most pronounced changes occur for parents' education. The multivariate analysis finds higher prevalence rates for the sons of high school graduates than sons whose parents had not completed high school—just the opposite of the bivariate results.

LONGITUDINAL VERSUS CROSS-SECTIONAL METHODS

Table 17.3 presents the estimated fatherhood rates by age 20 using longitudinal and cross-sectional data. We compared the prevalence of teen fatherhood using data from the 1991 follow-up, the first interview after which the respondent turned 20 (1991 or 1995), and the 1995 follow-up. For each of the three data sources, the recall time from age 20 to the survey date is indicated. The best estimate is also reported.

A comparison of the overall prevalence rates finds that as the length of recall increases, self-reported teen fatherhood decreases. The estimated prevalence of fatherhood by age 20 using data from the first follow-up is 7.8%, compared with 6.9% using data from the first interview after the respondent turned 20, and 6.7% using data from the second follow-up. Only the second follow-up estimate is significantly smaller than the best estimate.

For White respondents, the estimated fatherhood rate ranges from 6% at the 1991 follow-up to 5.1% at the 1995 follow-up. None of the alternative estimates is significantly different from the best estimate. Among African Americans, the difference between the cross-sectional and longitudinal estimates is slightly higher. The alternative estimates of teen fatherhood range from 14.2% using data from the first interview after age 20, to 14.6% using data from the 1991 follow-up. The latter estimate is significantly lower than the best estimate.

TABLE 17.3
Longitudinal Versus Cross-Sectional Estimates of Fatherhood
by Age 20

Interview (Recall Period)	Best	1991 Follow-Up (0–2 yrs)[a]	First Interview After Respondent Turned 20 (0–4 yrs)	1995 Follow-Up (2–6 yrs)
All	8.3	7.8 (0.6554)	6.9 (0.1345)	6.7 (0.0975)
White	5.9	6.0 (0.9627)	5.0 (0.4993)	5.1 (0.5327)
African American	17.9	14.6 (0.2071)	14.2 (0.0953)	14.4 (0.1318)
Hispanic	9.9	9.2 (0.8282)	9.5 (0.8888)	7.0 (0.2054)
N (unweighted)	1,554	777	1,554	1,377

[a]Only respondents who were age 20 at the time of the first follow-up were used in this analysis. p values are in parentheses. Values refer to t test of difference between cross-sectional and best estimate.

Among Hispanic respondents, 9.2% report being a father by age 20 in 1991, 9.5% at the first survey after they turned 20, and 7% at the second follow-up. Although the latter rate is almost 3 percentage points lower than the best estimate, none of the alternative estimates is significantly different from the best estimate.

DISCUSSION AND CONCLUSION

Among a nationally representative cohort of unmarried teen males in 1988, we estimate that about 2% reported becoming a father prior to age 18, and 8.3% acknowledged paternity prior to age 20. Although more than one third of fathers had some reporting inconsistency across survey waves, our estimated rates are robust to these inconsistencies. These rates, however, belie much diversity among key subgroups of males. Nearly one in five African American men became fathers before turning 20, compared with only 5.9% of Whites. This difference attenuates in multivariate models but remains significant. In the bivariate models, teen fatherhood is significantly more common among males whose parents had less education and whose mother was a teen mom. Although these racial and background differences are similar to those found for teen motherhood (Liebowitz, Eisen, & Chow, 1986; Zelnik, Kantner, & Ford, 1980), our estimates are predictably lower than similar estimates of teen motherhood. According to life table estimates from the 1995 National Survey of Family Growth, a woman has a 9% chance of giving birth prior to age 18 and a 19% chance of giving birth prior to age 20 (Moore, Driscoll, & Lindberg, 1998), rates that are more than four and two times that, respectively, of the corresponding rates for males. This is not unexpected, given that roughly two thirds of the fathers of babies born to teen mothers are aged 20 or older (Lindberg et al., 1998).

Our findings suggest that teen fatherhood is a far more common experience than previously estimated. Our estimates of 1.9% by age 18 and 8.3% by age 20 are 46% and 41% higher than Mott's 1982 NLSY estimates of 1.3% and 5.9%. Other evidence suggests that these differences cannot be ascribed solely to changes over time in young men's behavior. According to data from the National Vital Statistics System, the birth rate for 15- to 19-year-old men increased by only 33% between 1982 (the year of Mott's estimates) and 1993 (the year by which all the NSAM respondents were at least 20) (Ventura, Martin, et al., 1998). Assuming that any reporting bias in these measures remained constant over time, the vital statistics would indicate a smaller increase between 1982 and 1993 than our estimates reflect. Although the higher estimated rates of teen fatherhood in the NSAM likely reflect, in part, a secular increase in the rate of teen fatherhood from 1982 to 1993, we also believe it derives from more complete paternity reporting in the NSAM than in the NLSY.

Although further research is needed to investigate the pattern of male reports described here, we can identify certain aspects of the NSAM design that may have contributed to more complete fertility reports from its male respondents. Generally, fathers in a survey may be misclassified as non-fathers through either unintentional or intentional misreporting of their fertility experiences. If young men do not know they are fathers, they will unintentionally misclassify themselves. This can also occur if a proxy respondent reports on the young man's fertility and does not know his actual experiences. Although other surveys, such as the Current Population Survey and the Survey of Income and Program Participation, use proxy reporting (i.e., having one member of the household, usually a woman, report on the behaviors of all household members), the NSAM interviews young males directly, thus reducing the risk of unintentional misclassification.

Men may also unintentionally misclassify themselves as nonfathers if they do not remember, at the time of the interview, their past fertility experiences. Certain design aspects of the NSAM likely reduce this problem. Researchers have shown that the general context in which questions appear affects how respondents answer (Sudman & Bradburn, 1974). This may occur by helping to improve recall of key events. By asking questions about pregnancy immediately following a series of partner-specific questions about sexual and contraceptive behaviors, the survey design may have increased the salience of acts that produced a child and improved men's memory of related events. Previous research on the quality of reports about sexual activity by adolescent females found that respondents in surveys with a focus on sexual and reproductive behaviors reported more sexual activity than respondents in the NLSY, which focuses on employment behaviors (Kahn, Kalsbeek, & Hofferth, 1988). The short interval between birth and the interview in the NSAM also probably reduced the problem of misclassification owing to men not remembering their fertility experiences.

Men also may intentionally misclassify themselves as nonfathers, presumably because of concerns about social desirability. Many surveys ask male-fertility questions as part of a series of questions about payment of child support. Fathers may not provide information about nonresident children because they fear punishment for not paying support (Schaeffer, Seltzer, & Klawitter, 1991), and this could contribute to underreporting births. In contrast, the NSAM asks questions about fertility as part of a series of questions about sexual behavior. This likely reduces concerns about the social desirability associated not only with child support payments but with nonmarital childbearing more generally.

In our analysis, more than one third of teen fathers had one or more reporting inconsistencies across the three waves of the survey. The most common error was reporting a birth in one of the first two survey waves but failing to report the birth in subsequent waves, a phenomenon we refer to as lost children. Although the number of inconsistent reports was significant, they did not have a large effect on our estimated rates of teen fatherhood. In the majority of cases, the difference between the low and high estimates was 2 percentage points or less, and only rarely did the difference exceed 3 percentage points.

Although the overall rates of misreporting do not have a dramatic effect on the overall rates of teen fatherhood, we do find significantly higher rates of misreporting for certain types of fathers. We also find significant differences in the rates of misreporting by race-ethnicity. More than one half of the African American fathers gave inconsistent reports, compared with 26.8% of Whites and 17.5% of Hispanic fathers. These results are consistent with other surveys that find African American men to be much less reliable reporters of information on fertility and sexual activity than White men (Lauritsen & Swicegood, 1997; Mott, 1983). In addition, younger fathers, those who did not live with their first child, and those who were not married to the child's mother were more likely to provide conflicting data, characteristics also associated with underreporting in the validity studies. Most disturbing is the fact that roughly 10% of marital first births and 20% of nonmarital first births went unreported in one or more the subsequent waves.

The differences in the rates of misreporting by child's residence are also noteworthy given that it is these fathers, and their willingness to acknowledge paternity and ability to pay child support, who are often of greatest interest to policymakers. Among fathers coresiding with their child at the first report of birth, only 17% misreported that birth, and none had a lost child. On the other hand, one half of the nonresident fathers inconsistently reported events, with lost children by far the most common problem. The finding that nonresident fathers often lose contact with their children is not surprising in and of itself (see Furstenberg, 1990). What is both surprising and worrisome, however, is how extensive this phenomenon is, given that the vast majority of our lost children are under age 10. This strongly suggests the need to identify nonmarital and nonresident fathers as early as possible if children are to receive adequate financial and emotional support from these men.

Finally, these results indicate that we can obtain much more accurate estimates of fatherhood for certain types of fathers, particularly nonresident and unmarried fathers, by using longitudinal rather than cross-sectional data. If the only alternative is a cross-sectional survey, we must do a better job of collecting paternity information, particularly about fathers' nonresident children.

ACKNOWLEDGMENTS

This chapter was funded by a grant from the Office of Population Affairs, grant FPR 000057-05-1. The authors wish to thank Leighton Ku, Joe Pleck, and Freya Sonenstein for their comments and suggestions on earlier drafts. Any remaining errors are, of course, our own.

APPENDIX: DESCRIPTION OF VARIABLES USED IN LOGISTIC REGRESSION ANALYSIS

Variable	Categories (Comparison Group)[a]	% in Sample[b]
Individual characteristics		
Race	Non-Hispanic Black	17.6
	Hispanic	9.3
	(Non-Hispanic White)	73.0
Region of residence (1988)	Midwest	23.8
	South	36.5
	West	19.8
	(Northeast)	19.9
Urbanicity of residence (1988)	Urban	18.6
	Rural	35.1
	(Suburban)	46.3
Behind in school (1988)[c]	Yes	12.1
	No	87.9
Attended religious services less than once per month at age 14 (1988)	Yes	32.5
	No	67.5
Ever used alcohol before age 16	Yes	39.3
	No	51.5
	Missing	9.3
Ever used marijuana before age 16	Yes	18.7
	No	71.1
	Missing	10.2
Family characteristics		
Education level of most educated parent	(Less than high school)	9.7
	High school	37.3
	Some college	13.3
	College graduate	35.7
	Missing	4.0
Did not live with both biological parents at age 14	Yes	29.6
	No	70.4

(Continued)

Variable	Categories (Comparison Group) [a]	% in Sample [b]
Family received cash assistance (AFDC, food stamps, Social Security) in the last 12 months (1988)	Yes	14.4
	No	83.6
	Missing	2.1
Mother was a teen mother	Yes	31.0
	No	66.1
	Missing	2.9
Rules at home (staying out late, dating, alcohol, etc.) at age 14	Very strict	32.7
	Somewhat strict	54.5
	(Not strict/no rules)	12.8
Annual household income in the last 12 months (1988)	(Less than $10,000)	6.5
	$10,000–$30,000	34.0
	$30,000–$50,000	30.9
	More than $50,000	24.5
	Missing	4.1
Mother's employment while growing up	(Not working)	25.0
	Full-time	46.3
	Part-time	28.2
	Missing	0.6

[a]Categories in parentheses are the comparison groups in the logistic regression. [b]Among males observed until age 20 (N = 1,554). [c]Age minus last grade completed is greater than or equal to 8.

18

Qualitative Insights for Studying Male Fertility

William Marsiglio
University of Florida

Whether measuring aspects of male fertility using standard survey items or exploring men's procreative lives using qualitative, in-depth interviews, researchers face significant methodological challenges. The challenges, stemming in part from the gendered realities of reproductive physiology, vary in form and magnitude with the basic research objectives of survey (demographic) and qualitative (interpretive) methods. For example, precisely documenting male fertility is impossible because men's sexual partners sometimes withhold information about their sexual history (multiple partners near the time of conception) and fertility events (abortion, miscarriage, birth) that may involve the men. Demographers also have long argued that men's self-reported fertility histories are less consistent over time (and thus less reliable) than those of women (Mott, Baker, Haurin, & Marsiglio, 1983; Mott & Gryn, 2001). In addition, social psychologists stress that the complexity of men's subjective experiences surrounding procreation has been inadequately conceptualized and studied (Marsiglio & Hutchinson, 2002).

Obviously, verifiable genetic paternity, legal paternity, and social fatherhood (informal types of caring for or claiming children as one's own) represent different and important ways of capturing men's experiences

303

with children. Researchers, therefore, should provide men opportunities to define their circumstances as clearly and fully as possible, while also minimizing interviewing conditions that might foster intentional or unintentional reporting bias. This latter effort will hinge, in part, on interviewers—particularly those doing qualitative work—recognizing and effectively managing men's strategies for presenting a masculine image that emphasizes control, autonomy, and rationality (Marsiglio, 2004a; Schwalbe & Wolkomir, 2002).

Viewing fertility and fatherhood broadly, I assess survey and qualitative approaches for studying male fertility while underscoring the context and processes of men's varied experiences with procreation and children. I frame my insights, gleaned in part from my selective use of qualitative, in-depth interviews with men, by drawing on phenomenological, interactionist, and life course theoretical perspectives. My broad objectives speak primarily to conceptual and methodological concerns, although substantive issues are addressed also. I seek to show how insights generated from qualitative work can inform survey strategies for studying male fertility experiences. Furthermore, I argue that qualitative research can produce unique insights, significant in their own right, about the subjective experiences related to men's fertility.

More specifically, I begin by identifying and discussing three forms of knowledge men can possess related to their procreative abilities: basic understanding of male reproductive physiology, perceptions of personal potency, and "confirmed" paternity status (Marsiglio & Hutchinson, 2002). I emphasize the latter. Next, I explore, from both a quantitative and qualitative perspective, the merits of developing permutations of two concepts, paternity confidence and fatherhood readiness, to expand and refine the conceptualization and assessment of how men subjectively experience their procreative lives. I highlight men's cognitive orientation toward their experiences while acknowledging the relevance of emotional, symbolic, and social dimensions. Finally, because the social-demographic, cultural, and technological landscapes have changed rapidly in recent decades, I illustrate how these changes affect the context for men's fertility perceptions and behaviors. In particular, I use my stepfather research to emphasize how discussions about measurement and assessment issues should acknowledge the complexity of current demographic patterns (such as shifting family forms) and the dynamic qualities of men's personal lives. By introducing the concept *paternal claiming,* this discussion showcases how individuals negotiate the meaning of relationships and family. I then conclude by noting that any comprehensive assessment of births and infertility must account for the effect on male fertility of new male-oriented technological developments (e.g., infertility treatments and contraceptive methods). Although it is critical to measure and assess the full complement of fertility-related experiences that men may encounter (e.g., sex, contraception, infertility, pregnancy scare, conception, pregnancy, abortion, miscarriage, and birth), I restrict my observations to pregnancies, births, and infertility.

In short, I emphasize here how focusing on men's cognitive orientation, life course circumstances, and romantic-relationship dynamics can enhance the quality of research on men's reported and projected fertility experiences. I also emphasize the value of developing methodologies that foster opportunities to study the processes surrounding men's procreative experiences. Qualitative researchers are ideally suited to explore these experiences. Using multiple methods, researchers will be better equipped to fashion a more compelling story about men's procreative and family lives.

PRIMARY DATA SOURCES

What follows is based, in part, on primary data from a combined sample of 106 men who participated in in-depth interviews for two studies I have conducted during the past 6 years (see Marsiglio, 2004b, and Marsiglio & Hutchinson, 2002, for extensive methods discussions). These participants were involved in either a study of 70 men (69 single, one married [owing to a recruitment error]) exploring the procreative identities (i.e., self-perceptions based on men's perceived ability or inability to create human life) of men aged 16 to 30; or a study of 36 men who were acting as "stepfathers" to their romantic partner's children. Given my selective purposes here, I combine these samples; participants were recruited originally to help develop concepts, not to generate a representative sample. The overall mean age for this pooled sample is 26.5. Of the men in this group, 66 identified themselves as White, 27 were African American (including two biracial), 8 were Hispanic, 2 were Native American, 2 were Native African, and 1 was Asian American. At the time of the interview, 3 participants were still in high school, 4 were high school dropouts, 21 had completed high school but had no college experience, 53 had some college experience, and 25 had graduated from college. Because the eligibility criteria for the first study required men to be single, only 25 of the participants in the combined pool of participants were married, 14 were cohabiting with a partner, and the rest were single.

My research team asked 70 men in the initial study extensive questions regarding their procreative histories. Among these men, 40 had no pregnancy or fertility experience; 15 had partners who had aborted a pregnancy; 8 were involved with a partner currently pregnant with their child; 5 had experienced a partner's miscarriage; and 9 had biological children prior to the interview. Among the 36 men in the stepfather study, 5 had formally adopted their partner's child, and 22 had fathered their own biological child—3 with the birth mother of the stepchild.

I recruited men for the first study using a combination of strategies designed to maximize diversity in participants' procreative life experiences. I contacted men through a local department of motor vehicles office, abortion clinics, a prenatal clinic, a childbirth class, a local employment agency, a homeless shelter, personal contacts, and word of mouth. To be eligible, men had to have dated a woman or been divorced within the previous 3 years. I recruited men in the stepfather study through announcements in a university hospital newsletter, a listserv directed at various university departments, and a local parenting magazine. The research team posted flyers at a variety of sites throughout the community (e.g., community health center, fire station, homeless shelter, and churches), and we recruited several participants through word of mouth. To be included, the men had to describe themselves as being actively involved in the lives of their partner's children, who were younger than age 20 and living with the mother. All men resided in either north central Florida or Jacksonville.

Interviews followed a semistructured interview guide, were audiotaped, and transcribed. They lasted 90 minutes, on average. Participants were paid $20 in the first study and $25 in the second. Most interviews were conducted in university offices, but some were conducted at libraries, in a church, or in the participant's office or home. I personally conducted a total of 42 interviews, 32 for the second study alone. A colleague, two graduate research assistants, and a number of undergraduate students conducted the remaining interviews in the first study, whereas a different research assistant interviewed four stepfathers. Previous analyses with these data were guided by a grounded theory methodology, including the constant comparative method (Strauss & Corbin, 1998). I focused on various aspects of men's social and psychological experiences with either becoming and being aware of their ability to procreate or becoming involved with stepchildren.

COGNITIVE ORIENTATION AND ASSESSING MALE FERTILITY

Assessing male fertility in a broad and nuanced way necessitates that researchers address the contextual and subjective-emotional dimensions of men's procreative lives, including their involvement with pregnancies and births for which they claim full or tentative responsibility. This approach attends to how men frame their views on paternity, social fathering, family, and the "package deals" involving romantic relationships and children.

From an interpretive and qualitative perspective, an important objective in studying male fertility experiences is to better understand the subjective, emotional, and psychosocial dimensions of how men orient themselves toward their ability or inability to procreate. Researchers have explored men's knowledge, attitudes, beliefs, intentions, motivations, emotions, and symbolic meanings related to various experiences within the procreative realm (Jaccobs, 1995; Marsiglio, 1998; Marsiglio & Hutchinson, 2002; W. B. Miller, 1992; Webb & Daniluk, 1999). This domain of research addresses key individual and interpersonal processes not captured by typical demographic fertility variables. I review some of these dimensions here.

Procreative Consciousness

Some of my work (Marsiglio & Hutchinson, 2002) focuses on how young men become aware of their presumed ability to procreate and how men express aspects of this knowledge in their everyday lives. Informing my framework is Schutz's (1970a, 1970b) phenomenological approach to consciousness, with its emphasis on understanding how cognitive "relevance structures" and "stocks of knowledge" guide individuals' information processing. Similarly, the symbolic interactionist and life course perspectives provide useful insights. The former highlights processes by which individuals construct, negotiate, and assign meanings to particular situations, events, acts, others, and themselves. Social interaction is typically viewed as the basis from which these definitions spring. Because these meanings are socially constructed, men's procreative identities are often affected by their relationships. The life course perspective highlights the sequence of significant life events related to marriage, childbearing or infertility, education, and work while noting cultural expectations about the "appropriateness" and consequences of particular events and their sequence. Together, the two perspectives accentuate the merits of studying how some men experience turning points that fundamentally alter their procreative identity (Strauss, 1969). From a theoretical and programmatic perspective, much can be gained by developing a more nuanced conceptual and empirical understanding of how men develop, activate, and express their procreative consciousness.

Simply put, procreative consciousness is a broad and multilayered concept that includes the varied cognitive and emotional expressions of awareness that men experience about their ability to procreate, including perceptions of future children. Elsewhere I have discussed the significance of differentiating between how men's procreative consciousness is expressed in specific situations versus in a more global, enduring way (Marsiglio, 1998; Marsiglio & Hutchinson, 2002). Similarly, I distinguish between a consciousness molded by men's interactions with a romantic partner and one stemming from individual reflection. An important form of procreative consciousness—with significant program relevance—addresses the varied responsibilities (defined in multiple ways) associated with the ability to create human life.

Forms of Procreative Knowledge

An important subjective aspect of procreative consciousness includes three forms of knowledge: a basic understanding of male reproductive physiology, perceptions of personal potency, and confirmed paternity status.

Understanding Male Reproductive Physiology. This type of knowledge refers to men's basic understanding of male reproductive physiology and their presumed ability to procreate given the "right" set of circumstances. My research revealed that young men typically develop this knowledge sometime between ages 12 and 15, and they gain this understanding primarily from sex education and discussions with parents and friends (Marsiglio & Hutchinson, 2002). Although it is seldom a remarkable transition for young men, some suggest that it significantly affected how they thought of themselves, with some indicating that it scared them.

Personal Potency Perceptions. A second, and related, form of knowledge involves men's view of their own level of potency. Although many men simply take it for granted that they are capable of impregnating someone without having a clear sense of how potent they are, others may have a more decisive view that they are either extra potent, below average, or infertile—views that are subject to change based on personal experiences. This latter point is illustrated by two divorced men, who discussed how they came to believe that they were incapable of impregnating a woman owing to several years of unprotected intercourse with their former wives. In both cases, this belief led them to be nonchalant about using contraceptives in their most recent committed sexual relationships, a decision that presumably led to their partners becoming pregnant. One of these men, 27-year-old Jack, describes his current partner as having helped reinforce his self-perceived infertility by making it "real easy not to wrap up [use condoms]. She was like maybe you need to go to a doctor and get checked out. . . . I was embarrassed to go down and get something like that done. It's hard to think that something's wrong with ya, but then a couple of weeks after that she was pregnant."

Men's procreative self-knowledge and views of their fecundity, including their emotional reactions to it, become increasingly important to consider in light of what appears to be a large and growing proportion of men experiencing individual, partner, or couple-based infertility (Pasch & Christensen, 2000; Pressinger & Sinclair, 1998). More should be learned about what types of men experience these conditions and what it means to them

(Greil, 1997). No doubt it will be challenging to obtain high-quality survey data from a representative national sample of men about their struggles with male infertility, given the stigma associated with it and some men's penchant for presenting a masculine image during interviews (Mason, 1993; Schwalbe & Wolkomir, 2002). However, the issue's significance, as well as the paucity of social-science data on male infertility (Greil, 1997; Marsiglio & Hinojosa, 2004), warrants gathering survey data that would provide a social demographic portrait of those who have experienced it. It may even be possible to measure men's psychosocial reactions to their infertility (and female or couple-based infertility) using survey items. Webb and Daniluk's (1999) in-depth interviews with six men reveal that men have valuable things to say. These men talk about what infertility has meant to them and how they have dealt with it. This select sample of White men expressed "intense feelings of grief and loss, powerlessness and lack of control, inadequacy, isolation, and betrayal in response to being unable to father a child" (p. 20).

"Confirmed" Paternity Status.   Men also often acquire knowledge of their procreative status by communicating with one or more of their partners or, increasingly, through DNA testing. Thus, paternity confirmation defined in a loose sense can be based on either subjective or objective information. From an interactionist perspective emphasizing subjective perceptions, the process of having paternity "confirmed," vis–à–vis communication with a partner, is based on an individual's claim, which may or may not be factual. Moreover, the communication may or may not involve active negotiation. Prior to or after a birth, most partners agree, without dispute, that the man is the genetic father. Simply put, from the man's perspective, he is likely to assume he is the father if he trusts that he is the only eligible progenitor. Sometimes, though, an explicit negotiation takes place in which the man challenges the woman's claim, or vice versa. Challenges can range from mild questioning or doubting to aggressive denial. Ultimately, the evolution and implications of such challenges can vary considerably. The process can be complicated if an individual seeks or threatens to seek objective confirmation in the form of DNA testing. My research (see also Waller, 2002) indicates that uncontested understandings and explicit discussions are critical to how men launch their relationships with children, and manage their involvement with the mothers of the children.

These discussions sometimes are prompted and influenced by family members who have a vested interest in establishing or refuting a man's paternity. Ed, a 22-year-old, self-proclaimed father of five with three different mothers, provides an example of how a mother can play a prominent role in shaping her son's thinking about his paternity. When asked about his degree of confidence that the children were in fact his biological children, he shared how his mother has played a decisive role in determining his paternity status:

> When it's about a baby, the first thing I say is take it [to] my mamma's . . . cuz my mamma, she'll know . . . like this one girl tried to say I, she [made] my baby, my mamma looked at her, looked at the baby, and told her, "Girl, if you don't get up out my house bout this my damn son child, this ain't my son child" . . . My mama, she look at the nose, the eyes, and the ears, and sometimes she look at the set of teeth because she, I don't know what is, but she be knowing. She know all along though.

Here, we see how an informal family ritual provides this young man a boost of confidence in determining his paternity status in specific cases. Although presumably rare, this scenario highlights the fluid and negotiated nature of the paternity confirmation process. Understanding the informal practices by which a man realizes his degree of paternity confidence is important because they are embedded within a larger social and community context that can influence a man's emotional and legal connections to a child (Furstenberg, 1995b; M. Sullivan, 1989).

Prior to the accessibility of DNA testing, men had limited practical options for refuting a partner's paternity claim, aside from relying on visible postbirth evidence (e.g., racial discrepancies). Today, DNA technology has reshaped those parameters and enabled the government to assume a more prominent role in establishing legal paternity (Anderlik & Rothstein, 2002; Howe, 1993; Myricks, 2003; Wattenberg, 1993).

Unfortunately, demographers' standardized, closed-ended questions asking men to report on the children they have had are not well-suited to sorting out the rich complexities associated with men's multifaceted, and sometimes muddled, interpretations of their fertility history. Men's certainty, for example, may vary on whether they are the biological fathers of particular children. They can also acknowledge particular children as theirs in various ways. In a survey format, men may claim to have two children, but be convinced that only one is their biological child. Without exploring men's certainty about their paternity, and without clarifying aspects of whether and how they acknowledge children as theirs, demographic surveys may miss any differential perception of those children. Aside from their legal responsibilities, men's subjective willingness to claim children as their own may have subtle and not so subtle consequences for how they treat those children (e.g., abuse, financial support, nurturance, protection). Although most of the men in my research apparently felt confident that their current or former partner's child was theirs, this is not always the case. I did not systematically ask all participants about their degree of confidence in their paternity, but the confusion about paternity that sometimes emerges is illustrated by 20-year-old Reginald:

> I feel like it [child] ain't, and sometimes then, I don't know why. But, then, it show little mannerisms, and a little of my charisma sometimes, as young as it is, but maybe it just might be that the baby is bein' like that, so it might not be my mannerisms. . . . She [partner] say if I want to take a blood test, take it, but she might be usin' reverse psychology on me.

Later in this interview, Reginald admitted that he would probably feel closer to this child if he knew for sure that he was the biological father.

The nuances of paternity confidence are exemplified further by the unusual set of circumstances Allen faced with two children. This 27-year-old high school dropout presumed he was the biological father to a child produced in a one-night stand with a woman who was engaged to someone else—Norman—at the time. While pregnant, the woman told Allen that she was pregnant with his child and they agreed to secrecy, allowing Norman to marry her and claim the child as his. Allen, known as a friend of the family by the child, Donny, chose not to have a DNA test because he did not want to disrupt Donny's son–father relationship with Norman—a relationship that has persisted even though Norman and Donny's mother are now divorced. Asked how he knew that Donny was his biological son when he met the 5-year-old boy for the first time, Allen says, "[B]ecause, I think when you look into your own eyes and you can tell, you know, that's my biological son." Even though Allen became romantically involved temporarily with Donny's mother after she and Norman divorced, Allen has never sought to claim Donny as his child in a fully public way. However, Allen's mother and another girlfriend, Barbara, are aware of his predicament. With Barbara, Allen also chose to assume responsibility for her child, who, he was pretty sure initially, was not his, but whom he hoped was his child:

> I gave him his first bath like dads do in the hospital. . . . I knew that he might not be [mine], but I looked at him and swore that he was because he had those toes, little crooked toes, like everyone in my family has. . . . He looked like a little Sicilian baby, like I remember my brothers and sisters looking. . . . And I said "Man he's mine." . . . The possibility was still there that it wasn't. I didn't, at that point, even see a reason to do a DNA test . . . you know, look at him.

A few months after the child's birth, Barbara convinced Allen to take a paternity test. Allen reluctantly obliged. Even though the DNA test confirmed that he was not the child's genetic father, he asserted that he wanted to treat the child as though he were his son. He downplayed the praise he received from Barbara's family for claiming her son as his: "It ain't about being a big man, it's I love him, and that's the bottom line. . . . It doesn't matter to me that he is somebody's else's. Every baby deserves a father. . . . I've got a choice to do what I'm gonna do, and I did it out of pure love."

Although Reginald's and Allen's stories alert us to the complexity of how men can think about their paternity status, it is difficult to assess the value of developing paternity confidence as a descriptive or theoretical concept. Researchers have yet to determine the scope and demographic portrait of men's paternity uncertainty, measure the ways paternity confidence is expressed, or consider the extent to and in which ways paternity confidence affects men's relationships with their children.

However, various trends have coalesced in recent years to raise this concept's visibility and potential utility. Some scholars have considered paternity confidence in the context of different types of societies (Betzig, 1993; Cronin & Curry, 2000; Gaulin & Schlegel, 1980; see also Baker, 1996). Its value is also heightened given recent debates in medical ethics (Lucassen & Parker, 2001) and family law (Anderlik & Rothstein, 2002; Myricks, 2003) regarding misattributed paternity. Paternity confidence is relevant to recent U.S. federal welfare policy promoting genetic testing for the purpose of establishing paternity for nonmarital children and collecting child support. Paternity testing has become a burgeoning business enterprise. The United States spent $31.5 million on laboratory testing for paternity in 1998 (Anderlik & Rothstein, 2002), and parentage cases reported by accredited laboratories housed primarily in the United States increased more than fourfold, from 77,000 in 1988 to 340,798 in 2002 (American Association of Blood Banks, 2002). Grassroots organizations in numerous states have emerged to challenge false paternity claims using legal and advertising strategies. In addition, the media appear to be expanding coverage of disputed paternity cases (Andrlik & Rothstein, 2002; Cohen, 1997; DeCloet, 1998; Schneider & McLean, 2000). As a consequence, the media may be affecting public awareness by widely disseminating estimates of the relatively large proportion of children whose supposed fathers may have been duped into thinking they are the biological fathers (see Birks, 2002; Pearson, 2003). Although firm evidence is lacking, some suggest that misattributed paternity may be higher among lower income populations, with estimates ranging widely from 1% to 30% of specific population groups, with most in the range of between 2% and 5% (Baker, 1996; McDonald, 1999; Sykes & Irven, 2000). Over time, growing numbers of men, as well as social service and legal professionals working with families, are likely to become more sensitive to the prospects of false paternity claims in situations involving an unplanned pregnancy and a separation or divorce.

Both survey and qualitative researchers can engage in pilot research to explore the utility of paternity confidence. For example, national or regional surveys might include items, using a scaled set of responses, that would ask men to indicate how much confidence they have that specific children are related to them biologically. Such an item could prove useful because paternity confidence issues may contribute to the vexing problem documented in longitudinal survey data in which men report having a certain number of biological children during one interview, then report a lower number in a subsequent wave of data collection (Mott & Gryn, 2001). Although some of this misreporting is likely owing to men's inclination to not acknowledge children born to a previous romantic partner, especially when the child lives elsewhere, the reporting error may also be influenced by men's evolving interpretation of and response to their degree of confidence that particular children are their biological offspring. If data on the subjective assessment of paternity confidence were collected from representative samples, demographers could document how men's reports of paternity uncertainty correlated with social demographic and partner-relationship patterns. Analyses of this sort would augment efforts to develop a demographic profile of male fertility records that have been deemed "low confidence" (Mott & Gryn, 2001; see also chap. 16, this volume). Assigning a "confidence level" to paternity claims is based on the consistency of cross-linked data elements in multiple waves of survey data. Another data element that could be added to the mix, then, is men's self-reports of how confident they are that a particular child is theirs.

Qualitative researchers can bring their expertise to this question by asking men to discuss in depth the level of confidence they have that they are the biological father and how varying degrees of uncertainty make them feel. Where uncertainty is an issue, interviews could explore how it has been negotiated or "resolved" over time. In addition, interviewers could explore how particular circumstances or understandings affect men's approach to using objective information from the new DNA technologies to resolve paternity uncertainty.

In light of men's inclination to project a masculine self in an interview, survey and qualitative interviewers should consider using gender-sensitive strategies to foster candid responses when asking about paternity confidence and other issues that may implicate men's masculine identity. They might, for instance, preface their question about paternity confidence with an acknowledgment that other men have voiced uncertainty about whether children are their own. Sequencing comments and questions in this fashion can provide men with a safer space to share their vulnerable feelings about having a partner they believe cheated on them. In addition, my previous work suggests that when asked, slightly more than one third of young men aged 16 to 30 state a preference for a male interviewer, but most indicate their answers would not be altered in any significant way if they were interviewed by a woman (Marsiglio & Hutchinson, 2002). Young men tend to be receptive to experienced and attentive interviewers, irrespective of the interviewer's gender. Those interested in doing qualitative research in this area might recruit volunteers from genetic-testing services, including men with positive or negative results, and ask them to talk about their perceptions and feelings concerning their paternity status prior to and after the test.

A secondary issue related to paternity confidence involves men's certainty that they have *not* fathered children in past relationships, particularly fleeting ones. In other words, paternity confidence could be conceptualized as applying not only to children known to men but to potential children of whose existence men have no knowledge. Though perhaps of marginal significance, perceptions about procreative uncertainty for having fathered unknown children may influence some men's contraceptive practices in current relationships in which having a child is unintended, or moderate men's investment in children whom they believe to be theirs.

FATHERHOOD READINESS: BRIDGING FERTILITY CONCEPTS AND FATHERING

Fatherhood readiness (Marsiglio & Hutchinson, 2002) can be viewed as a conceptual bridge for studying subjective aspects of male fertility and fathering. Currently, the fertility field uses fertility intention (number of children desired) and fertility intendedness (whether a particular child was "planned" when pregnancy occurred). Thus, an implicit assumption of planned fertility is that actual fertility is less than fertility intention. In this scenario of planned fertility, fatherhood readiness represents the mediating concept, in that fertility intentions lead to fertility only in the context of a readiness for fatherhood. It captures the degree to which men feel prepared at a particular point in time to assume the varied responsibilities they associate with being a father. Some feel extremely ready, others have a muddled view, and others perceive themselves as decidedly unready.

Questions about readiness can be asked prior to a pregnancy, during a pregnancy, or after a child has been born. Of course, the meaning of the survey or qualitative data gathered at different points will be open to various interpretations, but it should help to expand the conceptualization and measurement of key concepts related to fertility and pregnancy intentions (Bachrach & Newcomer, 1999; Luker, 1999; L. S. Peterson & Mosher, 1999; Santelli et al., 2003).

My qualitative research highlights several prominent themes related to how men determine and express their sense of readiness. I mention two here. First, men's *degree and form of collaboration* highlights the extent to which and how men jointly construct their sense of readiness by discussing key issues with someone else (e.g., partner, parent, friend). Although men often appear to construct their views by themselves, some incorporate others into the process. Of particular importance are situations in which men's discussions with their partners help them clarify their sense of readiness.

Second, men's *focus of attention* can be on either themselves, the potential child, their partner, or some combination. In a related vein, men are free to attend to certain types of substantive issues, such as potential loss of leisure time, financial responsibilities, and emotional and psychological well-being. Insights about how men use these and other mechanisms to frame their views about becoming a father will sharpen understanding about the subjective context within which men approach fertility issues.

Terrance, a 25-year-old man who reported being poor, illustrates how perceptions about male fertility and fathering are related. Reflecting on his readiness to become a father, Terrance says:

[When] I was younger I didn't, definitely didn't, want to have one [a child], and it was like definitely no possibilities of me being able to take care of one, or supporting one, or teaching one, a baby, anything. But now I'm a little older, and I think that if I could support one, now would be, like 25 to 30 would be an excellent time to have, excellent time to have a kid. But only if I would, if I could give them anything I wanted to. If I could give my kid whatever I chose to give him, without a problem. If I saw something and I was like, "All right, I want you to have this," I could get it for him. I don't want to have one until I can definitely do that.

For Terrance, the father role of breadwinner is paramount to his sense of being ready to produce and rear a child. His perception of readiness, which he appears to have constructed on his own, is anchored in his feelings toward his prospective child's well-being.

CAPTURING STEPFATHERS' FAMILY-BUILDING EXPERIENCES

Assessing aspects of male fertility is particularly complicated in a society where family formation, family interaction, and dissolution patterns deviate from a traditional nuclear-family model. I highlight several key issues involving stepfathers while showing how subjective dimensions to creating "family" are negotiated with reference to genetic, social, and legal aspects of paternity and social fatherhood.

Stepfather Fertility Perceptions

As more men form relationships with women who have given birth to another man's child, understanding the relationship between single men and stepfathers' parental and fertility motivations takes on greater importance. The life course and symbolic interactionist traditions provide a valuable lens to consider male fertility within a context that emphasizes stepfathers' experiences. Although relatively little is known about stepfathers' fertility motivations (Stewart, 2002), my qualitative work reveals men's wide-ranging perceptions (Marsiglio, 2004b).

For stepfathers who are not fathers, their motivations to have biological children may be similar to first-time fathers. Meanwhile, stepfathers with or without biological children may feel that having a new child with their partner who is already a mother may help integrate them into and expand their stepfamily. In other words, having a child can provide a way to negotiate and reconfigure the parameters of their family. Alternatively, some men report that loving a stepchild satisfies their paternal desires and that they are reluctant to have a biological child because they fear that doing so would limit what they could do with and for their stepchild.

Carl's situation illustrates how some stepfathers think about having children and define their stepfamily. Having no biological children of his own, Carl describes his powerful feelings for his 8-year-old stepchild, Vicky: "I wanted a child biologically, but now it just seems that there's no need for it because I have everything I want and could ever possibly imagine having in a nonbiological child. I don't see Vicky as anything but my child." Asked if he wants to go through a pregnancy with his wife, Carl responds, "We've talked on and off about it. The main reason for us not doing anything at this point is just—is almost purely a financial—just because having an extra child would not allow us to do some of the things that we do for Vicky now—private school and some of the shopping and things like that." Carl has even resisted his wife's gesture to have a child with him if he wanted one.

In contrast, 26-year-old Alan, a stepfather to a 7-year-old boy, Danny, feels comfortable around the boy, but is eager to have his own child. As he says:

> I don't have any kids, and I wasn't really trying to have no kids 'cause I'm still young. I still got about a lot to learn; a lot to live. And since we've been together she's been pregnant, but she lost the baby, so I'm still trying. I'm married so I'm tryin' to have a kid—it's hard. Real hard. And she say, she like to say, 'cause I always be tellin' her you know, you got to get pregnant but I want a little girl. That's what I really want. Well you don't love Danny. Yeah I love Danny. But I also want something I made.

For Alan, biological paternity is firmly rooted in his "wide-awake" consciousness and in some ways may be activated often because of his daily interactions with Danny.

Carl's and Alan's comments highlight the challenge of studying complex fertility intentions and behavior in stepfamilies. Recent theoretical discussions coupled with survey data analyses raise issues about the relative symbolic and practical value of children and stepchildren (Stewart, 2002) and possible preferences for investing more in genetic offspring based on a biosocial model of fertility (K. G. Anderson, 2000). One key assumption in this line of thought is that, all things being equal, stepchildren are not viewed as full substitutes for having biological offspring. Anderson also suggests that, consistent with his findings from the Panel Study of Income Dynamics, "some men become stepfathers to procure mates and fertility benefits that they would otherwise have been unlikely to obtain," (p. 307) and these men are more likely to be "lowly ranked" in the mating market due to lower human capital.

Stewart's (2002) analysis, using two waves of data from the National Survey of Families and Households (1987–1988; 1992–1994), suggests that spouses think about each other's children when they develop their own fertility intentions. She finds that "children of one's spouse influence intentions to the same degree as one's own previous biological children (in the case of men, more so)" (p. 193). In addition, the value of stepchildren in predicting fertility intentions is moderated by family structure, such that, "intentions remain high until each partner has had a biological child" (p. 193). At the same time, "men's previous biological children did not affect their intentions of having a child" (p. 193).

Although Anderson's and Stewart's survey findings begin to address key issues associated with changing family formation patterns, detailed comments from men such as Carl and Alan illustrate how the complete story about stepfather fertility requires a more refined qualitative analysis of stepfathers' perceptions about family relationships, particularly the meaning of stepchildren and biological children. Consistent with Stewart's finding, Carl, middle class and college educated, takes his partner's child into account when thinking about having children. But, despite acknowledging his previous desire to become a biological father, Carl appears willing to forgo this status now because, as he observes, being a stepfather provides "[me with] everything I want and could ever possibly imagine." For some men, then, stepchildren represent a desirable alternative to biological fathering. Perhaps when stepfathers relate well to their stepchildren, they may have less incentive to procreate. Alternatively, in some stepfamilies with high-quality stepfather–stepchild relationships, men (and their partners) may experience less role strain and feel more at ease with having a child together. Unlike Carl, Alan did not see his stepchild as a replacement for his own prospective child, and his involvement with the stepchild may have intensified his desire to become a biological father. Given his criminal background, low education, and spotty work history, Alan's profile is consistent with Anderson's thesis that lower ranking men are more willing to marry a woman who has had another man's child. Alan's willingness to do so, may, in the long run, afford him the opportunity to have his own child, though he admittedly believes his wife is less enthralled with the idea.

Questions about stepfather fertility can also be informed by research showing that stepfathers who have children of their own, compared with those who do not, "feel more companionship with their stepchildren, experience more intimate stepfather–stepchild interactions, are more involved with their stepchildren's friends, feel fewer negative feelings about stepchildren, and have fewer desires to escape" (Ganong & Coleman, 1994, p. 83). In addition, an earlier analysis of national data found that stepfathers who lived with both stepchildren and biological children, compared with their counterparts who lived only with stepchildren, were more likely to report perceptions consistent with having a fatherlike identity (Marsiglio, 1995). Clearly, there is much to learn about how various relationship and stepfamily processes affect the way men form and alter their fertility intentions once they get involved in a stepfamily. Future research should focus on differentiating stepfathers' views on social fathering and biological paternity while exploring the extent to which they are intertwined and expressed through their fertility experiences within stepfamilies.

Claiming Stepchildren

Although male fertility assumes a biological link between men and their offspring, a more nuanced discussion of paternity and fathering calls for a broader treatment of men's relationships to and responsibilities for children. Toward this end, I recently used a sample of stepfathers to develop a detailed conceptual analysis of a state of mind and relationship orientation that I label *paternal claiming* (Marsiglio, 2004c). By focusing on how a man expresses his readiness to nurture, provide for, protect, and view a child as though the child were his own, paternal claiming includes emotional, psychological, practical, and often symbolic aspects. Although paternal claiming for biological fathers is closely tied to procreative knowledge and paternity confidence as described previously, it extends beyond those ways of "knowing" because it implies men's willingness to invest some combination of time, energy, resources, and emotions into their relationship with their child. In some ways, it may also be affected by men's fatherhood readiness, and provide insights relevant to what has been loosely defined as social fathering by men romantically involved with a woman who has had a child with another man.

Obviously, knowledge of genetic paternity compels most men to engage in some form of paternal claiming, but other interpersonal and familial processes can lead men to claim other men's children as their own, too. Much can be learned by focusing on how stepfathers develop and express paternal claiming and act as social, sometimes legal, fathers to children who are not their biological offspring.

My previous theoretical work generated 10 properties clarifying the way some stepfathers orient toward stepchildren as their own (Marsiglio,

2004c). It also suggested several conditions that may foster this orientation. Three interrelated properties among the 10 are of particular interest when advocating for an integrated approach to improve contemporary assessments of male fertility and fathering. They are degree of identity conviction, paternal-role range, and solo-shared identity.

In my research, men were likely to express, on their own and in response to my questions, the extent to which and how they fit into their stepchildren's lives. They often relied on a paternal or quasi-paternal frame of reference as they described their connections with stepchildren both in general terms and in more practical terms involving money, discipline, protection, guidance, child care, and affection. Some of their stories included implicit references to their desires to develop and sustain a familial sense of "we-ness." Vern, a father of three and stepfather to two, simplifies his everyday reality in a manner not uncommon for other stepfathers: "We [Vern and his wife] have since dropped that little fiction of I have three and she has two. We have five children and we just kind of treat it that way." Herman, speaking of his expectation that his stepchildren would be well-behaved, reasons, "maybe they didn't come from my loins, but now they belong to me, so I expect the same behavior from them that I put forth." Although these expressions of paternal claiming are not representations of male fertility per se, they do represent important opportunities for men to commit to and invest in children within the context of the men's romantic relationships. In some instances, this type of paternal claiming is experienced as a substitute for male procreation and biological fatherhood.

Degree of Identity Conviction.   Among stepfathers in particular, men differ in how fully they embrace a child as theirs. The depth of men's convictions may be expressed in terms of them feeling only partially like a father or perhaps having an intermediate level of conviction. Some stepfathers express a deep, unconditional commitment to their stepchildren and see them as their own, whereas others have much weaker convictions.

What accounts for men's varying perceptions? Some may be affected by how they feel about specific roles (e.g., disciplinarian, provider, legal guardian) or a stepchild's physical proximity to them at a given point in time, including whether their stepchild is presently residing with them. Stepfathers involved with stepchildren who split much of their time between the biological father's and birth mother's home may have a much more heightened sense of "claiming" a stepchild when the child is currently under their roof, and subject to their rules and financial circumstances. Robby, referring to his stepchildren, says: "To me, they are mine, when they're with me they are mine. So I, I treat them just like I would my own daughter, buying them things and whatever." This type of sentiment reflects the potentially fluid nature of men's perceptions. Comments like this should also inspire survey researchers to consider how they might augment their household roster questions to address in a more substantive manner stepfathers' perceptions about their stepchildren and their living circumstances.

Paternal Role Range. Men's degree of conviction for claiming a step-child or biological child may depend on which stepfather-father roles are in question. Consequently, assessing men's perceptions about the range of ways they can experience a sense of claiming may be valuable. Whereas some men may feel like fathers because they help children dress, pack their lunches, read bedtime stories, or supervise their schoolwork, men may not be comfortable disciplining children or providing for them financially if they are not their own biological offspring. For example, Tim is a 31-year-old father of two preschool boys whose mother has physical custody of them while he lives with his fiancée and her two youngest daughters, ages 2 and 3. The girls call Tim "daddy," and he admits to feeling like and acting like a father to them: He changes diapers, dresses them, feeds them, and disciplines them as though they were his own children. However, Tim is reluctant to assume official financial responsibility for the girls because it would terminate the biological father's child support obligations. He is also worried because he is not yet married to their mother. Although Tim has come to see himself as a father to these two girls, his conviction is only partial because he is still contemplating whether it makes sense to take on the financial role completely.

Solo or Shared Father Identity. An intriguing property of claiming a stepchild involves whether a man believes he is solely responsible for a stepchild or shares a paternal status with the biological father. Similarly, a biological father may or may not believe a stepfather shares a paternal status with him. When the biological father is not involved with the child or is involved only minimally, a stepfather will tend to have more leeway asserting a strong paternal claim. A stepfather, however, can still claim a child symbolically as "his" even if the father is actively involved. Eddie, age 35, found himself in this situation with his 8-year-old stepdaughter:

> Sometimes I feel like I'm on the outside looking in because—sometimes I wish she was mine. I guess because we're just that close . . . in my heart, I feel like I'm her father. . . . I know in reality, I'm not, but I'm going to give her all the benefit that a father should. I'm going to make sure she gets those benefits. Even though her dad is giving them to her, she is given a little extra and I figure that extra go a long way.

Recognizing that his stepdaughter is not really his, and that her father is there for her, providing her with benefits, Eddie nevertheless feels like a father who can supplement the biological father's contributions. The positive consequences of this shared father identity for the child are likely to be significant if the biological father is active and the stepfather respects the father's place in the child's life while simultaneously making a concerted effort to help the child in a fatherly way (White & Gilbreth, 2001).

Some stepfathers even make it easier for biological fathers to maintain contact and a positive relationship with their children. Using both overt and subtle means, stepfathers can act as allies to the fathers (Marsiglio, 2004b; Marsiglio & Hinojosa, 2004). How and why men construct this role is likely to influence and be affected in complex ways by men's orientation toward claiming stepchildren as their own.

Thus, some of the stepfathers, such as Eddie, construct their own understanding of "family" by assuming that it is fine for children to have two fathers. Terry, for example, was open to helping his now 9-year-old stepson, Zack, recognize a few years ago that it was okay to have two dads—even though he despised the biological father's lifestyle and approach to fathering. Terry, with his wife by his side, recalls telling Zack:

> "Look, it's okay to have two dads. You have a couple sets of grandparents and whatever. It's okay to have two different fathers. I'm the one that's here with you all the time and he's the one up there. If he gets more involved in your life, then great! If he doesn't, nothing changes. I'm still here. I'm the one that's going to be here every day." So I said, "don't be afraid to call me whatever you want to call me."

For Terry and his wife, the notion of Zack having two dads was rather mundane because it reflected many people's everyday reality. Not all stepfathers share this sentiment, however. Some want much clearer lines drawn between the biological father and stepfather statuses.

By emphasizing properties such as degree of identity conviction, paternal-role range, and solo or shared identity, survey and qualitative researchers can help capture men's diverse experiences in claiming children. Information about these properties can also reveal which men are involved with stepchildren but do not embrace their stepfather identity as fully. Providing biological fathers and stepfathers opportunities to define their relationships with their children in greater detail is consistent with the increasingly complex and fluid nature of men's family relationships.

In a related vein, the varied and dynamic aspects of relationship formation and family household structures (Cherlin, 1990) offer researchers ample opportunities to study the intersection between the demographic and social psychological aspects of men's fertility. For example, men increasingly are having children with multiple partners, both within committed unions and outside them. Men who have opportunities to develop coparenting roles with different women may have different experiences from men who restrict their fertility to one woman. Researchers should consider ways to gather data that will enable them to answer the question, How do men manage their fertility decision making and fathering when faced with this type of life course trajectory?

In addition, men who forge new romantic relationships after they have fathered a child with someone else often become involved with a woman who is in the twilight of her reproductive years or has already given birth. The family context for fertility decision making in this situation may be quite different from that among partners in which neither has had a child. How, then, do fertility and parenting experiences with previous partners (for both men and women) influence men's motivations for future fertility with their current partner? How are men's fertility intentions affected when they experience stepfatherhood first, then leave that relationship and have an opportunity to become a biological father with someone else? Framing fertility questions such that men can answer them directly while linking them to their involvement in particular relationship trajectories is important to advancing research.

MALE FERTILITY AND NEW TECHNOLOGIES

As scholars consider ways to improve research on male fertility, they should recognize the influence that new technologies will likely have on men's fertility experiences. For example, because delayed childbearing has become more prevalent in recent decades (Hewlett, 2002), questions focusing on men's perception of and involvement with assisted reproductive technologies (ARTs) are timely. As noted earlier, some research has explored men's experiences with ARTs, but little is known about how men deal with these forms of reproduction. Techniques that depend on donor semen are of particular interest because they raise issues for men about their sense of adequacy, concerns that may be related to or confounded by perceptions of sexual dysfunction. Research that generates a deeper understanding of men's individual concerns about ARTs and their interactions with their partner can offer fertility specialists and staff useful insights for assisting couples cope with their stressful attempts to address infertility. This research will likely require recruitment strategies that target specific populations; as such, national surveys may be unsuitable for collecting these data. However, large-scale surveys that use a nonhousehold sampling frame and qualitative projects can contribute to a better understanding of men's concerns and reactions to the diagnosis of infertility and subsequent treatments.

To reiterate an earlier point, because DNA technologies offer a more objective means to establish paternity, they will continue to alter the social and cultural landscape for how men perceive procreation. Using survey and qualitative methods to explore men's experiences with and perceptions about this technique could generate unique insights about the extent to which this technology has affected men's lives. Although most men are currently unaffected by it, I suspect that men increasingly will take note of the DNA-testing procedure as it becomes less expensive and unfamiliar.

In the area of contraception, recent advances in surgical techniques for vasectomy (Waites, 1993) that improve its reversibility are likely to alter men's experiences as well. Typically, men and their partners have perceived vasectomy to be a permanent form of birth control. As new technologies improve the reversibility of the procedure, however, vasectomies can provide an alternative temporary birth control strategy. Readily reversible vasectomies will allow men to have sex more freely without the fear of impregnating their partner, while being more confident that they can regain their procreative abilities should they choose to pursue that option with their current or future partner. Survey and qualitative researchers should therefore ask men to share their perceptions about vasectomy and their reasons for using or not using it. In particular, researchers can consider how using it affects men's procreative consciousness.

CONCLUSION

As scholars consider ways to improve the measurement and assessment of male fertility and fatherhood, they should be mindful of the emerging research questions arising from changes in family demography and technology. These wide-ranging questions raise important conceptual issues, implicating both social demographic and social psychological approaches. Efforts to develop a more nuanced understanding of male fertility and fatherhood will be most productive if they are guided by theoretical traditions sensitive to the interrelated conditions affecting men's perceptions of their fertility.

Theoretically grounded perspectives can showcase how male-fertility research can be connected to research on fathering and the meaning of children, both living and imaginary, in men's lives. Men's complex and multilayered views on fertility, and their orientation toward family life, provide powerful conceptual tools to frame the study of male fertility. This approach accentuates the meaning and context associated with the choices men make in reporting, describing, and interpreting their fertility-related experiences.

Survey researchers can experiment with strategies to capture more accurately men's diverse and potentially fluid fertility experiences and family relationships. Survey questions can be crafted to develop a broader and more refined sense of men's experiences with paternity confidence, fatherhood readiness, and paternal claiming. Questions should explore various aspects of men's "knowing" (most important, perceptions of personal potency, degree of paternity confidence, and methods for confirming paternity status) and the way fathers and stepfathers approach their conviction toward fatherhood, the range of their paternal roles, and their experience with a solo or shared father identity. Meanwhile, qualitative researchers should be aware of these concepts when assessing how men initially develop their identities as persons (presumably) capable of creating human life, then negotiate those identities once they have children or choose not to have them, navigate stepfamily life, or struggle to make sense of their own or their partner's infertility.

Ideally, future data collection should incorporate multimethod strategies that allow interpretive researchers to augment demographic detail about men's fertility. Conducting qualitative interviews with a subset of respondents in national surveys is one obvious way to achieve this diversity. Survey researchers can help document the pervasiveness of men's subjective experiences while profiling the individual and family characteristics associated with those experiences. Theoretically informed survey and qualitative strategies can each contribute to a broader, more refined understanding of men's subjective experiences of procreation.

19

Taking Stock: Do Surveys of Men's Fertility Deliver?

Christine Bachrach
*National Institute of Child Health
and Human Development*

In any discussion about improving measurement, it is important to begin with basic questions. What exactly are we trying to measure, and why? In the case of male fertility, the answers are somewhat ambiguous. This chapter explores possible answers to these questions and examines whether the recent surveys that have attempted to measure men's fertility have provided useful information.

What does it mean to measure men's fertility? Demographers use the term *fertility* to refer to the rate at which births occur in a population, usually either an entire population or a population of reproductive-age women. For an individual woman, fertility refers to the number of babies she has ever produced. Male fertility, by analogy, is the number of a man's biological offspring. By this definition, a man experiences fertility when he becomes a biological father. Male fertility is not the same as a man's ability to cause pregnancy, nor is it equivalent to becoming a parent. Assistive reproductive technologies and surrogate motherhood have enabled men to overcome infertility, expanding the ways in which they can become biological fathers. Broadening family forms have diversified the ways in which men can assume the social role of parenthood, without becoming biological fathers:

through stepparenthood, adoption, cohabitation, and visiting relationships with mothers (Marsiglio, 1998). Despite these diverse alternative pathways, male fertility remains a fundamental route to parenthood and an important construct for demographers to understand.

WHY DO WE CARE ABOUT MALE FERTILITY AND WHAT DO WE NEED TO KNOW?

Interest in measuring male fertility spans a variety of audiences with varying needs and priorities. Demographers have a fundamental interest in fertility because of its importance for population growth and structure. Measures of male fertility are unnecessary for describing population change, however, because the necessary information on counts of births can be obtained from vital statistics or surveys in which women report their births (Greene & Biddlecom, 2000). Information from men is potentially more useful when attempting to understand the long-range implications of behavioral patterns for population trends. Demographers have developed "two-sex" models that demonstrate that the intrinsic rate of growth in a population depends on female age-specific birth rates, male age-specific birth rates, and the joint age distribution of male-female reproduction (Das Gupta, 1978; Pollak, 1986). Demographers have thoroughly explored the causes and consequences of women's birth timing, but they have paid less attention to the tempo of male fertility, and very little to the relative ages of mothers and fathers. Studying these behaviors would require information that links births to the characteristics of their biological fathers.

Policy audiences and researchers concerned with families and human development have an interest in both male fertility and social fatherhood. Much of the recent attention to male fertility and fatherhood grows out of a broad set of concerns stemming from changes in individual and family behaviors and their implications for the well-being of children, adults, and society. Responding to rising rates of nonmarital childbearing and single parenthood, policymakers have sought information about the men who sire children, the men who parent them, and the extent and quality of men's investments in children (U.S. Department of Health and Human Services, 1998). This set of questions has profound implications for policy related to welfare dependency, child support, marriage, and other aspects of family life.

Past research on fertility and parenthood has emphasized the experience and roles of women, resulting in a major imbalance in basic knowledge about these topics from the male and female perspectives. Correcting this imbalance is important not only for answering policy questions, but also for addressing broader questions of human development. Becoming a parent is a fulfilling and socially meaningful part of adult life, and becoming a biological father has special meaning for many men. The ways in which men become biological fathers—whether within a stable relationship, as a result of a casual sexual encounter, or as a result of an unplanned birth—are likely to have implications for their experience and behaviors as fathers. Furthermore, men and women typically experience parenthood differently with respect to both parenting behaviors and the time spent parenting biological and nonbiological children (R. B. King, 1999). Finally, to the extent that fertility is increasingly occurring in the context of unstable couple relationships, men's and women's fertility experiences and trajectories are likely to diverge (Greene & Biddlecom, 2000). Thus, we need to know whether and how men become fathers and how satisfactorily men manage their reproductive lives and their relationships with the children they bring into the world and parent. We need to learn more about the diverse social, economic, cultural, and experiential factors that influence male paternity and parenting, and the ways in which pathways to becoming a father shape male parenting.

To answer these questions requires information about when, under what circumstances, and how men are becoming parents; it requires, in other words, information on what births occur to men at what ages, what children they parent, and in what kinds of relationships. It requires knowing whether pregnancies and births are wanted or planned—by the couple or by one or another partner. It requires knowing what resources parents bring to paternity and to parenthood—such as maturity, health, education, job skills, and extended family—that allow parents to rear children according to locally accepted standards.

In conjunction with other data on individuals and families, this information can help us examine the factors affecting whether men become parents and under what circumstances. Does growing up in poverty or an unstable family affect how one becomes a father? This information also helps us understand the consequences of becoming a biological or social father at a certain age or under certain circumstances for the men, the children, the children's mothers, and society at large.

Progress and Problems in Measuring Male Fertility

The *Nurturing Fatherhood* report (U.S. Department of Health and Human Services, 1998) identified five national studies that had collected recent information on male fertility: the 1991 National Survey of Men; the 1979 and 1997 cohorts of the National Longitudinal Survey of Youth (NLSY); the National Survey of Adolescent Males (NSAM); the National Survey of Families and Households (NSFH); and the Survey of Income and Program Participation (SIPP) (which accepted proxy reports on men's fertility from women). The report neglected the Panel Study of Income Dynamics, which began collecting men's fertility histories in 1985 (Rendall, Clarke, Peters, Ranjit, & Verropoulou, 1999). All five of the noted surveys were time limited, limited to a narrow age cohort, or limited in the extent of information collected about male fertility. The report concluded that "there are no reliable data on trends in pregnancies or births to males nor about the intendedness of these pregnancies or births. . . . Currently there is no institutionalized survey that provides information about the fertility and fertility-related behaviors of American men" (p. 58). Vital registration data, which collect the age of the father, were limited by the high rate of missing information on fathers' ages (Landry & Forrest, 1995).

Efforts to improve information on male fertility have shown some success. The National Survey of Family Growth, the federal survey responsible for producing statistics on many fertility-related topics, included a large sample of men in its 2002 survey. The National Longitudinal Study of Adolescent Health (Add Health) collected information on male fertility in its third wave of interviews (see chap. 3, this volume, for more on Add Health). Research on the completeness and quality of male-fertility data collected in surveys has continued to grow (Mott & Gryn, 2001; Rendall et al., 1999; see also chaps. 16 and 17, this volume). Birth certificate data on the age of fathers have become more complete. The percentage of births in which the father's age was unknown was 17% in 1992 and 13% a decade later. The percentage of births to teens with unknown information about the father's age declined from 41% to 34% in the same decade (Stephanie Ventura, personal communication, May 20, 2004). However, no changes were made to improve the recording of the mother's and father's marital status and living arrangements in the most recent revision of the birth certificate.

Two chapters in this volume explore data quality on male fertility and offer useful new analyses. Mott, Hurst, and Gryn (chap. 16) evaluate male reports of biological paternity in NLSY79. Boggess and coauthors (chap. 17) analyze inconsistencies across survey waves in the reporting of births in the NSAM. The analyses support the claim that it is possible to collect information on fertility from men. Evaluation of NLSY79 data finds that only 8% of the births reported at some point as the man's own are of uncertain or unlikely paternity. Furthermore, the correlates and patterns of male fertility this analysis reveals appear reasonable, mirroring patterns well established in the research on female fertility. The analysis shows that early male fertility tends to occur more often among men whose mothers were less educated or single and among racial and ethnic minorities. The sharp decline in African American early fatherhood between the 1979 and 1997 cohorts of the NSLY reflects trends seen in women (J. Martin et al., 2003).

However, these analyses also provide red flags about data quality and its correlates. Some type of inconsistency affected 34% of the births reported in NSAM. In the NLSY79, some fathers claimed biological paternity of children for the first time years after the children were born. These and other studies provide a consistent warning that inconsistencies or errors in male reports of fertility are more likely among very young fathers, Black fathers, men who are neither married to nor in a relationship with the mother at the time of birth, and men who do not consistently live with the child (Mott, 1985; Rendall et al., 1999; see also chaps. 16 and 17, this volume).

Neither of the chapters in this volume addresses the most difficult question about men's fertility reports: How complete are they? Beginning with the June 1980 Current Population Survey (CPS), researchers have recognized underreported male fertility as a problem (Cherlin et al., 1983). Evaluations of survey after survey have found male fertility to be underreported (Bachu, 1996; Mott, 1985; Rendall et al., 1999; Seltzer & Brandreth, 1994; Sorensen, 1997). The only analysis that fails to document significant underreporting is based on the NSAM, but even this shows fairly substantial (although statistically insignificant) underreporting among Black men (Lindberg et al., 1998).

Mott (1985, 1998) documented the underreporting of male births in prior rounds of the NLSY79, along with a tendency for completeness of recent birth reports to increase somewhat as the men aged. A crude calculation based on NLSY data from the 1998 round illustrates that underreporting remains a problem. In this round, men reported an average of 1.4 children. At the time, most of the men were aged 33 to 41. Men tend to be older than their sexual partners, so we can use the fertility of women aged 30 to 34 as a minimal standard of comparison. We can approximate the average number of children women have by ages 30 to 34 by calculating a partial *total fertility rate* (TFR). The partial TFR indicates the average number of children women would have had by their early 30s if they had given birth at the age-specific rates for a given year. The partial TFR was 1.7 in 1985 when the cohort was aged 20 to 28, and 1.8 in 1998 when the cohort was aged 33 to 41. Regardless of the specific value, the comparison suggests that a nontrivial proportion of births are missing in the male reports.

CAVEAT EMPTOR: THE PROMISE AND PITFALLS OF USING SURVEY DATA ON MALE FERTILITY

The field has learned some valuable lessons in the past decades about men's reproductive lives. One consistent lesson is that self-report surveys do not produce accurate data on male fertility. Because women become pregnant and give birth, they can be certain of their biological parenthood. Because men's biological contribution occurs 9 months prior to birth, men cannot always be certain and, in some cases, may not even know that they have caused a pregnancy. Because of these differences, men's reports of fertility will, in the aggregate, always contain some error.

We also know that the errors in survey data can go both ways; men may erroneously claim children as their biological offspring and they may omit their true biological children. In the past two decades, the errors of omission have greatly outweighed the errors of misclaimed paternity, resulting in substantial undercounts of births.

The field has also accumulated a large body of evidence that points to systematic sources of error in male-fertility histories. Error is more likely if the father is younger, not in a relationship with the mother, and not living in the same household as the child. The evidence in Mott and coauthors' chapter (chap. 16, this volume) on the turnover in fatherhood status for births that occur at early ages suggests that important social processes are underway that reinterpret biological parenthood when the biological parent is unprepared to parent. Marsiglio (chap. 18, this volume) describes the doubts men have about biological paternity, the various ways they address those doubts, and the consequences they can have for men's fathering. He also articulates various concepts related to men's readiness for fatherhood and their relation to paternal claiming. These social and psychological processes contribute to differences in reporting male fertility by age, race, and marital status, but likely play out differently depending on the age and situation of the biological father.

In short, the field has learned that men's reporting of their fertility strongly relates to its consequences for their lives, their identities, and their relationships with their children. This means that the less connected men are with their children, the more their fertility will be misrepresented. The same trends that have heightened interest in male fertility—the disconnect between men and children, and between men and the mothers of their children—have also undermined men's ability to report their own fertility.

Can we improve survey data on male fertility? Undoubtedly. Survey designers have a wealth of knowledge about response errors and techniques that work to minimize them. Event history calendars, probing techniques, and the careful ordering of questions have proved helpful in enhancing reporting of fertility and other retrospective data from women. Approaches that embed questions about fertility in relationship histories, as in NSAM, may make a unique difference for male fertility reporting (see chap. 17, this volume). Frequent assessment of fatherhood status in longitudinal surveys increases the likelihood of identifying births, but creates challenges for analysts who must resolve year-to-year inconsistencies in reports. Future developments in survey research may yield new ways to improve accuracy, especially if these developments incorporate knowledge of the psychological and social processes that influence whether biological fathers recognize and claim their children (see chap. 18, this volume). New developments in survey research could also reduce the undercount of men, a substantial component of missing male births (Rendall et al., 1999). However, it is unlikely that measuring men's fertility will ever be completely accurate in the absence of radical social and demographic change, change that ensures a close and enduring relationship between each man who causes a pregnancy and the person he helps to create.

Could we improve survey data on male fertility by obtaining information from women? Women's reports of their fertility tend to be much more complete (Abma, Chandra, Mosher, Peterson, & Piccinino, 1997; Mott, 1998). Women could potentially provide rich data about birth fathers, if able and willing to correctly identify the fathers and their characteristics. These conditions are most likely to hold when the woman has a continuing relationship with the father, and the characteristics in question can be easily observed and recalled.

Fortunately, we may not need accurate data for all our purposes. We do not need survey data to estimate aggregate levels of male fertility and describe gross population trends. When our interest is focused on an individual's entry into the social role of father via biological paternity, survey data do provide meaningful information; omitted births tend to be those that do not lead to meaningful father roles. However, when our interest is in understanding what happens to children sired by men under various circumstances or deciding how to reduce the prevalence of unclaimed children, omitted births are a major problem. For these purposes, survey data on male fertility may be highly misleading.

Demographers are good at applying what they have learned about data imperfections to the task of making better estimates. Armed with a strong understanding of the strengths and weaknesses of different types of data, they can triangulate. They can draw on vital registration data, strengthening it to the extent possible to include information on fathers. They can use mothers' survey reports of fathers' ages to assess, and if necessary correct, survey estimates based on fathers' reports (as in Lindberg et al., 1998). Researchers can use different study designs, such as the Fragile Families study (Reichman, Teitler, Garfinkel, & McLanahan, 2001), to better capture men missing from conventional household surveys. However, the field still needs to collect more data on mothers' attributes from the fathers and more data on the fathers' attributes from mothers, and then align them. Moving beyond men's experience of social fatherhood depends on the field's creativity in developing ways to make the data complete, or at least more valid, after the fact.

Researchers can enhance efforts to piece together an accurate story of men's fertility if they continue to address the social and psychological processes that underlie men's paternity and their involvement with the children they father. Doing so may help them design surveys in psychologically sensitive ways that will improve the reporting of male fertility; it will certainly help to identify and model threats to the validity of the data.

The processes that create differences between biological paternity and a "claimed" child will continue to evolve. DNA testing now makes it possible to know definitively whose sperm fertilized what egg. Recent social policies emphasize the importance of making the biological father responsible for his child. There is also, however, a long tradition, embedded in vital statistics, of assuming that a child born to a married woman is the biological product of her husband. Clearly this is not the case when donor sperm help conceive the child, and there is good reason to suspect it is not the case in other circumstances as well. The field's success in measuring and understanding male fertility will depend on its ability to keep its fingers on the pulse of cultural and technological changes that affect the path between fertilizing an egg and being a father.

PART VI

Fathers and Fathering

20

Resident Father Involvement
and Social Fathering

Sandra L. Hofferth
Natasha Cabrera
University of Maryland at College Park

Marcia Carlson
Columbia University

Rebekah Levine Coley
Boston College

Randal Day
Brigham Young University

Holly Schindler
Boston College

In the recent past, interest in fathers was occasioned by their absence and driven mainly by growing divorce and separation rates. This early research focused on how father absence affected the financial condition of the family (for a review of this early research, see McLanahan & Sandefur, 1994). More recently, changes in families' lives, including increased labor force participation of mothers and increased family involvement of fathers, again heightened interest in fathers' roles, ranging from the causes of father involvement and its effects on children to the variety of roles that fathers play in their children's lives (Day & Lamb, 2004; Lamb, 1997, 2004; Tamis-LeMonda & Cabrera, 2002).

Some of this recent research has challenged the stereotype of the un-involved, unmarried father. Research from the Fragile Families and Child Wellbeing study (2000) suggests that unmarried fathers are more involved with their families than popularly believed, at least in the early years of a new child's life. Other research has challenged the stereotype of the unin-terested stepfather, suggesting that such fathers spend substantial time with stepchildren and show considerable warmth and involvement (Hofferth & Anderson, 2003; Marsiglio, 2004b). As Frances Goldscheider pointed out in her comments on this chapter, integrating different types of fathers, such as stepfathers, raises the question of commitment: Are they as committed as are married biological fathers (Goldscheider, 2003)? Although we usu-ally assume that they are not, a variety of conditions, such as cohabitation, unemployment, low income, conflict, or commitment to children in other families, may affect fathers' involvement with resident children.

As more studies extend their data collection to the current partner of the mother, how to define and measure father involvement is becoming a major question (Day & Lamb, 2004). The objective of this chapter is to compare estimates in five recent data sets of father engagement, accessibility, respon-sibility, and positive emotional involvement across different child ages and family structures. The five data sets are the Fragile Families and Child Well-being Study (FF); the Welfare, Children, and Families: A Three-City Study (Three-City); the National Longitudinal Survey of Youth, 1997 (NLSY97); the Panel Study of Income Dynamics—Child Development Supplement (PSID-CDS); and the Early Head Start National Research and Evaluation Study (Early Head Start).

We first introduce methodological issues in measuring father involvement and discuss the parameters we use in our comparisons across data sets. Specifi-cally, we address who the father is, which includes defining the father types of interest to us. We then explore what father involvement is, which factors may affect involvement, and how to obtain the best data on fathers. This in-cludes who reports the information and the types of information reported.

Second, we compare resident fathers' involvement across the five data sets based on their marital relationship to the mother and their biological relationship to the child. We conclude with recommendations for future data collection on fathering in large-scale surveys.

DEFINING "FATHER"

Resident or Nonresident Fathers

The definition of a father is an open debate in research. Are fathers strictly those who have sired a biological child or are the men who have assumed the responsibilities of parenting a child also considered fathers, regardless of their biological link? There are cogent arguments for each definition.

The argument for studying biological fathers is that stepfathers and boyfriends may be temporary figures in a child's life and, thus, not as invested in the child's well-being, but biological fathers will continue to be relevant and invested, regardless of residence, and they are legally financially responsible for their children. The argument for studying nonbiological fathers is that biological fathers leave households and, increasingly, nonbiological fathers enter. In addition, the involvement of a nonresident biological father changes over time. Although two thirds of children under age 13 who were living apart from their biological father had been in touch with him in the past year, and one half in the past month (Hofferth et al., 2002), the nonresident father's involvement is likely to decline over time as he develops new attachments and, perhaps, a new family (Manning & Smock, 1999).

Given the configuration of today's families, the biological father may not be the most important father figure, and in fact he may have very little input or link to the child if he leaves the home. Resident nonbiological males may have a larger impact on children (positive or negative) simply because they are living with the child. Although children are very likely to be living with both biological parents at or around the time of birth (in 1994, 67% of children under age 6 were living with both parents [U.S. Department of Health and Human Services, 2000]), the proportion declines sharply as children age. By age 12 to 17, only 52% were living with both biological parents. Resident fathers (regardless of biological status) spend substantial time accessible to children or engaged with them. Over the course of a year, this time adds up (Hofferth & Anderson, 2003). In contrast, one third of nonresident biological fathers had no contact with their children during the prior year, and children who had any contact in the prior year spent an hour per week, on average, with their father (Hofferth et al., 2002).

Research has recently focused on positive father involvement and positive outcomes for children (Moore & Halle, 2001). An often overlooked feature of these important relationships, however, is that father involvement is not always positive, and negative involvement can have long-term consequences. A father, for example, may be cranky and depressed if he is home with children because he is unemployed, and this may lead to poorer parenting (Conger & Elder, 1994). More serious outcomes such as physical or sexual abuse may also be a risk, especially among stepfathers. Compared with biological children, stepchildren are 40 times more likely to be abused (Daly & Wilson, 1998). In addition, fathers who have recently returned from prison may bring with them both inappropriate behavior and contact with a variety of diseases such as hepatitis C, sexually transmitted diseases, and tuberculosis (Hammett, Roberts, & Kennedy, 2001).

In this chapter, we focus on the resident father or father figure for the following reasons. First, resident father figures other than the married biological father have been infrequently studied. Second, the types of information available and relevant to nonresident and resident fathers' relationships with children differ, making comparison difficult. Third, we suspect there may be unique family dynamics in families in which a primary parent figure is transitory, or in cases in which the child may experience confusion about familial membership. For the sake of parsimony and because later chapters in this volume focus on that topic, we exclude nonresident fathers in our analysis.

TYPES OF RESIDENT FATHERS OF INTEREST

During the past several decades, increased nonmarital childbearing and divorce have led to larger proportions of children living with a stepfather, and increased partner cohabitation has led to larger proportions of children living with two unmarried biological parents or with a biological mother and her partner (Smock, 2000). Research has shown that the level of commitment exhibited by married parents and by biological parents affects investments in children (Hofferth & Anderson, 2003). Comparisons that ignore these two crucial dimensions will be unable to judge fathers on the other dimensions that may affect investments. Therefore, throughout the analyses, we consistently divide the sample by the marital relationship of the child's resident parents and by the biological relationship of child to father.

Using two of the studies (NLSY97 and PSID-CDS), we compare to married biological fathers: (a) stepfathers married to the child's mother, and (b) unmarried partners. This permits a comparison of biological father versus nonbiological father involvement, and married versus unmarried father involvement. Three of the five studies reviewed here (Early Head Start, FF, and the Three-City study) either collected insufficient information on resident nonbiological fathers to provide a picture of their parenting, or the children were not yet old enough for sufficient numbers to be living with nonbiological fathers. For these three studies and the PSID-CDS, we compare resident biological fathers who are and are not married to the mother. These latter comparisons contribute to discussions of the importance of marriage to fathering. The important point of all these comparisons is that our discussion is not restricted to married fathers residing with their biological children, which is the focus of the bulk of prior research.

Identifying Social Fathers

In many cases in which the two biological parents separate, one or both parents remarry or repartner. As a result, many children are reared by nonbiological fathers. However, not all of these men consider themselves to be fathers, act as fathers, or are seen as fathers by children. Although most of the studies compare married and unmarried biological fathers (in both cases a biological mother is also present), two data sets used here (NLYS97 and the PSID-CDS) also collected information on resident, married, and unmarried nonbiological fathers.

In the PSID-CDS, we examine the stepfather and biological mother family and the biological mother and cohabiting partner family. The PSID-CDS considers the cohabiting partner of the mother to be a type of father figure; however, neither the man nor the child may consider the relationship to be fatherlike. In the NLSY97, we examine the biological mother and stepfather family, the mother and partner family, and the biological mother and related father figure family. In asking the adolescent about his or her relationship to family members, the NLSY97 offers a clear definition of a father figure: "a relative/nonrelative who is like a father to you." The survey used this, along with his relationship to the child, to identify the related father figure family. The NLSY97, which surveyed youth aged 12 to 17 in 1997, found no adolescent children living with a mother and an unmarried biological father; therefore, this data set does not contain that subgroup. Such living arrangements are likely to have dissolved or resulted in marriage prior to the child entering adolescence.

What Is Father Involvement?

We use Lamb, Pleck, Charnov, and Levine's (1987) three-dimensional model of father involvement (engagement, accessibility, responsibility) and two dimensions that are derived from the parenting literature, that is, warmth and monitoring/control. Paternal engagement includes direct interaction with children, and accessibility includes time the father is available to children, but not directly interacting with them. Responsibility encompasses the management of the child's welfare: ensuring the child is fed, clothed, housed, monitored, managed, examined by physicians, and cared for when needed. Warmth includes a father's affection toward his children, and monitoring/control includes paternal behaviors that lead to restricting, controlling, or managing children's behaviors.

Most developmental psychologists argue that the quality of parenting and the parent–child relationship are crucial to healthy development in children. Historically, research has focused on the mother–child dyad, although recent evidence suggests that the quality of the father–child relationship is also important for healthy child development (Lamb, 2004; Pleck, 1997). A combination of responsiveness and appropriate control is believed to create the best environment for child development (Maccoby & Martin, 1983). In this chapter, we measure responsiveness by examining the emotional content of the parent–child interaction, including warmth and closeness. Monitoring and control measure the demands of the parent on the child and are the second aspect of quality of the relationship measured in the chapter.

Correlates of Father Involvement

Parental involvement, such as warmth, tends to decline as children age. Comparisons, therefore, should be based on similar age groups. Because the five data sets include children of different ages, we created age groups that facilitate cross-sample comparisons. Children were about age 1 in the FF study; therefore, we include an age category 0 to 1. In contrast, the Early Head Start children were all about 2 years old. In the Three-City study, children were aged 0 to 5 and 10 to 14. The PSID-CDS children, in contrast, were aged 0 to 12.

To better compare across studies, we divided the 0 to 5 age groups into categories 0 to 1, 2 to 3, 4 to 5, and alternatively 0 to 2 and 3 to 5. Only the PSID-CDS included 6- to 12-year-olds. We divided the NLSY97 adolescents into younger (12 to 13) and older (14 to 16) adolescents in our comparisons with the PSID-CDS data.

Another important variable is a child's gender. Research on young children has suggested that fathers spend more time playing with boys than girls (Yeung, Sandberg, Davis-Kean, & Hofferth, 2001), and thus we compare the involvement of fathers with boys and with girls. Studies have also suggested that fathers of different race-ethnicities differ in their fathering behavior (Hofferth, 2003). Because different data sets have different ethnic-race composition, we examine fathering by race-ethnicity. To compare with other data, we must ensure that our ethnic mixes are similar or that race-ethnicity does not matter.

We also expect differences in father involvement by family income. High-income fathers may be better able than low-income fathers to adjust their schedules to spend more time with children. Alternatively, high-income fathers may be less involved with children because of time demands in their jobs. Our samples differ in income levels: Early Head Start and the Three-City study represent low-income and disadvantaged populations, and the FF study oversamples unmarried parents, who are disproportionately low income. The NLSY97 and PSID-CDS are nationally representative.

To compare father involvement across these studies, we used the same income groupings across the samples, specified as monthly income.[1] Father involvement is also likely to vary by the father's education. Better educated fathers may place a higher value on involvement with their children and may spend more time and be warmer with them. Although any father can express warmth, more highly educated fathers may better understand its importance to child development (Sandberg & Hofferth, 2001).

When examining nonbiological and biological fathers, it is important to consider how long this particular resident father has lived with the child (Hofferth & Anderson, 2003). Unfortunately, this information is rarely available. The length of coresidence would have to be asked directly in each survey wave, or, if data were collected over time, unique identifiers might be associated with each household member so that household members could be identified across data collection points and their total time in that household or family determined. This variable is available only for children in the PSID-CDS, which has residence information for children from birth to 1997, and so was not included in the comparisons shown here.

OBTAINING THE BEST INFORMATION ON FATHERS

Fathers are difficult to study and are usually undercounted in national surveys (Federal Interagency Forum on Child and Family Statistics, 1998). Many men are loosely connected to households and are simply not included in household enumerations. They may be living in several residences, on the street, in jail, or in the military (see, e.g., chap. 15, this volume). Even if they are identified, their fertility is often underestimated (see chap. 16, this volume).

One way to obtain direct information about fathers is by starting with the man as the study respondent and following him as he becomes an adult. A primary problem with this approach is that it is difficult to obtain accurate reports of when a man has fathered a child. For example, men without a high school degree, who are African American, who fathered a child at a young age, or who did not consistently live with the child from birth were less likely to be verified as children's fathers in the NLSY79 (chap. 16, this volume). A strategy that has worked well is to interview a couple at the "magic moment" of the birth of their baby (Cabrera et al., 2002). The FF study took this approach with unmarried couples, interviewing parents in the hospital just after the birth, and the resulting initial response rates were 87% for mothers and 75% for fathers; fathers' response rates varied by relationship to the baby's mother (M. Carlson & McLanahan, 2004).

Although timing the interview to coincide with a birth solves the problem of determining whether a man has fathered a child at all, it does not ensure that male-fertility reports are complete and accurate. In the Survey of Income and Program Participation (SIPP), 8% of men who reported having ever fathered a child declined to report the number of children ever born (Bachu, 1996). (For more information about male fertility, see chap. 16, this volume.)

Who Reports the Information

In earlier studies, researchers usually obtained information about fathers and father involvement by asking mothers. However, mothers' reports of fathers' involvement with children may be affected by the nature of the adult relationship (Amato & Rivera, 1999; for more on this topic, see chap. 21, this volume). Thus, it is important to talk with fathers themselves. Although it is easier to locate resident than nonresident fathers, the former are much less likely to participate than mothers. Because they work longer hours than mothers and because mothers play a gatekeeping role, it is more difficult to schedule interviews with them. Obtaining an interview with a second family member is expensive and time-consuming because it takes additional contact and interview time. The alternative, a self-administered questionnaire, is also less than completely satisfactory. The self-administered questionnaire in the 1997 PSID-CDS resulted in a response rate of only about 60% of resident fathers (Hofferth et al., 1999).

One issue that has not been carefully examined is whether the story differs depending on the reporter. In the studies reviewed here, *who* reports depends on children's ages. The experience of the parent–child relationship may be best reported by the child, and adolescents often report for themselves in surveys. In the NLSY97, children were 12 to 17 in 1997 and they reported on father involvement. In the PSID-CDS, children were aged 0 to 12 in 1997. For this group, mothers reported on fathers' time and activities with young children, and both mother and child reported on fathers' time and activities with older children. For the measures of warmth, activities, and responsibility, resident biological fathers, stepfathers, and cohabiting partners reported on their own behavior.

Two of our data sets offer reports from both parents on the father's behavior, and one study offers reports from both mothers and adolescents. In the Three-City study, mothers reported on biological father behavior for children and adolescents, and adolescents reported on the accessibility of and closeness to their father. Early Head Start reports are for children aged 2 to 3. In this study, biological fathers reported and, in one instance, the biological mother and father both reported, on father involvement. The FF study selected a sample of families at the birth of a child and about 1 year later. Reports at the 1- to 2-year mark are from both father and mother, and they provide an opportunity to test whether the report about father involvement differs depending on the reporter.

DATA DESCRIPTIONS AND MEASURES

The five data sets used in this chapter are summarized in Table 20.1. The following describes the measures of father involvement. Descriptive statistics from each data set are provided in the Appendix.

Child Development Supplement to the Panel Study of Income Dynamics

In 1997, researchers collected information on up to two randomly selected children in a family aged 0 to 12. The sources of information were primary caregivers, other caregivers, and the children themselves in families participating in the PSID, a nationally representative sample of U.S. men, women, children, and the families in which they reside. The PSID has followed families for more than 35 years. The PSID-CDS completed interviews with 2,394 child households and about 3,600 children from birth to age 13, given that a few had turned 13 by the date of interview. The sample used in this chapter consists of children aged 13 or younger living with a biological mother and a father or father figure.

The sample used to analyze parental time spent with children consists of 1,993 children with data from time diaries, reported by the child and the primary caregiver. Because fewer fathers than mothers responded, the sample size for father-reported measures of warmth is 1,226 children, and the sample size is 1,185 for father-reported measures of responsibility for managing the care of children. The survey asked these questions of fathers of children of all ages. For questions on activities, which included only fathers of children aged 3 and older, the sample size was 925. We used weights to adjust for differing probabilities of selection into the sample and for different response across instruments.

Measure 1: Time Children Spend Engaged With Their Fathers. The PSID-CDS collected a complete time diary for one weekday and one weekend day for each child aged 0 to 12 in the family. The time diary, which the mother, or mother and child, primarily, answered, asked several questions about the child's flow of activities during a 24-hour period beginning at midnight of the randomly assigned, designated day. These questions ask about the primary activity going on at that time, when it began and ended, and whether any other activity was taking place. An additional question—"Who was doing the activity with child?"—when linked to activity codes such as "playing" or "being read to," provides details on the extent of one-on-one interactions of others with the child (Hofferth, 1999).

We used the question, "Who else was there (but not engaged)?" to determine the amount of time the father was accessible but not engaged. For this analysis, we coded as *father engaged* times in which the father (biological father, stepfather, foster, or adoptive father) was engaged (present but not engaged in activities) with a child, and we coded as *father accessible* the time the father was present but not engaged in activities with a child. We summed times engaged and accessible over all activities for weekdays and weekends for each child. We also computed weekly time by multiplying weekday time by 5 and weekend time by 2, with no time = 0.

TABLE 20.1
Description of Five Data Sets

Study	Purpose	Population	Sample	Periodicity	Response Rates	Family Members Interviewed	Proxy Reports	Web Address
Panel Study of Income Dynamics Child Development Supplement	This omnibus study examines the causes and consequences of child health and development.	American children 0–12 in 1997 and their families	Families in the core PSID with children under age 13 in 1997; 3,563 children in 2,394 families; low-income families overrepresented in PSID	Wave 1: 1997; Wave 2, 2002–2003	Response rate: Wave 1, 88%, Wave 2, 91%	Primary caregiver, second caregiver (60%RR), child, childcare provider, teacher, nonresident parent	Primary caregiver reports on nonresidential parent; mother reports about up to two target children	psidonline.isr.umich.edu/
Fragile Families and Child Wellbeing	This study was designed to better understand new unwed parents and father participation in his child's life.	Population of children born to unmarried parents in U.S. cities with populations over 200,000; comparison groups of children born to married parents	3,700 children born to unmarried parents and 1,200 born to married parents	Wave 1: 1 year; Wave 2, 3 years; Wave 3: 4 years	Wave 1: 89% of married fathers, 75% of unmarried fathers; Wave 2: 86%, 77% reinterview	Mothers, fathers	Mother reports on father of child	http://crcw.princeton.edu/fragilefamilies/index.asp/

Early Head Start Evaluation, Father Involvement With Toddlers component	This was designed as a random assignment experiment to evaluate the effectiveness of EHS; fathers were added to learn more about their role in low-income families.	Infants and toddlers in low-income families	3,000 low-income families with children born between 9/95 and 7/98	Wave 1: 1 month; Wave 2, 6 months; Wave 3, 14 months; Wave 4, 24 months; Wave 5, 36 months	Response rate: 60% of fathers of children still in survey at 24 months	Mothers, fathers, children	Mother reports on father of child	www.acf.hhs.gov/programs/core/ongoing_research/ehs/ehs_intro.html/
Welfare, Children, and Families: A Three-City Study	This study was designed to evaluate the effects of welfare reform on low-income families.	Families with children 0–4 or 10–14 in low-income urban neighborhoods	2,402 families with children 0–4 or 10–14 in low-income neighborhoods in Boston, Chicago, and San Antonio	Wave 1: 1999; Wave 2: 2000–2001	Response rate: 74%	Primary caregivers; fathers also in a subset of 630 2- to 4-yr-old children; children	Mother reports on father of child	www.jhu.edu/~welfare/
National Longitudinal Survey of Youth, 1997	This study was designed to understand the transitions of youth into adulthood.	Youth 12–16 in Dec. 1996	8,984 youth in 6,819 households; oversample of African American and Hispanic youth	Wave 1: 1997; annual data collection	Response rate: 97% annually	Respondent, parent	Respondent reports on partners, spouse, children	www.bls.gov/nls/home.htm/

Measure 2: Responsibility. The eight responsibility items we use focus on the father's report of his child care: bathing and changing diapers; disciplining; choosing children's activities; buying clothes; driving children to activities; selecting a pediatrician and making appointments; selecting a child-care program, preschool, or school; and playing with children. Response categories are: 1= I do this, 2 = another household member does this, 3 = I share this task, and 4 = someone else does this task. If the respondent did the task, we coded the response as 2; if the respondent shared it, we coded it 1; otherwise, we coded the task 0. We summed scores over all items. Overall scale reliability using Cronbach's alpha was 0.73.

Measure 3: Types of Activities With Parents. In addition to gathering data in a time diary, the PSID-CDS asked fathers directly about 13 different activities they may have done with each of up to two children aged 3 and older in the past month (1 = did the activity, 0 = did not do the activity). These include washing or folding clothes; doing dishes; cleaning house; preparing food; looking at books or reading stories; talking about the family; working on homework; building or repairing something; playing computer or video games; playing a board game or card game, or doing a puzzle; and playing sports or outdoor activities. The total score, which reflects the number of activities fathers reported doing with each child, has a reliability coefficient (Cronbach's alpha) of 0.78. Sample sizes are smallest for these activity items.

Measure 4: Parental Warmth. Six items measure the warmth of the relationship between child and father by asking how often in the past month the father hugged each child, expressed his love, spent time with child, joked or played with child, talked with child, and told the child he appreciated what he or she did. The five response categories range from 1 = not in the past month, to 5 = every day, with a mean greater than 4. To distinguish high from low responders, we dichotomized each response into 1 = the father did this at least several times a week, or 0 = the father did this less frequently. We summed the scores on the six items to create a scale with a reliability coefficient (Cronbach's alpha) of 0.77.

National Longitudinal Survey of Youth, 1997

The NLSY97 is a nationally representative sample of 8,984 respondents in 6,819 unique households, composed of 6,748 youth aged 12 to 16 as of December 31, 1996, and a supplemental sample of 2,236 Hispanic and Black youth living in the United States at the same time. The survey collected data annually, beginning in 1997. The data for the present analysis come from youth reports in the first, 1997, wave. Of all youth who were

12 to 17 when interviewed in 1997, 6,440 lived with a father or father figure, and 2,541 did not, with 3 missing. Almost 80% lived with a biological father, 14% lived with a stepfather, 2% lived with a boyfriend of the mother, and 2% lived with a relative who was "like a father." In the present study, the NLSY97 identifies a biological father as "your biological father"; a stepfather includes both "your adoptive stepfather" and "a stepfather who did not adopt you." A cohabiting father is "your mother's boyfriend"; and a fatherlike person is "a relative who is like a father to you." This categorization does not include adoptive, foster, and unrelated father figures. Unique to this study is the inclusion of *related* father figures. The concepts related to father involvement are parental monitoring and child's affection for the father.

Definitions differ slightly between the PSID-CDS and the NLSY97. The PSID-CDS includes a few adoptive children as biological children, whereas the NLSY97 sample used here excludes adoptive children. Notably, neither data set includes foster children. In both data sets, "stepfather" includes men who may or may not have formally adopted their stepchildren. The NLSY97 has separate categories for partners of the mother and for related and unrelated father figures; we do not, in this chapter, consider unrelated father figures. The warmth, responsibility, and activities measures from the CDS were asked only of unrelated cohabiting partners, comparable to the NLSY97 partner category.

Measure 1: Parental Monitoring. Monitoring assesses the degree to which the parent has knowledge of the youth's activities, friends, friends' families, school teachers, and school performance. The concept was assessed by summing four items, which asked the youth respondents if their parents: (a) knew their close friends, (2) knew their friends' parents, (c) knew whom they were with when not at home, and (d) knew their teachers and what they were doing in school. The five response categories are 0 = knows nothing, 1 = knows just little things, 2 = knows some, 3 = knows most things, and 4 = knows everything. The reliability coefficient (Cronbach's alpha) is 0.81.

Measure 2: Child's Affection for the Father. A key feature of father involvement is whether the child holds much affection for the father. Although a perfect match is unlikely between involvement and affection, a long-term sense of affection should influence the father's investment in the child. We created the scale by summing the responses to three items: "I think highly of him," "He is a person I want to be like," and "I really enjoy spending time with him." Response categories are 0 = strongly disagree, 1 = disagree, 2 = neutral or mixed, 3 = agree, and 4 = strongly agree. This scale produced an alpha score of 0.81.

Fragile Families and Child Wellbeing Study

The FF follows a cohort of nearly 5,000 births in 20 large U.S. cities in 15 states. The data are representative of nonmarital births in cities with populations greater than 200,000 and nearly representative of marital births in large cities. The survey interviewed mothers (and most fathers) in the hospital within 48 hours after the birth of their child. Parents undergo further interviews when their child is about 1, 3, and 5 years old. We rely on mothers' reports of the couple's relationship at the 1-year survey to determine our sample. Our analysis includes 1,309 married resident fathers and 1,364 cohabiting resident fathers; of these, 1,166 married fathers and 1,176 cohabiting fathers were themselves interviewed.

Measures. We include four measures of the frequency of fathers' involvement with their 1-year-old children: (a) spending 1 or more hours per day with the child, (b) showing warmth, (c) engaging in cognitive-stimulation activities, and (d) providing direct caregiving. Both mothers' and fathers' reports contribute to the parental-warmth and cognitive-stimulation measures; only mothers' reports contribute to the measures of time spent per day with the child and engagement in caregiving activities.

The frequency of spending 1 or more hours a day with the child is based on the question asked of mothers: "In the past month, how often has [father] spent 1 or more hours a day with [child]?" Response choices were: 1 = not at all, 2 = only once or twice, 3 = a few times in the past month, 4 = a few times a week, and 5 = every day or nearly every day. The father–child activity items are based on reports by fathers or mothers, or both, about how often the father participated in the following seven activities with the child in the week before the survey: played games like "peek-a-boo" or "gotcha"; played inside with toys such as blocks or Legos; hugged or showed physical affection to the child; read stories; told stories; fed or gave the child a bottle; or changed the child's diaper. We divided responses into four categories: 1 = never, 2 = less than a few times per week, 3 = a few times a week, and 4 = every day or nearly every day.[2]

To assess whether we could combine the items in some fashion, we conducted factor analysis (using varimax rotation), and identified three factors that could be combined. The first factor includes three items that reflect fathers' parental warmth: playing games such as "peek-a-boo" or "gotcha," playing inside with toys, and hugging or showing physical affection (Cronbach's alpha = 0.84 for mothers' reports, and 0.80 for fathers' reports). The second factor includes two items of cognitive stimulation: reading and telling stories to the child (alpha = 0.818 for mothers' reports, and 0.79 for fathers' reports). The third factor includes the two activities of direct caregiving: feeding or giving a bottle, and changing the child's diaper (alpha = 0.83 for mothers' reports). The father interview did not include these items.

Welfare, Children, and Families: A Three-City Study

The Three-City study is a longitudinal, multimethod study of the well-being of low-income, urban children, families, and communities in the wake of federal welfare reform. The survey sample of the Three-City study includes a stratified, random sample of 2,402 children and their primary female caregivers in low-income families (family incomes less than 200% of the federal poverty line), who live in low-income, urban neighborhoods in Boston, Chicago, and San Antonio. The current analyses focus on a subsample of the survey families with a child aged 0 to 4 or 10 to 14, in which the biological father of the focal child was residing in the child's household according to household rosters and marital-status information drawn from mother reports ($n = 372$, or 15.5% of the full Three-City survey sample). We applied probability weights, which adjust for nonresponse and the sampling strategy, which led to a sample that is representative of low-income children in low-income families with resident biological fathers in the three cities. All data derive from in-person interviews with mothers or early-adolescent children.

Measure 1: Father Accessibility. Mothers reported on fathers' accessibility to each child by responding to the question, "How often can you count on [father] if you need him to take care of [child]?" Young adolescents also reported on their fathers' accessibility by answering two questions: "How often can you count on your father if you need him for something?" and "How often can you find your father pretty quickly if you want to talk to him?" Responses ranged on a Likert scale from 1 = no contact, to 6 = always.

Measure 2: Father Responsibility. We analyzed the concept of father responsibility from responses by the mother to two questions on discipline and basic care; developmentally appropriate wording varied by the age of the child. The discipline question asked, "How much responsibility does [father] take for making sure [child] behaves?" The care questions asked, "How much responsibility does [father] take in [child's] daily care, such as feeding, changing diapers, or bathing [child]?" (children aged 0-1); preparing food for [child], helping [him/her] get dressed, or giving [child] a bath?" (aged 2-5 years); preparing food for [child], or making sure [he/she] goes to school?" (aged 10-14). Responses ranged on a Likert scale from 1 = no contact, to 4 = complete responsibility. We also include a measure of parents' conflict based on the question, "How often do you and [father] disagree over issues concerning [child]?" Responses ranged from 1 = no contact, to 6 = always.

Measure 3: Father Warmth.   Mothers reported on fathers' warmth based on the question, "Overall, how close would you say [father] is to [child]?" Responses ranged from 1 = no contact, to 5 = extremely close. Adolescents answered a short version of Armsden and Greenberg's (1987) *Inventory of Parent and Peer Attachment*, a measure designed to assess the affective and cognitive dimensions of adolescents' relationships with their parents and friends. Based on previous research with low-income African American adolescents (Coley, 2003), we formed two subscales. The first, "trust and communication" (six items, alpha = .90), assesses adolescents' perceptions of the responsiveness, accessibility, and warmth of their fathers. The scale of responses ranges from 1 = never true, to 5 = always true. Examples of questions are: "I tell my father about my problems and troubles," or "When we discuss things, my father cares about my point of view." The second subscale is "anger and alienation" (six items, alpha = .66), which assesses adolescents' perceptions of their fathers' hostility, unresponsiveness, and inconsistency. Examples of questions are: "I feel angry with my father," or "My father doesn't understand what I'm going through these days."

The 1995 Early Head Start National Research and Evaluation Study

Early Head Start studies the implementation and effects of the Early Head Start program, a program of services from before birth until age 3 that includes a longitudinal study of infants and toddlers in low-income families. Early Head Start includes approximately 3,000 eligible families living in 17 communities across the country who had a child younger than 12 months at enrollment. Early Head Start first enrolled families, and later interviewed 820 fathers after mothers identified them. The primary caregiver in 95% of the families was the child's mother. The study included questions for the mother about father and father figure involvement with the children at baseline, again at the first follow-up parent interviews, and in child assessments conducted when the children were 14, 24, and 36 months old. The data used here come primarily from one component, FITS, a study of Father Involvement with Toddlers when children were about 2 years old.

Measure 1: Demographic Characteristics.   We used mothers' reports to identify the mother–father relationship and father residency status as married, cohabiting, boyfriend (nonresident but romantically involved with the mother), friend (nonresident but divorced or separated), or no relationship (mother reports having no relationship, romantic or otherwise, with the biological father). We selected only married and cohabiting fathers for this analysis.

Measure 2: Father Involvement. We assessed father involvement using a quantitative interview that included two constructs related to those used by Lamb (1987): engagement and responsibility. We measured engagement based on the question, asked of mothers, "How frequently has your child's father done the following four activities with your child: (a) read, (b) feed/prepare meals, (c) play with child, and (d) go for a walk outside/ take child to the playground?" Responses rated on a 6-point scale from 1 (not at all) to 4 (a few times a year) to 6 (several times a week). Also, fathers answered a series of 33 questions about the activities they did with their children in the past month. The questions included the following: "How often did you read to your child?" "How often did you take your child to visit relatives?" "How often did you feed your child?" and "How often did you play chasing games with your child?" We rated items on a 6-point scale from 1 (not at all) to 4 (a few times a week) to 6 (more than once a day). We then divided these items into four subscales, with alphas ranging from .77 to .86. The average score across these subscales was used.

We measured responsibility based on fathers' responses to the question, "How much influence do you have in making major decisions about your child's education, religion, and health care needs?" We rated responses using a 3-point Likert scale, ranging from 0 (no influence) to 2 (a great deal of influence). Finally, we measured warmth based on responses from fathers to the statement, "Holding and cuddling [child] is fun." We rated this item on a 4-point scale from 1 (never) to 4 (all of the time).

UNMARRIED VERSUS MARRIED BIOLOGICAL FATHERS

We first compare the engagement, availability, warmth, and responsibility that married and unmarried resident fathers express toward their biological children. The results summarized in Table 20.2 indicate whether father involvement was greater in married (M) or in unmarried (U) father families, or whether there was no difference (blank). All results are statistically significant at the .10 level; results significant at .05 to .10 are marked with a "+" sign, and the rest are significant at $p < .05$.

Engagement and Activities

The results from the PSID-CDS show that, generally, married biological fathers spend significantly more time with their children than unmarried resident biological fathers (Table 20.2, column 1). This distinction was most pronounced for moderate-income fathers, fathers with some college education, and African American fathers. This distinction was also evident for time spent with boys and with younger children. The study found no difference, however, between married and unmarried low-income fathers, or among fathers with only a high school diploma or less. The study also found no difference between these two groups in time spent with adolescent children, or White and Hispanic children.

In contrast, the PSID-CDS reveals neither an overall difference between married and unmarried biological fathers in reported frequency of activities with children in the last month (Table 20.2, column 2), nor any significant subgroup differences.

Results from the FF for time with father (Table 20.2, column 3) are generally consistent with those from the PSID-CDS. Where there are significant differences, married fathers spend more time with their children than do unmarried fathers, as reported by mothers. Married fathers also spend marginally more time with male children than do unmarried fathers. Married fathers with more education and higher incomes are somewhat more likely to spend at least an hour a day with their children than are unmarried fathers, which could be because unmarried fathers (who have less education) may have to work more hours to earn that higher income, and more hours at work means less time with children (Hofferth & Anderson, 2003). More education is generally linked to more time with children. Why there should be a difference in time spent with children among married and unmarried fathers with similarly high levels of education is puzzling. Unmarried fathers with a college degree are atypical; only 4% of unmarried fathers have a college degree compared with more than one quarter of married fathers. There may be other, unmeasured differences between the two groups.

The results from the FF analysis show no overall difference between the frequency of activities with children of married and unmarried biological fathers, and only a few subgroup comparisons are significant (Table 20.2, columns 4 and 5). The results are inconsistent. Based on mother reports, *unmarried* fathers with less education and with lower monthly household income more frequently engage in cognitively stimulating activities with their children. Based on father reports, *married* African American fathers more frequently engage in stimulating activities than do unmarried African American fathers.

Based on the fathers' reports, the only significant difference in Early Head Start data (not shown in table) was that unmarried fathers with some college education tend to be more involved with their children than are married fathers with some college education. Based on the mothers' reports, there were no significant differences. The conclusion is that differences in time engagement favor married fathers, whereas differences in reported

TABLE 20.2
Differences Between Unmarried (U) and Married (M)
Biological Fathers in Level of Engagement With Children

| | PSID-CDS | | Fragile Families | | |
| | Time | Activities | Time[a] | Activities | Activities |
	Mother Report	Father Report	Mother Report	Mother Report	Father Report
All	M				
Income (monthly)					
0–$1000		—		U	
$1,001–2,000	M				
$2,001–3,600	M+		M		
$3,601–5,600		—	M+		
$5,601+	—	—			
Education					
Less than high school		—		U+	
High school graduate				U	
Some college	M+	—	M		
College+	—	—	M		
Age of child					
0–1	M	—			
2–3	M				
4–5		—			
6–13					
0–2	M	—			
3–5	M+				
6–9	M				
10–14		—			
Gender of child					
Male	M		M+		
Female					
Race					
White					
Black	M				M+
Hispanic	—				
Other	—	—	M+		U

Note. This table reports findings from two of the four relevant studies. The unreported studies (Early Head Start and Three-City) had no, or only one, measures to report. The one measure in the Early Head Start study not reported in the table was for fathers with some college; unmarried fathers in this group spent more time with their children than did married fathers. CDS children were 0 to 12; Fragile Families children were age 1. All results significant at $p < .10$; + indicates $.05 < p < .10$. NA = not available. — = fewer than 10 cases. Blank cells = no difference.

[a] = spent 1 or more hours per day with 1-year-old child.

activity frequency do not consistently favor married or unmarried biological fathers.

Accessibility to Father

Although we found no overall difference in accessibility between married and unmarried biological fathers, we did find differences by subgroups in the PSID-CDS (Table 20.3, column 1). For example, African American married fathers are much more accessible to children than are African American unmarried fathers. In addition, married fathers with a high school education are much more accessible than are comparable unmarried fathers. Finally, married fathers of 6- to 9-year-olds are more accessible than are unmarried fathers of these children.

Adolescents in the Three-City study score married biological fathers higher than cohabiting biological fathers on availability and on being able to count on them (Table 20.3, columns 3 and 4). The differences for whether the father can be found quickly are significant overall, including for African American and female children.

We found only one significant difference for younger children in the Three-City study, and this was opposite of what was expected: Hispanic mothers report greater accessibility of unmarried than married biological fathers to their younger children (Table 20.3, column 2).

Warm Behaviors

We find no overall difference in warmth in any age group between unmarried and married biological fathers in the PSID-CDS, but we find a few differences by subgroups (Table 20.4, column 1). For example, married biological fathers with children aged 0 to 2 or 3 to 5 are warmer than comparable unmarried biological fathers. Married fathers with male children and married fathers with less than a high school education are warmer than their unmarried counterparts. African American fathers are the sole exception to the generally greater warmth of married fathers.

The FF measures the number of activities in the last week involving expressions of warmth between father and child (Table 20.4, columns 2 and 3). Two results are clear. First, mother and father reports are generally similar. The only exception is that mothers report African American unmarried fathers to be warmer than married fathers, but African American married fathers report themselves to be warmer than do unmarried fathers. Second, overall, unmarried biological fathers report that they engage in significantly more warm activities than do married biological fathers (column 3), a phenomenon that is also true for Hispanic fathers, less-educated fathers, low-income fathers (earning less than $2,000 per month), and fathers of girls. Although statistically significant, none of these differences is large.

TABLE 20.3
Differences in Accessibility Between Unmarried (U) and Married (M) Biological Fathers

| | PSID-CDS | Three-City | | |
| | | Children Can Count on | Adolescents Can Count on | Adolescents Can Find Quickly |
	Mother Report	Mother Report	Adol. Report	Adol. Report
All				M
Income (monthly)				
0–$1,000				
$1,001–2,000				
$2,001–3,600				
$3,601–5,600				
$5,601+	—			
Education				
Less than high school				
High school graduate	M			
Some college				
College+	—			
Age of child				
0–1				
2–3				
4–5				
6–13(14)	M+			
0–2				
3–5				
6–9	M+			
10–14				M
Gender of child				
Male				
Female				M
Race				
White				
African American	M		M	M
Hispanic		U		
Other	—			

Note. PSID-CDS children were 0 to 12; Three-City children were 0 to 4 and 10 to 14. All results significant at $p < .10$; + indicates $.05 < p < .10$. — = fewer than 10 cases. Blank cell = no difference.

TABLE 20.4
Differences in Warmth Between Unmarried (U)
and Married (M) Biological Fathers

| | PSID-CDS | Fragile Families | | EHS | Three-City | |
	Father Report	Mother Report	Father Report	Father Report	Mother Report, Children	Adolescent Report
All			U+			M
Income (monthly)						
0–$1,000		U	U			
$1,001–2,000			U		U[a]	M[a]
$2,001–3,600					—	—
$3,601–5,600	—			U	—	—
$5,601+	—				—	—
Education						
Less than high school	M	U+	U			
High school graduate						
Some college				U		
College+	—					
Age of child						
0–1						
2–3						
4–5	—				U	
6–13					U	M
0–2	M					
3–5	M					
6–9						
10–14	—				U	M
Gender of child						
Male	M+					
Female			U+			M
Race						
White						
Black	U	U	M+			M
Hispanic			U			
Other	—					

Note. PSID-CDS children were 0 to 12; Fragile Families children were age 1; EHS children were 0 to 4 and 10 to 14. EHS children were 2 years old. All results significant at $p < .10$; + indicates $.05 < p < .10$. — = fewer than 10 cases. Blank cell = no difference.

[a]The highest income category is $1,000 plus.

The mean frequency of warm activities averages 3.59 to 3.75, which lies between every day and a few times per week. Low-income (under $1,000) married fathers' self-reported warmth averages 3.56, and unmarried fathers' warmth averages 3.73.

We find no overall difference in average levels of warmth between unmarried and married biological fathers in Early Head Start (Table 20.4, column 4). In a few cases (moderately high income and some college education), unmarried fathers show greater warmth than married fathers. Differences are small, however. Regardless of education, income, race, and child's gender, both married and unmarried fathers report that "holding and cuddling their child" is fun almost "all of the time" (married: mean = 3.81; unmarried: mean = 3.86).

Similarly, in the Three-City study, mothers report few significant differences in father closeness to child for the sample as a whole (Table 20.4, columns 5 and 6). Among certain subgroups (e.g., relatively higher income fathers within this low-income sample [$1,000 or more per month]; fathers of 4- to 5-year-olds; and fathers of adolescents), mothers report that unmarried biological fathers have closer relationships with their children than do married biological fathers.

In contrast, adolescents consistently report greater warmth with married than cohabiting fathers, using a standardized measure of the trust and communication in the adolescent–parent relationship. This married versus unmarried father difference is particularly large among African American and female adolescents (not shown). Only one significant subgroup difference emerges within adolescent reports of the negative aspects of their relationships: Adolescents living in very low-income families report higher levels of anger and alienation if they live with their mother and an unmarried father than with their mother and a married father (as captured by a standardized measure of anger and alienation, not shown). Otherwise, anger and alienation do not differ between married and unmarried fathers.

Responsibility

In the PSID-CDS, unmarried biological fathers report significantly greater managerial responsibility for their children than do married biological fathers, which holds across the majority of subgroups (Table 20.5, column 1). The few exceptions are African American fathers, fathers with low incomes (less than $1,000 per month), fathers with a high school education or less, and fathers of very young children (aged 0–1). In these four subgroups, we find no significant difference in responsibility between married and unmarried biological fathers. However, sample sizes are small in some subgroups.

Table 20.5 shows no overall differences between married and unmarried biological fathers in the mean frequency of caregiving activities with

TABLE 20.5
**Differences in Responsibility Between Unmarried (U)
and Married (M) Biological Fathers**

| | PSID-CDS | Fragile Families | EHS | Three-City | | |
| | | | | Mother Report | | |
	Father Report	Mother Report	Father Report	Child Care	Behavior	Parental Agreement
All	U				M	M
Income (monthly)						
0–$1,000			M		M	M
$1,001–2,000	U	U	M			M
$2,001–3,600	U					
$3,601–5,600	—					
$5,601+	—		—			
Education						
Less than high school		U+	M			
High school graduate		U				
Some college	U		M			
College+	—					
Age of child						
0–1				M	M	
2–3	U					M
4–5	—					U
6–13						M
0–2						M
3–5	U					
6–9						
10–14	—					M
Gender of child						
Male	U	U+	M			
Female	U		M		M	M
Race						
White	U		M			
Black						
Hispanic	—	U+	M	M	M	M
Other	—					

Note. PSID-CDS children were 0 to 12; Fragile Families children were age 1; EHS children were 0 to 4 and 10 to 14. EHS children were 2 years old. All results significant at $p < .10$; + indicates $.05 < p < .10$. — = fewer than 10 cases. Blank cell = no difference.

children, as reported by mothers in the FF (column 2). However, we find some differences within subgroups. Generally, unmarried fathers take on more caregiving responsibility than do married fathers. For instance, unmarried Hispanic fathers assume more caregiving responsibility than do married Hispanic fathers. Unmarried fathers participate in more caregiving with boys than do married fathers. In addition, less-educated, unmarried fathers and those with incomes from $1,000 to $2,000 per month also engage in significantly more caregiving than do comparable married fathers. The average frequency of caregiving is high, between a few times per week and every day.

In Early Head Start, we find that, as perceived by fathers, married biological fathers consistently take more responsibility for their children than do unmarried biological fathers (Table 20.5, column 3). Both married and unmarried fathers report that they have "a great deal of influence" in making decisions about such things as education, religion, and health care for their child. However, unmarried fathers with the lowest incomes, those with some college education, those with less than a high school education, and White and Hispanic unmarried men perceive themselves as having less influence than their counterpart married fathers. We find no apparent differences between the responsibility levels of married and unmarried African American men.

In the Three-City study, mothers report no difference in biological fathers' responsibility for basic child care, whether married or unmarried (Table 20.5, column 4). Among specific subgroups of families, however (Hispanic families and families with infants), mothers report married fathers to be more involved in child care than are cohabiting fathers.

Overall differences do appear in responsibility for children's behavior and in parental agreement in the Three-City study. Mothers report married fathers to be significantly more responsible for children's behavior than are cohabiting fathers. Subgroup differences are significant for Hispanic and low-income families, and for fathers of infants and of girls. Finally, mothers report significantly fewer disagreements over children with married than cohabiting biological fathers. This holds for the entire group and for most subgroups.

NONBIOLOGICAL VERSUS BIOLOGICAL FATHERS

In this section, we compare children living with a nonbiological resident father (either cohabiting or step), or a nonbiological father figure, to those living with a married biological father.

Engagement and Activities

Because only the PSID-CDS collected time diary data and activities, we have no comparison data set for this measure of involvement. Married biological fathers spend significantly more time with their children than do married stepfathers or cohabiting partners (Table 20.6). A few categories show no differences between the two groups, such as low-income stepfathers, moderate-income cohabiting fathers, African American cohabiting fathers, and cohabiting fathers of adolescent children. However, overall,

TABLE 20.6
Differences in Levels of Engagement Between Married Biological
Fathers (MB) and Married Stepfathers (S) and Between Married
Biological Fathers (MB) and Cohabiting (C) Partners

	PSID-CDS	
	Step vs. Married Bio	Cohabiting vs. Married Bio
All	MB	MB
Income (monthly)		
0–$1,000		MB
$1,001–2,000	MB	
$2,001–3,600	MB	MB
$3,601–5,600	MB	—
$5601+		—
Education		
Less than high school	MB	—
High school graduate	MB	MB
Some college	MB	MB
College+	MB	—
Age of child		
0–2	—	MB
3–5	MB	MB
6–9	MB	MB
10–13	MB	
14+		
Gender of child		
Male	MB	MB
Female	MB	MB
Race		
White	MB	MB
Black	MB	
Hispanic		—
Other	—	—

Note. PSID-CDS children were 0 to 12, NLSY97 children were 12 to 16. All results significant at $p < .10$; + indicates $.05 < p < .10$. — - fewer than 10 cases. Blank cell = no difference.

married biological fathers are more involved than either married nonbiological stepfathers or cohabiting nonbiological partners. These results seem to indicate that biology is important.

To test whether marriage is important, we also compared stepfathers to unmarried partners, which revealed no statistically significant differences (not shown). This suggests that marriage does not increase engagement among nonbiological fathers. Sample sizes were small, however, so that moderate differences were not statistically significant. Research comparing different types of nonbiological fathers is needed.

Warmth and Affection

Married biological fathers in the PSID-CDS are consistently warmer than either married stepfathers or unmarried cohabiting partners (Table 20.7, columns 1 and 2). Similarly, in the NLSY97, adolescents report significantly greater affection for married biological fathers than for stepfathers or cohabiting partners (columns 3 and 4). However, among low-income families, adolescents report no difference in affection between married biological fathers, stepfathers, and partners of the mother. Teens also report no difference in warmth between married biological fathers and stepfathers who have a college education. Equalizing families' resources and education helps reduce differences in warmth. We also find no differences in affection between related father figures and biological fathers (column 5). None of the subgroups shows a significant difference.

Responsibility

In the PSID-CDS, married biological fathers report taking more responsibility than stepfathers for children (Table 20.8, column 1). No significant differences arose between married biological fathers and cohabiting partners, but sample sizes were too small for precise estimation in most categories (column 2).

In the NLSY97, married biological fathers are reported to monitor their children more than do stepfathers and cohabiting partners (Table 20.8, columns 3 and 4). We did find a few exceptions to these general trends. High-income cohabiting partners (incomes of $3,600 or more per month) monitor their children as well as biological fathers, as do Hispanic cohabiting fathers and stepfathers. Cohabiting fathers with at least some college education also monitor as well as biological fathers. Overall, father figures monitor their children to the same degree as married biological fathers. However, married biological White and African American fathers and married biological fathers of younger adolescents monitored their children more than did comparable father figures.

DISCUSSION

This chapter examined differences in father involvement with children of different ages according to whether the father was biological and married to the child's mother. With all but one of the data sets, we were able to compare the involvement with their children of married and unmarried biological fathers. We chose to focus on men who were fathers not only because they sired children, but also because they lived with them, had a relationship

TABLE 20.7
Differences in Warmth Between Married Biological Fathers (MB)
and Stepfathers (S) and Between Married Biological Fathers (MB)
and Cohabiting (C) Partners

	PSID-CDS		NLSY 97		
	Step vs. Married Bio	Cohabiting vs. Married Bio	Step vs. Married Bio	Cohabiting vs. Married Bio	Father Figure vs. Married Bio
All	MB				
Income (monthly)					
0–$1,000	—	—			
$1,001–2,000	MB	—	MB		
$2,001–3,600	MB	MB	MB	MB	
$3,601–5,600			MB	MB	
$5,601+			MB		
Education					
Less than high school	—	—	MB	MB	
High school graduate		MB	MB	MB	
Some college	MB	MB	MB	—	
College+		—		—	
Age of child					
0–2	—	—	NA	NA	
3–5		—	NA	NA	
6–9	MB	—	NA	NA	
10–13		—	MB	MB	
14+		—	MB	MB	
Gender of child					
Male		—	MB	MB	
Female	MB	MB	MB	MB	
Race					
White	MB	MB	MB	MB	
Black	MB	—	MB	MB	
Hispanic	—	—	MB	MB	
Other	—	—	—	—	

Note. PSID-CDS children were 0 to 12, NLSY97 children were 12 to 16. All results significant at $p < .10$; + indicates $.05 < p < .10$. — = fewer than 10 cases. Blank cell = no difference. NA = not available.

with them, spent time with them, and had some degree of responsibility for their care. Two of the data sets also included stepfathers and partners of the mother, and one included relatives who were father figures. In these latter data sets, we addressed the importance of biology. Here we address how the results can help us better define fathers and father involvement. We focus on how to best define and measure father involvement, who should report it, critical types of fathers to examine, and important subgroups to study.

TABLE 20.8
Differences in Responsibility Between Married Biological Fathers (MB)
and Stepfathers (S) and Between Married Biological Fathers (MB)
and Cohabiting (C) Partners

	PSID-CDS		NLSY 97		
	Step vs. Married Bio	Cohabiting vs. Married Bio	Step vs. Married Bio	Cohabiting vs. Married Bio	Father Figure vs. Married Bio
All					
Income (monthly)		—			
0–$1,000	—	—			
$1,001–2,000			MB	MB	—
$2,001–3,600	MB		MB	MB	
$3,601–5,600		—	MB		
$5,601+		—	MB	—	—
Education					
Less than high school	—	—	MB	MB	
High school graduate			MB		—
Some college	MB+		MB	—	—
College+	—	—		—	—
Age of child					
0–2	—	—	NA	NA	NA
3–5		—	NA	NA	NA
6–9		—	NA	NA	NA
10–13		—	MB	MB	MB
14+	—	—	MB	MB	
Gender of child					
Male		—	MB	MB	
Female	MB		MB	MB	
Race					
White	MB+		MB	MB	MB
Black		—	MB	MB	MB
Hispanic	—	—			—
Other	—	—	—	—	

Note. PSID-CDS children were 0 to 12; NLSY97 children were 12 to 16. All results significant at $p < .10$; + indicates $.05 < p < .10$. — = fewer than 10 cases. Blank cell = no difference. NA - not available.

The Biological Relationship Is Important

It is important to know the biological relationship between each parent and each child in the household because the father–child relationship differs by biology. In general, biological fathers are more involved with children and more accessible than nonbiological fathers. Here, however, the generalizations on fatherhood end. Warmth does not universally favor biological fathers. The two studies that interviewed nonbiological fathers found that, in college-educated families, married nonbiological stepfathers were equally as warm as married biological fathers. Furthermore, in high-income families, married stepfathers were equally responsible as married biological fathers. And, in one of these two studies, high-income stepfathers were just as warm as married biological fathers.

Biology may influence gender differences in parenting. Stepfathers and married biological fathers were equally responsible for male children but not female children, which might represent an example of the gender taboo in stepfamilies. To avoid at least the perception of inappropriate behavior toward stepdaughters, stepfathers may be less involved with daughters, particularly as they mature.

However, we found no evidence that *only* biological fathers contribute to parenting children. Some resident nonbiological fathers and father figures provide substantial fathering to children.

Distinguishing Between Unmarried and Married Fathers Is Important

We found surprising and important differences in fathering based on whether the parents were married. These differences sometimes favored married and sometimes favored unmarried fathers. Although we did not conduct controlled multivariate analyses, and therefore cannot rule out the possibility that the distinctions would disappear if we controlled for demographic characteristics of fathers, we did control for some of these differences and found several significant subgroup distinctions in the influence of marital status on father involvement. We cannot therefore assume that fathering by unmarried biological fathers is equal to fathering by married biological fathers.

The results show that married fathers spend more time with children than unmarried biological fathers. Fathers and adolescents also report that married fathers are more accessible to children. However, unmarried biological fathers in low-income and disadvantaged families are as warm as or warmer than married biological fathers. Although this is surprising, lack of marriage in these groups probably reflects financial constraints as much or more than lack of desire for marriage and involvement with children. In the nationally representative PSID-CDS, married biological fathers rated themselves as warmer than did unmarried biological fathers. Interestingly, adolescents in low-income families report having greater trust in and less alienation from married biological fathers than unmarried biological fathers. The lack of an institutionalized marital relationship is associated with adolescents being more suspicious and less trusting of their fathers. That said, it is rare for teens to be living with a biological father who has not yet married his or her mother. The results for responsibility are completely different from those for warmth. In the Three-City and Early Head Start studies, marriage was associated with greater responsibility of biological fathers for children, but in the national PSID-CDS sample, unmarried biological fathers appear more responsible. The explanation could be an economic one; the PSID-CDS contains higher income families. The fact that the FF, with family income levels higher than Three-City and Early Head Start, also showed more involvement for unmarried fathers, supports the economic argument.

Results may also depend on who provides the information. It seems reasonable that unmarried biological fathers perceive themselves as assuming considerable responsibility for children; however, this may not be the perception of the mother. In the PSID-CDS, the father provided the information, and unmarried father involvement was higher than that of married fathers; whereas in the Three-City study, which showed greater married father responsibility, it was the mother. However, Early Head Start, which showed more involvement for married fathers, also relied on father reports.

Finally, the questions vary in their conceptualization of responsibility. The FF measure was based on mothers' reports of caregiving for their young children, whereas the PSID-CDS and Early Head Start included managerial responsibility. The type of responsibility and age of the child may influence the parent's response to the question. The context of the survey is also likely to affect fathers' and mothers' responses to the question. More work is needed to develop a better set of items on responsibility. In addition, we must place the responses in the broader context of their family circumstances, such as income of the family, culture, and developmental stage of the child.

Including Father Figures Is Important

The important roles of father figures in the lives of children, as shown in the PSID-CDS and the NLSY97, suggest that studies should do a better job of measuring the contributions of these men. It is likely that the presence of father figures will affect children's outcomes. When we think of father figures, we typically think of cohabiting men, and these men do spend time with and father children. However, adolescent children do not report the same level of affection and trust in cohabiting fathers, biological or not, as in married fathers. Adolescents' opinions differ from those of mothers, who report the relationship with a cohabiting, biological father more positively. Research should particularly address the relationship with cohabiting non-biological father figures, related or not. This is not typically done unless this person is the guardian of the child. Typically, mothers are asked to nominate a father figure, but without a confirmation from the father figure that he sees himself as such. However, it is worth more research to identify the best approaches to studying father figures.

Socioeconomic Status and Cultural Differences Are Important

Fathering is likely to differ by the economic situation of the family. The five studies differed in the socioeconomic status of the participants. Although the results show substantial similarities between the parenting involvement of resident married and unmarried biological fathers, the FF results suggest that, in the most disadvantaged families (in particular, those with a high school education or less and those with low monthly incomes), unmarried biological fathers spend more time than married biological fathers in activities with children. This may reflect differences in the work schedules and availability of these disadvantaged married and unmarried fathers; the latter may be working nights or evenings or fewer hours than married fathers. Other research has shown that fathers who spend more time working spend less time with—and take less responsibility for—their children (Hofferth & Anderson, 2003). However, it may also reflect differences in the expectations of and constraints faced by low-income parents in the rearing of children.

Hispanic, African American, and White fathers may also have different expectations for father involvement because of cultural differences. In contrast to other groups, marriage seemed to be associated with greater involvement overall (except for warmth) for African American than for other fathers. Marriage was an important factor contributing to Hispanic fathers assuming responsibility for their children. African American fathers are much less likely, and Hispanic fathers are more likely, than White fathers to be married (Hofferth, 2003).

Response Rates and Representativeness of Fathers

Fathers' cooperation in survey research affects the appearance of their involvement with their children. Those studies that are the most selective in their coverage of fathers will interview the most involved fathers. One way to determine whether this is a problem is to obtain information from the mother about the demographic characteristics of the father so that researchers can compare those who participate with those who do not. Several of our studies made such comparisons.

A major limitation of most of these studies was the small number of men in some of the father categories, such as unmarried biological fathers and cohabiting partners of the mother. We need substantial sample sizes or targeted sampling to capture these important father groups.

Measuring Father Involvement Requires Additional Study

Engagement. Measuring engagement by the reported number of activities in the past month is not the same as calculating it from time diaries or observations (e.g., videotape). This chapter provides evidence that the time diary measures more comprehensively capture the amount of time that children spend with their father and mother than parent reports. In our analyses, we find greater differences between married and unmarried biological father involvement through diary data than stylized activities lists. Time diaries also likely reflect less social desirability bias than stylized measures. The diary takes time to fill out, but it captures a significant amount of information relatively reliably. Videotaped observations are the most accurate way to collect information about what occurs between parents and children at a particular time. Yet, again, they are burdensome to respondents and can capture only a small proportion of a day.

Accessibility. The accessibility measure used in the Three-City study seems to be a reasonably good measure of maternal perceptions of father availability for child care and adolescent perceptions of father accessibility. The accessibility measure drawn from the time diaries in the PSID-CDS presents some problems because the diaries require editing to ensure that everyone present during each time period is mentioned in the diary. This is time-consuming, and its omission can result in underreporting the presence of multiple persons. Additionally, physical and emotional accessibility may be different constructs. Just because a father is physically accessible does not mean that a child in need will turn to him.

Warmth. The frequency of warm behaviors reported by parents distinguishes differences in paternal emotional involvement for younger, but not older, children. Older children should report this for themselves. Mothers' reports may be a measure of her trust in her partner rather than the actual warmth experienced by the child. Moreover, mothers cannot observe the relationship when they are not there.

Responsibility. Finally, responsibility is a promising measure to explore. The measures used across studies are quite different, with some focusing on caregiving (FF, Three-City study) and others focusing on managerial decisions (Early Head Start, PSID-CDS). Ideally, such a measure has the potential to distinguish among fathers who coparent and those who do not. Most of the studies used a question format to measure responsibility, but a degree of standardization in what is included would be useful. That is, researchers should tap not just activities, but also managerial responsibility. The results differ across studies, and it was not possible to explain whether this is because of different questions or different samples.

Reports From Both Fathers and Mothers on Father Behavior Are Useful

Having both mother and father reports was helpful when comparing the implications of different reporters. Studies that offered reports from both parents (FF and Early Head Start) show similar conclusions across reporters. However, when comparing mothers and adolescent reporters (as in the NLSY97), the reporter appears to make a difference; mothers typically paint a much rosier picture of relationships.

Given the difficulty of obtaining reports from fathers, the evidence that mothers are relatively reliable reporters of certain types of father involvement is reassuring. However, maternal reports will often differ from adolescents' reports of their relationship with their father. The study's purpose can help determine the most accurate reporter. Alternatively, more sophisticated study designs should build in assessments of multiple family members' opinions.

Obtain Similar Measures for Mothers and for Fathers

One conclusion seems clear: Measures used for both mothers and fathers should be the same. There is little justification for different measures for the two reporters. Including different measures makes comparing responses difficult.

CONCLUSIONS

The five studies analyzed for this chapter are some of the first to examine father involvement in different family types and, as such, they are pioneering. The results suggest that, generally, married biological fathers tend to be more involved with children than do unmarried biological fathers, and biological fathers tend to be more involved than do nonbiological fathers. However, there are important exceptions to these generalizations for subgroups of the population. These results also suggest, therefore, that fathering is not a simple concept and that context matters.

Notes

1. This was defined as monthly family income for four of the studies (PSID-CDS, Early Head Start, FF, and NLSY97) and monthly paternal income in the Three-City study.
2. Response choices on the activity items varied in two versions of the survey. In the initial cities, the survey offered five categorical responses, ranging from "never" to "every day." In the later cities, the survey asked respondents the number of days in the past week that the father engaged in the activity, ranging from 0 to 7. For this analysis, we analyzed the frequencies on the responses and integrated them into the four categories noted.

APPENDIX

TABLE A1
Descriptive Characteristics, 1997 PSID-CDS

| | | | Type of Father | | | | | | | |
	Total Sample	%	Married Bio N	%	Unmarried N	%	Step N	%	Cohab N	%
All	1,993		1,650	82.8	142	7.12	129	6.47	72	3.61
FAMILY INCOME										
0–$1,000	126	6.3	70	4.2	32	22.5	12	9.3	12	16.7
$1,001–$2,000	294	14.8	190	11.5	40	28.2	37	28.7	27	37.5
$2,001–$3,600	557	27.9	460	27.9	41	28.9	33	25.6	23	31.9
$3,601–$5,600	492	24.7	445	27.0	20	14.1	23	17.8		0.0
$5,601+	524	26.3	485	29.4		0.0	24	18.6		0.0
EDUCATION										0.0
High school	308	15.5	254	15.4	36	25.4	13	10.1		0.0
High school graduate	637	32.0	529	32.1	43	30.3	42	32.6	23	31.9
Some college	557	27.9	399	24.2	56	39.4	63	48.8	39	54.2
College plus	491	24.6	468	28.4		0.0	11	8.5		0.0
CHILD'S AGE										
0–1 years	306	15.4	252	15.3	47	33.1	—			0.0
2–3 years	312	15.7	252	15.3	40	28.2	10	7.8	10	13.9
4–5 years	309	15.5	261	15.8	17	12.0	19	14.7	12	16.7
6–13 years	1,066	53.5	885	53.6	38	26.8	97	75.2	46	63.9
0–2 years	479	24.0	394	23.9	68	47.9	—		11	15.3
3–5 years	448	22.5	371	22.5	36	25.4	26	20.2	15	20.8
6–9 years	581	29.2	484	29.3	24	16.9	46	35.7	27	37.5
10–13 years	485	24.3	401	24.3	14	9.9	51	39.5	19	26.4
MONTHS WITH FATHER										
0–25%	81	4.1		0.0		0.0	46	35.7	35	48.6
26–75%	106	5.3	37	2.2	26	18.3	39	30.2		0.0
76–100%	1806	90.6	1613	97.8	116	81.7	44	34.1	33	45.8
CHILD'S GENDER		0.0		0.0		0.0		0.0		
Male	1,016	51.0	841	51.0	72	50.7	70	54.3	33	45.8
Female	977	49.0	809	49.0	70	49.3	59	45.7	39	54.2
RACE		0.0		0.0						
Non-Hispanic White	1,228	61.6	1087	65.9	46	32.4	53	41.1	42	58.3
Non-Hispanic Black	510	25.6	351	21.3	74	52.1	60	46.5	25	34.7
Hispanic	172	8.6	144	8.7	16	11.3	11	8.5		0.0
Other	83	4.2	68	4.1		0.0		0.0		0.0

Note. Means weighted by population weights. Blank = fewer than 10 cases.

TABLE A2
Descriptive Statistics, Fragile Families Study

	Total Sample	%	Married Bio N	Married Bio %	Unmarried N	Unmarried %
			Type of Father			
All	2,673	100.0	1,309	49.0	1,364	51.0
FAMILY INCOME						
0–$1,000	469	20.0	132	11.3	337	28.7
$1,001–$2,000	495	21.1	171	14.7	324	27.6
$2,001–$3,600	543	23.2	258	22.1	285	24.2
$3,601–$5,600	449	19.2	285	24.4	164	14.0
$5,601+	386	16.5	320	27.4	66	5.6
EDUCATION						
High school	778	29.4	258	19.8	520	38.6
High school graduate	866	32.7	334	25.7	532	39.5
Some college	605	22.8	354	27.2	251	18.6
College plus	400	15.1	356	27.3	44	3.3
CHILD'S GENDER						
Male	1,403	52.6	697	53.3	706	51.9
Female	1,266	47.4	611	46.7	655	48.1
RACE						
Non-Hispanic White	679	25.5	508	38.9	171	12.6
Non-Hispanic Black	1,074	40.3	365	28.0	709	52.1
Hispanic	797	29.9	354	27.1	443	32.5
Other	118	4.4	79	6.1	39	2.9

Note. All data are unweighted from the 1-year follow-up survey. Categories may not sum to totals because of missing data.

TABLE A3
Descriptive Characteristics, Three-City Study

| | | | Total Sample | | | | Adolescent Sample[a] | | | |
| | | | Married Bio | | Unmarried | | Married Bio | | Unmarried | |
	Total Sample	%	N	%	N	%	N	%	N	%
All	372		257	69.09	115	30.91	112	0.30	20	5.38
PATERNAL INCOME										
0–$501	185	49.7	105	40.9	80	69.6	44	39.3	13	65.0
$501–$1,000	77	20.7	58	22.6	19	16.5	22	19.6	7	35.0
$1,001+	110	29.6	94	36.6	16	13.9	46	41.1		0.0
CHILD'S AGE										
0–1 years	97	26.1	49	19.1	48	41.7	NA	NA	NA	NA
2–3 years	91	24.5	60	23.3	31	27.0	NA	NA	NA	NA
4–5 years	48	12.9	34	13.2	14	12.2	NA	NA	NA	NA
6–9 years	NA	NA	NA	NA	NA	NA	NA	NA	NA	NA
10–14 years	136	36.6	114	44.4	22	19.1	112	100.0	20	100.0
0–2 years	144	38.7	79	30.7	65	56.5	NA	NA	NA	NA
3–5 years	92	24.7	64	24.9	28	24.3	NA	NA	NA	NA
6–9 years	NA	NA	NA	NA	NA	NA	NA	NA	NA	NA
10–14 years	136	36.6	114	44.4	22	19.1	112	100.0	20	100.0
CHILD'S GENDER										
Male	187	50.3	130	50.6	57	49.6	54	48.2	8	40.0
Female	185	49.7	127	49.4	58	50.4	58	51.8	12	60.0
RACE										
Non-Hispanic White	37	9.9	22	8.6	15	13.0	10	8.9	9	45.0
Non-Hispanic Black	113	30.4	57	22.2	56	48.7	22	19.6	11	55.0
Hispanic	222	59.7	178	69.3	44	38.3	80	71.4		0.0
Other										

Note. Cells with n < 5 are not included in statistical comparisons. NA = not applicable.
[a]For variables drawn from adolescent reports.

Descriptive Characteristics, Early Head Start

	Total Sample	%	Type of Father			
			Married Bio		Unmarried	
			N	%	N	%
All	458		338		120	
FAMILY INCOME						
0–$1,000	141	30.8	98	29.0	43	35.8
$1,001–$2,000	216	47.2	163	48.2	53	44.2
$2,001–$3,600	85	18.6	66	19.5	19	15.8
$3,601–%5,600	15	3.3	10	3.0		0.0
$5,601+		0.0		0.0		0.0
EDUCATION						
High school	236	51.5	157	46.4	79	65.8
High school graduate	93	20.3	65	19.2	28	23.3
Some college	145	31.7	124	36.7	21	17.5
College plus						
CHILD'S GENDER						
Male	245	53.5	173	51.2	72	60.0
Female	232	50.7	175	51.8	57	47.5
RACE						
Non-Hispanic White	237	51.7	185	54.7	51	42.5
Non-Hispanic Black	75	16.4	38	11.2	38	31.7
Hispanic	152	33.2	112	33.1	38	31.7
Other	14	3.1	12	3.6		0.0

Note. Blank = fewer than 10 cases.

Descriptive Characteristics, NLSY97

	Total Sample	%	Type of Father							
			Married Bio		Step		Cohab		Fatherlike	
			N	%	N	%	N	%	N	%
All	3,885		3,138		542		107		98	
FAMILY INCOME										
0–$1,000	279	7.2	188	6.0	49	9.0	32	29.9	10	10.2
$1,001–$2,000	387	10.0	288	9.2	74	13.7	19	17.8		0.0
$2,001–$3,600	685	17.6	550	17.5	106	19.6	21	19.6		0.0
$3,601–%5,600	735	18.9	619	19.7	89	16.4	13	12.1	14	14.3
$5,601+	791	20.4	691	22.0	90	16.6		0.0		0.0
Missing	971	25.0	796	25.4	131	24.2	17	15.9	27	27.6
EDUCATION										
High school	1,275	32.8	915	29.2	156	28.8	85	79.4	89	90.8
High school grad	1,100	28.3	887	28.3	196	36.2	12	11.2		0.0
Some college	1,153	29.7	1,012	32.2	128	23.6		0.0		0.0
College plus	357	9.2	324	10.3	32	5.9		0.0		0.0
CHILD'S AGE										
LE 14 years	2,608	67.1	2,103	67.0	377	69.6	73	68.2	55	56.1
GT 14 years	1,277	32.9	1,035	33.0	165	30.4	34	31.8	43	43.9
CHILD'S GENDER										
Male	2,060	53.0	1,665	53.1	281	51.8	55	51.4	59	60.2
Female	1,825	47.0	1,473	46.9	261	48.2	52	48.6	39	39.8
RACE										
Non-Hispanic White	2,539	65.4	2,130	67.9	325	60.0	42	39.3	42	42.9
Non-Hispanic Black	753	19.4	519	16.5	142	26.2	47	43.9	45	45.9
Hispanic	453	11.7	373	11.9	56	10.3	15	14.0		0.0

Note. Blank = fewer than 10 cases.

21

Measuring Contact Between Children and Nonresident Fathers

Laura Argys

University of Colorado–Denver

Elizabeth Peters

Cornell University

Steven Cook

University of Wisconsin–Madison

Steven Garasky

Iowa State University

Lenna Nepomnyaschy

Columbia University

Elaine Sorensen

The Urban Institute

High rates of divorce and nonmarital childbearing in the United States mean that many children will spend some of their childhood in a single-parent family. Data from the General Social Survey (Ellwood & Jencks, 2002) show that 44% of respondents who turned 16 in the 1990s reported that they were not living with both of their own parents at age 16. In their 1994 landmark study, McLanahan and Sandefur documented the differences in outcomes for children who grew up in an intact family and those who did not. Children from intact families had higher test scores, more education, higher wages, and a lower incidence of teen childbearing. Their analysis shows that about one half of the differences in outcomes can be attributed to differences in economic circumstances between the two groups, but the other one half stems from other factors.

Reduced interaction with the nonresident parent, most often the father, is one factor that could explain the poorer outcomes for children of single parents. Data from a variety of sources show that a large minority of children with nonresident fathers have not seen their fathers at all in the past year. There is also some evidence that contact drops off over time.

Various theories have been developed to explain the potential impact of father involvement on the outcomes of children of single parents. Economic theories stress the idea that fathers who have contact with their children can more easily monitor how their child support dollars are being spent, and are thus more willing to provide that support (Argys & Peters, 2003; Y. Weiss & Willis, 1985). Additional child support, in turn, increases the resources available to the children. Sociologists stress the potential loss of social capital from reduced involvement of fathers (J. Coleman, 1988). Psychologists suggest that more involved fathers can contribute to their children's well-being by acting as positive role models, maintaining effective discipline and supervision, and providing support for the mother. Specifically, emotional closeness to fathers can strengthen children's emotional security and help them cope with stress, and authoritative parenting helps children develop self-regulation and internalize social norms (Amato & Gilbreth, 1999; Lamb, 1997).

A few small-scale studies found positive benefits from contact with non-resident fathers (Hetherington, Cox, & Cox, 1978; Wallerstein & Kelly, 1980). Surprisingly, however, most studies based on large-scale, nationally representative data have found very little correlation between measures of child well-being (both behavioral and cognitive outcomes) and the amount of contact children have with their nonresident fathers (Amato & Gilbreth, 1999; Furstenberg & Harris, 1993; Furstenberg, Morgan, & Allison, 1987; V. King, 1994).

One possible explanation is that existing data sets may not measure the quantity of the father–child interaction very well. For example, father–child interactions are likely to change over the life cycle or even over the calendar year (e.g., children of divorce spending summer months with their father), and a point-in-time measure may not accurately capture the amount of contact. Also, the resident mother usually reports contact, and it is possible that she may underestimate the amount of interaction between the nonresident father and his children. In addition, most data sets, at best, try to measure the quantity of time nonresident fathers spend with their children, but they do not measure the quality of that interaction. Yet the few studies that have investigated the quality of father–child interactions find that it is quality rather than quantity that matters (Amato & Gilbreth, 1999). Finally, some studies find that the relationship between the two parents moderates the effect of father contact. When parental conflict is low, contact with nonresident fathers is more likely to have beneficial effects on children (Amato & Rezac, 1994; Hetherington et al., 1982).

Another important aspect of contact that is often ignored in studies is the legal context in which this occurs. This is important because policymakers cannot directly legislate the nature of the father–child relationship, but they do have some policy tools available (e.g., laws regarding custody and visitation and child support enforcement). Seltzer (1998) found that having a joint legal custody agreement led to increased father involvement, even after controlling for his predivorce level of involvement.

In this chapter, we document substantial differences in reported levels of contact between nonresident fathers and their children across several data sets. We highlight the difficulties in measuring this dynamic, complex, and multidimensional behavior, and we discuss the ways in which surveys have attempted to measure the quality of the time that children spend with their nonresident fathers.

We first describe the six data sets we use in our analysis and then begin the analysis with a discussion of legal-custody agreements. The next section compares basic measures of father–child contact in these data sets. We then document and discuss measurement difficulties that arise from differences in the definitions of contact, differences in reports of contact by mothers and fathers, and differences in patterns of irregular contact. Finally, we focus on measures of the quality of father–child contact. This chapter concludes with recommendations about the collection of data on contact between children and their nonresident parent.

DATA

Four of the six data sets we use are nationally representative (after weighting), and the other two target specific populations. The National Survey of America's Families (NSAF) and the Survey of Income and Program Participation (SIPP) are nationally representative, family-level data sets. The National Longitudinal Survey of Youth 1997 (NLSY97) cohort is nationally representative of adolescents who were aged 12 to 16 in 1997. The National Longitudinal Survey of Youth 1979 child data are representative of children ever born to mothers who were aged 35 to 43 in 2000. We also analyze the Fragile Families and Child Wellbeing Study (FF), a survey of new parents with nonmarital births in large U.S. cities, and the Wisconsin Child Support Demonstration Evaluation (WCSDE) survey data, which surveyed women who entered Wisconsin's Temporary Assistance for Needy Families (TANF) program during a 9-month period in the late 1990s.

The NSAF surveyed U.S. civilian, noninstitutionalized residents under age 65 with the intent of assessing child, adult, and family well-being in America. We focus on households with children up to the age of 18 who live with their mothers and have nonresident, living fathers, and we use mothers' reports of contact from the 1999 interviews. Because of the sampling design, these data are representative of households, not children. (For more information on the NSAF data, see http://www.urban.org/Content/ Research/NewFederalism/NSAF/Overview/NSAFOverview.htm.)

The SIPP data are from the 1996 panel, which includes a nationally representative sample of approximately 36,000 households. The households were interviewed every 4 months for 4 years. Core information gathered at each interview (or wave) included basic demographic and economic data. Each wave also collected detailed information about specific topics. Our analyses use data from the child support module (Wave 5 in 1997), which also included questions about how much contact the child had with the nonresident father in the past year and data about custody arrangements. Although the sampling unit in the SIPP is a family, mothers reported contact information separately for individual children. (See http://www.sipp .census.gov/sipp for further information.)

The NLSY79 child data consists of more than 10,000 children who were ever born to the original 6,289 female respondents from the NLSY79 cohort. The NLSY79 was designed to be nationally representative of the cohort born between 1957 and 1964, with an oversample of African American, Hispanic, and economically disadvantaged adolescents. Children born to the female respondents were followed in a supplement to this survey, and information about these children, provided by the mothers in the 2000 survey, compose the samples for our analyses. The NLSY79 child data are representative of 90% of all children born to mothers who were aged 35 to 43 in 2000. (Additional information can be found at http://www.bls .gov/nls/nlsy79.htm.)

The 1997 cohort of the NLSY consists of a sample of nearly 9,000 young men and women between ages 12 and 16 at the time of sample selection at the end of 1996. These adolescents undergo interviews annually and provide their own reports of contact with their nonresident fathers and their attitudes toward their fathers. Their resident parent was also interviewed in 1997, and provided information on legal agreements between parents (i.e., child support, paternity establishment, and legal- and physical-custody agreements). These are child-level data provided from a nationally representative sample of adolescents born between 1980 and 1984. (See http://www.bls.gov/nls/nlsy97.htm for additional information.)

Fragile Families is a longitudinal survey of parents with nonmarital births between 1998 and 2000. Mothers and fathers were interviewed in the hospital shortly after their child was born and were reinterviewed when the child was 1, 3, and 5 years old. All respondents were located in 20 U.S. cities, and the data are nationally representative of parents with nonmarital births in cities with populations of 200,000 or more. We use both mother and father reports of contact from the 1-year follow-up, conducted between 1999 and 2002. Children were, on average, 15 months old at the time of the FF 1-year follow-up. (FF information can be found at http://crcw.princeton.edu/fragilefamilies/index.asp.)

The WCSDE offers data on child support dating back more than 20 years. We use data from a 1999 survey of mothers who entered Wisconsin's TANF program, called "Wisconsin Works," between September 1997 and June 1998. The WCSDE obtains information from both a resident parent and a legally adjudicated, nonresident parent of a focal child, but it is representative only of families that entered the TANF program in Wisconsin during a 9-month period. (See http://www.irp.wisc.edu/research/childsup/csde.htm for additional information.)

It should be noted that other data sets could be used to examine father–child contact. The Panel Study of Income Dynamics: Child Development Supplement (Hofferth et al., 2002), the National Longitudinal Survey of Adolescent Health (Harris & Ryan, 2004), and the Current Population Survey Child Support Supplement are nationally representative and provide information on contact between children and their nonresident fathers. The Stanford Child Custody Study and the Arizona State Survey of Separating Families are examples of other geographically restricted data sets that sample previously married parents and could yield insights into father–child contact.

In the descriptive statistics that follow, we often divide our samples by race (White, non-Hispanic, or non-White), and by reason for father's absence. We classify children into two groups by reason for father's absence: those whose parents were unmarried at the time of the child's birth and who never married each other; and those whose parents were married at one time, but subsequently divorced or separated. Table A1 in the Appendix reports sample sizes separated by race and age group.

LEGAL CHILD CUSTODY

We begin with a discussion of legal, or de jure, child custody arrangements because the policies that regulate and enforce those legal agreements are the only direct way for the state to affect parents' decisions about their child's residence. De jure custody agreements can specify three aspects of custody: legal custody, physical custody, and, less often, visitation. We focus on physical custody, or which parent has primary residential responsibility for the child.

De jure physical custody usually falls into one of four categories: mother as sole custodian, father as sole custodian, joint custody in which the children spend some time with each parent, or split custody in which some children live primarily with their mother and others live primarily with their father. More than 80% of the agreements in the NLSY97 identified the mother as the sole custodian, but fathers are the primary custodian in more than 12% of the cases. Joint custody was awarded in 4% of the cases, and the remainder fell into "other" or "no custody" categories.

These agreements can change as a result of changes in parents' economic circumstances, age of the child, marital status of the parents, or other conditions (Peters, Argys, Maccoby, & Mnookin, 1993). Of the 1,614 adolescents in the NLSY97 for whom an original custody agreement was reached, 105 (6.5%) at some point made a legal change to that agreement. Of those, 14 experienced a third change in custody. The most common change in custody (44%) entailed a switch from the father as the sole custodian to the mother; 18% switched sole custody from the mother to the father. More than 11% of changes shifted from joint custody to sole custody by the mother. Very few agreements shifted from sole custody by either parent to joint custody.

Another example of the fluid nature of children's residential arrangements is that the actual de facto residence of the child may vary substantially from the de jure agreement. The NLSY97 data allow us to compare the de jure physical custody mandated by the custody agreement with the actual overnight stays with the father. For this analysis, our sample includes all children who have a legal agreement indicating their custody arrangement. Figure 21.1 shows the distribution of the reports of the number of nights the children in the NLSY97 stay with their fathers by the three de jure custody categories: sole-mother, sole-father, and joint custody. Among children with sole-mother custody arrangements, more than 70% never stay overnight with their fathers, but more than one quarter spend at least 50 nights per year at their fathers' homes, indicating a substantial amount of residential contact between a father and child within this custody category.

Of children whose parents were awarded joint custody, about two thirds spend at least 100 nights per year with their father, as expected. However, more than 20% of children never stayed overnight with their father in the past year. Unsurprisingly, in nearly 90% of cases in which fathers have sole custody, children stay overnight with their fathers more than 100 nights per year. However, 10% of children whose fathers have sole custody spend 25 nights or fewer per year with their fathers, and most of this group report never having spent the night with their father throughout the year. These

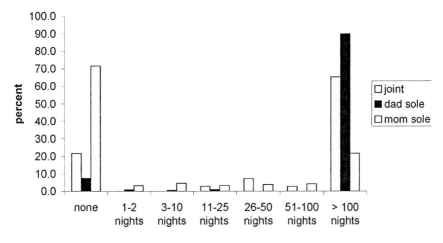

FIG. 21.1.   Number of overnights with father by custody type, NLSY97.

results suggest that, although legal, physical-custody categories reflect actual residential patterns for most children, for a substantial minority of children current residential arrangements may deviate substantially from the original de jure physical custody agreement.

Legal modifications to child support awards are much more prevalent than changes to custody agreements (Peters et al., 1993; see also chap. 22, this volume). This difference may stem from the fact that child support agreements are legally enforceable, and both the federal and state governments have invested substantial resources toward collecting child support, but, as yet, many states are reluctant to enforce custody and visitation arrangements. Although infrequent, these changes in custody agreements, and more informal changes in de facto residential arrangements, have been found to cause changes in other parent–child interactions. Alterations in child support payments, either legal or informal, often accompany changes in custody arrangements as the out-of-pocket expenditures associated with residence shift from one parent to the other (Peters et al., 1993).

Data on de jure custody arrangements are available in only a few data sets, but data on actual contact between children and their nonresident parents are more common, and all of our data sets measure some aspect of that contact. The samples for our analysis of contact consist of children from each data set who at the time of the survey were living with their biological mothers, and whose fathers were alive but are not residing in the same home. We focus on nonresident fathers because, even in those data sets that provide the information, the samples of nonresident mothers are too small for independent analyses.

BASIC MEASURES OF NONRESIDENT
PARENT–CHILD CONTACT

All data sets used in these analyses allow us to identify whether the child had any contact with his or her nonresident father and, if so, to measure the frequency of contact. However, the variation in the phrasing of the questions is significant. Consequently, the variation in the patterns of reported contact is also significant. Differences in patterns of contact may also result from differences in whether the sample is representative of children or families.

Table 21.1 highlights differences among our six data sets in sample design and in the wording of the questions used to ascertain the amount of contact between a father and his child. The FF and SIPP surveys both ask parents about the amount of contact and allow them to report the number of days of contact, or in the case of SIPP, the number of days, weeks, or months. In contrast, the other surveys only allow respondents to report the amount of contact within broad categories indicating regular, repeated contact, such as once a week or one to three times per month. The NLSY79 child data and the WCSDE follow these questions about frequency of contact with a question about the length of the visits. To measure the annual amount of contact, we assign a numeric equivalent, usually the midpoint, for each re-ported category. For example, in the NSAF data, "more than once a week" equals 104 days of contact; "about once a week" equals 52 days of contact; "1 to 3 times per month" equals 24 days of contact; "1 to 11 times per year" equals 6 days of contact; and "less than 3 months" equals 45 days.

Using the conversions of the information from these questions, Table 21.2 categorizes the amount of father–child contact according to reason for the father's absence and by the child's race and age for children who reside with their mother. For each data set, the first column indicates the proportion of children who report having had any contact with their fathers in the past year. The second column lists the mean number of days of annual contact for children with any contact. (The children represented in the FF data set are asked about any contact and amount of contact with the father in the past 30 days rather than in the past year. We multiply the amount of contact in the past 30 days by 12 to make it comparable to the other data sets.)

Patterns of contact vary by the reason for the father's absence. In gen-eral, contact is more likely among children whose parents were married than among those whose parents never married, and the difference is much more pronounced for White children. For example, in the NLSY97, 79% of White children aged 12 to 17/18 whose parents were divorced or separated saw their father in the past year, compared with only 41% of White children aged 12 to 17/18 whose parents never married. As mentioned previously, the low incidence of children living primarily with their fathers limits our analysis to children who reside with their mothers. Thus, the incidence of contact between children and their fathers reported here is an understatement of father–child contact for all children of unmarried parents.

Racial differences are also evident. Most of the data sets indicate that, among children whose parents are divorced or separated, White children are more likely to have contact with their parents. This difference is particularly pronounced in the SIPP data. The pattern is less clear for children whose parents never married. Typically, more non-White children whose parents never married report having some contact with their fathers than do White children whose parents never married. In the NSAF, for example, non-White children are 11 to 14 percentage points more likely than White children to report having seen their fathers in the past year. It is interesting that the average number of days of contact between father and child, conditional on any contact, does not differ strikingly by race and reason for father's absence. However, this finding is unsurprising, given that having any contact is selective of fathers who want to be involved in their children's lives, and this reduces variation across the characteristics that are associated with this selection.

What is most striking about the reports of father–child contact in Table 21.2, and perhaps most alarming to researchers, are the large differences across survey results, even among surveys that use similar sampling frameworks and within the same race and age groups and by reason for father's absence. For each of the rows in Table 21.2, we compared the lowest mean level of any contact with the highest. In all cases but one, the difference is significant at the 5% level and often at 1%. For example, the NSAF reports that 79% to 84% of White children whose parents were previously married reported some contact during the past year. In contrast, the SIPP data suggest that only 63% to 73% of White children whose parents were previously married saw their fathers in the past year. The differences between the reports of contact in these two surveys, both of which are nationally representative of families, are even more pronounced for non-White children whose parents never married. Should we be concerned that, according to the SIPP data, fewer than one half of these children under age 6 see their fathers each year? Or should we be reassured by the NSAF statistics that nearly three quarters of these non-White children report annual contact with their fathers?

OTHER ASPECTS OF NONRESIDENT PARENT–CHILD CONTACT

Despite the fact that few studies have been able to demonstrate that contact per se or the amount of contact has an effect on children, interactions between a nonresident father and his child are most often summarized by

TABLE 21.1

Survey Questions on Nonresident Parent–Child Contact

Fragile Families and Child Wellbeing (FF)	Since (CHILD) was born, has (FATHER) seen (him/her)? During the past 30 days, how many days has (FATHER) seen (CHILD)? Since (CHILD's) birth, has (CHILD) ever stayed overnight with (FATHER)? How many nights altogether has (CHILD) spent with (FATHER)?	Representative of parents with a nonmarital birth in 20 large U.S. cities between 1998 and 2000
Children of the National Longitudinal Survey of Youth 1979 (NLSY79 Child Data)	In the past 12 months (or since separated from mother/father) how often has (BIO CHILD 01) seen his/her mother/father? *Almost every day, 2–5 times a week, about once a week, 1–3 times a month, 7–11 times in past 12 months, 2–6 times in past 12 months, once in past 12 months, never* How long do these visits usually last?	Representative of children of mothers who were ages 35–43 in 2000
National Longitudinal Survey of Youth, 1997 (NLSY97)	Thinking about the last 12 months or since you began living apart: How many times have you received a card, letter, or phone call from your biological father? *Never, once or twice, less than once a month, about twice a month, about once a week, several times a week, every day* How many times have YOU contacted or tried to contact your biological father either by mail or phone? *Same responses as above* How many times have you visited your biological father either at his house, your house, or somewhere else without spending the night? *Same responses as above* Thinking only about the last 12 months or since you began living apart, have you ever stayed overnight at your biological father's house? *Same responses as above*	Representative of children born between 1980 and 1984

	How many nights have you stayed over at your biological father's house during the past 12 months or since you began living apart? Think about visits at holidays, during vacations, and other times like weekends. *Once or twice, 3–10 nights, 11–25 nights, 26–50 nights, 51–100 nights, more than 100 nights*	
National Survey of America's Families (NSAF)	Does (CHILD) have (a biological/an adoptive/a biological or adoptive) father who lives somewhere else? During the last 12 months how often has (CHILD) seen (his/her) father? [If child lived with father in last 12 months, record the times the father has seen the child since child and father no longer lived together.] *Not at all, more than once a week, about once a week, one to three times a month, one to 11 times a year, other (specify)*	Representative of families in 1999
Survey of Income and Program Participation (SIPP)	Did all of the children visit the other parent about the same number of days in the past 12 months? What is the total amount of time (the child/all children/the oldest child) spent visiting the other parent in the past 12 months? ____ days ____ weeks ____ months	Representative of families in 1996
Wisconsin Child Support Demonstration Evaluation—Mother Survey (WCSDE)	During the time you and (focal child's) father lived apart in 1998, did (focal child) spend time with his/her father, even one time? *yes no* During the time you and (focal child's) father lived apart in 1998, did (focal child) spend time with his/her father? *About every week, about every other week, about every month, less than that* Next, I'd like to know about how many days (focal child) spent time with his/her father on each of these visits. Count each day when they saw each other at all, even for a short time. During the time you and (focal child's) father lived apart in 1998, on about how many days every [week/other week/month] did (focal child) spend with his/her father?	Representative of families entering the TANF program in Wisconsin between September 1997 and June 1998

385

TABLE 21.2
Contact Between Children and Their Nonresident Fathers Within the Past Year, by Race, Age, and Reason for Father's Absence

	Fragile Families (1st Year Follow-Up)		NLSY 1979 Child (2000 Interview)		NLSY 1997 (1997 Interview)		NSAF (1997 Interview)		SIPP (1997 Interview)		Wisconsin Mother Survey	
	Any Contact (%)[a]	Days of Contact (Mean)[a]	Any Contact (%)	Days of Contact (Mean)	Any Contact (%)	Days of Contact (Mean)	Any Contact (%)	Days of Contact (Mean)	Any Contact (%)	Days of Contact (Mean)	Any Contact (%)	Days of Contact (Mean)
Children of divorced or separated parents												
Non-White Age 0–5	—	—	86	89.7	—	—	90	66.5	44	50.0	67[b]	80.9[b]
Age 6–11	—	—	84	100.0	—	—	82	42.0	44	33.4	83	81.7
Age 12–17/18	—	—	74	107.0	67	65.6	76	40.8	43	86.6	59	72.4
White Age 0–5	—	—	89[b]	112.3[b]	—	—	84	63.7	71	66.9	90	70.4
Age 6–11	—	—	89	91.3	—	—	79	50.7	73	62.9	71	49.5
Age 12–17/18	—	—	79	71.3	79	88.2	79	42.0	63	49.0	64	58.5
Children born to unmarried parents												
Non-White Age 0–5	65	176.4	81	165.4	—	—	72	58.2	39	110.2	69	116.6
Age 6–11	—	—	65	104.9	—	—	57	37.5	48	99.5	59	87.9
Age 12–17/18	—	—	61	79.4	52	67.9	57	38.2	38	51.7	51	55.0
White Age 0–5	55	127.2	60[b]	130.7[b]	—	—	61	55.6	45	77.0	62	81.6
Age 6–11	—	—	61	83.3	—	—	45	45.0	46	70.0	57	74.0
Age 12–17/18	—	—	62	64.8	41	74.4	43	34.4	46	45.3	44[b]	24.4[b]

Note. Average days of contact is calculated only for those who report any contact. The number of days of contact for NSAF, NLSY79, NLSY97, and WCSDE are calculated by assigning numeric equivalents (usually midpoints) to the response categories.

[a] The Fragile Families data reports any contact in the past 30 days. The amount of contact is the number of days in the past 30 days multiplied by 12. All other data sets report any contact and days of contact in the past year.

[b] Indicates means calculated from a sample of less than 50 observations.

the statistics described earlier. In this section, we examine other measures of contact that might also matter.

Type of Contact

In four of our six data sets, the questions described previously about basic contact between parents and children are followed by questions about overnight visits. Patterns are similar to those in Table 21.2 by race and reason for father's absence, but striking differences emerge by the age of the child (Table 21.3). Specifically, older children are much less likely to stay overnight with their fathers, and those who do stay substantially fewer nights than their younger counterparts.

As noted earlier, in five of the six data sets, contact questions refer to either the number of times the child has "seen" his or her nonresident parent, or the amount of time "spent with" the parent. In both cases, these questions seem to imply that the only contact being measured is face-to-face contact. The NLSY97, however, uses more detailed categories. Adolescents are asked to indicate whether and how much contact they have had with their father (a) by card, letter, or phone, (b) in face-to-face, but not overnight contact, and (c) by staying overnight. Conditional on having any contact with their nonresident father, it is striking that, of adolescents whose parents divorced or separated, more than 10% interacted with their father only by card, letter, or telephone. Nearly 8% of adolescents whose parents never married reported this exclusive means of contact. Nearly one half of children in both groups who had contact with their fathers reported all three types of contact during the past year.

Irregular or Infrequent Contact

As illustrated by the majority of the questions on contact between a father and his nonresident child, respondents are often expected to select a single category that suggests regular contact. The NLSY79 child data, for example, classifies contact as almost every day; 2 to 5 times a week; about once a week; 1 to 3 times a month; 7 to 11 times in the past 12 months; 2 to 6 times in the past 12 months; once in the past 12 months; or never.

Anecdotal evidence suggests that children often spend every other weekend with their nonresident parent, and some children spend longer periods of time with their fathers during breaks from school, during holidays, and during the summer. Because it is difficult to know whether respondents report number of visits or number of days, it is unclear which of the aforementioned categories one would select to indicate such visits. Only the NSAF data and the WCSDE offer an option that could accommodate longer, less frequent visits. The NSAF, for example, includes an "other" category as a

TABLE 21.3
Overnight Stays with Nonresident Fathers Within the Past Year, by Race, Age, and Reason for Father's Absence

	Fragile Families (1st Year Follow-Up)		NLSY 1979 Child (2000 Interview)		NLSY 1997 (1997 Interview)		Wisconsin Mother Survey	
	Any Overnights (%)	No. of Nights (Mean)	Any Overnights (%)	No. of Nights (Mean)	Any Overnights (%)	No. of Nights (Mean)	Any Overnights (%)	No. of Nights (Mean)
Children of divorced or separated parents:								
Non-White Age 0–5	—	—	57	102.3	—	—	44[a]	—
Age 6–11	—	—	51	108.0	—	—	56	—
Age 12–17/18	—	—	39	90.5	22	32.7	28	—
White Age 0–5	—	—	75[a]	161.4[a]	—	—	60[a]	—
Age 6–11	—	—	65	88.8	—	—	55	—
Age 12–17/18	—	—	52	65.4	35	52.9	45[a]	—
Children born to unmarried parents:								
Non-White Age 0–5	51	72.6	33	185.8	—	—	44	—
Age 6–11	—	—	32	97.7	—	—	41	—
Age 12–17/18	—	103.3	24	68.2	16	36.9	28	—
White Age 0–5	38	—	27[a]	150.8[a]	—	—	31	—
Age 6–11	—	—	42	87.7	—	—	40	—
Age 12–17/18	—	—	42	71.9	13	32.5	16[a]	—

Note. Average number of nights is calculated only for those who report any contact. Number of overnights for NLSY79 child data and NLSY97 are calculated by assigning numeric equivalents (usually midpoints) to the response categories. In the FF data, any overnights and number of nights are measured since the child's birth. All other data sets report any overnights and number of nights in the past year.

[a] Indicates means calculated from a sample of fewer than 50 observations.

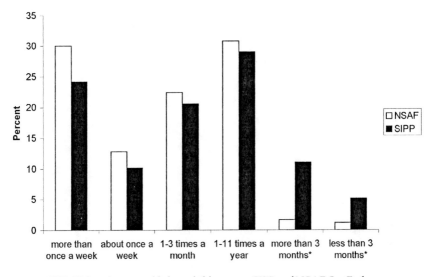

FIG. 21.2.   Amount of father–child contact, SIPP and NSAF. See Endnote 1 for an explanation of the asterisk (*).

possible response to the question asking how often the child has seen his or her nonresident father in the past 12 months. Using detailed information that is not included in the public-release data, we can classify respondents in the "other" category into two additional groups (3 months or more, or less than 3 months) that capture the longer, less frequent visitation just described.[1] Figure 21.2 shows that approximately 3% of children in NSAF who have contact with their fathers reported patterns that could fall into these two categories. In addition, this longer, less frequent visitation is more likely among White families than non-White families (not shown).

Information from SIPP provides additional evidence that allowing respondents to indicate larger, more infrequent periods of contact may substantially improve accuracy of data. The SIPP question allows the resident parent to indicate the amount of contact in the past 12 months in one of three ways: number of days, number of weeks, or number of months. Figure 21.3 shows the amount of contact based on these responses.

Of respondents who indicated any contact between the nonresident father and his child, a substantial proportion appears to have irregular contact. More than 16% of respondents chose to report contact in number of months, rather than days or weeks. Thirteen percent reported contact in number of weeks, and the remaining 71% indicated the number of days of annual contact. These responses can be seen as spikes in Fig. 21.3 at, for instance, 30 or 60 days, which represent 1 or 2 months per year, respectively.

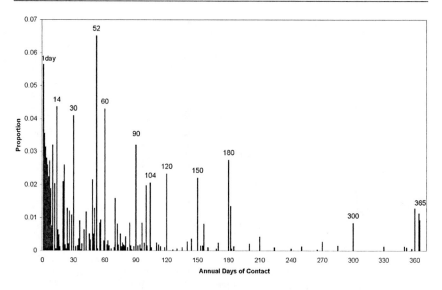

FIG. 21.3.   Frequency of annual father–child contact among children with
any contact: SIPP.

To better understand how reports of father–child contact differ with
differences in response options, we compare the categorical responses in
NSAF with those in the SIPP by converting the SIPP data into groups
comparable to the NSAF categories. (See Table A2 in the Appendix for
details of the conversion.) Figure 21.2 shows that the most striking differences occur among parents reporting contact in durations of months. Only
1.7% of NSAF parents reported contact of 3 months or more, whereas 11%
of SIPP parents indicated that the child saw his nonresident father 3 or
more months per year. Similarly, slightly more than 1% of NSAF respondents report less than 3 months of contact per year, whereas 5% of SIPP
respondents reported this length of contact.

The WCSDE survey asks separate questions about regular and irregular
visits. The survey first asks respondents to indicate the amount of regular
contact as detailed above, and then asks mothers: "In addition to these
regular visits, did <focal child> spend time with <his/her> father on other
days, for example, during holidays or summer vacation or at other times,
during <the time you and <focal child>'s father lived apart in> 1998?" If
yes, then: "During <the time you and <focal child>'s father lived apart in>
1998, on about how many additional days did they spend time together,
during holidays or summer vacations or at other times?" These questions
evoke more reports of longer, less frequent contact. Specifically, of all of

the Wisconsin respondents who reported some regular contact, nearly 25% indicated that there was also some contact during holidays, summer vacations, or at other times. A small fraction, 2.4%, reported substantial contact (more than 50 days per year) outside of regular visitation. These data highlight the importance of providing parents with responses that capture longer, less frequent contact. More detailed questions also allow researchers not only to examine the effect that the amount of contact has on the relationship between children and their fathers, but to investigate whether there is a difference between regular and irregular contact, or frequent and infrequent contact.

DIFFERENCES IN REPORTS OF CONTACT BY MOTHERS AND FATHERS

Because of difficulties in locating and interviewing nonresident fathers, most data sets obtain information about child support and visitation from mothers. The FF study collects information from both the mother and father about contact between the father and child for the entire sample, and we report differences between mothers' and fathers' reports of father contact in Table 21.4. Without exception, mothers report significantly lower levels of contact between the father and child than do fathers. This pattern is similar to reports of child support payments by mothers and fathers (Peters & Argys, 1992; Schaeffer et al., 1991; Smock & Manning, 1997; Sonenstein & Calhoun, 1990). Mothers' reports of father contact in the past month are more than 10 percentage points lower than fathers' reports. Among those who report any contact, fathers report 2 to 4 more days per month of contact than do mothers.

It is possible that these differences are simply the result of recall error or differences in the timing of mothers' and fathers' interviews, although in that case one would not expect the consistent underreporting by mothers relative to fathers. To determine whether there are characteristics that predict differences in parents' reports of contact, we regress the difference between parents' reports on parental characteristics such as the mother's race and both parents' ages and education levels. In addition, to assess whether animosity between the parents may foster a self-serving bias, we include a dichotomous indicator (as reported by the mother) of the level of conflict between the parents. The results generally indicate that none of these explanatory variables systematically predicts differences in the reports. Despite our inability to identify the causes of these reporting differences, the relatively large size of the differences highlights the potential importance of gathering information from both parents.

TABLE 21.4
Differences in Mother's and Father's Reports of Father's Contact:
Fragile Families Survey

	All Unmarried at Birth[a]	Race	
		White	Non-White
Saw child in past 30 days[b]			
Mother's report of father's contact	.75	.71	.75
Father's report of his contact	.86	.79	.87
Difference (F–M)	.11***	.08*	.12***
No. of days for all[c]			
Mother	7.1	4.7	7.5
Father	9.5	6.9	9.9
Difference (F–M)	2.4***	2.1*	2.4***
No. of days if any			
Mother	11.4	8.6	11.7
Father	13.8	12.8	13.9
Difference (F–M)	2.4***	4.1**	2.2**
Had overnight w/ child since birth[b]			
Mother	.60	.50	.61
Father	.78	.74	.79
Difference (F–M)	.18***	.24***	.18***

***$p < .001$. **$p < .01$. *$p < .05$.
[a]Parents with unwed births who were both interviewed and not cohabiting at the one-year follow-up.
[b]Fathers who reported that they lived with the child all/most or half of the time were not asked about contact and were coded as having contact in the past 30 days and as having had overnight visits.
[c]Fathers were only asked about number of days if they reported that they lived with the child some or none of the time. Fathers and mothers in Oakland and Austin were not asked about overnight visits or number of days of contact.

QUALITY OF PARENT–CHILD CONTACT

Although few studies have found substantial benefits to children from increases in the amount of contact with the nonresident parent, the quality of father–child interactions appears to matter (Amato & Gilbreth, 1999). However, questions about quality of contact are often missing from surveys because, for a number of reasons, it is even more difficult to measure than the amount of contact. First, researchers differ about which aspects of the parent–child relationship are important to measure. One measure chronicles the activities in which the child and the nonresident parent engage (e.g., going on outings, helping with homework, playing with child, or reading to child). A second type of measure asks the child about feelings of closeness to the nonresident parent. What constitutes the most viable type of measure depends on the availability of different respondents. For example, the most common respondents in data sets, residential mothers, are likely to be the least accurate reporters of both the activities in which the child engages with the father and feelings the child has about the father. Fathers and children would be better reporters, but nonresident fathers are often difficult to locate and include in surveys, and children must be old enough to report reliably.

The NLSY97 is one of the few data sets that asks adolescents to assess their relationship with their father. These measures exist whether or not the father and child reside together, so long as they had some contact within the past year. Respondents were asked whether their father knows their friends, whether he blames them for his problems, whether he is permissive, whether he is supportive or helpful, and whether they enjoy spending time with him and want to be like him.

Table 21.5 reports the weighted averages of adolescents' assessment of their relationship with their nonresident fathers, conditional on having some contact. In general, children whose parents divorced view their fathers somewhat more favorably than children whose parents never married. For example, 73% of children of divorced parents report that they enjoy spending time with their nonresident father compared with only 66% of children whose parents never married. Reports of undesirable father behaviors also vary by reason for father's absence: 18% of nonmarital children indicated that their father always or usually cancels, compared with slightly more than 8% of children of divorced fathers.

The FF survey provides insight into activities that fathers and their very young children share. Specifically, if the father has had contact with his child, the mother is asked how often the father engages in entertaining activities, such as playing peek-a-boo, telling stories, or playing with toys, and how many days he assists with child-care activities, such as changing a diaper, feeding the child, or putting him or her to bed. On average, fathers participate in most of these activities 2 to 4 days per month (Table 21.6). Non-White fathers more actively assist with changing diapers, feeding their child, and putting their child to bed. Non-White fathers also hug their children more frequently.

Although not detailed here, the WCSDE data also include questions about specific father–child activities (e.g., doing homework, going to the zoo, going to a doctor's appointments). The NSAF, NLSY79 child data, and SIPP contain no information on the quality of children's interactions with their nonresident parent.

Researchers have begun using these data to examine activities parents engage in with their children (Lundberg & Rose, 2003). The responses to these questions will allow researchers to investigate whether these

TABLE 21.5
Father Involvement (Mean) by Reason for Father's Absence: NLSY97

	Parents Divorced (%)	Parents Separated (%)	Parents Never Married Each Other (%)
Father-child relationship			
Father was very supportive[a]	45.46	54.20	43.92
Father was permissive[a]**	49.50	44.34	54.94
Wants to be like father**	37.04	44.42	25.75
Thinks highly of father	62.13	71.38	58.54
Enjoys time with father*	72.53	73.82	65.82
Father usually/always praises youth[b]	57.20	66.67	52.98
Father usually/always critical[b]	7.16	3.27	11.20
Father usually/always helpful[b]	46.82	57.64	37.08
Father usually/always blames youth[b]	4.59	0	4.35
Father usually/always cancels[b]***	8.53	13.01	18.27
Father knows youth's friends	14.19	21.22	15.17
Father knows friend's parents	9.86	20.52	8.37
Father knows who youth is with	36.06	55.56	33.62
Father familiar with school issues*	43.52	59.17	34.12
Sample Size	1,132	253	1,084

Note. This table appeared originally as part of Table 2 in Peters and Argys (2001). Means are weighted to population totals.

[a]Asked of all youths who have had any contact with their father. All others are asked of all youths between age 12 and 14 who had any contact with their father.

[b]Percentage represents the fraction of youth who indicated that their father usually or always engaged in a behavior relative to those who indicated that their father sometimes, rarely, or never engaged in that behavior.

***Difference between divorced and never married is significant at the 1% level.
**Difference between divorced and never married is significant at the 5% level.
*Difference between divorced and never married is significant at the 10% level.

dimensions of contact between parent and child have an impact on various child outcomes.

CONCLUSION

Current data do not yet provide a consistent or clear picture of either the quantity or quality of interactions between children and their nonresident parents. Different data sets provide strikingly different estimates of the proportion of children who see their nonresident father, and each provides some insight into particular aspects of father–child contact. Our analyses suggest some important issues to consider when designing survey questions, and we offer seven recommendations based on our findings.

TABLE 21.6
Mean Number of Days Fathers Engaged in Activities With Child:
Fragile Families Survey, Mother's Report at 1-Year Follow-Up

Days/Week Father Did Following w/ Child (Range = 0–7)	All Fathers[a]	White	Non-White
Play games like peek-a-boo or gotcha	3.45	3.70	3.42
Sing songs or nursery rhymes	1.96	1.68	1.99
Read stories	1.52	1.49	1.53
Tell stories	1.64	1.68	1.63
Play inside w/ toys	2.93	2.63	2.96
Take to visit relatives	1.76	1.44	1.80
Change diaper*	2.82	2.28	2.89
Feed or bottle**	3.22	2.52	3.30
Hug or show affection***	4.07	3.11	4.18
Put to bed**	2.28	1.62	2.36

Note. Significant differences by race: *$p < .05$. **$p < .01$. ***$p < .001$.
[a]Only asked of fathers who reported seeing child more than once in past month.

Recommendation #1: Our results indicate that contact between children and their nonresident parents is not well defined. Is it only face-to-face contact that matters? Can e-mail or phone calls sustain a relationship between fathers and children who do not live in the same city or country? Do overnight stays with the father lead to greater benefits than just daytime contact? To address these questions, data about contact between children and their nonresident parents should include information about various types of contact, including contact by phone, e-mail, or text messaging, as well as face-to-face contact. Overnight contact should remain distinct.

Recommendation #2: Not only may different types of contact matter, but the timing of contact may be important. Unlike financial support for children, visitation may not be fungible. That is, longer periods of irregular contact, experienced by as many as 22% of the children who have contact with their nonresident fathers, may or may not be a good substitute for the same amount of contact spread more evenly throughout the year. Therefore, we recommend that contact questions allow respondents the opportunity to report not only a total amount of contact, but the frequency and timing of contact.

Recommendation #3: The type of father–child contact varies throughout a child's life. Longer, less frequent visitation and phone calls or e-mail may replace more regular daytime contact as a child reaches adolescence. Even legally specified living arrangements may change. It may be important to determine the patterns of contact at different ages. Therefore, visitation and custody data should be collected repeatedly over a child's life, and longitudinal or retrospective reports of agreements and contact should be collected.

Recommendation #4: Agencies that most frequently interact with parents and children from nonintact families often focus on establishing and enforcing a child support award. However, legal agreements between parents often go far beyond this measure of financial contribution. Legal agreements specify custody and often include an agreement regarding physical custody and visitation. Current data collection, which provides measures of compliance with child support awards, is inadequate to measure compliance with visitation. We are unable to determine if parents are complying with visitation orders, much less understand why. Are residential parents interfering with visitation? Is this in response to nonpayment of child support? Or are nonresident parents willingly reducing their visitation? Until we can match visitation with the visitation agreement, these questions will remain unanswered. Therefore, we recommend gathering reports that document visitation agreements and the degree to which actual visitation complies with these agreements.

Recommendation #5: We recommend collecting data on structural constraints that preclude contact, especially information about where the father lives in relation to the child (e.g., number of miles) and the degree of conflict between biological parents. These variables may help researchers to separate factors that lead to any contact from those that affect the amount of contact conditional on any contact. In addition, it has been suggested that the relationship between the parents can moderate the effect on children of infrequent contact with the nonresident father.

Recommendation #6: Statistics indicating the prevalence and frequency of contact between a nonresident father and his child vary substantially depending on the source of the information. Mothers consistently report that fathers are less likely to see their children at all. Conditional on having some father–child contact, mothers also report fewer days of contact than do fathers. Therefore, we recommend interviewing both mothers and fathers about the relationship between the nonresident parent and the child.

Recommendation #7: Although there is currently no consensus on which measures of the quality of parent–child interaction matter most, quantifying the nature of the relationship between nonresident parents, their children, and their shared activities is paramount. Therefore, surveys designed to examine child well-being should incorporate questions about the activities nonresident parents and their children share and the quality of their relationship.

ACKNOWLEDGMENTS

The Fragile Families and Child Wellbeing Study is funded by: the National Institute of Child Health and Human Development (NICHD), the

California Healthcare Foundation, the Commonwealth Fund, the Ford Foundation, the Foundation for Child Development, the Fund for New Jersey, the William T. Grant Foundation, the Healthcare Foundation of New Jersey, the William and Flora Hewlett Foundation, the Hogg Foundation, the Christina A. Johnson Endeavor Foundation, the Kronkosky Charitable Foundation, the Leon Lowenstein Foundation, the John D. and Catherine T. MacArthur Foundation, the A.L. Mailman Family Foundation, the Charles S. Mott Foundation, the National Science Foundation, the David and Lucille Packard Foundation, the Public Policy Institute of California, the Robert Wood Johnson Foundation, the St. David's Hospital Foundation, the St. Vincent Hospital and Health Services, and the U.S. Department of Health and Human Services (ASPE and ACF). Peters and Argys gratefully acknowledge the support of NICHD grant HD30944 and the programming assistance of Suzann Eshleman.

Note

1. All of the responses that were coded into these two new categories reported an extended visit, such as 6 weeks in the summer. If the extended visit plus the weekly visits summed to less than 3 months, we coded it less than 3 months. On the other hand, if the extended visit plus the weekly visits summed to more than 3 months, we coded it that way. Thus, for example, if someone responded that the child saw her father every other week and 4 weeks during the summer, we coded it "less than 3 months." If someone responded that the child saw her father 3 months during the summer, plus Christmas and Easter, we coded it "3 months or more."

APPENDIX

TABLE A1
Sample Sizes by Race, Age, and Reason for Father's Absence

	FF (1st-Year Follow-Up)	NLSY 1979 Child (2000 Interview)	NLSY 1997 1997 (Interview)	NSAF (1997 Interview)	SIPP	Wisconsin Mother Survey
		Children of Divorced or Separated Parents				
Non-White						
Age 0–5	—	63	—	166	94	20
6–11	—	243	—	280	173	52
12–18	—	475	558	375	208	54
White						
Age 0–5	—	35	—	696	550	45
6–11	—	191	—	1,470	1,222	59
12–18	—	335	823	1,857	1,299	51
		Children Born to Parents Who Never Married Each Other				
Non-White						
Age 0–5	1,393	99	—	1,100	526	617
6–11	—	277	—	847	351	438
12–18	—	479	859	548	272	183
White						
Age 0–5	194	15	—	1,236	655	268
6–11	—	57	—	973	514	103
12–18	—	101	212	622	266	31

Note. FF = Fragile Families survey; NLSY = National Longitudinal Survey of Youth; NSAF = National Survey of America's Families; SIPP = Survey of Income and Program Participation.

TABLE A2
Conversion of Days of Contact Reported in SIPP to NSAF Contact Categories

NSAF categories	More than 1 time per week	About 1 time per week	1–3 times per month	1–11 times per year	3+ months	Less than 3 months
SIPP responses	60+ days and 9+ weeks	44–59 days and 7–8 weeks	12–43 days and 2–6 weeks	1–11 days and 1 week	3–12 months	1 or 2 months

22

Measuring Support to Children by Nonresident Fathers

Steven Garasky
Iowa State University

Elizabeth Peters
Cornell University

Laura Argys
University of Colorado–Denver

Steven Cook
University of Wisconsin–Madison

Lenna Nepomnyaschy
Columbia University

Elaine Sorensen
The Urban Institute

Gathering data from parents living separately presents many challenges. For example, it is often difficult to locate both parents, and when they are interviewed, they tend to provide different accounts of the nonresident parent's involvement with the same child (Schaeffer et al., 1991; Sonenstein & Calhoun, 1990). Furthermore, family and household configurations are complicated by the addition of new relationships (e.g., step-relationships) that evolve over time and the dynamic nature of the residential patterns of children who often reside with different parents at different times of the year or at different times in their childhood (Manning & Smock, 2000).

Within this challenging context, we examine the support provided by nonresident parents (specifically fathers, owing to data limitations) to their children. We focus on how questions about support are asked and the results that are found. We examine eight separate data sets: six survey-based data sets, one compilation of data from court records, and an extract of data from administrative records of a state public-assistance program. Although other research has used these and other data to examine a wide range of policy-relevant questions regarding child support, the overriding objective of our chapter is to gain a better understanding of the strengths and weaknesses of the current data-gathering approaches (Freeman & Waldfogel, 2001; Sorensen & Hill, 2004). Our goal is to provide insights into how we can improve surveys in this important area of family demography.

We explore three facets of providing support. First, we examine the concept of support. We begin with the strictest measure, formal cash support provided in response to an established legal support order. We also consider informal cash support and in-kind support (e.g., food and toys) in an effort to obtain a more complete picture of what nonresident parents provide to their children. Second, we examine the complexity of the families with whom we are dealing. A key question asks: How many relationships are in play when considering the support provided by a specific nonresident parent to a specific child? Clearly, the broader context of relationships will affect the support that is provided. Finally, in a preliminary effort to understand the dynamic nature of these relationships, we examine the extent in which legal orders to provide support are modified over time. We construe the modification of an order as a sign of change in the resident parent–nonresident parent–child relationship; however, we also understand that an award modification may result from a change in circumstances other than a child's change in residence (e.g., a change in one parent's income).

Before exploring the various facets of support with our eight data sets, we first briefly review what is known about child support from another widely used data set, the Current Population Survey Child Support Supplement (CPS-CSS). The CPS-CSS has provided national-level information in this area for more than 20 years, and has been the data source for numerous policy-relevant studies (e.g., Beller & Graham, 1993; Garfinkel & Robins, 1994; Lerman & Sorensen, 2003). Because the CPS-CSS has been well covered in the research, we choose not to replicate those studies here, and instead focus on other data sets that examine child-support outcomes.

THE CURRENT POPULATION SURVEY
CHILD SUPPORT SUPPLEMENT

The CPS is a monthly survey of approximately 50,000 U.S. households that the government has conducted for more than 50 years. (This overview of the Current Population Survey draws heavily from Herz, 2003.) The CPS provides cross-sectional characteristics of the U.S. labor force as well as of other aspects of family life. Each month, interviewers ask a core set of questions. In addition, they ask a set of topical modules on a regular, but less frequent basis. The CPS uses a rolling sample (families are interviewed for 4 consecutive months, not interviewed for 8 months, and then interviewed for another 4 months) so that responses to the core and topical module questions may be compared across months for more detailed analyses. The Child Support Supplement (CSS) to the CPS is conducted in April every 2 years and is sponsored, in part, by the Office of Child Support Enforcement of the U.S. Department of Health and Human Services. The survey collects additional supplemental information in the March interview, such as income, employment, program participation, and health insurance coverage in the preceding year. Researchers can link this information to responses to the CSS for families who were interviewed in both months.

The Census Bureau reported:

> In the spring of 2002, an estimated 13.4 million parents had custody of 21.5 million children under 21 years of age whose other parent lived somewhere else. Of all custodial parents, 84.0% were mothers and 16.0% were fathers. . . . Overall, about 27.6% of all children under 21 living in families had a parent not living in the home. (Grall, 2003, p. 1)

Among the custodial mothers interviewed in 2002, 63.0% indicated that they had some type of support agreement or award for one or more of their children, whereas 55.0% of all custodial mothers reported being owed some child support. About three fourths (74.7%) of mothers who were owed support received some support, with slightly less than one half (45.4%) receiving the full amount due. The average amount of support owed to these parents was $5,138 for the year; the average amount received by all mothers owed support was $3,192, or 62.1% of what was owed.

In terms of other support, the Census Bureau (Grall, 2003) found that 5.5 million custodial parents (mothers and fathers) without current awards or agreements reported receiving $900 million in 2001 directly from the nonresident parent. These parents may have awards for children past the age of eligibility, awards officially starting after 2001, or no legal awards at all. Furthermore, 61.0% of all custodial parents received some type of non-cash (in-kind) support. Parents with support agreements were more likely to receive some type of noncash support than were those without awards (65.8% vs. 54.1%).

STUDY DATA SETS

We summarize the data sets we use in this chapter in Table 22.1. The Survey of Income and Program Participation (SIPP) and the National Survey of America's Families (NSAF) most resemble the CPS in sample coverage. The SIPP, also conducted by the Census Bureau, is a nationally representative sample (when weighted) of the U.S. civilian, noninstitutionalized population. Panels are initiated at regular intervals and are followed typically for 2.5 to 4 years, with interviews taking place every 4 months. Data examined here are from the 1996 panel and represent 1997, a time period slightly earlier than that of the April 2002 CPS-CSS.

The NSAF is a cross-sectional survey that is nationally representative of the U.S. civilian, noninstitutionalized population under age 65. The NSAF, SIPP, and CPS-CSS represent the same population when the analyses focus on parents and their children under age 18. Unique to the NSAF is its child support module, which is administered to adults such as grandparents, foster parents, and close relatives who have custody of children who are not their own. This approach can potentially identify more children with absent parents who are eligible for child support. In contrast, the CPS-CSS and SIPP are limited to children who live with one biological or adoptive parent and have one nonresident parent. We examine data from the 1999 (second) wave of the NSAF, a time period most compatible with the most recent CPS findings.

The National Longitudinal Survey of Youth for 1979 (NLSY79) and 1997 (NLSY97) also are national in their sample coverage, but they are limited to more narrow cohorts of the full population. When weighted, the responses of participants for the NLSY79 can be considered representative of all men and women born in the late 1950s and early 1960s and living in the United States when the survey began in 1979. Similarly, the NLSY97 is representative of young men and women who were ages 12 to 16 on December 31, 1996. As a result, the analyses of the NSLY79 and NLSY97 reported here are not directly comparable to the published CPS-CSS findings for all resident and nonresident parents and their children. We examine data from the 2000 wave of the NLSY79 and the 1997 wave of the NLSY97.

The Fragile Families and Child Wellbeing Study (FF) offers information for another cohort of the U.S. population. Different from the age-based cohorts of the NLSY, the FF follows a birth cohort of mostly unwed parents and their children. The total sample includes both unmarried and married parents in 20 cities in the United States. These data represent nonmarital

TABLE 22.1
Summary of Data Sets Used in this Study

Data Set	Acronym	Survey Years for This Study	Survey Is Representative of:
Fragile Families and Child Wellbeing Study	FF	Baseline (1998–2000) and 3-year follow-up (2001–2003)	Nonmarital births in U.S. cities with populations over 200,000 between 1998 and 2000.
National Longitudinal Survey of Youth, 1979 cohort	NLSY79	2000	All persons born between 1957 and 1964 and living in the United States when the survey began in 1979.
National Longitudinal Survey of Youth, 1997 cohort	NLSY97	1997	All Americans living in the United States in 1997 and born between 1980 and 1984.
National Survey of America's Families	NSAF	1999	U.S. civilian, noninstitutionalized population under age 65.
Survey of Income and Program Participation, 1996 panel	SIPP	1997	U.S. civilian, noninstitutionalized population at the time of the start of the panel in 1996.
Wisconsin Child Support Demonstration Evaluation, administrative data	WCSDE-ADMIN	1998	Complete collection of Wisconsin administrative data for all parents who were receiving or had applied for welfare (AFDC or TANF) from August 1997 to June 2003.
Wisconsin Child Support Demonstration Evaluation, survey data	WCSDE-SURVEY	1998	Mothers who entered Wisconsin's TANF program between September 1997 and June 1998.
Wisconsin court record data	WISC-CRD	1996–1998	Court records in 21 Wisconsin counties between 1980 and 1998.

Note. Additional information about these data sets can be obtained from the authors. AFDC = Aid to Families with Dependent Children (the precursor to TANF); TANF = Temporary Assistance for Needy Families. The families in the Wisconsin data set were receiving Wisconsin's version of TANF, called Wisconsin Works.

births in each of the 20 cities and also represent nonmarital births in U.S. cities with populations greater than 200,000. As with the NLSY, the results from the FF are not directly comparable to the published CPS findings. Nevertheless, the survey provides an opportunity to explore many unique aspects of data collection involving nonmarital births. In this chapter, we examine FF data from both the baseline (1998–2000) and the 3-year follow-up (2001–2003).

Finally, we review data from one particular state, Wisconsin. Wisconsin has more than a 20-year history of data collection and research in the area of child support. We examine data from the Wisconsin court records data set (WISC-CRD), which includes court records in 21 Wisconsin counties. Our two other data sources—one based on administrative data and the other a survey—are from the Wisconsin Child Support Demonstration Evaluation (WCSDE). The administrative data (WCSDE-ADMIN) cover all parents who were receiving or had applied for cash assistance (Aid to Families with Dependent Children [AFDC] or the state's Temporary Assistance for Needy Families [TANF] program called "Wisconsin Works") from August 1997 to June 2003. The survey (WCSDE-SURVEY) included mothers who entered Wisconsin's TANF program between September 1997 and June 1998. The two nonsurvey data sources (WISC-CRD and WCSDE-ADMIN) provide this study with a unique perspective on data available for research in this area. In addition, the Wisconsin survey is unique in that it offers perspectives obtained from both a resident and a legally adjudicated nonresident parent of a specific case.

In the following sections, we first examine formal awards of support as indicated in the eight data sets. We then examine receipt of support, including formal support payments, informal support payments, and noncash or in-kind support. After exploring aspects of support provision, we examine the complexity of families and their dynamic nature.

ASSESSING CHILD SUPPORT

The Child Support Module Screener

Typically, the lead-in to the child support module of a survey is a screener to determine whether the respondent is eligible for the module. The screener is very important, given that it dictates the coverage universe of the module responses. The CPS-CSS seeks to identify whether the household has a parent with children whose other parent is living elsewhere. Similarly, the NLSY79 asks only about children of the respondent and his or her spouse or partner and whether the other biological parent of the child lives in the household. The SIPP asks whether the respondent has any children of his or her own in the household who have a parent living elsewhere. The NLSY97 identifies adolescent respondents who do not live with one of their parents (biological or adopted) and then gathers support information from the residential parent. The NSAF also does not limit its inquiry to biological parents, but includes other types of parents, such as grandparents and relatives who have children in their home whose parents live elsewhere. Our analyses of NSAF data indicate that about 10% of the children surveyed do not live with either biological parent and have at least one nonresident parent who may be eligible to provide, or actually does provide, support for the child.

The Unit of Analysis

In the CPS-CSS, the unit of analysis is the custodial parent. The screener identifies parents who have at least one child under age 21 with a parent living elsewhere. The NLSY79 uses this approach as well, but the NSAF, the FF, and the NLSY97 use the child as the unit of analysis. The NSAF randomly selects two children from each family for in-depth questioning. The guardian for each randomly selected child, called a focal child, answers questions about that child's status regarding child support. The NLSY97 also asks the guardian of the adolescent about the adolescent's eligibility for and receipt of child support. The FF asks the mother about her child's child support status. The SIPP and Wisconsin data have the flexibility to use either the parent or the child as the unit of analysis.

TYPES OF CHILD SUPPORT AGREEMENTS

Formal Child Support Agreements

After screening for respondent eligibility, the module typically begins with a question asking the respondent about child support agreements. For example, the CPS-CSS asks: "Did R ever have any type of child support agreement or ever attempt to have any type of child support agreement with CHILD's mother/father?" Similarly, the NLSY79 asks: "Are you [or spouse/partner] currently legally entitled to receive child support payments through a court order or any other type of legal agreement?" When asked in this manner, having an order for *any* child results in an affirmative response.

The NSAF and SIPP allow for more child-specific responses. The NSAF asks the guardian of each randomly selected child: "Is CHILD covered by a child support order?" The NSAF is the only survey we examine that uses the word *order* rather than *agreement*. The SIPP asks a series of questions

designed to determine whether each child who has a parent living elsewhere is covered by a child support agreement. The battery of questions
flows as follows:

- "Have child support payments ever been agreed to or awarded for
  (this child/any of these children)?
- How many children are covered by a child support agreement?
- Are _____'s children that we have just listed covered by dif-
  ferent child support agreements? By that we mean separate agree-
  ments involving different absent parents?
- How many different child support agreements cover these children?
- Which of these children are covered by the most recent agreement?
- Which of these children are covered by other child support agree-
  ments, either written or verbal?
- Which child/children is/are covered by the agreement?
- Which of these children are not covered by any child support agree-
  ments?"

Table 22.2 reports formal child support agreement rates across our eight
data sets. Recall that the Census Bureau reported that 63.0% of custodial
mothers of children younger than age 21 have some type of child support
agreement for at least one child, whether formal or informal. In contrast,
according to NSAF results (not reported in Table 22.2), 53% of children

TABLE 22.2

**Percentage Reporting a Formal Child Support Agreement
in Place, by Age of Youngest Child**

	Age of Youngest Child			
Data Set	3	0–5	6–11	12–17/18
FF	30.3	—	—	—
NLSY79	—	65.5	69.4	69.1
NLSY97	—	—	—	66.9
NSAF[a]	—	41.2	56.2	59.0
SIPP[b]	—	33.9	50.6	54.0
WCSDE-ADMIN	—	69.1	63.2	48.0
WCSDE-SURVEY	—	—	—	—
WISC-CRD	—	86.6	81.0	80.6

Note. See Table 22.1 for list of data set abbreviations and
titles.
[a]NSAF reports age of focal children. [b]SIPP figures include
all eligible children.

aged 18 or younger with a father living elsewhere have a child support order, which probably reflects only formal agreements. An important implication regarding the difference in the unit of analysis—custodial parent or child—is that analyses of custodial parents with awards will overstate the prevalence of awards for children eligible for child support to the extent that not all of the children are covered by an award. We report our findings in Table 22.2 by the age of the youngest child in the family to demonstrate another aspect of having an award: Except for the Wisconsin court and administrative data sets, the likelihood of having a child support order increases with the age of the child. As one might expect, the proportions reported using the WISC-CRD are highest (more than 80%), given that all of these children are in the legal system. The proportion in the FF sample is lowest (30%), as would be expected from a sample of very young children born outside of marriage. Interestingly, the results from the NLSY79 and NLSY97 are quite similar to those of the CPS-CSS. SIPP rates include all eligible children and are about 5 to 7 percentage points lower than those of the NSAF.

Table 22.3 explores formal child support agreements more fully, taking advantage of information on multiple children in these data sets. The unit of observation for this table is a child, who is not necessarily the youngest child. Table 22.3 categorizes children by the same ages as Table 22.2, except for the exclusion of those only aged 3. Interestingly, it is only for the subgroup of parents not married at the birth of the child that the likelihood of having a formal child support order increases with the age of the child. Generally, if the parents of the child were not married when the child was born, the proportion of children with a formal child support order increases from birth to age 11 and is lower for the oldest group, those aged 12 to 18. The latter most likely represents a birth cohort effect. The proportion increases through age 11 for children born to married parents as well. The trend is mixed, however, across data sets for the oldest group. When examining agreement rates by welfare receipt status, resident parents who did not receive welfare in the last 12 months had higher agreement rates for children in all age groups than did those who did receive welfare. This difference can be attributed to the higher number of never-married parents in the welfare population whose children also must have paternity established.

Informal Child Support Agreements

Our understanding of the cash support provided by nonresident parents has grown as surveys inquire about support beyond formal (that is, legal) child support payments. The CPS-CSS distinguishes between legal agreements, nonlegal agreements that say the noncustodial parent should make child support payments, and no agreement. The survey then asks detailed

TABLE 22.3
Percentage With a Formal Child Support Agreement,
by Marital and Welfare Status

Sample Population/Data Set	Age of Child		
	0–5	6–11	12–17/18
Parents not married at birth of child			
NSAF	34.8	47.9	41.0
SIPP	28.4	35.8	32.7
WCSDE-ADMIN	54.8	54.0	34.8
Parents married at birth of child			
NSAF	58.3	65.2	68.2
SIPP	45.9	64.3	66.9
WCSDE-ADMIN	54.9	58.0	60.5
Resident parent receives welfare			
NSAF[a]	37.4	46.7	46.2
SIPP[b]	31.5	35.9	35.3
WCSDE-ADMIN[c]	53.7	53.9	39.1
Resident parent does not receive welfare			
NSAF	42.0	57.4	59.8
SIPP	36.5	59.3	60.5
WCSDE-ADMIN	57.3	56.7	47.3

Note. NSAF = National Survey of America's Families; SIPP = Survey of Income and Program Participation; WCSDE-ADMIN = Wisconsin Child Support Demonstration Evaluation, administrative data

[a]Resident parent is or is not receiving welfare at the time of the survey. [b]Resident parent received or did not receive welfare in the last month. [c]All cases in the WCSDE samples had been in Wisconsin's TANF program sometime in the last year, but some received benefits and some received only employment assistance (no cash). Those receiving cash benefits are included in the "received welfare" group and those not receiving cash benefits are in the "did not receive welfare" group.

questions about legal and nonlegal agreements. Grall (2003) reported that 4% of custodial parents have a nonlegal, or informal, agreement, and 41% have no agreement. Unfortunately, Grall did not report amounts due and received separately for legal and nonlegal agreements; instead, he reported these statistics as a whole for all agreements.

The SIPP child support module includes informal (nonlegal) agreements. Specifically, the module asks the respondent: "Was this agreement a voluntary written agreement ratified by the court, a court-ordered agreement, some other type of written agreement, or a nonwritten (verbal) agreement?" The module then asks specific questions about the nonlegal agreement, including:

- In what year was this agreement/understanding first reached?

TABLE 22.4
Percentage With a Verbal Child Support Agreement From the
1996 Panel of the Survey of Income and Program Participation

	Age of Child		
Sample Population	0–5	6–11	12–18
All children	5.9	4.4	2.7
Parents not married at birth of child	4.1	2.3	1.7
Parents married at birth of child	9.7	6.4	3.3
Resident parent received welfare in the last month	2.3	1.9	0.4
Resident parent did not receive welfare in the last month	9.7	5.9	3.5

- What was the dollar amount of that agreement/understanding?
- Has the dollar amount ever been changed?
- In what year was the amount last changed?
- What was the dollar amount of the agreement/understanding after the last change?

Table 22.4 reports proportions of mothers with verbal child support agreements in the SIPP by the age of the child. Keep in mind that SIPP respondents are asked about other agreements *only if they report having no formal support agreements*. Consistent with the CPS-CSS and Grall (2003), we find that about 6% of the youngest children (aged birth to 5) have a verbal support agreement. This proportion decreases with age, to 3% for children aged 12 to 18. This declining likelihood of verbal support agreements with age is evident in each group considered. Worth exploring is whether this decrease is a result of an increase in formal support agreements or a decrease in contact between the nonresident parent and the child. Overall, children born to married parents and children with a resident parent who did not receive welfare in the last month were more likely to have a verbal support agreement. Nevertheless, the SIPP finds few children with verbal agreements. None of the groups had verbal agreement rates greater than 10%.

RECEIPT OF FORMAL
CHILD SUPPORT PAYMENTS

Surveys investigate the receipt of formal child support payments in a variety of ways. For example, FF asks: "Has (father) paid anything toward (child's) support since the legal agreement was made (or in the last 12 months if legal agreement was before that)?" In a relatively simple approach, the NLSY79, after asking detailed questions about the amount of child support the respondent is supposed to receive, asks: "In total, how much child support did you actually receive during (year)?"[1] Similarly, the NLSY97 asks: "How much did you [your spouse/partner] receive in child support during (year)?" The NSAF again asks for an amount for a specific year, but allows the amount to be annual or monthly: "How much child support did you receive in (year)? This can be either a monthly amount or the total for the year."

At the other extreme are the CPS-CSS and SIPP, which explore a variety of issues related to the amount of formal support received, including whether the local welfare agency passed on any support to the family, whether any payments were to be deducted from the noncustodial parent's paycheck, and whether any of the amount paid was for back support. Clearly, the depth of the CPS-CSS questioning reflects its partial sponsorship by the Federal Office of Child Support Enforcement.

Another aspect of formal support receipt examined by some surveys is compliance. That is, surveys ask respondents to compare the amount received to the amount ordered. Although one can often calculate the ratio of the amount paid to the amount ordered from other responses, some surveys follow questions about the amount paid with questions on how the amount compares with the ordered amount and how timely the payments are. For example, the NSAF asks: "During the last 12 months, how much of the child support order was actually paid? Would you say (1) the full amount, (2) a partial amount, or (3) none?" The CPS-CSS asks for similar details for individual payments: "And for the child support payments you received, how many of them were for the full amount you were supposed to receive? Would you say all of them, most of them, some of them, or none of them?" Finally, the SIPP attempts to capture the frequency of payments, asking, "How regularly were child support payments received over the past 12 months? Were they received (a) all of the time; (b) most of the time; (c) some of the time; (d) none of the time?"

We examine the receipt of formal child support payments in three ways. First, we are interested in the prevalence of receipt. That is, we want to know what proportion of mothers received some formal child support. The Census Bureau reports that about 4.6 million of 11.3 million custodial mothers (41%) were due child support and received it in 2001. The NSAF reports similar rates for older children; only about one in four (25.5%) younger children received some formal support (see Table 22.5). The NLSY reports rates slightly higher than the CPS-CSS, ranging from 44.7% (NLSY79, youngest child aged 0–5) to 59.7% (NLSY97, youngest child aged 12–17). The rates from Wisconsin data are higher in the court records and the administrative data than in the WCSDE survey. This difference is likely due to inaccurate parent recall about child support payments. The FF and SIPP rates are lowest and comparable for the youngest children.

TABLE 22.5
Percentage Who Received a Formal Child Support
Payment, by Age of Youngest Child

		Age of Youngest Child		
Data Set	3	0–5	6–11	12–17/18
FF	16.6	—	—	—
NLSY79	—	44.7	50.7	49.8
NLSY97	—	—	—	55.7
NSAF[a]	—	25.5	40.2	42.0
SIPP[b]	—	19.9	33.8	36.0
WCSDE-ADMIN	—	50.0	47.6	42.4
WCSDE-SURVEY	—	28.6	32.9	28.0
WISC-CRD	—	59.7	57.3	63.2

Note. See Table 22.1 for list of data set abbreviations and titles.
[a]NSAF figures include all children (not the youngest).
[b]SIPP figures include all eligible children (not the youngest).

We also examine the average amount of formal support received among mothers who received some support. The Census Bureau reported that custodial mothers who were due child support payments and who received them received an average of $4,274 in 2001 (Grall, 2003; see http://www.bls.census.gov/cps/overmain.htm). Generally speaking, our results for the SIPP are consistent with those of the CPS-CSS. We find that the mean amount of formal support received increased with the age of the youngest child, from $2,603 for the youngest SIPP children (aged 0–5) to $3,888 for the oldest group (aged 12–18) (see Table 22.6). Results from the FF mothers indicate that mothers averaged $1,832 (in 2002 dollars) in formal support for their young children. Results from the other data sets are inconsistent. Mean payments from the Wisconsin court records and NSAF are consistent with the CPS-CSS for the youngest children, and increase with the age of the youngest child, to more than $7,000 for the oldest Wisconsin children and more than $5,000 for the oldest NSAF children. Mean amounts from the NLSY79 are higher than those of the CPS-CSS, but do not steadily increase with age. The mean amount for children in the NLSY97 ($4,542) also is higher than the mean for mothers in the CPS-CSS. The means from the Wisconsin CSDE data sets are much lower than those of other data sets. This is clearly a function of the population covered, public-assistance recipients.

Finally, we are interested in compliance with support orders. We examine whether mothers received all, some, or none of the ordered support. Grall (2003) reported from the CPS-CSS that, among custodial mothers

TABLE 22.6
Average Formal Child Support Payment Received,
If Any Formal Payment Received ($2002)

| | | Age of Youngest Child | | |
Data Set	3	0–5	6–11	12–17/18
FF	1,832	—	—	—
NLSY79	—	4,473	5,280	3,988
NLSY97	—	—	—	4,542
NSAF[a]	—	3,265	4,635	5,585
SIPP[b]	—	2,603	3,766	3,888
WCSDE-ADMIN	—	2,020	2,174	2,098
WCSDE-SURVEY	—	1,288	1,565	1,742
WISC-CRD	—	3,327	6,056	7,036

Note. See Table 22.1 for list of data set abbreviations and titles.
[a]NSAF figures include all children (not the youngest).
[b]SIPP figures include all eligible children (not the youngest).

with agreements in 2001, slightly less than one half (45.4%) received their full amount. About one fourth (29.3%) received some, but not all, of the amount that was due. The remainder (25.3%) received nothing. Interestingly, these results are quite similar to the NSAF question of how much of the owed support was paid (see Table 22.7). Among all families in the NSAF, about one half (47.3%) received the full amount. Another one fifth (20.2%) received some of the ordered amount. The remainder (32.5%) received nothing. Full-payment compliance increases with the age of the youngest child. Full compliance also is greater for children whose parents were married at their birth and is slightly higher for children who are not currently receiving welfare.

RECEIPT OF INFORMAL
CHILD SUPPORT PAYMENTS

As the Census Bureau (Grall, 2003) noted, a nonresident parent might provide cash support to his or her children for a number of reasons, even when a child support agreement is not in place. The parent may continue to make payments even though an order is no longer in effect. Also, the parent may pay before an order for support officially starts.

Two of our data sets ask about informal child support (in the form of cash) without an agreement. The FF survey asks respondents with no formal or informal agreement: "Has (father) paid anything toward (child's) support

TABLE 22.7
Families Receiving All, Some, or None of the Ordered Child Support
Payment Amount From the 1999 Wave of the National Survey
of America's Families (%)

Sample Population	Received Full Ordered Amount	Received Some of the Ordered Amount	Received None of the Ordered Amount
All families	47.3	20.2	32.5
Families whose youngest child is age 0–5	38.0	22.6	39.4
Families whose youngest child is age 6–11	47.5	20.9	31.7
Families whose youngest child is age 12–17/18	52.0	18.2	29.8
Families whose focal child was born outside of marriage	37.9	20.2	41.9
Families whose focal child was born within marriage	53.5	20.1	26.4
Families who are receiving welfare at time of survey	16.5	17.7	65.8
Families who are not receiving welfare at time of survey	50.7	20.4	28.9

since (he/she) was born?" Similarly, the SIPP asks: "Were any payments received from the other parent in the last 12 months for the child(ren) with no child support agreement?" In contrast, though the Wisconsin CSDE survey asks whether the respondent received various types of in-kind support, it also asks the respondent to calculate the total value of all informal support (both cash and in-kind). There is neither a way to separate the value of cash and in-kind payments nor to distinguish informal support that resulted from an informal agreement from informal support provided without an agreement. The values shown in Table 22.8 for the Wisconsin survey refer to this total estimated value of cash and in-kind benefits received from the father, independent of the presence of an informal agreement. Finally, NSAF does not explicitly ask about informal support, but it can be inferred from those who receive support, yet lack a child support order.

Table 22.8 reports the percentage of resident mothers receiving child support payments (or in-kind support for the WCSDE survey) among all resident mothers with either a nonlegal (e.g., verbal) support agreement or no agreement. We refer to these payments as informal support. Over one half (58.9%) of the FF mothers reported receiving informal support for their child. Similar rates exist for the WCSDE survey mothers, all of whom receive welfare. The rate of informal support receipt declines with the age of the youngest child. Results from the SIPP and NSAF indicate much

TABLE 22.8
Received an Informal Child Support Payment (%)

Sample Population, Data Set	Age of Child			
	3	0–5	6–11	12–17/18
All children				
FF	58.9	—	—	—
NSAF[a]	—	27.1	17.6	11.9
SIPP[b]	—	10.9	5.8	4.1
WCSDE-SURVEY[c]	—	55.4	44.7	36.5
Parents not married at birth of child				
FF	58.9	—	—	—
NSAF	—	28.3	14.6	11.6
SIPP	—	8.8	3.4	3.5
WCSDE-SURVEY	—	55.5	42.3	29.8
Parents married at birth of child				
FF	—	—	—	—
NSAF	—	23.8	20.8	12.1
SIPP	—	15.4	8.1	4.5
WCSDE-SURVEY	—	54.5	56.0	55.9
Resident parent received welfare in the last 12 months				
FF	48.0	—	—	—
NSAF[d]	—	16.0	7.8	12.5
SIPP[e]	—	6.4	3.0	3.0
WCSDE-SURVEY[f]	—	56.5	45.0	34.6
Resident parent did not receive welfare in the last 12 months				
FF	63.9	—	—	—
NSAF	—	29.5	18.8	11.8
SIPP	—	15.8	7.5	4.5
WCSDE-SURVEY	—	53.5	44.2	39.8

Note. See Table 22.1 for list of data set abbreviations and titles.

[a]NSAF reports are based on all focal children. [b]SIPP reports are based on all eligible children. [c]The Wisconsin CSDE Survey asks about the value of all payments (cash and in-kind) other than official child support and asks the respondent to estimate the total of value of all these contributions received from the father. Reported by age of youngest child. [d]Resident parent's welfare status determined at the time of the survey. [e]Receipt of welfare is in the last month. [f]All cases in the WCSDE samples had been on Wisconsin's TANF program sometime in the last year, but some received benefits and some received only employment assistance (no cash). Those receiving cash benefits are included in the "received welfare" group and those not receiving cash benefits are in the "did not receive welfare" group.

lower rates of informal support, but exhibit the same pattern of decline with the child's age as the Wisconsin survey. Clearly, some of the differences in receipt rates across data sets reflect differences in study populations. The decline in informal support receipt as the child ages is consistent with reduced contact with the nonresident parent over time (for more information, see chap. 21, this volume).

Table 22.8 also examines child support receipt in the absence of a legal agreement by samples of resident mothers. The WCSDE survey data show that the pattern of declining informal support as the child ages holds for children born to unmarried parents, and for children of resident parents who received and who did not receive welfare in the last 12 months. The rates of informal support as the child ages are remarkably stable for children born to married parents. The NSAF data show much lower rates of informal support than the Wisconsin data. These rates decline as the child ages for all groups, except those receiving welfare. The NSAF resident parents who receive welfare have much lower informal support rates, which do not vary much by the age of the child. Again, SIPP patterns follow those of the NSAF, but SIPP rates are lower overall. The FF study shows similar results for children with resident parents receiving welfare; their support rates are much lower than those of children with resident parents who no longer receive welfare.

Table 22.9 shows that, among those who receive support without an official agreement, the amount paid (as reported by resident parents) is nontrivial. The FF parents receive about $200 per month ($2,461 annually) on average. The SIPP amounts are even higher, ranging from $2,345 to $2,897 annually, depending on the age of the child. The WCSDE survey amounts are much lower than those of the FF young children and the SIPP, which is not surprising, considering that all of the surveyed mothers are drawn from the state welfare program. The WCSDE estimates indicate that the amount of informal support declines as children age. This pattern is not found with the SIPP.

Next, we examine the amount of support received in more detail among those without an official agreement. Parents in the FF study who are not receiving welfare currently receive almost $1,600 more in informal support than parents who are receiving welfare. There is also a large difference in informal support by welfare status among SIPP parents of the youngest and oldest group of children. Among the Wisconsin survey respondents, support amounts are higher for younger children across all groups. In contrast to the other two data sets, when examined by welfare status, amounts are higher for all WCSDE survey children with resident parents who received welfare in the last 12 months than for children whose resident parents did not. In sum, informal support is an important component of the support provided to children with nonresident parents.

TABLE 22.9
Average Informal Child Support Payment Received, If Any Informal
Payment Received ($2002)

Sample Population, Data Set		Age of Youngest Child		
	3	0–5	6–11	12–17/18
All children				
FF	2,461	—	—	—
SIPP[a]	—	2,345	2,897	2,735
WCSDE-SURVEY	—	499	371	326
Parents not married at birth of child				
FF	2,461	—	—	—
SIPP	—	2,077	2,237	1,636
WCSDE-SURVEY	—	500	370	346
Parents married at birth of child				
FF	—	—	—	—
SIPP	—	2,672	3,161	3,254
WCSDE-SURVEY	—	482	375	296
Resident parent received welfare in the last 12 months				
FF	1,289	—	—	—
SIPP	—	1,291	2,891	1,704
WCSDE-SURVEY[b]	—	525	387	359
Resident parent did not receive welfare in the last 12 months				
FF	2,884	—	—	—
SIPP[c]	—	2,812	2,898	2,989
WCSDE-SURVEY	—	451	348	280

Note. See Table 22.1 for list of data set abbreviations and titles.

[a]SIPP reports are based on all eligible children. [b]All cases in the WCSDE samples had been on Wisconsin's TANF program sometime in the last year, but some received benefits and some received only employment assistance (no cash). Those receiving cash benefits are included in the "received welfare" group and those not receiving cash benefits are in the "did not receive welfare" group. [c]Receipt of welfare is in the last month.

RECEIPT OF ANY (FORMAL OR INFORMAL) CHILD SUPPORT PAYMENTS

When we examine formal and informal support payments together, we find that the percentage providing support is much greater than when we consider only formal support payments (see Table 22.10.) The FF study, for example, reports that nearly two thirds (64.1%) of the families with very young children receive some cash support from the nonresident parent. The NSAF reports that combined formal and informal payment receipt rates are

TABLE 22.10
Received Any Child Support Payment,
by Age of Youngest Child (%)

	Age of Youngest Child			
Data Set	3	0–5	6–11	12–17/18
FF	64.1	—	—	—
NSAF[a]	—	34.8	49.1	48.7
SIPP[b]	—	30.7	39.6	40.1
WCSDE-SURVEY	—	64.2	58.9	46.4

Note. See Table 22.1 for list of data set abbreviations and titles.
[a]NSAF figures are based on the question that asks whether the child's family received child support. [b]SIPP figures are based on all eligible children.

about 10 percentage points higher than formal payments alone. SIPP rates of formal and informal payments combined increase slightly as the child ages and are between 30% and 40%, about 4 to 11 percentage points higher than formal payments alone. The parents surveyed as part of the WCSDE report a support payment rate consistent with the FF study for youngest children, a rate that declines steadily with the increasing age of the youngest child. The proportion of WCSDE survey parents who receive any cash support is about 25 percentage points higher than the rate reported in Table 22.5, which accounts for only formal payments. As seen in Table 22.9, however, the average amount these parents received in informal payments is relatively small.

The results reported in Table 22.11 demonstrate that, in general, the average amount of support received is lower for parents receiving *any* support than just formal support alone. This outcome is consistent with the finding that parents who receive only informal support receive lower average amounts of support than parents who receive formal support (see Table 22.6). The average amount FF parents receive, however, increases by nearly $800 annually when we include informal support in the computation. The NSAF reports the highest mean amounts of child support, but that may be because it includes any child support paid to the family, not necessarily from a single child support agreement alone. The SIPP mean total (formal and informal) payments are lower than those of the NSAF, but both data sets show a pattern of increasing payments with the age of the child. Wisconsin survey mean amounts are lowest among the four data sets, but increase with the age of the child as well.

TABLE 22.11
Average Amount of Any Child Support Payment
Received, If Any Payment Received,
by Age of Youngest Child ($2002)

		Age of Youngest Child		
Data Set	3	0–5	6–11	12–17/18
FF	2,620	—	—	—
NSAF[a]	—	3,234	4,359	5,307
SIPP[b]	—	2,512	3,639	3,771
WCSDE-SURVEY	—	1,000	1,148	1,282

Note. See Table 22.1 for list of data set abbreviations and titles.

[a]NSAF reports the average amount of child support received by the child's family. [b]SIPP reports are based on all eligible children.

IN-KIND SUPPORT

Not all support provided by nonresident parents is in the form of cash. Recently, surveys have begun to examine the provision of noncash or in-kind support to children. CPS-CSS employs the most common approach to capturing this information. The Census Bureau asks (yes/no):

> Other than the child support you told me about, did CHILD's mother/father do any of the following for CHILD:
> - Give any birthday, holiday, or other gifts to the CHILD?
> - Provide clothes, diapers, or shoes?
> - Provide food or groceries?
> - Pay for child care or summer camp?
> - Pay for medical expenses such as medicine or visits to the doctor or dentist, other than health insurance?

The FF study has a similar roster of items with an opening statement that reads: "I am going to read you a list of things that children need. Please tell me how often (father) buys these for (child)?" Valid responses include "never," "rarely," "sometimes," and "often." The SIPP, on the other hand, asks an open-ended question: "Were any non-cash items or services for child support received for any of _____'s children?" If the response is yes, the SIPP asks the respondent to specify which items or services were provided. Finally, the WCSDE survey asks about the types of in-kind support received, such as gifts and clothing. The WCSDE also asks respondents to estimate the total value of all contributions (cash and in-kind) other than official child support.

TABLE 22.12
Received Any In-Kind Support for Children (%)

		Age of Child		
Data Set	3	0–5	6–11	12–18
FF	69.3	—	—	—
SIPP[a]	—	27.3	26.2	22.3

Note. FF = Fragile Families study; SIPP = Survey of
Income and Program Participation.
[a]SIPP figures are based on all eligible children.

The Census Bureau (Grall, 2003) reported from the CPS-CSS that 61.0% of all custodial parents receive at least one type of noncash support. Receipt rates were higher for parents with child support agreements or awards (65.8% vs. 54.1%). The fact that receipt rates were higher for parents with child support agreements or awards can be interpreted to mean that formal support and in-kind support are complements rather than substitutes as has been discussed in past research. Gifts for birthdays, holidays, or other occasions were the most common type of noncash support (58.2%), followed by clothes (39.3%), and food or groceries (28.5%).

The FF study (Table 22.12) indicates that parents of these young children receive in-kind support at rates somewhat higher (69.3%) than parents in the CPS-CSS. If receipt rates of in-kind support decline with the age of the child, then results across these two surveys are consistent. FF parents not receiving welfare were slightly more likely to receive in-kind support than those receiving welfare (71.4% vs. 65.5%, not reported in Table 22.12). Recall that the FF study asked parents how often they received in-kind support. On a scale of 1 to 4 where 1 is "never," 2 is "rarely," 3 is "sometimes," and 4 is "often," nonresident parents provide clothes, toys, medicine, and food rarely to sometimes. Rates of in-kind support among SIPP mothers are much lower: 27% for children aged 0 to 5; 26% for children aged 6 to 11; and 22% for children aged 12 to 18. The discrepancy may be because the SIPP uses an open-ended question to inquire about in-kind support.

FAMILY COMPLEXITY
AND SUPPORT PROVISION

As noted earlier, the Census Bureau (Grall, 2003) estimated that in spring 2002, 13.4 million parents had custody of 21.5 million children under age 21 who had a nonresident parent. Of these 13.4 million parents, 3.2 million (23.9%) were married. Of those married custodial parents, 26.2% were married for the first time. The remaining couples (73.8%) remarried follow-ing a divorce or death of a spouse. An unreported number of the unmarried custodial parents were cohabitating. In short, these families are complex, especially considering interactions between parents and children who were born into prior and current relationships.

Surveys such as the CPS-CSS capture many aspects of the respondent's relationships. However, as we seek to understand relationships beyond the respondent that affect child support payment and receipt, many of the major surveys are less useful. The FF study, however, offers a unique opportunity to examine the effects of the relationships of the mother and the father on child support provision. Table 22.13 reports findings from the FF 3-year follow-up. We focus on the effect that having children from other relationships has on child support outcomes, keeping in mind that multiple-partner fertility likely correlates with a number of other factors (nonmarital births, low in-come, etc.), which may relate to child support outcomes. Given this, we urge caution in interpreting the bivariate statistics presented in Table 22.13.

We find that 30.3% of the children in the FF sample (nearly all FF par-ents were unmarried at their child's birth) have a child support agreement, although the percentage of parents with a support agreement varies slightly depending on parenting history. Children with fathers who have children from other partners are slightly more likely to have an agreement (35.1%), as are children with mothers who do not have children from other partners (32.1%). Least likely to have support agreements are children whose fathers have no children with other partners (26.7%). In short, no obvious pattern arises to determine whether a child born to unmarried parents in the FF study is more or less likely to have a child support agreement if the child's parents have children from other partners.

The likelihood of receiving formal support follows the same pattern as having a support agreement. Overall, 16.6% of the children in the FF sample received support payments, and the likelihood of receiving payments was slightly higher (18.9%) for children whose fathers have children from other partners. Again, children whose mothers have children from other partners were less likely (15.3%) to receive formal support than children whose mothers who had no other children from past relationships (18.2%).

Having a formal child support agreement increases the odds of receiving support substantially. Among children with a formal support agreement, the likelihood of receiving a payment is highest for those whose parents do not have children from other relationships. Among children whose fathers have no children from other partners, 59.2% received a child support payment, whereas 56.7% of children whose mothers have no children from other partners received a payment (Table 22.13). In general, however, the rates do not differ substantially by parenting history. The lowest rate (53.1%) is for children with mothers who have children from other partners.

TABLE 22.13
Child Support Outcomes for Parents With Multiple Partners
From Fragile Families 3-Year Follow-Up Mother's Report

Child Support Outcome	All Children Unmarried at Birth	Children With Fathers Who Have Children From Other Partners	Children With Fathers Who Do Not Have Children From Other Partners	Children With Mothers Who Have Children From Other Partners	Children With Mothers Who Do Not Have Children From Other Partners
Have child support agreement (%)	30.3	35.1	26.7	28.8	32.1
Received formal child support payments (%)	16.6	18.9	15.8	15.3	18.2
Received formal child support payments if had a support agreement (%)	54.8	53.8	59.2	53.1	56.7
Average formal payment if any formal payments received ($2002)	1,832	1,844	1,829	1,851	1,814
Received informal child support payments (%)	58.9	51.8	69.2	52.2	65.8
Average informal payment if any informal payments received ($2002)	2,461	2,355	2,661	2,515	2,419
Received any child support payments (%)	64.1	60.9	75.6	56.7	72.3
Average total payment if any payments received ($2002)	2,620	2,392	2,918	2,481	2,747
Received any in-kind support (%)	69.3	65.6	77.8	64.3	75.2

The annual amount of formal child support received by children is relatively similar across groups, at $1,832 on average (Table 22.13). Interestingly, although the highest average amount was for children whose mothers had children from other partners, this group had the lowest rate of formal support receipt after controlling for a support agreement.

Informal-support receipt rates are slightly higher than formal receipt rates among children with support agreements. The overall rate is 58.9%. As with formal support, the rate of informal receipt is highest among children whose fathers do not have children from other partners (69.2%). The next highest rate is for mothers without children from other partners (65.8%). The rate of informal support receipt falls to just over one half when the child's parents have children from other partners.

As with formal support, children with fathers without other children receive the highest average amount, $2,661. Children with mothers who have children with other partners are next, receiving $2,515. Children whose fathers have other children received $2,355, on average, whereas children whose mothers do not have children from other partners received an average of $2,419.

Our examination of the receipt of any child support demonstrates that many children receive both formal and informal support. About two thirds (64.1%) of the FF children received support payments. This rate is less than the sum of the rates of children who received formal (16.6%) and informal (58.9%) support as some children receive both. The patterns of receipt across groups, however, are consistent with our separate examinations of formal and informal support. Children with fathers who do not have children from other partners have the highest rate of receipt of any support (75.6%), followed closely by children with mothers who do not have other children from other partners (72.3%). The rates of support decline when parents have children from other partners. Receipt rates are about 15 percentage points lower when a parent has children from another partner.

The average total payment, if any payments are received, is higher ($2,620) when we consider all support as a whole than when we consider formal and informal support separately (Table 22.13). Children with parents who do not have children from other partners receive more support than children with parents who have children from other partners.

The receipt of in-kind support follows this same pattern. Approximately two thirds (69.3%) of the children receive in-kind support (Table 22.13). Children with parents without children from other partners are more likely to receive in-kind support than children with parents who have children from other partners.

It is clear from the FF study that understanding patterns in child support receipt requires understanding parental relationships beyond those of the resident parent and within that parent's household. In particular, evidence suggests that whether the mother or father has children from another relationship affects the payment of formal, informal, and in-kind child support.

FAMILY DYNAMICS AND SUPPORT PROVISION

As we study families within the context of child support provision, it becomes clear that they are not only complex, but also dynamic. Being a resident parent changes over the short term with periodic visits and overnight stays with the other parent. Changes occur seasonally, as children who reside with one parent during the school year live with the other parent during the summer. Finally, the status of resident parent can change on a permanent basis; a child may choose at some point to live with the nonresident parent.

Capturing family dynamics requires analyses of longitudinal data beyond the scope of this chapter. Nevertheless, we briefly consider a potential indicator of change in family living arrangements: modification of a formal child support agreement. We understand that an award modification may result from a change in circumstances other than a child's change in residence. For example, a support order may become modified if one or both parents have a change in income. Thus, we recommend considering the results presented next as merely informational.

Table 22.14 reports the percentage of agreements modified by the age of the child at the time of the SIPP interview. The results indicate that the likelihood that an agreement has been modified increases with the age of the child to the point that over one fourth (28%) of the agreements have undergone modification for children between ages 12 and 18. Furthermore, the rate of modification was similar for the two youngest age

TABLE 22.14
Child Support Agreement Ever Modified Among Those With a
Child Support Agreement From the 1996 Panel of the
Survey of Income and Program Participation (%)

	Age of Child		
Sample Population	0–5	6–11	12–18
All children	14.5	21.1	28.1
Parents not married at birth of child	15.4	21.3	19.2
Parents married at birth of child	13.3	21.1	30.9
Resident parent received welfare in the last month	16.5	22.9	24.0
Resident parent did not receive welfare in the last month	12.7	20.5	28.9

groups of children born within and outside of marriage. However, the rate of modification was over 50% higher (30.9%) for children aged 12 to 18 born within marriage than for those born outside of marriage (19.2%). The reason for this divergence is unclear, but could relate to the fact that this older cohort of children was born when child support policies were more focused on children of divorce rather than those born outside of marriage. Finally, younger (aged 0–5) and older (aged 12–18) children with a resident parent who did not receive welfare in the last month had slightly higher modification rates than children with a resident parent receiving welfare; this was not true for children in the middle (aged 6–11) age group.

DISCUSSION AND RECOMMENDATIONS

Data collection occurs within time and budget constraints. In a perfect world, in which data collection related to the support of children by nonresident parents would be unrestricted, we might collect very detailed information about all types and amounts of support. Similarly, we would collect information from every person in the resident parent's household and everyone outside that household who might affect the support the child receives. Finally, we would gather this information frequently to capture the dynamics of child support provision.

Real-world constraints, however, require data gatherers to compromise. For example, instead of asking about all types of support received, we often focus only on cash support, and sometimes only on cash support paid in response to a formal support agreement. When asking about amounts, we often aggregate them over all children and over a specified time period, usually 12 months, asking, "Did the respondent ever receive support type 'X' over this period, and if so, how much in total was received?" In the real world, we may not inquire about the support due or received by every eligible child. Alternatively, we may limit questioning to the youngest child, or the focal child. Finally, we may not question everyone involved in the child's life, but may limit the interview to one individual, usually the child's resident parent. This chapter examined various data-gathering approaches employed across a variety of data sets, seeking to understand child support provision by nonresident parents. The goal of this exercise was to identify ways to improve data gathering. Following are our recommendations based on this effort.

Recommendation #1: Researchers should gather data on child support provision from both resident parents and nonresident parents whenever possible. The support provided to children takes many forms. Prior research shows that resident mothers tend to underreport the support provided by nonresident fathers, whereas nonresident parents tend to overreport what they have provided. Thus, both sides should be interviewed. Ideally, the mothers and fathers of the same child would be interviewed, but this has proved extremely difficult to accomplish and quite costly. Nonetheless, household surveys can easily interview nonresident parents about the support they provide with little additional cost.

Recommendation #2: Regardless of a resident parent's agreement status, surveys must better capture all types of support provided, formal and informal, cash and in-kind. The battery of questions surveys use to understand whether and how much formal support is ordered and how much is actually paid is well established. Unfortunately, surveys less frequently ask about informal support. Our analyses indicate that informal support for children is a significant form of support for many populations. Similarly, nonresident parents also provide important in-kind supports, such as food, medicine, toys, and transportation.

Recommendation #3: Future studies should strive to understand the regularity of support payments by nonresident parents, especially informal and in-kind support. Not only does support for nonresident children take a variety of forms, support often is provided at irregular intervals. Most surveys attempt to assess the amount of paid formal support and compare it to the ordered amount. In addition, some surveys try to understand how much was provided via informal and in-kind support. Few surveys, however, attempt to understand the consistency with which nonresident parents make these payments.

Recommendation #4: Child support module screeners must allow all adults with children who have nonresident parents to respond to the module. Families are complex. At times, children do not reside with either biological parent, but with another relative or guardian. Surveys that focus only on children living with one parent may miss a small but important group of children who are eligible for child support—children living with neither parent.

Recommendation #5: Researchers should gather child support data for each eligible child in a household, recognizing that children may have different nonresident parents who provide support by differing means, at differing levels, and with differing frequency. We know that many parents have children from multiple partners. Often, children residing in the same home have different parents. Frequently, however, the child support survey instrument asks about support provided to the resident parent in total or about a particular agreement, such as the latest agreement. When examining aspects of support provision by the age of the child, researchers must categorize responses by a proxy measure such as the age of the youngest child. Focal child–based surveys inquire about support provided to a particular child. Clearly, although these studies may omit children eligible for support, this approach allows for direct categorization of children by age. Surveys that ask about all children in a household who are eligible for support provide the clearest picture of the family situation and allow for the most accurate assessment of support.

ACKNOWLEDGMENTS

The Fragile Families and Child Wellbeing Study is funded by the National Institute of Child Health and Human Development (NICHD), the California Healthcare Foundation, the Commonwealth Fund, the Ford Foundation, the Foundation for Child Development, the Fund for New Jersey, the William T. Grant Foundation, the Healthcare Foundation of New Jersey, the William and Flora Hewlett Foundation, the Hogg Foundation, the Christina A. Johnson Endeavor Foundation, the Kronkosky Charitable Foundation, the Leon Lowenstein Foundation, the John D. and Catherine T. MacArthur Foundation, the A.L. Mailman Family Foundation, the Charles S. Mott Foundation, the National Science Foundation, the David and Lucille Packard Foundation, the Public Policy Institute of California, the Robert Wood Johnson Foundation, the St. David's Hospital Foundation, the St. Vincent Hospital and Health Services, and the U.S. Department of Health and Human Services (ASPE and ACF). Peters and Argys gratefully acknowledge the support of NICHD grant HD30944 and the programming assistance of Suzann Eshleman.

Note

1. Note that prior to 1993, the NLSY79 asked about child support receipt only in the income section, the same way they collected information about welfare income, unemployment compensation, and regular earnings. In earlier unpublished analyses, Argys and Peters found that the child support amounts collected in that way were much different (as a fraction of the amount due) from when receipt was asked immediately following questions about the amount due.

PART VII

Conclusion

23

Progress Made, Gaps Remain: Final Observations

Sandra L. Hofferth
University of Maryland at College Park

Lynne M. Casper
University of Southern California

Men and women have been marrying, bearing and rearing children, and dissolving their families for many millennia. What new light has this volume shed on this process? Among other things, it emphasizes how dynamic family formation is. Although men and women form intimate unions, bear and rear children, separate, and re-form unions, how this happens changes over time. Our measuring tools often lag substantially behind the phenomena that we would like to describe. The rise of cohabitation without a formal legal marital tie is one of those phenomena. Although cohabitation is not new, the rise in the proportion of marriages that are preceded by such unions—ranging from 50% to 60%—is new. The proportion of cohabiting unions in which children reside also is substantial—more than two out of five. The definition of out-of-wedlock childbearing is no longer meaningful, given that more than one half of children born out of wedlock are living with both biological parents.

This volume has focused on how these family phenomena have been measured in large-scale surveys and the implications of different measurement methods for their prevalence and nature. In this chapter, we highlight the volume's important findings that represent the progress we have made in improving measures in family research. We also summarize the volume's key recommendations for improving measures for family research; these recommendations point to the gaps that remain. For purposes of this discussion, we have divided the volume into three parts. The first part focuses on family formation, including marriage, cohabitation, and union dissolution; the second part focuses on relationships within and across households; and the third part focuses on fatherhood and fathering.

MARRIAGE, COHABITATION, SEPARATION, AND DIVORCE

Although living together seems like a fairly straightforward concept, the boundaries and meaning of cohabitation for many couples are ambiguous. Whether two persons are identified as cohabiting varies by the criteria used to define coresidence in different surveys, including the number of nights couples spend together, whether they maintain separate residences, whether they live together in a "marriage-like" relationship, and how long they have lived together. Cohabitors are diverse in their marriage intentions, residence patterns, and reasons for living together. Measurement is complicated even further when we consider that two individuals may have different perceptions of the same relationship. Therefore, cohabitation rates also may vary, depending on whether the man or the woman is asked to report on the couple's living arrangement. In this volume, Knab and McLanahan (chap. 2) and Pollard and Harris (chap. 3) describe how different ways of measuring cohabitation lead to different prevalence estimates.

Even more remarkably, *marriage* has come to have some ambiguity, particularly in the case of same-gender couples who, in some states, have registered a civil union or domestic partnership that may qualify them for the same protections married couples enjoy. How such couples would respond to the standard marital-status question asked in most surveys is unknown.

For many people, the nature of the relationship matters as much or more than its legal status and is often a more important factor in whether a relationship remains intact or dissolves. However, most surveys do not collect detailed information on relationship quality, and the measures that are used may be sorely outdated. Chapters 4, 5, 6, and 7 examine the measurement of marital quality. Each chapter begins with the standard marital happiness/satisfaction measure and proceeds beyond it to define what each set of authors views as the key unmeasured aspects of marriage. These new concepts include commitment, personal and interpersonal virtues, and group loyalty. Moore and colleagues (chap. 7) propose a set of 10 basic concepts that could be developed to create a single measure of healthy marriages or relationships to be included in surveys or intervention studies. More psychometric work that tests the reliability and validity of such a measure will be useful.

Finally, chapter 8 addresses measurement of marriage, separation, and divorce. Knowing the timing of these events is critical to establishing the extent of stability in the lives of families. The most critical omission in most surveys is a cohabitation history. However, even establishing accurate dates of marriage, separation, and divorce is difficult. The authors point out a major limitation of the Survey of Income and Program Participation (SIPP) data for examining marital patterns: Events are dated only to the year and not to the month in the public-use files. On one hand, this limitation may be necessary for protecting the confidentiality of the respondents; on the other hand, it severely curtails the usefulness of this data set for establishing sequences of events. Whereas vital statistics no longer regularly collect data on divorces, survey data do a relatively good job of measuring them. This is a very encouraging finding. However, the dating and sequencing of events, including divorce, remain problematic, according to both Bumpass and Raley (chap. 8) and O'Connell (chap. 9). The Census Bureau has crafted innovative methods to impute missing dates. Persistent and targeted efforts to improve the reporting of dates of events in surveys are needed. We have more research than ever before that could uncover the factors that help individuals remember events; we should draw on such research in designing our surveys. Finally, Bumpass and Raley also recommend that the National Survey of Family Growth expand its range of ages to include older respondents up to age 64. Expanding the age range would improve the accuracy of marriage, cohabitation, divorce, and separation measures.

RELATIONSHIPS WITHIN
AND ACROSS HOUSEHOLDS

Several chapters address issues of measuring household and interpersonal relationships, focusing on the use of the household roster, measuring cross-household family ties, and the policy implications of how family units are defined within a household.

Chapters 10 and 13 by Brandon and Iceland, respectively, demonstrate that how individuals are related within households is crucial information affecting important policy issues such as poverty levels and eligibility for public programs. That the incomes of cohabiting partners are not included in the poverty measure means that children and their families may appear less well off than they actually are, given that some cohabitors benefit from economies of scale and income pooling. Single individuals living as housemates may benefit to some extent from these economies as well, but they are not usually included in family income when calculating poverty levels. Yet many of our data sets do not have the information that we need to sort out who contributes to household income, how much they contribute, and whether their contribution represents a net gain or loss to the household.

Individuals may be better off than they seem if they are receiving child support and income from other households. Few studies include economic and social ties with other households in examining child well-being, with one major exception: The receipt of child support is considered in calculating household income and, therefore, poverty. Hill and Callister's chapter 11 is important in its recommendation that research include families that extend across households rather than be restricted to individuals who live together. This chapter makes a convincing case that researchers should broaden survey questions to include a variety of nonhousehold family members in measuring the well-being of children.

In chapter 12, Manning and Bulanda emphasize that not only the family type in which children reside affect their behavior, but those children's experience with family types throughout their childhood has an effect as well. Measures that indicate the extent of stability of a child's family structure between early and later childhood better represent the true experience of the child and are more closely associated with early-adulthood outcomes than are measures at any one point in time. Children reared in stable environments, regardless of family type, face similar odds of being expelled or suspended from school, and these odds are lower than those for children in less stable environments. However, the number of transitions does not appear to be important.

Measuring relationships between same-gender partners has taken on a new urgency, given changes in state laws permitting same-gender marriage, civil unions, and domestic partnerships. The new options make it more important to word questions correctly in our surveys. These new types of relationships mean that more same-gender couples will check "married." It will no longer be sufficient either to assign these relationships to same-gender partnerships (i.e., assuming misreported marital status) or to assign them to heterosexual marriages (assuming misreported gender). In chapter 14, Gates and Sell make a strong case for thinking through the implications of changing lifestyles for measuring families.

The increased interest in family formation behaviors of men, particularly minority men, means that we may have to seriously consider expanding our samples to include institutionalized populations, such as men and women in the military, jail, or prison. Mosher (chap. 15) points out that a substantial proportion—one third—of Black men is or has been incarcerated. Although the proportion in the military is small at any given point in time, it affects many households over time.

FATHERHOOD AND FATHERING

The final topic addressed in this book focuses on fathering and men's role in rearing children. Two chapters provide important quantitative data on estimates of paternity obtained from men. Mott, Hurst, and Gryn's chapter 16 clearly shows that stable coresidence of a father and child is the best indicator of biological fatherhood. Reports are most consistent when children have lived with their father for an extended period of time.

For the majority of men, reports of paternity are relatively consistent. However, we must be cautious in interpreting studies of fathering behavior among minorities and young men. Boggess, Martinez, Jasik, and Lindberg (chap. 17) found significant differences in the rates of misreporting by race-ethnicity (as did Mott et al.). More than one half of the African American fathers gave inconsistent paternity reports compared with 26.8% of Whites and 17.5% of Hispanic fathers. These results are consistent with other surveys that find African American men to be much less reliable reporters of information on fertility and sexual activity than White men. This difference likely stems from the fathers' age and the differing circumstances surrounding birth. Younger fathers, those who did not live with their first child, and those who were not married to the child's mother were more likely to provide conflicting data—characteristics also associated with underreporting among minorities in the validity studies.

Marsiglio's chapter 18 demonstrates that we have a substantial task ahead if we want to include the male perspective on fertility in our studies. Men's experiences with children range from genetic fatherhood to social fatherhood. Researchers should provide men opportunities to define their circumstances as clearly and fully as possible, while also minimizing interviewing conditions that might foster intentional or unintentional reporting bias. Data collectors must recognize the importance of managing interviews so as to allow men to maintain a masculine image of control, autonomy, and rationality.

The last three chapters focus on the involvement of resident and nonresident fathers with children. Although some progress has been made in measuring the involvement of resident biological fathers in terms of warmth, closeness, and engagement, additional research is needed on the extent to which resident biological and nonbiological fathers are involved in managing their children, that is, taking more active responsibility for their well-being. There is substantial evidence that a relationship between father and mother is crucial for the involvement of the father, and that the biological relationship also increases father involvement. Hofferth and colleagues (chap. 20) recommend that more information be gathered directly from nonbiological fathers as well as biological fathers, including asking father figures about their relationships with individual children.

Among biological fathers estranged from their child's mother, the measurement of contact and involvement is in its early stages, according to chapter 21 by Argys and colleagues. Substantial research is needed to reconcile different ways of measuring involvement during the course of a year. Total type and amount of contact and its timing during a year or during the child's lifetime are critical elements. The extent of contact between nonresident fathers and their children must be placed in the context of legal visitation agreements; that is, there may be limits on the extent to which fathers are permitted to contact their children. What is the agreed-upon extent of visitation? In addition, we need to learn more about the nature of the relationship between father and child as well as between father and ex-spouse.

Finally, financial contributions of nonresident fathers are important given that about one quarter of all children under the age of 21 have a nonresident parent. Chapter 22 by Garasky and colleagues recommends gathering data on child support from all parents, capturing the amount and regularity of informal as well as formal support, collecting data for children not necessarily living with a biological parent, and gathering data for each eligible child in a household. These recommendations would greatly improve our ability to understand the resources available to children.

IMPLICATIONS

Four key implications emerge from this volume. First, before the next round of the Decennial Census and the American Community Survey, researchers, policymakers, and government employees should advise the Census Bureau to revise its current data collection methods to provide better and more inclusive data on marriage and cohabitation. There has been no marital-status question on the long form, for example. This revision should permit us to more accurately identify cohabiting couples and same-gender couples. The current methods of collecting these data are outdated and will cause problems in the future if they are not improved soon.

Second, identifying all biological parents and any social parents in the household is essential, and this type of data should be collected for each child in all major family surveys. Although a relationship matrix is useful, information may be collected more efficiently and succinctly with a household roster that contains follow-up questions regarding each child's parents. Information about nonhousehold family members and their role in rearing children and supporting the family is critical. However, it is not just the structure of the family at a single point in time that is important. As Bumpass and Raley (chap. 8), Manning and Bulanda (chap. 12), and others point out, it is critical to obtain marital and cohabitation histories for adults of all ages, and the need to include them as a standard part of our surveys is an important implication of this volume.

A third implication is that we must obtain better family formation information from minority men. This will require more sensitivity on the part of interviewers and surveys, more focus on getting accurate paternity information, and more attention to the contested area of father involvement and whether fathers are inside or outside the household or in prison or jail. Any information should be asked equally of mothers and fathers. Parallel data collection on children would also help clarify these issues.

Fourth and finally, future issues include defining relationship quality such that the questions are asked in a meaningful way and are valid across a variety of populations. Such measurement is in its early stages, pioneered by some of the authors who contributed to this volume.

These four key implications also were included in the 14 targets of opportunity recommended by the participants in the Counting Couples conference (see the Preface) for improving measures of family research. On one hand, the emergence of only four key implications indicates that we have made and are making progress. Today some researchers are conducting qualitative research to uncover nuances in the meaning of cohabitation and fertility for the individuals involved. Others have begun to develop measures that more accurately reflect families and family life in the new millennium. On the other hand, that this volume's four major recommendations parallel those that were made 4 years ago indicates that gaps remain.

We conclude with a quote by Christine Bachrach from this volume (chap. 19):

> In any discussion about improving measurement, it is important to begin with basic questions. What exactly are we trying to measure, and why? In the case of male fertility, the answers are somewhat ambiguous. . . . The processes that create differences between biological paternity and a "claimed" child will continue to evolve. DNA testing now makes it possible to know definitively whose sperm fertilized what egg. Recent social policies emphasize the importance of making the biological father responsible for his child. There is also, however, a long tradition, embedded in vital statistics, of assuming that a child born to a married woman is the biological product of her husband. Clearly this is not the case when donor sperm help conceive the child, and there is good reason to suspect it is not the case in other circumstances as well. The field's success in measuring and understanding male fertility will depend on its ability to keep its fingers on the pulse of cultural and technological changes that affect the path between fertilizing an egg and being a father.

We believe that the field's success in measuring and understanding the other structures and processes covered in this volume also depends on its ability to keep its fingers on the pulse of cultural, economic, and technological changes.

References

Abma, J., Chandra, A., Mosher, W. D., Peterson, L., & Piccinino, L. (1997). Fertility, family planning, and women's health: New data from the 1995 National Survey of Family Growth. National Center for Health Statistics. *Vital and Health Statistics, Series 23*(19).

Acs, G., & Nelson, S. (2001). *Honey I'm home: Changes in living arrangements in the late 1990s.* Washington, DC: Urban Institute.

Acs, G., & Nelson, S. (2002). *The kids are alright? Children's well-being and the rise in cohabitation* (New Federalism B-48). Washington, DC: Urban Institute.

Agnew, C. R., Van Lange, P. A. M., Rusbult, C. E., & Langston, C. A. (1998). Cognitive interdependence: Commitment and the mental representation of close relationships. *Journal of Personality and Social Psychology, 63*, 596–612.

Ahrons, C. (1981). The continuing coparental relationship between divorced spouses. *American Journal of Orthopsychiatry, 51*, 415–428.

Ahrons, C., & Perlmutter, M. (1982). The relationship between former spouses: A fundamental subsystem in the remarriage family. In J. C. Hansen & L. Messinger (Eds.), *Therapy with remarriage families* (pp. 31–46). Rockville, MD: Aspen.

Albrecht, C., & Teachman, J. (2004). Childhood living arrangements and the risk of premarital intercourse. *Journal of Family Issues, 24*, 667–894.

Allport, G. W., & Ross, J. M. (1967). Personal religious orientation and prejudice. *Journal of Personality and Social Psychology, 5*, 432–443.

Amato, P. R. (1993). Children's adjustment to divorce: Theories, hypotheses, and empirical support. *Journal of Marriage and the Family, 55*, 23–38.

Amato, P. R. (1996). Explaining the intergenerational transmission of divorce. *Journal of Marriage and the Family, 58*, 628–641.

Amato, P. R. (2000). Consequences of divorce for adults and children. *Journal of Marriage and the Family, 62*, 1269–1287.

Amato, P. R., & Booth, A. (1997). *A generation at risk: Growing up in an era of family upheaval.* Cambridge, MA: Harvard University Press.

Amato, P. R., & Booth, A. (2001). The legacy of marital discord: Consequences for children's marital quality. *Journal of Personality and Social Psychology, 81*, 627–638.

Amato, P. R., & DeBoer, D. (2001). The transmission of divorce across generations: Relationship skills or commitment to marriage? *Journal of Marriage and Family, 63*, 1038–1051.

Amato, P. R., & Gilbreth, J. G. (1999). Nonresident fathers and children's well-being: A meta-analysis. *Journal of Marriage and the Family, 61,* 557–573.

Amato, P. R., & Rezac, S. (1994). Contact with nonresident parents, interparental conflict, and children's behavior. *Journal of Family Issues, 15,* 191–207.

Amato, P., & Rivera, F. (1999). Paternal involvement and children's behavior problems. *Journal of Marriage and the Family, 61,* 375–384.

Amato, P. R., & Rogers, S. (1997). A longitudinal study of marital problems and subsequent divorce. *Journal of Marriage and the Family, 59*(3), 612–624.

Amato, P., & Rogers, S. (1999). Do attitudes toward divorce affect marital quality? *Journal of Family Issues, 20*(1), 69–86.

American Association of Blood Banks. (2003, November). *Annual report summary for testing in 2002.* Retrieved August 26, 2004, from http://www.aabb.org/About_the_AABB/Stds_and_Accred/ptannrpt02.pdf

Anderlik, M. R., & Rothstein, M. A. (2002). DNA-based identity testing and the future of the family: A reseach agenda. *American Journal of Law & Medicine, 28,* 215–232.

Anderson, E. (1990). *Streetwise: Race, class, and change in an urban community.* Chicago: University of Chicago Press.

Anderson, E. (1993). Sex codes and family life among poor inner-city youths. In R. Lerman & T. Ooms (Eds.), *Young unwed fathers: Changing roles and emerging policies* (pp. 74–98). Philadelphia: Temple University Press.

Anderson, E. A. (2003). *Measurement and family demography.* Unpublished memo commissioned by Child Trends.

Anderson, K. G. (2000). The life histories of American stepfathers in evolutionary perspective. *Human Nature, 11,* 307–333.

Andersson, G., & Phillipov, D. (2002). Life-table representations of family dynamics in Sweden, Hungary, and 14 other FFS countries. *Demographic Research, 7*(4). Retrieved January 24, 2005, from http://www.demographic-research.org/

Argys, L., & Peters, H. E. (2001). Interactions between unmarried fathers and their children: The role of paternity establishment and child-support policies. *American Economic Review, 91,* 125–129.

Argys, L., & Peters, H. E. (2003). Can adequate child support be legislated?: A model of responses to child support guidelines and enforcement efforts. *Economic Inquiry, 41,* 463–479.

Armsden, G., & Greenberg, M. (1987). The inventory of parent and peer attachment: Individual differences and their relationship to psychological well-being in adolescence. *Journal of Youth and Adolescence, 16,* 427–454.

Auriat, N. (1993). "My wife knows best": A comparison of event dating accuracy between the wife, the husband, the couple, and the Belgium Population Register. *Public Opinion Quarterly, 57,* 165–190.

Australian Bureau of Statistics. (2004). *Family characteristics.* Retrieved January 24, 2005, from www.abs.gov.au/AUSSTATS/abs%40.nsf/mf/4442.0?OpenDocument

Axinn, W. G., & Thornton, A. (1992). The relationship between cohabitation and divorce: Selectivity or causality? *Demography, 29*(3), 357–374.

Bachrach, C. A., & Newcomer, S. (1999). Intended pregnancies and unintended pregnancies: Distinct categories or opposite ends of a continuum? *Family Planning Perspectives, 5,* 251–252.

Bachrach, C. A., Ventura, S. J., Newcomer, S. F., & Mosher, W. D. (1995). *Why have births among unmarried teens increased?* (Sexuality and American Social Policy: A Seminar Series). Menlo Park, CA: Henry J. Kaiser Foundation.

Bachu, A. (1996). *Fertility of American men* (Population Division Working Paper No. 14). Washington, DC: U.S. Bureau of the Census.

Badgett, M. V. L., & Rogers, M. A. (2003). *Left out of the count: Missing same-sex couples in Census 2000*. Amherst, MA: Institute for Gay and Lesbian Strategic Studies.

Baker, R. (1996). *Sperm wars: The science of sex*. New York: Basic Books.

Baron, R. M., & Kenny, D. A. (1986). The moderator-mediator variable distinction in social psychological research: Conceptual, strategic, and statistical considerations. *Journal of Personality and Social Psychology, 51*(6), 1173–1182.

Baughman, R., Dickert-Conlin, S., & Houser, S. (2002). How well can we track cohabitation using the SIPP? A consideration of direct and inferred measures. *Demography, 39*, 455–465.

Bauman, K. J. (1999). Shifting family definitions: The effect of cohabitation and other non-family household relationships on measures of poverty. *Demography, 36*, 315–326.

Bauserman, R. (2002). Child adjustment in joint-custody versus sole-custody arrangements: A meta-analytic review. *Journal of Family Psychology, 16*, 91–102.

Beach, S. R., & O'Leary, K. D. (1993). Marital discord and dysphoria: For whom does the marital relationship predict depressive symptomatology? *Journal of Social and Personal Relationships, 10*(3), 405–420.

Bellah, R. N., Madsen, R., Sullivan, W., Swidler, A., & Tipton, S. N. (1985). *Habits of the heart: Individualism and commitment in American life*. Berkeley: University of California Press.

Beller, A. H., & Graham, J. W. (1993). *Small change: The economics of child support*. New Haven, CT: Yale University Press.

Belli, R. F. (1998). The structure of autobiographical memory and the event history calendar: Potential improvements in the quality of retrospective reports in surveys. *Memory, 6*, 383–406.

Belli, R., Shay, W., & Stafford, F. (2001). Event history calendars and question list surveys. *Public Opinion Quarterly, 65*, 45–75.

Berkey, B. R., Perelman-Hall, T., & Kurdek, L. A. (1990). The multidimensional scale of sexuality. *Journal of Homosexuality, 19*(4), 67–87.

Betzig, L. (1993). Where are the bastard's daddies? *Behavioural and Brain Sciences, 285*, 16.

Bianchi, S. M., & Casper, L. M. (2000). American families. *Population Bulletin, 55*, 1–42.

Binstock, G., & Thornton, A. (2003). Separations, reconciliations, and living apart in cohabiting and marital unions. *Journal of Marriage and Family, 65*, 432.

Birchler, G., Weiss, R., & Vincent, J. (1975). Multimethod analysis of social reinforcement exchange between maritally distressed and nondistressed spouse and stranger dyads. *Journal of Personality and Social Psychology, 31*, 349–360.

Birks, S. (2000). *Submission to the Justice and Electoral Committee on the House of Representatives Supplementary Order Paper No. 25, Matrimonial Property Amendment Bill*. Retrieved August 8, 2002, from http://econ.massey.ac.nz/cppe/issues/sop25sub.htm

Birks, S. (2001). NZSCHF definition of "family" and its implications. *Child and family: Children in families as reflected in statistics, research and policy* (Issues Paper No. 11) (S. Birks, Ed.) (pp. 53–62). Centre for Public Policy Evaluation. Retrieved January 24, 2005, from http://econ.massey.ac.nz/cppe/papers/cppeip11/cppeip11.pdf

Birks, S. (2002, March 5). *Who is the father?* Retrieved August 24, 2004, from http://www.massey.ac.nz/~kbirks/gender/whosdad.htm

Black, D., Gates, G. J., Sanders, S. G., & Taylor, L. (2000). Demographics of the gay and lesbian population in the United States: Evidence from available systematic data sources. *Demography, 37*, 139–154.

Black, D. Gates, G. J., Sanders, S. G., & Taylor, L. (2003). *Same-sex unmarried partner couples in Census 2000: How many are gay and lesbian?* (Working paper, The Urban Institute, prepared for Population Association of American Meetings, Minneapolis, MN).

Blank, R. M., & Ellwood, D. T. (2002). The Clinton legacy for America's poor. In J. Frankel & P. Orsag (Eds.), *American economic policy in the 1990s* (pp. 749–800). Cambridge, MA: MIT Press.

Blankenhorn, D. (1995). *Fatherless America: Confronting our most urgent social problem.* New York: Basic Books.

Boggess, S., Martinez, G., & Bradner, C. (1998, May). *Counting dads: New estimates of teen fatherhood in the U.S.* Paper presented at the annual meeting of the Population Association of America, Minneapolis, MN.

Bolger, N., Zuckerman, A., & Kessler, R. C. (2000). Invisible support and adjustment to stress. *Journal of Personality and Social Psychology, 79*(6), 953–961.

Bonczar, T. P. (2003, August). Prevalence of imprisonment in the U.S. population, 1974–2001 (Bureau of Justice Statistics Special Report). Retrieved from www.ojp.usdoj.gov/bjs/pub/pdf/piusp01.pdf

Booth, A., & Amato, P. R. (2001). Parental predivorce relations and offspring postdivorce well-being. *Journal of Marriage and the Family, 63,* 197–212.

Booth, A., Amato, P. R., Johnson, D., & Rogers, S. (2003). *Conceptualizing and measuring healthy marriages and positive relationships.* Unpublished memo commissioned by Child Trends.

Booth, A., & Crouter, A. (2002). *Just living together: Implications of cohabitation on families, children, and social policy.* Mahwah, NJ: Lawrence Erlbaum Associates.

Booth, A., & Edwards, J. N. (1985). Age at marriage and marital instability. *Journal of Marriage and the Family, 47,* 67–75.

Booth, A., & Johnson, D. R. (1994). Declining health and marital quality. *Journal of Marriage and the Family, 56,* 218–223.

Booth, A., Johnson, D., & Edwards, J. N. (1983). Measuring marital instability. *Journal of Marriage and the Family, 42*(2), 387–394.

Booth, A., Johnson, D. R., White, L. K., & Edwards, J. N. (1981). *Female labor force participation and marital instability: Methodology report.* Lincoln: University of Nebraska, Bureau of Sociological Research.

Booth, A., Johnson, D. R., White, L. K., & Edwards, J. N. (1985). Predicting divorce and permanent separation. *Journal of Family Issues, 6,* 331–346.

Bradbury, T., & Fincham, F. (1990). Attributions in marriage: Review and critique. *Psychological Bulletin, 107,* 3–33.

Bradbury, T., & Fincham, F. (1992). Attributions and behavior in marital interaction. *Journal of Personality and Social Psychology, 63*(4), 613–628.

Bradbury, T. N., Fincham, F. D., & Beach, S. R. H. (2000). Research on the nature and determinants of marital satisfaction: A decade in review. *Journal of Marriage and the Family, 62,* 964–980.

Bramlett, M. D., & Mosher, W. D. (2001). First marriage dissolution, divorce, and remarriage: United States. *Advance Data From Vital and Health Statistics, 323.*

Bramlett, M. D., & Mosher, W. D. (2002). Cohabitation, marriage, divorce and remarriage in the United States. *Vital Health Statistics, 23*(22).

Brandon, P. (2003). *Entries onto welfare among children living with grandparents in the United States.* Unpublished manuscript, University of Massachusetts at Amherst: Department of Sociology.

Brandon, P., & Bumpass, L. (2001). Children's living arrangements, Coresidence of umarried fathers, and welfare receipt. *Journal of Family Issues, 22,* 3–26.

Braver, S. L., & Griffin, W. A. (2000). Engaging fathers in the post-divorce family. In H. E. Peters, G. W. Peterson, S. K. Steinmetz, & R. D. Day (Eds.), *Fatherhood: Research, interventions and policies* (pp. 247–267). New York: Haworth.

Braver, S., Wolchik, S., Sandler, I., Fogas, B., & Zvetina, D. (1991). Frequency of visitation by divorced father: Differences in reports by fathers and mothers. *American Journal of Orthopsychiatry, 61*, 448–454.

Bray, J. H., & Jouriles, E. N. (1995). Treatment of marital conflict and prevention of divorce. *Journal of Marital and Family Therapy, 21*, 461–473.

Brien, M. J., & Willis, R. J. (1997). Costs and consequences for the fathers. In R. Maynard (Ed.), *Kids having kids: Economic costs and social consequences of teen pregnancy* (pp. 95–143). Washington, DC: Urban Institute.

Brindis, C., Boggess, J., Katsuranis, F., Mantell, M., McCarter, V., & Wolfe, A. (1998). A profile of the adolescent male family planning client. *Family Planning Perspectives, 30*(2), 63–66, 88.

Brines, J., & Joyner, K. (1999). The ties that bind: Commitment and stability in the modern union. *American Sociological Review, 64*, 333–356.

Bronte-Tinkew, J. (2004a). The measurement of marital relationships in incarcerated populations. In *Conceptualizing and measuring "healthy marriage" for empirical research and evaluation studies: A review of the literature and annotated bibliography* (pp. 163–178) Washington, DC: Child Trends.

Bronte-Tinkew, J. (2004b). Measures used in the measurement of marital relationships in military populations. In *Conceptualizing and measuring "healthy marriage" for empirical research and evaluation studies: A review of the literature and annotated bibliography* (pp. 133–162). Washington, DC: Child Trends.

Brown, S. (2002). Child well-being in cohabiting families. In A. Booth & A. Crouter (Eds.), *Just living together: Implications for children, families, and public policy* (pp. 173–188). Mahwah, NJ: Lawrence Erlbaum Associates.

Brown, S. L. (2004). Family structure and child well-being: The significance of parental cohabitation. *Journal of Marriage and the Family, 66*, 351–367.

Brown, S. L., & Booth, A. (1996). Cohabitation versus marriage: A comparison of relationship quality. *Journal of Marriage and the Family, 58*, 668–678.

Brown, S. S., & Eisenberg, L. (1995). *The best intentions: Unintended pregnancy and the well-being of children and families.* Washington, DC: National Academy Press.

Buchanan, C., Maccoby, E., & Dornbusch, S. (1996). *Adolescents after divorce.* Cambridge, MA: Harvard University Press.

Buehlman, K. T., Gottman, J. M., & Katz, L. F. (1992). How a couple views their past predicts their future: Predicting divorce from an oral history interview. *Journal of Family Psychology, 5*, 295–318.

Bumpass, L. L. (1990). What's happening to the family? Interactions between demographic and institutional change. *Demography, 27*, 483–498.

Bumpass, L. L., & Lu, H.-H. (2000). Trends in cohabitation and implications for children's family contexts in the United States. *Population Studies, 54*, 29–41.

Bumpass, L. L., Martin, T. C., & Sweet, J. A. (1991). The impact of family background and early marital factors on marital disruption. *Journal of Family Issues, 12*, 22–44.

Bumpass, L., & Raley, R. K. (1995). Redefining single-parent families: Cohabitation and changing family reality. *Demography, 32*, 97–109.

Bumpass, L., Raley, R. K., & Sweet, J. (1995). The changing character of stepfamilies: Implications of cohabitation and nonmarital childbearing. *Demography, 32*, 425–436.

Bumpass, L., & Sweet, J. (1989a). Children's experience in single-parent families: Implications of cohabitation and marital transitions. *Family Planning Perspectives, 21*, 256–260.

Bumpass, L., & Sweet, J. (1989b). National estimates of cohabitation. *Demography, 26*, 615–625.

Bumpass, L., Sweet, J., & Castro Martin, T. (1990). Changing patterns of remarriage in the U.S. *Journal of Marriage and the Family, 52*, 747–756.

Bumpass, L. L., Sweet, J. A., & Cherlin, A. (1991). The role of cohabitation in declining rates of marriage. *Journal of Marriage and the Family, 53*, 91–127.

Burchett-Patel, D., Gryn, T., & Mott, F. (1999, March). *The families of men: Exploring relationship dynamics with the National Longitudinal Survey of Youth.* Paper presented at the annual meeting for the Population Association of America, New York.

Busby, D. M., Crane, D. R., Larson, J. H., & Christensen, C. (1995). A revision of the Dyadic Adjustment Scale for use with distressed and nondistressed couples: Construct hierarchy and multidimensional scales. *Journal of Marital and Family Therapy, 21*, 289–308.

Busby, D. M., Holman, T. B., & Taniguchi, N. (2001). RELATE: Relationship evaluation of the individual, family, cultural, and couple contexts. *Family Relations, 50*, 308–316.

Cabrera, N., Brooks-Gunn, J., Moore, K., West, J., Boller, K., & Tamis-LeMonda, C. (2002). Bridging research and policy: Including fathers of young children in national studies. In C. Tamis-LeMonda & N. Cabrera (Eds.), *Handbook of father involvement: Multidisciplinary perspectives* (pp. 489–523). Mahwah, NJ: Lawrence Erlbaum Associates.

Call, V., & Heaton, T. (1997). Religious influence on marital stability. *Journal for the Scientific Study of Religion, 36*, 382–392.

Callister, P., & Hill, M. (2002). Are "two-parent" and "single-parent" families misnomers misdirecting policies and family/work research? (Working Paper No. 02-18). Cornell University, Cornell Careers Institute. Retrieved January 24, 2005, from http://www.blcc.cornell.edu/cci/workpap_all.html

Card, J., & Wise, L. (1978). Teenage mothers and teenage fathers: The impact of early childbearing on parent's personal and professional lives. *Demography, 10*(4), 137–156.

Carlson, E. J. (1994). *Marriage and the English Reformation.* Oxford, England: Blackwell.

Carlson, M., & Corcoran, M. (2001). Family structure and children's behavioral and cognitive outcomes. *Journal of Marriage and Family, 63*, 779–792.

Carlson, M., & McLanahan, S. (2002). *Do good partners make good parents?* (Working Paper #02-16-FF). Princeton, NJ: Center for Research on Child Wellbeing.

Carlson, M., & McLanahan, S. (2004). Early father involvement in fragile families. In R. Day & M. Lamb (Eds.), *Conceptualizing and measuring father involvement* (pp. 241–271). Mahwah, NJ: Lawrence Erlbaum Associates.

Carlson, M., McLanahan, S., & Brooks-Gunn, J. (2003, May). *Father involvement among fragile families one year later.* Presented at the Annual Population Association of America Meeting, Minneapolis, MN.

Carlson, M., McLanahan, S., & England, P. (2003). *Union formation in fragile families* (Working Paper # 01-06-FF). Princeton, NJ: Center for Research on Child Wellbeing.

Carmines, E. G., & Zeller, R. A. (1979). *Reliability and validity assessment.* Beverly Hills, CA: Sage.

Carpenter, C. (2004). New evidence on gay and lesbian household incomes. *Contemporary Economic Policy, 22*, 78–94.

Carpenter, C., & Gates, G. J. (2004, August 11). *Benchmarking census same-sex unmarried partner data with other GLBT survey data.* Paper presented at the Joint Statistical Meetings, Toronto, Canada.

Carrere, S., Buehlman, K. T., Gottman, J. M., Coan, J. A., & Ruckstuhl, L. (2000). Predicting marital stability and divorce in newlywed couples. *Journal of Family Psychology, 14*, 42–58.

Carroll, J. S. (2004). *The ability to negotiate or the ability to love: An investigation of interpersonal competence in marriage.* Manuscript under review.

Carroll, J. S., & Doherty, W. J. (2003). Evaluating the effectiveness of premarital prevention programs: A meta-analytic review of outcome research. *Family Relations, 52*, 105–118.

Casper, L. M., & Bianchi, S. M. (2002). *Continuity and change in the American family.* Thousand Oaks, CA: Sage.

Casper, L. M., & Bryson, K. (1998a). *Co-resident grandparents and their grandchildren: Grandparent maintained families* (Working Paper No. 26). Washington, DC: Population Division, Bureau of the Census.

Casper, L. M., & Bryson, K. (1998b). *Household and family characteristics: March 1998 (Update)* (U.S. Census Bureau, Current Population Reports, Population Characteristics, P20–515). Washington, DC: U.S. Government Printing Office.

Casper, L. M., & Cohen, P. N. (2000). How does POSSLQ measure up? Historical estimates of cohabitation. *Demography, 37,* 237–245.

Casper, L. M., & Sayer, L. (2000, March). *Cohabitation transitions: Different attitudes and purposes, different paths.* Paper presented at the annual meeting of the Population Association of America, Los Angeles.

Casper, L. M., & Sayer, L. C. (2002, May). *Cohabitation transitions: Different purposes and goals, different paths.* Paper presented at the annual meeting of the Population Association of America.

Castro Martin, T., & Bumpass, L. (1989). Recent trends in marital disruption. *Demography, 26,* 37–51.

Center for Human Resource Research. (1999). *NYLS79 User's guide: A guide to the 1979–1998 National Longitudinal Survey of Youth Data.* Columbus: Ohio State University, CHRR User Services.

Center for Human Resource Research. (2003). *The National Longitudinal Surveys NLSY97 User's Guide 2003.* Columbus: Ohio State University.

Center for Marriage and the Family. (1995). *Marriage preparation in the Catholic church: Getting it right.* Omaha, NE: Creighton University.

Cherlin, A. (1990). Recent changes in American fertility, marriage, and divorce. In S. H. Preston (Ed.), *World population: Approaching the year 2000* (pp. 145–154). Newbury Park, CA: Sage.

Cherlin, A. J. (1992). *Marriage, divorce, remarriage.* Cambridge, MA: Harvard University Press.

Cherlin, A., & Griffith, J. (1998). Methodological issues in improving data on fathers: Report of the working group on the methodology of studying fathers. In *Nurturing fatherhood: Improving data and research on male fertility* (pp. 75–211). Washington, DC: Federal Interagency Forum on Child and Family Statistics.

Cherlin, A., Griffith, J., & McCarthy, J. (1983). A note on maritally-disrupted men's reports of child support in the June 1980 Current Population Survey. *Demography, 20*(3), 385–389.

Child Trends. (2002). *Charting parenthood: A statistical portrait of fathers and mothers in America.* Washington, DC: Author.

Christensen, A., & Heavey, C. (1990). Gender and social structure in the demand/withdraw pattern of marital conflict. *Journal of Personality and Social Psychology, 59,* 73–82.

Christensen, A., & Jacobsen, N. S. (2000). *Reconcilable differences.* New York: Guilford.

Citro, C., & Kalton, G. (1993). *The future of the Survey of Income and Program Participation.* Washington, DC: National Academy Press.

Clark, M. S., Mills, J., & Powell, M. C. (1986). Keeping track of needs in communal and exchange relationships. *Journal of Personality and Social Psychology, 51,* 333–338.

Clements, M. L., Stanley, S. M., & Markman, H. J. (2004). Before they said "I Do": Discriminating among marital outcomes over 13 years based on premarital data. *Journal of Marriage and the Family, 66,* 613–626.

Cohan, C., & Kleinbaum, S. (2002). Toward a greater understanding of the cohabitation effect: Premarital cohabitation and marital communication. *Journal of Marriage and Family, 64,* 180–192.

Cohen, W. (1997, January 27). Kid looks like the mailman? *U.S. News & World Report,* p. 62.

Coleman, E. (1990). Toward a synthetic understanding of sexual orientation. In D. P. Mc-Whirter, S. A. Sanders & J. M. Reinisch (Eds.), *Homosexuality/heterosexuality: Concepts of sexual orientation* (pp. 267–276). New York: Oxford University Press.

Coleman, J. (1988). Social capital in the creation of human capital. *American Journal of Sociology, 94,* 95–120.

Coleman, M., Ganong, L., & Fine, M. (2000). Reinvestigating remarriage: Another decade of progress. *Journal of Marriage and the Family, 62,* 1288–1307.

Coley, R. L. (2001). (In)visible men: Emerging research on low-income, unmarried, and minority fathers. *American Psychologist, 56,* 743–753.

Coley, R. L. (2003). Daughter–father relationships and adolescent psychosocial functioning in low-income African American families. *Journal of Marriage and Family, 65,* 867–875.

Coley, R. L., & Chase-Lansdale, P. L. (1999). Stability and change in paternal involvement among urban African American fathers. *Journal of Family Psychology, 13,* 416–435.

Coley, R. L., & Morris, J. E. (2002). Comparing father and mother reports of father involvement among low-income minority families. *Journal of Marriage and the Family, 64,* 982–997.

Colter, M. S. (2003). *Examining the accuracy of divorce: Comparing divorce records and survey data.* Unpublished master's thesis, Brigham Young University, Provo, UT.

Conger, R., & Elder, G. H., Jr. (1994). *Families in troubled times: Adapting to changes in rural America.* New York: Aldine de Gruyter.

Conger, R. D., Elder, G. H., Lorenz, F. O., Conger, K. J., Simons, R. L., Whitbeck, L. B., Huck, S., & Melby, J. (1990). Linking economic hardship to marital quality and instability. *Journal of Marriage and the Family, 52,* 643–656.

Cooksey, E. (1997). Consequences of young mothers' marital histories for children's cognitive development. *Journal of Marriage and the Family, 59,* 245–261.

Cowan, C. P., & Cowan, P. A. (2003). *The conceptualization and measurement of "Healthy Marriages/Couple Relationships."* Unpublished memo commissioned by Child Trends.

Cronin, H., & Curry, O. (2000, January). *The evolved family.* London School of Economics. Retrieved September 28, 2003, from http://www.lse.ac.uk/Depts./cpnss/Darwin/family.htm

Cummings, E. M., & Davies, P. T. (1994). *Children and marital conflict: The impact of family dispute and resolution.* New York: Guilford.

Cutrona, C. E. (1996). *Social support in couples: Marriage as a resource in times of stress.* Thousand Oaks, CA: Sage.

Daly, M., & Wilson, M. (1998). *The truth about Cinderella: A Darwinian view of parental love.* New Haven, CT: Yale University Press.

Das Gupta, P. (1978). An alternative formulation of the birth function in a two-sex model. *Population Studies, 32,* 367–379.

DaVanzo, J., & Rahman, M. O. (1993). American families: Trends and correlates. *Population Index, 59*(3), 350–386.

Davila, J., & Bradbury, T. N. (2001). Attachment insecurity and the distinction between unhappy spouses who do and do not divorce. *Journal of Family Psychology, 15,* 371–393.

Day, R. D. (2003). *Couple relationships when one partner is in prison.* Unpublished memo commissioned by Child Trends.

Day, R. D., Gavazzi, S., & Acock, A. (2001). Compelling family processes. In A. Thornton (Ed.), *The well-being of children and families: Research and data needs* (pp. 103–126). Ann Arbor: The University of Michigan Press.

Day, R. D., & Lamb, M. E. (2004). *Conceptualizing and measuring father involvement.* Mahwah, NJ: Lawrence Erlbaum Associates.

De Leeuw, E., & de Heer, W. (2002). Trends in household survey nonresponse: A longitudinal and international comparison. In R. M. Groves, D. A. Dillman, J. L. Eltinge, & R. A. Little (Eds.), *Survey nonresponse* (pp. 41–54). New York: Wiley.

DeCloet, D. (1998). The strands of adultery. *Alberta Report, 25*(34), 36.

DeLeire, T., & Kalil, A. (2002). Good things come in threes: Single-parent multigenerational family structure and adolescent adjustment. *Demography, 39*, 393–413.

DeLeire, T., & Kalil, A. (2005). How do cohabiting couples with children spend their money? *Journal of Marriage and the Family, 67*, 286–295.

DeMaris, A., & Rao, V. (1992). Premarital cohabitation and subsequent marital stability in the United States: A reassessment. *Journal of Marriage and Family, 54*, 178–190.

Dench, G., & Thomson, K. (1999). Family breakdown and the role of grandparents. *Family Policy, Winter*, 7–21.

Devins, G. M., & Orme, C. M. (1985). Center for Epidemiologic Studies depression scale. In D. J. Keyser & R. C. Sweetland (Eds.), *Test critiques* (pp. 144–160). Kansas City, MO: Test Corporation of America.

Doherty, W. J. (1981). Cognitive processes in intimate conflict, II: Efficacy and learned helplessness. *American Journal of Family Therapy, 9*(2), 35–44.

Doyle, P., Czajka, J., Boldin, P., Beebout, H., & Hirabayashi, S. (1987). *Conceptual studies of SIPP-based simulation of the Food Stamp Program, Part 1. Uniform eligibility measures* (Final Report to the Food and Nutrition Service, U.S. Department of Agriculture). Washington, DC: Mathematica Policy Research.

Dubow, E., Roecker, C., & D'Imperio, R. (2001). Mental health. In R. Ammerman & M. Hershon (Eds.), *Handbook of prevention and treatment with children and adolescents: Intervention in the real world context* (pp. 259–286). New York: Wiley.

Dugoni, B., Lee, L., & Tourangeau, R. (1997). *Report on the NLSY Round 16 Recall Experiment* (NLS 97–34). Washington, DC: Bureau of Labor Statistics, Office of Economic Research.

Duncan, S., & Edwards, R. (1997). Lone mothers and paid work: Rational economic man or gendered moral rationalities? *Feminist Economics, 3*, 29–61.

Dunifon, R., & Kowalski-Jones, L. (2002). Who's in the house? Race differences in cohabitation, single-parenthood, and child development. *Child Development, 73*, 1249–1264.

Dunn, J. (2004). Children's relationships with their nonresident fathers. *Journal of Child Psychology and Psychiatry and Allied Disciplines, 45*, 659–671.

Ellwood, D. T., & Jencks, C. (2002). The uneven spread of single parent families in the United States since 1960: What do we know? Where do we look for answers? In K. Neckerman (Ed.), *Social inequity* (pp. 3–77). New York: Russell Sage Foundation.

Ellwood, D. T., & Jencks, C. (2004). *The spread of single-parent families in the United States since 1960* (KSG Faculty Research Working Paper Series No. RWP04-008). Cambridge, MA: Harvard University.

Elster, A. B., Lamb, M. E., & Tavare, J. (1987). Association between behavioral and school problems and fatherhood in a national sample of adolescent fathers. *Journal of Pediatrics, 111*, 932–936.

Emery, R. (1982). Interparental conflict and the children of discord and divorce. *Psychological Bulletin, 92*, 310–330.

Emery, R. E. (1988). *Marriage, divorce and children's adjustment*. Thousand Oaks, CA: Sage.

England, P., Edin, K., & Linnenberg, K. (2003, September). *Love and distrust among unmarried parents*. Paper presented at the symposium, Marriage and Family Formation Among Low-Income Couples: What Do We Know From Research? National Poverty Center, Ann Arbor, MI.

Fabricius, W. V. (2003). Listening to children of divorce: New findings that diverge from Wallerstein, Lewis, & Blakeslee. *Family Relations, 52*, 385–396.

Fagan, P. F. (2003). *Healthy marriage measures*. Unpublished memo commissioned by Child Trends.

Federal Interagency Forum on Child and Family Statistics. (1998). *Nurturing fatherhood: Improving data and research on male fertility, family formation and fatherhood*. Washington, DC: Author.

Federal Interagency Forum on Child & Family Statistics. (2001). *Counting couples: Improving marriage, divorce, remarriage, and cohabitation data in the federal statistical system*. Highlights from a National Workshop. Bethesda, MD: National Institutes of Health.

Federal Register Notice. 60 Fed. Reg. 241 64437 (1995).

Fein, D. J. (2004). *Married and poor: Basic characteristics of economically disadvantaged married couples in the U.S.* (Supporting Health Marriage Demonstration Working Paper No. SHM-04-01). Bethesda, MD: Abt Associates.

Fields, J. (2001). *Living arrangements of children* (Current Population Reports P70-74). Washington, DC: U.S. Census Bureau.

Fields, J. (2003). Children's living arrangements and characteristics: March 2002. In *Population Characteristics* (U.S. Census Bureau, Current Population Reports, Population Characteristics, P20-547). Washington, DC: U.S. Government Printing Office.

Fields, J., & Casper, L. M. (2001). *America's families and living arrangements: March 2000* (Current Population Reports, P-20-537). Washington, DC: U.S. Bureau of the Census.

Fields, J., & Kreider, R. (2000, October). *Marriage and divorce rates in the U.S.: A multistate life table analysis, Fall 1996 SIPP*. Paper presented at the annual meeting of the presented at the Southern Demographic Association, New Orleans, LA.

Fincham, F. (2000). The kiss of the porcupines: From attributing responsibility to forgiving. *Personal Relationships, 7*, 1–23.

Fincham, F. (2003). Marital conflict: Correlates, structure, and context. *Current Directions in Psychological Science, 12*(1), 23–27.

Fincham, F., & Beach, S. (1999). Marital conflict: Implications for working with couples. *Annual Review of Psychology, 50*, 47–77.

Findlay, J., & Wright, R. (1992). *Gender, poverty and intra-household distribution of resources* (Working Paper No. 83). Luxembourg Income Study, University of Glasgow, Scotland.

Fitch, C. A., & Ruggles, S. (2000). Historical trends in marriage formation: The United States 1850–1990. In L. J. Waite (Ed.), *The ties that bind: Perspectives on marriage and cohabitation* (pp. 59–88). New York: Aldine de Gruyter.

Fleming, R., & Atkinson, T. (1999). *Families of a different kind: Life in the households of couples who have children from previous marriages or marriage-like relationships*. Waikanae, New Zealand: Families of Remarriage Project.

Fowers, B. J. (1993). Psychology as public philosophy: An illustration of the moral dimension of psychology with marital research. *Journal of Theoretical and Philosophical Psychology, 13*, 124–126.

Fowers, B. J. (1998). Psychology and the good marriage: Social theory as practice. *American Behavioral Scientist, 41*, 516–541.

Fowers, B. J. (2000). *Beyond the myth of marital happiness: How embracing the virtues of loyalty, generosity, justice, and courage can strengthen your relationship*. San Francisco: Jossey-Bass.

Fowers, B. J. (2001). The limits of a technical concept of a good marriage: Examining the role of virtues in communication skills. *Journal of Marital and Family Therapy, 27*, 327–340.

Fowers, B. J. (2003). *Conceptualizing and measuring healthy marriages and positive relationships*. Unpublished memo commissioned by Child Trends.

Fowers, B. J., Bucker, J., Calbeck, K. B., & Harrigan, P. (2003). *How do social scientists define a good marriage?* Unpublished manuscript.

Fowers, B. J., Lyons, E. M., & Montel, K. H. (1996). Positive marital illusions: Self-enhancement or relationship enhancement? *Journal of Family Psychology, 2,* 192–208.

Fowers, B., & Olson, D. (1986). Predicting marital success with PREPARE: A predictive validity study. *Journal of Marital and Family Therapy, 12,* 403–413.

Fragile Families and Child Wellbeing. (2000). *Dispelling myths about unmarried fathers* (Fragile Families Research Brief No. 1). Princeton, NJ: Bendheim-Thoman Center for Research on Child Wellbeing.

Freedman, D., Thornton, A., Camburn, D., Alwin, D., & Young-DeMarco, L. (1988). The life history calendar: A technique for collecting retrospective data. In C. C. Clogg (Ed.), *Sociological methodology* (Vol. 18, pp. 37–68). San Francisco: Jossey-Bass.

Freeman, R. B., & Waldfogel, J. (2001). Dunning delinquent dads. *Journal of Human Resources, 36,* 207–225.

Furstenberg, F. F., Jr. (1990). Divorce and the American family. *Annual Review of Sociology, 16,* 379–403.

Furstenburg, F. F., Jr. (1995a). Dealing with dads: The changing roles of fathers. In P. Chase-Landsdale & J. Brook-Gunn (Eds.), *Escape from poverty: What makes a difference for children?* (pp. 189–210). Cambridge, England: Cambridge University Press.

Furstenberg, F. F., Jr. (1995b). Fathering in the inner city: Paternal participation and public policy. In W. Marsiglio (Ed.), *Fatherhood: Contemporary theory, research, and social policy* (pp. 119–147). Thousand Oaks, CA: Sage.

Furstenberg, F. F., Jr., & Cherlin, A. J. (1991). *Divided families: What happens to children when parents part.* Cambridge, MA: University of Harvard Press.

Furstenberg, F. F., & Harris, K. M. (1993). When and why fathers matter: Impacts of father involvement on the children of adolescent mothers. In R. L. Lerman & T. J. Ooms (Eds.), *Young unwed fathers* (pp. 117–138). Philadelphia: Temple University Press.

Furstenberg, F. F., Morgan, S. P., & Allison, P. D. (1987). Paternal participation and children's well-being after marital dissolution. *American Sociological Review, 52,* 695–701.

Furukawa, S. (1994). The diverse living arrangements of children: Summer 1991. In *Current Population Reports* (Series P70-38). Washington, DC: U.S. Government Printing Office.

Gable, S. (2003, October). *Accentuating the positives: Supportive responses to expressions of positive events.* Presented at the International Positive Psychology Summit, Washington, DC.

Ganong, L. H., & Coleman, M. M. (1994). *Remarried family relationships.* Thousand Oaks, CA: Sage.

Ganong, L., & Coleman, M. (2003). *Couples in stepfamilies.* Unpublished memo commissioned by Child Trends.

Garasky, S. (1995). The effects of family structure on educational attainment: Do the effects vary by the age of the child? *American Journal of Economics & Sociology, 54,* 89–105.

Garfinkel, I., Glei, D., & McLanahan, S. S. (2002). Assortative mating among unmarried parents: Implications for ability to pay child support. *Journal of Population Economics, 15,* 417–432.

Garfinkel, I., McLanahan, S. S., & Hanson, T. L. (1998). A patchwork portrait of nonresident fathers. In I. Garfinkel, S. McLanahan, D. Meyer, & J. Seltzer (Eds.), *Fathers under fire: The revolution in child support enforcement* (pp. 31–60). New York: Russell Sage.

Garfinkel, I., & Oellerich, D. (1989). Noncustodial fathers' ability to pay child support. *Demography, 26,* 219–233.

Garfinkel, I., & Robins, P. (2004). The relationship between child support enforcement tools and child support outcomes. In I. Garfinkel, S. McLanahan, & P. Robins (Eds.), *Child support and child well-being* (pp. 133–170). Washington, DC: Urban Institute.

Gates, G. J., & Ost, J. (2004). *The gay and lesbian atlas.* Washington, DC: Urban Institute Press.

Gaulin, S. J., & Schlegel, A. (1980). Paternal confidence and paternal investment: A cross-cultural test of a sociobiological hypothesis. *Ethology and Sociobiology, 1*, 301–309.

Gibbs, J. (1988). Young Black males in America: Endangered, embittered, and embattled. In J. Gibbs (Ed.), *Young, Black, and male in America: An endangered species* (pp. 1–36). Dover, MA: Auburn House.

Giblin, P., Sprenkle, D., & Sheehan, R. (1985). Enrichment outcome research: A meta-analysis of premarital, marital, and family interventions. *Journal of Marital and Family Therapy, 11*(3), 257–271.

Glenn, N. D. (1990). Quantitative research on marital quality in the 1980s: A critical review. *Journal of Marriage and the Family, 52*, 818–831.

Goldscheider, F. (2003, November). *Remarks re measuring father involvement.* Paper presented at workshop on measurement issues in family demography, Bethesda, MD.

Goldscheider, F. K., & Kaufman, G. (1996). Fertility and committment: Bringing men back in. *Population and Development Review, 22*(Suppl), 87–99.

Goldstein, J. R. (1999). The leveling of divorce in the United States. *Demography, 36*, 409–414.

Gordon, K. C., & Baucom, D. H. (2003). *Forgiveness and marriage: Preliminary support for a measure based on a model of recovery from marital betrayal.* Unpublished manuscript, University of Tennessee, Knoxville.

Gordon, K. C., Baucom, D. H., & Snyder, D. K. (2003). *An integrative intervention for promoting recovery from extramarital affairs.* Unpublished manuscript, University of Tennessee, Knoxville.

Gorsuch, R. L., & McPherson, S. E. (1989). Intrinsic/extrinsic measurement: I/E revised and single item scales. *Journal for the Scientific Study of Religion, 28*, 348–354.

Gottman, J. M. (1993). A theory of marital dissolution and stability. *Journal of Family Psychology, 7*, 57–75.

Gottman, J. M. (1994). *What predicts divorce? The relationship between marital processes and marital outcomes.* Hillsdale, NJ: Lawrence Erlbaum Associates.

Gottman, J. M. (1999). *The marriage clinic: A scientifically based marital therapy.* New York: Norton.

Gottman, J. (2003). *The sound relationship house questionnaires.* Unpublished memo commissioned by Child Trends.

Gottman, J. M., Coan, J., Carrere, S., & Swanson, C. (1998). Predicting marital happiness and stability from newlywed interactions. *Journal of Marriage and the Family, 60*, 5–22.

Gottman, J. M., Driver, J., & Tabares, A. (2002). Building the sound marital house: An empirically derived couple therapy. In A. S. Gurman & N. S. Jacobson (Eds.), *Clinical handbook of couple therapy* (3rd ed., pp. 373–399). New York: Guilford.

Gottman, J. M., & Notarius, C. I. (2000). Decade review: Observing marital interaction. *Journal of Marriage and the Family, 62*, 927–948.

Gottman, J. M., Murray, J. D., Swanson, C. C., Tyson, R., & Swanson, K. R. (2002). *The mathematics of marriage: Dynamic nonlinear models.* Cambridge, MA: MIT Press.

Gottman, J. M., Ryan, K. D., Carrere, S., & Erley, A. M. (2002). Toward a scientifically based marital therapy. In H. A. Liddle, D. A. Santisteban, R. F. Levant, & J. H. Bray (Eds.), *Family psychology: Science-based interventions* (pp. 147–174). Washington, DC: American Psychological Association.

Gottman, J. M., & Silver, N. (1994). *Why marriages succeed or fail.* New York: Simon & Schuster.

Graefe, D. R., & Lichter, D. T. (1999). Life course transitions of American children: Parental cohabitation, marriage, and single motherhood. *Demography, 36*, 205–217.

Grall, T. S. (2003, October). *Custodial mothers and fathers and their child support: 2001* (Current Population Reports No. P60-225). Washington, DC: U.S. Census Bureau.

Greene, M. E., & Biddlecom, A. E. (2000). Absent and problematic men: Demographic accounts of male reproductive roles. *Population and Development Review, 26*, 81–115.

Greil, A. L. (1997). Infertility and psychological distress: A critical review of the literature. *Social Science Medicine, 45*, 1679–1704.

Groves, R., & Couper, M. (1998). *Nonresponse in household interview surveys.* New York: John Wiley and Sons.

Groves, R., Dillman, D., Eltinge, J., & Little, R. (Eds.). (2002). *Survey nonresponse.* New York: John Wiley and Sons.

Grych, J. H., & Fincham, F. D. (1990). Marital conflict and children's adjustment: A cognitive contextual framework. *Psychological Bulletin, 108*, 267–290.

Gryn, T., Mott, F., & Burchett-Patel, D. (2000, March). *Relationship trajectories for a contemporary cohort of men in early middle age: Evidence from the NLSY79.* Paper presented at the annual meeting of the Population Association of America, Los Angeles.

Guerney, B. G., Jr. (1977). *Relationship enhancement.* San Francisco: Jossey-Bass.

Guzman, L. (2004). Measures used in the measurement of marital relationships in stepfamily populations. In *Conceptualizing and measuring "healthy marriage" for empirical research and evaluation studies: A review of the literature and annotated bibliography* (pp. 55–92). Washington, DC: Child Trends.

Haddock, S. A., Zimmerman, T. S., Ziemba, S. J., & Current, L. R. (2001). Ten adaptive strategies for work and family balance: Advice from successful families. *Journal of Marital and Family Therapy, 27*, 445–458.

Hahlweg, K., & Markman, H. J. (1988). The effectiveness of behavioral marital therapy: Empirical status of behavioral techniques in preventing and alleviating marital distress. *Journal of Consulting and Clinical Psychology, 56*, 441–447.

Hahlweg, K., Markman, H., Thurmaier, F., Engl, J., & Eckert, V. (1998). Prevention of marital distress: Results of a German prospective longitudinal study. *Journal of Family Psychology, 12*, 543–556.

Halford, W. K., Markman, H. J., Kline, G., & Stanley, S. M. (2003). Best practice in couple relationship education. *Journal of Marital and Family Therapy, 29*(3), 385–406.

Halford, W. K., Sanders, M. R., & Behrens, B. C. (2000). Repeating the errors of our parents? Family of origin spouse violence and observed conflict management in engaged couples. *Family Process, 39*, 219–235.

Halford, W. K., Sanders, M. R., & Behrens, B. C. (2001). Can skills training prevent relationship problems in at-risk couples? Four-year effects of a behavioral relationship education program. *Journal of Family Psychology, 15*, 797–801.

Hammett, T., Roberts, C., & Kennedy, S. (2001). Health-related issues in prisoner reentry. *Crime and Delinquency, 47*, 390–409.

Hanson, S., Morrison, D., & Ginsburg, A. (1989). The antecedents of teenage fatherhood. *Demography, 26*, 579–596.

Hanson, T. L., McLanahan, S., & Thomson, E. (1997). Economic resources, parental practices, and children's well-being. In G. J. Duncan & J. Brooks-Gunn (Eds.), *Consequences of growing up poor* (pp. 190–238). New York: Russell Sage Foundation.

Hao, L., & Xie, G. (2001). The complexity of endogeneity of family structure in explaining children's misbehavior. *Social Science Research, 31*, 1–28.

Hargrave, T. D. (2000). *The essential humility of marriage: Honoring the third identity in couple therapy.* Phoenix, AZ: Zeig, Tucker and Theisen.

Harlow, C. W. (2003). *Education and correctional populations* (Bureau of Justice Statistics Special Report; Publication NCJ 195670). Retrieved from www.ojp.usdoj.gov/bjs

Harris, K. M., Florey, F., Tabor, J., Bearman, P. S., Jones, J., & Udry, J. R. (2003). *The National Longitudinal Study of Adolescent Health: Study design.* Retrieved November 1, 2003, from http://www.cpc.unc.edu/projects/addhealth/

Harris, K. M., Heard, H., & King, V. (2000, March). *Resident father involvement: Differences by family structure, race and ethnicity, and social class.* Presented at the annual meeting of the Population Association of America, Los Angeles.

Harris, K. M., & Ryan, S. (2004). Father involvement and the diversity of family context. In R. D. Day & M. E. Lamb (Eds.), *Conceptualizing and measuring father involvement* (pp. 292–319). Mahwah, NJ: Lawrence Erlbaum Associates.

Harrison, P., & Karberg, J. (2004). Prison and jail inmates at midyear 2003 (Bureau of Justice Statistics report). Retrieved from www.ojp.usdoj.gov/bjs

Hawkins, A. J., Marshall, C. M., & Allen, S. M. (1998). The Orientation Toward Domestic Labor Questionnaire: Understanding dual-earner wives' sense of fairness about family work. *Journal of Family Psychology, 12,* 244–258.

Heaton, T. B., & Albrecht, S. L. (1991). Stable unhappy marriages. *Journal of Marriage and the Family, 53,* 747–758.

Heaton, T. B., & Pratt, E. L. (1990). The effects of religious homogamy on marital satisfaction and stability. *Journal of Family Issues, 11,* 191–207.

Herdt, G. (1998). *Same sex, different cultures: Exploring gay and lesbian lives.* New York: Westview Press.

Hernandez, D. (1993). *America's children: Resources from family, government, and the economy.* New York: Russell Sage Foundation.

Hernandez, D., & Brandon, P. (2002). Who are the fathers of the 1990s? In C. Tames-LeMonda & N. Cabrera (Eds.), *Fatherhood involvement: Multidisciplinary perspectives* (pp. 33–62). Mahwah, NJ: Lawrence Earlbaum Associates.

Hertz, R. (2002). The father as an idea: A challenge to kinship boundaries by single mothers. *Symobolic Interaction, 25,* 1–31.

Herz, D. (2003). CPS overview. In *Current Population Survey.* The Bureau of Labor Statistics and Census joint project Web site. Retrieved January 24, 2005, from http://www.bls.census.gov/cps/overmain.htm

Hetherington, E. M., Cox, M., & Cox, R. (1978). The aftermath of divorce. In J. H. J. Stevens & M. Matthews (Eds.), *Mother–child father–child relations* (pp. 149–176). Washington, DC: National Association for the Education of Young Children.

Hetherington, E. M., Cox, M. J., & Cox, R. (1982). Effects of divorce on parents and children. In M. D. Tucker & C. Mitchell-Kernan (Eds.), *Nontraditional families: Parenting and child development* (pp. 233–288). Hillsdale, NJ: Lawrence Erlbaum.

Hetherington, E. M., & Kelly, J. (2002). *For better or for worse: Divorce reconsidered.* New York: Norton.

Hetherington, E. M., & Stanley-Hagen, M. M. (1995). Parenting in divorced and remarried families. In M. H. Bornstein (Ed.), *Handbook of parenting* (Vol. 3, pp. 233–254).

Hewlett, S. A. (2002). *Creating a life: Professional women and the quest for children.* New York: Talk Miramax Books.

Heyman, R. E. (2001). Observation of couple conflicts: Clinical assessment applications, stubborn truths, and shaky foundations. *Psychological Assessment, 13*(1), 5–35.

Heyman, R. E. (2003). *Healthy relationships: Definitional and measurement issues.* Unpublished memo commissioned by Child Trends.

Hill, C. T., & Peplau, L. A. (1999). Premarital predictors of relationship outcomes: A 15-year follow-up of the Boston Couples Study. In T. N. Bradbury (Ed.), *The developmental course of marital dysfunction* (pp. 237–278). New York: Cambridge University Press.

Hill, M. S. (1992). The role of economic resources and remarriage in financial assistance for children of divorce. *Journal of Family Issues, 13,* 158–178.

Hill, M. S., Yeung, W. J., & Duncan, G. J. (2001). Childhood family structure and young adult behaviors. *Journal of Population Economics, 14,* 271–299.

Hodgson, R., & Birks, S. (2002). *Statistics New Zealand's definition of family, its implications for the accuracy of data and effectiveness of policy targeting.* Student Paper No. 4. Centre for Public Policy Evaluation. Retrieved August 8, 2002, from http://econ.massey.ac.nz/cppe/papers/cppesp04/cppesp04.htm

Hofferth, S. (in press). Response bias in a popular indicator of reading to children. *Sociological Methodology.*

Hofferth, S. L. (2003). Race/ethnic differences in father involvement in two-parent families: Culture, context, or economy. *Journal of Family Issues, 24,* 185–216.

Hofferth, S. L., & Anderson, K. G. (2003). Are all dads equal? Biology versus marriage as a basis for parental investment. *Journal of Marriage and Family, 65,* 213–232.

Hofferth, S., Davis-Kean, P., Davis, J., & Finkelstein, J. (1999). *1997 User Guide: The Child Development Supplement to the Panel Study of Income Dynamics.* Ann Arbor: University of Michigan, Institute for Social Research.

Hofferth, S., & Phillips, D. (1987). Child care in the United States, 1970–1995. *Journal of Marriage and the Family, 49,* 559–571.

Hofferth, S. L., Pleck, J., Stueve, J., Bianchi, S., & Sayer, L. (2002). The demography of fathers: What fathers do. In C. S. Tamis-LeMonda & N. Cabrera (Eds.), *Handbook of father involvement: Multidisciplinary perspectives* (pp. 63–70). Mahwah, NJ: Lawrence Erlbaum Associates.

Holman, T. R. (2003). *Thought on "Healthy Marriage."* Unpublished memo commissioned by Child Trends.

Holmbeck, G. N. (1997). Toward terminological, conceptual, and statistical clarity in the study of mediators and moderators: Examples from the child-clinical and pediatric psychology literatures. *Journal of Consulting and Clinical Psychology, 65,* 599–610.

Holtzworth-Munroe, A., & Stuart, G. (1994). Typologies of male batterers: Three subtypes and the differences among them. *Psychological Bulletin, 116,* 467–497.

Horn, W. (2003, June). *Going to the chapel: The president's healthy marriage initiative.* Keynote address to the seventh annual meeting of Smart Marriages in Reno, NV.

Horwitz, A. V., Raskin, H., & Howell-White, S. (1996). Becoming married and mental health: A longitudinal study of a cohort of young adults. *Journal of Marriage and the Family, 58*(4), 895–907.

Howe, R. A. W. (1993). Legal rights and obligations: An uneven evolution. In R. I. Lerman & T. J. Ooms (Eds.), *Young unwed fathers: Changing roles and emerging policies* (pp. 141–169). Philadelphia: Temple University Press.

Hunter, J. (2003). *Report on cognitive testing of cohabitation questions.* Center for Survey Methods Research, Statistical Research Division, U.S. Census Bureau.

Iceland, J. (2000). The "family/couple/household" unit of measurement in poverty estimation. *Journal of Economic and Social Measurement, 26,* 253–265.

Iceland, J. (2003). *The dynamics of economic well-being: Poverty, 1996–1999* (U.S. Census Bureau, Current Population Reports, Population Characteristics, P70–91). Washington, DC: U.S. Goverment Printing Office.

Jaccobs, M. J. G. (1995). The wish to become a father: How do men decide in favour of parenthood? In M. C. P. van Dongen, G. A. B. Frinking, & M. J. G. Jacobs (Eds.), *Changing fatherhood: An interdisciplinary perspective* (pp. 67–83). Amsterdam: Thesis.

Jekielek, S. M. (2004). Synopsis of measures used in studies of relationship quality for couple co-parenting after relationship dissolution. In *Conceptualizing and measuring "healthy marriage" for empirical research and evaluation studies: A review of the literature and annotated bibliography.* Washington, DC: Child Trends.

Johnson, C. (1985). The impact of illness on later-life marriages. *Journal of Marriage and the Family, 47,* 165–172.

Johnson, C., Stanley, S., Glenn, N., Amato, P., Nock, S., Markman, H., & Dion, M. R. (2001). *Marriage in Oklahoma: 2001 baseline statewide survey on marriage and divorce*. Oklahoma City: Oklahoma Department of Human Services.

Johnson, C. A., Stanley, S. M., Glenn, N. D., Amato, P. A., Nock, S. L., Markman, H. J., & Dion, M. R. (2002). *Marriage in Oklahoma: 2001 baseline statewide survey on marriage and divorce* (S02096 OKDHS). Oklahoma City: Oklahoma Department of Human Services.

Johnson, D., & Rusbult, C. (1989). Resisting temptation: Devaluation of alternative partners as a means of maintaining commitment in close relationships. *Journal of Personality and Social Psychology, 57*, 967–980.

Johnson, M. P. (2003). *Intimate violence and relationship health*. Unpublished memo commissioned by Child Trends.

Johnson, M. P., Caughlin, J. P., & Huston, T. L. (1999). The tripartite nature of marital commitment: Personal, moral, and structural reasons to stay married. *Journal of Marriage and the Family, 61*, 160–177.

Johnson, M. P., & Ferraro, K. J. (2000). Research on domestic violence in the 1990s: Making distinctions. *Journal of Marriage and the Family, 62*, 948–963.

Johnson, W. E. (2003). *Conceptualization and measurement of positive couple relationships*. Unpublished memo commissioned by Child Trends.

Jones, W., & Adams, J. (1999). *Handbook of interpersonal commitment and relationship stability*. New York: Plenum.

Jordan, P., Stanley, S., & Markman, H. (1999). *Becoming parents*. San Francisco: Jossey-Bass.

Kahn, J. R., Kalsbeek, W. D., & Hofferth, S. L. (1988). National estimates of teenage sexual activity: Evaluating the comparability of three national surveys. *Demography, 25*(2), 189–204.

Karney, B., & Bradbury, T. (1995). The longitudinal course of marital quality and stability: A review of theory, method, and research. *Psychological Bulletin, 118*, 3–34.

Katzev, A., Warner, R., & Acock, A. (1994). Girls or boys? Relationship of child gender to marital instability. *Journal of Marriage and the Family, 56*, 89–100.

Kauffman Early Education Exchange. (2002). *Set for success: Building a strong foundation for school readiness based on the social-emotional development of young children*. Kansas City, MO: Ewing Marion Kauffman Foundation.

Kenney, C. (2003, May). *Who pays for rent? Who pays for kids? Dividing expenses for the household and the child when the couple keeps separate purses*. Paper presented at the annual meeting of the Population Association of America, Minneapolis, MN.

Kiecolt-Glaser, J. K., & Newton, T. L. (2001). Marriage and health: His and hers. *Psychological Bulletin, 127*, 472–503.

King, R. B. (1999). Time spent in parenthood status among adults in the United States. *Demography, 36*, 377–385.

King, V. (1994). Nonresident father involvement and child well-being: Can dads make a difference? *Journal of Family Issues, 15*, 78–96.

Kinsey, A. C., Pomery, W. B., & Martin, C. E. (1948). *Sexual behavior in the human male*. Philadelphia: Saunders.

Kitzmann, K., Nicholson, L., & Schum, L. (2003). *Conceptualization and measurement of co-parenting after divorce*. Unpublished memo commissioned by Child Trends.

Klein, F., Sepekoff, B., & Wolf, T. J. (1985). Sexual orientation: A multi-variable dynamic process. *Journal of Homosexuality, 11*, 35–49.

Kline, G. H., Julien, D., Baucom, B., Hartman, S. G., Gilbert, K., Gonzales, T., et al. (2004). The Interactional Dimensions Coding System: A global system for couple interactions. In P. K. Kerig & D. H. Baucom (Eds.), *Couple observational coding systems* (pp. 113–127). Mahwah, NJ: Lawrence Erlbaum Associates.

Kline, G. H., Stanley, S. M., & Markman, H. J. (2002, November). Pre-engagement cohabitation and increased risk for poor marital outcomes. In *Understanding the association between cohabitation and poor relationship outcomes: Implications for preventive education and couples therapy.* Symposium presented at the meeting of the Association for the Advancement of Behavioral Therapy, Reno, NV.

Kline, G. H., Stanley, S. M., Markman, H. J., Olmos-Gallo, P. A., St. Peters, M., Whitton, S. W., & Prado, L. M. (2004). Timing is everything: Pre-engagement cohabitation and increased risk for poor marital outcomes. *Journal of Family Psychology, 18*, 311–318.

Knab, J. (2005). *Cohabitation: Sharpening a fuzzy concept* (Working Paper No. 04-05-FF). Princeton, NJ: Princeton University, Center for Research on Child Wellbeing.

Krieder, R., & Fields, J. (2002). *Number, timing, and duration of marriages and divorces: 1996* (Household Economic Studies, Series P70-80). Washington, DC: U.S. Census Bureau.

Krosnick, J. A. (2003, Summer). Response rates, Huffington, and more: Reflections on the 58th annual conference. *AAPOR News, 31*(2).

Kurdek, L. A. (1995). Predicting change in marital satisfaction from husbands' and wives' conflict resolution styles. *Journal of Marriage and the Family, 57*(1), 153–165.

L'Abate, L. (1997). *The self in the family: A classification of personality, criminality, and psychopathology.* New York: Wiley.

Lamb, M. (1987). *The father's role: Cross-cultural perspectives.* Hillsdale, NJ: Lawrence Erlbaum Associates.

Lamb, M. (1997). *The role of the father in child development* (3rd ed.). (M. Lamb, Ed.). New York: Wiley.

Lamb, M. (2002). Nonresidential fathers and their children. In C. S. Tamis-LeMonda & N. Cabrera (Eds.), *Handbook of father involvement: Multidisciplinary perspectives* (pp. 169–184). Mahwah, NJ: Lawrence Erlbaum Associates.

Lamb, M. (2004). *The role of the father in child development* (4th ed.). Hoboken, NJ: Wiley.

Lamb, M. E., Pleck, J. H., Charnov, E. L., & Levine, J. A. (1985). Paternal behavior in humans. *American Zoologist, 25*, 883–894.

Landry, D. J., & Forrest, J. D. (1995). How old are U.S. fathers? *Family Planning Perspectives, 27*, 159–161, 165.

Larsen, A. S., & Olson, D. H. (1989). Predicting marital satisfaction using PREPARE: A replication study. *Journal of Marital and Family Therapy, 15*, 311–322.

Laumann, E. O., Gagnon, J. H., Michael, R. T., & Michaels, S. (1994). *The social organization of sexuality: Sexual practices in the United States.* Chicago: University of Chicago Press.

Lauritsen, J. L., & Swicegood, C. G. (1997). The consistency of self-reported initiation of sexual activity. *Family Planning Perspectives, 29*, 215–221.

Lerman, R. I. (1993). Unwed fathers: Who are they? *The American Enterprise, 4*, 32–35.

Lerman, R., & Ooms, T. (1993). Introduction: Evolution of unwed fatherhood as a policy issue. In R. Lerman & T. Ooms (Eds.), *Young unwed fathers: Changing roles and emerging policies* (pp. 1–26). Philadelphia: Temple University Press.

Lerman, R., & Sorensen, E. (2000). Father involvement with their nonmarital children: Patterns, determinants, and effects on their earnings. In H. G. Peters, G. W. Peterson, S. Steinmetz, & R. D. Day (Eds.), *Fatherhood: Research, interventions and policies* (pp. 137–158). New York: Haworth.

Lerman, R. I., & Sorensen, E. (2003). Child support: Interactions between private and public transfers. In R. Moffitt (Ed.), *Means-tested transfer programs in the United States* (pp. 587–628). Chicago: University of Chicago Press.

Levinger, G. (1976). A socio-psychological perspective on marital dissolution. *Journal of Social Issues, 52*, 21–47.

Lichter, D. T., Batson, C. D., & Mellott, L. M. (2003). *Conceptualization and measurement of positive couple relationships.* Unpublished memo commissioned by Child Trends.

Lichter, D. T., & Graefe, D. R. (2001). Finding a mate? The marital and cohabitation histories of unwed mothers. In L. L. Wu & B. Wolfe (Eds.), Out of wedlock: Causes and consequences of nonmarital fertility (pp. 317–343). New York: Russell Sage Foundation.

Lichter, D. T., Zhenchao, Q., & Crowley, M. L. (2004). Child poverty among racial minorities and immigrants: Explaining trends and differentials. Unpublished manuscript.

Liebowitz, A., Eisen, M., & Chow, W. K. (1986). An economic model of teenage pregnancy decision-making. Demography, 23, 67–77.

Liker, J. K., Elder, G. H., Jr. (1983). Economic hardship and marital relations in the 1930s. American Sociological Review, 48, 343–359.

Lillard, L. A., Brien, M. J., & Waite, L. J. (1995). Premarital cohabitation and subsequent marital dissolution: A matter of self-selection? Demography, 32, 437–457.

Lillard, L. A., & Waite, L. J. (1989). Panel versus retrospective data on marital histories: Lessons from the PSID. In H. V. Beaton, D. A. Ganni, & D. T. Frankel (Eds.), Individuals and families in transition: Understanding change through longitudinal data (pp. 243–253). Washington, DC: U.S. Dept. of Commerce, Bureau of the Census.

Lin, I. F., Schaeffer, N. C., Seltzer, J. A., & Tuschen, K. L. (2004). Divorced parents' qualitative and quantitative reports of children's living arrangements. Journal of Marriage and Family, 66, 385–397.

Lin, I., & McLanahan, S. S. (2001). Norms about nonresident fathers' obligations and rights. Children & Youth Services Review, 23, 485–512.

Lindberg, L. D., Sonenstein, L. K., Ku, L., & Martinez, G. (1997). Age differences between minors who give birth and their adult partners. Family Planning Perspectives, 29(2), 61–66.

Lindberg, L. D., Sonenstein, F. L., Martinez, G., & Marcotte, J. (1998). Completeness of young father's reports of fertility. Journal of Economic and Social Measurement, 24, 15–23.

Links, P. S., & Stockwell, M. (2002). The role of couple therapy in the treatment of narcissistic personality disorder. American Journal of Psychotherapy, 56(4), 522–539.

Long, J. S., & Freese, J. (2003). Regression models for categorical dependent variables using Stata. College Station, TX: Stata Press.

Lucassen, A., & Parker, M. (2001). Revealing false paternity: Some ethical considerations. Lancet, 357, 1033–1035.

Luker, K. C. (1999). A reminder that human behavior frequently refuses to conform to models created by researchers. Family Planning Perspectives, 5, 248–249.

Lund, M. (1985). The development of investment and commitment scales for predicting continuity of personal relationships. Journal of Social and Personal Relationships, 2, 3–23.

Lundberg, S., & Rose, E. (2003, January). Child gender and father involvement with nonmarital children. Paper presented at the 2003 annual meeting of the American Economic Association, Washington, DC.

Maccoby, E., & Martin, J. (1983). Socialization in the context of the family: Parent–child interaction. In E. M. Hetherington (Ed.), Handbook of child psychology (Vol. 4, pp. 1–101). New York: Wiley.

Macklin, E. (1972). Heterosexual cohabitation among unmarried college students. The Family Coordinator, 21, 463–472.

Mahoney, A., Pargament, K., Jewell, T., Swank, A., Scott, E., Emery, E., & Rye, M. (1999). Marriage and the spiritual realm: The role of proximal and distal religious constructs in marital functioning. Journal of Family Psychology, 13(3), 321–338.

Manning, W. D. (1993). Marriage and cohabitation following premarital conception. Journal of Marriage and the Family, 55, 839–850.

Manning, W. D., & Brown, S. L. (2003). Children's economic well-being in cohabiting parent families: An update and extension (Working Paper Series No. 03-05). Bowling Green, OH: Bowling Green State University, Center for Family and Demographic Research.

Manning, W., & Lamb, K. (2003). Adolescent well-being in cohabiting, married, and single-parent families. Journal of Marriage and Family, 65, 876–893.

Manning, W. D., & Lichter, D. T. (1996). Parental cohabitation and children's economic well-being. *Journal of Marriage and the Family, 58*, 998–1010.

Manning, W. D., & Smock, P. J. (1995). Why marry? Race and the transition to marriage among cohabitors. *Demography, 32*, 509–520.

Manning, W. D., & Smock, P. J. (1999). New families and nonresident father–child visitation. *Social Forces, 78*, 87–116.

Manning, W. D., & Smock, P. J. (2000). "Swapping" families: Serial parenting and economic support for children. *Journal of Marriage and the Family, 62*, 111–122.

Manning, W. D., & Smock, P. J. (2005). Measuring and modeling cohabitation: New perspectives from qualitative data. *Journal of Marriage and the Family, 67*, 989–1002.

Manning, W. D., Smock, P. J., & Majumdar, D. (2004). The relative stability of cohabiting and marital unions for children. *Population Research and Policy Review, 23*, 135–159.

Manning, W. D., Stewart, S. D., & Smock, P. J. (2001). *The complexity of fathers' parenting responsibilities and involvement with nonresident children* (PSC Research Report No. 01-478). Ann Arbor, MI: Population Studies Center at the Institute for Social Research.

Marcil-Gratton, N. (1998). *Growing up with mom and dad? The intricate family life courses of Canadian children.* Ottowa, Canada: Statistics Canada.

Markman, H., Floyd, F., Stanley, S., & Storaasli, R. (1988). The prevention of marital distress: A longitudinal investigation. *Journal of Consulting and Clinical Psychology, 56*, 210–217.

Markman, H., & Hahlweg, K. (1993). The prediction and prevention of marital distress: An international perspective. *Clinical Psychology Review, 13*(3), 29–43.

Markman, H. J., & Notarius, C. I. (1987). Coding marital and family interaction: Current status. In T. Jacob (Ed.), *Family interaction and psychopathology: Theories, methods, and findings* (pp. 329–390). New York: Plenum.

Markman, H. J., Resnick, M. J., Floyd, F. J., Stanley, S. M., & Clements, M. (1993). Preventing marital distress through communication and conflict management training: A four- and five-year follow-up. *Journal of Consulting and Clinical Psychology, 61*, 70–77.

Markman, H., Stanley, S., & Blumberg, S. (2001). *Fighting for your marriage: New and revised version.* San Francisco: Jossey-Bass.

Marsiglio, W. (1987). Adolescent fathers in the United States: Their initial living arrangements, marital experiences and educational outcomes. *Family Planning Perspectives, 19*, 240–251.

Marsiglio, W. (1995). Stepfathers with minor children living at home: Parenting perceptions and relationship quality. In W. Marsiglio (Ed.), *Fatherhood: Contemporary theory, research, and social policy* (pp. 211–229). Thousand Oaks, CA: Sage.

Marsiglio, W. (1998). *Procreative man.* New York: New York University Press.

Marsiglio, W. (2004a). *Qualitative insights for studying male fertility: Assessing the procreative man.* Paper presented November 13, 2003, at the Measurement Issues in Family Demography workshop, sponsored by the National Institute of Child Health and Human Development and the Marlyand Population Research Center, Bethesda, MD.

Marsiglio, W. (2004b). *Stepdads: Stories of love, hope, and repair.* Boulder, CO: Rowman & Littlefield.

Marsiglio, W. (2004c). Studying fathering trajectories: In-depth interviewing and sensitizing concepts. In R. D. Day & M. E. Lamb (Eds.), *Conceptualizing and measuring father involvement* (pp. 61–82). Mahwah, NJ: Lawrence Erlbaum Associates.

Marsiglio, W., Amato, P., & Day, R. D. (2000). Scholarship on fatherhood in the 1990s and beyond. *Journal of Marriage and the Family, 62*, 1173–1191.

Marsiglio, W., & Hinojosa, R. (in press). Social and psychological influences on male reproductive function. In F. R. Kandeel, R. Swerdloff & J. Pryor (Eds.), *Male reproductive dysfunction: Pathophysiology and treatment.* New York: Marcel Dekker.

Marsiglio, W., & Hinojosa, R. (2004, November). *Managing the multi-father family: Stepfathers as father allies.* Paper presented at the National Council on Family Relations, Orlando FL.

Marsiglio, W., & Hutchinson, S. (2002). *Sex, men, and babies: Stories of awareness and responsibility.* New York: New York University Press.

Martin, J., Hamilton, B. E., Sutton, P. D., Ventura, R., Menacker, R., & Munson, M. L. (2003, December). Births: Final data for 2002. *National Vital Statistics Reports, 52*(10).

Maruschak, L. (1999, November). HIV in Prisons 1997. (*Bureau of Justice Statistics Bulletin,* Publication Number NCJ 178284). Retrieved November 1999 from www.ojp.usdoj.gov/bjs

Mason, M. C. (1993). *Male infertility—men talking.* New York: Routledge.

Massachusetts Department of Education. (2004). *Massachusetts high school students and sexual orientation: Results of the 1999 Youth Risk Behavior Survey.* Retrieved March 14, 2004, from www.doe.mass.edu/hsss/yrbs99/glb_rslts.html

May, E. T. (1980). *Great expectations: Marriage and divorce in post-Victorian America.* Chicago: University of Chicago.

Maynard, R. A. (1997). *Kids having kids: Economic costs and social consequences of teen pregnancy.* Washington, DC: Urban Institute.

McCarthy, J. (1978). A comparison of the probability of the dissolution of first and second marriages. *Demography, 15,* 345–359.

McCarthy, J., Pendleton, A., & Cherlin, A. (1989). The quality of marriage and divorce data from surveys (No. PHS 90-1214). *Proceedings of the 1989 Public Health Conference on Records and Statistics.* Washington, DC: U.S. Government Printing Office.

McCullough, M., Worthington, E., Jr., & Rachal, K. (1997). Interpersonal forgiving in close relationships. *Journal of Personality and Social Psychology, 73,* 321–336.

McDonald, M. A. (1999, April 9). Shared paternity in South American tribes confounds biologists and anthropologists. *Chronicle of Higher Education, 45,* A19-A20.

McLanahan, S. (1988). Family structure and dependency: Early transitions to female household headship. *Demography, 25,* 1–16.

McLanahan, S., & Casper, L. (1995). Growing diversity and inequality in the American family. In R. Farley (Ed.), *State of the union: America in the 1990s* (pp. 1–45). New York: Russell Sage Foundation.

McLanahan, S. S., Garfinkel, I., & Mincy, R. B. (2001). *Fragile families, welfare reform, and marriage* (Policy Brief No. 10). Brookings Institution. Retrieved August 8, 2002, from www.brook.edu/dybdocroot/wrb/publications/pb/pb10.pdf

McLanahan, S., Garfinkel, I., Reichman, N., Teitler, J., Carlson, M., & Audigier, C. (2003). *The Fragile Families and Child Wellbeing Study Baseline National Report.* Princeton, NJ: Princeton University, Center for Research on Child Wellbeing.

McLanahan, S., & Sandefur, G. (1994). *Growing up with a single parent: What hurts, what helps.* Cambridge, MA: Harvard University Press.

McLaughlin, D. K., & Lichter, D. T. (1997). Poverty and the marital behavior of young women. *Journal of Marriage and the Family, 59*(3), 582–594.

Menaghan, E. G. (1991). Work experiences and family interaction processes: The long reach of the job? *American Review of Sociology, 17,* 419–444.

Meng, X.-L., Rosenthal, R., & Rubin, D. B. (1992). Comparing correlated correlation coefficients. *Psychological Bulletin, 111,* 172–175.

Miller, K. (2002). *Cognitive analysis of sexual identity, attraction, and behavior questions* (Cognitive Methods Staff Working Paper Series No. 32). Washington, DC: Office of Research and Technology, National Center for Health Statistics.

Miller, S., Wackman, D., & Nunnally, E. (1976). A communication training program for couples. *Social Casework, 57*(1), 9–18.

Miller, W. B. (1992). Personality traits and developmental experiences as antecedents of childbearing motivation. *Demography, 29*, 265–285.

Mincy, R. B. (2002). *Who should marry whom? Multiple partner fertility among new parents* (Working paper No. 02-03-FF). Center for Research on Child Well-being. Retrieved January 24, 2005, from http://crcw.princeton.edu/workingpapers/WP02-03-FF-Mincy .pdf

Mintz, S., & Kellogg, S. (1988). *Domestic revolutions: A social history of American family life.* New York: The Free Press.

Mirowsky, J., Goldsteen, K., & Ross, C. E. (1990). The impact of the family on health: The decade in review. *Journal of Marriage and the Family, 52*(4), 1059–1079.

Moffitt, R., Reville, R., & Winkler, A. E. (1998). Beyond single mothers: Cohabitation and marriage in the AFDC program. *Demography, 35*, 259–278.

Moore, K. (1995). Nonmarital childbearing in the United States. In K. Moore (Ed.), *Report to Congress on out-of-wedlock childbearing* (pp. v–xxii). Washington, DC: U.S. Department of Health and Human Services.

Moore, K. A., Driscoll, A. K., & Lindberg, L. D. (1998). *A statistical portrait of adolescent sex, contraception, and childbearing.* Washington, DC: National Campaign to Prevent Teen Pregnancy.

Moore, K. A., Driscoll, A. K., & Ooms, T. (1997). *Not just for girls: The roles of boys and men in teen pregnancy prevention.* Washington, DC: National Campaign to Prevent Teen Pregnancy.

Moore, K., & Halle, T. (2001). Preventing problems vs. promoting the positive: What do we want for our children? In S. Hofferth & T. Owens (Eds.), *Children at the millennium: Where have we come from, where are we going?* (pp. 141–170). Oxford, England: Elsevier.

Morgan, S., Lye, D., & Condron, G. (1988). Sons, daughters and the risk of marital disruption. *American Journal of Sociology, 94*, 110–129.

Morrison, D. R., & Cherlin, A. J. (1995). The divorce process and young children's well-being: A prospective analysis. *Journal of Marriage and the Family, 57*, 800–812.

Morrison, D. R., & Ritualo, A. (2000). Routes to children's economic recovery after divorce: Are maternal cohabitation and remarriage equivalent? *American Sociological Review, 65*, 560–580.

Mosher, W. D. (1998). Design and operation of the 1995 National Survey of Family Growth. *Family Planning Perspectives, 30*(1), 43–46. Also available at: www.agi-usa.org

Mosher, W. D., Bachrach, C. A. (1996, January/February). Understanding U.S. fertility: Continuity and change in the National Survey of Family Growth, 1988–1995. *Family Planning Perspectives, 28*(1), 4–12. Also available at: www.agi-usa.org

Mott, F. L. (1985). *Evaluation of fertility data and preliminary analytical results from the 1983 (5th round) Survey of the National Longitudinal Surveys of Work Experience of Youth.* Columbus, OH: Center for Human Resources Research.

Mott, F. L. (1998). *Male data collection: Inferences from the National Longitudinal Surveys.* Columbus, OH: Center for Human Resources Research.

Mott, F. L., Baker, P. C., Haurin, R. J., & Marsiglio, W. (1983). *Fertility related data in the 1982 National Longitudinal Survey of Youth: An evaluation of data quality and some preliminary analytical results.* Columbus, OH: Center for Human Resource Research, The Ohio State University.

Mott, F. L., & Gryn, T. A. (2001, March). *Evaluating male fertility data: Who reports consistently and what are the analytical implications?* Paper presented at the meeting of the Population Association of America, Washington, DC.

Mott, F., Gryn, T., & Burchett-Patel, D. (2002). *Augmented male fertility variables for all NLSY79 male respondents 1979–1998.* Columbus, OH: Center for Human Resource Research.

Mumola, C. (2000). Incarcerated parents and their children. In *Bureau of Justice statistics special report* (pp. 1–12). Washington, DC: U.S. Government Printing Office.

Murray, S. L., Holmes, J. G., & Griffin, D. W. (1996). The benefits of positive illusions: Idealization and the construction of satisfaction in close relationships. *Journal of Personality and Social Psychology, 70*, 79–98.

Murry, V. M. (2003). *Conceptualization and measurement of positive marital and marital-analogous relationships among African American couples.* Unpublished memo commissioned by Child Trends.

Murry, V. M., Brown, A. P., Brody, G. H., & Cutrona, C. E. (2001). Racial discrimination as a moderator of links among stress, maternal psychological functioning, and family relationships. *Journal of Marriage and the Family, 63*, 915–936.

Murstein, B., & MacDonald, M. (1983). The relationship of "exchange-orientation" and "commitment" scales to marriage adjustment. *International Journal of Psychology, 18*, 297–311.

Myricks, N. (2003). DNA testing and child support: Can the truth really set you free? *American Journal of Family Law, 17*, 31–35.

Nathanson, C. A. (1991). *Dangerous passage: The social control of sexuality in women's adolescence.* Philadelphia: Temple University Press.

National Center for Education Statistics. (1998). *Nonresident fathers can make a difference in children's school performance* (Issue brief, June). Retrieved January 24, 2005, from http://nces.ed.gov/pubs98/98117.pdf

National Center on Fathers and Families. (n.d.). *The fathering indicators framework: A tool for quantitative and qualitative analysis.* Philadelphia: University of Pennsylvania.

National Center for Health Statistics. (1996). *Vital statistics of the United States, 1988: Vol. 3. Marriage and divorce.* Washington, DC: Public Health Service.

National Research Council. (1995). *Measuring poverty: A new approach* (C. F. Citro & R. T. Michael, Eds.). Washington, DC: National Academy Press.

Nock, S. L. (1995). A comparison of marriages and cohabiting relationships. *Journal of Family Issues, 16*, 53–76.

Nock, S. (1998). *Marriage in men's lives.* New York: Oxford University Press.

Nock, S. L. (2003). *Conceptualizing and measuring healthy marriages and positive relationships.* Unpublished memo commissioned by ChildTrends.

Nolan, F. (2001). Statistical families. In S. Birks (Ed.), *Child and family: Children in families as reflected in statistics, research and policy.* Issues Paper No. 11 (26-33). Centre for Public Policy Evaluation. Retrieved January 24, 2005, from http://econ.massey.ac.nz/cppe/papers/cppeip11/cppeip11.pdf

Nord, C., & Zill, N. (1996). *Non-custodial parents' participation in their children's lives: Evidence from the survey of income and program participation: Vol. 2. Final report.* Washington, DC: Department of Health and Human Services, Office of Human Services Policy.

Notarius, C., & Vanzetti, N. (1984). The Marital Agendas Protocol. In E. Filsinger (Ed.), *Marital and family assessment* (pp. 209–227). Beverly Hills, CA: Sage.

O'Dea, D. (2000). *The changes in New Zealand's income distribution* (Working Paper No. 00/13). Wellington, New Zealand: The Treasury.

Olson, D. H., & Knutson, L. (2003). *Healthy marriages and positive couple relationships: Conceptualization and measurement.* Unpublished memo commissioned by Child Trends.

Ooms, T. (1998). *Toward more perfect unions: Putting marriage on the public agenda.* Washington, DC: Family Impact Seminar.

Oropesa, R. S., Landale, N. S., & Kenkre, T. (2003). Income allocation in marital and cohabiting unions: The case of mainland Puerto Ricans. *Journal of Marriage and Family, 65*, 910–926.

Osborne, C. (2002). *Diversity among unmarried parents: The importance of marriage expectations*

(Working Paper No. 2002-01-FF). Princeton, NJ: Princeton University, Center for Research on Child Wellbeing.

Padilla, Y. C., & Reichman, N. E. (2001). Low birthweight: Do unwed fathers help? *Children & Youth Services Review, 23*, 427–452.

Parkinson, P., Cashmore., J., & Single, J. (2003). *Adolescents' views on the fairness of parenting and financial arrangements after separation.* Faculty of Law, University of Sydney, Australia. Retrieved January 24, 2005, from http://www.law.usyd.edu.au/staff/PatrickParkinson/AIFSFairness2003.pdf

Pasch, L. A., & Bradbury, T. N. (1998). Social support, conflict, and the development of marital dysfunction. *Journal of Consulting and Clinical Psychology, 66*, 219–230.

Pasch, L. A., & Christensen, A. (2000). Couples facing fertility problems. In L. Hammer Burns & S. N. Covington (Eds.), *Infertility counseling: A comprehensive handbook for clinicians* (pp. 241–267). New York: Parthenon.

Pasley, K., & Braver, S. (2004). Measuring father involvement in divorced, nonresident fathers. In R. D. Day & M. E. Lamb (Eds.), *Conceptualizing and measuring father involvement* (pp. 217–240). Mahwah, NJ: Lawrence Erlbaum Associates.

Pastore, A. L., & Maguire, K. (Eds.). (2002). *Sourcebook of criminal justice statistics* (online). Available at: http://www.albany.edu/sourcebook

Pearson, B. (2003). *Misattributed paternity.* Child Support Analysis. Retrieved August 24, 2004, from http://www.childsupportanalysis.co.uk/analysis_and_opinion/choices_and_behaviours/misattributed_paternity.htm

Peters, H. E. (1988). Retrospective versus panel data in analyzing lifecycle events. *The Journal of Human Resources, 23*, 488–513.

Peters, H. E., & Argys, L. M. (1992, January). *Testing a behavioral model of compliance with child support awards* (Final Report for Grant No. 89ASPE225A). Washington, DC: Department of Health and Human Services.

Peters, H. E., Arys, L. M., Maccoby, E. E., & Mnookin, R. H. (1993). Enforcing divorce settlements: Evidence from child support compliance and award modifications. *Demography, 30*, 719–735.

Peters, H. E., & Day, R. D. (2000). Fatherhood: Research, interventions, and policies: Parts I & II. *Marriage & Family Review, 29*, 2–4.

Peterson, L. S., & Mosher, W. D. (1999). Options for measuring unintended pregnancy in Cycle 6 of the National Survey of Family Growth. *Family Planning Perspectives, 5*, 252–253.

Peterson, P. E., & Zill, N. (1986). Marital disruption, parent–child relationships, and behavior problems in children. *Journal of Marriage and the Family, 62*(4), 1269–1287.

Phillips, R. (1988). *Putting asunder.* Cambridge, England: Cambridge University Press.

Pirog-Good, M. A. (1992). Teen fathers and the child support enforcement system. In *Paternity establishment: A public policy conference: Vol. 2. Studies of the circumstances of mothers and fathers* (SR No. 56B). Madison: University of Wisconsin, Institute for Research on Poverty.

Pirog-Good, M. A. (1995). The family background and attitudes of teen fathers. *Youth and Society, 26*, 351–376.

Pleck, J. H. (1997). Paternal involvement: Levels, sources, and consequences. In M. E. Lamb (Ed.), *The role of the father in child development* (pp. 66–103). New York: Wiley.

Pollak, R. A. (1986). A reformation of the two-sex problem. *Demography, 23*, 247–259.

Popenoe, D., & Whitehead, B. D. (2001). *Who wants to marry a soul mate?* Piscataway, NJ: National Marriage Project.

Powell, M. A., & Parcel, T. L. (1997). Effects of family structure on the earnings attainment process: Differences by gender. *Journal of Marriage and the Family, 59*, 419–433.

Pressinger, R. W., & Sinclair, W. (1998, August). *Environmental causes of infertility.* Retrieved January 24, 2005, from http://www.chem-tox.com/infertility/download/InfertilityFacts.pdf

Preston, S., & McDonald, J. (1979). The incidence of divorce with cohorts of American marriages contracted since the Civil War. *Demography, 16*, 1–24.

Pryor, J., & Rodgers, B. (2001). *Children in changing families: Life after parental separation.* Oxford, England: Blackwell.

Radosh, P. (2002). Reflections on women's crime and mothers in prison: A peacemaking approach. *Crime & Delinquency, 48*, 300–315.

Raley, R. K. (1999, March). *Then comes marriage? Recent changes in women's response to a non-marital pregnancy.* Paper presented at the annual meeting of the Population Association of America, New York.

Raley, R. K. (2000). Recent trends and differentials in marriage and cohabitation. In L. J. Waite (Ed.), *The ties that bind: Perspectives on marriage and cohabitation* (pp. 19–39). New York: Aldine de Gruyter.

Raley, R. K., & Bumpass, L. (2003). The topography of the divorce plateau: Levels and trends in union stability since 1980. *Demographic Research, 8*(8). Retrieved January 24, 2005, from http://www.demographic-reseach.org.

Raley, R. K., & Wildsmith, E. (2004). Cohabitation and children's family instability. *Journal of Marriage and the Family, 66*, 210–219.

Reichert, D. (1999). *Broke but not deadbeat: Reconnecting low-income fathers and children.* Washington, DC: National Conference of State Legislatures.

Reichman, N., Teitler, J., Garfinkel, I., & McLanahan, S. (2001). The Fragile Families and Child WellBeing Study: Sample and design. *Children and Youth Services Review, 23*, 303–326.

Reis, H. T., Sheldon, K. M., Gable, S., Roscoe, J., & Ryan, R. M. (2000). Daily well-being: The role of autonomy, competence, and relatedness. *Personality and Social Psychology Bulletin, 26*, 419–435.

Rendall, M. S., Clarke, L., Peters, H. E., Ranjit, N., & Verrapoulou, G. (1999). Incomplete reporting of men's fertility in the United States and Britain: A research note. *Demography, 36*(1), 135–144.

Research Triangle Institute. (1993). *SUDAAN survey data analysis software, Release 6.34.* Research Triangle Park, CA: Author.

Resnick, M. D., Bearman, P. S., Blum, R. K., Bauman, K. E., Harris, K. M., Jones, J., Tabor, J., Beuhring, T., Sieving, R. E., Shew, M., Ireland, M., Bearinger, L. H., & Udry, J. R. (1997). Protecting adolescents from harm: Findings from the National Study on Adolescent Health. *Journal of the American Medical Association, 278*(10), 823–832.

Richardson, F. C., Fowers, B. J., & Guignon, C. (1999). *Re-envisioning psychology: Moral dimensions of theory and practice.* San Francisco: Jossey-Bass.

Ridley, C., Jorgenson, S., Morgan, A., & Avery, A. (1982). Relationship enhancement with premarital couples: An assessment of effects on relationship quality. *The American Journal of Family Therapy, 10*, 41–48.

Rindfuss, R. R., & VandenHeuvel, A. (1990). Cohabitation: A precursor to marriage or an alternative to being single. *Population and Development Review, 16*, 703–726.

Rogge, R. D., & Bradbury, T. N. (1999). Recent advances in the prediction of marital outcomes. In R. Berger & M. T. Hannah (Eds.), *Handbook of preventive approaches in couples therapy* (pp. 331–360). New York: Brunner/Mazel.

Rokach, A., & Spomenka, K. (1997). Loneliness in jail: A study of the loneliness of incarcerated men. *International Journal of Offender Therapy and Comparative Criminology, 41*(2), 168–179.

Rusbult, C. E., Bissonnette, V. L., Arriaga, X. B., & Cox, C. L. (1998). Accommodation processes during the early years of marriage. In T. N. Bradbury (Ed.), *The developmental course of marital dysfunction* (pp. 74–113). Cambridge, England: Cambridge University Press.

Russell, S. T., & Joyner, K. (2001). Adolescent sexual orientation and suicide risk: Evidence from a national study. *American Journal of Public Health, 91*(8), 1276–1281.

Ryan, S. (2004). Synopsis of measures used in studies of relationship quality among cohabiting and visiting couples. In *Conceptualizing and measuring "healthy marriage" for empirical research and and evaluation studies: A review of the literature and annotated bibliography* (pp. 11–54). Washington, DC: Child Trends.

Sacco, W. P., & Phares, V. (2001). Partner appraisal and marital satisfaction: The role of self-esteem and depression. *Journal of Marriage and the Family, 63*(2), 504–513.

Sambrooks, J. E., & MacCulloch, M. J. (1973). A modification of the sexual orientation method and automated technique for presentation and scoring. *British Journal of Social and Clinical Psychology, 12,* 163–174.

Sandberg, J. F., & Hofferth, S. L. (2001). Changes in parental time with children. *Demography, 38,* 423–436.

Sandefur, G. D., McLanahan, S., & Wojtkiewicz, R. A. (1992). The effects of parental marital status during adolescence on high school graduation. *Social Forces, 71,* 103–121.

Santelli, J., Rochat, R., Hatfield-Timajchy, K., Gilbert, B. C., Curtis, K., Cabral, R., Hirsch, J. S., & Schieve, L. (2003). The measurement and meaning of unintended pregnancy. *Perspectives on Sexual and Reproductive Health, 35,* 94–101.

Sarre, S. (1996). *A place for fathers: Fathers and social policy in the post-war period* (Discussion Paper No. WSP 125). London: London School of Economics.

Sassler, S. (2004). The process of entering into cohabiting unions. *Journal of Marriage and Family, 66,* 491–505.

Sayer, L., Cohen, P., & Casper, L. (2004). *Women, men and work* (Census Bulletin). Washington, DC: Population Reference Bureau.

Schaeffer, N., Seltzer, J., & Dykema, J. (1998). *Methodological and theoretical issues in studying nonresident fathers: A selective review* (Working Paper No. WP-98-02). Philadelphia: University of Pennsylvania, National Center on Fathers and Familes.

Schaeffer, N. C., Seltzer, J. A., & Klawitter, M. (1991). Estimating nonresponse and response bias: Resident and nonresident parents' reports about child support. *Sociological Methods and Research, 20,* 30–59.

Schneider, W. H., & McLean, C. (2000, April 24). Pregnant on the sly. *The Report, 26,* 52–53.

Schoen, R., & Standish, N. (2001). The retrenchment of marriage in the U.S. *Population and Development Review, 27,* 553–563.

Schutz, A. (1970a). *Alfred Schutz on phenomenology and social relations.* Chicago: University of Chicago Press.

Schutz, A. (1970b). *Reflections on the problem of relevance.* New Haven, CT: Yale University Press.

Schwalbe, M., & Wolkomir, M. (2002). Interviewing men. In J. F. Gubrium & J. A. Holstein (Eds.), *Handbook of interview research: Context & method* (pp. 203–219). Thousand Oaks, CA: Sage.

Schwartz, L. K. (2002). The American Time Use Survey: Cognitive pretesting. *Monthly Labor Review, 125,* 34–45.

Segrin, C., & Flora, J. (2001). Perceptions of relational histories, marital quality, and loneliness when communication is limited: An examination of married prison inmates. *Journal of Family Communication, 1*(3), 151–173.

Sell, R. L. (1997). Defining and measuring sexual orientation: A review. *Archives of Sexual Behavior, 26,* 643–658.

Sell, R. L. (1998). The Sell Assessment of Sexual Orientation: Background and scoring. *Journal of Gay, Lesbian, and Bisexual Identity, 1,* 295–310.

Sell, R. L., & Becker, J. B. (2001a). *Sexual orientation data: Inclusion in information systems and databases of the Department of Heath and Human Services* (Report prepared for the Office of the Assistant Secretary for Planning and Evaluation).

Sell, R. L., & Becker, J. B. (2001b). Sexual orientation data: Inclusion in health information systems used to monitor HP2010. *American Journal of Public Health*, 91(6), 876–882.

Sell, R. L., & Petrulio, C. (1996). Sampling homosexuals, bisexuals, gays and lesbians for public health research: A review of the literature from 1990–1992. *Journal of Homosexuality*, 30(4), 31–47.

Sell, R. L., Wells, J. A., & Wypij, D. (1995). The prevalence of homosexual behavior and attraction in the United States, the United Kingdom and France: Results of national population-based samples. *Archives of Sexual Behavior*, 24, 235–248.

Seltzer, J. A. (1991). Relationships between fathers and children who live apart: The father's role after separation. *Journal of Marriage and the Family*, 53, 79–101.

Seltzer, J. A. (1994). Consequences of marital dissolution for children. *Annual Review of Sociology*, 20, 235–266.

Seltzer, J. A. (1998). Father by law: Effects of joint legal custody on nonresident fathers' involvement with children. *Demography*, 35, 135–146.

Seltzer, J. A. (2000). Families formed outside of marriage. *Journal of Marriage and the Family*, 62(4), 1247–1268.

Seltzer, J. A., & Bianchi, S. M. (1988). Children's contact with absent parents. *Journal of Marriage and the Family*, 50, 663–677.

Seltzer, J. A., & Brandreth, Y. (1994). What father's say about involvement with children and separation. *Journal of Marriage and the Family*, 15, 49–77.

Shively, M. G., & DeCecco, J. P. (1977). Components of sexual identity. *Journal of Homosexuality*, 3, 41–48.

Silenzio, V. M. B. (1997). Lesbian, gay and bisexual health in cross-cultural perspective. *Journal of the Gay and Lesbian Medical Association*, 1, 75–86.

Silliman, B., & Schumm, W. R. (1989). Topics of interest in premarital counseling: Clients' views. *Journal of Sex and Marital Therapy*, 15(3), 199–204.

Silliman, B., Stanley, S., Coffin, W., Markman, H., & Jordan, P. (2001). Preventive interventions for couples. In H. Liddle, D. Santisteban, R. Levant, & J. Bray (Eds.), *Family psychology: Science-based interventions* (pp. 123–146). Washington DC: American Psychological Association.

Smart, C., Neale, B., & Wade, A. (2001). *The changing experience of childhood: Families and divorce*. Cambridge, England: Polity.

Smock, P. J. (2000). Cohabitation in the United States: An appraisal of research themes, findings, and implications. *Annual Review of Sociology*, 26, 1–20.

Smock, P. J., & Gupta, S. (2002). Cohabitation in contemporary North America. In A. Booth & A. C. Crouter (Eds.), *Just living together: Implications of cohabitation on families, children, and social policy* (pp. 53–84). Mahwah, NJ: Lawrence Erlbaum Associates.

Smock, P. J., & Manning, W. D. (1997). Nonresidential parents' characteristics and child support. *Journal of Marriage and the Family*, 59, 798–808.

Smock, P. J., & Manning, W. D. (2003a). *The conceptualization and measurement of relationship quality: Insights from a qualitative study of cohabiting young adults*. Unpublished memo commissioned by Child Trends.

Smock, P., & Manning, W. D. (2003b, May). *The formation of cohabiting unions: New perspectives from qualitative data*. Paper presented at the annual meeting of the Population Association of America, Minneapolis, MN.

Sonenstein, F. L., & Calhoun, C. A. (1990). Determinants of child support: A pilot survey of absent parents. *Contemporary Policy Issues*, 8, 75–94.

Sonenstein, F., Ku, L., & Pleck, J. (1997). Measuring sexual behavior among teenage males in the U.S. In J. Bancroft (Ed.), *Researching sexual behavior* (pp. 87–105). Bloomington: Indiana University Press.

Sonenstein, F. L., Pleck, J. H., & Ku, L. C. (1993). Paternity risk among adolescent males. In

R. Lerman & T. Ooms (Eds.), *Young unwed fathers: Changing roles and emerging policies* (pp. 99–116). Philadelphia: Temple University Press.

Sonenstein, F. L., Stewart, K., Lindberg, L. D., Pernas, M., & Williams, S. (1997). *Involving males in preventing teen pregnancy: A guide for program planners*. Washington, DC: Urban Institute.

Sorensen, E. (1997). A national profile of nonresident fathers and their ability to pay child support. *Journal of Marriage and the Family, 59*, 785–797.

Sorensen, E., & Hill, A. (2004). Single mothers and their child support receipt: How well is child support enforcement doing? *Journal of Human Resources, 39*, 135–154.

Spingarn, R. W., & Durant, R. H. (1996). Male adolescents involved in pregnancy: Associated health risk and problem behaviors. *Pediatrics, 98*, 262–268.

Stagner, M., Ehrle, J., Kortenkamp, K., & Reardon-Anderson, J. (2003, September). *Systematic review of the impact of marriage and relationship programs*. Paper presented at the National Poverty Center Conference on Marriage and Family Formation Among Low-Income Couples: What Do We Know From Research?, Washington, DC.

Stanley, S. (1998). *The heart of commitment: Compelling research that reveals the secrets of a lifelong, intimate marriage*. Nashville, TN: Thomas Nelson.

Stanley, S. (2001). Making the case for premarital education. *Family Relations, 50*, 272–280.

Stanley, S., Allen, E. S., Markman, H. J., Saiz, C. C., Bloomstrom, G., Thomas, R., Schumm, W. R., & Baily, A. E. (2005). Dissemination and evaluation of marriage education in the Army. *Family Process, 44*, 187–201.

Stanley, S., Blumberg, S., & Markman, H. (1999). Helping couples fight for their marriages: The PREP Approach. In R. Berger & M. Hannah (Eds.), *Handbook of preventive approaches in couple therapy* (pp. 279–303). New York: Brunner/Mazel.

Stanley, S., Bradbury, T., & Markman, H. (2000). Structural flaws in the bridge from basic research on marriage to interventions for couples: Illustrations from Gottman, Coan, Carrere, and Swanson (1998). *Journal of Marriage and the Family, 62*, 256–264.

Stanley, S., Lobitz, W., & Dickson, F. (1999). Using what we know: Commitment and cognitions in marital therapy. In W. Jones & J. Adams (Eds.), *Handbook of interpersonal commitment and relationship stability* (pp. 411–424). New York: Plenum.

Stanley, S., & Markman, H. (1992). Assessing commitment in personal relationships. *Journal of Marriage and the Family, 54*, 595–608.

Stanley, S. & Markman, H. (1998). Acting on what we know: The hope of prevention. In T. Ooms (Ed.), *Strategies to strengthen marriage: What we know, what we need to know*. Washington DC: The Family Impact Seminar.

Stanley, S., Markman, H., Prado, L., Olmos-Gallo, P., Tonelli, L., St. Peters, M., Leber, B. D., Bobulinski, M., Cordova, A., & Whitton, S. W. (2001). Community based premarital prevention: Clergy and lay leaders on the front lines. *Family Relations, 50*, 67–76.

Stanley, S., Markman, H., & Whitton, S. (2002). Communication, conflict, and commitment: Insights on the foundations of relationship success from a national survey. *Family Process, 41*, 659–675.

Stanley, S., Prado, L., St. Peters, M., Olmos-Gallo, P., Whitton, S., Markman, H., et al. (2000, November). *The development of female depression early in marriage: A path analysis looking at the role of commitment variables and female relational confidence*. Paper presented at the 34th Annual Meeting for the Association for the Advancement of Behavior Therapy, New Orleans, LA.

Stanley, S., Trathen, D., McCain, S., & Bryan, M. (1998). *A lasting promise*. San Francisco: Jossey-Bass.

Stanley, S., Whitton, S. W., & Markman, H. J. (2004). Maybe I do: Interpersonal commitment and premarital or non-marital cohabitation. *Journal of Family Issues, 25*, 496–519.

Stewart, S. D. (1999). Nonresident mothers' and fathers' social contact with children. *Journal of Marriage and the Family*, 61, 894–907.

Stewart, S. D. (2002). The effect of stepchildren on childbearing intentions and births. *Demography*, 39, 181–197.

Stone, L. (1979). *The family, sex and marriage in England 1500–1800*. New York: Harper.

Straus, M. A. (1992). Sociological research and social policy: The case of family violence. *Sociological Forum*, 7(2), 211–238.

Straus, M. A., & Gelles, R. J. (1990). *Physical violence in American families: Risk factors and adaptations to violence in 8145 families*. New Brunswick, NJ: Transaction Books.

Straus, M. (1979). Measuring intra family conflict and violence: The Conflict Tactics (CT) Scales. *Journal of Marriage and the Family*, 41, 75–88.

Strauss, A. (1969). Turning points in identity. In A. Strauss (Ed.), *Mirrors and masks: Transformations of identity* (pp. 92–100). New York: Macmillan.

Strauss, A. L. (1959). *Mirrors and masks: The search for identity*. Glencoe, IL: The Free Press.

Strauss, A., & Corbin, J. (1998). *Basics of qualitative research: Grounded theory procedures and techniques*. Thousand Oaks, CA: Sage.

Strom, B. (2003). Communicator virtue and relation to marriage quality. *Journal of Family Communication*, 3(1), 21–40.

Sudman, S., & Bradburn, N. M. (1974). *Response effects in surveys*. Chicago: Aldine.

Sullivan, K., & Anderson, C. (2002). Recruitment of engaged couples for premarital counseling: An empirical examination of the importance of program characteristics and topics to potential participants. *The Family Journal*, 10, 388–397.

Sullivan, M. (1989). Absent fathers in the inner city. *Annals of the American Academy of Political and Social Science*, 501, 48–58.

Sullivan, M. L. (1993). Young fathers and parenting in two inner-city neighborhoods. In R. Lerman & T. Ooms (Eds.), *Young unwed fathers: Changing roles and emerging policies* (pp. 52–73). Philadelphia: Temple University Press.

Sweet, J., & Bumpass, L. (1987). *American families and households*. New York: Russell Sage Foundation.

Sykes, B., & Irven, C. (2000). Surnames and the Y chromosome. *American Journal of Human Genetics*, 66, 1417–1419.

Talvi, S. J. A. (2002). "Deadbeat" dads—or just "dead broke?" *The Christian Science Monitor*. Retrieved October 13, 2003, from http://www.csmonitor.com/2002/0204/p20s01-wmgn.html

Tamis-LeMonda, C., & Cabrera, N. (2002). *Handbook of father involvement: Multidisciplinary perspectives*. Mahwah, NJ: Lawrence Erlbaum Associates.

Teachman, J. (2002). Stability across cohorts in divorce risk factors. *Demography*, 39, 331–351.

Teachman, J. T., & Paasch, K. (1991). Legal status and the stability of coresidential unions. *Demography*, 28, 571–586.

Teachman, J., Tedrow, L., & Crowder, K. (2000). The changing demography of America's families. *Journal of Marriage and Family*, 62, 1234–1246.

Teitler, J. O. (2001). Father involvement, child health and maternal health behavior. *Children & Youth Services Review*, 23, 403–425.

Teitler, J., & Reichman, N. (2001). *Cohabitation: An elusive concept* (Working Paper No. 2001-07-FF). Princeton, NJ: Princeton University, Center for Research on Child Well-being.

Teitler, J. O., Reichman, N., & Koball, H. (forthcoming). Contemporaneous versus retrospective reports of cohabitation in the Fragile Families Survey. *Journal of Marriage and the Family*.

Thibaut, J., & Kelly, H. (1959). *The social psychology of groups*. New York: Wiley.

Thomas, A., & Sawhill, I. (2002). Incentives, challenges, and dilemmas of TANF: A case study for richer or for poorer: Marriage as an antipoverty strategy. *Journal of Policy Analysis Management, 21,* 587–599.

Thomson, E., McLanahan, S. S., & Curtin, R. B. (1992). Family structure, gender, and parental socialization. *Journal of Marriage and the Family, 54,* 368–378.

Thornberry, T., Smith, C., & Howard, G. (1997). Risk factors for teenage fatherhood. *Journal of Marriage and the Family, 59,* 505–522.

Thornton, A., Axinn, W. G., & Teachman, J. D. (1995). The influence of school enrollment and accumulation on cohabitation and marriage in early adulthood. *American Sociological Review, 60,* 762–774.

Turcotte, P., Renaud, V., & Cunningham, R. (2003, May). *Same-sex relationships and sexual orientation in Canada: Data, concepts, and methodological issues.* Paper presented at the annual meeting of the Population Association of America, Minneapolis, MN.

Uhlenberg, P. (1980). Death and the family. *Journal of Family History, 5,* 313–320.

Umberson, D., & Williams, C. (1993). Divorced fathers: Paternal role strain and psychological distress. *Journal of Family Issues, 14,* 378–400.

United Nations. (1989). *Convention on the rights of the child.* Office of the High Commissioner for Human Rights, Geneva, Switzerland. Retrieved August 8, 2002, from http://www.unhchr.ch/html/menu3/b/k2crc.htm

United Nations. (1998). *Principles and recommendations for population and housing censuses* (Revision 1). New York: United Nations.

U.S. Census Bureau. (1999a). *Living arrangements of children under 18 years old: 1960 to present* (Internet Historical Time Series of Living Arrangements of Children, Table CH-1). Retrieved January 24, 2005, from http://www.census.gov/population/socdemo/ms-la/tabch-1.txt

U.S. Census Bureau. (1999b). *Living arrangements of White children under 18 years old: 1960 to present* (Internet Historical Time Series of Living Arrangements of Children, Table CH-2). Retrieved January 25, 2005, from http://www.census.gov/population/socdemo/ms-la/tabch-2.txt

U.S. Census Bureau. (2000a). *Statistical abstract of the U.S., 2000.* Washington, DC: U.S. Government Printing Office.

U.S. Census Bureau. (2000b). *Table US-EST90INT-04—Intercensal Estimates of the United States Resident Population by Age Groups and Sex, 1990–2000: Selected Months.* Washington, DC: Author.

U.S. Census Bureau. (2001). *Statistical abstract of the U.S., 2001.* Washington, DC: U.S. Government Printing Office.

U.S. Census Bureau. (2002). *Statistical abstract of the United States: 2002.* Washington, DC: U.S. Government Printing Office. Tables 12, 14, 61, 322–324, 327, 494. Also available at www.census.gov

U.S. Department of Defense. (2002a, July). *Status of forces survey report* (Table 1). Retrieved from www.dmdc.mil

U.S. Department of Defense. (2002b). *2002 Status of forces survey of active-duty members* (Table 1). Retrieved from www.dmdc.osd.mil

U.S. Department of Health and Human Services. (1998). *Nurturing fatherhood: Improving data and research on male fertility, family formation, and fatherhood.* Washington, DC: Federal Interagency Forum on Child and Family Statistics.

U.S. Department of Health and Human Services. (2000). *Trends in the well-being of America's children & youth.* Washington, DC: U.S. Government Printing Office.

Van Lange, P. A. M., Rusbult, C. E., Drigotas, S. M., Arriaga, X. B., Witcher, B. S., & Cox, C. L. (1997). Willingness to sacrifice in close relationships. *Journal of Personality and Social Psychology, 72,* 942–966.

Ventura, S. J., Abma, J. C., Mosher, W. D., & Henshaw, S. (2003). Revised pregnancy rates, 1990–97, and new rates for 1998–99: United States. *National Vital Statistics Reports*, *52*.

Ventura, S. J., Martin, J. A., Curtin, S. C., & Matthews, T. J. (1998). *Report of final natality statistics, 1996* (Monthly Vital Statistics Report No. 47). Hyattsville, MD: National Center for Health Statistics.

Waite, L., Bachrach, C. Hindin, M., Thomson, E., & Thornton, A. (Eds.). (2000). *Ties that bind: Perspectives on marriage and cohabitation*. Hawthorne, NY: Aldine de Gruyter.

Waite, L. J. (1995). Does marriage matter? *Demography*, *32*, 483–508.

Waite, L. J., & Joyner, K. (2001). Emotional satisfaction and physical pleasure in sexual unions: Time horizon, sexual investment, and sexual exclusivity. *Journal of Marriage and the Family*, *63*, 247–264.

Waites, G. M. H. (1993). Male fertility regulation: The challenges for the year 2000. *British Medical Bulletin*, *49*, 210–221.

Waller, M. R. (2002). *My baby's father: Unmarried parents and paternal responsibility*. Ithaca, NY: Cornell University Press.

Waller, M., & McLanahan, S. (2005). "His" and "her" marriage expectations: Determinants and consequences. *Journal of Marriage and Family*, *67*, 53–67.

Wallerstein, J. S., & Kelly, J. B. (1980). *Surviving the breakup*. New York: Basic Books.

Wampler, K. (1990). An update of research on the Couple Communication Program. *Family Science Review*, *3*(1), 21–40.

Wasserman, S., & Faust, K. (1999). *Social network analysis: Methods and applications*. Cambridge, England: Cambridge University Press.

Watson, N., & Wooden, M. (2002). *The Household, Income, and Labour Dynamics in Australia (HILDA) Survey: Wave 1 Survey Methodology* (HILDA Project Technical Paper Series No. 1 /02). Melbourne, Australia: University of Melbourne, Melbourne Institute of Applied Economic and Social Research.

Wattenberg, E. (1993). Paternity actions and young fathers. In R. I. Lerman & R. J. Ooms (Eds.), *Young unwed fathers: Changing roles and emerging policies* (pp. 213–234). Philadelphia: Temple University Press.

Webb, R. E., & Daniluk, J. C. (1999). The end of the line: Infertile men's experiences of being unable to produce a child. *Men and Masculinities*, *2*, 6–25.

Weed, J. (1980). National estimates of marriage dissolution and survivorship. In *Vital Health Statistics*, Ser. 3, No. 19 IV (DHS Pub. No. PHS-81-1403). Washington, DC: U.S. Department of Health and Human Services.

Weiss, R. L., & Cerreto, M. C. (1980). The Marital Status Inventory: Development of a measure of dissolution potential. *American Journal of Family Therapy*, *8*(2), 80–85.

Weiss, Y., & Willis, R. (1985). Children as collective goods in divorce settlements. *Journal of Labor Economics*, *3*, 268–702.

Westoff, C. F. (1975). The yield of the imperfect: The 1970 National Fertility Study. *Demography*, *12*, 573–580.

Whisman, M. A., & Bruce, M. L. (1999). Marital dissatisfaction and incidence of major depressive episode in a community sample. *Journal of Abnormal Psychology*, *4*, 674–678.

White, L., & Gilbreth, J. G. (2001). When children have two fathers: Effects of relationships with stepfathers and noncustodial fathers on adolescent outcomes. *Journal of Marriage and the Family*, *63*, 155–167.

White, L., & Rogers, S. (2000). Economic circumstances and family outcomes: A review of the 1990s. *Journal of Marriage and the Family*, *62*, 1035–1051.

Whitehead, B. D. (1997). *The divorce culture*. New York: Knopf.

Whitton, S. W., Stanley, S. M., & Markman, H. J. (2002). Sacrifice in romantic relationships: An exploration of relevant research and theory. In H. T. Reiss, M. A. Fitzpatrick & A. L. Vangelisti (Eds.), *Stability and change in relationship behavior across the lifespan* (pp. 156–181). Cambridge, England: Cambridge University Press.

Wieselquist, J., Rusbult, C. E., Foster, C. A., & Agnew, C. R. (1999). Commitment, pro-relationship behavior, and trust in close relationships. *Journal of Personality and Social Psychology, 77*, 942–966.

Williams, R., & Thomson, E. (1985). Can spouses be trusted? A look at husband/wife proxy reports. *Demography, 22*, 115–123.

Willis, R. J. (1999). A theory of out-of-wedlock childbearing. *Journal of Political Economy, 107*(S6), S33–S64.

Wojtkiewicz, R. (1993). Simplicity and complexity in the effects of high school graduation. *Demography, 30*, 701–717.

Wu, L., & Martinson, B. (1993). Family structure and the risk of a premarital birth. *American Sociological Review, 58*, 210–232.

Wu, L., & Thomson, E. (2001). Race differences in family experience sexual initiation: Dynamic models of family structure and family change. *Journal of Marriage and the Family, 63*, 682–696.

Wu, Z., & Balakrishnan, T. R. (1995). Dissolution of premarital cohabitation in Canada. *Demography, 32*, 521–532.

Yeung, W. J., Sandberg, J., Davis-Kean, P. E., & Hofferth, S. L. (2001). Children's time with fathers in intact families. *Journal of Marriage and the Family, 63*(1), 136–154.

Zelnik, M., Kantner, J., & Ford, K. (1980). *Determinants of fertility behavior among U.S. females aged 15–19, 1971 and 1976* (Final Report to National Institute of Child Health and Human Development). Baltimore: Johns Hopkins University Press.

Zill, N. (1996). Family change and student achievement: What we have learned, what it means for schools. In A. Booth & J. F. Dunn (Eds.), *Family–School Links: How do they affect educational outcomes?* (pp. 139–174). Mahwah, NJ: Lawrence Erlbaum Associates.

Author Index

Subject Index